THE LITTLE, BROWN READER

THE LITTLE, BROWN READER

Short Fifth Edition

Edited by

MARCIA STUBBS
Wellesley College

SYLVAN BARNET
Tufts University

Scott, Foresman and Company
Glenview, Illinois   Boston   London

Library of Congress Cataloging-in-Publication Data

The Little, Brown reader / edited by Marcia Stubbs, Sylvan Barnet. —
    Short 5th ed.
        p.   cm.
    Includes index.
    ISBN 0-673-39679-7
    1. College readers.   I. Stubbs, Marcia.   II. Barnet, Sylvan.
PE1122.L56 1989b
808′.0427–dc19   88–38047
                                                              CIP

1 2 3 4 5 6 7 8 9 10 — RRC — 94 93 92 91 90 89 88

Cover art: *"A Day at the Race," Richard Diebenkorn, 1953. The Carnegie Museum of Art,
Pittsburgh; Patrons Art Fund, 1953.*

Printed in the United States of America

Acknowledgments begin on page 708.

PREFACE

Books have been put to all sorts of unexpected uses. Tolstoy used Tatishef's dictionaries as a test of physical endurance, holding them in his outstretched hand for five minutes, enduring "terrible pain." Books (especially pocket-sized Bibles) have served as armor by deflecting bullets. And they have served as weapons: two hundred years ago the formidable Dr. Johnson knocked a man down with a large book.

In a course in writing, what is the proper use of the book in hand? This anthology contains more than ninety essays, together with a few poems, stories, and fables, and numerous paragraphs and aphorisms. But these readings are not the subject matter of the course; the subject matter of a writing course is writing, particularly the writing the students themselves produce. The responsibilities we felt as editors, then, were to include selections that encourage and enable students to write well, and to exclude selections that do not.

To talk of "enabling" first: Students, like all other writers, write best when they write on fairly specific topics that can come within their experience and within their command in the time that they have available to write. A glance at the first three thematic sections of our table of contents—these follow Chapter 1, which offers an overview of "Reading (and Writing About) Essays"—will reveal the general areas within which, we believe, students can find topics they have already given some thought to and are likely to be encountering in other courses as well: family relationships, love and courtship; schools; work, sports, and play. Although the next three sections ("Open for Business," "Messages," and "Networks") are also on familiar subjects—entrepreneurship, language, and popular culture—the selections themselves offer ways of thinking about these subjects that may be less familiar. Television commercials and films, for example, can be thought of as networks that articulate and transmit values implicit in a culture. The last two sections are about areas of experience that, while hardly remote from students' interest, are perhaps more difficult for all of us to grasp concretely: the tension between civil rights and liberties and the need for law and order and the nature of religious faith—Hebrew, Christian, and Muslim. In these last sections, therefore, we have taken particular care to exclude writing that is, for our purposes, too abstract, or too technical, or too elaborate.

This returns us to the need we felt as editors to think carefully about whether selections we were inclined to use—because they were beautifully written or on a stimulating topic—would encourage students to write. Such encouragement does not come, we feel, solely from the subject of an essay or from its excellence; it comes when the essay engenders in the reader a confidence in the writing process itself. No one quality in essays automatically teaches such confidence: not length or brevity, not difficulty or simplicity, not necessarily clarity, and almost certainly not brilliance. But essays that teach writing demonstrate, in some way, that the writers had some stake in what they were saying, took some pains to say what they meant, and took pleasure in having said it. The selections we include vary in length, complexity, subtlety, tone, and purpose. Most were written by our contemporaries, but not all. The authors include historians, sociologists, architects, scientists, saints, and philosophers, as well as journalists and other professional writers. And we have included some pictures in each section. But we hope that everything here will allow students, including those who have previously read very little, to establish helpful connections between the activities that produced the words (and pictures) in these pages and their own work in putting critical responses to them on paper.

Although any arrangement of the selections—thematic, rhetorical, alphabetical, chronological, or random—would have suited our purposes, we preferred the thematic arrangement. For one thing, by narrowing our choices it helped us to make decisions. But more important, we know that in the real world what people write about is subjects, and we didn't want to miss any opportunity to suggest that what goes on in writing courses is something like what goes on outside. The thematic categories are not intended to be rigid, however, and they do not pretend to be comprehensive; some of the questions following the selections suggest that leaping across boundaries is permitted, even encouraged. And, for instructors who prefer to organize their writing courses rhetorically, we have added a selective table of contents organized rhetorically. Finally, we append a glossary of terms for students of writing and a brief essay on looking at and writing about pictures. The pictures (beautiful things in themselves, we think), like the essays, stories, and poems, suggest or provide immediate or nearly immediate experiences for students to write about.

As usual, we are indebted to readers-in-residence. Morton Berman, William Burto, and Judith Stubbs have often read our material and then told us what we wanted to hear.

While we were selecting the essays, we received helpful advice from Eric D. Brown, Kenneth Cooney, William Devlin, George D. Haich, Ruth C. Hege, William E. Lucas, William Lutz, Mary Shesgreen, Judith Stanford, Michael West, and Harvey Vetstein.

We thank those instructors who generously offered suggestions based on their classroom experience with the first four editions: Bonnie Alexander, Kenneth Alrutz, Marianne Antczack, Norman Sidney Ashbridge, Andrew Aung, Donald Babcock, James Barcus, Lloyd Becker, Frank Bidart, Joseph Blimm, Frank Bliss, Beverly Boone, Grant Boswell, George Branam, Lillian Broderick, Ruth Brown, Jean Young Brunk, Beth Burch, Debra L. Burgauet, Anne Burley, Carol Burns, D. G. Campbell, J. V. Chambers, John Clifford, Ann Connor, Anne Cooney, Marion Copeland, Robert Cosgrove, Helene Davis, Donald DeSulis, John A. R. Dick, Fiona Emde, Robert Erickson, Richard Fahey, Evelyn Farbman, Michael Feehan, Linda Feldmeier, Gretchen Fillmore, Sister Jeremy Finnegan, Kathleen P. Flint, Martha Flint, William Ford, Joseph S. Frany, James French, Charles Frey, Yvonne Frey, David Gadziola, George Griffith, Steve Hamelman, Bettina Hanlon, Brian O. Hannon, Hymen H. Hart, Pat Hart, Steven Harvey, Mal Haslett, Stephen Hathaway, Mark Hawkins, George Hayhoe, Zelda Hedden-Sellman, Kathryn Hellerstein, Dr. Elbert R. Hill, Maureen Hoal, David Hoddeson, Kathryn Holms, John Howe, William Howrath, Morris Husted, Lois B. Janzer, Johanna Jung, F. A. Kachur, Michael Kalter, Robert D. Keohan, Richard Kirchoffer, Walt Klarner, Robert Knox, Karl Kumm, Sandra M. Lee, Dorinda Lemaire, Claudia Limbert, Joyce D. Lipkis, Marie M. McAllister, Anne McCormick, Charles McLaughlin, Garry Merritt, George Miller, John Milstead, Mary F. Minton, Chris M. Mott, Abigail Mulcahy, John Nesselhof, Robert Ohafson, Terry Otten, Jewyl Pallette, Linda Pelzer, Richard Price, Richard Priebe, Phyllis Reed, Karyn Riedell, Leo Rockas, Duncan Rollo, Harriet Rosenblum, Ronald Ruland, Ralph St. Louis, Jack Seltzer, Emerson Shuck, Carol Sicherman, James Smith, Larry Smith, Mark Smith, Harry Solomon, John Stahl, Judith Stanford, Carol Starikoff, Petra Steele, William B. Stone, Mary Lee Strode, William L. Stull, Tereatha Taylor,

David Templeman, Elizabeth Tentarelli, Robert Thompson, Leatrice Timmons, Pamela Topping, Marilyn Valention, J. Keith Veizer, Brother Roland Vigeant, Lorraine Viscardi, Anthony Vital, Carolyn Wall, Don Wall, Doug Watson, Mary Weinkauf, Mark Wenz, Richard Whitworth, Lyn Yonack, Lee Yosha, and Thomas Young.

We owe a special debt to Professor John Harwood and other teachers in the composition program at Pennsylvania State University for suggesting ways in which *The Little, Brown Reader* can be used in a course that emphasizes persuasive writing.

We are grateful to colleagues at Wellesley College—Michael David Coogan, Katheryn H. Doran, Lidwien Kapteijns, Louise Marlow, Robert Umans, Winifred Jane Wood, and Teresa Amott—who suggested materials for the new sections on science and religion, or who otherwise assisted us with this new edition.

People at Scott, Foresman/Little, Brown have been unfailingly helpful; we would especially like to thank Cynthia Chapin and Joseph Opiela.

A Note on the Fifth Edition

"Never read a book that is not old." Thus Emerson. It's good advice, but we are of course pleased that when *The Little, Brown Reader* was published it immediately found a receptive audience. Second, third, and fourth editions allowed us to strengthen the book by adding some recent essays, and now the publisher has asked for a fifth edition in order to meet the needs of instructors who wish to continue to use the book but who also want something new. William Hazlitt, Emerson's older contemporary, said that he always read an old book when a new one was published. We hope that this new edition allows instructors to read both at once, for although we have now (1) provided an introductory chapter on reading and writing essays, (2) substituted many essays within the thematic chapters—for instance four new essays in "Networks," including one by Woody Allen on colorizing film—and (3) added two new thematic sections ("Open for Business" and "Articles of Faith"), we have also tried to preserve the original character of the book.

CONTENTS

1 READING (AND WRITING ABOUT) ESSAYS

2   ALL IN THE FAMILY

3   TEACHING AND LEARNING

---

* Denotes fiction.
** Denotes poetry.

4   WORK AND PLAY

6   MESSAGES

8   LAW AND ORDER

9 ARTICLES OF FAITH

RHETORICAL GUIDE

Analogy

Analysis or Classification

Argument
(See *Persuasion*)

Autobiography
(See *Journal and Personal Report*)

Cause and Effect

Comparison and Contrast

Definition

Description

Diction

Evaluation

Examples, Illustrations

Exposition

Irony
(See also *Persuasion*)

Journal and Personal Report

Narration

Persuasion

Style

1
READING
(AND WRITING ABOUT)
ESSAYS

Getting Started: Skimming and Reading

"Some books are to be tasted, others to be swallowed, and some few to be chewed and digested." You may already have encountered this wise remark by Francis Bacon, a very good reader (and a good writer too, though he did not write Shakespeare's plays). Bacon puts his finger on an important truth: not all books (or essays) are to be read in the same way. We occasionally see advertisements for courses in speed reading; one ad claimed that President Kennedy took such a course and learned to read a couple of hundred pages in an hour. That's about the right speed for most of the stuff that crossed his desk. But (despite the advertisements) he wasn't reading, he was skimming. The art of skimming is essential if we are to survive the daily deluge of paper loosed upon us, and most of us develop the art satisfactorily: we get through junk mail in a matter of seconds, the newspaper and *Time* or *Newsweek* in a matter of minutes. We skim, perhaps taking in only the captions, and then, when an item catches our interest, we stop skimming and really read; possibly we even go back and reread the opening paragraphs that we had skimmed.

Skimming has its place in academic life too; in studying for an examination or in doing a research paper you probably will skim many pages to find the material that is relevant and that will require close reading. Even if you know at the outset that an article or book is important, you may skim it first, to get the gist, so that you can then more easily read it a second time (really a first time) and take notes on it. Skimming may reveal, for instance, that each chapter ends with a summary, and so even before you begin to read closely you know that you will not have to take very general notes later when you inch through each page.

Inevitably, however, and especially in a composition course, much of the assigned reading and every essay that you intend to write about must be read slowly and with all of your powers of attention. Only by reading attentively do we hear in the mind's ear the writer's *tone*— whether it is ironic or earnestly straightforward, indignant or genial. Perhaps you know the line from Owen Wister's novel *The Virginian:* "When you call me that, smile." Words spoken with a smile mean something different from the same words forced through clenched teeth. But while speakers can communicate by body language and by gestures, by facial expressions and by changes in tone of voice, writers have only words in ink on paper. As a writer, you are learning control of tone as you learn to take pains in your choice of words, in the way you arrange sentences, and even in the punctuation marks you may find yourself changing in your final draft. These skills will pay off doubly if you apply them to your reading, by putting yourself in the place of the writer whose work you are reading. As a reader—a thoughtful reader—you must also make some effort to "hear" the writer's tone as part of the meaning the words communicate. Skimming is not adequate to that task.

Close reading begins with reading the title, and thinking about it, at least briefly. If we pick up an essay called "Do-It-Yourself Brain Surgery" we ought to know at once that we can prepare to be amused. Such a title must be ironic; it simply cannot be taken straight by a thoughtful reader. What about Judy Syfers's "Why I Want a Wife"? That title on an essay by a woman demands at least a double take and, very likely, a glance at the biographical note at the bottom of the page. There, as it happens (page 40 in this book), you'll find the information that the essay first appeared in the premier issue of *Ms.* magazine. If that means nothing to you, reading the first paragraph, just three brief sentences, should confirm your hunch that Syfers's title is not exactly straightforward and it should prepare you for the essay's ironic content.

We say "should" because a surprising number of college students persist, despite these clues, in reading this and other essays containing irony as if the essays were perfectly straightforward or even solemn. Perhaps such students have been conditioned to expect only "fact" in a printed text, and thus miss what is more usually there—a particular writer's opinions, beliefs, and attitudes, which may or may not be based on facts or supported by facts. Or, it may be that such students, whose own conversation and even writing are often richly ironic, fail to detect irony in what they read because they have come to expect that anything in a textbook, certainly anything in a textbook for an English class, is solemn and boring, and that a safe tack is to fake a kind of pious interest in it, whatever it is. If you have fallen into that trap yourself, we recommend two remedies: first, consciously question your own assumptions about what you read; and second, at least in reading this book, be prepared for some surprises.

Many titles in this anthology *are* perfectly straightforward and informative. Paul Goodman's "A Proposal to Abolish Grading" is one, and Paul Robinson's "TV Can't Educate" is a terse summary of the essay's argument, or thesis. But some titles convey very little: E. B. White's "Education" hardly prepares us for his rather genial comparison of a public elementary school with a private school, or for the argumentative edge of the comparison. We will have to read further to get even the faintest idea of what he is up to. Orwell's "Shooting an Elephant" deliberately misleads us, for the title suggests some sort of hunting tale, though if we know that Orwell is fundamentally a social critic we suspect he is not really going to give us a yarn about an Englishman's pleasure in shooting big game.

Identifying the Topic and Thesis

If the writer's *thesis* is not stated or implied in the title, it ought to become increasingly evident as you work your way into the essay. This thesis is a point, an argument; and a point or argument implies an *attitude* toward a *topic*. In reading, then, try to identify the topic (not really do-it-yourself brain surgery, but do-it-yourself books) and the attitude (amused contempt for such books). Even an essay that is largely narrative, recounting a personal experience or a bit of history, will usually include an attitude toward the event being narrated, and it is the attitude—the interpretation of the event—rather than the event itself that is usually the richest part of the essay. "Shooting an Elephant" does in fact recount an episode in which Orwell shot an elephant, but the essay is really about *why* he shot the elephant, and what the experience revealed. His analysis of the episode brought him, he says, to an understanding of "the real nature of imperialism— the real motives for which despotic governments act."

Here is Orwell's essay. Since we refer to it several times in later pages, we suggest that you read the essay now. Note, as you read, passages that clearly reveal Orwell's *attitude* toward imperialism. Note particularly passages that seem ironic.

George Orwell

Shooting an Elephant

In Moulmein, in Lower Burma, I was hated by large num- 1
bers of people—the only time in my life that I have been important
enough for this to happen to me. I was sub-divisional police officer of
the town, and in an aimless, petty kind of way anti-European feeling
was very bitter. No one had the guts to raise a riot, but if a European
woman went through the bazaars alone somebody would probably
spit betel juice over her dress. As a police officer I was an obvious
target and was baited whenever it seemed safe to do so. When a nimble
Burman tripped me up on the football field and the referee (another
Burman) looked the other way, the crowd yelled with hideous laughter. This happened more than once. In the end the sneering yellow
faces of young men that met me everywhere, the insults hooted after
me when I was at a safe distance, got badly on my nerves. The young
Buddhist priests were the worst of all. There were several thousands
of them in the town and none of them seemed to have anything to do
except stand on street corners and jeer at Europeans.

All this was perplexing and upsetting. For at that time I had already 2
made up my mind that imperialism was an evil thing and the sooner
I chucked up my job and got out of it the better. Theoretically—and
secretly, of course—I was all for the Burmese and all against their
oppressors, the British. As for the job I was doing, I hated it more
bitterly than I can perhaps make clear. In a job like that you see the
dirty work of Empire at close quarters. The wretched prisoners huddling in the stinking cages of the lock-ups, the grey, cowed faces of
the long-term convicts, the scarred buttocks of the men who had been
flogged with bamboos—all these oppressed me with an intolerable
sense of guilt. But I could get nothing into perspective. I was young
and ill-educated and I had had to think out my problems in the utter

George Orwell (1903–1950) was the pen name adopted by Eric Blair, an Englishman born in India. Orwell was educated at Eton, in England, but in 1921 he went
back to the East and served for five years as a police officer in Burma. He then
returned to Europe, doing odd jobs while writing novels and stories. In 1936 he
fought in the Spanish Civil War on the side of the Republicans, an experience
reported in *Homage to Catalonia* (1938). His last years were spent writing in
England.

silence that is imposed on every Englishman in the East. I did not even know that the British Empire is dying, still less did I know that it is a great deal better than the younger empires that are going to supplant it. All I knew was that I was stuck between my hatred of the empire I served and my rage against the evil-spirited little beasts who tried to make my job impossible. With one part of my mind I thought of the British Raj as an unbreakable tyranny, as something clamped down, in *saecula saeculorum*,[1] upon the will of the prostrate peoples; with another part I thought that the greatest joy in the world would be to drive a bayonet into a Buddhist priest's guts. Feelings like these are normal by-products of imperialism; ask any Anglo-Indian official, if you can catch him off duty.

One day something happened which in a roundabout way was 3
enlightening. It was a tiny incident in itself, but it gave me a better glimpse than I had had before of the real nature of imperialism—the real motives for which despotic governments act. Early one morning the sub-inspector at a police station the other end of town rang me up on the 'phone and said that an elephant was ravaging the bazaar. Would I please come and do something about it? I did not know what I could do, but I wanted to see what was happening and I got on to a pony and started out. I took my rifle, an old .44 Winchester and much too small to kill an elephant, but I thought the noise might be useful *in terrorem*.[2] Various Burmans stopped me on the way and told me about the elephant's doings. It was not, of course, a wild elephant, but a tame one which had gone "must." It had been chained up, as tame elephants always are when their attack of "must" is due, but on the previous night it had broken its chain and escaped. Its mahout, the only person who could manage it when it was in that state, had set out in pursuit, but had taken the wrong direction and was now twelve hours' journey away, and in the morning the elephant had suddenly reappeared in the town. The Burmese population had no weapons and were quite helpless against it. It had already destroyed somebody's bamboo hut, killed a cow and raided some fruit-stalls and devoured the stock; also it had met the municipal rubbish van and, when the driver jumped out and took to his heels, had turned the van over and inflicted violences upon it.

The Burmese sub-inspector and some Indian constables were wait- 4
ing for me in the quarter where the elephant had been seen. It was a

[1] World without end. (Editors' note)
[2] As a warning. (Editors' note)

very poor quarter, a labyrinth of squalid bamboo huts, thatched with palmleaf, winding all over a steep hillside. I remember that it was a cloudy, stuffy morning at the beginning of the rains. We began questioning the people as to where the elephant had gone and, as usual, failed to get any definite information. That is invariably the case in the East; a story always sounds clear enough at a distance, but the nearer you get to the scene of events the vaguer it becomes. Some of the people said that the elephant had gone in one direction, some said that he had gone in another, some professed not even to have heard of any elephant. I had almost made up my mind that the whole story was a pack of lies, when we heard yells a little distance away. There was a loud, scandalized cry of "Go away, child! Go away this instant!" and an old woman with a switch in her hand came round the corner of a hut, violently shooing away a crowd of naked children. Some more women followed, clicking their tongues and exclaiming; evidently there was something that the children ought not to have seen. I rounded the hut and saw a man's dead body sprawling in the mud. He was an Indian, a black Dravidian coolie, almost naked, and he could not have been dead many minutes. The people said that the elephant had come suddenly upon him round the corner of the hut, caught him with its trunk, put its foot on his back and ground him into the earth. This was the rainy season and the ground was soft, and his face had scored a trench a foot deep and a couple of yards long. He was lying on his belly with arms crucified and head sharply twisted to one side. His face was coated with mud, the eyes wide open, the teeth bared and grinning with an expression of unendurable agony. (Never tell me, by the way, that the dead look peaceful. Most of the corpses I have seen looked devilish.) The friction of the great beast's foot had stripped the skin from his back as neatly as one skins a rabbit. As soon as I saw the dead man I sent an orderly to a friend's house nearby to borrow an elephant rifle. I had already sent back the pony, not wanting it to go mad with fright and throw me if it smelt the elephant.

The orderly came back in a few minutes with a rifle and five car- 5
tridges, and meanwhile some Burmans had arrived and told us that the elephant was in the paddy fields below, only a few hundred yards away. As I started forward practically the whole population of the quarter flocked out of the houses and followed me. They had seen the rifle and were all shouting excitedly that I was going to shoot the elephant. They had not shown much interest in the elephant when he was merely ravaging their homes, but it was different now that he was going to be shot. It was a bit of fun to them, as it would be to an

English crowd; besides they wanted the meat. It made me vaguely uneasy. I had no intention of shooting the elephant—I had merely sent for the rifle to defend myself if necessary—and it is always unnerving to have a crowd following you. I marched down the hill, looking and feeling a fool, with the rifle over my shoulder and an ever-growing army of people jostling at my heels. At the bottom, when you got away from the huts, there was a metalled road and beyond that a miry waste of paddy fields a thousand yards across, not yet ploughed but soggy from the first rains and dotted with coarse grass. The elephant was standing eight yards from the road, his left side towards us. He took not the slightest notice of the crowd's approach. He was tearing up bunches of grass, beating them against his knees to clean them and stuffing them into his mouth.

I had halted on the road. As soon as I saw the elephant I knew   6
with perfect certainty that I ought not to shoot him. It is a serious matter to shoot a working elephant—it is comparable to destroying a huge and costly piece of machinery—and obviously one ought not to do it if it can possibly be avoided. And at that distance, peacefully eating, the elephant looked no more dangerous than a cow. I thought then and I think now that his attack of "must" was already passing off; in which case he would merely wander harmlessly about until the mahout came back and caught him. Moreover, I did not in the least want to shoot him. I decided that I would watch him for a little while to make sure that he did not turn savage again, and then go home.

But at that moment, I glanced round at the crowd that had followed   7
me. It was an immense crowd, two thousand at the least and growing every minute. It blocked the road for a long distance on either side. I looked at the sea of yellow faces above the garish clothes—faces all happy and excited over this bit of fun, all certain that the elephant was going to be shot. They were watching me as they would watch a conjuror about to perform a trick. They did not like me, but with the magical rifle in my hands I was momentarily worth watching. And suddenly I realized that I should have to shoot the elephant after all. The people expected it of me and I had got to do it; I could feel their two thousand wills pressing me forward, irresistibly. And it was at this moment, as I stood there with the rifle in my hands, that I first grasped the hollowness, the futility of the white man's dominion in the East. Here was I, the white man with his gun, standing in front of the unarmed native crowd—seemingly the leading actor of the piece; but in reality I was only an absurd puppet pushed to and fro by the will of those yellow faces behind. I perceived in this moment that when

the white man turns tyrant it is his own freedom that he destroys. He becomes a sort of hollow, posing dummy, the conventionalized figure of a sahib. For it is the condition of his rule that he shall spend his life in trying to impress the "natives," and so in every crisis he has got to do what the "natives" expect of him. He wears a mask, and his face grows to fit it. I had got to shoot the elephant. I had committed myself to doing it when I sent for the rifle. A sahib has got to act like a sahib; he has got to appear resolute, to know his own mind and do definite things. To come all that way, rifle in hand, with two thousand people marching at my heels, and then to trail feebly away, having done nothing—no, that was impossible. The crowd would laugh at me. And my whole life, every white man's life in the East, was one long struggle not to be laughed at.

But I did not want to shoot the elephant. I watched him beating [8] his bunch of grass against his knees, with that preoccupied grandmotherly air that elephants have. It seemed to me that it would be murder to shoot him. At that age I was not squeamish about killing animals, but I had never shot an elephant and never wanted to. (Somehow it always seems worse to kill a *large* animal.) Besides, there was the beast's owner to be considered. Alive, the elephant was worth at least a hundred pounds; dead, he would only be worth the value of his tusks, five pounds, possibly. But I had got to act quickly. I turned to some experienced-looking Burmans who had been there when we arrived, and asked them how the elephant had been behaving. They all said the same thing: he took no notice of you if you left him alone, but he might charge if you went too close to him.

It was perfectly clear to me what I ought to do. I ought to walk [9] up to within, say, twenty-five yards of the elephant and test his behavior. If he charged, I could shoot; if he took no notice of me, it would be safe to leave him until the mahout came back. But also I knew that I was going to do no such thing. I was a poor shot with a rifle and the ground was soft mud into which one would sink at every step. If the elephant charged and I missed him, I should have about as much chance as a toad under a steam-roller. But even then I was not thinking particularly of my own skin, only of the watchful yellow faces behind. For at that moment, with the crowd watching me, I was not afraid in the ordinary sense, as I would have been if I had been alone. A white man mustn't be frightened in front of "natives"; and so, in general, he isn't frightened. The sole thought in my mind was that if anything went wrong those two thousand Burmans would see me pursued, caught, trampled on and reduced to a grinning corpse like that Indian up the hill. And if that happened it was quite probable that some of them would laugh. That would never do. There was only one alternative. I shoved the cartridges into the magazine and lay down on the road to get a better aim.

The crowd grew very still, and a deep, low, happy sigh, as of 10 people who see the theatre curtain go up at last, breathed from innumerable throats. They were going to have their bit of fun after all. The rifle was a beautiful German thing with cross-hair sights. I did not then know that in shooting an elephant one would shoot to cut an imaginary bar running from ear-hole to ear-hole. I ought, therefore, as the elephant was sideways on, to have aimed straight at his earhole; actually I aimed several inches in front of this, thinking the brain would be further forward.

When I pulled the trigger I did not hear the bang or feel the kick— 11 one never does when a shot goes home—but I heard the devilish roar of glee that went up from the crowd. In that instant, in too short a time, one would have thought, even for the bullet to get there, a mysterious, terrible change had come over the elephant. He neither stirred nor fell, but every line of his body had altered. He looked suddenly stricken, shrunken, immensely old, as though the frightful impact of the bullet had paralysed him without knocking him down. At last, after what seemed a long time—it might have been five seconds, I dare say—he sagged flabbily to his knees. His mouth slobbered. An enormous senility seemed to have settled upon him. One could have imagined him thousands of years old. I fired again into the same spot. At the second shot he did not collapse but climbed with desperate slowness to his feet and stood weakly upright, with legs sagging and head drooping. I fired a third time. That was the shot that did for him. You could see the agony of it jolt his whole body and knock the last remnant of strength from his legs. But in falling he seemed for a moment to rise, for as his hind legs collapsed beneath him he seemed to tower upward like a huge rock toppling, his trunk reaching skywards like a tree. He trumpeted, for the first and only time. And then down he came, his belly towards me, with a crash that seemed to shake the ground even where I lay.

I got up. The Burmans were already racing past me across the 12 mud. It was obvious that the elephant would never rise again, but he was not dead. He was breathing very rhythmically with long rattling gasps, his great mound of a side painfully rising and falling. His mouth was wide open. I could see far down into caverns of pale pink throat. I waited a long time for him to die, but his breathing did not weaken. Finally I fired my two remaining shots into the spot where I thought his heart must be. The thick blood welled out of him like red velvet, but still he did not die. His body did not even jerk when the shots hit him, the tortured breathing continued without a pause. He was dying, very slowly and in great agony, but in some world remote from me where not even a bullet could damage him further. I felt I had to put an end to that dreadful noise. It seemed dreadful to see the great beast lying there, powerless to move and yet powerless to die, and not even to be able to finish him. I sent back for my small rifle and poured shot after shot into his heart and down his throat. They seemed to make no impression. The tortured gasps continued as steadily as the ticking of a clock.

In the end I could not stand it any longer and went away. I heard 13 later that it took him half an hour to die. Burmans were bringing dahs and baskets even before I left, and I was told they had stripped his body almost to the bones by the afternoon.

Afterwards, of course, there were endless discussions about the 14 shooting of the elephant. The owner was furious, but he was only an Indian and could do nothing. Besides, legally I had done the right thing, for a mad elephant has to be killed, like a mad dog, if its owner fails to control it. Among the Europeans opinion was divided. The older men said I was right, the younger men said it was a damn shame to shoot an elephant for killing a coolie, because the elephant was worth more than any damn Coringhee coolie. And afterwards I was very glad that the coolie had been killed; it put me legally in the right and it gave me sufficient pretext for shooting the elephant. I often wondered whether any of the others grasped that I had done it solely to avoid looking a fool.

Underlining, Highlighting, Summarizing

Reading with a pencil in hand is a great aid to thinking. As you read, underline or highlight key expressions and those sentences that strike you as especially important, for instance topic sentences or sentences that seem to summarize. But beware of underlining and highlighting so much material that you merely make the text unread-able. For an especially complex or detailed essay, you probably will find it helpful to jot down a sentence summarizing each paragraph, or each group of closely related paragraphs, thus giving yourself a sort of outline of the essay you are reading.

Orwell's first two paragraphs, for instance, might be summarized thus:

1. Orwell, a police officer in Lower Burma, like other Europeans was assaulted in minor ways (unfairly tripped during a game) by the Burmans.
2. He was upset because he was anti-imperialist and pro-Burmese, but he was not educated enough to understand how to reconcile his hatred of empire with his hatred of the Burmese who made his life difficult.

Whether you will want—or need—to make an outline-summary of Orwell's essay depends on how difficult you found it. If you found "Shooting an Elephant" difficult to follow, you will get a better grasp of it by rereading it and making summaries of this sort. The act of summarizing each paragraph will, of course, help you grasp the meaning of the paragraphs. You won't want to write so much for an essay that strikes you as extremely easy, but at the very least you will want to jot down some key words and phrases. Making a list of key phrases or ideas or making an outline and writing a summary are laborious activities, but they are worth the effort; you will gain a closer knowledge of the material than can be gained by merely letting your eye run over the page, or even than can be gained by underlining or highlighting.

Asking Questions, Taking Notes

"It is thinking," the philosopher John Locke wrote, "that makes what we read ours." But when do you start writing about what you have read? And how do you begin? The answer is that if you have been reading closely you have already begun writing. You have had a pen or pencil in hand, a notebook or sheets of paper beside your book, probably a dictionary within arm's reach, perhaps a handbook, and, of course, a wastebasket. You have read with pen in hand not simply to record what you think, but to help you think. Assuming that you are reading a book that you own, as you read begin making discreet marks in the margins of the text. Not broad yellow lines through every other sentence—those will only distract you later and impede thoughtful rereading—but little checks, or brackets, or question marks next to passages that you find especially interesting, or puzzling, or quotable. On rereading, paying special attention to those passages, you may begin to detect a pattern that will disclose a topic and may eventually lead you to formulate a thesis.

Suppose you are going to write on "Shooting an Elephant." Possibly at this stage of the course your instructor is concerned with teaching a particular topic—let's say organization, or narration, or description, or the uses of foreshadowing—and therefore he or she limits the scope of your study of Orwell's essay to an examination of this topic. Perhaps the topic is organization. In reading or rereading the essay you notice that from the third paragraph through the next-to-last paragraph, Orwell is telling a story, but in the middle—not the end—he tells us the significance of the story. And so you mark the passage, perhaps with a question mark, perhaps with a pair of square brackets:

> And it was at this moment, as I stood there with the rifle in my hands, that I first grasped the hollowness, the futility of the white man's dominion in the East. . . . I perceived in this moment that when the white man turns tyrant it is his own freedom that he destroys. He becomes a sort of hollow, posing dummy, the conventionalized figure of a sahib.

You might even jot down some questions in your notebook. Why does Orwell spill the beans here, and why—pages later—does he describe at length the death throes of the elephant, since even without the elephant's lingering death he had come to his insight? Answers will vary (perhaps good reasons can be offered, or perhaps Orwell bungled the essay), but in noting and questioning this apparently unusual organization you may come to a fuller understanding of Orwell's essay (and you may also learn something about strategies of organization that you can apply to your own writing in other courses and after you leave college).

Of course, the passages that you mark, in one way or another, will depend largely on the assigned topic. For example, if your instructor's assignment includes words such as "summarize," "compare," "define," "evaluate," you will be alerted to think in particular directions. It's important to read the assignment carefully before you begin to work. It's equally important to consult and reread the assignment at various stages in your work to be sure you haven't wandered off the track—into summarizing or into writing a personal narrative, for example, when an analysis—a careful examination—was called for. If you don't understand the assignment, you should not hesitate to ask your instructor or a peer advisor for help. And you should start early enough so that you have time to know what your questions about the assignment are and get help with them.

Let's say, however, that the instructor has not assigned a topic but has left the choice up to you. Again, your jottings of various sorts (lists of key phrases, underlinings, formulation of Orwell's thesis, and perhaps a summary) should suggest various possibilities. Perhaps you were puzzled by Orwell's depiction of the Burmese, which doesn't seem terribly sympathetic for someone who claims to be on their side. "Sneering yellow faces," "no one had the guts to raise a riot"—such passages may be worth thinking about and writing about. Looking at the essay again you notice that although Orwell begins with more or less the conventional attitudes of the white oppressor, he increasingly reveals his sympathy for the Burmese without sentimentalizing them. An essay on Orwell's way of depicting the Burmese (and therefore to some extent on his way of depicting his own changing attitudes) as it develops in his essay is a possibility. At this point you might try writing a few sentences in your notebook.

Let's assume that on thinking further about "Shooting an Elephant" you come to feel that your greatest interest is in Orwell's political interpretation of his action. Now, in other words, you are *settling on a topic*. You keep coming back to that passage, in the middle, about his recognition of the nature of imperialism, and somehow you don't quite feel that Orwell has correctly interpreted his own experience. For one thing, you are bothered by what seems to you to be an act of cowardice on his part. Yes, the pressure on him was great—that mob at his back, his fear of losing face—and you see that Orwell has from the beginning of the essay carefully depicted the plight of the white man in Burma. But you still think that a person of greater moral fiber would have resisted the pressure and would not have shot the elephant. That is to say (and this is crucial in feeling your way toward your essay), you are beginning to *formulate a thesis statement*.

Free Writing

Perhaps now is the time to engage in what is called "free writing," or "free associating," or "pre-writing," scribbling away so that one idea on paper will help to call up another. What you produce at this stage is not so much a first draft as a zero draft, but it is invaluable as a means of developing your thoughts. Free writing is especially easy if you use a word processor; you can enter material with much less physical effort than is expended in pushing a pen across paper, and you will thus find that you can put down a good many ideas, some of which really will turn out to be good. Orwell, you may come to feel, is explaining away his own failure by giving it a grand significance, by inflating it with political meaning. And so now you are *refining the thesis*. (Almost surely, however, you will want to refine it further, when your ideas become somewhat clarified during the process of writing your first draft.)

The step after this will be to work out, at least tentatively, *strategies for putting forth this thesis*. How will you begin? With a quotation from Orwell? With a statement of your initial reaction to the essay? Which passages will you quote? What tone will you adopt? Will a comparison be useful? How personal should you get? You can't hope to settle all of these questions at once, and it will almost certainly be impossible for you to write an introductory paragraph. Fortunately, the only thing you need to do at this point is to *start writing*. With a topic in mind, an idea about it (your tentative thesis), and some rough notes, you start getting as many of your ideas on paper as you can.

Listing and Outlining

At this point it might be useful to sketch a very rough outline, a sort of shopping list of the points you want to make. Here is the outline with which one student began. Notice, by the way, how one idea gave rise to another. Making a list is not so much a matter of putting down ideas that you already have as a matter of *generating* ideas that you didn't know you had.

```
Sympathy for Orwell--how he creates it
His interpretation of shooting ("the system")
Why I don't buy it
Was he a "tyrant"?
Was he a "dummy"?
Maybe a coward?
How I interpret shooting: guilt
Why he misinterprets: Guilt
(End with something good?)
```

The First Draft

With some such rough outline in front of you, simply begin writing sentences. Don't worry about mechanical matters, such as spelling, or getting every word exactly right. Leave gaps in your sentences if you need to. What you are doing is writing a *rough draft* that no one else need ever see and that even you must not regard as sacred. You can always add or delete, or change a word, or even your mind. If you have written a rough outline you will probably tinker with that too as your ideas take clearer shape because you find more and more evidence to support or to modify the thesis.

When you reach this point, you are probably ready to try writing your introductory paragraph. If you own a word processor, you'll probably be ready now to open a file for your first draft. But if you share a word processor with many others, at a computer center, for example, it's probably more efficient, and certainly more courteous, to work through at least one draft by hand, or on your own typewriter. If you don't compose on a word processor, take a fresh sheet of paper for this job. If you find that your first effort is a false start, crumple the page and throw it away. Your next attempt, or your next after your next, will be better and will show you what parts of your draft can be used, what must be added, deleted, or rearranged.

Imagining Your Audience

When you reread your draft, try to imagine someone else reading it. You may have received, with your assignment, instructions about the audience your essay should address. If not, you must define for yourself the reader you intend to persuade, and then you must keep that reader in mind as you compose and revise. We suggest that you imagine your reader to be someone like you, a classmate perhaps. But it's helpful to imagine that your reader has *not* read the essay you're writing about; it is essential to imagine that your reader knows and understands the essay less well than you do. Your reader certainly does not know what assignment you are fulfilling, and could not have arrived, unassisted, at the thesis you are prepared to argue.

With such a reader in mind—obviously not your instructor—you will be careful to be clear and to be consistent. You will take care, for example, probably in your first paragraph, to identify, at least by author and title, the essay you are analyzing. A footnote following your first quotation from the essay will usually suffice to give your reader further details of where and when the essay was published.

Keeping your reader in mind will also help you to decide how much summary to include, where the summary is needed, how much detail it should contain, and at what points in your analysis—your examination of the essay you are responding to—an additional sentence or two of summary would be helpful. Imagining a real reader may also help to remind you that it is your job to analyze and to persuade, that is, to set forth a thoughtful response to the essay and not offer a mere synopsis. Summarize only enough to keep your real reader with you, following you step by step and, we hope, agreeing with each point you make.

Reading Your Draft

To write a good essay you must be a good reader not only of the essay you are writing about but also of the essay you yourself are writing. We're not talking about proofreading or correcting spelling errors, though of course you must engage also in those activities.

As you read your draft, keep in mind the fact that your essay should contain two theses and two voices—Orwell's thesis and voice, and your own thesis and voice. That is, the reader should be told, early and fairly, what Orwell's point is, and should get some sense of the way Orwell makes the point. The reader should also perceive *your* point, and be able to take some pleasure in the way in which you make your point. Note, too, that the point or thesis and the voice that predominates in the essay are yours (unless the assignment has been merely to summarize a published essay). That is, your essay is, finally, *your* essay—a thoughtful *response* to someone else's essay. It probably will begin with an introductory comment, and will then give a brief summary of the essay you are responding to, but chiefly it will set forth your own views.

Revising and Editing Your Draft

And then, of course, you revise (preferably after giving the manuscript a day's rest) and revise again, perhaps adding or deleting some quotations, and checking the quotations for accuracy. Perhaps now you are ready to give your essay a title. Your title may prompt you to make still further changes: substituting one quotation for another, finding more exact verbs for your draft, perhaps even adding new material, and almost certainly revising your conclusion.

At this point, try reading your essay aloud, preferably to a roommate, friend, or classmate. But if it is 3:00 A.M. and you alone are awake, read it aloud anyway (quietly). Again, imagine a real reader, or listener. You'll almost certainly find yourself deleting unnecessary repetitions and adding necessary transitions such as "but," "furthermore," and "on the other hand."

Finally, check spellings of words you're not sure of in a dictionary, and check doubtful constructions in a handbook. In short, you laboriously do all the things that will make your essay seem effortless to your reader. This includes typing (or writing legibly) and, after giving yourself and your manuscript as much rest as time allows, proofreading (and making final corrections as necessary).

Sample Essay

We have just described (partly by imagining them) the thought processes and the work of a student who wrote the following essay. We suggest that first you reread Orwell's essay. Then read the student's essay. Finally, reread her essay, this time glancing back at her rough outline and our marginal notes.

Title is provocative, and implies the thesis	Is Orwell's Elephant Big Enough to Hold Orwell's Interpretation?
Essay begins by identifying Orwell and showing appreciation of Orwell, i.e., shows fair-mindedness	George Orwell's "Shooting an Elephant" is a memorable essay about his experience as a British police officer in Burma, and it is almost the exciting story the title seems to promise. The beginning of the first sentence compels our attention: "In Moulmein, in Lower Burma, I was hated by large numbers of people." And, so
Identifies Orwell's tone	that on second thought this will not seem egotistical to the reader, Orwell wryly adds that this was "the only time in my life that I have been important enough for this to happen to
Reference to note citing source	me."[1] We can hardly fail to like the writer of this sentence. The next paragraph, too, with its sympathy for
Citation of source, and explanation of subsequent references	1. In The Little, Brown Reader, 5th ed., Marcia Stubbs and Sylvan Barnet, eds. (Glenview, Ill.: Scott, Foresman, 1989), p. 5. Subsequent references will be made parenthetically within the text.

Summary in which brief, relevant quotations let us hear Orwell's voice

Transition ("But") lets us know that essayist will now take a somewhat different view

Student's thesis statement

Repetition of "interpretation" provides transition

Relevant summary

Student clearly sets forth Orwell's thesis

Relevant summary

Page reference given

"the wretched prisoners huddling in the stinking cages of the lock-ups" presents us with a man who, because of his sympathy for the oppressed and because of his "intolerable sense of guilt," gains our sympathy. But to say that we sympathize with Orwell is not to say that we have to share all of his opinions. Although we have to take his word for what happened when he shot the elephant, and we recognize that he has first-hand experience of imperialism, we do not have to believe that his interpretation of his experience gives us the truth about the nature of imperialism.

He first presents his interpretation just beyond the middle of the essay—just as Orwell is about to shoot the elephant (page 8). He explains not one but two things. He explains why he shot the elephant, and he also explains, or claims to explain, the contradiction of imperialism: "When the white man turns tyrant it is his own freedom that he destroys. He becomes a sort of hollow, posing dummy." Now, in "Shooting an Elephant" Orwell admits that he became a sort of dummy. He felt that he was forced to shoot the elephant because the Burmese wanted him to shoot it, and he was afraid not to live up to their expectations. He was afraid, he says, that if he didn't shoot the elephant "the crowd would laugh at me" (p. 9). Orwell has effectively prepared us for the terrible power of contemptuous laughter when, in his first paragraph, he says, "The crowd yelled with hideous laughter." Nevertheless the generalization about what happens "when the white man turns tyrant" is not really

supported. In the first place, Orwell
does not give us any reason to believe that he was a tyrant. True, he
was a British police officer in
Burma, and thus he was a representative of imperial England, but nothing
in the essay suggests that he was
cruel or even unfair. We do know,
however, that his work as a policeman
produced in him "an intolerable sense
of guilt" (page 5), and this, I
think, is a clue to Orwell's interpretation of his act.

First sentence of new
paragraph offers a
clear transition

What was his act? Under pressure
from a crowd, he needlessly killed an
elephant. He certainly should feel
guilt for killing a harmless beast,
and also for depriving the owner of
valuable property. And he should feel
guilt, I think, for yielding to the
pressure of the crowd. I am not saying that I wouldn't have yielded too,

Student does not
overstate her criticism

but I am saying that it was wrong to
yield and that a stronger person
would have said to himself or herself, "Never mind what all of these
people think; the elephant is harmless and I won't shoot it." Perhaps
if he had refused to shoot the elephant the malicious jeers would soon
have turned into cheers for the brave
sahib who dared to face a crazy elephant and then walked calmly away.

Clarification of
student's thesis

But Orwell did yield to the mob,
and he felt guilty for doing so. It
is probably this guilt, this awareness of his weakness, rather than the
guilt about being a policeman in
Burma, that is at the heart of the
essay. But apparently he couldn't
face it. Despite his modesty and his
no doubt genuine sympathy for the
victims of imperialism, he shifts the
blame from himself to, as we now say,

"the system." It isn't really his fault, Orwell says in effect, that he was a coward; it is the nature of imperialism to turn the imperialist into a coward, a "dummy."

Again essayist tries to be fair and not seem superior to author she is analyzing; good tone

Let me say again that, judging from this essay, Orwell was in many ways a decent person, and we can admire his honesty when he admits, in the last line, that he killed the elephant "solely to avoid looking a fool." This humble confession certainly gains our sympathy, and if the essay were entirely about his deed and his awareness of his weakness there would be nothing to complain about. But Orwell tries to explain away his failure by seeing himself as (no less than the Burmese) the victim of imperialism. Finally, then for all of his good nature and his modesty and his confession of weakness, he presents himself as innocent. He <u>had</u> to shoot the elephant, he wants us to believe, because imperialists <u>have</u> to do what their victims want them to do. His comments about the nature of imperialism may or may not be true. But it seems clear, even from his own essay, that Orwell's action in the last analysis resulted not from "the nature of imperialism," as he claims, but from Orwell's own failure of nerve.

Forceful ending

Restatement of student's thesis

Our marginal comments offer our chief views, but a brief restatement and amplification may be useful:

1. Although the title may be a trifle strained, it at least provides the reader with a focus, and thus it is far better than such an unhelpful title as "George Orwell's 'Shooting an Elephant' " or "On 'Shooting an Elephant.' "
2. Keeping her audience in mind, the student helpfully identifies and summarizes Orwell's essay.

3. The writer's tone is satisfactory. She is critical of Orwell, but she avoids overstating her case or condescending to him.

Using Quotations

Our marginal comments call your attention to some of the essay's strengths as well as to some of the conventions of editing your final draft. Here we remind you of procedures for using quotations (covered in detail in most handbooks). These procedures are not noteworthy when handled properly, but they become noticeable and even ruinous to your essay when bungled. Read the following reminders over, check them against the student's essay you just read, and consult them again the first few times you write about an essay.

1. *Quote.* Quotations from the work under discussion provide indispensable support for your thesis.
2. *Don't overquote.* Most of the essay should consist of your own words.
3. *Quote briefly.* Use quotations as evidence, not as padding.
4. *Comment on what you quote,* immediately before or immediately after the quotation. Make sure your reader understands why you find the quotation relevant. Don't count on the quotation to make your point for you.
5. *Take care with embedded quotations* (quotations within a sentence of your own). A quotation must fit grammatically into the sentence of which it is a part.

Incorrect:

> The first sentence does not sound egotistical because "the only time in my life that I have been important enough for this to happen to me."

Correct:

> The first sentence does not sound egotistical because Orwell adds that this was "the only time in my life that I have been important enough for this to happen to me."

Don't try to fit a long quotation into the middle of one of your own sentences. It is almost impossible for the reader to come out of the quotation and pick up the thread of your sentence. It is better to lead into a long quotation with "Orwell says," and then, after quoting, to begin a new sentence of your own.

6. *Quote exactly.* Any material that you add (to make the quotation coherent with your sentence) must be in square brackets. Thus:

> Orwell says the torture of prisoners "oppressed [him] with an intolerable sense of guilt."

An ellipsis (any material that you omit from within a quotation) must be indicated by three spaced periods:

> He knew that "a sahib has got to . . . know his own mind and do definite things."

If a quotation ends before the end of the author's sentence, add a period and then three spaced periods to indicate the omission:

> As Orwell claims, "it was a tiny incident in itself. . . ."

(Orwell's sentence followed the word "itself" with "but it gave me a better glimpse than I had had before of the real nature of imperialism—the real motives for which despotic governments act.")

7. *Quote fairly.* It would not be fair, for example, to say "Orwell claims he 'had done the right thing' " when in fact he says "legally I had done the right thing." His qualification "legally" is important, and it would be unfair to omit it.

8. *Identify the quotation* clearly for your reader. Notice in this essay such helpful expressions as "Orwell . . . adds," and "The next paragraph . . . represents," as well as references to pages.

9. *Identify the source of quotations in a footnote,* or in a list of Works Cited if you are using more than one source.

10. *Check your punctuation.* Remember: Periods and commas go inside of quotation marks, semicolons and colons go outside. Question marks and exclamation points go inside if they are part of the quotation, outside if they are your own.

A Checklist for Analyzing and Evaluating an Essay That You Are Writing About

When you read, try to read sympathetically, opening yourself to the writer's vision of things. But when you have finished a sympathetic reading, and an attentive reading, and you have made various sorts of notes, probably including an outline and a summary of the essay you are reading, you are ready to *analyze* the writer's methods and to *evaluate* the piece.

In analyzing, you will examine the relationships between the parts; that is, you will ask such questions as:

What is the *topic* of the essay (see page 4). Try to state it, preferably in writing, as specifically as possible. For example, broadly speaking one might say that the subject of Orwell's "Shooting an Elephant" (page 5) is British imperialism in India, but within this subject his topic, more specifically, is the effects of imperialism on the imperialists themselves.

What is the essay's *thesis* (either stated or implied)? If you have located a *thesis sentence* in the essay, underline it and write *thesis* in the margin. If the thesis is implied, try to formulate it in a sentence of your own.

What does the title do? What *purpose* does it suggest the writer holds?

What is the function of the opening paragraph (or paragraphs)? What claim on our attention or beliefs does it make?

What speaker or *persona* (see pages 704–705) does the writer create, and how does the writer create it?

Does the tone (page 2) shift as the essay progresses? If so, why does it shift?

What *audience* is the writer addressing? The general, literate public, or a more specialized group?

How is the argument set forth? By logic? By drawing on personal experience? What evidence is there that the writer is an authority on the topic? Are there other appeals to authority? What other kinds of evidence support the essay's claim? What are the author's underlying assumptions? Are they stated or implied, and are they acceptable to you, or can you challenge them?

If there is a formal, explicit conclusion, underline or restate it. If the conclusion is not stated, but is implied, what does the writer want us to conclude?

In evaluating, you will ask such questions as:

Is the essay as clear as it can be, given the complexity of the material? For example, do specific examples help to make the generalizations clear? Are crucial terms adequately defined? If the thesis is not explicitly stated, is the essay unclear or is it perhaps better because of the indirectness?

If the conclusion is not stated but implied, why does the writer not
     state it?
Is the argument (if the essay is chiefly an argument) convincing, or is
     it marred by faulty thinking? If statistics are used, are they sound
     and relevant? If authorities are quoted, are they indeed authorities
     (rather than just big names) on this topic?
Is the essay interesting? If so, in what ways, and if not, why not?—
     which gets us back to analysis. If there are passages of undisguised
     argument, for instance, are they clear without being repetitious
     and boring? Do specific examples clarify and enliven general as-
     sertions?
If the essay includes narrative or descriptive passages, are they per-
     tinent? Should they have been amplified, or should they have been
     reduced or even deleted?
How is the essay organized? Is the organization effective? Does the
     essay build to a climax?

Another way of thinking about the criteria for evaluating an essay
is this:

Is the essay persuasive (whether because of its logic or because of the
     power of the speaker's personality)? and,
Does the essay give pleasure?

Don't hesitate to demand that an essay give you pleasure. The
author probably thought that he or she was writing well, and certainly
hoped to hold your interest throughout the essay and to make you
feel that you were learning something of interest. In short, the author
hoped that you would like the essay. You have every right to evaluate
the essay partly by considering the degree of pleasure that it affords.
Of course, in *your* essay you cannot simply say that you enjoyed an
essay or that you were bored by it. You will have to support your
assertions with reasons based on evidence. To support your assertions
you must have read the writer's words carefully, so we are back to an
earlier point: the first thing to do if you are going to write about a piece
of writing is to read it attentively, pen or pencil in hand.
     As you read and reread the material that you are writing about,
subjecting it to the kinds of questions we have mentioned, your understanding of it will almost surely deepen. You will probably come
to feel that it is better—or worse—than you had thought at first, or
in any case somewhat different.

As you prepare to write your own essay, and as you draft it, you are learning, feeling your way toward a considered analysis. All writers are in the position of the little girl who, told by an adult that she should think before she spoke, replied, "How do I know what I think until I say it?" But once having said something—whether in a mental question to yourself or in a note or a draft—you have to evaluate your thought, and improve it if it doesn't stand up under further scrutiny.

2
ALL IN THE FAMILY

"*While we're at supper, Billy, you'd make Daddy and Mommy very happy if you'd remove your hat, your sunglasses, and your earring.*"

Courtesy of the Göteborgs Konstmuseum

Feeding Time
Paul Martin, 1892

Short Views

After a certain age, the more one becomes oneself, the more obvious one's family traits become.
Marcel Proust

All happy families resemble one another; every unhappy family is unhappy in its own fashion.
Leo Tolstoy, *Anna Karenina*

On Tuesday, March 31, he and I dined at General Paoli's. A question was started, whether the state of marriage was natural to man. Johnson. "Sir, it is so far from being natural for a man and woman to live in a state of marriage, that we find all the motives which they have for remaining in that connection, and the restraints which civilized society imposes to prevent separation, are hardly sufficient to keep them together." The General said, that in a state of nature a man and woman uniting together would form a strong and constant affection, by the mutual pleasure each would receive; and that the same causes of dissension would not arise between them, as occur between husband and wife in a civilized state. Johnson. "Sir, they would have dissensions enough, though of another kind. One would choose to go a hunting in this wood, the other in that; one would choose to go a fishing in this lake, the other in that; or, perhaps, one would choose to go a hunting, when the other would choose to go a fishing; and so they would part. Besides, Sir, a savage man and a savage woman meet by chance; and when the man sees another woman that pleases him better, he will leave the first."
James Boswell

Marriage is the best of human statuses and the worst, and it will continue to be. And that is why, though its future in some form or other is as assured as anything can be, this future is as equivocal as its past. The demands that men and women make on marriage will never be fully met; they cannot be.
Jessie Bernard

32

A slavish bondage to parents cramps every faculty of the mind; and Mr. Locke very judiciously observes, that "if the mind be curbed and humbled too much in children, if their spirits be abased and broken much by too strict an hand over them, they lose all their vigour and industry." This strict hand may in some degree account for the weakness of women; for girls, from various causes, are more kept down by their parents, in every sense of the word, than boys. The duty expected from them is, like all the duties arbitrarily imposed on women, more from a sense of propriety, more out of respect for decorum, than reason; and thus taught slavishly to submit to their parents, they are prepared for the slavery of marriage. I may be told that a number of women are not slaves in the marriage state. True, but they then become tyrants; for it is not rational freedom, but a lawless kind of power resembling the authority exercised by the favourites of absolute monarchs, which they obtain by debasing means.
Mary Wollstonecraft

Twenty years from now humanity will be in the midst of one of its most painful and difficult social changes. This century will be the last in which families of more than two children can be tolerated; everyone knows this, and the only argument is over the means of achieving the goal. But there is another aspect of the matter which is seldom given much serious consideration.

The two-child family is not large enough to generate the interactions that develop a good personality; this is why single children are often monsters. Probably the optimum number of siblings is four or five—twice the permissible quota. This means that, somehow, several families must be psychologically fused together for the health of the child, and of society. Working out ways of doing this will raise the blood pressure of a whole generation of lawyers and moralists.
Arthur C. Clarke

Nobody who has not been in the interior of a family can say what the difficulties of any individual of that family may be.
Jane Austen, *Emma*

Lewis Coser

The Family

Following the French anthropologist Claude Lévi-Strauss,   1
we can define the family as a group manifesting these characteristics:
it finds its origin in marriage; it consists of husband, wife and children
born in their wedlock—though other relatives may find their place
close to that nuclear group; and the members of the group are united
by moral, legal, economic, religious, and social rights and obligations.
These include a network of sexual rights and prohibitions and a variety
of socially patterned feelings such as love, attraction, piety, awe, and
so on.

The family is among the few universal institutions of mankind.   2
No known society lacks small kinship groups of parents and children
related through the process of reproduction. But recognition of the
universality of this institution must immediately be followed by the
acknowledgment that its forms are exceedingly varied. The fact that
many family organizations are not monogamic, as in the West, led
many nineteenth-century observers to the erroneous conclusion that
in "early" stages of evolution there existed no families, and that "group
marriage," institutionalized promiscuity, prevailed. This is emphatically not the case; even though patterned wife-lending shocked the
sensibilities of Victorian anthropologists, such an institution is evidently predicated on the fact that men have wives in the first place.
No matter what their specific forms, families in all known societies
have performed major social functions—reproduction, maintenance,
socialization, and social placement of the young.

Families may be monogamous or polygamous—there are systems   3
where one man is entitled to several wives and others where several
husbands share one wife. A society may recognize primarily the small
nuclear conjugal unit of husband and wife with their immediate de-
scendants or it may institutionalize the large extended family linking
several generations and emphasizing consanguinity more than the conjugal bond. Residence after marriage may be matrilocal, patrilocal or

Lewis Coser, born in Berlin, in 1913, was educated at the Sorbonne in Paris and
at Columbia University, where he received a Ph.D. in sociology in 1954. He now
teaches at the State University of New York, Stony Brook, and holds the title
Distinguished Professor.

neolocal; exchanges of goods and services between families at the time of marriage may be based on bride price, groom price or an equal exchange; endogamous or exogamous regulations may indicate who is and who is not eligible for marriage; the choice of a mate may be controlled by parents or it may be left in large measure to the young persons concerned. These are but a few of the many differences which characterize family structures in variant societies.

Questions

1. At the end of paragraph 2, Coser writes: "No matter what their specific forms, families in all known societies have performed major social functions—reproduction, maintenance, socialization, and social placement of the young." What does "socialization" mean? How does it differ from "social placement of the young"? What specific forms does each take in our society?
2. Can you give examples of "moral, legal, economic, religious, and social rights and obligations" (paragraph 1) that unite members of a family?
3. Compare Coser and Plumb (pages 35–39) on the social functions of the family. According to Plumb, what responsibility does the family in our society have in performing the social functions Coser lists? How do other institutions compete with the family in performing some of these functions?

J. H. Plumb

The Dying Family

I was rather astonished when a minibus drove up to my   1 house and out poured ten children. They had with them two parents, but not one child had them both in common as mother and father,

J[ohn] H[arold] Plumb, born in England in 1911, was professor of modern English history at the University of Cambridge until his retirement. He also taught at universities in the United States.

and two of them belonged to neither parent, but to a former husband of the wife who had died. Both parents, well into middle age, had just embarked, one on his fourth, the other on her third marriage. The children, who came in all sizes, and ranged from blonde nordic to jet-haired Greek, bounded around the garden, young and old as happy as any children that I have seen. To them, as Californians, their situation was not particularly odd; most of their friends had multiple parents. Indeed to them perhaps the odd family was the one which Western culture has held up as a model for two thousand years or more—the lifelong union of man and wife. But it took me a very long time to believe that they could be either happy or adjusted. And yet, were they a sign of the future, a way the world was going?

Unlike anthropologists or sociologists, historians have not studied   2
family life very closely. Until recently we knew very little of the age at which people married in Western Europe in the centuries earlier than the nineteenth or how many children they had, or what the rates of illegitimacy might be or whether, newly wed, they lived with their parents or set up a house of their own. Few of these questions can be answered with exactitude even now, but we can make better guesses. We know even less, however, of the detailed sexual practices that marriage covered: indeed this is a subject to which historians are only just turning their attention. But we do know much more of the function of family life—its social role—particularly if we turn from the centuries to the millennia and pay attention to the broad similarities rather than the fascinating differences between one region and another: and, if we do, we realize that the family has changed far more profoundly than even the bus load of Californians might lead us to expect.

Basically the family has fulfilled three social functions—to provide   3
a basic labor force, to transmit property and to educate and train children not only into an accepted social pattern, but also in the work skills upon which their future subsistence would depend. Until very recent times, the vast majority of children never went to any school: their school was the family, where they learned to dig and sow and reap and herd their animals, or they learned their father's craft of smith or carpenter or potter. The unitary family was particularly good at coping with the small peasant holdings which covered most of the world's fertile regions from China to Peru. In the primitive peasant world a child of four or five could begin to earn its keep in the fields, as they still can in India and Africa: and whether Moslem, Hindu, Inca or Christian, one wife at a time was all that the bulk of the world's population could support, even though their religion permitted them

more. Indeed, it was the primitive nature of peasant economy which gave the family, as we know it, its wide diffusion and its remarkable continuity.

Whether or not it existed before the neolithic revolution we shall never know, but certainly it must have gained in strength as families became rooted to the soil. Many very primitive people who live in a pre-agrarian society of hunting and food-gathering often tend to have a looser structure of marriage and the women a far greater freedom of choice and easier divorce, as with the Esquimaux, than is permitted in peasant societies. There can be little doubt that the neolithic revolution created new opportunities for the family as we know it, partly because this revolution created new property relations. More importantly it created great masses of property, beyond anything earlier societies had known. True, there were a few hunting peoples, such as the Kwakiutl Indians, who had considerable possessions—complex lodges, great pieces of copper and piles of fibre blankets, which periodically they destroyed in great battles of raging pride—but the property, personal or communal, of most primitive hunting people is usually trivial.

After the revolution in agriculture, property and its transmission lay at the very heart of social relations and possessed an actuality which we find hard to grasp. Although we are much richer, possessions are more anonymous, often little more than marks in a ledger, and what we own constantly changes. Whereas for the majority of mankind over this last seven thousand years property has been deeply personal and familial: a plot of land, if not absolute ownership over it, then valuable rights in it; sometimes a house, even though it be a hovel by our standards; perhaps no more than the tools and materials of a craft, yet these possessions were the route both to survival and to betterment. Hence they were endowed with manna, bound up with the deepest roots of personality. In all societies the question of property became embedded in every aspect of family life, particularly marriage and the succession and rights of children. Because of property's vital importance, subservience of women and children to the will of the father, limited only by social custom, became the pattern of most great peasant societies. Marriage was sanctified not only by the rites of religion, but by the transmission of property. Few societies could tolerate freedom of choice in marriage—too much vital to the success or failure of a family depended on it: an ugly girl with five cows was a far fairer prospect than a pretty girl with one. And because of the sexual drives of frail human nature, the customs of marriage and of family relationships needed to be rigorously enforced. Tradition sanctified them; religion blessed them. Some societies reversed the sexually restrictive nature of permanent marriage and permitted additional wives, but such permission was meaningless to the mass of the peasantry who fought a desperate battle to support a single family. And, as we shall see, the patterns of family life were always looser for the rich and the favored.

But a family was always more than property expressed clearly and 6
visibly in real goods; it was for thousands of years both a school and a tribunal, the basic unit of social organization whose function in modern society has been very largely taken over by the state. In most peasant societies, life is regulated by the village community, by the patriarchs of the village, and the only officer of the central government these villagers see with any regularity is the tax-gatherer; but in societies that have grown more complex, and this is particularly true of the West during the last four hundred years, life has become regulated by the nation state or by the growth in power and importance of more generalized local communities—the town or county.

This has naturally weakened the authority of heads of families, a 7
fact that can be symbolically illustrated by change in social custom. No child in Western Europe would sit unbidden in the presence of its parents until the eighteenth century: if it did it could be sure of rebuke and punishment. No head of a household would have thought twice about beating a recalcitrant young servant or apprentice before the end of the nineteenth century. For a younger brother to marry without the consent of his eldest brother would have been regarded as a social enormity; and sisters were disposable property. All of this power has vanished. Indeed the family ties of all of us have been so loosened that we find it hard to grasp the intensity of family relationships or their complexity, they have disintegrated so rapidly this last hundred years. Now nearly every child in the Western world, male or female, is educated outside the family from five years of age. The skills they learn are rarely, if ever, transmitted by parents: and what is more they learn about the nature of their own world, its social structure and its relationships in time outside the family. For millennia the family was the great transmitter and formulator of social custom; but it now only retains a shadow of this function, usually for very young children only.

Although the economic and education functions of the family have 8
declined, most of us feel that it provides the most satisfactory emotional basis for human beings; that a secure family life breeds stability, a capacity not only for happiness, but also to adjust to society's demands. This, too, may be based on misjudgment, for family life in the

past was not remarkable for its happiness. We get few glimpses into the private lives of men and women long dead, but when we do we often find strain, frustration, petty tyranny. For so many human beings family life was a prison from which they could not escape. And although it might create deep satisfactions here and there, the majority of the rich and affluent classes of the last four hundred years in Western Europe created for themselves a double standard, particularly as far as sex was concerned. In a few cities such as Calvin's Geneva, the purity of family life might be maintained, but the aristocracies of France, Italy and Britain tolerated, without undue concern, adultery, homosexuality and that sexual freedom which, for better or worse, we consider the hallmark of modern life. Indeed the family as the basic social group began firstly to fail, except in its property relations, amongst the aristocracy.

But what we think of as a social crisis of this generation—the rapid 9 growth of divorce, the emancipation of women and adolescents, the sexual and educational revolutions, even the revolution in eating which is undermining the family as the basis of nourishment, for over a hundred years ago the majority of Europeans never ate in public in their lives—all of these things, which are steadily making the family weaker and weaker, are the inexorable result of the changes in society itself. The family as a unit of social organization was remarkably appropriate for a less complex world of agriculture and craftsmanship, a world which stretches back some seven thousand years, but ever since industry and highly urbanized societies began to take its place, the social functions of the family have steadily weakened—and this is a process that is unlikely to be halted. And there is no historical reason to believe that human beings could be less or more happy, less or more stable. Like any other human institution the family has always been molded by the changing needs of society, sometimes slowly, sometimes fast. And that bus load of children does no more than symbolize the failure, not of marriage, but of the role of the old-fashioned family unit in a modern, urbanized, scientific and affluent society.

Questions

1. In paragraph 3 Plumb uses the term "unitary family," but he does not define it. How might it be defined? Explain how you arrived at your definition.
2. Paraphrase the sentence (in paragraph 5) "Hence they were endowed with manna, bound up with the deepest roots of personality."

3. Plumb says (paragraph 9) that "the revolution in eating" is "undermining the family as the basis of nourishment." Explain. To what extent do you agree that a family's eating habits reveal its stability?

Judy Syfers

Why I Want a Wife

I belong to that classification of people known as wives. I   1
am A Wife. And, not altogether incidentally, I am a mother.

Not too long ago a male friend of mine appeared on the scene   2
fresh from a recent divorce. He had one child, who is, of course, with
his ex-wife. He is looking for another wife. As I thought about him
while I was ironing one evening, it suddenly occurred to me that I,
too, would like to have a wife. Why do I want a wife?

I would like to go back to school so that I can become economically   3
independent, support myself, and, if need be, support those dependent upon me. I want a wife who will work and send me to school.
And while I am going to school I want a wife to take care of my children. I want a wife to keep track of the children's doctor and dentist
appointments. And to keep track of mine, too. I want a wife to make
sure my children eat properly and are kept clean. I want a wife who
will wash the children's clothes and keep them mended. I want a wife
who is a good nurturant attendant to my children, who arranges for
their schooling, makes sure that they have an adequate social life with
their peers, takes them to the park, the zoo, etc. I want a wife who
takes care of the children when they are sick, a wife who arranges to
be around when the children need special care, because, of course I
cannot miss classes at school. My wife must arrange to lose time at
work and not lose the job. It may mean a small cut in my wife's income

Judy Syfers was born in San Francisco in 1937. She received a bachelor's degree
from the University of Iowa in 1960 and wanted to do the graduate work that
would qualify her for teaching in a university, but she was dissuaded by her male
teachers. "Why I Want a Wife" originally appeared in the first issue of Ms.

from time to time, but I guess I can tolerate that. Needless to say, my wife will arrange and pay for the care of the children while my wife is working.

I want a wife who will take care of *my* physical needs. I want a   4
wife who will keep my house clean. A wife who will pick up after my children, a wife who will pick up after me. I want a wife who will keep my clothes clean, ironed, mended, replaced when need be, and who will see to it that my personal things are kept in their proper place so that I can find what I need the minute I need it. I want a wife who cooks the meals, a wife who is a *good* cook. I want a wife who will plan the menus, do the necessary grocery shopping, prepare the meals, serve them pleasantly, and then do the cleaning up while I do my studying. I want a wife who will care for me when I am sick and sympathize with my pain and loss of time from school. I want a wife to go along when our family takes a vacation so that someone can continue to care for me and my children when I need a rest and a change of scene.

I want a wife who will not bother me with rambling complaints   5
about a wife's duties. But I want a wife who will listen to me when I feel the need to explain a rather difficult point I have come across in my course of studies. And I want a wife who will type my papers for me when I have written them.

I want a wife who will take care of the details of my social life.   6
When my wife and I are invited out by my friends, I want a wife who will take care of the babysitting arrangements. When I meet people at school that I like and want to entertain, I want a wife who will have the house clean, will prepare a special meal, serve it to me and my friends, and not interrupt when I talk about things that interest me and my friends. I want a wife who will have arranged that the children are fed and ready for bed before my guests arrive so that the children do not bother us. I want a wife who takes care of the needs of my guests so that they feel comfortable, who makes sure that they have an ashtray, that they are passed the hors d'oeuvres, that they are offered a second helping of the food, that their wine glasses are replenished when necessary, that their coffee is served to them as they like it. And I want a wife who knows that sometimes I need a night out by myself.

I want a wife who is sensitive to my sexual needs, a wife who   7
makes love passionately and eagerly when I feel like it, a wife who makes sure that I am satisfied. And, of course, I want a wife who will not demand sexual attention when I am not in the mood for it. I want

a wife who assumes the complete responsibility for birth control, because I do not want more children. I want a wife who will remain sexually faithful to me so that I do not have to clutter up my intellectual life with jealousies. And I want a wife who understands that *my* sexual needs may entail more than strict adherence to monogamy. I must, after all, be able to relate to people as fully as possible.

If, by chance, I find another person more suitable as a wife than 8
the wife I already have, I want the liberty to replace my present wife with another one. Naturally, I will expect a fresh, new life; my wife will take the children and be solely responsible for them so that I am left free.

When I am through with school and have a job, I want my wife 9
to quit working and remain at home so that my wife can more fully and completely take care of a wife's duties.

My God, who *wouldn't* want a wife?   10

Questions

1. Does the second sentence of the essay mean anything different from the first? If so, what? If not, why is it there?
2. Describing a recently divorced man, Syfers says in paragraph 2: "He had one child, who is, of course, with his ex-wife." What information does "of course" convey? What attitude or tone?
3. If the constant repetition of "I want a wife who . . ." is not boring, what keeps it from being boring?
4. Syfers is attacking sexual stereotyping. Do you find in her essay any assumptions or details that limit the stereotyping to an economic class, or to an ethnic or racial group? Explain.

Julie Matthaei

Political Economy and Family Policy

O*ur current, "natural" family system, based on biological sim-* 1
ilarities and differences, is in crisis. Not only are its institutions breaking
down, they are also under attack as unjust, unequal, and unfree. The "natural"
family system needs to be replaced by a consciously social family system; this
means socializing parenting costs and pursuing policies which attack the sexual
division of labor and better integrate economic and family life.

The family plays a central role in the distribution of income and 2
wealth in our society, reproducing class, race, and gender inequalities.
This paper will 1) present a radical and feminist analysis of the "traditional" family system, 2) discuss the recent breakdown of this system, 3) present a radical and feminist critique of the traditional family
system, and 4) indicate social policies which would build a family system more consistent with the principles of equality, freedom, and social justice.

The "Natural" Family

The development of capitalism and wage labor in the nineteenth-cen- 3
tury U.S. brought with it new familial institutions. The family continued to be patriarchal—ruled by the husband/father—but was less
defined by and involved in commodity production, either as a family
firm, or as a family enslaved to producing for others. The family
emerged as an increasingly personal and feminine sphere, physically
separate and distinct from the competitive and masculine economy
(Matthaei 1982). Since, in the nineteenth century, "scientific" explanations of social life were replacing the former religious ones, the new
familial institutions were viewed as "natural," and stress was placed

Julie Matthaei teaches economics at Wellesley College and is active with the
Economic Literacy Project of Women for Economic Justice of Boston. She is
the author of *An Economic History of Women in America* and is working on a
book entitled *Beyond Sex and Blood: Economy, Family, and the Breakdown of
the "Natural" Family.*

on their determination by biological similarities and differences. This "natural"[1] family system has three, interconnected parts:

1. *"Natural" Marriage.* Marriage is seen as a union of naturally different and complementary beings: men/males and women/females (biological sex and social gender are equated). Men and women are believed to be instinctually heterosexual; those who form homosexual liaisons are viewed as unnatural and perverted.[2] Men are seen as natural bread-winners, competing in the economy, and women as natural homemakers, caring for their husbands and children in the home, and segregated into dead-end, low paid "women's jobs." Forced into this sexual division of labor, men and women need one another to be socially complete, and in order to undertake the essential function of marriage, which is seen as . . .

2. *"Natural" Parenting.* Parenting is seen as the biological production of offspring, a process in which adults pass on their identities and wealth to their children, to "their own flesh and blood." Children are seen as the responsibility and property of their parents. Women/females are seen as naturally endowed with special maternal instincts which make them more qualified than men/males for parenting.

3. *"Natural" Community.* Connected to the view of family life as natural is a white racist view of society which divides people into races and views whites as the biologically superior race. Whites rationalize their political and economic domination of people of color not only as natural but also as part of "white man's burden to civilize the savages."[3] Races and white supremacy are perpetuated as social entities by the prohibition of racial intermarriage; by the passing down of wealth or poverty, language and culture to one's children; and by racially segregated institutions such as housing and job markets.

The Breakdown of the "Natural" Family System

In the last fifteen years, the "natural" family system has been breaking down and coming under increasing attack by feminists and others.   4

1. *Married women have entered the labor force and "men's jobs" in growing*   5

---

[1] Natural is in quotes because the "natural" family system is actually a social product.

[2] In contrast, previous times viewed homosexual attractions as natural (and shared by all) but immoral and not to be acted on (Weeks 1979).

[3] Similarly, whites in the Eugenics movement argued that poor whites had inferior genes, and worked to limit their reproduction (Gould 1981).

numbers, challenging the "natural" sexual division of labor. Now over half of married women are in paid jobs at any one time. Women are demanding entry into the better-paid "men's jobs," and pressing their husbands to do "women's work" in the home. The "natural" marriage union between a bread-winning husband and a homemaking wife has become the exception rather than the rule, characterizing only 29% of husband/wife couples in 1985 (Current Population Reports March 1985).

2. *Married women's labor force participation has created a crisis in day*   6
care: there is a severe shortage of day care facilities, especially affordable ones.
In New York, for example, between 830,000 and 1.2 million preschool and school-age children vie for the fewer than 135,000 available licensed child care placements (Select Committee on Children 1987). The shortage of day care, combined with the absence of flexible jobs, forces parents to use make-shift arrangements: 2.1 million or 7% of 5–13 year olds whose mothers work outside the home are admittedly left unsupervised; actual numbers are much higher (Children's Defense Fund 1987).

3. *Growing numbers are not living in husband/wife families;* only 57%   7
of all households include married couples. Adults are marrying later, spending more time living alone (23.4% of all households) or with friends or lovers. Homosexuality appears to be on the rise, and gays are coming out of the closet and demanding their rights. Marriages have become very unstable; divorce rates more than tripled between 1960 and 1982, more than doubling the number of female-headed households (1986 and 1987 Statistical Abstracts).

4. *"Natural" parenting is on the wane.* Divorces create "unnatural"   8
female-headed households, most with dependent children. Unwed mothering has increased to comprise 1 in 5 births and over half of all births among blacks (1987 Statistical Abstract). Remarriages create "unnatural" families, with step-parents and -siblings. More "unnatural" is the trend for sterile couples, gays, and singles to obtain children through artificial insemination, surrogate mothers, and inter-country inter-racial adoptions.

What do these trends mean? Members of the so-called Moral Majority interpret them as the breakdown of *the* family; their solution,   9
embodied in the Family Protection Act of the late 1970s and early 1980s, is to put the "natural" family back together: encourage marriage; discourage divorce, unwed mothering, homosexuality; and get married women out of men's jobs and back into the home. The radical perspective is the opposite; the "natural" family is only one of many pos-

sible family systems, a very oppressive and ineffective one at that, as the next section will show. Growing numbers are rejecting the "natural" family system, and trying to create alternative family structures. What society needs is a radical family policy to focus and facilitate this process of dismantling of the old family system and constructing a new and more liberated one.

The Radical Critique of the "Natural" Family

The radical critique of the "natural" family has many prongs. All of these are underlain by a common claim—the "natural" family is not natural, necessary, or optimal, and a more adequate family system needs to be developed.

1. *The "natural" family system is not natural.* Biological differences in skin color or sex organs, and biological similarities between parent and child, do not necessitate a particular family form, or hierarchy and difference between the sexes and races. Past family systems have been very different from the "natural" family.[4] It is not nature but our society which is producing and reproducing the "natural" family, and its associated institutions of gender and race difference and inequality, through parenting practices, laws, labor market structures, and culture.

2. *The "natural" family system is classist and racist.* The conception of the "natural" family is generated by the dominant culture of upperclass, native-born whites, who then claim it applies to all. Since being a man means bread-winning and supporting a homebound home maker and children, men without "family wage" jobs due to unemployment, class, or race discrimination are seen (and often see themselves) as less than manly. Black women, forced into the labor force to compensate for their husbands' lack of economic opportunity, are viewed as unfeminine, castrating "matriarchs," and the extended and

---

[4] Among the Rangiroa, adopted children were given equal status and rights as biological offspring, and considered "one belly" (from the same mother) with one another and with their other siblings (Sahlins 1976). In the New England and Southern colonies, mothering among the wealthy was essentially biological, producing one's husband's children, who were then nursed and cared for by poor white or slave women. Mead (1935) found societies where men and women shared the early care of children. Many societies see polygamy as the norm for marriage; others have allowed females to live as men and take wives after having cross-sex dreams (Blackwood 1984). Among the ancient Greeks, the highest form of love for an adult man was homosexual love for a younger man.

The numbers 10, 11, 12 appear in the right margin beside the corresponding paragraphs.

chosen family system which blacks have developed to combat poverty and economic insecurity is condemned as deviant (Stack 1974). The inability of the poor to properly parent their children because of their meager resources is seen as a fault in their characters, and they are criticized for having children at all, as if the poor do not have a right to parent.

3. *The "natural" family system impoverishes female-headed households.* Women and children face high risks of poverty. Married women are to specialize in unpaid homemaking and mothering, complementing their husbands' bread-winning. Divorce or widowhood leaves women with little access to income, but with major if not full emotional and financial responsibility for the children.[5] "Women's jobs" do not pay enough to cover child care and keep female households with young children out of poverty. The present welfare system (Aid to Families with Dependent Children), structured to support the "natural" family system, does not even provide female-headed families with poverty-level income. The result: the majority of black and Hispanic female-headed families (50 and 53%, respectively), and 27% of white female-headed families, are poor. Children are penalized the most: 54% of children in such families are poor (Current Population Reports 1985).

4. *"Natural" marriage creates inequality between the sexes.* Since wives are relegated to unpaid housework and low paid jobs, they are economically dependent upon their husbands. Fear of losing this financial support can force women into subservience to their husbands, and into staying in unsatisfying marriages. Indeed, some feminists see "natural" marriage as a struggle in which men have gained the upper hand by monopolizing the higher-paid jobs (Hartmann 1981). Whatever its origins, "natural" marriage is clearly unequal, making mutual love and respect difficult.

5. *"Natural" parenting is oppressive and unjust.* Along with financial responsibility, parents are given almost total power over children. Children have no rights, and no system through which they can complain about mistreatment or find alternative parents (Rodham 1976). In a society where most men are under the power of bosses, and women under that of their husbands, parenting provides an arena where adults have total power and authority. It is easy to forget one's chil-

---

[5] In 1983, only 35% of mothers caring for their children with absent fathers received any child-support, and the average yearly payment was only $2,341; only 6% of separated or divorced women received any alimony (1987 Statistical Abstract).

dren's needs and use or abuse them to fill one's own needs. What results is not only an epidemic of child physical and sexual abuse,[6] but also the training of each child to accept and participate in hierarchical and authoritarian systems, from schools to workplaces to politics (Miller 1981).

6. *The "natural" family perpetuates inequality between families* through the generations, because parents pass down their economic position to their children. Inheritance keeps ownership of the means of production in the hands of a few, mostly white, families.[7] Children born into higher-income families receive better nutrition, housing, health care, and schooling than their poor counterparts, have the "insurance" of wealthy relatives to back them up and encourage risk-taking, and can expect to inherit wealth. On the other hand, 11 million children (one in five) must live without even the most basic goods and services (Current Population Reports 1985). This is not only unjust but also irrational: it is in society's interest to guarantee quality health care and education to its future workers and citizens.

7. *The "natural" family system discourages the formation of alternative families, while forcing many into unwanted "natural" families.* Its broad and virulent anti-gay discrimination—from education, employment, housing, and marriage laws to media images—makes it very difficult for people to love and share their lives with people of the same sex. It discriminates against couples who are unable to have children biologically by treating adoption and artificial insemination as "unnatural" and undesirable options. On the other hand, the "natural" family's equation of sex, reproduction, and marriage creates unwanted children by creating opposition to sex education, birth control for unmarried teens, and abortion. Forty percent of all births are mistimed or unwanted—for those under 24, a disastrous 53%—forcing millions of women into premature or unwanted motherhood and/or marriages (1987 Statistical Abstract).

Conceptualizing a Social Family System

The "natural" family system is inadequate, oppressive, and is coming apart at the seams. At the same time, all need the love and warmth

---

[6] The media have focussed on child abuse by strangers—on day care scandals and missing children—whereas the vast majority of children are abused by their parents or relatives (Eliasoph 1986).

[7] The wealthiest 2.4% of households owns 65% of the income-producing wealth (Edwards, Reich, Weisskopf 1986).

and sharing and parenting which family relationships provide.[8] Hence criticism is not enough; an *alternative* and better vision of family life needs to be delineated, along with a set of concrete policies to bring such a new family system into being.

The oppressiveness of the "natural" family system was accepted   19 because its institutions were seen as natural and inevitable. Our new family system would be a *consciously* social one, its institutions developed through study, discussion, struggle and compromise, and continually criticized and improved so as to maximize freedom, equality, self-fulfillment, democracy, and justice. Here are some of the central principles of such a system; while it may appear utopian, many are living out parts of this vision now.

Social Marriage. Marriage would become a *symmetrical* relationship   20 between whole, equal, and socially independent human beings, each participating in a similar range of familial, economic and political activities.[9] Its basis would be mutual love of the other, i.e., liking of, respect for, and sexual attraction to the person the other is, as providing the reason for intimate sharing of lives and living spaces and, if desired, parenting. Couples would not be expected to stay together "for better or for worse . . . as long as ye both shall live"; nor would they need to, since each would have earnings.

Social Parenting. Parenting would be recognized as a quintessen-   21 tially *social* activity which, by shaping our unconsciousnesses, bodies, and minds, shapes the future of our society. Society would ensure that each child is well cared for and educated, since the upbringing of children as physically and psychologically healthy, creative, educated, and socially-conscious citizens is essential both to society's well-being, and to our belief in equal opportunity. This would include providing children and their parents with economic and institutional support, as well as seeking out optimal parenting practices and educating prospective parents in them.

Social Community. Cultural and economic differences between   22 groups of people would be acknowledged to be social rather than natural products. All human beings would be recognized as equally

---

[8] Some feminists and gays have taken an "anti-family" position, as if the "natural" family is the only family form (Barrett and McIntosh 1982); however they usually advocate some alternative, family-like institutions.

[9] If this seems far-fetched, an October 1977 CBS–*New York Times* National Survey found that 50% of 30–44 year olds, and 67% of 18–29 year olds, preferred a symmetrical marriage (of a man and woman who both had jobs, did housework, and cared for the children) over the traditional, complementary one.

human citizens of the world, and a concept of basic human rights, both political and economic, developed. Intercultural marriages would be encouraged to further social understanding.

Bringing the Social Family into Being: A Policy Check-list

Although the "natural" family system is in decline, the social family 23 system cannot replace it unless there are many changes in our economic and social institutions. Here are some of the policies which will help bring about these changes; many are now in place in other countries.

1. *Policies which socialize parenting* 24

a. *Policies which establish the right of all adults to choose when and if they wish to parent.* Universal sex education and parenting training for adolescents, as well as access of all to free, safe, 100% effective birth control, abortions, and adoption placement, are needed to make every child a wanted child. At the same time, society must recognize the right of those who are infertile, gay, or single to parent, and support the development of alternative modes of obtaining children from adoption to artificial insemination and in-vitro fertilization.[10] The right to parent must also be protected by programs to help low-income parents with the costs of child-rearing (see 1b). Finally, the right to parent must be seen as socially established, rather than inhering in the genetic connection between a parent and a child; parenting rights must be revocable if a parent neglects or abuses a child, and society should seek to prevent child abuse through an effective system of child advocates and parenting support and training.

b. *Policies which ensure a basic, social inheritance for every child.* The best way to ensure healthy and provided-for children is to ensure this health and income to all families through a system of national health insurance and a combination of anti-poverty measures, from full employment, to comparable worth, to a guaranteed annual income. In addition, since having children does increase a family's poverty risk,

---

[10] Most doctors refuse to artificially inseminate single or lesbian women. The developing practice of surrogate mothering is very controversial among feminists and radicals. Since eggs can be fertilized outside of a womb, and embryos can be raised in incubators from the age of a few months, there are many other possibilities, including impregnating men, or even producing infants entirely outside of human bodies, as Marge Piercy (1976) and Shulamith Firestone (1970) have envisioned.

family allowances should be provided to parents according to need.[11] Furthermore, all children need to have access to high quality, free or sliding-scale education, from preschool day care when their parents are at work, to elementary and secondary school and college. This "social inheritance" program would be paid for by high inheritance taxes and very progressive income and/or luxury taxes. Such taxes would, in themselves, help reduce the present gross inequalities of opportunity among children.[12]

c. *Policies which socialize child-care costs: government- and business-subsidized day care.* Making quality child care available and affordable to all should be the joint financial responsibility of business and government, since it benefits both employers and society at large. A few trend-setting employers now provide child-care benefits to their workers, having found that these more than pay for themselves by decreasing worker absenteeism, increasing productivity, and attracting top workers (Blau and Ferber 1986). Current federal funding through Title 20 is woefully inadequate; many states are serving less than 30% of their eligible populations (Select Committee on Children 1987). One survey found that ¼ of all full-time homemakers, and ½ of all single parents, were kept from employment and training programs by the unavailability of child care (Cal. Governor's Task Force on Child Care 1986). Again, Sweden provides the example to follow: the government pays 90% of the child-care costs of public day care centers, which are used by over half of children with employed mothers (Blau and Ferber 1986).

On the other hand, to permit parents with job commitments to spend more time with their children, especially their infants, a system of paid leaves from work without loss of one's job or seniority must be established. The U.S. does not even have laws guaranteeing prospective parents an *unpaid* leave when they have or adopt a child.[13]

[11] Sweden and France give housing allowances to parents (Kamerman and Kahn 1979); many European countries have national health insurance and family allowances. Swedish policy is to guarantee all citizens a minimum standard of living (Ibid.); in the U.S., the needy only receive support through "entitlement" programs, which require certain qualifications (such as being a female household head with children) other than being poor, and which do not, in any event, raise incomes up to the poverty level.

[12] See Chester (1982) for a review of Western thought on inheritance.

[13] Kamerman and Kingston (in Kamerman and Hayes 1982) found that paid maternity leave was available to fewer than one-third of all employed women in 1978, and averaged only about six weeks of benefits.

In a few states, women can use their temporary disability insurance to pay for 4 to 10 weeks of pregnancy/infant care leave (Kamerman et al. 1983). Again, Sweden is the model in this area, with 1) paid, year-long parental leaves, 2) up to 60 days a year paid leave to care for sick children, and 3) the right for all full-time employed parents with children under 8 to reduce their work weeks (with reduced pay) to 30 hours a week (Ginsberg 1983). Radicals have advocated a shorter work week without reduction in pay as a solution to unemployment and low productivity, for it would create more jobs, reduce unemployment, and increase output (Bowles, Gordon, and Weisskopf 1983); a consideration of the needs of parents makes such policies even more desirable. Other innovations which allow adults to combine work with parenting are flex-time and flex-place (working at home); the extension of health, pension, and other benefits to part-time workers; and the cafeteria benefit plan, which allows dual-career couples to eliminate doubly-covered benefits in favor of more of other benefits, such as leaves or child-care support (Farley 1983; Kamerman and Hayes 1982).

2. *Policies to support egalitarian, symmetrical marriages* in which partners participate equally in parenting, housework, the labor force, and political life.[14]

a. *Comparable worth, affirmative action, increased unionization.* Comparable worth would increase the pay of women's jobs to that of men's jobs requiring comparable skill, effort, and responsibility. Affirmative action encourages women to enter into traditionally masculine jobs. Women need to organize in unions to fight for the above, and for general wage increases; one platform is "solidarity wages," again practiced in Sweden, in which workers agree to take part of their wage increase to reduce inequalities among them. Together these policies would stop the segregation of women into low-paid, dead end, less-satisfying jobs, reduce women's economic dependence upon men, and encourage more similar work and family participation by the sexes.

b. *Socialization of parenting* (see #1 above) would support symmetrical marriage, for it would allow adults to combine parenting with labor force commitments, reducing the pressure to specialize as in "natural" marriage.

c. *Repeal of the laws that discourage formation of "unnatural" marriages and non-traditional households.* This includes repealing sodomy laws and advocating legislation prohibiting discrimination against gays in em-

[14] Cuba encourages such marriages through its "Family Code," adopted in 1975 (Randall 1981); however, it still discriminates against gay couples.

ployment, housing, insurance, foster parenting, adoption, and other areas.[15] Gay relationships must be legitimized in marriage laws, to give spouses health insurance, pension, inheritance, and other benefits and rights enjoyed by heterosexual spouses.[16] The repeal of co-residence laws, which in many states prohibit the cohabitation of more than two unrelated adults, is needed to allow the formation of non-biologically–based extended families.

d. *Individual rather than joint taxation of married couples.* Our present income tax system is progressive and married couples are taxed on the basis of their combined incomes. This discourages wives from entering the labor force since, when a woman's earnings raise the household's tax bracket, much of her earnings are paid to the government in taxes.[17] Taxing adults individually (as is currently done in Sweden), rather than jointly, would instead encourage both members of a couple to participate in the labor force.

e. *Policies to aid the casualties of the "natural" marriage system.* Until the above changes are achieved, women and children will continue to face high poverty risks when they live in female-headed households. Many feminists advocate the strengthening of alimony and child-support laws; however, this both reinforces the "natural" marriage notion that husbands should be the main providers, and reproduces class and race inequality, because wives' and children's incomes depend on that of their husbands/fathers. Extensive welfare reform, combined with the policies above, is a better solution.

3. *Policies to create social community.* Labor market reforms (2a) must always aim at eliminating both race and sex segregation and discrimination. These, along with social inheritance policies, will go far in stopping the economic reproduction of racial inequality in the U.S. The decline of "natural" parenting views of children as "one's own

27

---

[15] Sodomy laws, which outlaw forms of "unnatural sex" (e.g., anal intercourse and oral/genital sex, either heterosexual or homosexual), still exist in many states, and were recently upheld by the Supreme Court, although they are seldom enforced. Many cities and a few states have passed gay rights legislation, and more and more employers have extended their non-discrimination policy to include sexual preference or orientation.

[16] In June 1987, the Swedish Parliament approved a bill which gave gay couples the same rights as heterosexuals married by common law; it will allow couples to sign housing leases as couples, regulate the division of property after a break-up, and grant lovers the right to inherit property in the absence of a will (*Gay Community News,* June 14–20, 1987).

[17] Even though the recent tax reform reduced the progressivity of the tax system, and a 1983 reform exempted 10% of the income of the lower-earning partner from taxation, the "marriage penalty" persists (Blau and Ferber 1986).

flesh and blood" will foster, and in turn be fostered by, the decline of conceptions of race, as both are replaced by a view of a human community reproduced through social parenting.

Bibliography

Barrett, Michele, and McIntosh, Mary. 1982. *The Anti-Social Family*. London: New Left Books.

Blackwood, Evelyn. 1984. Sexuality and Gender in Certain Native Tribes: The Case of Cross-Gender Females. *Signs* 10(1):27–42.

Blau, Francine, and Ferber, Marianne. 1986. *The Economics of Women, Men, and Work*. Englewood Cliffs, N.J.: Prentice-Hall.

Bowles, Samuel, David M. Gordon, and Thomas E. Weisskopf. 1983. *Beyond the Wasteland: A Democratic Alternative to Economic Decline*. New York: Anchor/Doubleday.

Chester, Ronald. 1982. *Inheritance, Wealth, and Society*. Bloomington: Indiana University Press.

Children's Defense Fund. 1987. Unpublished paper.

Edwards, Richard, Reich, Michael, and Weisskopf, Thomas. 1986. *The Capitalist System*. Englewood Cliffs, N.J.: Prentice-Hall. Third Edition.

Eliasoph, Nina. 1986. Drive-In Mortality, Child Abuse, and the Media. *Socialist Review* #90, 16(6):7–31.

Farley, Jennie, ed. 1983. *The Woman in Management*. New York: ILR Press.

Firestone, Shulamith. 1970. *The Dialectic of Sex*. New York: Morrow.

Ginsberg, Helen. 1983. *Full Employment and Public Policy: The United States and Sweden*. Lexington, Mass.: D.C. Heath and Co.

Gould, Steven J. 1981. *The Mismeasure of Men*. New York: Norton.

Hartmann, Heidi. 1981. The Unhappy Marriage of Marxism and Feminism. In *Women and Revolution: A Discussion of the Unhappy Marriage of Marxism and Feminism*, Lydia Sargent (ed.), pp. 1–41. Boston: South End Press.

Kamerman, Sheila, and Kahn, Alfred. 1979. *Family Policy: Government and Families in Fourteen Countries*. New York: Columbia University Press.

Kamerman, Sheila, and Hayes, Cheryl, eds. 1982. *Families that Work: Children in a Changing World*. Washington: National Academy Press.

Kamerman, Sheila, et al., eds. 1983. *Maternity Policies and Working Women*. New York: Columbia University Press.

Matthaei, Julie. 1982. *An Economic History of Women in America: Women's Work, the Sexual Division of Labor, and the Development of Capitalism*. New York: Schocken Books.

Mead, Margaret. 1935. *Sex and Temperament in Three Primitive Societies*. New York: William Morrow and Co.

Miller, Alice. 1981. *The Drama of the Gifted Child*. trans. by Ruth Ward. New York: Basic Books.

Piercy, Marge. 1976. *Woman on the Edge of Time.* New York: Fawcett.

Randall, Margaret. 1981. *Women in Cuba: Twenty Years Later.* New York: Smyrna Press.

Rodham, Hilary. 1976. Children under the Law. In *Rethinking Childhood* Arlene Skolnick (ed.). Boston: Little, Brown and Co.

Sahlins, Marshall. 1976. *The Use and Abuse of Biology: An Anthropological Critique of Sociobiology.* Ann Arbor: University of Michigan Press.

Select Committee on Children, Youth and Families, U.S. House of Representatives. 1987. Fact Sheet: Hearing on Child Care, Key to Employment in a Changing Economy. March 10.

Stack, Carol. 1974. *All Our Kin.* New York: Harper & Row.

U.S. Bureau of the Census, Current Population Reports. 1985. Household and Family Characteristics: March 1985.

—. 1985. Money Income and Poverty Status of Families and Persons in the United States.

—. 1986. 1987. Statistical Abstract of the United States.

Weeks, Jeffrey. 1979. *Coming Out: Homosexual Politics in Britain, from the Nineteenth Century to the Present.* London: Quartet Books.

Questions

1. What, if anything, strikes you as "radical" in Matthaei's "radical analysis" of the "'natural' family" (paragraph 3)? Do any parts of this analysis strike you as unfair, misleading, or wrong? If so, which parts, and what do you find wrong with them?

2. In paragraph 7 Matthaei says that "adults are marrying later." Assuming this statement to be true, what do you think are the causes? What do you think may be the consequences, good and bad?

3. In paragraph 10 Matthaei denies that the "natural" family is natural. Do you think she proves her case? If not, in what way(s) does she fail?

4. Matthaei argues (paragraph 15) that the idea of the "natural" family can lead easily to child abuse. Can one argue, in response, that the "natural" family is better suited to assist children in growing into healthy, responsible, happy adults than is any conceivable alternative arrangement? If you think so, what arguments might you offer? (For an interesting argument that children should be granted legal rights to escape impossible families, see "Confessions of an Erstwhile Child," pages 87–91.)

5. In paragraph 17 Matthaei argues that the idea of the "natural" family "discriminates against couples who are unable to have children biologically." Is she saying that all adults—including the sterile, the infertile, and those who do not wish to engage in heterosexual

sex—have a right to have children? If she is saying this, on what might she base this right? (In her next paragraph she says, "All need the love and warmth and sharing and parenting which family relationships provide." Is this need perhaps the basis for a right— possessed by all adults—to have children? (See also the discussion in paragraph 24.)

6. Much of the essay is devoted to arguing on behalf of various kinds of equality. For example, in paragraph 20, in discussing "social marriage," Matthaei says that "marriage would become a sym- metrical relationship between whole, equal, and socially indepen- dent human beings." The two persons involved would participate "in a similar range of familial, economic and political activities." But what if both persons do not share an interest in, for example, political activities? Should they therefore not marry? Or suppose that one person enjoyed the world of paid work and the other pre- ferred to engage, at least for a while, chiefly in the role of parenting and housekeeping. Do you think such a marriage would be inher- ently unstable?

7. In point 1b of paragraph 24, Matthaei argues for programs and pol- icies that would redistribute wealth—for example, a guaranteed an- nual income. Suppose someone argued (or at least asserted) that he or she saw no reason to support the families of the poor. What reply might you make?

8. Matthaei apparently sees marriage as involving only two adults. Do you assume that she rejects polygamy (a practice not unknown in the United States and elsewhere)? And what about polyandry (one woman with two or more husbands)? If you accept Matthaei's ar- guments, or most of them, how do *you* feel about polygamy and polyandry? Arguments for polygamy can be found in the essay by B. Aisha Lemu (pages 64–66). What argument(s) for polyandry can you imagine?

Richard John Neuhaus

Renting Women, Buying Babies and Class Struggles

Quite suddenly, it seems, we have a new form of trade in 1
human beings. It is called surrogate motherhood, and several states
have already declared it legitimate by establishing regulations for the
trade. Voices have been raised to oppose the baby traders before their
business becomes a fait accompli.[1] It may already be too late for that.
The *New York Times* has editorially pronounced that regulation is the
only way to go since, after all, "the business is probably here to stay."
Numerous objections of a moral, legal, and commonsensical nature
have been raised to surrogate motherhood. One aspect that has not
been sufficiently explored is the way in which the baby trade so rudely
rips the veil off class divisions and hostilities in American life.

Surrogating Today and Yesterday

The most celebrated, or notorious, case of surrogate motherhood is the 2
one that has swirled around "Baby M" in a New Jersey courtroom.
Some of the details are by now well known. Mr. William Stern, a
biochemist married to Dr. Elizabeth Stern, a pediatrician who thought
pregnancy might be bad for her health, contracted with Mrs. Mary
Beth Whitehead to have his baby in return for $10,000 plus an equal

---

[1] Fait accompli: thing already done, so that opposition is useless (French). (Editors'
note).

Richard John Neuhaus, a Lutheran clergyman who for seventeen years served
as senior pastor in a black and Hispanic parish in Brooklyn, New York, is now
director of the Rockford Institute Center on Religion and Society in New York
City. He is editor of *Religion and Society Report* and editor-in-chief of *This World:
A Journal of Religion and Public Life.* He is also the author of several books,
including *The Naked Public Square: Religion and Democracy in America.*

amount in expenses. Mrs. Whitehead and her husband Richard, a sanitation worker, agreed. The surrogate contract is not uninteresting, including as it does provisions for amniocentesis and obligatory abortion if Mr. Stern did not like the results of the test. Also, Mrs. Whitehead would not receive the $10,000 but only a small payment for her troubles "in the event the child is miscarried, dies, or is stillborn." The Sterns were taking no chances. But they could not prevent Mary Beth Whitehead from changing her mind. "It's such a miracle to see a child born," she said. "The feeling is overwhelming. All the pain and suffering you've gone through is all gone." Within five minutes she is breastfeeding the baby, the bonding is effected, she runs away to avoid having to turn the baby over to the Sterns, the Sterns hire detectives to snatch the baby, and it all ends up in a court trying to decide who gets to keep the baby.

The liberal Catholic journal, *Commonweal,* observes: "Surrogate   3
motherhood is a simple idea. It has become a critical issue today not because of the breakthrough in technology but because of a breakdown in moral understanding—namely, the understanding that human reproduction should be firmly placed in the matrix of personal sexuality, marital love, and family bonds." The point is an important one. Also in religious circles today, there is much prattle about changing moral rules because of technological advances and new discoveries about sexuality. It is highly doubtful that we know anything very significant about sexuality that, say, Saint Augustine did not know. As to surrogate motherhood, long before the dawn of modern science human males had mastered the technique of impregnating women other than their wives. Genesis 16 tells how Sarah and Abraham chose Hagar to be the surrogate mother of Ishmael. That too turned out badly, although Hagar did get to keep the child. Hagar, of course, was a slave.

Today it is at least gauche to speak of buying or renting women.   4
The Sterns got over that awkwardness by hiring a Manhattan clinical psychologist who testified, "In both structural and functional terms, Mr. and Mrs. Stern's role as parents to Baby M was achieved by a surrogate uterus and not a surrogate mother." The contract did not call for Mrs. Whitehead to get involved. In fact *she* was supposed to stay out of this deal altogether. Mary Beth's problem, it would seem, is that she was not able to disaggregate herself from her uterus. She did not understand that she could rent out her uterus just as the Manhattan doctor could rent out his certified expertise. The capable lawyers hired by the Sterns had made it all very clear, and for a while she

thought she understood, but then somehow the whole thing began to seem surreal. (Not being an educated person, she did not say it seemed surreal. She said it just seemed wrong.)

Taking Advantage

True, there are those who argue that there is nothing new in the rich 5
renting the nonrich, whether in whole or in part. A servant or employee, they say, is in effect a rented person. It is hard to argue with people who say such things. More often than not, they are the kind of people who also say that property is theft and tolerance is oppression. One can point out that the employee is free to quit, that a person's work "belongs" to him even if he is paid to do it, that the worker may find fulfillment in the work, and so forth. But such wrongheaded people do have one undeniable point: with respect to the negotiation of worldly affairs, rich people do generally have the advantage of nonrich people. That said, one can only hope it will be acknowledged that there is something singular about the connections between a woman, her sexuality, and her procreative capacity. It is not the kind of acknowledgment people can be argued into, and those to whom it must be explained probably cannot understand. Proabortion proponents of a woman's "reproductive rights" regularly appeal to the uniquely intimate relationship between a woman and her body. Strangely enough, many of them also approve surrogate motherhood as a further step in rationalizing sexual relationships and liberating society from the oppression of traditional mores. The recently discovered constitutional doctrine of "privacy," it would seem, is absolute—unless you have accepted money to have it violated. The inviolably intimate sphere of sexuality is one thing, but a deal is a deal.

As with abortion, there is another party involved. As is not the 6
case with abortion, everyone here recognizes the other party involved. Baby M, having passed the quality-control tests, is certified as a Class-A member of the species. The question is who owns this valuable product. Presumably ownership is fifty-fifty between Mrs. Whitehead and Mr. Stern. Mr. Stern's case is that Mrs. Whitehead had agreed to sell her share of the baby for $10,000 and then reneged on the deal. A Solomonic decision may be required, except Solomon's proposed solution would likely be found unconstitutional. Mary Beth is perplexed by the ownership conundrum. The following is from a taped telephone conversation admitted in evidence: "WHITEHEAD: I gave her

life. I did. I had the right during the whole pregnancy to terminate it, didn't I? STERN: It was your body. WHITEHEAD: That's right. It was my body and now you're telling me that I have no right. STERN: Because you made an agreement . . . you signed an agreement." It is not that nothing is sacred anymore. It is simply that the sacred has been re-located, away from realities such as life and motherhood and placed in a contract signed and sealed by money. Some simplistic types who have not kept up with the demands of cultural change find this re-pugnant. For example, William Pierce, president of the National Com-mittee for Adoption, flatly says: "If you regulate surrogate mother-hood, that is making a public statement that it's all right. We decided a hundred years ago we didn't want people bought and sold in this country."

That is not the question, says the judge in the Baby M case. The   7 question, the only question, is what is "in the best interest" of Baby M. In other words, who can offer Baby M the better prospect for the good things in life, the Whiteheads or the Sterns? Here, although the word is never used, the question of class takes center stage in the courtroom drama. The relative stability of American society is due in part to our kindly veiling of class distinctions and hostilities. People making $20,000 and people making $100,000 or more have tacitly agreed to say they are middle class. In fact, some are rich and some are not rich and some are poor. In terms of income, the Sterns are upper-middle or upper class, the Whiteheads are low–low-middle class and have at times been poor. Perhaps more important than the criterion of income, the Sterns and their allies in the New Jersey court-room represent the new knowledge class. The disputes are over sym-bolic knowledge; that is to say, over how to establish the "meaning" of ideas such as parenthood, love, stability, life opportunity, and psy-chological well-being. In the symbolic knowledge showdown, Mary Beth Whitehead is pitifully outgunned. She has never even heard of the transvaluation of values, which is what the Baby M trial is all about.

Class Struggle

It is not simply that the Sterns can hire a battery of lawyers, detectives,   8 psychological experts and social workers, while Mary Beth must get along with a lawyer three years out of school whose main experience has been in liability cases. No, the greater disparity is that the Sterns, their hired experts, the judge, and almost everyone else involved rep-resents the new class arrayed against the world of the Whiteheads who represent the bottom side of the working class. In the class war being waged in the courtroom, the chief weapon of the new class is contempt for the world of their cultural inferiors, a world so blatantly represented by the Whiteheads. Mrs. Whitehead must be criticized for her decision to enter into the agreement in the first place. But that is not a criticism employed in the courtroom to discredit Mrs. Whitehead, for it might reflect unfavorably on the other party to the agreement, even suggesting that perhaps Mr. Stern took advantage.

Rather, Mary Beth Whitehead is to be discredited and declared an 9 unfit mother because the world of which she is part is unfit for Mr. Stern's baby, or at least not nearly so fit as the world of the Sterns. So extensive evidence is presented that the Whiteheads have had a hard time of it financially, even living in a house trailer for a time. More than that, Mrs. Whitehead received welfare payments for a few months and her husband underwent a bout with alcoholism some years ago. The mandatory new class attitude under usual circumstances is that there is absolutely no stigma whatsoever attached to welfare or alcoholism. But that is under usual circumstances. In the class war being fought in the New Jersey courtroom such things are sure evidence of moral turpitude and the Whiteheads' "unsuitability" as parents for the 50 percent wellborn Baby M. In addition, a team of mental health experts has testified that Mrs. Whitehead shows definite signs of "distress," and one psychiatrist bluntly says she is suffering from "mixed personality disorder." That presumed illness is defined as "traits from several personality disorders but not all the criteria of any one disorder." It is a kind of catchall category in which, one fears, most human beings might be caught. Yet another psychiatrist in the new class alliance attempts to come up with harder evidence. Dr. Judith Brown Greif said that Mrs. Whitehead "often is unable to separate out her own needs from the needs of the baby." Well, there you have it. Mary Beth, in her pathetic ignorance, probably thought that was a sign of being a good mother. Little does she know about the need-fulfilling autonomy of the psychologically mature.

In order to get empirical support for their class biases, a group of 10 mental health and child development experts visited "for several hours" in the Whitehead and Stern homes to observe firsthand how Baby M "related" to the respective parties. At the Whiteheads, Baby M seemed very happy, but their other two children, ages eleven and twelve, were vying for her attention and Mrs. Whitehead exhibited "an inflated sense of self." This, according to Dr. Marshall Schechter, psychiatrist at the University of Pennsylvania, was revealed in her making "an assumption that because she is the mother, the child, Baby M, belongs to her. This gives no credence to or value to the genetic contribution of the birth father." Things were different at the quiet and spacious Stern home. There were no other children to interrupt and, as Dr. and Mrs. Stern sat on the living room floor chatting with their mental health visitors, Baby M gave every sign of relating very well to Mr. Stern. Of Mr. Stern one psychiatrist reported. "He is a thoughtful, sensitive man with a deep sense of responsibility and a respect for privacy." He did not need to add that none of those nice things could be said of Mrs. Whitehead.

Another expert (the one who contributed the distinction between   11 renting the woman and renting the uterus), unequivocally declared that the Sterns are "far and away more capable of meeting the baby's needs than the Whiteheads." This includes of course his professional evaluation of Dr. Elizabeth, the wife. She is also, the experts told the court, very good at relating. In Dr. Stern's extensive court testimony, according to the *Times*, "she spoke of her delights at home with the baby and her disdain for Mrs. Whitehead." Often, she testified, she takes the baby shopping. "She's the cutest thing around. She's always pulling at the clothes in Bloomingdale's, trying to get them off the rack." At Bloomies, of course. You can bet that Mary Beth Whitehead probably doesn't even know where it is.

We Americans have a way of declaring something outrageous,   12 repugnant, odious, and beyond the pale—and then concluding that we should regulate it. Surrogate motherhood should not be regulated, it should be outlawed. Some think the buying and selling of human beings was outlawed with the abolition of slavery, and the renting of women with laws against prostitution. But those big questions are bypassed if one agrees with the court that the only question is, "What is in the best interest of the child?" Then enters the ugly factor of naked class advantage. If "interest" is defined by material wellbeing, life opportunities, professionally certified mental and emotional health, and a "lifestyle" approved by the new knowledge class, then clearly the baby must go to the Sterns. By the criteria by which Mary Beth Whitehead is declared an unsuitable mother, millions of (dare we use the term?) lower-class women are unsuitable mothers. (One waits to see whether the court would take her other two children into custody.) By the criteria by which the Sterns are found to be "far and away more capable of meeting the baby's needs," people of recognized achievement and approved attitudes have a right to the best babies that money can buy.

Questions

1. In paragraph 2 what words or phrases convey Neuhaus's antipathy for the Sterns?

2. What words, phrases, or sentences in paragraph 4 are examples of verbal (conscious) irony, or even of sarcasm? (On irony, see pages 702–703 in the Glossary.) Do you consider the paragraph effective? Why, or why not? As you reread the essay, what other striking instances of verbal irony do you note?

3. In paragraph 5 Neuhaus finds it strange that many people who approve of abortion "also approve surrogate motherhood as a further step in rationalizing sexual relationships and liberating society from the oppression of traditional mores." If you do *not* find it strange, explain why. (For instance, you might try to argue that if a woman has a right to abort a fetus, she also has the right to rent out her uterus, on the grounds that it is *her* body. Do you imagine that Neuhaus would find this explanation acceptable? Why, or why not?)

4. In paragraph 6 Neuhaus quotes Stern as reminding Mary Beth Whitehead that she "made an agreement." Does Neuhaus believe that the agreement—the contract—settles the issue? Do you?

5. In his opening paragraph Neuhaus claims that "the baby trade" exposes class conflict in American life. How does he support this point? If you agree that his main point is that surrogacy arrangements are immoral, does this secondary point support his thesis or dilute it?

6. In his final paragraph Neuhaus bluntly states: "Surrogate motherhood should not be regulated, it should be outlawed." Do you agree or disagree? Why?

7. In the week after the birth of the baby, the Whiteheads and the Sterns passed the baby back and forth. Later the Whiteheads kept the baby for four months, until, on March 31, 1987, a court awarded custody of the child to the Sterns and terminated Ms. Whitehead's custody rights. Ten months later the New Jersey Supreme Court declared the surrogacy contract illegal and voided, and also voided the adoption of the baby by Dr. Stern, allowing her no parental rights. Ms. Whitehead was given visitation rights. The child is now legally the daughter of Ms. Whitehead and Mr. Stern, who must negotiate visitation rights, as a divorced couple must. What do you think of the court's decision?

B. Aisha Lemu

In Defense of Polygamy

Perhaps the aspect of Islam in respect of women which 1
is most prominent in the Western mind is that of polygamy. Firstly let
me clarify that Islam does not impose polygamy as a universal practice.
The Prophet himself was a monogamist for the greater part of his married life, from the age of twenty-five when he married Khadija until
he was fifty when she died.

One should therefore regard monogamy as the norm and polyg- 2
amy as the exception.

One may observe that, although it has been abused in some times 3
and some places, polygamy has under certain circumstances a valuable
function. In some situations it may be considered as the lesser of two
evils, and in other situations it may even be a positively beneficial
arrangement.

The most obvious example of this occurs in times of war when 4
there are inevitably large numbers of widows and girls whose fiances
and husbands have been killed in the fighting. One has only to recall
the figures of the dead in the first and second world wars to be aware
that literally millions of women and girls lost their husbands and fiances and were left alone without any income or care or protection for
themselves or their children. If it is still maintained that under these
circumstances a man may marry only one wife, what options are left
to the millions of other women who have no hope of getting a husband?
Their choice, bluntly stated, is between a chaste and childless old maid-
enhood, or becoming somebody's mistress—that is, an unofficial second wife with no legal rights for herself or for her children. Most
women would not welcome either of these since most women have
always wanted and still do want the security of a legal husband and
family.

The compromise therefore is for women under these circumstances 5

B. Aisha Lemu comes from an English background. She is now a Muslim. We
print here part of a talk she gave (and part of the discussion that followed) at
the International Islamic Conference held in London in April 1976.

to face the fact that if given the alternative many of them would rather share a husband than have none at all. And there is no doubt that it is easier to share a husband when it is an established and publicly recognised practice than when it is carried on secretly along with attempts to deceive the first wife.

And it is no secret that polygamy of a sort is widely carried on in 6 Europe and America. The difference is that while the Western man has no legal obligations to his second, third or fourth mistresses and their children, the Muslim husband has complete legal obligations towards his second, third or fourth wife and their children.

There may be other circumstances unrelated to war—individual 7 circumstances, where marriage to more than one wife may be preferable to other available alternatives—for example, where the first wife is chronically sick or disabled. There are of course some husbands who can manage this situation, but no one would deny its potential hazards. A second marriage in some cases could be a solution acceptable to all three parties.

Again there are cases in which a wife is unable to have children, 8 while the husband very much wants them. Under Western laws a man must either accept his wife's childlessness if he can, or if he cannot he must find a means of divorce in order to marry again. This could be avoided in some cases if the parties agreed on a second marriage.

There are other cases where a marriage has not been very suc- 9 cessful and the husband loves another woman. This situation is so familiar that it is known as the Eternal Triangle. Under Western laws the husband cannot marry the second woman without divorcing the first one. But the first wife may not wish to be divorced. She may no longer love her husband, but she may still respect him and wish to stay with him for the security of marriage, for herself and their children. Similarly the second woman may not wish to break up the man's first family. There are certain cases such as this where both women could accept a polygamous marriage rather than face divorce on the one hand or an extra-marital affair on the other.

I have mentioned some of these examples because to the majority 10 of Westerners polygamy is only thought of in the context of a harem of glamorous young girls, not as a possible solution to some of the problems of Western society itself. I have given some time to it not in order to advocate its indiscriminate use, but in an attempt to show that it is a practice not to be condemned without thinking of its uses and possible benefits in any community.

[A slightly edited version of the discussion that followed Lemu's talk   11
is given below.]

Discussion

Question: I would like to ask a question in relation to polygamy.   12
If one concedes the arguments you have given in support of a man
having more than one wife in certain circumstances, would the same
arguments be extended to the situation of a woman in relation to her
husband/husbands? To be more precise, if a woman becomes invalid
and sexually incapacitated and because of that the husband is allowed
to have a second wife, why should not the same hold good in respect
of men? If a husband becomes invalid, would it be permitted for the
wife to have a second husband?

B. Aisha Lemu: The instances which I quoted were examples of   13
human circumstances where there is a genuine problem and I mentioned that in the Western world the options are limited. That is, either
you stay with it or you obtain divorce, you cannot bring the third
alternative of another wife. Now the question of a woman having more
than one husband raises a number of other problems. One of them is
the question of inheritance. If a woman has more than one husband,
there is no certainty of the paternity of the child, and I think this is
something which will be very disturbing to men, not to be sure that
a certain child is their own, that it might be the child of another husband. Another problem that one could foresee here is that for a woman
to look after one husband is, generally speaking, considered to be quite
enough trouble (laughter and applause) without bringing upon herself
more than one.

Questions

1. Lemu says that polygamy is sometimes the lesser of two evils, and
   sometimes "a positively beneficial arrangement." What are some
   examples she gives of each category? Does polygamy strike you
   as a practical solution in the circumstances she describes?
2. In paragraph 10 Lemu suggests that polygamy is a possible solution
   to some problems of Western society itself. To what problems does
   she refer? Does polygamy strike you as a practical solution to these

problems? Whether or not you think polygamy practical, do you think it should be a legal option in our society? Why, or why not?
3. In her response to a question about polyandry, Lemu does not answer the specific question she was asked. What question does she answer, and how does she answer it? What objection might be made to her answer?

Jane Howard

All Happy Clans Are Alike
In Search of the Good Family

Call it a clan, call it a network, call it a tribe, call it a 1 family. Whatever you call it, whoever you are, you need one. You need one because you are human. You didn't come from nowhere. Before you, around you, and presumably after you, too, there are others. Some of these others must matter a lot—to you, and if you are very lucky, to one another. Their welfare must be nearly as important to you as your own. Even if you live alone, even if your solitude is elected and ebullient, you still cannot do without a clan or a tribe.

The trouble with the clans and tribes many of us were born into 2 is not that they consist of meddlesome ogres but that they are too far away. In emergencies we rush across continents and if need be oceans to their sides, as they do to ours. Maybe we even make a habit of seeing them, once or twice a year, for the sheer pleasure of it. But blood ties seldom dictate our addresses. Our blood kin are often too remote to ease us from our Tuesdays to our Wednesdays. For this we must rely on our families of friends. If our relatives are not, do not wish to be, or for whatever reasons cannot be our friends, then by

Jane Howard, born in Springfield, Illinois, in 1935, was educated at the University of Michigan. She served as reporter, writer, and editor for *Life* magazine, and she is the author of several books.

some complex alchemy we must try to transform our friends into our relatives. If blood and roots don't do the job, then we must look to water and branches, and sort ourselves into new constellations, new families.

These new families, to borrow the terminology of an African tribe   3 (the Bangwa of the Cameroons), may consist either of friends of the road, ascribed by chance, or friends of the heart, achieved by choice. Ascribed friends are those we happen to go to school with, work with, or live near. They know where we went last weekend and whether we still have a cold. Just being around gives them a provisional importance in our lives, and us in theirs. Maybe they will still matter to us when we or they move away; quite likely they won't. Six months or two years will probably erase us from each other's thoughts, unless by some chance they and we have become friends of the heart.

Wishing to be friends, as Aristotle, wrote, is quick work, but   4 friendship is a slowly ripening fruit. An ancient proverb he quotes in his *Ethics* had it that you cannot know a man until you and he together have eaten a peck of salt. Now a peck, a quarter of a bushel, is quite a lot of salt—more, perhaps, than most pairs of people ever have occasion to share. We must try though. We must sit together at as many tables as we can. We must steer each other through enough seasons and weathers so that sooner or later it crosses our minds that one of us, God knows which or with what sorrow, must one day mourn the other.

We must devise new ways, or revive old ones, to equip ourselves   5 with kinfolk. Maybe such an impulse prompted whoever ordered the cake I saw in my neighborhood bakery to have it frosted to say "Happy Birthday Surrogate." I like to think that this cake was decorated not for a judge but for someone's surrogate mother or surrogate brother: Loathsome jargon, but admirable sentiment. If you didn't conceive me or if we didn't grow up in the same house, we can still be related, if we decide we ought to be. It is never too late, I like to hope, to augment our families in ways nature neglected to do. It is never too late to choose new clans.

The best-chosen clans, like the best friendships and the best blood   6 families, endure by accumulating a history solid enough to suggest a future. But clans that don't last have merit too. We can lament them but we shouldn't deride them. Better an ephemeral clan or tribe than none at all. A few of my life's most tribally joyous times, in fact, have been spent with people whom I have yet to see again. This saddens me, as it may them too, but dwelling overlong on such sadness does no good. A more fertile exercise is to think back on those times and try to figure out what made them, for all their brevity, so stirring. What can such times teach us about forming new and more lasting tribes in the future?

New tribes and clans can no more be willed into existence, of 7 course, than any other good thing can. We keep trying, though. To try, with gritted teeth and girded loins, is after all American. That is what the two Helens and I were talking about the day we had lunch in a room up in a high-rise motel near the Kansas City airport. We had lunch there at the end of a two-day conference on families. The two Helens were social scientists, but I liked them even so, among other reasons because they both objected to that motel's coffee shop even more than I did. One of the Helens, from Virginia, disliked it so much that she had brought along homemade whole wheat bread, sesame butter, and honey from her parents' farm in South Dakota, where she had visited before the conference. Her picnic was the best thing that happened, to me at least, those whole two days.

"If you're voluntarily childless and alone," said the other Helen, 8 who was from Pennsylvania by way of Puerto Rico, "it gets harder and harder with the passage of time. It's stressful. That's why you need support systems." I had been hearing quite a bit of talk about "support systems." The term is not among my favorites, but I can understand its currency. Whatever "support systems" may be, the need for them is clearly urgent, and not just in this country. Are there not thriving "megafamilies" of as many as three hundred people in Scandinavia? Have not the Japanese for years had an honored, enduring—if perhaps by our standards rather rigid—custom of adopting nonrelatives to fill gaps in their families? Should we not applaud and maybe imitate such ingenuity?

And consider our own Unitarians. From Santa Barbara to Boston 9 they have been earnestly dividing their congregations into arbitrary "extended families" whose members are bound to act like each other's relatives. Kurt Vonnegut, Jr., plays with a similar train of thought in his fictional *Slapstick.* In that book every newborn baby is assigned a randomly chosen middle name, like Uranium or Daffodil or Raspberry. These middle names are connected with hyphens to numbers between one and twenty, and any two people who have the same middle name are automatically related. This is all to the good, the author thinks, because "human beings need all the relatives they can get—as possible donors or receivers not of love but of common decency." He envisions these extended families as "one of the four greatest inventions by Americans," the others being *Robert's Rules of Order*, the Bill of Rights, and the principles of Alcoholics Anonymous.

This charming notion might even work, if it weren't so arbitrary. 10 Already each of us is born into one family not of our choosing. If we're going to devise new ones, we might as well have the luxury of picking the members ourselves. Clever picking might result in new families whose benefits would surpass or at least equal those of the old. As a member in reasonable standing of six or seven tribes in addition to the one I was born to, I have been trying to figure which characteristics are common to both kinds of families.

1. Good families have a chief, or a heroine, or a founder—someone 11 around whom others cluster, whose achievements, as the Yiddish word has it, let them *kvell*, and whose example spurs them on to like feats. Some blood dynasties produce such figures regularly; others languish for as many as five generations between demigods, wondering with each new pregnancy whether this, at last, might be the messianic baby who will redeem them. Look, is there not something gubernatorial about her footstep, or musical about the way he bangs with his spoon on his cup? All clans, of all kinds, need such a figure now and then. Sometimes clans based on water rather than blood harbor several such personages at one time. The Bloomsbury Group in London six decades ago was not much hampered by its lack of a temporal history.

2. Good families have a switchboard operator—someone who can- 12 not help but keep track of what all the others are up to, who plays Houston Mission Control to everyone else's Apollo. This role is assumed rather than assigned. The person who volunteers for it often has the instincts of an archivist, and feels driven to keep scrapbooks and photograph albums up to date, so that the clan can see proof of its own continuity.

3. Good families are much to all their members, but everything to 13 none. Good families are fortresses with many windows and doors to the outer world. The blood clans I feel most drawn to were founded by parents who are nearly as devoted to what they do outside as they are to each other and their children. Their curiosity and passion are contagious. Everybody, where they live, is busy. Paint is spattered on eyeglasses. Mud lurks under fingernails. Person-to-person calls come in the middle of the night from Tokyo and Brussels. Catcher's mitts,

ballet slippers, overdue library books, and other signs of extrafamilial concerns are everywhere.

4. Good families are hospitable. Knowing that hosts need guests as much as guests need hosts, they are generous with honorary memberships for friends, whom they urge to come early and often and to stay late. Such clans exude a vivid sense of surrounding rings of relatives, neighbors, teachers, students, and godparents, any of whom at any time might break or slide into the inner circle. Inside that circle a wholesome, tacit emotional feudalism develops: you give me protection, I'll give you fealty. Such pacts begin with, but soon go far beyond, the jolly exchange of pie at Thanksgiving or cake on a birthday. They mean that you can ask me to supervise your children for the fortnight you will be in the hospital, and that however inconvenient this might be for me, I shall manage to do so. It means I can phone you on what for me is a dreary, wretched Sunday afternoon and for you is the eve of a deadline, knowing you will tell me to come right over, if only to watch you type. It means we need not dissemble. ("To yield to seeming," as Martin Buber wrote, "is man's essential cowardice, to resist it is his essential courage . . . one must at times pay dearly for life lived from the being, but it is never too dear.")

5. Good families deal squarely with direness. Pity the tribe that doesn't have, and cherish, at least one flamboyant eccentric. Pity too the one that supposes it can avoid for long the woes to which all flesh is heir. Lunacy, bankruptcy, suicide, and other unthinkable fates sooner or later afflict the noblest of clans with an undertow of gloom. Family life is a set of givens, someone once told me, and it takes courage to see certain givens as blessings rather than as curses. It surely does. Contradictions and inconsistencies are givens, too. So is the battle against what the Oregon patriarch Kenneth Babbs calls malarkey. "There's always malarkey lurking, bubbles in the cesspool, fetid bubbles that pop and smell. But I don't put up with malarkey, between my stepkids and my natural ones or anywhere else in the family."

6. Good families prize their rituals. Nothing welds a family more than these. Rituals are vital especially for clans without histories, because they evoke a past, imply a future, and hint at continuity. No line in the seder service at Passover reassures more than the last: "Next year in Jerusalem!" A clan becomes more of a clan each time it gathers to observe a fixed ritual (Christmas, birthdays, Thanksgiving, and so on), grieves at a funeral (anyone may come to most funerals; those who do declare their tribalness), and devises a new rite of its own. Equinox breakfasts can be at least as welding as Memorial Day parades.

Several of my colleagues and I used to meet for lunch every Pearl Harbor Day, preferably to eat some politically neutral fare like smorgasbord, to "forgive" our only ancestrally Japanese friend, Irene Kubota Neves. For that and other things we became, and remain, a sort of family.

"Rituals," a California friend of mine said, "aren't just externals and holidays. They are the performances of our lives. They are a kind of shorthand. They can't be decreed. My mother used to try to decree them. She'd make such a goddamn fuss over what we talked about at dinner, aiming at Topics of Common Interest, topics that celebrated our cohesion as a family. These performances were always hollow, because the phenomenology of the moment got sacrificed for the *idea* of the moment. Real rituals are discovered in retrospect. They emerge around constitutive moments, moments that only happen once, around whose memory meanings cluster. You don't choose those moments. They choose themselves." A lucky clan includes a born mythologizer, like my blood sister, who has the gift for apprehending such a moment when she sees it, and who cannot help but invent new rituals everywhere she goes.

7. Good families are affectionate. This of course is a matter of style. I know clans whose members greet each other with gingerly handshakes or, in what pass for kisses, with hurried brushes of jawbones, as if the object were to touch not the lips but the ears. I don't see how such people manage. "The tribe that does not hug," as someone who has been part of many *ad hoc* families recently wrote to me, "is no tribe at all. More and more I realize that everybody, regardless of age, needs to be hugged and comforted in a brotherly or sisterly way now and then. Preferably now."

8. Good families have a sense of place, which these days is not achieved easily. As Susanne Langer wrote in 1957, "Most people have no home that is a symbol of their childhood, not even a definite memory of one place to serve that purpose . . . all the old symbols are gone." Once I asked a roomful of supper guests if anyone felt a strong pull to any certain spot on the face of the earth. Everyone was silent, except for a visitor from Bavaria. The rest of us seemed to know all too well what Walker Percy means in *The Moviegoer* when he tells of the "genie-soul of a place, which every place has or else is not a place [and which] wherever you go, you must meet and master or else be met and mastered." All that meeting and mastering saps plenty of strength. It also underscores our need for tribal bases of the sort which soaring real estate taxes and splintering families have made all but obsolete.

So what are we to do, those of us whose habit and pleasure and 20
doom is our tendency, as a Georgia lady put it, to "fly off at every
other whipstitch?" Think in terms of movable feasts, that's what. Live
here, wherever here may be, as if we were going to belong here for
the rest of our lives. Learn to hallow whatever ground we happen to
stand on or land on. Like medieval knights who took their tapestries
along on Crusades, like modern Afghanis with their yurts, we must
pack such totems and icons as we can to make short-term quarters feel
like home. Pillows, small rugs, watercolors can dispel much of the
chilling anonymity of a motel room or sublet apartment. When we can,
we should live in rooms with stoves or fireplaces or at least candlelight.
The ancient saying is still true: Extinguished hearth, extinguished family.

Round tables help too, and as a friend of mine once put it, so do 21
"too many comfortable chairs, with surfaces to put feet on, arranged
so as to encourage a maximum of eye contact." Such rooms inspire
good talk, of which good clans can never have enough.

9. Good families, not just the blood kind, find some way to connect 22
with posterity. "To forge a link in the humble chain of being, encircling
heirs to ancestors," as Michael Novak has written, "is to walk within
a circle of magic as primitive as humans knew in caves." He is talking
of course about babies, feeling them leap in wombs, giving them suck.
Parenthood, however, is a state which some miss by chance and others
by design, and a vocation to which not all are called. Some of us, like
the novelist Richard P. Brickner, look on as others "name their children
and their children in turn name their own lives, devising their own
flags from their parents' cloth." What are we who lack children to do?
Build houses? Plant trees? Write books or symphonies or laws? Perhaps, but even if we do these things, there should be children on the
sidelines if not at the center of our lives.

It is a sadly impoverished tribe that does not allow access to, and 23
make much of, some children. Not too much, of course; it has truly
been said that never in history have so many educated people devoted
so much attention to so few children. Attention, in excess, can turn
to fawning, which isn't much better than neglect. Still, if we don't
regularly see and talk to and laugh with people who can expect to
outlive us by twenty years or so, we had better get busy and find some.

10. Good families also honor their elders. The wider the age range, 24
the stronger the tribe. Jean-Paul Sartre and Margaret Mead, to name
two spectacularly confident former children, have both remarked on
the central importance of grandparents in their own early lives. Grandparents are now in much more abundant supply than they were a

generation or two ago, when old age was more rare. If actual grand-parents are not at hand, no family should have too hard a time finding substitute ones to whom to pay unfeigned homage. The Soviet Union's enchantment with day-care centers, I have heard, stems at least in part from the state's eagerness to keep children away from their presumably subversive grandparents. Let that be a lesson to clans based on interest as well as to those based on genes.

Of course there are elders and elders. Most people in America, as   25
David T. Bazelon has written, haven't the slightest idea of what to do with the extra thirty years they have been given to live. Few are as briskly secure as Alice Roosevelt Longworth, who once, when I visited her for tea, showed a recent photograph and asked whether I didn't think it made her look like "a malevolent Eurasian concubine—an *aged* malevolent Eurasian concubine." I admitted that it did, which was just what she wanted to hear. But those of us whose fathers weren't Pres-idents may not grow old, if at all, with such style.

Sad stories abound. The mother of one friend of mine languished   26
for years, never far from a coma, in a nursing home. Only when her husband and children sang one of her favorite old songs, such as "Lord Jeffrey Amherst," would a smile fleet across her face. But a man I know of in New Jersey, who couldn't stand the state of Iowa or babies, changed his mind on both counts when his daughter, who lived in Iowa, had a baby. Suddenly he took to inventing business trips to St. Louis, by way of Cedar Rapids, phoning to say he would be at the airport there at 11:31 P.M. and "Be sure to bring Jake!" That cheers me. So did part of a talk I had with a woman in Albuquerque, whom I hadn't seen since a trip some years before to the Soviet Union.

"Honey," she said when I phoned her during a short stopover   27
and asked how she was, "if I were any better I'd blow up and *bust!* I can't *tell* you how *neat* it is to put some age on! A lot of it, of course, has to do with going to the shrink, getting uncorked, and of course it doesn't hurt to have money—no, we *don't* have a ranch; it's only 900 acres, so we call it a farm. But every year, as far as age is concerned, I seem to get better, doing more and more stuff I love to do. The only thing I've ever wanted and don't have is a good marriage. Nothing I do ever pleases the men I marry. The only reason I'm still married now is it's too much trouble not to be. But my girls are growing up to be just *neat* humans, and the men they're sharing their lives with are too. They pick nice guys, my girls. I wish I could say the same. But I'm a lot better off than many women my age. I go to parties where

sixty-year-olds with blue bouffant hairdos are still telling the same jokes they told twenty-five or thirty years ago. Complacent? No, that's not it, exactly. What they are is sad—sad as the dickens. They don't seem to be *connected*."

Some days my handwriting resembles my mother's, slanting hope- 28
fully and a bit extravagantly eastward. Other days it looks more like my father's: resolute, vertical, guardedly free of loops. Both my parents will remain in my nerves and muscles and mind until the day I die, and so will my sister, but they aren't the only ones. If I were to die tomorrow, the obituary would note that my father and sister survived me. True, but not true enough. Like most official lists of survivors, this one would be incomplete.

Several of the most affecting relationships I have ever known of, 29
or been part of, have sprung not from genes or contracts but from serendipitous, uncanny bonds of choice. I don't think enough can be said for the fierce tenderness such bonds can generate. Maybe the best thing to say is nothing at all, or very little. Midwestern preachers used to hold that "a heavy rain doesn't seep into the ground but rolls off— when you preach to farmers, your sermon should be a drizzle instead of a downpour." So too with any cause that matters: shouting and lapel-grabbing and institutionalizing can do more harm than good. A quiet approach works better.

"I wish it would hurry up and get colder," I said one warm af- 30
ternoon several Octobers ago to a black man with whom I was walking in a park.

"Don't worry," he told me. "Like my grandmother used to say 31
when I was a boy, 'Hawk'll be here soon enough.' "

"What did she mean by 'hawk'?" 32

"Hawk meant winter, cold, trouble. And she was right: the hawk 33
always came."

With regard to families, many would say that the hawk has long 34
been here, hovering. "I'd rather put up with being lonely now than have to put up with being still more lonely in the future," says a character in Natsume Soseki's novel *Kokoro*. "We live in an age of freedom, independence, and the self, and I imagine this loneliness is the price we have to pay for it." Seven decades earlier, in *Either/Or*, Sören Kierkegaard had written, "Our age has lost all the substantial categories of family, state, and race. It must leave the individual entirely to himself, so that in a stricter sense he becomes his own creator."

If it is true that we must create ourselves, maybe while we are 35 about it we can also devise some new kinds of families, new connections to supplement the old ones. The second verse of a hymn by James Russell Lowell says,

New occasions bring new duties;
Time makes ancient good uncouth.

Surely one outworn "good" is the maxim that blood relatives are the only ones who can or should greatly matter. Or look at it another way: go back six generations, and each one of us has sixty-four direct ancestors. Go back twenty—only four or five centuries, not such a big chunk of human history—and we each have more than a million. Does it not stand to reason, since the world population was then so much smaller, that we all have a lot more cousins—though admittedly distant ones—than we were brought up to suspect? And don't these cousins deserve our attention?

One day after lunch at a friend's apartment I waited in his lobby while he collected his mail. Out of the elevator came two nurses supporting a wizened, staring woman who couldn't have weighed much more than seventy pounds. It was all the woman could do to make her way down the three steps to the sidewalk and the curb where a car was waiting. Those steps must have been to that woman what a steep mountain trail would be to me. The nurses guided her down them with infinite patience. 36

"Easy, darlin'," one nurse said to the woman. 37

"That's a good girl," said the other. The woman, my friend's doorman told us, was ninety. That morning she had fallen and hurt herself. On her forehead was something which, had it not been a bruise, we might have thought beautiful: a marvel of mauve and lavender and magenta. This woman, who was then being taken to a nursing home, had lived in my friend's apartment building for forty years. All her relatives were dead, and her few surviving friends no longer chose to see her. 38

"But how can that be?" I asked my friend. "We could never be that alone, could we?" 39

"Don't be so sure," said my friend, who knows more of such matters than I do. "Even if we were to end up in the same nursing home, if I was in markedly worse shape than you were, you might not want to see me, either." 40

"But I can't imagine not wanting to see you." 41

"It happens," my friend said.

42

Maybe we can keep it from happening. Maybe the hawk can be kept at bay, if we give more thought to our tribes and our clans and our several kinds of families. No aim seems to me more urgent, nor any achievement more worthy of a psalm. So *hosanna in excelsis,* and blest be the tie that binds. And please pass the salt.

43

Questions

1. Howard begins paragraph 7 by saying: "New tribes and clans can no more be willed into existence, of course, than any other good thing can." What other passages in the essay support this view? What passages contradict it? Does Howard succeed in reconciling the contradiction?
2. In her last paragraph Howard suggests that we might prevent loneliness by giving "more thought to our tribes and our clans and our several kinds of families." How might Julie Matthaei (pages 43–54) respond to her suggestion? Did either Howard's or Matthaei's essay stimulate your thoughts on families? Which did you find more useful in thinking about family relationships?

Laura Cunningham

The Girls' Room

When I heard she was coming to stay with us I was pleased. At age eight I thought of "grandmother" as a generic brand. My friends had grandmothers who seemed permanently bent over

1

Laura Cunningham was born in 1947. Orphaned at the age of eight, she was brought up by two unmarried uncles, both of whom were writers. She says that she became a writer because she didn't know that one could become anything else. Had she known of other possibilities, she says, she would have become a ballerina.

cookie racks. They were a source of constant treats and sweets. They were pinchers of cheeks, huggers and kissers. My own grandmother had always lived in a distant state; I had no memory of her when she decided to join the household recently established for me by my two uncles.

But with the example of my friends' grandmothers before me, I 2 could hardly wait to have a grandmother of my own—and the cookies would be nice too. For while my uncles provided a cuisine that ranged from tuna croquettes to Swedish meatballs, they showed no signs of baking anything more elegant than a potato.

My main concern on the day of my grandmother's arrival was: 3 How soon would she start the cookies? I remember her arrival, my uncles flanking her as they walked down the apartment corridor. She wore a hat, a tailored navy blue suit, an ermine stole. She held, tucked under her arm, the purple leather folder that contained her work in progress, a manuscript entitled "Philosophy for Women." She was preceded by her custom-made white trunk packed with purses, necklaces, earrings, dresses and more purple-inked pages that stress "the spiritual above the material."

She was small—at 5 feet 1 inch not much taller than I was—thin 4 and straight, with a pug nose, one brown eye (the good eye) and one blue eye (the bad eye, frosted by cataracts). Her name was "Esther in Hebrew, Edna in English, and Etka in Russian." She preferred the Russian, referring to herself as "Etka from Minsk." It was not at once apparent that she was deaf in her left ear (the bad ear) but could hear with the right (the good ear). Because her good ear happened to be on the opposite side from the good eye, anyone who spoke to her had to run around her in circles, or sway to and fro, if eye contact and audibility were to be achieved simultaneously.

Etka from Minsk had arrived not directly from Minsk, as the black- 5 eyed ermine stole seemed to suggest, but after many moves. She entered with the draft of family scandal at her back, blown out of her daughter's home after assaults upon her dignity. She held the evidence: an empty-socketed peacock pin. My cousin, an eleven-year-old boy, had surgically plucked out the rhinestone eyes. She could not be expected to stay where such acts occurred. She had to be among "human beings," among "real people" who could understand. We seemed to understand. We—my two uncles and I—encircled her, studied her vandalized peacock pin and vowed that such things would never happen with "us."

She patted my head—a good sign—and asked me to sing the Is- 6
raeli national anthem. I did, and she handed me a dollar. My uncles
went off to their jobs, leaving me alone with my grandmother for the
first time. I looked at her, expecting her to start rolling out the cookie
dough. Instead she suggested: "Now maybe you could fix me some
lunch?"

It wasn't supposed to be this way, I thought, as I took her order: 7
"toasted cheese and a sliced orange." Neither was she supposed to
share my pink and orange bedroom, but she did. The bedroom soon
exhibited a dual character—stuffed animals on one side, a hospital bed
on the other. Within the household this chamber was soon referred
to as "the girls' room." The name, given by Uncle Abe, who saw no
incongruity, only the affinity of sex, turned out to be apt, for what
went on in the girls' room could easily have been labeled sibling rivalry
if she had not been eighty and I eight. I soon found that I had acquired
not a traditional grandmother but an aged kid sister.

The theft and rivalry began within days. My grandmother had 8
given me her most cherished possession, a violet beaded bag. In return
I gave her my heart-shaped "ivory" pin and matching earrings. That
night she stole back the purse but insisted on keeping the pin and
earrings. I turned to my uncles for mediation and ran up against un-
foreseen resistance. They thought my grandmother should keep the
beaded bag; they didn't want to upset her.

I burned at the injustice of it and felt the heat of an uncomfortable 9
truth: where I once had my uncles' undivided indulgence, they were
now split as my grandmother and I vied for their attention. The household, formerly geared to my little-girl needs, was rearranged to accommodate hers. I suffered serious affronts—my grandmother, in a
fit of frugality, scissored all the household blankets, including what a
psychiatrist would have dubbed my "security" blanket, in half.
"Now," she said, her good eye gleaming, "we have twice as many."
I lay under my narrow slice of blanket and stared hopelessly up at the
ceiling. I thought evilly of ways of getting my grandmother out of the
apartment.

Matters worsened, as more and more of my trinkets disappeared. 10
One afternoon I came home from school to find her squeezed into my
unbuttoned favorite blouse. Rouged and beribboned, she insisted that
the size 3 blouse was hers. Meanwhile, I was forced to adapt to her
idiosyncracies: she covered everything black—from the dog to the telephone—with white doilies. She left saucers balanced on top of glasses.
She sang nonstop. She tried to lock my dog out of the apartment.

The word that explained her behavior was "arteriosclerosis." She   11
had forgotten so much that sometimes she would greet me with "You
look familiar." At other times she'd ask, "What hotel is this?" My
answer, shouted in her good ear, was: "We're not in a hotel! This is
our apartment!" The response would be a hoot of laughter: "Then why
are we in the ballroom?"

Finally we fought: arm-to-arm combat. I was shocked at her grip,   12
steely as the bars that locked her into bed at night. Her good eye burned
into mine and she said, "I'll tell." And she did. For the first time I was
scolded. She had turned their love to disapproval, I thought, and how
it chafed.

Eventually our rivalry mellowed into conspiracy. Within months   13
we found we had uses for each other. I provided the lunches and
secret, forbidden ice cream sundaes. She rewarded me with cold cash.
She continued to take my clothes; I charged her competitive prices. I
hated school; she paid me not to go. When I came home for lunch I
usually stayed.

Our household endured the status quo for eight years: my uncles,   14
my grandmother and I. Within the foursome rivalries and alliances
shifted. I became my grandmother's friend and she became mine. We
were the source of all the family comedy. When she said she wanted
a college diploma we gave her one—with tinfoil stars and a "magna
magna summa summa cum laude" inscription. We sang and performed skits. We talcum-powdered hair and wearing one of her old
dresses, I would appear as her "long-lost friend." We had other
themes, including a pen pal, "The Professor."

Of course, living with an elderly person had its raw aspects. When   15
she was ill our girls' room took on the stark aura of a geriatrics ward.
I imagined, to my shame, that neighbors could stare in through cur-
tainless windows as I tended to my grandmother's most personal
needs.

Yet, in these times of age segregation, with grandmothers sent off   16
to impersonal places, I wonder if the love and the comedy weren't
worth the intermittent difficulties? Certainly I learned what it might
be to become old. And I took as much comfort as my grandmother did
in a nightly exchange of Russian endearments—"Ya tebya lyublyu,"
"Ya tebya tozhe lyublyu—"I love you," "I love you, too."

If I sold my grandmother blouses and baubles, maybe she gave   17
me the truth in exchange. Once, when we were alone in the girls'
room, she turned to me, suddenly lucid, her good eye as bright as it

would ever be—a look I somehow recognized as her "real" gaze—and said, "My life passes like a dream."

Questions

1. In the second sentence, what does Cunningham mean by "a generic brand"?
2. What is the title of Esther's manuscript? What is it about? Do you detect any irony in the way Cunningham conveys this information? Explain.
3. In the second sentence of paragraph 4, what is conveyed by putting the names within quotation marks?
4. Is paragraph 4—about Esther's physical disabilities—in bad taste? Explain.
5. In her last paragraph Cunningham says that perhaps her grandmother gave her "the truth." What does she mean?
6. "I burned at the injustice of it and felt the heat of an uncomfortable truth." Where in the narrative does Cunningham say this? What was the "truth"? If you remember a similar experience, write a narrative that discloses both the experience and the truth on which it was based. Or, write an essay of 500 words on your own most potent experience of living with or near an elderly person.

Black Elk

High Horse's Courting

You know, in the old days, it was not very easy to get a girl when you wanted to be married. Sometimes it was hard work for a young man and he had to stand a great deal. Say I am a young

Black Elk, a *wichasha wakon* (holy man) of the Oglala Sioux, as a small boy witnessed the battle of the Little Bighorn (1876). He lived to see his people all but annihilated and his hopes for them extinguished. In 1931, toward the end of his life, he told his life story to the poet and scholar John G. Neihardt to preserve a sacred vision given him.

"High Horse's Courting" is a comic interlude in *Black Elk Speaks*, a predominantly tragic memoir.

man and I have seen a young girl who looks so beautiful to me that
I feel all sick when I think about her. I cannot just go and tell her about
it and then get married if she is willing. I have to be a very sneaky
fellow to talk to her at all, and after I have managed to talk to her,
that is only the beginning.

   Probably for a long time I have been feeling sick about a certain   2
girl because I love her so much, but she will not even look at me, and
her parents keep a good watch over her. But I keep feeling worse and
worse all the time; so maybe I sneak up to her tepee in the dark and
wait until she comes out. Maybe I just wait there all night and don't
get any sleep at all and she does not come out. Then I feel sicker than
ever about her.

   Maybe I hide in the brush by a spring where she sometimes goes   3
to get water, and when she comes by, if nobody is looking, then I jump
out and hold her and just make her listen to me. If she likes me too,
I can tell that from the way she acts, for she is very bashful and maybe
will not say a word or even look at me the first time. So I let her go,
and then maybe I sneak around until I can see her father alone, and
I tell him how many horses I can give him for his beautiful girl, and
by now I am feeling so sick that maybe I would give him all the horses
in the world if I had them.

   Well, this young man I am telling about was called High Horse,   4
and there was a girl in the village who looked so beautiful to him that
he was just sick all over from thinking about her so much and he was
getting sicker all the time. The girl was very shy, and her parents
thought a great deal of her because they were not young any more
and this was the only child they had. So they watched her all day long,
and they fixed it so that she would be safe at night too when they were
asleep. They thought so much of her that they had made a rawhide
bed for her to sleep in, and after they knew that High Horse was
sneaking around after her, they took rawhide thongs and tied the girl
in bed at night so that nobody could steal her when they were asleep,
for they were not sure but that their girl might really want to be stolen.

   Well, after High Horse had been sneaking around a good while   5
and hiding and waiting for the girl and getting sicker all the time, he
finally caught her alone and made her talk to him. Then he found out
that she liked him maybe a little. Of course this did not make him feel
well. It made him sicker than ever, but now he felt as brave as a bison
bull, and so he went right to her father and said he loved the girl so
much that he would give two good horses for her—one of them young
and the other one not so very old.

But the old man just waved his hand, meaning for High Horse to 6
go away and quit talking foolishness like that.

High Horse was feeling sicker than ever about it; but there was 7
another young fellow who said he would loan High Horse two ponies
and when he got some more horses, why, he could just give them
back for the ones he had borrowed.

Then High Horse went back to the old man and said he would 8
give four horses for the girl—two of them young and the other two
not hardly old at all. But the old man just waved his hand and would
not say anything.

So High Horse sneaked around until he could talk to the girl again, 9
and he asked her to run away with him. He told her he thought he
would just fall over and die if she did not. But she said she would not
do that; she wanted to be bought like a fine woman. You see she
thought a great deal of herself too.

That made High Horse feel so very sick that he could not eat a 10
bite, and he went around with his head hanging down as though he
might just fall down and die any time.

Red Deer was another young fellow, and he and High Horse were 11
great comrades, always doing things together. Red Deer saw how High
Horse was acting, and he said: "Cousin, what is the matter? Are you
sick in the belly? You look as though you were going to die."

Then High Horse told Red Deer how it was, and said he thought 12
he could not stay alive much longer if he could not marry the girl pretty
quick.

Red Deer thought awhile about it, and then he said: "Cousin, I 13
have a plan, and if you are man enough to do as I tell you, then
everything will be all right. She will not run away with you; her old
man will not take four horses; and four horses are all you can get. You
must steal her and run away with her. Then afterwhile you can come
back and the old man cannot do anything because she will be your
woman. Probably she wants you to steal her anyway."

So they planned what High Horse had to do, and he said he loved 14
the girl so much that he was man enough to do anything Red Deer or
anybody else could think up. So this is what they did.

That night late they sneaked up to the girl's tepee and waited until 15
it sounded inside as though the old man and the old woman and the
girl were sound asleep. Then High Horse crawled under the tepee with
a knife. He had to cut the rawhide thongs first, and then Red Deer,
who was pulling up the stakes around that side of the tepee, was going
to help drag the girl outside and gag her. After that, High Horse could

put her across his pony in front of him and hurry out of there and be happy all the rest of his life.

When High Horse had crawled inside, he felt so nervous that he 16 could hear his heart drumming, and it seemed so loud he felt sure it would 'waken the old folks. But it did not, and afterwhile he began cutting the thongs. Every time he cut one it made a pop and nearly scared him to death. But he was getting along all right and all the thongs were cut down as far as the girl's thighs, when he became so nervous that his knife slipped and stuck the girl. She gave a big, loud yell. Then the old folks jumped up and yelled too. By this time High Horse was outside, and he and Red Deer were running away like antelope. The old man and some other people chased the young men but they got away in the dark and nobody knew who it was.

Well, if you ever wanted a beautiful girl you will know how sick 17 High Horse was now. It was very bad the way he felt, and it looked as though he would starve even if he did not drop over dead sometime.

Red Deer kept thinking about this, and after a few days he went 18 to High Horse and said: "Cousin, take courage! I have another plan, and I am sure, if you are man enough, we can steal her this time." And High Horse said: "I am man enough to do anything anybody can think up, if I can only get that girl."

So this is what they did. 19

They went away from the village alone, and Red Deer made High 20 Horse strip naked. Then he painted High Horse solid white all over, and after that he painted black stripes all over the white and put black rings around High Horse's eyes. High Horse looked terrible. He looked so terrible that when Red Deer was through painting and took a good look at what he had done, he said it scared even him a little.

"Now," Red Deer said, "if you get caught again, everybody will 21 be so scared they will think you are a bad spirit and will be afraid to chase you."

So when the night was getting old and everybody was sound 22 asleep, they sneaked back to the girl's tepee. High Horse crawled in with his knife, as before, and Red Deer waited outside, ready to drag the girl out and gag her when High Horse had all the thongs cut.

High Horse crept up by the girl's bed and began cutting at the 23 thongs. But he kept thinking, "If they see me they will shoot me because I look so terrible." The girl was restless and kept squirming around in bed, and when a thong was cut, it popped. So High Horse worked very slowly and carefully.

But he must have made some noise, for suddenly the old woman 24 awoke and said to her old man: "Old Man, wake up! There is somebody in this tepee!" But the old man was sleepy and didn't want to be bothered. He said: "Of course there is somebody in this tepee. Go to sleep and don't bother me." Then he snored some more.

But High Horse was so scared by now that he lay very still and   25
as flat to the ground as he could. Now, you see, he had not been sleeping very well for a long time because he was so sick about the girl. And while he was lying there waiting for the old woman to snore, he just forgot everything, even how beautiful the girl was. Red Deer who was lying outside ready to do his part, wondered and wondered what had happened in there, but he did not dare call out to High Horse.

Afterwhile the day began to break and Red Deer had to leave with   26
the two ponies he had staked there for his comrade and girl, or somebody would see him.

So he left.   27

Now when it was getting light in the tepee, the girl awoke and   28
the first thing she saw was a terrible animal, all white with black stripes on it, lying asleep beside her bed. So she screamed, and then the old woman screamed and the old man yelled. High Horse jumped up, scared almost to death, and he nearly knocked the tepee down getting out of there.

People were coming running from all over the village with guns   29
and bows and axes, and everybody was yelling.

By now High Horse was running so fast that he hardly touched   30
the ground at all, and he looked so terrible that the people fled from him and let him run. Some braves wanted to shoot at him, but the others said he might be some sacred being and it would bring bad trouble to kill him.

High Horse made for the river that was near, and in among the   31
brush he found a hollow tree and dived into it. Afterwhile some braves came there and he could hear them saying that it was some bad spirit that had come out of the water and gone back in again.

That morning the people were ordered to break camp and move   32
away from there. So they did, while High Horse was hiding in his hollow tree.

Now Red Deer had been watching all this from his own tepee and   33
trying to look as though he were as much surprised and scared as all the others. So when the camp moved, he sneaked back to where he had seen his comrade disappear. When he was down there in the brush, he called, and High Horse answered, because he knew his friend's voice. They washed off the paint from High Horse and sat down on the river bank to talk about their troubles.

High Horse said he never would go back to the village as long as   34 he lived and he did not care what happened to him now. He said he was going to go on the war-path all by himself. Red Deer said: "No, cousin, you are not going on the war-path alone, because I am going with you."

So Red Deer got everything ready, and at night they started out   35 on the war-path all alone. After several days they came to a Crow camp just about sundown, and when it was dark they sneaked up to where the Crow horses were grazing, killed the horse guard, who was not thinking about enemies because he thought all the Lakotas were far away, and drove off about a hundred horses.

They got a big start because all the Crow horses stampeded and   36 it was probably morning before the Crow warriors could catch any horses to ride. Red Deer and High Horse fled with their herd three days and nights before they reached the village of their people. Then they drove the whole herd right into the village and up in front of the girl's tepee. The old man was there, and High Horse called out to him and asked if he thought maybe that would be enough horses for his girl. The old man did not wave him away that time. It was not the horses that he wanted. What he wanted was a son who was a real man and good for something.

So High Horse got his girl after all, and I think he deserved   37 her.

Questions

Although High Horse's behavior is amusing and at times ridiculous, how does Black Elk make it clear that he is not ridiculing the young man, but is instead in sympathy with him? Consider the following questions:

1. What is the effect of the first three paragraphs? Think about the first two sentences, and then the passage beginning "Say I am a young man . . ." and ending ". . . I would give him all the horses in the world if I had them."
2. Describe the behavior of the young girl, and of her father and mother. How do they contribute to the comedy? How does their behavior affect your understanding of Black Elk's attitude toward High Horse?
3. What is the function of Red Deer?
4. The narrative consists of several episodes. List them in the order in which they occur, and then describe the narrative's structure. How does this structure affect the tone?

Anonymous

Confessions of an Erstwhile Child

Some years ago I attempted to introduce a class of Upward   1
Bound students to political theory via More's *Utopia*. It was a mistake:
I taught precious little theory and earned More a class full of undying
enemies on account of two of his ideas. The first, that all members of
a Utopian family were subject to the lifelong authority of its eldest
male. The second, the Utopian provision that should a child wish to
follow a profession different from that of his family, he could be transferred by adoption to a family that practiced the desired trade. My
students were not impressed with my claim that the one provision
softened the other and made for a fair compromise—for what causes
most of our quarrels with our parents but our choice of life-patterns,
of occupation? In objecting to the first provision my students were
picturing themselves as children, subject to an unyielding authority.
But on the second provision they surprised me by taking the parents'
role and arguing that this form of ad lib adoption denied them a fundamental right of ownership over their children. It occurred to me that
these reactions were two parts of the same pathology: having suffered
the discipline of unreasonable parents, one has earned the right to be
unreasonable in turn to one's children. The phenomenon has well-
known parallels, such as frantic martinets who have risen from the
ranks. Having served time as property, my Upward Bound students
wanted theirs back as proprietors. I shuddered. It hardly takes an advanced course in Freudian psychology to realize that the perpetuation,
generation after generation, of psychic lesions must go right to this
source, the philosophically dubious notion that children are the property of their biological parents, compounded with the unphilosophic
certitude so many parents harbor, that their children must serve an
apprenticeship as like their own as they can manage.

The idea of the child as property has always bothered me, for   2
personal reasons I shall outline. I lack the feeling that I own my children and I have always scoffed at the idea that what they are and do

---

The anonymous author of this essay has revealed only that he was forty when
he wrote it, is married, and is the father of three children.

is a continuation or a rejection of my being. I like them, I sympathize with them, I acknowledge the obligation to support them for a term of years—but I am not so fond or foolish as to regard a biological tie as a lien on their loyalty or respect, nor to imagine that I am equipped with preternatural powers of guidance as to their success and happiness. Beyond inculcating some of the obvious social protocols required in civilized life, who am I to pronounce on what makes for a happy or successful life? How many of us can say that we have successfully managed our own lives? Can we do better with our children? I am unimpressed, to say no more, with parents who have no great track record, presuming to oracular powers in regard to their children's lives.

The current debate over the Equal Rights Amendment frequently 3 turns to custody questions. Opponents of ERA have made the horrifying discovery that ERA will spell the end of the mother's presumed rights of custody in divorce or separation cases, and that fathers may begin custody rights. Indeed a few odd cases have been so settled recently in anticipation of the ratification of ERA. If ratified, ERA would be an extremely blunt instrument for calling the whole idea of custody into question, but I for one will applaud anything that serves to begin debate. As important as equal rights between adults may be, I think that the rights of children are a far more serious and unattended need. To me, custody by natural parents, far from being a presumed right only re-examined in case of collapsing marriages, should be viewed as a privilege.

At this point I have to explain why I can so calmly contemplate 4 the denial of so-called parental rights.

I am the only child of two harsh and combative personalities who 5 married, seemingly, in order to have a sparring partner always at hand. My parents have had no other consistent or lasting aim in life but to win out over each other in a contest of wills. They still live, vigorous and angry septuagenarians, their ferocity little blunted by age or human respect. My earliest memories—almost my sole memories—are of unending combat, in which I was sometimes an appalled spectator, more often a hopeless negotiator in a war of no quarter, and most often a bystander accused of covert belligerency on behalf of one side or the other, and frequently of both! I grew up with two supposed adults who were absorbed in their hatreds and recriminations to the exclusion of almost all other reality. Not only did I pass by almost unnoticed in their struggle, the Depression and World War II passed them by equally unnoticed. I figured mainly as a practice target for sarcasm and invective, and occasionally as the ultimate culprit responsible for their unhappiness. ("If it weren't for you," my mother would sometimes say, "I could leave that SOB," a remark belied by her refusal to leave the SOB during these 20 long years since I left their "shelter.")

The reader may ask, "How did you survive if your parents' house 6 was all that bad?" I have three answers. First, I survived by the moral equivalent of running away to sea or the circus, i.e., by burying myself in books and study, especially in the history of faraway and (I thought) more idealistic times than our own, and by consciously shaping my life and tastes to be as different as possible from those of my parents (this was a reproach to them, they knew, and it formed the basis of a whole secondary area of conflict and misunderstanding). Second, I survived because statistically most people "survive" horrible families, but survival can be a qualified term, as it is in my case by a permanently impaired digestive system and an unnatural sensitivity to raised voices. And third, though I found solace in schooling and the rationality, cooperation and basic fairness in teachers that I missed in my parents, I must now question whether it is healthy for a child to count so heavily on schooling for the love and approval that he deserves from his home and family. Even if schooling can do this well, in later life it means that one is loyal and affectionate toward schooling, not toward parents, who may in some sense need affection even if they don't "deserve" it. I am not unaware that however fair and rational I may be in reaction to my parents' counter-examples, I am a very cold-hearted man. I might have done better transferred to a new family, not just by receiving love, but through learning to give it—a lack I mourn as much or more than my failure to receive.

It is little wonder then that I have an acquired immunity to the 7 notion that parental custody is by and large a preferable thing. In my case, almost anything else would have been preferable, including even a rather callously run orphanage—anything for a little peace and quiet. Some people are simply unfit, under any conditions, to be parents, even if, indeed especially if, they maintain the charade of a viable marriage. My parents had no moral right to custody of children, and I cannot believe that my experience is unique or particularly isolated. There are all too many such marriages, in which some form of horror, congenial enough to adults too sick or crazed to recognize it, works its daily ruination on children. Surely thousands of children conclude at age 10 or 11, as I did, that marriage is simply an institution in which people are free to be as beastly as they have a mind to, which may lead either to a rejection of marriage or to a decision to reduplicate a sick marriage a second time, with another generation of victims. It is time to consider the rights of the victims.

How to implement a nascent theory of justice for children is difficult to say. One cannot imagine taking the word of a five-year-old against his parents, but what about a 10- or 12-year-old? At *some* point, children should have the right to escape the dominance of impossible parents. The matter used to be easier than it has been since World War I. The time-honored solution—for boys—of running away from home has been made infeasible by economic conditions, fingerprints, social security and minimum wage laws. No apprenticeship system exists any more, much less its upper-class medieval version—with required exchange of boys at puberty among noble families to serve as pages and so forth. The adoption system contemplated in More's *Utopia* is a half-remembered echo of a medieval life, in which society, wiser than its theory, decreed a general exchange of children at or just before puberty, whether through apprenticeship or page-service, or more informal arrangements, like going to a university at 14 or running away with troubadors or gypsies.

Exchanging children is a wisely conceived safety valve against a too traumatic involvement between the biological parent and the child. Children need an alternative to living all their formative life in the same biological unit. They should have the right to petition for release from some sorts of families, to join other families, or to engage in other sorts of relationships that may provide equivalent service but may not be organized as a family. The nuclear family, after all, is not such an old or proven vehicle. Phillippe Aries' book, *Centuries of Childhood,* made the important point that the idea of helpless childhood is itself a notion of recent origin, that grew up simultaneously in the 16th and 17th centuries with the small and tight-knit nuclear family, sealed off from the world by another recent invention, "privacy." The older *extended* family (which is the kind More knew about) was probably more authoritarian on paper but much less productive of dependency in actual operation. There ought to be more than one way a youngster can enter adult society with more than half of his sanity left. At least no one should be forced to remain in a no-win game against a couple of crazy parents for 15–18 years. At 10 or 12, children in really messy situations should have the legal right to petition for removal from impossible families, and those rights should be reasonably easy to exercise. (This goes on de facto among the poor, of course, but it is not legal, and usually carries both stigma and danger.) The minimum wage laws should be modified to exempt such persons, especially if they wish to continue their education, working perhaps for public agencies, if they have no other means of support. If their parents can support them, then the equivalent of child support should be charged them to maintain their children, not in luxury, but adequately. Adoption of older children should be facilitated by easing of legal procedures (designed mainly to govern the adoption of *infants*) plus tax advantages for those willing to adopt older children on grounds of goodwill. Indeed children wishing to escape impossible family situations should be allowed a fair degree of initiative in finding and negotiating with possible future families.

Obviously the risk of rackets would be very high unless the exact terms of such provisions were framed very carefully, but the possibility of rackets is less frightening to anyone who thinks about it for long than the dangers of the present situation, which are evident and unrelieved by any signs of improvement. In barely a century this country has changed from a relatively loose society in which Huckleberry Finns were not uncommon, to a society of tense, airless nuclear families in which unhealthy and neurotic tendencies, once spawned in a family, tend to repeat themselves at a magnifying and accelerating rate. We may soon gain the distinction of being the only nation on earth to need not just medicare but "psychi-care." We have invested far too heavily in the unproved "equity" called the nuclear family; that stock is about to crash and we ought to begin finding escape options. In colonial days many New England colonies passed laws imposing fines or extra taxes on parents who kept their children under their own roofs after age 15 or 16, on the sensible notion that a person of that age ought to be out and doing on his own, whether going to Yale or apprenticing in a foundry. Even without the benefit of Freud, the colonial fathers had a good sense of what was wrong with a closely bound and centripetal family structure—it concentrates craziness like compound interest, and so they hit it with monetary penalties, a proper Protestant response, intolerant at once of both mystery and excuses. But this was the last gasp of a medieval and fundamentally Catholic idea that children, God help them, while they may be the children of *these* particular parents biologically, spiritually are the children of God, and more appositely are the children of the entire community, for which the entire community takes responsibility. The unguessed secret of the middle ages was not that monasteries relieved parents of unwanted children; more frequently, they relieved children of unwanted parents!

Questions

1. What is the author's thesis? (Quote the thesis sentence.) Apart from his own experience, what evidence or other means does he offer to persuade you to accept his thesis?
2. What part does the *tone* of his article play in persuading you to agree with him, or in alienating you? Does his tone strike you, perhaps, as vigorous or belligerent, as ironic or bitter, as reasonable or hysterical?
3. The author admits (paragraph 6) that he is "a very cold-hearted man." Do you remember your initial reaction to that sentence? What was it? Overall, does the author strengthen or jeopardize his argument by this admission? Explain.
4. If you did not find the article persuasive, did you find it interesting? Can you explain why?

Jonathan Swift

A Modest Proposal

For Preventing the Children of Poor People
in Ireland from Being a Burden to Their
Parents or Country, and for Making Them
Beneficial to the Public

It is a melancholy object to those who walk through this   1
great town or travel in the country, when they see the streets, the
roads, and cabin doors, crowded with beggars of the female sex, fol-

Jonathan Swift (1667–1745) was born in Ireland of an English family. He was
ordained in the Church of Ireland in 1694, and in 1714 he became dean of St.
Patrick's Cathedral, Dublin. He wrote abundantly on political and religious topics, often motivated (in his own words) by "savage indignation." It is ironic that
Gulliver's Travels, the masterpiece by this master of irony, is most widely thought
of as a book for children.

From the middle of the sixteenth century the English regulated the Irish
economy so that it would enrich England. Heavy taxes and other repressive
legislation impoverished Ireland, and in 1728, the year before Swift wrote "A
Modest Proposal," Ireland was further weakened by a severe famine. Swift,
deeply moved by the injustice, the stupidity, and the suffering that he found in
Ireland, adopts the disguise or persona of an economist and offers an ironic
suggestion on how Irish families may improve their conditions.

lowed by three, four, or six children, all in rags and importuning every passenger for an alms. These mothers, instead of being able to work for their honest livelihood, are forced to employ all their time in strolling to beg sustenance for their helpless infants: who as they grow up either turn thieves for want of work, or leave their dear native country to fight for the pretender in Spain, or sell themselves to the Barbadoes.

I think it is agreed by all parties that this prodigious number of 2 children in the arms, or on the backs, or at the heels of their mothers, and frequently of their fathers, is in the present deplorable state of the kingdom a very great additional grievance; and, therefore, whoever could find out a fair, cheap, and easy method of making these children sound, useful members of the commonwealth, would deserve so well of the public as to have his statue set up for a preserver of the nation.

But my intention is very far from being confined to provide only 3 for the children of professed beggars; it is of a much greater extent, and shall take in the whole number of infants at a certain age who are born of parents in effect as little able to support them as those who demand our charity in the streets.

As to my own part, having turned my thoughts for many years 4 upon this important subject, and maturely weighed the several schemes of our projectors, I have always found them grossly mistaken in their computation. It is true, a child just dropped from its dam may be supported by her milk for a solar year, with little other nourishment; at most not above the value of 2s.,[1] which the mother may certainly get, or the value in scraps, by her lawful occupation of begging; and it is exactly at one year old that I propose to provide for them in such a manner as instead of being a charge upon their parents or the parish, or wanting food and raiment for the rest of their lives, they shall on the contrary contribute to the feeding, and partly to the clothing, of many thousands.

There is likewise another great advantage in my scheme, that it 5 will prevent those voluntary abortions, and that horrid practice of women murdering their bastard children, alas! too frequent among us! sacrificing the poor innocent babes I doubt more to avoid the expense than the shame, which would move tears and pity in the most savage and inhuman breast.

The number of souls in this kingdom being usually reckoned one 6 million and a half, of these I calculate there may be about 200,000 couple whose wives are breeders; from which number I subtract 30,000 couple

---

[1] 2s. = two shillings. Later in the essay, "£" and "l" stand for pounds and "d" for pence. (Editors' note)

who are able to maintain their own children (although I apprehend there cannot be so many, under the present distress of the kingdom); but this being granted, there will remain 170,000 breeders. I again subtract 50,000 for those women who miscarry, or whose children die by accident or disease within the year. There only remain 120,000 children of poor parents annually born. The question therefore is, how this number shall be reared and provided for? which, as I have already said, under the present situation of affairs, is utterly impossible by all the methods hitherto proposed. For we can neither employ them in handicraft or agriculture; we neither build houses (I mean in the country) nor cultivate land; they can very seldom pick up a livelihood by stealing, till they arrive at six years old, except where they are of towardly parts; although I confess they learn the rudiments much earlier; during which time they can, however, be properly looked upon only as probationers; as I have been informed by a principal gentleman in the county of Cavan, who protested to me that he never knew above one or two instances under the age of six, even in a part of the kingdom so renowned for the quickest proficiency in that art.

I am assured by our merchants, that a boy or a girl before twelve   7
years old is no saleable commodity; and even when they come to this age they will not yield above 31. or 31. 2s. 6d. at most on the exchange; which cannot turn to account either to the parents or kingdom, the charge of nutriment and rags having been at least four times that value.

I shall now therefore humbly propose my own thoughts, which I   8
hope will not be liable to the least objection.

I have been assured by a very knowing American of my acquaint-   9
ance in London, that a young healthy child well nursed is at a year old a most delicious, nourishing, and wholesome food, whether stewed, roasted, baked, or broiled; and I make no doubt that it will equally serve in a fricassee or a ragout.

I do therefore humbly offer it to public consideration that of the   10
120,000 children already computed, 20,000 may be reserved for breed, whereof only one-fourth part to be males; which is more than we allow to sheep, black cattle, or swine; and my reason is, that these children are seldom the fruits of marriage, a circumstance not much regarded by our savages; therefore one male will be sufficient to serve four females. That the remaining 100,000 may, at a year old, be offered in sale to the persons of quality and fortune through the kingdom; always advising the mother to let them suck plentifully in the last month, so

as to render them plump and fat for a good table. A child will make two dishes at an entertainment for friends; and when the family dines alone, the fore or hind quarter will make a reasonable dish, and seasoned with a little pepper or salt will be very good boiled on the fourth day, especially in winter.

I have reckoned upon a medium that a child just born will weigh 11 12 pounds, and in a solar year, if tolerably nursed, will increase to 28 pounds.

I grant this food will be somewhat dear, and therefore very proper 12 for landlords, who, as they have already devoured most of the parents, seem to have the best title to the children.

Infant's flesh will be in season throughout the year, but more plen- 13 tiful in March, and a little before and after: for we are told by a grave author, an eminent French physician, that fish being a prolific diet, there are more children born in Roman Catholic countries about nine months after Lent than at any other season; therefore, reckoning a year after Lent, the markets will be more glutted than usual, because the number of popish infants is at least three to one in this kingdom: and therefore it will have one other collateral advantage, by lessening the number of papists among us.

I have already computed the charge of nursing a beggar's child (in 14 which list I reckon all cottagers, laborers, and four-fifths of the farmers) to be about 2s. per annum, rags included; and I believe no gentleman would repine to give 10s. for the carcass of a good fat child, which, as I have said, will make four dishes of excellent nutritive meat, when he has only some particular friend or his own family to dine with him. Thus the squire will learn to be a good landlord, and grow popular among the tenants; the mother will have 8s. net profit, and be fit for work till she produces another child.

Those who are more thrifty (as I must confess the times require) 15 may flay the carcass; the skin of which artificially dressed will make admirable gloves for ladies, and summer boots for fine gentlemen.

As to our city of Dublin, shambles may be appointed for this pur- 16 pose in the most convenient parts of it, and butchers we may be assured will not be wanting: although I rather recommend buying the children alive, and dressing them hot from the knife as we do roasting pigs.

A very worthy person, a true lover of his country, and whose 17 virtues I highly esteem, was lately pleased in discoursing on this matter to offer a refinement upon my scheme. He said that many gentlemen of this kingdom, having of late destroyed their deer, he conceived that the want of venison might be well supplied by the bodies of young lads and maidens, not exceeding fourteen years of age nor under twelve; so great a number of both sexes in every country being now ready to starve for want of work and service; and these to be disposed of by their parents, if alive, or otherwise by their nearest relations. But with due deference to so excellent a friend and so deserving a patriot, I cannot be altogether in his sentiments; for as to the males, my American acquaintance assured me from frequent experience that their flesh was generally tough and lean, like that of our schoolboys by continual exercise, and their taste disagreeable; and to fatten them would not answer the charge. Then as to the females, it would, I think, with humble submission be a loss to the public, because they soon would become breeders themselves: and besides, it is not improbable that some scrupulous people might be apt to censure such a practice (although indeed very unjustly), as a little bordering upon cruelty; which, I confess, has always been with me the strongest objection against any project, how well soever intended.

But in order to justify my friend, he confessed that this expedient 18 was put into his head by the famous Psalmanazar, a native of the island Formosa, who came from thence to London about twenty years ago: and in conversation told my friend, that in his country when any young person happened to be put to death, the executioner sold the carcass to persons of quality as a prime dainty; and that in his time the body of a plump girl of fifteen, who was crucified for an attempt to poison the emperor, was sold to his imperial majesty's prime minister of state, and other great mandarins of the court, in joints from the gibbet, at 400 crowns. Neither indeed can I deny, that if the same use were made of several plump young girls in this town, who without one single groat to their fortunes cannot stir abroad without a chair, and appear at the playhouse and assemblies in foreign fineries which they never will pay for, the kingdom would not be the worse.

Some persons of a desponding spirit are in great concern about 19 that vast number of poor people, who are aged, diseased, or maimed, and I have been desired to employ my thoughts what course may be taken to ease the nation of so grievous an encumbrance. But I am not in the least pain upon that matter, because it is very well known that they are every day dying and rotting by cold and famine, and filth and vermin, as fast as can be reasonably expected. And as to the young laborers, they are now in as hopeful a condition: they cannot get work, and consequently pine away for want of nourishment, to a degree that if at any time they are accidentally hired to common labor, they have not strength to perform it; and thus the country and themselves are happily delivered from the evils to come.

I have too long digressed, and therefore shall return to my subject. 20 I think the advantages by the proposal which I have made are obvious and many, as well as of the highest importance.

For first, as I have already observed, it would greatly lessen the 21 number of papists, with whom we are yearly overrun, being the principal breeders of the nation as well as our most dangerous enemies; and who stay at home on purpose to deliver the kingdom to the Pretender, hoping to take their advantage by the absence of so many good Protestants, who have chosen rather to leave their country than stay at home and pay tithes against their conscience to an Episcopal curate.

Secondly, The poor tenants will have something valuable of their 22 own, which by law may be made liable to distress and help to pay their landlord's rent, their corn and cattle being already seized, and money a thing unknown.

Thirdly, Whereas the maintenance of 100,000 children from two 23 years old and upward, cannot be computed at less than 10s. a-piece per annum, the nation's stock will be thereby increased £50,000 per annum, beside the profit of a new dish introduced to the tables of all gentlemen of fortune in the kingdom who have any refinement in taste. And the money will circulate among ourselves, the goods being entirely of our own growth and manufacture.

Fourthly, The constant breeders beside the gain of 8s. sterling per 24 annum by the sale of their children, will be rid of the charge of maintaining them after the first year.

Fifthly, This food would likewise bring great custom to taverns, 25 where the vintners will certainly be so prudent as to procure the best receipts for dressing it to perfection, and consequently have their houses frequented by all the fine gentlemen, who justly value themselves upon their knowledge in good eating; and a skilful cook who understands how to oblige his guests, will contrive to make it as expensive as they please.

Sixthly, This would be a great inducement to marriage, which all 26 wise nations have either encouraged by rewards or enforced by laws and penalties. It would increase the care and tenderness of mothers toward their children, when they were sure of a settlement for life to the poor babes, provided in some sort by the public, to their annual profit instead of expense. We should see an honest emulation among the married women, which of them would bring the fattest child to the market. Men would become as fond of their wives during the time of their pregnancy as they are now of their mares in foal, their cows in calf, their sows when they are ready to farrow; nor offer to beat or kick them (as is too frequent a practice) for fear of a miscarriage.

Many other advantages might be enumerated. For instance, the 27 addition of some thousand carcasses in our exportation of barreled beef, the propagation of swine's flesh, and improvement in the art of making good bacon, so much wanted among us by the great destruction of pigs, too frequent at our table; which are no way comparable in taste or magnificence to a well-grown, fat, yearling child, which roasted whole will make a considerable figure at a lord mayor's feast or any other public entertainment. But this and many others I omit, being studious of brevity.

Supposing that 1,000 families in this city would be constant cus- 28 tomers for infants' flesh, besides others who might have it at merry-meetings, particularly at weddings and christenings, I compute that Dublin would take off annually about 20,000 carcasses; and the rest of the kingdom (where probably they will be sold somewhat cheaper) the remaining 80,000.

I can think of no one objection that will possibly be raised against 29 this proposal, unless it should be urged that the number of people will be thereby much lessened in the kingdom. This I freely own, and it was indeed one principal design in offering it to the world. I desire the reader will observe, that I calculate my remedy for this one individual kingdom of Ireland and for no other that ever was, is, or I think ever can be upon earth. Therefore let no man talk to me of other expedients: of taxing our absentees at 5s. a pound: of using neither clothes nor household furniture except what is of our own growth and manufacture: of utterly rejecting the materials and instruments that promote foreign luxury: of curing the expensiveness of pride, vanity, idleness, and gaming in our women: of introducing a vein of parsimony, prudence, and temperance: of learning to love our country, in the want of which we differ even from Laplanders and the inhabitants of Topinamboo: of quitting our animosities and factions, nor acting any longer like the Jews, who were murdering one another at the very moment their city was taken: of being a little cautious not to sell our country and conscience for nothing: of teaching landlords to have at least one degree of mercy toward their tenants: lastly, of putting a spirit of honesty, industry, and skill into our shopkeepers; who, if a resolution could now be taken to buy only our native goods, would immediately unite to cheat and exact upon us in the price, the measure, and the goodness, nor could ever yet be brought to make one fair proposal of just dealing, though often and earnestly invited to it.

Therefore, I repeat, let no man talk to me of these and the like 30 expedients, till he has at least some glimpse of hope that there will be ever some hearty and sincere attempt to put them in practice.

But as to myself, having been wearied out for many years with 31 offering vain, idle, visionary thoughts, and at length utterly despairing of success, I fortunately fell upon this proposal; which, as it is wholly new, so it has something solid and real, of no expense and little trouble, full in our own power, and whereby we can incur no danger in disobliging England. For this kind of commodity will not bear exportation, the flesh being of too tender a consistence to admit a long continuance in salt, although perhaps I could name a country which would be glad to eat up our whole nation without it.

After all, I am not so violently bent upon my own opinion as to 32 reject any offer proposed by wise men, which shall be found equally innocent, cheap, easy, and effectual. But before something of that kind shall be advanced in contradiction to my scheme, and offering a better, I desire the author or authors will be pleased maturely to consider two points. First, as things now stand, how they will be able to find food and raiment for 100,000 useless mouths and backs. And secondly, there being a round million of creatures in human figure throughout this kingdom, whose subsistence put into a common stock would leave them in debt 200,000,000l. sterling, adding those who are beggars by profession to the bulk of farmers, cottagers, and laborers, with the wives and children who are beggars in effect; I desire those politicians who dislike my overture, and may perhaps be so bold as to attempt an answer, that they will first ask the parents of these mortals, whether they would not at this day think it a great happiness to have been sold for food at a year old in the manner I prescribe, and thereby have avoided such a perpetual scene of misfortunes as they have since gone through by the oppression of landlords, the impossibility of paying rent without money or trade, the want of common sustenance, with neither house nor clothes to cover them from the inclemencies of the weather, and the most inevitable prospect of entailing the like or greater miseries upon their breed for ever.

I profess, in the sincerity of my heart, that I have not the least 33 personal interest in endeavoring to promote this necessary work, having no other motive than the public good of my country, by advancing our trade, providing for infants, relieving the poor, and giving some pleasure to the rich. I have no children by which I can propose to get a single penny; the youngest being nine years old, and my wife past child-bearing.

Questions

1. In paragraph 4, Swift speaks of "projectors." Check the *Oxford English Dictionary* to see the implications of this word in the eighteenth century. Keeping these implications in mind, characterize the pamphleteer (not Swift but his persona, an invented "projector") who offers his "modest proposal." What sort of man does he think he is? What sort of man do we regard him as? Support your assertions with evidence.
2. In the first paragraph the speaker says that the sight of mothers begging is "melancholy." In this paragraph what assumption does the speaker make about women that in part gives rise to this melancholy? Now that you are familiar with the entire essay, explain Swift's strategy in his first paragraph.
3. Explain the function of the "other expedients" (listed in paragraph 29).
4. How might you argue that although this satire is primarily ferocious, it also contains some playful touches? What specific passages might support your argument?
5. In the speaker's view, what underlies good family relationships?

Peter Singer

Animal Liberation

I

We are familiar with Black Liberation, Gay Liberation, and a variety of other movements. With Women's Liberation some thought we had come to the end of the road. Discrimination on the

Peter Singer teaches philosophy at Monash University in Melbourne, Australia. This essay originally appeared, in 1973, as a review of *Animals, Men and Morals*, edited by Stanley and Roslind Godlovitch and John Harris.

basis of sex, it has been said, is the last form of discrimination that is universally accepted and practiced without pretense, even in those liberal circles which have long prided themselves on their freedom from racial discrimination. But one should always be wary of talking of "the last remaining form of discrimination." If we have learned anything from the liberation movements, we should have learned how difficult it is to be aware of the ways in which we discriminate until they are forcefully pointed out to us. A liberation movement demands an expansion of our moral horizons, so that practices that were previously regarded as natural and inevitable are now seen as intolerable.

Animals, Men and Morals is a manifesto for an Animal Liberation 2 movement. The contributors to the book may not all see the issue this way. They are a varied group. Philosophers, ranging from professors to graduate students, make up the largest contingent. There are five of them, including the three editors, and there is also an extract from the unjustly neglected German philosopher with an English name, Leonard Nelson, who died in 1927. There are essays by two novelist/critics, Brigid Brophy and Maureen Duffy, and another by Muriel the Lady Dowding, widow of Dowding of Battle of Britain fame and the founder of "Beauty Without Cruelty," a movement that campaigns against the use of animals for furs and cosmetics. The other pieces are by a psychologist, a botanist, a sociologist, and Ruth Harrison, who is probably best described as a professional campaigner for animal welfare.

Whether or not these people, as individuals, would all agree that 3 they are launching a liberation movement for animals, the book as a whole amounts to no less. It is a demand for a complete change in our attitudes to nonhumans. It is a demand that we cease to regard the exploitation of other species as natural and inevitable, and that, instead, we see it as a continuing moral outrage. Patrick Corbett, Professor of Philosophy at Sussex University, captures the spirit of the book in his closing words:

> . . . We require now to extend the great principles of liberty, equality and fraternity over the lives of animals. Let animal slavery join human slavery in the graveyard of the past.

The reader is likely to be skeptical. "Animal Liberation" sounds 4 more like a parody of liberation movements than a serious objective. The reader may think: We support the claims of blacks and women for equality because blacks and women really are equal to whites and males—equal in intelligence and in abilities, capacity for leadership, rationality, and so on. Humans and nonhumans obviously are not equal in these respects. Since justice demands only that we treat equals equally, unequal treatment of humans and nonhumans cannot be an injustice.

This is a tempting reply, but a dangerous one. It commits the non- 5 racist and non-sexist to a dogmatic belief that blacks and women really are just as intelligent, able, etc., as whites and males—and no more. Quite possibly this happens to be the case. Certainly attempts to prove that racial or sexual differences in these respects have a genetic origin have not been conclusive. But do we really want to stake our demand for equality on the assumption that there are no genetic differences of this kind between the different races or sexes? Surely the appropriate response to those who claim to have found evidence for such genetic differences is not to stick to the belief that there are no differences, whatever the evidence to the contrary; rather one should be clear that the claim to equality does not depend on IQ. Moral equality is distinct from factual equality. Otherwise it would be nonsense to talk of the equality of human beings, since humans, as individuals, obviously differ in intelligence and almost any ability one cares to name. If possessing greater intelligence does not entitle one human to exploit another, why should it entitle humans to exploit nonhumans?

Jeremy Bentham expressed the essential basis of equality in his 6 famous formula: "Each to count for one and none for more than one." In other words, the interests of every being that has interests are to be taken into account and treated equally with the like interests of any other being. Other moral philosophers, before and after Bentham, have made the same point in different ways. Our concern for others must not depend on whether they possess certain characteristics, though just what that concern involves may, of course, vary according to such characteristics.

Bentham, incidentally, was well aware that the logic of the demand 7 for racial equality did not stop at the equality of humans. He wrote:

The day *may* come when the rest of the animal creation may acquire those rights which never could have been withholden from them but by the hand of tyranny. The French have already discovered that the blackness of the skin is no reason why a human being should be abandoned without redress to the caprice of a tormentor. It may one day come to be recognized that the number of the legs, the villosity of the skin, or the termination of the *os sacrum*, are reasons equally insufficient for abandoning a sensitive being to the same fate. What else is it that should trace the insuperable line? Is it the faculty of reason, or perhaps the faculty of discourse? But a full-grown horse or dog is beyond comparison a more rational, as well as a more conversable animal, than an infant of a day, or a week, or even a month, old. But suppose they were otherwise, what would it avail? The question is not, Can they *reason?* nor Can they *talk?* but, Can they *suffer?*[1]

Surely Bentham was right. If a being suffers, there can be no moral justification for refusing to take that suffering into consideration, and, indeed, to count it equally with the like suffering (if rough comparisons can be made) of any other being.

So the only question is: Do animals other than man suffer? Most people agree unhesitatingly that animals like cats and dogs can and do suffer, and this seems also to be assumed by those laws that prohibit wanton cruelty to such animals. Personally, I have no doubt at all about this and find it hard to take seriously the doubts that a few people apparently do have. The editors and contributors of *Animals, Men and Morals* seem to feel the same way, for although the question is raised more than once, doubts are quickly dismissed each time. Nevertheless, because this is such a fundamental point, it is worth asking what grounds we have for attributing suffering to other animals. 8

It is best to begin by asking what grounds any individual human has for supposing that other humans feel pain. Since pain is a state of consciousness, a "mental event," it can never be directly observed. No observations, whether behavioral signs such as writhing or screaming or physiological or neurological recordings, are observations of pain itself. Pain is something one feels, and one can only infer that others are feeling it from various external indications. The fact that only philosophers are ever skeptical about whether other humans feel pain shows that we regard such inference as justifiable in the case of humans. 9

Is there any reason why the same inference should be unjustifiable for other animals? Nearly all the external signs which lead us to infer pain in other humans can be seen in other species, especially "higher" animals such as mammals and birds. Behavioral signs—writhing, yelping, or other forms of calling, attempts to avoid the source of pain, and many others—are present. We know, too, that these animals are biologically similar in the relevant respects, having nervous systems like ours which can be observed to function as ours do. 10

So the grounds for inferring that these animals can feel pain are nearly as good as the grounds for inferring other humans do. Only 11

[1] *The Principles of Morals and Legislation*, ch. XVII, sec. 1, footnote to paragraph 4.

nearly, for there is one behavioral sign that humans have but non-humans, with the exception of one or two specially raised chimpanzees, do not have. This, of course, is a developed language. As the quotation from Bentham indicates, this has long been regarded as an important distinction between man and other animals. Other animals may communicate with each other, but not in the way we do. Following Chomsky, many people now mark this distinction by saying that only humans communicate in a form that is governed by rules of syntax. (For the purposes of this argument, linguists allow those chimpanzees who have learned a syntactic sign language to rank as honorary humans.) Nevertheless, as Bentham pointed out, this distinction is not relevant to the question of how animals ought to be treated, unless it can be linked to the issue of whether animals suffer.

This link may be attempted in two ways. First, there is a hazy line 12 of philosophical thought, stemming perhaps from some doctrines associated with Wittgenstein, which maintains that we cannot meaningfully attribute states of consciousness to beings without language. I have not seen this argument made explicit in print, though I have come across it in conversation. This position seems to me very implausible, and I doubt that it would be held at all if it were not thought to be a consequence of a broader view of the significance of language. It may be that the use of a public, rule-governed language is a precondition of conceptual thought. It may even be, although personally I doubt it, that we cannot meaningfully speak of a creature having an intention unless that creature can use a language. But states like pain, surely, are more primitive than either of these, and seem to have nothing to do with language.

Indeed, as Jane Goodall points out in her study of chimpanzees, 13 when it comes to the expression of feelings and emotions, humans tend to fall back on non-linguistic modes of communication which are often found among apes, such as a cheering pat on the back, an exuberant embrace, a clasp of hands, and so on.[2] Michael Peters makes a similar point in his contribution to *Animals, Men and Morals* when he notes that the basic signals we use to convey pain, fear, sexual arousal, and so on are not specific to our species. So there seems to be no reason at all to believe that a creature without language cannot suffer.

The second, and more easily appreciated way of linking language 14 and the existence of pain is to say that the best evidence that we can have that another creature is in pain is when he tells us that he is. This is a distinct line of argument, for it is not being denied that a non-

---

[2] Jane van Lawick-Goodall, *In the Shadow of Man* (Houghton Mifflin, 1971), p. 225.

language-user conceivably could suffer, but only that we could know that he is suffering. Still, this line of argument seems to me to fail, and for reasons similar to those just given. "I am in pain" is not the best possible evidence that the speaker is in pain (he might be lying) and it is certainly not the only possible evidence. Behavioral signs and knowledge of the animal's biological similarity to ourselves together provide adequate evidence that animals do suffer. After all, we would not accept linguistic evidence if it contradicted the rest of the evidence. If a man was severely burned, and behaved as if he were in pain, writhing, groaning, being very careful not to let his burned skin touch anything, and so on, but later said he had not been in pain at all, we would be more likely to conclude that he was lying or suffering from amnesia than that he had not been in pain.

Even if there were stronger grounds for refusing to attribute pain   15 to those who do not have a language, the consequences of this refusal might lead us to examine these grounds unusually critically. Human infants, as well as some adults, are unable to use language. Are we to deny that a year-old infant can suffer? If not, how can language be crucial? Of course, most parents can understand the responses of even very young infants better than they understand the responses of other animals, and sometimes infant responses can be understood in the light of later development.

This, however, is just a fact about the relative knowledge we have   16 of our own species and other species, and most of this knowledge is simply derived from closer contact. Those who have studied the behavior of other animals soon learn to understand their responses at least as well as we understand those of an infant. (I am not referring to Jane Goodall's and other well-known studies of apes. Consider, for example, the degree of understanding achieved by Tinbergen from watching herring gulls.[3] Just as we can understand infant human behavior in the light of adult human behavior, so we can understand the behavior of other species in the light of our own behavior (and sometimes we can understand our own behavior better in the light of the behavior of other species).

The grounds we have for believing that other mammals and birds   17 suffer are, then, closely analogous to the grounds we have for believing that other humans suffer. It remains to consider how far down the evolutionary scale this analogy holds. Obviously it becomes poorer when we get further away from man. To be more precise would require a detailed examination of all that we know about other forms of life.

[3] N. Tinbergen, *The Herring Gull's World* (Basic Books, 1961).

With fish, reptiles, and other vertebrates the analogy still seems strong, with molluscs like oysters it is much weaker. Insects are more difficult, and it may be that in our present state of knowledge we must be agnostic about whether they are capable of suffering.

If there is no moral justification for ignoring suffering when it occurs, and it does occur in other species, what are we to say of our attitudes toward these other species? Richard Ryder, one of the contributors to *Animals, Men and Morals,* uses the term "speciesism" to describe the belief that we are entitled to treat members of other species in a way in which it would be wrong to treat members of our own species. The term is not euphonious, but it neatly makes the analogy with racism. The non-racist would do well to bear the analogy in mind when he is inclined to defend human behavior toward nonhumans. "Shouldn't we worry about improving the lot of our own species before we concern ourselves with other species?" he may ask. If we substitute "race" for "species" we shall see that the question is better not asked. "Is a vegetarian diet nutritionally adequate?" resembles the slave-owner's claim that he and the whole economy of the South would be ruined without slave labor. There is even a parallel with skeptical doubts about whether animals suffer, for some defenders of slavery professed to doubt whether blacks really suffer in the way whites do.

I do not want to give the impression, however, that the case for Animal Liberation is based on the analogy with racism and no more. On the contrary, *Animals, Men and Morals* describes the various ways in which humans exploit nonhumans, and several contributors consider the defenses that have been offered, including the defense of meat-eating mentioned in the last paragraph. Sometimes the rebuttals are scornfully dismissive, rather than carefully designed to convince the detached critic. This may be a fault, but it is a fault that is inevitable, given the kind of book this is. The issue is not one on which one can remain detached. As the editors state in their Introduction:

> Once the full force of moral assessment has been made explicit there can be no rational excuse left for killing animals, be they killed for food, science, or sheer personal indulgence. We have not assembled this book to provide the reader with yet another manual on how to make brutalities less brutal. Compromise, in the traditional sense of the term, is simple unthinking weakness when one considers the actual reasons for our crude relationships with the other animals.

The point is that on this issue there are few critics who are genuinely detached. People who eat pieces of slaughtered nonhumans every day find it hard to believe that they are doing wrong; and they also find it hard to imagine what else they could eat. So for those who do not place nonhumans beyond the pale of morality, there comes a stage when further argument seems pointless, a stage at which one can only accuse one's opponent of hypocrisy and reach for the sort of sociological account of our practices and the way we defend them that is attempted by David Wood in his contribution to this book. On the other hand, to those unconvinced by the arguments, and unable to accept that they are merely rationalizing their dietary preferences and their fear of being thought peculiar, such sociological explanations can only seem insultingly arrogant.

II

The logic of speciesism is most apparent in the practice of exper-   21
imenting on nonhumans in order to benefit humans. This is because the issue is rarely obscured by allegations that nonhumans are so different from humans that we cannot know anything about whether they suffer. The defender of vivisection cannot use this argument because he needs to stress the similarities between man and other animals in order to justify the usefulness to the former of experiments on the latter. The researcher who makes rats choose between starvation and electric shocks to see if they develop ulcers (they do) does so because he knows that the rat has a nervous system very similar to man's, and presumably feels an electric shock in a similar way.

Richard Ryder's restrained account of experiments on animals   22
made me angrier with my fellow men than anything else in this book. Ryder, a clinical psychologist by profession, himself experimented on animals before he came to hold the view he puts forward in his essay. Experimenting on animals is now a large industry, both academic and commercial. In 1969, more than 5 million experiments were performed in Britain, the vast majority without anesthetic (though how many of these involved pain is not known). There are no accurate U.S. figures, since there is no federal law on the subject, and in many cases no state law either. Estimates vary from 20 million to 200 million. Ryder suggests that 80 million may be the best guess. We tend to think that this is all for vital medical research, but of course it is not. Huge numbers of animals are used in university departments from Forestry to Psychology, and even more are used for commercial purposes, to test whether cosmetics can cause skin damage, or shampoos eye damage, or to test food additives or laxatives or sleeping pills or anything else.

A standard test for foodstuffs is the "LD50." The object of this test   23
is to find the dosage level at which 50 percent of the test animals will

die. This means that nearly all of them will become very sick before finally succumbing or surviving. When the substance is a harmless one, it may be necessary to force huge doses down the animals, until in some cases sheer volume or concentration causes death.

Ryder gives a selection of experiments, taken from recent scientific journals. I will quote two, not for the sake of indulging in gory details, but in order to give an idea of what normal researchers think they may legitimately do to other species. The point is not that the individual researchers are cruel men, but that they are behaving in a way that is allowed by our speciesist attitudes. As Ryder points out, even if only 1 percent of the experiments involve severe pain, that is 50,000 experiments in Britain each year, or nearly 150 every day (and about fifteen times as many in the United States, if Ryder's guess is right). Here then are two experiments: 24

> O. S. Ray and R. J. Barrett of Pittsburgh gave electric shocks to the feet of 1,042 mice. They then caused convulsions by giving more intense shocks through cup-shaped electrodes applied to the animals' eyes or through pressure spring clips attached to their ears. Unfortunately some of the mice who "successfully completed Day One training were found sick or dead prior to testing on Day Two." [*Journal of Comparative and Physiological Psychology,* 1969, vol. 67, pp. 110–116]

> At the National Institute for Medical Research, Mill Hill, London, W. Feldberg and S. L. Sherwood injected chemicals into the brains of cats—"with a number of widely different substances, recurrent patterns of reaction were obtained. Retching, vomiting, defaecation, increased salivation and greatly accelerated respiration leading to panting were common features." . . .
>
> The injection into the brain of a large dose of Tubocuraine caused the cat to jump "from the table to the floor and then straight into its cage, where it started calling more and more noisily whilst moving about restlessly and jerkily . . . finally the cat fell with legs and neck flexed, jerking in rapid clonic movements, the condition being that of a major [epileptic] convulsion . . . within a few seconds the cat got up, ran for a few yards at high speed and fell in another fit. The whole process was repeated several times within the next ten minutes, during which the cat lost faeces and foamed at the mouth."
>
> This animal finally died thirty-five minutes after the brain injection. [*Journal of Physiology,* 1954, vol. 123, pp. 148–167]

There is nothing secret about these experiments. One has only to open any recent volume of a learned journal, such as the *Journal of Comparative and Physiological Psychology,* to find full descriptions of experiments of this sort, together with the results obtained—results that 25 are frequently trivial and obvious. The experiments are often supported by public funds.

It is a significant indication of the level of acceptability of these 26 practices that, although these experiments are taking place at this moment on university campuses throughout the country, there has, so far as I know, not been the slightest protest from the student movement. Students have been rightly concerned that their universities should not discriminate on grounds of race or sex, and that they should not serve the purposes of the military or big business. Speciesism continues undisturbed, and many students participate in it. There may be a few qualms at first, but since everyone regards it as normal, and it may even be a required part of a course, the student soon becomes hardened and, dismissing his earlier feelings as "mere sentient," comes to regard animals as statistics rather than sentiment beings with interests that warrant consideration.

Argument about vivisection has often missed the point because it 27 has been put in absolutist terms: Would the abolitionist be prepared to let thousands die if they could be saved by experimenting on a single animal? The way to reply to this purely hypothetical question is to pose another: Would the experimenter be prepared to experiment on a human orphan under six months old, if it were the only way to save many lives? (I say "orphan" to avoid the complication of parental feelings, although in doing so I am being overfair to the experimenter, since the nonhuman subjects of experiments are not orphans.) A negative answer to this question indicates that the experimenter's readiness to use nonhumans is simple discrimination, for adult apes, cats, mice, and other mammals are more conscious of what is happening to them, more self-directing, and, so far as we can tell, just as sensitive to pain as a human infant. There is no characteristic that human infants possess that adult mammals do not have to the same or a higher degree.

(It might be possible to hold that what makes it wrong to exper- 28 iment on a human infant is that the infant will in time develop into more than the nonhuman, but one would then, to be consistent, have to oppose abortion, and perhaps contraception, too, for the fetus and the egg and sperm have the same potential as the infant. Moreover, one would still have no reason for experimenting on a nonhuman rather than a human with brain damage severe enough to make it impossible for him to rise above infant level.)

The experimenter, then, shows a bias for his own species when- 29 ever he carries out an experiment on a nonhuman for a purpose that he would not think justified him in using a human being at an equal or lower level of sentience, awareness, ability to be self-directing, etc. No one familiar with the kind of results yielded by these experiments can have the slightest doubt that if this bias were eliminated the number of experiments performed would be zero or very close to it.

III

If it is vivisection that shows the logic of speciesism most clearly, it is   30 the use of other species for food that is at the heart of our attitudes toward them. Most of *Animals, Men and Morals* is an attack on meat-eating—an attack which is based solely on concern for nonhumans, without reference to arguments derived from considerations of ecology, macrobiotics, health, or religion.

The idea that nonhumans are utilities, means to our ends, per-   31 vades our thought. Even conservationists who are concerned about the slaughter of wild fowl but not about the vastly greater slaughter of chickens for our tables are thinking in this way—they are worried about what we would lose if there were less wildlife. Stanley Godlovitch, pursuing the Marxist idea that our thinking is formed by the activities we undertake in satisfying our needs, suggests that man's first classification of his environment was into Edibles and Inedibles. Most animals came into the first category, and there they have remained.

Man may always have killed other species for food, but he has   32 never exploited them so ruthlessly as he does today. Farming has succumbed to business methods, the objective being to get the highest possible ratio of output (meat, eggs, milk) to input (fodder, labor costs, etc.). Ruth Harrison's essay "On Factory Farming" gives an account of some aspects of modern methods, and of the unsuccessful British campaign for effective controls, a campaign which was sparked off by her *Animal Machines* (Stuart: London, 1964).

Her article is in no way a substitute for her earlier book. This is a   33 pity since, as she says, "Farm produce is still associated with mental pictures of animals browsing in the fields . . . of hens having a last forage before going to roost. . . ." Yet neither in her article nor elsewhere in *Animals, Men and Morals* is this false image replaced by a clear idea of the nature and extent of factory farming. We learn of this only indirectly, when we hear of the code of reform proposed by an advisory committee set up by the British government.

Among the proposals, which the government refused to imple-   34 ment on the grounds that they were too idealistic, were: "*Any animals should at least have room to turn around freely.*"

Factory farm animals need liberation in the most literal sense. Veal 35
calves are kept in stalls five feet by two feet. They are usually slaughtered when about four months old, and have been too big to turn in
their stalls for at least a month. Intensive beef herds, kept in stalls only
proportionately larger for much longer periods, account for a growing
percentage of beef production. Sows are often similarly confined when
pregnant, which, because of artifical methods of increasing fertility,
can be most of the time. Animals confined in this way do not waste
food by exercising, nor do they develop unpalatable muscle.

"A dry bedded area should be provided for all stock." Intensively kept 36
animals usually have to stand and sleep on slatted floors without straw,
because this makes cleaning easier.

"Palatable roughage must be readily available to all calves after one week 37
of age." In order to produce the pale veal housewives are said to prefer,
calves are fed on an all-liquid diet until slaughter, even though they
are long past the age at which they would normally eat grass. They
develop a craving for roughage, evidenced by attempts to gnaw wood
from their stalls. (For the same reason, their diet is deficient in iron.)

"Battery cages for poultry should be large enough for a bird to be able to 38
stretch one wing at a time." Under current British practice, a cage for
four or five laying hens has a floor area of twenty inches by eighteen
inches, scarcely larger than a double page of the *New York Review of
Books*. In this space, on a sloping wire floor (sloping so the eggs roll
down, wire so the dung drops through) the birds live for a year or
eighteen months while artificial lighting and temperature conditions
combine with drugs in their food to squeeze the maximum number of
eggs out of them. Table birds are also sometimes kept in cages. More
often they are reared in sheds, no less crowded. Under these conditions
all the birds' natural activities are frustrated, and they develop "vices"
such as pecking each other to death. To prevent this, beaks are often
cut off, and the sheds kept dark.

How many of those who support factory farming by buying its 39
produce know anything about the way it is produced? How many have
heard something about it, but are reluctant to check up for fear that
it will make them uncomfortable? To non-speciesists, the typical consumer's mixture of ignorance, reluctance to find out the truth, and
vague belief that nothing really bad could be allowed seems analogous
to the attitudes of "decent Germans" to the death camps.

There are, of course, some defenders of factory farming. Their 40
arguments are considered, though again rather sketchily, by John Harris. Among the most common: "Since they have never known anything

else, they don't suffer." This argument will not be put by anyone who knows anything about animal behavior, since he will know that not all behavior has to be learned. Chickens attempt to stretch wings, walk around, scratch, and even dustbathe or build a nest, even though they have never lived under conditions that allowed these activities. Calves can suffer from maternal deprivation no matter at what age they were taken from their mothers. "We need these intensive methods to provide protein for a growing population." As ecologists and famine relief organizations know, we can produce far more protein per acre if we grow the right vegetable crop, soy beans for instance, than if we use the land to grow crops to be converted into protein by animals who use nearly 90 percent of the protein themselves, even when unable to exercise.

There will be many readers of this book who will agree that factory   41
farming involves an unjustifiable degree of exploitation of sentient creatures, and yet will want to say that there is nothing wrong with rearing animals for food, provided it is done "humanely." These people are saying, in effect, that although we should not cause animals to suffer, there is nothing wrong with killing them.

There are two possible replies to this view. One is to attempt to   42
show that this combination of attitudes is absurd. Roslind Godlovitch takes this course in her essay, which is an examination of some common attitudes to animals. She argues that from the combination of "animal suffering is to be avoided" and "there is nothing wrong with killing animals" it follows that all animal life ought to be exterminated (since all sentient creatures will suffer to some degree at some point in their lives). Euthanasia is a contentious issue only because we place some value on living. If we did not, the least amount of suffering would justify it. Accordingly, if we deny that we have a duty to exterminate all animal life, we must concede that we are placing some value on animal life.

This argument seems to me valid, although one could still reply   43
that the value of animal life is to be derived from the pleasures that life can have for them, so that, provided their lives have a balance of pleasure over pain, we are justified in rearing them. But this would imply that we ought to produce animals and let them live as pleasantly as possible, without suffering.

At this point, one can make the second of the two possible replies   44
to the view that rearing and killing animals for food is all right so long as it is done humanely. This second reply is that so long as we think that a nonhuman may be killed simply so that a human can satisfy his

taste for meat, we are still thinking of nonhumans as means rather than as ends in themselves. The factory farm is nothing more than the application of technology to this concept. Even traditional methods involve castration, the separation of mothers and their young, the breaking up of herds, branding or ear-punching, and of course transportation to the abattoirs and the final moments of terror when the animal smells blood and senses danger. If we were to try rearing animals so that they lived and died without suffering, we should find that to do so on anything like the scale of today's meat industry would be a sheer impossibility. Meat would become the prerogative of the rich.

I have been able to discuss only some of the contributions to this book, saying nothing about, for instance, the essays on killing for furs and for sport. Nor have I considered all the detailed questions that need to be asked once we start thinking about other species in the radically different way presented by this book. What, for instance, are we to do about genuine conflicts of interest like rats biting slum children? I am not sure of the answer, but the essential point is just that we *do* see this as a conflict of interests, that we recognize that rats have interests too. Then we may begin to think about other ways of resolving the conflict—perhaps by leaving out rat baits that sterilize the rats instead of killing them.

I have not discussed such problems because they are side issues compared with the exploitation of other species for food and for experimental purposes. On these central matters, I hope that I have said enough to show that this book, despite its flaws, is a challenge to every human to recognize his attitudes to nonhumans as a form of prejudice no less objectionable than racism or sexism. It is a challenge that demands not just a change of attitudes, but a change in our way of life, for it requires us to become vegetarians.

Can a purely moral demand of this kind succeed? The odds are certainly against it. The book holds out no inducements. It does not tell us that we will become healthier, or enjoy life more, if we cease exploiting animals. Animal Liberation will require greater altruism on the part of mankind than any other liberation movement, since animals are incapable of demanding it for themselves, or of protesting against their exploitation by votes, demonstrations, or bombs. Is man capable of such genuine altruism? Who knows? If this book does have a significant effect, however, it will be a vindication of all those who have believed that man has within himself the potential for more than cruelty and selfishness.

Questions

1. Reread Singer's first seven paragraphs carefully, observing how he leads us to see that "animal liberation" is not a joke. It will help you to understand his strategy if for each of his paragraphs you write one sentence either summarizing the paragraph or commenting on what it accomplishes in his argument.
2. What grounds does Singer find for attributing suffering to non-humans? List the arguments he offers to dismiss the relevance of a developed language. Why does he find it necessary to offer these arguments?
3. Does Singer attribute the capacity to feel pain to all species? Explain.
4. How does Singer define speciesism? To what extent does he use the analogy of speciesism to racism?
5. What is vivisection? Why, according to Singer, *must* defenders of vivisection also defend speciesism? Why do many of us who would not be willing to defend speciesism tolerate or even participate in experiments on animals?
6. What use of animals does Singer analyze beginning with paragraph 30? Why does he reserve this discussion for the last part of his essay? Why does he offer more detailed and more concrete examples in this section than in the second part, beginning with paragraph 21?

Jamaica Kincaid

Girl

Wash the white clothes on Monday and put them on the stone heap; wash the color clothes on Tuesday and put them on the clothesline to dry; don't walk barehead in the hot sun; cook pump- 1

Jamaica Kincaid, born in St. Johns, Antigua, in 1949 and educated there at the Princess Margaret School, is a writer for *The New Yorker*. Ms. Kincaid informs us that "benna," mentioned early in this piece, refers to "songs of the sort your parents didn't want you to sing, at first calypso and later rock and roll."

kin fritters in very hot sweet oil; soak your little cloths right after you take them off; when buying cotton to make yourself a nice blouse, be sure that it doesn't have gum in it, because that way it won't hold up well after a wash; soak salt fish overnight before you cook it; is it true that you sing benna in Sunday school?; always eat your food in such a way that it won't turn someone else's stomach; on Sundays try to walk like a lady and not like the slut you are so bent on becoming; don't sing benna in Sunday school; you mustn't speak to wharf-rat boys, not even to give directions; don't eat fruits on the street—flies will follow you; *but I don't sing benna on Sundays at all and never in Sunday school;* this is how to sew on a button; this is how to make a buttonhole for the button you have just sewed on; this is how to hem a dress when you see the hem coming down and so to prevent yourself from looking like the slut I know you are so bent on becoming; this is how you iron your father's khaki shirt so that it doesn't have a crease; this is how you iron your father's khaki pants so that they don't have a crease; this is how you grow okra—far from the house, because okra tree harbors red ants; when you are growing dasheen, make sure it gets plenty of water or else it makes your throat itch when you are eating it; this is how you sweep a corner; this is how you sweep a whole house; this is how you sweep a yard; this is how you smile to someone you don't like too much; this is how you smile to someone you don't like at all; this is how you smile to someone you like completely; this is how you set a table for tea; this is how you set a table for dinner; this is how you set a table for dinner with an important guest; this is how you set a table for lunch; this is how you set a table for breakfast; this is how to behave in the presence of men who don't know you very well, and this way they won't recognize immediately the slut I have warned you against becoming; be sure to wash every day, even if it is with your own spit; don't squat down to play marbles—you are not a boy, you know; don't pick people's flowers—you might catch something; don't throw stones at blackbirds, because it might not be a blackbird at all; this is how to make a bread pudding; this is how to make doukona; this is how to make pepper pot; this is how to make a good medicine for a cold; this is how to make a good medicine to throw away a child before it even becomes a child; this is how to catch a fish; this is how to throw back a fish you don't like, and that way something bad won't fall on you; this is how to bully a man; this is how a man bullies you; this is how to love a man, and if this doesn't work there are other ways, and if they don't work don't feel too bad about giving up; this is how to spit up in the air if you feel like it, and this is how to move quick so that it doesn't fall on you; this is how to make ends meet; always squeeze bread to make sure it's fresh; *but what if the baker won't let me feel the bread?;* you mean to say that after all you are really going to be the kind of woman who the baker won't let near the bread?

Question

In a paragraph, identify the two characters whose voices we hear in this story. Explain what we know about them (their circumstances and their relationship). Cite specific evidence from the text. For example, what is the effect of the frequent repetition of "this is how"? Are there other words or phrases frequently repeated?

Italo Calvino

The Aquatic Uncle

The first vertebrates who, in the Carboniferous period, aban- 1
doned aquatic life for terrestrial, descended from the osseous, pulmonate fish
whose fins were capable of rotation beneath their bodies and thus could be used
as paws on the earth.

By then it was clear that the water period was coming to an end,—
old Qfwfq recalled,—those who decided to make the great move were growing more and more numerous, there wasn't a family that didn't have some loved one up on dry land, and everybody told fabulous tales of the things that could be done there, and they called back to their relatives to join them. There was no holding the young fish; they

Italo Calvino (1923–1985) was of Italian descent, but he was born in Cuba, where his father was engaged in agricultural research. Soon after his birth, the family returned to Italy, where Calvino was educated. During World War II he was a member of the Anti-Fascist Resistance; later he edited an intellectual journal and wrote stories, novels, and essays.

We print here one of the twelve fanciful stories that constitute *Cosmicomics.*

slapped their fins on the muddy banks to see if they would work as paws, as the more talented ones had already discovered. But just at that time the differences among us were becoming accentuated: there might be a family that had been living on land, say, for several generations, whose young people acted in a way that wasn't even amphibious but almost reptilian already; and there were others who lingered, still living like fish, those who, in fact, became even more fishy than they had been before.

Our family, I must say, including grandparents, was all up on the shore, padding about as if we had never known how to do anything else. If it hadn't been for the obstinacy of our great-uncle N'ba N'ga, we would have long since lost all contact with the aquatic world.

Yes, we had a great-uncle who was a fish, on my paternal grandmother's side, to be precise, of the Coelacanthus family of the Devonian period (the fresh-water branch: who are, for that matter, cousins of the others—but I don't want to go into all these questions of kinship, nobody can ever follow them anyhow). So as I was saying, this great-uncle lived in certain muddy shallows, among the roots of some protoconifers, in that inlet of the lagoon where all our ancestors had been born. He never stirred from there: at any season of the year all we had to do was push ourselves over the softer layers of vegetation until we could feel ourselves sinking into the dampness, and there below, a few palms' lengths from the edge, we could see the column of little bubbles he sent up, breathing heavily the way old folk do, or the little cloud of mud scraped up by his sharp snout, always rummaging around, more out of habit than out of the need to hunt for anything.

"Uncle N'ba N'ga! We've come to pay you a visit! Were you expecting us?" we would shout, slapping our paws and tails in the water to attract his attention. "We've brought you some insects that grow where we live! Uncle N'ba N'ga! Have you ever seen such fat cockroaches? Taste one and see if you like it. . . ." 5

"You can clean those revolting warts you've got with your stinking cockroaches!" Our great-uncle's answer was always some remark of this sort, or perhaps even ruder: this is how he welcomed us every time, but we paid no attention because we knew he would mellow after a little while, accept our presents gladly, and converse in politer tones.

"What do you mean, Uncle? Warts? When did you ever see any warts on us?"

This business about warts was a widespread prejudice among the

old fish: a notion that, from living on dry land, we would develop
warts all over our bodies, exuding liquid matter: this was true enough
for the toads, but we had nothing in common with them; on the contrary, our skin, smooth and slippery, was such as no fish had ever
had; and our great-uncle knew this perfectly well, but he still couldn't
stop larding his talk with all the slanders and intolerance he had grown
up in the midst of.

We went to visit our great-uncle once a year, the whole family
together. It also gave us an opportunity to have a reunion, since we
were scattered all over the continent; we could exchange bits of news,
trade edible insects, and discuss old questions that were still unsettled.

Our great-uncle spoke his mind even on questions that were re-   10
moved from him by miles and miles of dry land, such as the division
of territory for dragonfly hunting; and he would side with this one or
that one, according to his own reasoning, which was always aquatic.
"But don't you know that it's always better to hunt on the bottom and
not on the water's surface? So what are you getting all upset over?"

"But, Uncle, you see: it isn't a question of hunting on the bottom
or on the surface. I live at the foot of a hill, and he lives halfway up
the slope. . . . You know what I mean by hill, Uncle. . . ."

And he said: "You always find the best crayfish at the foot of the
cliffs." It just wasn't possible to make him accept a reality different
from his own.

And yet, his opinions continued to exert an authority over all of
us; in the end we asked his advice about matters he didn't begin to
understand, though we knew he could be dead wrong. Perhaps his
authority stemmed from the fact that he was a leftover from the past,
from his way of using old figures of speech, like: "Lower your fins
there, youngster!," whose meaning we didn't grasp very clearly.

We had made various attempts to get him up on land with us,
and we went on making them; indeed, on this score, the rivalry among
the various branches of the family never died out, because whoever
managed to take our great-uncle home with him would achieve a position of pre-eminence over the rest of our relatives. But the rivalry
was pointless, because our uncle wouldn't dream of leaving the lagoon.

"Uncle, if you only knew how sorry we feel leaving you all alone,   15
at your age, in the midst of all that dampness. . . . We've had a wonderful idea . . ." someone would begin.

"I was expecting the lot of you to catch on finally," the old fish
interrupted, "now you've got over the whim of scraping around in
that drought, so it's time you came back to live like normal beings.

Here there's plenty of water for all, and when it comes to food, there's never been a better season for worms. You can all dive right in, and we won't have to discuss it any further."

"No, no, Uncle N'ba N'ga, you've got it all wrong. We wanted to take you to live with us, in a lovely little meadow. . . . You'll be nice and snug; we'll dig you a little damp hole. You'll be able to turn and toss in it, just like here. And you might even try taking a few steps around the place: you'll be very good at it, just wait and see. And besides, at your time of life, the climate on land is much more suitable. So come now, Uncle N'ba N'ga, don't wait to be coaxed. Won't you come home with us?"

"No!" was our great-uncle's sharp reply, and taking a nose dive into the water, he vanished from our sight.

"But why, Uncle? What have you got against the idea? We simply don't understand. Anyone as broad-minded as you ought to be above certain prejudices. . . ."

From an angry huff of water at the surface, before the final plunge 20 with a still-agile jerk of his tail fin, came our uncle's final answer: "He who has fleas in his scales swims with his belly in the mud!" which must have been an idiomatic expression (similar to our own, much more concise proverb: "If you itch, scratch"), with that term "mud" which he insisted on using where we would say "land."

That was about the time when I fell in love. Lll and I spent our days together, chasing each other; no one as quick as she had ever been seen before; in the ferns, which were as tall as trees in those days, she would climb to the top in one burst, and the tops would bend almost to the ground, then she would jump down and run off again; I, with slower and somewhat clumsier movements, followed her. We ventured into zones of the interior where no print had ever marked the dry and crusty terrain; at times I stopped, frightened at having come so far from the expanse of the lagoons. But nothing seemed so far from aquatic life as she, Lll, did: the deserts of sand and stones, the prairies, the thick forests, the rocky hillocks, the quartz mountains: this was her world, a world that seemed made especially to be scanned by her oblong eyes, to be trod by her darting steps. When you looked at her smooth skin, you felt that scales had never existed.

Her relatives made me a bit ill at ease; hers was one of those families who had become established on Earth in the earliest period and had finally become convinced they had never lived anywhere else, one of those families who, by now, even laid their eggs on dry terrain, protected by a hard shell, and Lll, if you looked at her when she jumped, at her flashing movements, you could tell she had been born the way she was now, from one of those eggs warmed by sand and sun, having completely skipped the swimming, wriggling phase of the tadpole, which was still obligatory in our less evolved families.

The time had come for Lll to meet my family: and since its oldest and most authoritative member was Great-Uncle N'ba N'ga, I couldn't avoid a visit to him, to introduce my fiancée. But every time an opportunity occurred, I postponed it, out of embarrassment; knowing the prejudices among which she had been brought up, I hadn't yet dared tell Lll that my great-uncle was a fish.

One day we had wandered off to one of those damp promontories that girdle the lagoon, where the ground is made not so much of sand as of tangled roots and rotting vegetation. And Lll came out with one of her usual dares, her challenges to feats: "Qfwfq, how long can you keep your balance? Let's see who can run closest to the edge here!" And she darted forward with her Earth-creature's leap, now slightly hesitant, however.

This time I not only felt I could follow her, but also that I could win, because my paws got a better grip on damp surfaces. "As close to the edge as you like!" I cried. "And even beyond it!"

"Don't talk nonsense!" she said. "How can you run beyond the edge? It's all water there!"

Perhaps this was the opportune moment to bring up the subject of my great-uncle. "What of that?" I said to her. "There are those who run on this side of the edge, and those who run on the other."

"You're saying things that make no sense at all!"

"I'm saying that my great-uncle N'ba N'ga lives in the water the way we live on the land, and he's never come out of it!"

"Ha! I'd like to meet this N'ba N'ga of yours!"

She had no sooner finished saying this than the muddied surface of the lagoon gurgled with bubbles, moved in a little eddy, and allowed a nose, all covered with spiky scales, to appear.

"Well, here I am. What's the trouble?" Great-Uncle said, staring at Lll with eyes as round and inexpressive as stones, flapping the gills at either side of his enormous throat. Never before had my great-uncle seemed so different from the rest of us: a real monster.

"Uncle, if you don't mind . . . this is . . . I mean, I have the pleasure to present to you my future bride, Lll," and I pointed to my fiancée, who for some unknown reason had stood erect on her hind paws, in one of her most exotic poses, certainly the least likely to be appreciated by that boorish old relative.

"And so, young lady, you've come to wet your tail a bit, eh?" my great-uncle said: a remark that in his day no doubt had been considered courtly, but to us sounded downright indecent.

I looked at Lll, convinced I would see her turn and run off with 35 a shocked twitter. But I hadn't considered how strong her training was, her habit of ignoring all vulgarity in the world around her. "Tell me something: those little plants there . . ." she said, nonchalantly, pointing to some rushes growing tall in the midst of the lagoon, "where do they put down their roots?"

One of those questions you ask just to make conversation: as if she cared about those rushes! But it seemed Uncle had been waiting only for that moment to start explaining the why and the wherefore of the roots of floating trees and how you could swim among them and, indeed, how they were the very best places for hunting.

I thought he would never stop. I huffed impatiently, I tried to interrupt him. But what did that saucy Lll do? She encouraged him! "Oh, so you go hunting among those underwater roots? How interesting!"

I could have sunk into the ground from shame.

And he said: "I'm not fooling! The worms you find there! You can fill your belly, all right!" And without giving it a second thought, he dived. An agile dive such as I'd never seen him make before. Or rather, he made a leap into the air—his whole length out of the water, all dotted with scales—spreading the spiky fans of his fins; then, when he had completed a fine half-circle in the air, he plunged back, head-first, and disappeared quickly with a kind of screw-motion of his crescentshaped tail.

At this sight, I recalled the little speech I had prepared hastily to 40 apologize to Lll, taking advantage of my uncle's departure ("You really have to understand him, you know, this mania for living like a fish has finally even made him look like a fish"), but the words died in my throat. Not even I had ever realized the full extent of my grandmother's brother's fishiness. So I just said: "It's late, Lll, let's go . . ." and already my great-uncle was re-emerging, holding in his shark's lips a garland of worms and muddy seaweed.

It seemed too good to be true, when we finally took our leave; but as I trotted along silently behind Lll, I was thinking that now she would begin to make her comments, that the worst was still to come. But then Lll, without stopping, turned slightly toward me: "He's very nice, your uncle," and that was all she said. More than once in the past her irony had disarmed me; but the icy sensation that filled me at this remark was so awful that I would rather not have seen her any more than to have to face the subject again.

Instead, we went on seeing each other, going together, and the lagoon episode was never mentioned. I was still uneasy: it was no use my trying to persuade myself she had forgotten; every now and then I suspected she was remaining silent in order to embarrass me later in some spectacular way, in front of her family, or else—and, for me, this was an even worse hypothesis—she was making an effort to talk about other things only because she felt sorry for me. Then, out of a clear sky, one morning she said curtly: "See here, aren't you going to take me to visit your uncle any more?"

In a faint voice I asked: "Are you joking?"

Not at all; she was in earnest, she couldn't wait to go back and have a little chat with old N'ba N'ga. I was all mixed up.

That time our visit to the lagoon lasted longer. We lay on a sloping 45
bank, all three of us: my great-uncle was nearest the water, but the two of us were half in and half out, too, so anyone seeing us from the distance, all close together, wouldn't have known who was terrestrial and who was aquatic.

The fish started in with one of his usual tirades: the superiority of water respiration to air breathing, and all his repertory of denigration. "Now Lll will jump up and give him what for!" I thought. Instead, that day Lll was apparently using a different tactic: she argued seriously, defending our point of view, but as if she were also taking old N'ba N'ga's notions into consideration.

According to my great-uncle, the lands that had emerged were a limited phenomenon: they were going to disappear just as they had cropped up or, in any event, they would be subject to constant changes: volcanoes, glaciations, earthquakes, upheavals, changes of climate and of vegetation. And our life in the midst of all this would have to face constant transformations, in the course of which whole races would disappear, and the only survivors would be those who were prepared to change the bases of their existence so radically that the reasons why living was beautiful would be completely overwhelmed and forgotten.

This prospect was in absolute contradiction to the optimism in which we children of the coast had been brought up, and I opposed the idea with shocked protests. But for me the true, living confutation of those arguments was Lll: in her I saw the perfect, definitive form, born from the conquest of the land that had emerged; she was the sum of the new boundless possibilities that had opened. How could my great-uncle try to deny the incarnate reality of Lll? I was aflame with polemical passion, and I thought that my fiancée was being all too patient and too understanding with our opponent.

True, even for me—used as I was to hearing only grumblings and abuse from my great-uncle's mouth—this logically arranged argumentation of his came as a novelty, though it was still spiced with antiquated and bombastic expressions and was made comical by his peculiar accent. It was also amazing to hear him display a detailed familiarity—though entirely external—with the continental lands.

But Lll, with her questions, tried to make him talk as much as possible about life under water: and, to be sure, this was the theme that elicited the most tightly knit, even emotional discourse from my great-uncle. Compared to the uncertainties of earth and air, lagoons and seas and oceans represented a future with security. Down there, changes would be very few, space and provender were unlimited, the temperature would always be steady; in short, life would be maintained as it had gone on till then, in its achieved, perfect forms, without metamorphoses or additions with dubious outcome, and every individual would be able to develop his own nature, to arrive at the essence of himself and of all things. My great-uncle spoke of the aquatic future without embellishments or illusions, he didn't conceal the problems, even serious ones, that would arise (most worrying of all, the increase of saline content); but they were problems that wouldn't upset the values and the proportions in which he believed.

"But now we gallop over valleys and mountains, Uncle!" I cried, speaking for myself but especially for Lll, who remained silent.

"Go on with you, tadpole, when you're wet again, you'll be back home!" he apostrophized, to me, resuming the tone I had always heard him use with us.

"Don't you think, Uncle, that if we wanted to learn to breathe under water, it would be too late?" Lll asked earnestly, and I didn't know whether to feel flattered because she had called my old relative uncle or confused because certain questions (at least, so I was accustomed to think) shouldn't even be asked.

"If you're game, sweetie," the fish said, "I can teach you in a minute!"

Lll came out with an odd laugh, then finally began to run away, to run on and on beyond all pursuit.

I hunted for her across plains and hills, I reached the top of a basalt spur which dominated the surrounding landscape of deserts and forests surrounded by the waters. Lll was there. What she had wanted to tell me—I had understood her!—by listening to N'ba N'ga and then by fleeing and taking refuge up here was surely this: we had to live in our world thoroughly, as the old fish lived in his.

"I'll live here, the way Uncle does down there," I shouted, stammering a bit; then I corrected myself: "The two of us will live here, together!" because it was true that without her I didn't feel secure.

But what did Lll answer me then? I blush when I remember it even now, after all these geological eras. She answered: "Get along with you, tadpole; it takes more than that!" And I didn't know whether she was imitating my great-uncle, to mock him and me at once, or whether she had really assumed the old nut's attitude toward his nephew, and either hypothesis was equally discouraging, because both meant she considered me at a halfway stage, a creature not at home in the one world or in the other.

Had I lost her? Suspecting this, I hastened to woo her back. I took to performing all sorts of feats: hunting flying insects, leaping, digging underground dens, wrestling with the strongest of our group. I was proud of myself, but unfortunately whenever I did something brave, she wasn't there to see me: she kept disappearing, and no one knew where she had gone off to hide.

Finally I understood: she went to the lagoon, where my great-uncle   60
was teaching her to swim under water. I saw them surface together: they were moving along at the same speed, like brother and sister.

"You know?" she said, gaily, "my paws work beautifully as fins!"

"Good for you! That's a big step forward," I couldn't help remarking, sarcastically.

It was a game, for her: I understood. But a game I didn't like. I had to recall her to reality, to the future that was awaiting her.

One day I waited for her in the midst of a woods of tall ferns which sloped to the water.

"Lll, I have to talk to you," I said as soon as I saw her, "you've   65
been amusing yourself long enough. We have more important things ahead of us. I've discovered a passage in the mountains: beyond it stretches an immense stone plain, just abandoned by the water. We'll be the first to settle there, we'll populate unknown lands, you and I, and our children."

"The sea is immense," Lll said.

"Stop repeating that old fool's nonsense. The world belongs to those with legs, not to fish, and you know it."

"I know that he's somebody who is somebody," Lll said.

"And what about me?"

"There's nobody with legs who is like him."   70

"And your family?"

"We've quarreled. They don't understand anything."

"Why, you're crazy! Nobody can turn back!"

"I can."

"And what do you think you'll do, all alone with an old fish?"   75

"Marry him. Be a fish again with him. And bring still more fish into the world. Good-by."

And with one of those rapid climbs of hers, the last, she reached the top of a fern frond, bent it toward the lagoon, and let go in a dive. She surfaced, but she wasn't alone: the sturdy, curved tail of Great-Uncle N'ba N'ga rose near hers and, together, they cleft the waters.

It was a hard blow for me. But, after all, what could I do about it? I went on my way, in the midst of the world's transformations, being transformed myself. Every now and then, among the many forms of living beings, I encountered one who "was somebody" more than I was: one who announced the future, the duck-billed platypus who nurses its young, just hatched from the egg; or I might encounter another who bore witness to a past beyond all return, a dinosaur who had survived into the beginning of the Cenozoic, or else—a crocodile—part of the past that had discovered a way to remain immobile through the centuries. They all had something, I know, that made them somehow superior to me, sublime, something that made me, compared to them, mediocre. And yet I wouldn't have traded places with any of them.

Questions

1. In paragraph 2 Old Qfwfq recalls "the great move." What is the great move, and who (or what) is old Qfwfq?
2. What is the conflict between Qfwfq and Uncle N'ba N'ga? In what ways does it strike you as realistic?
3. About midway through the story Qfwfq reports: "That was about the time when I fell in love" (paragraph 21). Reread the paragraph and jot down the details that convince you that Qfwfq was indeed in love.
4. The uncle predicts that the land will be subject to terrible changes and that "the only survivors would be those who were prepared to change the bases of their existence so radically that the reasons why living was beautiful would be completely overwhelmed and forgotten." What are "the reasons why living was beautiful"?

5. At what point do you become aware that N'ba N'ga and LII are flirting with each other? When does Qfwfq become aware of this? How do you feel when LII gives him the brush-off?
6. If the story has a hero, would you say the hero is N'ba N'ga or Qfwfq? Explain.
7. At the end of the story Qfwfq compares himself to others he meets as he goes on his way and confesses his mediocrity. In terms of the story, what does "mediocrity" mean? Why does Qfwfq say, referring to those others, that he wouldn't trade places with any of them?

Theodore Roethke

My Papa's Waltz

The whiskey on your breath
Could make a small boy dizzy;
But I hung on like death:
Such waltzing was not easy.   4

We romped until the pans
Slid from the kitchen shelf;
My mother's countenance
Could not unfrown itself.   8

The hand that held my wrist
Was battered on one knuckle;
At every step you missed
My right ear scraped a buckle.   12

You beat time on my head
With a palm caked hard by dirt,
Then waltzed me off to bed
Still clinging to your shirt.   16

Theodore Roethke (1908–1963), author of eight volumes of poetry, was born in Saginaw, Michigan. Roethke's father ran a greenhouse, but the son earned his living by teaching English literature, chiefly at the University of Washington, in Seattle.

Questions

1. Who is the speaker?
2. Summarize the scene presented. Which details suggest what has happened before the waltz began? Do any details suggest that there have been similar scenes before?
3. How does the speaker feel about his father?
4. Describe the rhythm of the poem. Is it appropriate to a waltz?

3
TEACHING AND LEARNING

Washoe Makes the Sign for "Drink"
T. J. Kaminski

Courtesy R. A. and B. T. Gardner

Short Views

Knowledge is power.
Francis Bacon

Hard students are commonly troubled with gouts, catarrahs, rheums, cachexia, bradypepsia, bad eyes, stone, and collick, crudities, oppilations, vertigo, winds, consumptions, and all such diseases as come by over-much sitting: they are most part lean, dry, ill-colored . . . and all through immoderate pains and extraordinary studies.
Robert Burton

In my opinion, the only justification for high schools is as therapeutic halfway houses for the deranged. Normal adolescents can find themselves and grow further only by coping with the jobs, sex, and chances of the real world—it is useless to feed them curricular imitations. I would simply abolish the high schools, substituting apprenticeships and other alternatives and protecting the young from gross exploitation by putting the school money directly in their pockets. The very few who have authentic scholarly interests will gravitate to their own libraries, teachers, and academies, as they always did in the past, when they could afford it. In organic communities, adolescents cluster together in their own youth houses, for their fun and games and loud music, without bothering sober folk. I see no reason whatsoever for adults to set up or direct such nests or to be there at all unless invited.
Paul Goodman

I can judge one of the main effects of personal grading by the attitudes of students who land in my remedial course in college. They hate and fear writing more than anything else they have had to do in school. If they see a blank sheet of paper on which they are expected to write something, they look as though they want to scream. Apparently they have never written anything that anyone thought was good. At least, no one ever *told* them that anything in their writing was good. All their teachers looked for were mistakes, and there are so many kinds of mistakes in writing that their students despair of ever learning to avoid them.

The attitude toward writing that these students have developed is well illustrated by a story told by the Russian writer Chekhov about a kitten that was given to his uncle. The uncle wanted to make the kitten a champion killer of mice, so while it was still very young, he showed it a live mouse in a cage. Since the kitten's hunting instinct had not yet developed, it examined the mouse curiously but without any hostility. The uncle wanted to teach it that such fraternizing with the enemy was wrong, so he slapped the kitten, scolded it, and sent it away in disgrace. The next day the same mouse was shown to the kitten again. This time the kitten regarded it rather fearfully but without any aggressive intent. Again the uncle slapped it, scolded it, and sent it away. This treatment went on day after day. After some time, as soon as the kitten saw or smelled that mouse, it screamed and tried to climb up the walls. At that point the uncle lost patience and gave the kitten away, saying that it was stupid and would never learn. Of course the kitten had learned perfectly, and had learned exactly what it had been taught, but unfortunately not what the uncle intended to teach. "I can sympathize with that kitten," says Chekhov, "because that same uncle tried to teach me Latin."
Paul B. Diederich

You go to a great school not for knowledge so much as for arts and habits; for the habit of attention, for the art of expression, for the art of assuming at a moment's notice a new intellectual posture, for the art of entering quickly into another person's thought, for the habit of submitting to censure and refutation, for the art of indicating assent or dissent in graduated terms, for the habit of regarding minute points of accuracy, for the habit of working out what is possible in a given time, for taste, for discrimination, for mental courage and mental soberness. Above all, you go to a great school for self-knowledge.
William Cory

How people keep correcting us when we are young! There's always some bad habit or other they tell us we ought to get over. Yet most bad habits are tools to help us through life.
Johann Wolfgang von Goethe

Supposing anyone were to suggest that the best results for the individual and society could be derived through compulsory feeding. Would not the most ignorant rebel against such a stupid procedure? And yet the stomach has far greater adaptability to almost any situation than the brain. With all that, we find it quite natural to have compulsory mental feeding.

Indeed, we actually consider ourselves superior to other nations, because we have evolved a compulsory brain tube through which, for a certain number of hours every day, and for so many years, we can force into the child's mind a large quantity of mental nutrition.

. . . The great harm done by our system of education is not so much that it teaches nothing worth knowing, that it helps to perpetuate privileged classes, that it assists them in the criminal procedure of robbing and exploiting the masses; the harm of the system lies in its boastful proclamation that it stands for true education, thereby enslaving the masses a great deal more than could an absolute ruler.

Emma Goldman

The education of women should always be relative to that of men. To please, to be useful to us, to make us love and esteem them, to educate us when young, to take care of us when grown up; to advise, to console us, to render our lives easy and agreeable. These are the duties of women at all times, and what they should be taught in their infancy.

Jean Jacques Rousseau, *Emile*

If Johnny can't learn because he is hungry, that's the fault of poverty. But if Johnny can't pay attention because he is sleepy, that's the fault of parents.

What does it matter if we have a new book or an old book, if we open neither?

Jesse Jackson

Education. An education in things is not. We all are involved in the condemnation of words, an age of words. We are shut up in schools and college recitation rooms for ten or fifteen years, and come out at last with a bellyfull of words and do not know a thing. We cannot use our hands, or our legs, or our eyes, or our arms. We do not know an edible root in the woods. We cannot tell our course by the stars, nor the hour of the day by the sun. It is well if we can swim and skate. We are afraid of a horse, of a cow, of a dog, of a

cat, of a spider. Far better was the Roman rule to teach a boy nothing that he could not learn standing. Now here are my wise young neighbors who, instead of getting, like the woodmen, into a railroad-car, where they have not even the activity of holding the reins, have got into a boat which they have built with their own hands, with sails which they have contrived to serve as a tent by night, and gone up the Merrimack to live by their wits on the fish of the stream and the berries of the wood. My worthy neighbor Dr. Bartlett expressed a true parental instinct when he desired to send his boy with them to learn something. The farm, the farm, is the right school. The reason of my deep respect for the farmer is that he is a realist, and not a dictionary. The farm is a piece of the world, the school-house is not. The farm, by training the physical, rectifies and invigorates the metaphysical and moral nature.
  Ralph Waldo Emerson

Universities are, of course, hostile to geniuses.
  Ralph Waldo Emerson

The man who can make hard things easy is the educator.
  Ralph Waldo Emerson

If then a practical end must be assigned to a University course, I say it is that of training good members of society. Its art is the art of social life, and its end is fitness for the world. It neither confines its views to particular professions on the one hand, nor creates heroes or inspires genius on the other. Works indeed of genius fall under no art; heroic minds come under no rule; a University is not a birthplace of poets or of immortal authors, of founders of schools, leaders of colonies, or conquerors of nations. It does not promise a generation of Aristotles or Newtons, of Napoleons or Washingtons, of Raphaels or Shakespeares, though such miracles of nature it has before now contained within its precincts. Nor is it content on the other hand with forming the critic or the experimentalist, the economist or the engineer, though such too it includes within its scope. But a University training is the great ordinary means to a great but ordinary end; it aims at raising the intellectual tone of society, at cultivating the public mind, at purifying the national taste, at supplying true principles to popular enthusiasm and fixed aims to popular aspiration, at giving enlargement and sobriety to the ideas of the age, at facilitating the exercise of political power, and refining the intercourse of private life. It is the education which gives a man a clear conscious view of his own opinions and judgments, a truth in developing them, an eloquence in expressing them, and a force in urging them. It teaches him to see things as they are, to go right to the point, to disentangle a skein of thought, to detect what is sophistical, and to discard what is irrelevant. It prepares him to fill any post with credit, and to master any subject with facility. It shows him how to accommodate himself to others, how to throw himself into their state of mind, how to bring before them his own, how to influence them, how to come to an understanding with them, how to bear with them.

John Henry Newman

Education! Which of the various me's do you propose to educate, and which do you propose to suppress?

D. H. Lawrence

Think about the kind of world you want to live and work in. What do you need to know to build the world? Demand that your teachers teach you that.

Prince Kropotkin

The entire object of true education is to make people not merely *do* the right things, but *enjoy* the right things.

John Ruskin

I think [Raymond Weaver] first attracted my attention as someone worth watching when, while we were both new instructors, I heard from a bewildered freshman about the quiz he had just given. The first question written on the blackboard was, "Which of the required readings in this course did you find least interesting?" Then, after members of the class had had ten minutes in which to expatiate on what was certainly to many a congenial topic, he wrote the second question: "To what defect in yourself do you attribute this lack of interest?"

Joseph Wood Krutch

Plato

The Myth of the Cave

And now, I said, let me show in a figure how far our nature   1
is enlightened or unenlightened—Behold! human beings living in an
underground den, which has a mouth open toward the light and reaching all along the den; here they have been from their childhood, and
have their legs and necks chained so that they cannot move, and can
only see before them, being prevented by the chains from turning

---

Plato (427–347 B.C.), born in Athens, the son of an aristocratic family, wrote thirty
dialogues in which Socrates is the chief speaker. Socrates, about twenty-five
years older than Plato, was a philosopher who called himself a gadfly to Athenians. For his efforts at stinging them into thought, the Athenians executed
him in 399 B.C. "The Myth of the Cave" is the beginning of Book VII of Plato's
dialogue entitled *The Republic*. Socrates is talking with Glaucon.

For Plato, true knowledge is philosophic insight or awareness of the Good,
not mere opinion or the knack of getting along in this world by remembering
how things have usually worked in the past. To illustrate his idea that awareness
of the Good is different from the ability to recognize the things of this shabby
world, Plato (through his spokesman Socrates) resorts to an allegory: men imprisoned in a cave see on a wall in front of them the shadows or images of
objects that are really behind them, and they hear echoes, not real voices. (The
shadows are caused by the light from a fire behind the objects, and the echoes
by the cave's acoustical properties.) The prisoners, unable to perceive the real
objects and the real voices, mistakenly think that the shadows and the echoes
are real, and some of them grow highly adept at dealing with this illusory world.
Were Plato writing today, he might have made the cave a movie theater: we see
on the screen in front of us images caused by an object (film, passing in front
of light) that is behind us. Moreover, the film itself is an illusory image, for it
bears only the traces of a yet more real world—the world that was photo-
graphed—outside of the movie theater. And when we leave the theater to go
into the real world, our eyes have become so accustomed to the illusory world
that we at first blink with discomfort—just as Plato's freed prisoners do when
they move out of the cave—at the real world of bright day, and we long for the
familiar darkness. So too, Plato suggests, dwellers in ignorance may prefer the
familiar shadows of their unenlightened world ("the world of becoming") to the
bright world of the eternal Good ("the world of being") that education reveals.

We have just used the word "education." You will notice that the first sentence in the translation (by Benjamin Jowett) says that the myth will show "how
far our nature is enlightened or unenlightened." In the original Greek the words
here translated "enlightened" and "unenlightened" are *paideia* and *apaideusia*.
No translation can fully catch the exact meanings of these elusive words. Depending on the context, *paideia* may be translated as "enlightenment," "education," "civilization," "culture," "knowledge of the good."

round their heads. Above and behind them a fire is blazing at a distance, and between the fire and the prisoners there is a raised way; and you will see, if you look, a low wall built along the way, like the screen which marionette players have in front of them, over which they show the puppets.

I see.   2

And do you see, I said, men passing along the wall carrying all   3
sorts of vessels, and statutes and figures of animals made of wood and stone and various materials, which appear over the wall? Some of them are talking, others silent.

You have shown me a strange image, and they are strange pris-   4
oners.

Like ourselves, I replied; and they see only their own shadows,   5
or the shadows of one another, which the fire throws on the opposite wall of the cave?

True, he said; how could they see anything but the shadows if they   6
were never allowed to move their heads?

And of the objects which are being carried in like manner they   7
would only see the shadows?

Yes, he said.   8

And if they were able to converse with one another, would they   9
not suppose that they were naming what was actually before them?

Very true.   10

And suppose further that the prison had an echo which came from   11
the other side, would they not be sure when one of the passersby spoke that the voice which they heard came from the passing shadow?

No question, he replied.   12

To them, I said, the truth would be literally nothing but the shad-   13
ows of the images.

That is certain.   14

And now look again, and see what will naturally follow if the   15
prisoners are released and disabused of their error. At first, when any of them is liberated and compelled suddenly to stand up and turn his neck round and walk and look toward the light, he will suffer sharp pains; the glare will distress him, and he will be unable to see the realities of which in his former state he had seen the shadows; and then conceive some one saying to him, that what he saw before was an illusion, but that now, when he is approaching nearer to being and his eye is turned toward more real existence, he has a clearer vision—what will be his reply? And you may further imagine that his instructor is pointing to the objects as they pass and requiring him to name

them—will he not be perplexed? Will he not fancy that the shadows which he formerly saw are truer than the objects which are now shown to him?

Far truer.

And if he is compelled to look straight at the light, will he not 17 have a pain in his eyes which will make him turn away to take refuge in the objects of vision which he can see, and which he will conceive to be in reality clearer than the things which are now being shown to him?

16

True, he said.

And suppose once more, that he is reluctantly dragged up a steep 19 and rugged ascent, and held fast until he is forced into the presence of the sun himself, is he not likely to be pained and irritated? When he approaches the light his eyes will be dazzled, and he will not be able to see anything at all of what are now called realities.

18

Not all in a moment, he said.

He will require to grow accustomed to the sight of the upper world. 21 And first he will see the shadows best, next the reflections of men and other objects in the water, and then the objects themselves; then he will gaze upon the light of the moon and the stars and the spangled heaven; and he will see the sky and the stars by night better than the sun or the light of the sun by day?

20

Certainly.

Last of all he will be able to see the sun, and not mere reflections 23 of him in the water, but he will see him in his own proper place, and not in another; and he will contemplate him as he is.

22

Certainly.

He will then proceed to argue that this is he who gives the season 25 and the years, and is the guardian of all that is in the visible world, and in a certain way the cause of all things which he and his fellows have been accustomed to behold?

24

Clearly, he said, he would first see the sun and then reason about 26 him.

And when he remembered his old habitation, and the wisdom of 27 the den and his fellow-prisoners, do you not suppose that he would felicitate himself on the change, and pity them?

Certainly, he would.

And if they were in the habit of conferring honors among them- 29 selves on those who were quickest to observe the passing shadows and to remark which of them went before, and which followed after, and which were together; and who were therefore best able to draw

28

conclusions as to the future, do you think that he would care for such honors and glories, or envy the possessors of them? Would he not say with Homer,

Better to be the poor servant of a poor master,

and to endure anything, rather than think as they do and live after their manner?

Yes, he said, I think that he would rather suffer anything than 30 entertain these false notions and live in this miserable manner.

Imagine once more, I said, such an one coming suddenly out of 31 the sun to be replaced in his old situation; would he not be certain to have his eyes full of darkness?

To be sure, he said. 32

And if there were a contest, and he had to compete in measuring 33 the shadows with the prisoners who had never moved out of the den, while his sight was still weak, and before his eyes had become steady (and the time which would be needed to acquire this new habit of sight might be very considerable), would he not be ridiculous? Men would say of him that up he went and down he came without his eyes; and that it was better not even to think of ascending; and if any one tried to loose another and lead him up to the light, let them only catch the offender, and they would put him to death.

No question, he said. 34

This entire allegory, I said, you may now append, dear Glaucon, 35 to the previous argument; the prison-house is the world of sight, the light of the fire is the sun, and you will not misapprehend me if you interpret the journey upwards to be the ascent of the soul into the intellectual world according to my poor belief, which, at your desire, I have expressed—whether rightly or wrongly God knows. But, whether true or false, my opinion is that in the world of knowledge the idea of good appears last of all, and is seen only with an effort; and, when seen, is also inferred to be the universal author of all things beautiful and right, parent of light and of the lord of light in this visible world, and the immediate source of reason and truth in the intellectual; and that this is the power upon which he who would act rationally either in public or private life must have his eye fixed.

I agree, he said, as far as I am able to understand you. 36

Moreover, I said, you must not wonder that those who attain to 37 this beatific vision are unwilling to descend to human affairs; for their souls are ever hastening into the upper world where they desire to dwell; which desire of theirs is very natural, if our allegory may be trusted.

Yes, very natural.

And is there anything surprising in one who passes from divine contemplations to the evil state of man, misbehaving himself in a ridiculous manner; if, while his eyes are blinking and before he has become accustomed to the surrounding darkness, he is compelled to fight in courts of law, or in other places, about the images or the shadows of images of justice, and is endeavoring to meet the conceptions of those who have never yet seen absolute justice?

Anything but surprising, he replied.

Any one who has common sense will remember that the bewilderments of the eyes are of two kinds, and arise from two causes, either from coming out of the light or from going into the light, which is true of the mind's eye, quite as much as of the bodily eye; and he who remembers this when he sees any one whose vision is perplexed and weak, will not be too ready to laugh; he will first ask whether that soul of man has come out of the brighter life, and is unable to see because unaccustomed to the dark, or having turned from darkness to the day is dazzled by excess of light. And he will count the one happy in his condition and state of being, and he will pity the other; or, if he have a mind to laugh at the soul which comes from below into the light, there will be more reason in this than in the laugh which greets him who returns from above out of the light into the den.

That, he said, is a very just distinction.

But then, if I am right, certain professors of education must be wrong when they say that they can put a knowledge into the soul which was not there before, like sight into blind eyes.

They undoubtedly say this, he replied.

Whereas, our argument shows that the power and capacity of learning exists in the soul already; and that just as the eye was unable to turn from darkness to light without the whole body, so too the instrument of knowledge can only by the movement of the whole soul be turned from the world of becoming into that of being, and learn by degrees to endure the sight of being, and of the brightest and best of being, or in other words, of the good.

Very true.

And must there not be some art which will effect conversion in the easiest and quickest manner; not implanting the faculty of sight, for that exists already, but has been turned in the wrong direction, and is looking away from the truth?

Yes, he said, such an art may be presumed.   48

And whereas the other so-called virtues of the soul seem to be   49
akin to bodily qualities, for even when they are not originally innate
they can be implanted later by habit and exercise, the virtue of wisdom
more than anything else contains a divine element which always remains, and by this conversion is rendered useful and profitable; or,
on the other hand, hurtful and useless. Did you never observe the
narrow intelligence flashing from the keen eye of a clever rogue—how
eager he is, how clearly his paltry soul sees the way to his end; he is
the reverse of blind, but his keen eyesight is forced into the service of
evil, and he is mischievous in proportion to his cleverness?

Very true, he said.   50

But what if there had been a circumcision of such natures in the   51
days of their youth; and they had been severed from those sensual
pleasures, such as eating and drinking, which, like leaden weights,
were attached to them at their birth, and which drag them down and
turn the vision of their souls upon the things that are below—if, I say,
they had been released from these impediments and turned in the
opposite direction, the very same faculty in them would have seen the
truth as keenly as they see what their eyes are turned to now.

Very likely.   52

Yes, I said; and there is another thing which is likely, or rather a   53
necessary inference from what has preceded, that neither the uned-
ucated and uninformed of the truth, nor yet those who never make
an end of their education, will be able ministers of State; not the former,
because they have no single aim of duty which is the rule of all their
actions, private as well as public; nor the latter, because they will not
act at all except upon compulsion, fancying that they are already dwelling apart in the islands of the blest.

Very true, he replied.   54

Then, I said, the business of us who are the founders of the State   55
will be to compel the best minds to attain that knowledge which we
have already shown to be the greatest of all—they must continue to
ascend until they arrive at the good; but when they have ascended
and seen enough we must not allow them to do as they do now.

What do you mean?   56

I mean that they remain in the upper world: but this must not be   57
allowed; they must be made to descend again among the prisoners in
the den, and partake of their labors and honors, whether they are
worth having or not.

But is not this unjust? he said; ought we to give them a worse life,   58
when they might have a better?

You have again forgotten, my friend, I said, the intention of the 59
legislator, who did not aim at making any one class in the State happy
above the rest; the happiness was to be in the whole State, and he
held the citizens together by persuasion and necessity, making them
benefactors of the State, and therefore benefactors of one another; to
this end he created them, not to please themselves, but to be his instruments in binding up the State.

True, he said, I had forgotten. 60

Observe, Glaucon, that there will be no injustice in compelling our 61
philosophers to have a care and providence of others; we shall explain
to them that in other States, men of their class are not obliged to share
in the toils of politics: and this is reasonable, for they grow up at their
own sweet will, and the government would rather not have them.
Being self-taught, they cannot be expected to show any gratitude for
a culture which they have never received. But we have brought you
into the world to be rulers of the hive, kings of yourselves and of the
other citizens, and have educated you far better and more perfectly
than they have been educated, and you are better able to share in the
double duty. Wherefore each of you, when his turn comes, must go
down to the general underground abode, and get the habit of seeing
in the dark. When you have acquired the habit, you will see ten thousand times better than the inhabitants of the den, and you will know
what the several images are, and what they represent, because you
have seen the beautiful and just and good in their truth. And thus our
State which is also yours will be a reality, and not a dream only, and
will be administered in a spirit unlike that of other States, in which
men fight with one another about shadows only and are distracted in
the struggle for power, which in their eyes is a great good. Whereas
the truth is that the State in which the rulers are most reluctant to
govern is always the best and most quietly governed, and the State in
which they are most eager, the worst.

Quite true, he replied. 62

And will our pupils, when they hear this, refuse to take their turn 63
at the toils of State, when they are allowed to spend the greater part
of their time with one another in the heavenly light?

Impossible, he answered; for they are just men, and the commands 64
which we impose upon them are just; there can be no doubt that every
one of them will take office as a stern necessity, and not after the
fashion of our present rulers of State.

Yes, my friend, I said; and there lies the point. You must contrive 65
for your future rulers another and a better life than that of a ruler, and
then you may have a well-ordered State; for only in the State which

offers this, will they rule who are truly rich, not in silver and gold, but in virtue and wisdom, which are the true blessings of life. Whereas if they go to the administration of public affairs, poor and hungering after their own private advantage, thinking that hence they are to snatch the chief good, order there can never be; for they will be fighting about office, and the civil and domestic broils which thus arise will be the ruin of the rulers themselves and of the whole State.

Most true, he replied. 66

And the only life which looks down upon the life of political am- 67 bition is that of true philosophy. Do you know of any other?

Indeed, I do not, he said. 68

And those who govern ought not to be lovers of the task? For, if 69 they are, there will be rival lovers, and they will fight.

No question. 70

Who then are those whom we shall compel to be guardians? Surely 71 they will be the men who are wisest about affairs of State, and by whom the State is best administered, and who at the same time have other honors and another and a better life than that of politics?

They are the men, and I will choose them, he replied. 72

And now shall we consider in what way such guardians will be 73 produced, and how they are to be brought from darkness to light— as some are said to have ascended from the world below to the gods?

By all means, he replied. 74

The process, I said, is not the turning over of an oyster-shell,[1] but 75 the turning round of a soul passing from a day which is little better than night to the true day of being, that is, the ascent from below which we affirm to be true philosophy?

Quite so. 76

Questions

1. Plato is not merely reporting one of Socrates' conversations; he is teaching. What advantages does a dialogue have over a narrative or an essay as a way of teaching philosophy? How is the form of a dialogue especially suited to solving a problem?

[1] An allusion to a game in which two parties fled or pursued according as an oyster-shell which was thrown into the air fell with the dark or light side uppermost.

2. If you don't know the etymology of the word "conversion," look it
   up in a dictionary. How is the etymology appropriate to Plato's idea
   about education.
3. In paragraph 19, describing the prisoner as "reluctantly dragged"
   upward and "forced" to look at the sun, Socrates asks: "Is he not
   likely to be pained and irritated?" Can you recall experiencing pain
   and irritation while learning something you later were glad to have
   learned? Can you recall learning something new *without* experiencing pain and irritation?
4. "The State in which the rulers are most reluctant to govern is always
   the best and most quietly governed, and the State in which they
   are most eager, the worst" (paragraph 61). What does Socrates
   mean? Using examples from contemporary politics, defend this
   proposition, or argue against it.
5. Can you account for the power of this myth or fable? In our introductory comment (page 139) we tried to clarify the message by
   saying that a movie theater might serve as well as a cave, but in
   fact if the story were recast using a movie theater, would the emotional power be the same? Why or why not?
6. The metaphors of education as conversion and ascent are linked
   by the metaphor of light. Consider such expressions as "I see"
   (meaning "I understand") and "Let me give an illustration" (from
   the Latin *in* = in, and *lustrare* = to make bright). What other expressions about light are used metaphorically to describe intellectual
   comprehension?

Ernesto Galarza

Growing into Manhood

Up to the time a boy was between five and six years old, 1
Jalcocotán was for the most part an easy place in which to live. The
neighbors and *compadres* and *comadres* who scolded you for your bad

---

Ernesto Galarza, a teacher, writer, and lecturer, lives in San Jose, California.
"Growing into Manhood" (editors' title) is from Part One of *Barrio Boy,* a book
that began, Galarza says, "as anecdotes I told my family about Jalcocotán, the
mountain village in western Mexico where I was born."

manners or sent you on errands did not interfere much if you were respectful and stayed out of the way. With my two cousins and other boys of my own age I always had something to watch or to do.

The near side of the pond was shallow and fringed with reeds and tall clumps of grass that blossomed with plumes of cream-colored fluff. Around them the pond was always muddy and cool. In your bare feet you sank up to the ankles and by wriggling your toes you could raise oozy, iridescent bubbles. Trampling and squishing the mud, we made plopping hollow sounds and pretended we had gas on our stomachs. Pulling your foot out of the soft gumbo while your friends listened closely made noise remarkably like the mules in the corrals when they dropped manure.

Although we never collected polliwogs or frogs or lizards we chased them along the mud flat until they hopped into deep water or slithered away in the grass. Water snakes were everywhere, which we imagined were poisonous *víboras* or copperheads, like those the *jalcocotecanos* found in the forest. We spiced our play with a legend about an alligator that had crawled all the way up from Miramar and lay in wait for us somewhere in a deep pool of the arroyo—a monster no less real because he lived only in our imagination.

When the older boys of the village came to the pond on Sunday afternoons we watched them swim and dive. From a high branch of the big *nogal* they dropped a swing made of bush vines we called *liana*, braided like the women of the pueblo did their hair. The boy who was to dive next waited up in the *nogal*. Another handed him the end of the *liana*. The diver kicked off and let go as high as he could swing, his naked brown body twisting through the air like a split string bean. On our side of the swimming hole the smaller boys stripped and paddled while the divers yelled instructions on strokes and kicks.

Once in a great while the older boys would also allow us to join them in the bullfights they organized in one corner of the pasture. The bulls, the matadores, and the picadores were the ten- to twelve-year-olds, and the master of the fight was the oldest of the gang. We were permitted to take part only as fans or *aficionados*, to provide the yelling, the catcalls and the cheers. The master of the *corrida* directed us to sit on the ground on the upper slope of the bullring, which was entirely imaginary.

From behind a tree a trumpeter stepped to the edge of the ring. Blowing on a make-believe bugle he sounded a call and the bull rushed in—a boy with a plain sarape over his shoulders, holding with both hands in front of his chest the bleached skull of a steer complete with horns. Between the horns a large, thick cactus leaf from which the thorns had been removed, was tied. It was at the cactus pad that the matadores and picadores aimed their wooden swords and bamboo spears.

If the fight went according to the rules, the master declared the bull dead after a few rushes, by counting the stabs into the cactus, and the dead bull was replaced by a live one. Sometimes a sword or a spear missed the cactus pad and poked the bull in the stomach or some more sensitive spot. If the bull suspected that the miss was on purpose and dropped his skull to charge the torero with his fists, there was a free-for-all. We *aficionados* fell on one another with grunts and kicks, wrestling on the ground to increase the bedlam. If the commotion got out of the hands of the master of the *corrida*, there was always an adult watching from the village across the arroyo, who would walk over to the ring to scatter the rioters and send them home. 7

The girls of the village, needless to say, did not take part in the swimming parties or in the action of the bullfights. Neither did we, the boys who were under seven years of age. 8

This by no means put us in the same class. Up to his third year, a boy could still be led by the hand or undressed by an older sister. He was a *chilpayate,* a toddler who could play on the street naked without anybody noticing it. Little by little the *chilpayates* became men of sorts. They noticed that only girls had their earlobes pierced, wearing bits of string until their parents could afford genuine rings. They had to sit for hours to have their hair braided. At five years of age girls began to learn to carry water up from the arroyo in *ollas,* holding them on top of their heads with both hands, something that no man in Jalco would think of doing. They played silly games like La Ronda, hopping around and around, we thought, like *zopilotes.* Boys did girls' chores only if, and everybody knew that it was only if, there were no girls in the family—like shaking and sunning the bed mats or sprinkling the street in front of your cottage. 9

Between five and six, the fact that girls belonged to a lower class became even more obvious. Boys went into the forest to gather firewood. If their father's *milpa* or banana patch was not too far away they would be sent off before noon with a hot lunch in the haversack. They picked coffee beans on the lower branches of the bushes. They were taught to halter the burros and water them at the arroyo. They cut and bundled weeds in the *milpa* to feed the hens and the stock. 10

When a Jalco boy was passing six years of age and had become used to such jobs, he spent more and more of his day with the men and less time with the women. He was given more important tasks, which had a great deal to do with his becoming a man: "para que se 11 vaya haciendo hombre." At six, a boy stood about as tall as a machete, but he would not be able to use one for several years. By the time he was fourteen he would be a man, complete with a machete of his own, working the *milpa* or the coffee patch or the banana stand by the side of his father, and able to do it by himself, if necessary.

Somewhere between seven and fourteen the village noticed other signs of his coming manhood. The surest of these was his watching the girls when they went to the arroyo to scrub clothes and bathe. We under-sixers could do this anyway without anyone paying attention or chasing us off. Sitting high on a boulder just above the pond I could see them, with a white skirt pulled up and pinned over one shoulder, slapping the clothes on the rocks, dipping them in the water and wringing them. When the washing was over they slipped off the skirt and slid into a pool, dunking themselves, chattering and laughing above the noise of the current. That was how I found out, without my folks making any particular fuss, that there were at least two important differences between boys and girls besides the braids and the perforated ears.   12

That was not, however, real girl watching. Around twelve years, boys stood away, behind a tree or a bush. If someone noticed, they pretended that they were going into the forest or to the *milpa* to work.   13

After you picked out a girl you began watching her in the village, coming closer step by step until everybody knew it. In this way the girl was staked out and every other young man in the pueblo was on notice. Any other watcher would have to fight for it sooner or later. All this took time; if you began watching when you were around twelve by the time you were sixteen you could propose, asking your parents to ask hers for permission to get married.   14

All this happened only if the parents of the girl liked you. If they didn't, her father would let you know. Jalco was a small, tight town and you could easily be caught shadowing the girl or even speaking to her. She would most likely get a beating, and you might be chased away by her father or brothers.   15

But you were not ready to take the risks of going steady in Jalco until you had proved yourself a man at work. At six years of age or thereabouts you stopped being a playmate and became an apprentice. Jacinto and his father were a good example of this.   16

Chinto, as we called him, became an apprentice *campesino* when he was only a little older than I. I saw them pass in front of our cottage in the early dawn, Chinto following his *jefe* to their cornpatch down the mountain. The man walked ahead, his cotton pants cinched tightly   17 to his waist, one side of the fly crossed over the other and tucked into the waistband. The legs of the *calzones* were wound snug to the ankles, like puttees. At this time of the day the grass along the path to the *milpa* would be heavy with dew; the puttees soaked up less moisture than the bell-bottoms of the pants legs when they were loose. The soles and leather thongs of the huaraches the father wore were the soiled brown color of his ankles and toes. The hat was the usual ice cream cone of straw set on a wide brim curving down over the eyes and upward above the neck. He carried a machete in a sheath with the rawhide loop over one shoulder, and over the other the lunch bag.

Jacinto walked behind, dressed exactly like his father, except that he did not carry a machete. Several paces behind, he trotted to keep up with the steady gait of the man, learning the first lesson of his life as a *campesino:* that he would spend the rest of his life walking, walking, walking. "Ay va Jacinto con su papá," someone said in the gloom of our kitchen. It was the end of another boy and the beginning of another man. 18

They came back at nightfall in the same way, the man leading the boy. Both had rolled their pants legs above the knees, their white cotton shirts open in front, their hats tilted back. The man carried his huaraches over his shoulder. When the trail had roughened and calloused the feet of the boy, he would do the same. 19

The daily rounds that Jacinto and his father made were either to the cornpatch, the *platanar* where they cultivated banana trees or to the few rows of peppers and *jitomate* they tended. We knew the day that Jacinto went to pick coffee berries with his father, because they both carried wicker baskets, the man a large one, Jacinto a small one. When they left the village for several days to herd cattle for a *patrón,* father and son carried rawhide slings, the father a long sling, the boy a short one. Rounding up heifers and calves, the father taught the boy to whirl the sling and let one end go, timing it so the pebble would strike the target. Jacinto showed us how, when he was practicing in the pasture. 20

Jacinto and the other seven-year-olds who were growing into manhood lost no time in making it clear to the rest of us that we were nothing but stay-at-homes. As we felt more important than girls, so Jacinto and his fellow apprentices felt more important than us. It took courage to walk toward the *milpa* through the forest where you could step on a rattler any moment, if you didn't see it coiled in the path or hear its tail buzzing. It took stamina to weed the corn hills and the banana trees under the broiling sun. Only a boy with manstuff in him 21 could walk down the mountain and up the next ridge to spend the night tending heaps of burning wood to make charcoal that the burros carried to Tepic and San Blas. At night from Jalco we could see the orange bonfires high up on the mountain to the east. We saw Jacinto come back with his father from such work—jaunty *carboneros* with rolled-up pants legs, hats tilted back, face and legs and arms smeared with charcoal, dust, and sweat.

It was in the cultivated patches in the forest that boys grew into   22
men. With machetes they cleared the steep slopes and the hollows, setting fire to the brush and the stumps. In the ashes they planted corn, beans, peppers, *jitomate*, and bananas. Under the shade of a tall tree they grew coffee bushes. The forest provided the rest of Jalcotán's living—timber, charcoal, wild fruit, herbs, bears, deer, and hides from alligators and cougars.

Out of the forest a man took out only what he and his family could   23
use. Not all the *campesinos* in Jalcocotán, or in all the pueblos on the mountain together took out so much that the *monte* and the arroyo could not replenish themselves. In the conversation of the townspeople they were ancient sayings—*dichos*—that showed how long the people and the forest had lived together: "Agua que no has de beber, déjala correr"—at the arroyo drink your fill, let the rest run down the hill. "El que a buen árbol se arrima buena sombra le da"—the shade beneath a goodly tree is good for you and good for me.

Other than the stone walls of their corrals, the *jalcocotecanos* did   24
not build fences to separate one man's property from another's. When the soil wore out in a *milpa* and another one was cleared, there were no old fences to take down or new ones to put up.

The world of work into which Jacinto and the other seven-year-   25
olds were apprenticed was within sight and sound of the pueblo. It was work under the blazing sun, in rainstorms, in pitch-black nights. It was work that you were always walking to or walking from, work without wages and work without end. It was work that gave you a bone-tired feeling at the end of the day, so you learned to swing a machete, to tighten a cinch, and to walk without lost motion. Between seven and twelve you learned all this, each lesson driven home when your *jefe* said with a scowl: "Así no, hombre; así." And he showed you how.

But he knew that there was another world of work beyond Jalco.   26
Over in Miramar, Los Cocos, Puga and such places there were haciendas where peasants from the pueblos could work for money. Some *jalcocotecanos* did this kind of hiring out. They cut sugarcane, herded

cattle, butchered steers, tended the crops, gathered coconuts for the soap works, and cleared land *a puro machetazo*—with your bare hands and a machete.

Boys who went with their fathers to the haciendas soon learned   27
the differences between making a living on the mountain and working for the *patrones*. One was that on the mountain you took home corn, bananas, peppers, coffee, and anything else you had raised, but never money. From the hacienda, when your contract ended, you never took anything to eat or wear except what you paid for at the *tienda de raya*, the company store. A peon could make as much as ten pesos a month at hard labor working from dawn to dusk, seven days a week, four weeks every month. It came to about two or three centavos per hour, plus your meals and a place to spread your straw sleeping mat.

The most important difference, however, was the *capataz*, the rid-   28
ing boss who watched the laborers all day long, just as the *guardia* watched them throughout the night. The business of the *capataz* was to keep the *peonanda*, as the crews of field hands were called, hustling at the assigned tasks. He carried a machete slung from his saddle, a whip, and often a pistol: the equipment of a top sergeant of the hacienda. The captain was the *Administrador*, who in turn took his orders from the *patrón* who probably lived in Tepic or Guadalajara or perhaps even in La Capital, as everyone called Mexico City.

The men who had worked on haciendas knew of these matters.   29
We heard snatches of firsthand reports from them but mostly we learned from Don Catarino, José, Don Cleofas, and the muleteers who passed through Jalco. Whoever had been there came back cursing it. The riding boss was the Devil on horseback; in the company store every centavo you earned was taken back by a clerk who kept numbers in a book that proved you always owed him something. If a peon left the hacienda before his contract was over and his debts were paid, he became a fugitive. He either returned to his pueblo, his *compadres* and his *milpa* in some far-off place in the mountains, or he scratched for a living, lost in the forest. Old men in the village talked of the time they had worked on a hacienda as if they had served a sentence in prison or on a chain gang. They remembered capataces who had whipped them or cursed them fifty years before, and they still murmured a phrase: "Algún día me la pagan." There were a hundred blood debts of this kind in Jalcocotán, Doña Esther said, thousands of them in all the villages of the Sierra Madre, and millions in all the pueblos of Mexico.

"Algún día me la pagan."

30

"Tía, what does that mean?" I asked her more than once. She 31
always sent me to my mother with the question. Her answer was: "It
means that somebody owes him something."

"But what does somebody owe him?" 32

The anger and the foreboding in "algún día me la pagan" was in 33
my mother's voice: "Something that hurts." She did not explain, just
as she would not tell me why Catalino the bandit hated the *rurales* and
shot so many of them.

Guessing at what people meant, I came to *feel* certain words rather 34
than to *know* them. They were words which came from the lips of the
jalcocotecanos with an accent of suspicion, of fear, and of hatred. These
words were *los rurales*, the *jefe politico*, the *señor gobernador, las autori-*
dades, el gobierno. When a stranger rode into Jalco, people stopped talking. Every detail about him and his horse was observed for a clue as
to whether he was one of the *autoridades*.

It was the same with all outsiders. They always came asking ques- 35
tions, which the *jalcocotecanos* answered politely but roundabout. For
me the world began to divide itself into two kinds of people—the men
on horseback and the men who walked.

Questions

1. Summarize the contents of paragraphs 1 through 7. How has Galarza organized his materials in these paragraphs? What other ways
   of organizing them can you imagine? What is the function of paragraph 8?
2. In this chapter from *Barrio Boy* Galarza reflects on several distinct
   areas in the education and indoctrination of the child into the world
   of the adult. What are they? Could you outline, with comparable
   distinctness, parts of your own education and indoctrination? If not,
   why not?

E. B. White

Education

I have an increasing admiration for the teacher in the country school where we have a third-grade scholar in attendance. She not only undertakes to instruct her charges in all the subjects of the first three grades, but she manages to function quietly and effectively as a guardian of their health, their clothes, their habits, their mothers, and their snowball engagements. She has been doing this sort of Augean task for twenty years, and is both kind and wise. She cooks for the children on the stove that heats the room, and she can cool their passions or warm their soup with equal competence. She conceives their costumes, cleans up their messes, and shares their confidences. My boy already regards his teacher as his great friend, and I think tells her a great deal more than he tells us. 1

The shift from city school to country school was something we worried about quietly all last summer. I have always rather favored public school over private school, if only because in public school you meet a greater variety of children. This bias of mine, I suspect, is partly an attempt to justify my own past (I never knew anything but public schools) and partly an involuntary defense against getting kicked in the shins by a young ceramist on his way to the kiln. My wife was unacquainted with public schools, never having been exposed (in her early life) to anything more public than the washroom of Miss Winsor's. Regardless of our backgrounds, we both knew that the change in schools was something that concerned not us but the scholar himself. We hoped it would work out all right. In New York our son went to a medium-priced private institution with semi-progressive ideas of education, and modern plumbing. He learned fast, kept well, and we were satisfied. It was an electric, colorful, regimented existence with moments of pleasurable pause and giddy incident. The day the Christ- 2

E[lwyn] B[rooks] White (1899–1985) wrote poetry and fiction, but he is most widely known as an essayist and as the coauthor (with William Strunk, Jr.) of *Elements of Style*. After a long career at *The New Yorker* he retired to Maine, but he continued to write until the year before his death at the age of 86.

mas angel fainted and had to be carried out by one of the Wise Men was educational in the highest sense of the term. Our scholar gave imitations of it around the house for weeks afterward, and I doubt if it ever goes completely out of his mind.

His days were rich in formal experience. Wearing overalls and an 3 old sweater (the accepted uniform of the private seminary), he sallied forth at morn accompanied by a nurse or a parent and walked (or was pulled) two blocks to a corner where the school bus made a flag stop. This flashy vehicle was as punctual as death: seeing us waiting at the cold curb, it would sweep to a halt, open its mouth, suck the boy in, and spring away with an angry growl. It was a good deal like a train picking up a bag of mail. At school the scholar was worked on for six or seven hours by half a dozen teachers and a nurse, and was revived on orange juice in mid-morning. In a cinder court he played games supervised by an athletic instructor, and in a cafeteria he ate lunch worked out by a dietitian. He soon learned to read with gratifying facility and discernment and to make Indian weapons of a semi-deadly nature. Whenever one of his classmates fell low of a fever the news was put on the wires and there were breathless phone calls to physicians, discussing periods of incubation and allied magic.

In the country all one can say is that the situation is different, and 4 somehow more casual. Dressed in corduroys, sweatshirt, and short rubber boots, and carrying a tin dinner-pail pail, our scholar departs at the crack of dawn for the village school, two and a half miles down the road, next to the cemetery. When the road is open and the car will start, he makes the journey by motor, courtesy of his old man. When the snow is deep or the motor is dead or both, he makes it on the hoof. In the afternoons he walks or hitches all or part of the way home in fair weather, gets transported in foul. The schoolhouse is a two-room frame building, bungalow type, shingles stained a burnt brown with weather-resistant stain. It has a chemical toilet in the basement and two teachers above the stairs. One takes the first three grades, the other the fourth, fifth, and sixth. They have little or no time for individual instruction, and no time at all for the esoteric. They teach what they know themselves, just as fast and as hard as they can manage. The pupils sit still at their desks in class, and do their milling around outdoors during recess.

There is no supervised play. They play cops and robbers (only 5 they call it "Jail") and throw things at one another—snowballs in winter, rose hips in fall. It seems to satisfy them. They also construct darts, pinwheels, and "pick-up sticks" (jackstraws), and the school itself does a brisk trade in penny candy, which is for sale right in the classroom and which contains "surprises." The most highly prized surprise is a fake cigarette, made of cardboard, fiendishly lifelike.

The memory of how apprehensive we were at the beginning is 6 still strong. The boy was nervous about the change too. The tension, on that first fair morning in September when we drove him to school, almost blew the windows out of the sedan. And when later we picked him up on the road, wandering along with his little blue lunch-pail, and got his laconic report "All right" in answer to our inquiry about how the day had gone, our relief was vast. Now, after almost a year of it, the only difference we can discover in the two school experiences is that in the country he sleeps better at night—and *that* probably is more the air than the education. When grilled on the subject of school-in-country vs. school-in-city, he replied that the chief difference is that the day seems to go so much quicker in the country. "Just like lightning," he reported.

Questions

1. Which school, public or private, does White prefer? Since White doesn't state his preference outright, from what evidence were you able to infer it?
2. In the first half of paragraph 2 White admits to a bias in favor of public schools, and he speculates, half-seriously, about the origins of his bias. If his intention here is not simply to amuse us, what is it?
3. What is White's strongest argument in favor of the school he prefers? Where in the essay do you find it?

Maya Angelou

Graduation

The children in Stamps trembled visibly with anticipation. 1
Some adults were excited too, but to be certain the whole young population had come down with graduation epidemic. Large classes were
graduating from both the grammar school and the high school. Even
those who were years removed from their own day of glorious release
were anxious to help with preparations as a kind of dry run. The junior
students who were moving into the vacating classes' chairs were tra-
dition-bound to show their talents for leadership and management.
They strutted through the school and around the campus exerting pressure on the lower grades. Their authority was so new that occasionally
if they pressed a little too hard it had to be overlooked. After all, next
term was coming, and it never hurt a sixth grader to have a play sister
in the eighth grade, or a tenth-year student to be able to call a twelfth
grader Bubba. So all was endured in a spirit of shared understanding.
But the graduating classes themselves were the nobility. Like travelers
with exotic destinations on their minds, the graduates were remarkably
forgetful. They came to school without their books, or tablets or even
pencils. Volunteers fell over themselves to secure replacements for the
missing equipment. When accepted, the willing workers might or
might not be thanked, and it was of no importance to the pregraduation
rites. Even teachers were respectful of the now quiet and aging seniors,
and tended to speak to them, if not as equals, as beings only slightly
lower than themselves. After tests were returned and grades given,
the student body, which acted like an extended family, knew who did
well, who excelled, and what piteous ones had failed.

Unlike the white high school, Lafayette County Training School 2
distinguished itself by having neither lawn, nor hedges, nor tennis
court, nor climbing ivy. Its two buildings (main classrooms, the grade
school and home economics) were set on a dirt hill with no fence to
limit either its boundaries or those of bordering farms. There was a
large expanse to the left of the school which was used alternately as

Maya Angelou was born in St. Louis in 1928. She has written books of poetry
and three autobiographic books.
    "Graduation" (editors' title) is from her first autobiography, *I Know Why the
Caged Bird Sings*, Chapter 23.

a baseball diamond or a basketball court. Rusty hoops on the swaying poles represented the permanent recreational equipment, although bats and balls could be borrowed from the P.E. teacher if the borrower was qualified and if the diamond wasn't occupied.

Over this rocky area relieved by a few shady tall persimmon trees   3
the graduating class walked. The girls often held hands and no longer bothered to speak to the lower students. There was a sadness about them, as if this old world was not their home and they were bound for higher ground. The boys, on the other hand, had become more friendly, more outgoing. A decided change from the closed attitude they projected while studying for finals. Now they seemed not ready to give up the old school, the familiar paths and classrooms. Only a small percentage would be continuing on to college—one of the South's A & M (agricultural and mechanical) schools, which trained Negro youths to be carpenters, farmers, handymen, masons, maids, cooks and baby nurses. Their future rode heavily on their shoulders, and blinded them to the collective joy that had pervaded the lives of the boys and girls in the grammar school graduating class.

Parents who could afford it had ordered new shoes and ready-   4
made clothes for themselves from Sears and Roebuck or Montgomery Ward. They also engaged the best seamstresses to make the floating graduating dresses and to cut down secondhand pants which would be pressed to a military slickness for the important event.

Oh, it was important, all right. Whitefolks would attend the cer-   5
emony, and two or three would speak of God and home, and the Southern way of life, and Mrs. Parsons, the principal's wife, would play the graduation march while the lower-grade graduates paraded down the aisles and took their seats below the platform. The high school seniors would wait in empty classrooms to make their dramatic entrance.

In the Store I was the person of the moment. The birthday girl.   6
The center. Bailey had graduated the year before, although to do so he had had to forfeit all pleasures to make up for his time lost in Baton Rouge.

My class was wearing butter-yellow piqué dresses, and Momma   7
launched out on mine. She smocked the yoke into tiny crisscrossing puckers, then shirred the rest of the bodice. Her dark fingers ducked in and out of the lemony cloth as she embroidered raised daisies around the hem. Before she considered herself finished she had added a crocheted cuff on the puff sleeves, and a pointy crocheted collar.

I was going to be lovely. A walking model of all the various styles   8 of fine hand sewing and it didn't worry me that I was only twelve years old and merely graduating from the eighth grade. Besides, many teachers in Arkansas Negro schools had only that diploma and were licensed to impart wisdom.

The days had become longer and more noticeable. The faded beige 9 of former times had been replaced with strong and sure colors. I began to see my classmates' clothes, their skin tones, and the dust that waved off pussy willows. Clouds that lazed across the sky were objects of great concern to me. Their shiftier shapes might have held a message that in my new happiness and with a little bit of time I'd soon decipher. During that period I looked at the arch of heaven so religiously my neck kept a steady ache. I had taken to smiling more often, and my jaws hurt from the unaccustomed activity. Between the two physical sore spots, I suppose I could have been uncomfortable, but that was not the case. As a member of the winning team (the graduating class of 1940) I had outdistanced unpleasant sensations by miles. I was headed for the freedom of open fields.

Youth and social approval allied themselves with me and we tram- 10 meled memories of slights and insults. The wind of our swift passage remodeled my features. Lost tears were pounded to mud and then to dust. Years of withdrawal were brushed aside and left behind, as hanging ropes of parasitic moss.

My work alone had awarded me a top place and I was going to 11 be one of the first called in the graduating ceremonies. On the classroom blackboard, as well as on the bulletin board in the auditorium, there were blue stars and white stars and red stars. No absences, no tardinesses, and my academic work was among the best of the year. I could say the preamble to the Constitution even faster than Bailey. We timed ourselves often: "WethepeopleoftheUnitedStatesinordertoformamoreperfectunion . . ." I had memorized the Presidents of the United States from Washington to Roosevelt in chronological as well as alphabetical order.

My hair pleased me too. Gradually the black mass had lengthened 12 and thickened, so that it kept at last to its braided pattern, and I didn't have to yank my scalp off when I tried to comb it.

Louise and I had rehearsed the exercises until we tired out our- 13 selves. Henry Reed was class valedictorian. He was a small, very black boy with hooded eyes, a long, broad nose and an oddly shaped head. I had admired him for years because each term he and I vied for the best grades in our class. Most often he bested me, but instead of being disappointed I was pleased that we shared top places between us. Like many Southern Black children, he lived with his grandmother, who was as strict as Momma and as kind as she knew how to be. He was courteous, respectful and soft-spoken to elders, but on the play-ground he chose to play the roughest games. I admired him. Anyone, I reckoned, sufficiently afraid or sufficiently dull could be polite. But to be able to operate at a top level with both adults and children was admirable.

His valedictory speech was entitled "To Be or Not to Be." The 14 rigid tenth-grade teacher had helped him to write it. He'd been working on the dramatic stresses for months.

The weeks until graduation were filled with heady activities. A 15 group of small children were to be presented in a play about buttercups and daisies and bunny rabbits. They could be heard throughout the building practicing their hops and their little songs that sounded like silver bells. The older girls (non-graduates, of course) were assigned the task of making refreshments for the night's festivities. A tangy scent of ginger, cinnamon, nutmeg and chocolate wafted around the home economics building as the budding cooks made samples for themselves and their teachers.

In every corner of the workshop, axes and saws split fresh timber 16 as the woodshop boys made sets and stage scenery. Only the graduates were left out of the general bustle. We were free to sit in the library at the back of the building or look in quite detachedly, naturally, on the measures being taken for our event.

Even the minister preached on graduation the Sunday before. His 17 subject was, "Let your light so shine that men will see your good works and praise your father, Who is in Heaven." Although the sermon was purported to be addressed to us, he used the occasion to speak to backsliders, gamblers, and general ne'er-do-wells. But since he had called our names at the beginning of the service we were mollified.

Among Negroes the tradition was to give presents to children 18 going only from one grade to another. How much more important this was when the person was graduating at the top of the class. Uncle Willie and Momma had sent away for a Mickey Mouse watch like Bailey's. Louise gave me four embroidered handkerchiefs. (I gave her three crocheted doilies.) Mrs. Sneed, the minister's wife, made me an underskirt to wear for graduation, and nearly every customer gave me a nickel or maybe even a dime with the instruction "Keep on moving to higher ground," or some such encouragement.

Amazingly the great day finally dawned and I was out of bed 19 before I knew it. I threw open the back door to see it more clearly, but

Momma said, "Sister, come away from that door and put your robe on."

I hoped the memory of that morning would never leave me. Sun- 20
light was itself still young, and the day had none of the insistence maturity would bring it in a few hours. In my robe and barefoot in the backyard, under cover of going to see about my new beans, I gave myself up to the gentle warmth and thanked God that no matter what evil I had done in my life He had allowed me to live to see this day. Somewhere in my fatalism I had expected to die, accidentally, and never have the chance to walk up the stairs in the auditorium and gracefully receive my hard-earned diploma. Out of God's merciful bosom I had won reprieve.

Bailey came out in his robe and gave me a box wrapped in Christ- 21
mas paper. He said he had saved his money for months to pay for it. It felt like a box of chocolates, but I knew Bailey wouldn't save money to buy candy when we had all we could want under our noses.

He was as proud of the gift as I. It was a soft-leather-bound copy 22
of a collection of poems by Edgar Allan Poe, or, as Bailey and I called him, "Eap." I turned to "Annabel Lee" and we walked up and down the garden rows, the cool dirt between our toes, reciting the beautifully sad lines.

Momma made a Sunday breakfast although it was only Friday. 23
After we finished the blessing, I opened by eyes to find the watch on my plate. It was a dream of a day. Everything went smoothly and to my credit. I didn't have to be reminded or scolded for anything. Near evening I was too jittery to attend to chores, so Bailey volunteered to do all before his bath.

Days before, we had made a sign for the Store and as we turned 24
out the lights Momma hung the cardboard over the doorknob. It read clearly: CLOSED. GRADUATION.

My dress fitted perfectly and everyone said that I looked like a 25
sunbeam in it. On the hill, going toward the school, Bailey walked behind with Uncle Willie, who muttered, "Go on, Ju." He wanted him to walk ahead with us because it embarrassed him to have to walk so slowly. Bailey said he'd let the ladies walk together, and the men would bring up the rear. We all laughed, nicely.

Little children dashed by out of the dark like fireflies. Their crepe- 26
paper dresses and butterfly wings were not made for running and we heard more than one rip, dryly, and the regretful "uh uh" that followed.

The school blazed without gaiety. The windows seemed cold and 27 unfriendly from the lower hill. A sense of ill-fated timing crept over me, and if Momma hadn't reached for my hand I would have drifted back to Bailey and Uncle Willie, and possibly beyond. She made a few slow jokes about my feet getting cold, and tugged me along to the now-strange building.

Around the front steps, assurance came back. There were my fel- 28 low "greats," the graduating class. Hair brushed back, legs oiled, new dresses and pressed pleats, fresh pocket handkerchiefs and little handbags, all homesewn. Oh, we were up to snuff, all right. I joined my comrades and didn't even see my family go in to find seats in the crowded auditorium.

The school band struck up a march and all classes filed in as had 29 been rehearsed. We stood in front of our seats, as assigned, and on a signal from the choir director, we sat. No sooner had this been accomplished that the band started to play the national anthem. We rose again and sang the song, after which we recited the pledge of allegiance. We remained standing for a brief minute before the choir director and the principal signaled to us, rather desperately I thought, to take our seats. The command was so unusual that our carefully rehearsed and smooth-running machine was thrown off. For a full minute we fumbled for our chairs and bumped into each other awkwardly. Habits change or solidify under pressure, so in our state of nervous tension we had been ready to follow our usual assembly pattern: the American National Anthem, then the pledge of allegiance, then the song every Black person I knew called the Negro National Anthem. All done in the same key, with the same passion and most often standing on the same foot.

Finding my seat at last, I was overcome with a presentiment of 30 worse things to come. Something unrehearsed, unplanned, was going to happen, and we were going to be made to look bad. I distinctly remember being explicit in the choice of pronoun. It was "we," the graduating class, the unit, that concerned me then.

The principal welcomed "parents and friends" and asked the Bap- 31 tist minister to lead us in prayer. His invocation was brief and punchy, and for a second I thought we were getting back on the high road to right action. When the principal came back to the dais, however, his voice had changed. Sounds always affected me profoundly and the principal's voice was one of my favorites. During assembly it melted and lowed weakly into the audience. It had not been in my plan to listen to him, but my curiosity was piqued and I straightened up to give him my attention.

He was talking about Booker T. Washington, our "late great 32 leader," who said we can be as close as the fingers on the hand, etc. . . . Then he said a few vague things about friendship and the friendship of kindly people to those less fortunate than themselves. With that his voice nearly faded, thin, away. Like a river diminishing to a stream and then to a trickle. But he cleared his throat and said, "Our speaker tonight, who is also our friend, came from Texarkana to deliver the commencement address, but due to the irregularity of the train schedule, he's going to, as they say, 'speak and run.' " He said that we understood and wanted the man to know that we were most grateful for the time he was able to give us and then something about how we were willing always to adjust to another's program, and without more ado—"I give you Mr. Edward Donleavy."

Not one but two white men came through the door offstage. The 33 shorter one walked to the speaker's platform, and the tall one moved over to the center seat and sat down. But that was our principal's seat, and already occupied. The dislodged gentleman bounced around for a long breath or two before the Baptist minister gave him his chair, then with more dignity than the situation deserved, the minister walked off the stage.

Donleavy looked at the audience once (on reflection, I'm sure that 34 he wanted only to reassure himself that we were really there), adjusted his glasses and began to read from a sheaf of papers.

He was glad "to be here and to see the work going on just as it 35 was in the other schools."

At the first "Amen" from the audience I willed the offender to 36 immediate death by choking on the word. But Amen's and Yes, sir's began to fall around the room like rain through a ragged umbrella.

He told us of the wonderful changes we children in Stamps had 37 in store. The Central School (naturally, the white school was Central) had already been granted improvements that would be in use in the fall. A well-known artist was coming from Little Rock to teach art to them. They were going to have the newest microscopes and chemistry equipment for their laboratory. Mr. Donleavy didn't leave us long in the dark over who made these improvements available to Central High. Nor were we to be ignored in the general betterment scheme he had in mind.

He said that he had pointed out to people at a very high level that 38 one of the first-line football tacklers at Arkansas Agricultural and Mechanical College had graduated from good old Lafayette County Training School. Here fewer Amen's were heard. Those few that did break through lay dully in the air with the heaviness of habit.

He went on to praise us. He went on to say how he had bragged   39
that "one of the best basketball players at Fisk sank his first ball right here at Lafayette County Training School."

The white kids were going to have a chance to become Galileos   40
and Madame Curies and Edisons and Gauguins, and our boys (the girls weren't even in on it) would try to be Jesse Owenses and Joe Louises.

Owens and the Brown Bomber were great heroes in our world,   41
but what school official in the white-goddom of Little Rock had the right to decide that those two men must be our only heroes? Who decided that for Henry Reed to become a scientist he had to work like George Washington Carver, as a bootblack, to buy a lousy microscope? Bailey was obviously always going to be small to be an athlete, so which concrete angel glued to what country seat had decided that if my brother wanted to become a lawyer he had to first pay penance for his skin by picking cotton and hoeing corn and studying correspondence books at night for twenty years?

The man's dead words fell like bricks around the auditorium and   42
too many settled in my belly. Constrained by hard-learned manners I couldn't look behind me, but to my left and right the proud graduating class of 1940 had dropped their heads. Every girl in my row had found something new to do with her handkerchief. Some folded the tiny squares into love knots, some into triangles, but most were wadding them, then pressing them flat on their yellow laps.

On the dais, the ancient tragedy was being replayed. Professor   43
Parsons sat, a sculptor's reject, rigid. His large, heavy body seemed devoid of will or willingness, and his eyes said he was no longer with us. The other teachers examined the flag (which was draped stage right) or their notes, or the windows which opened on our now-famous playing diamond.

Graduation, the hush-hush magic time of frills and gifts and con-   44
gratulations and diplomas, was finished for me before my name was called. The accomplishment was nothing. The meticulous maps, drawn in three colors of ink, learning and spelling decasyllabic words, memorizing the whole of *The Rape of Lucrece*—it was nothing. Donleavy had exposed us.

We were maids and farmers, handymen and washerwomen, and   45
anything higher that we aspired to was farcical and presumptuous.

Then I wished that Gabriel Prosser and Nat Turner had killed all white-folks in their beds and that Abraham Lincoln had been assassinated before the signing of the Emancipation Proclamation, and that Harriet Tubman had been killed by that blow on her head and Christopher Columbus had drowned in the *Santa Maria*.

It was awful to be Negro and have no control over my life. It was   46
brutal to be young and already trained to sit quietly and listen to charges brought against my color with no chance of defense. We should all be dead. I thought I should like to see us all dead, one on top of the other. A pyramid of flesh with the whitefolks on the bottom, as the broad base, then the Indians with their silly tomahawks and teepees and wigwams and treaties, the Negroes with their mops and recipes and cotton sacks and spirituals sticking out of their mouths. The Dutch children should all stumble in their wooden shoes and break their necks. The French should choke to death on the Louisiana Purchase (1803) while silkworms ate all the Chinese with their stupid pigtails. As a species, we were an abomination. All of us.

Donleavy was running for election, and assured our parents that   47
if he won we could count on having the only colored paved playing field in that part of Arkansas. Also—he never looked up to acknowledge the grunts of acceptance—also, we were bound to get some new equipment for the home economics building and the workshop.

He finished, and since there was no need to give any more than   48
the most perfunctory thank-you's, he nodded to the men on the stage, and the tall white man who was never introduced joined him at the door. They left with the attitude that now they were off to something really important. (The graduation ceremonies at Lafayette County Training School had been a mere preliminary.)

The ugliness they left was palpable. An uninvited guest who   49
wouldn't leave. The choir was summoned and sang a modern arrangement of "Onward, Christian Soldiers," with new words pertaining to graduates seeking their place in the world. But it didn't work. Elouise, the daughter of the Baptist minister, recited "Invictus," and I could have cried at the impertinence of "I am the master of my fate, I am the captain of my soul."

My name had lost its ring of familiarity and I had to be nudged   50
to go and receive my diploma. All my preparations had fled. I neither marched up to the stage like a conquering Amazon, nor did I look in the audience for Bailey's nod of approval. Marguerite Johnson, I heard the name again, my honors were read, there were noises in the audience of appreciation, and I took my place on the stage as rehearsed.

I thought about colors I hated: ecru, puce, lavender, beige and 51
black.

There was shuffling and rustling around me, then Henry Reed 52
was giving his valedictory address, "To Be or Not to Be." Hadn't he
heard the whitefolks? We couldn't *be*, so the question was a waste of
time. Henry's voice came out clear and strong. I feared to look at him.
Hadn't he got the message? There was no "nobler in the mind" for
Negroes because the world didn't think we had minds, and they let
us know it. "Outrageous fortune"? Now, that was a joke. When the
ceremony was over I had to tell Henry Reed some things. That is, if
I still cared. Not "rub," Henry, "erase." "Ah, there's the erase." Us.

Henry had been a good student in elocution. His voice rose on 53
tides of promise and fell on waves of warnings. The English teacher
had helped him to create a sermon winging through Hamlet's solilo-
quy. To be a man, a doer, a builder, a leader, or to be a tool, an unfunny
joke, a crusher of funky toadstools. I marveled that Henry could go
through with the speech as if we had a choice.

I had been listening and silently rebutting each sentence with my 54
eyes closed; then there was a hush, which in an audience warns that
something unplanned is happening. I looked up and saw Henry Reed,
the conservative, the proper, the A student, turn his back to the audience and turn to us (the proud graduating class of 1940) and sing,
nearly speaking,

> Lift ev'ry voice and sing
> Till earth and heaven ring
> Ring with the harmonies of Liberty . . .

It was the poem written by James Weldon Johnson. It was the music
composed by J. Rosamond Johnson. It was the Negro National Anthem. Out of habit we were singing it.

Our mothers and fathers stood in the dark hall and joined the 55
hymn of encouragement. A kindergarten teacher led the small children
onto the stage and the buttercups and daisies and bunny rabbits
marked time and tried to follow:

> Stony the road we trod
> Bitter the chastening rod
> Felt in the days when hope, unborn, had died.
> Yet with a steady beat
> Have not our weary feet
> Come to the place for which our fathers sighed?

Every child I knew had learned that song with his ABC's and along 56
with "Jesus Loves Me This I Know." But I personally had never heard
it before. Never heard the words, despite the thousands of times I had
sung them. Never thought they had anything to do with me.

On the other hand, the words of Patrick Henry had made such 57
an impression on me that I had been able to stretch myself tall and
trembling and say, "I know not what course others may take, but as
for me, give me liberty or give me death."

And now I heard, really for the first time: 58

We have come over a way that with tears has been watered,
We have come, trading our path through the blood of the slaughtered.

While echoes of the song shivered in the air, Henry Reed bowed 59
his head, said "Thank you," and returned to his place in the line. The
tears that slipped down many faces were not wiped away in shame.

We were on top again. As always, again. We survived. The depths 60
had been icy and dark, but now a bright sun spoke to our souls. I was
no longer simply a member of the proud graduating class of 1940; I
was a proud member of the wonderful, beautiful Negro race.

Oh, Black known and unknown poets, how often have your auc- 61
tioned pains sustained us? Who will compute the lonely nights made
less lonely by your songs, or the empty pots made less tragic by your
tales?

If we were a people much given to revealing secrets, we might 62
raise monuments and sacrifice to the memories of our poets, but slavery cured us of that weakness. It may be enough, however, to have
it said that we survive in exact relationship to the dedication of our
poets (include preachers, musicians and blues singers).

Questions

1. In paragraph 1 notice such overstatements as "glorious release,"
   "the graduating classes themselves were the nobility," and "exotic
   destinations." Find further examples in the next few pages. What
   is the function of this diction?
2. Characterize the writer as you perceive her up through paragraph
   28. Support your characterization with references to specific passages. Next, characterize her in paragraph 46, which begins "It was

awful to be Negro." Next, characterize her on the basis of the entire essay. Finally, in a sentence, try to describe the change, telling the main attitudes or moods that she goes through.

3.   How would you define "poets" as Angelou uses the word in the last sentence?

Pauline Kael

High School and Other Forms of Madness

Many of us grow to hate documentaries in school, because   1
the use of movies to teach us something seems a cheat—a pill disguised as candy—and documentaries always seem to be about something we're not interested in. But Wiseman's documentaries show what is left out of both fictional movies and standard documentaries that simplify for a purpose, and his films deal with the primary institutions of our lives: *Titicut Follies* (Bridgewater, an institution in which we lock away the criminally insane), *High School* (a high school in a large Eastern city), and *Law and Order* (the Kansas City police force). Television has been accustoming us to a horrible false kind of "involvement"; sometimes it seems that the only thing the news shows can think of is to get close to emotion. They shove a camera and a microphone in front of people in moments of stress and disaster and grief, and ram their equipment into any pores and cavities they can reach. Wiseman made comparable mistakes in *Titicut Follies,* but he learned better fast.

High School is so familiar and so extraordinarily evocative that a   2
feeling of empathy with the students floods over us. How did we live through it? How did we keep any spirit? When you see a kid trying to make a phone call and being interrupted with "Do you have a pass

Pauline Kael, born in 1919 in Petaluma, California, grew up in San Francisco and attended the University of California at Berkeley. She regularly writes film criticism for *The New Yorker.*

to use the phone?'' it all floods back—the low ceilings and pale-green walls of the basement where the lockers were, the constant defensiveness, that sense of always being in danger of breaking some pointless, petty rule. When since that time has one ever needed a pass to make a phone call? This movie takes one back to where, one discovers, time has stood still. Here is the girl humiliated for having worn a short dress to the Senior Prom, being told it was "offensive" to the whole class. Here it is all over again—the insistence that you be "respectful"; and the teachers' incredible instinct for "disrespect," their antennae always extended for that little bit of reservation or irony in your tone, the tiny spark that you desperately need to preserve your *self*-respect. One can barely hear it in the way a boy says "Yes, sir" to the dean, but the dean, ever on the alert, snaps, "Don't give me that 'Yes, sir' business!. . . . There's no sincereness behind it." Here, all over again, is the dullness of high-school education:

> *Teacher:* What on the horizon or what existed that forced labor to turn to collective bargaining? What was there a lack of?
> *Girl:* Communications?
> *Teacher:* Security, yes, communications, lack of security, concern for the job. The important thing is this, let's get to the beginning. First of all, there was the lack of security; second of all, there was a lack of communication. . . .

The same old pseudo-knowledge is used to support what the schools think is moral. The visiting gynecologist in a sex-education class lectures the boys:

> The more a fellow gets into bed with more different girls, the more insecure he is, and this shows up actually later in all the divorce statistics in America. . . . You can graph right on a graph, the more girls fellows got into bed with or vice-versa the higher the divorce rate, the greater the sexual inadequacy. . . .

And there's the beautiful military doubletalk when it's a question of a teacher's incompetence or unfairness. A boy protests a disciplinary action against him by a teacher, and after he has explained his innocence, the dean talks him into accepting the punishment "to establish that you can be a man and that you can take orders." The teachers are masters here; they're in a superior position for the only time in their lives, probably, and most of the petty tyrannies—like laying on the homework—aren't fully conscious. They justify each other's actions as a matter of course, and put the students in the wrong in the same indifferent way. They put a student down with "It's nice to be individualistic, but there are certain places to be individualistic," yet they never tell you where. How can one stand up against such bland authoritarianism? The teachers, crushing and processing, are the most insidious kind of enemy, the enemy with corrupt values who means well. The counsellor advising on college plans who says "You can have all your dream schools, but at the bottom you ought to have some college of last resort where you could be sure that you would go, if none of your dreams came through" certainly means to be realistic and helpful. But one can imagine what it must feel like to be a kid trudging off to the bottom college of last resort. There's a jolly good Joe of a teacher staging a fashion show who tells the girls, "Your legs are all too heavy. . . . Don't wear it too short; it looks miserable." And she's not wrong. But, given the beauty norms set up in this society, what are they to do? Cut off their legs? Emigrate? They're defeated from the legs up. Mediocrity and defeat sit in the offices and classrooms, and in those oppressive monitored halls.

We went through it all in order to graduate and be rid of passes 5 forever, and once it was over we put it out of our minds, and here are the students still serving time until graduation, still sitting in class staring out the windows or watching the crawling hands of those ugly school clocks. So much of this education is part of an obsolete system of authority that broke down long ago, yet the teachers and administrators are still out there, persevering, "building character." *High School* seems an obvious kind of film to make, but as far as I know no one before has gone into an ordinary, middle-class, "good" (most of the students go to college) high school with a camera and looked around to see what it's like. The students are even more apathetic than we were. Probably the conflicts over the restrictions come earlier now—in junior high—and by high school the kids either are trying to cool it and get through to college or are just beaten down and sitting it out. We may have had a few teachers who really got us interested in something—it was one of the disappointments of the movie *Up the Down Staircase* that, treating this theme, it failed to be convincing—and, remembering our good luck, we could always say that even if a school was rotten, there were bound to be a few great teachers in it. This movie shows competent teachers and teachers who are trying their best but not one teacher who really makes contact in the way that means a difference in your life. The students are as apathetic toward the young English teacher playing and analyzing a Simon & Garfunkel record as toward the English teacher reciting "Casey at the Bat," and, even granted that as poetry there might not be much to choose between them—and perhaps Casey has the edge—still, one might think the students would, just as a *courtesy*, respond to the young teacher's attempt, the way one always gave the ingénue in the stock company a special round of applause. But it's very likely that high schools no longer *are* saved by live teachers, if hostility and cynicism and apathy set in right after children learn their basic skills. The students here sit on their hands even when a teacher tries. That's the only visible difference between this school and mine. I think we would have responded appreciatively to obvious effort, even if we thought the teacher was a jerk; these kids are beyond that. So the teachers are trapped, too. The teachers come off much worse than the police do in *Law and Order*. *High School* is a revelation because now that we see school from the outside, the teachers seem to give themselves away every time they open their mouths—and to be unaware of it.

At the end, the principal—a fine-looking woman—holds up a letter from a former student, on stationery marked "U.S.S. Okinawa," and reads it to the faculty: 6

> I have only a few hours before I go. Today I will take a plane trip from this ship. I pray that I'll make it back but it's all in God's hands now. You see, I am going with three other men. We are going to be dropped behind the D.M.Z. (the Demilitarized Zone). The reason for telling you this is that all my insurance money will be given for that scholarship I once started but never finished, if I don't make it back. I am only insured for $10,000. Maybe it could help someone. I have been trying to become a Big Brother in Vietnam, but it is very hard to do. I have to write back and forth to San Diego, California, and that takes time. I only hope that I am good enough to become one. God only knows. My personal family usually doesn't understand me. . . . They say: "Don't you value life? Are you crazy?" My answer is: "Yes. But I value all the lives of South Vietnam and the free world so that they and all of us can live in peace." Am I wrong? If I do my best and believe in what I do, believe that what I do is right—that is all I can do. . . . Please don't say anything to Mrs. C. She would only worry over me. I am not worth it. I am only a body doing a job. In closing I thank everyone for what they all have done for me.

And the principal comments, "Now, when you get a letter like this, to me it means that we are very successful at [this] high school. I think you will agree with me."

It's a great scene—a consummation of the educational process 7
we've been watching: They are successful at turning out bodies to do
a job. Yet it's also painfully clear that the school must have given this
soldier more kindness and affection than he'd ever had before. There
must be other students who respond to the genuine benevolence behind the cant and who are grateful to those who labor to turn them
into men. For those students, this schooling in conformity is successful.

Wiseman extends our understanding of our common life the way 8
novelists used to—a way largely abandoned by the modern novel and
left to the journalists but not often picked up by them. What he's doing
is so simple and so basic that it's like a rediscovery of what we knew,
or should know. We often want more information about the people
and their predicaments than he gives, but this is perhaps less a criticism
of Wiseman's method than it is a testimonial to his success in making
us care about his subjects. With fictional movies using so little of our
shared experience, and the big TV news "specials" increasingly using
that idiot "McLuhanite" fragmentation technique that scrambles all
experience—as if the deliberate purpose were to make us indifferent
to the life around us—it's a good sign when a movie sends us out
wanting to know more and feeling that there is more to know. Wiseman is probably the most sophisticated intelligence to enter the documentary field in recent years.

Questions

1. In paragraph 2 Kael assumes that her readers share with her the
   view, based on experience, that high school is dull, dispiriting, and
   even humiliating. Is the assumption warranted?
2. At the end of paragraph 2 Kael quotes a bit of dialogue. Pinpoint
   examples of dullness in the dialogue.
3. The language of paragraph 4 suggests that high school is a battle-
   ground between teachers and students. Are the hostilities Kael cites
   familiar? If not, do you find them nevertheless convincing? With
   what weapons is each side armed?
4. In paragraph 1 Kael writes: "Many of us grow to hate documentaries
   in school." Did you? If so, why? What reasons might you offer to
   argue that the documentary films you saw in school were educational or anti-educational?

Nathan Glazer

Some Very Modest Proposals for the Improvement of American Education

That we can do a great deal for the sorry state of American 1
education with more money is generally accepted. Even apparently
modest proposals will, however, cost a great deal of money. Consider
something as simple as increasing the average compensation of American teachers—who are generally considered underpaid—by $2,000 a
year each. The bill would come to five billion dollars a year. A similar
figure is reached by the report of the highly qualified Twentieth Century Fund Task Force on Federal, Elementary, and Secondary Educational Policy, which proposes fellowships and additional compensation for master teachers. Reducing class size 10 percent, or increasing the number of teachers by the same percentage, would cost another
five billion dollars: With present-day federal deficits, these look like
small sums, but since education is paid for almost entirely by states
and local government, these modest proposals would lead to substantial and painful tax increases. (I leave aside for the moment the
views of skeptics who believe that none of these changes would
matter.)

But the occasional visitor to American schools will note some 2
changes that would cost much less, nothing at all, or even save
money—and yet would improve at least the educational *environment*
in American schools (once again, we ignore those skeptics who would
insist that even a better educational environment cannot be guaranteed
to improve educational achievement). In the spirit of evoking further
cheap proposals, here is a small list of suggestions that, to my mind
at least—and the mind I believe of any adult who visits American
public schools—would mean a clear plus for American education:

Nathan Glazer, born in 1923 in New York City, is a professor of education and
sociology at Harvard University. He is co-editor of *The Public Interest* magazine
and the co-author of *The Lonely Crowd* and *Beyond the Melting Pot*.

1. *Disconnect all loudspeaker systems in American schools—or at least* 3
reserve them, like the hotline between Moscow and Washington, for only the
gravest emergencies. The American classroom—and the American
teacher and his or her charges—is continually interrupted by announcements from central headquarters over the loudspeaker system.
These remind teachers to bring in some form or other; or students to
bring in some form or other; or students engaged in some activity to
remember to come to practice or rehearsal; or they announce a change
of time for some activity. There is nothing so unnerving to a teacher
engaged in trying to explain something, or a student engaged in trying
to understand something, as the crackle of the loudspeaker prepared
to issue an announcement, and the harsh and gravelly voice (the systems are not obviously of the highest grade) of the announcement
itself.

Aside from questions of personal taste, why would this be a good 4
idea? As I have suggested, one reason is that the loudspeaker interrupts efforts to communicate complicated material that requires undivided attention. Second, it demeans the teacher as professional:
every announcement tells her whatever she is doing is not very important and can be interrupted at any time. Third, it accentuates the
notion of hierarchy in education—the principal and assistant principal
are the important people, and command time and attention even in
the midst of instruction. Perhaps I have been softened by too many
years as a college teacher, but it would be unimaginable that a loudspeaker, if one existed, would ever interrupt a college class except
under conditions of the gravest and most immediate threat to life and
limb. One way of showing students that education is important is not
to interrupt it for band-rehearsal announcements.

2. *Disarm the school.* One of the most depressing aspects of the 5
urban school in the United States is the degree of security manifest
within it, and that seems to me quite contradictory to what a school
should be. Outer doors are locked. Security guards are present in the
corridors. Internal doors are locked. Passes are necessary to enter the
school or move within it, for outsiders and for students. Students are
marched in groups from classroom to classroom, under the eye of the
teachers. It is understandable that given the conditions in lower-class
areas in our large cities—and not only lower-class areas—some degree
of security-mindedness is necessary. There is valuable equipment—
typewriters, computers, audio-visual equipment—that can be stolen;
vandalism is a serious concern; marauders can enter the school in
search for equipment, or teachers' pocketbooks, or to threaten directly

personal safety in search of money or sex, and so on. School integration and busing, at least in their initial stages, have contributed to increased interracial tensions in schools and have in part severed the link between community and school. The difference in ethnic and racial composition of faculty, other staff, administrators, and students contributes to the same end.

Having acknowledged all this, I still believe the school should feel 6 less like a prison than it does. One should examine to what extent outside doors must be closed; to what extent the security guard cannot be replaced by local parents, volunteer or paid; the degree to which the endless bells indicating "stop" and "go" are really necessary. I suspect that now that the most difficult period of school integration has passed, now that teachers and administrators and staff more closely parallel in race and ethnic background students and community owing to the increase in black and Hispanic teachers and administrators, we may be saddled with more security than we need. Here we come to the sticky problem of *removing* security measures whose need has decreased. What school board will open itself to suit or to public criticism by deliberately providing *less* security? And yet one must consider the atmosphere of the school and a school's primary objective as a teaching agent: can this be reconciled with a condition of maximum security? Perhaps there are lessons to be learned from colleges and community colleges in older urban areas, which in my experience do seem to manage with less security. One reason is that there are more adults around in such institutions. Is that a hint as to how we could manage better in our public schools?

3. *Enlist the children in keeping the school clean.* Occasionally we see 7 a practice abroad that suggests possible transfer to the American scene. In Japan, the children clean the school. There is a time of day when mops and pails and brooms come out, and the children sweep up and wash up. This does, I am sure, suggest to the children that this is *their* school, that it is not simply a matter of being forced to go to a foreign institution that imposes alien demands upon them. I can imagine some obstacles in the way of instituting regular student clean-up in American schools—custodians' unions, for example, might object. But they can be reassured that children don't do that good a job, and they will still be needed. Once again, as in the case of the security problem, one wants to create in the school, if at all possible, a common enterprise of teachers and students, without the latter being bored and resistant, the former, in response, becoming equally indifferent. The school should be seen as everyone's workplace—and participation in cleaning the school will help.

4. *Save old schools*. Build fewer new ones. It has often surprised me [8] that while in schools such as Eton and Oxford—and indeed well-known private schools and colleges in the United States—old buildings are prized, in so many communities older public schools are torn down when to the naked eye they have many virtues that would warrant their maintenance and use. Only a few blocks from where I live, an excellent example of late nineteenth-century fine brickwork and carved stonework that served as the Cambridge Latin School came down for a remodeling. The carved elements are still displayed about the remodeled school, but why a building of such character should have deserved demolition escaped my understanding, particularly since one can take it almost as a given that a school building put up before the 1940s will be built of heavier and sturdier materials than one constructed today. Even the inconveniences of the old can possess a charm that makes them worthwhile. And indeed many of the reforms that seemed to require new buildings (for example, classrooms without walls, concentrated around activities centers in large open rooms) have turned out, on use, to be not so desirable. Our aim should be to give each school a history, a character, something that at least some students respond to. The pressures for new buildings are enormous, and sometimes perfectly legitimate (as when communities expand), but often illegitimate, as when builders and building-trades workers and contract-givers seek an opportunity or when state aid makes it appear as if a new building won't cost anything.

5. *Look on new hardware with a skeptical eye*. I think it likely that the [9] passion for the new in the way of teaching-hardware not only does not contribute to higher educational achievement but may well serve as a temporary means to evade the real and hard tasks of teaching—which really require almost no hardware at all, besides textbooks, blackboard, and chalk. Admittedly, when one comes to high-school science, something more is called for. And yet our tendency is to always find cover behind new hardware. It's *fun* to get new audio-visual equipment, new rooms equipped with them in which all kinds of things can be done by flicking a switch or twisting a dial, or, as is now the case, to decide what kind of personal computers and software are necessary for a good educational program. Once again, foreign experience can be enlightening. When Japanese education was already well ahead of American, most Japanese schools were in prewar wooden buildings. (They are now as up-to-date as ours, but neither their age nor up-to-dateness has much to do with their good record of achievement.) Resisting the appeal of new hardware not only saves money, and provides less in the way of saleable goods to burglarize,

but it also prevents distraction from the principal tasks of reading, writing, and calculating. When it turns out that computers and new software are shown to do a better job at these key tasks—I am skeptical as to whether this will ever be the case—there will be time enough to splurge on new equipment. The teacher, alone, up front, explaining, encouraging, guiding, is the heart of the matter—the rest is fun, and very helpful to corporate income, and gives an inflated headquarters staff something new to do. But students will have time enough to learn about computers when they get to college, and getting there will depend almost not at all on what they can do with computers, but how well they understand words and sentences, and how well they do at simple mathematics.

There is nothing wrong with old textbooks, too. Recently, review- 10 ing some recent high-school American history texts, I was astonished to discover they come out in new editions every two years or so, and not because the main body of the text is improved, but because the textbook wants to be able to claim it covers the very last presidential campaign, and the events of the last few years. This is a waste of time and energy and money. There is enough to teach in American history up to 1950 or 1960 not to worry about whether the text includes Reagan's tax cuts. I suspect many new texts in other areas also offer little advantage over the older ones. There is also a virtue in a teacher becoming acquainted with a particular textbook. When I read that a school is disadvantaged because its textbooks are old, I am always mystified. Even the newest advances in physics and biology might well be reserved for college.

6. *Expand the pool from which we draw good teachers.* This general 11 heading covers a number of simple and concrete things, such as: if a teacher is considered qualified to teach at a good private school, that teacher should be considered qualified to teach at a public school. It has always seemed to me ridiculous that teachers accepted at the best private schools in New York City or top preparatory schools in the country would not be allowed to teach in the public school system of New York or Boston. Often, they are willing—after all, the pay is better in public schools and there are greater fringe benefits. They might, it is true, be driven out of those schools by the challenge of lower- and working-class children. But when they are willing, it seems unbelievable that the teacher qualified (or so Brearley thinks) for Brearley will not be allowed to teach at P.S. 122. Greater use of part-time teachers might also be able to draw upon people with qualities that we are told the average teacher unfortunately doesn't possess—such as a higher level of competence in writing and mathematics.

Our recurrent concern with foreign-language teaching should lead us to recruit foreign-born teachers. There are problems in getting teaching jobs today in Germany and France—yet teachers there are typically drawn from pools of students with higher academic skills than is the case in this country. Paradoxically, we make it easy for teachers of Spanish-language background to get jobs owing to the expansion of bilingual programs—but then their teaching is confined to children whose Spanish accent doesn't need improvement. It would make more sense to expose children of foreign-language background more to teachers with native English—and children from English-speaking families to teachers who speak French, German, Spanish, and, why not, Japanese, and Chinese natively. This would mean that rules requiring that a teacher must be a citizen, or must speak English without an accent, should be lifted for special teachers with special tasks. Perhaps we could make the most of the oversupply of teachers in some foreign countries by using them to teach mathematics—a subject where accent doesn't count. The school system in Georgia is already recruiting from Germany. Colleges often use teaching assistants whose English is not native and far from perfect, including Asians from Korea and China, to assist in science and mathematics courses. (There are many state laws which would not permit them to teach in elementary and secondary schools.)   12

All the suggestions above eschew any involvement with some great issues of education—tradition or reform, the teaching of values, the role of religion in the schools—that have in the past dominated arguments over education and still do today. But I add one more proposal that is still, I am afraid, somewhat controversial: 13

7. *Let students, within reason, pick their schools, or let parents choose them for them.* All those informed on school issues will sense the heaving depths of controversy under this apparently modest proposal. Does this mean they might choose parochial schools, without being required to pay tuition out of their own pockets? Or does this mean black children would be allowed to attend schools in black areas, and whites in white areas, or the reverse if each is so inclined? As we all know, the two great issues of religion and race stand in the way of any such simple and commonsensical arrangement. Students are regularly bused from one section of a city to another because of their race, and students cannot without financial penalty attend that substantial sector of schools—30 percent or so in most Northern and Midwestern cities—that are called "private." I ignore the question of whether, holding all factors constant, students do "better" in private or public schools, in racially well-mixed or hardly mixed schools. The evidence   14

will always be uncertain. What is perhaps less arguable is that students will do better in a school that forms a community, in which teachers, parents, and students all agree that *that* is the school they want to teach in, to attend, to send their children to. I would guess that this is the kind of school most of the readers of this article have attended; it is the kind of school, alas, that our complex racial and religious history makes it harder and harder for those of minority race or of lower- and working-class status to attend.

I have eschewed the grand proposals—for curriculum change, for 15 improving the quality of entering teachers, for checking on the competence of teachers in service, for establishing national standards for achievement in different levels of education—all of which now form the agenda for many state commissions of educational reform and all of which seem reasonable to me. Rather, I have concentrated on a variety of other things that serve to remove distraction, to open the school to those of quality who would be willing to enter it to improve it, to concentrate on the essentials of teaching and learning as I (and many others) have experienced it. It would be possible to propose larger changes in the same direction: for example, reduce the size of the bureaucracies in urban school systems. Some of my modest proposals are insidiously intended to do this—if there were less effort devoted to building new schools, buying new equipment, evaluating new textbooks, or busing children, there would be no need to maintain quite so many people at headquarters. Or so I would hope.

In the meantime, why not disconnect the loudspeakers?   16

Questions

1. What does "modest" mean in Glazer's second sentence?
2. Glazer's third proposal is to have children clean their schools. How do you imagine high school students would respond to this proposal? How would you and your friends have responded?
3. Analyze the arrangement of Glazer's proposals. Do you discern any order or pattern in them?
4. If you disagree with one of Glazer's proposals, set forth your disagreement in a paragraph or two.
5. What proposals can you add to Glazer's list of "modest proposals"? Take one of your proposals and argue for it, in a paragraph or two.

Neil Postman

Order in the Classroom

William O'Connor, who is unknown to me in a personal 1
way, was once a member of the Boston School Committee, in which
capacity he made the following remark: "We have no inferior education
in our schools. What we have been getting is an inferior type of student."

The remark is easy to ridicule, and I have had some fun with it 2
in the past. But there are a couple of senses in which it is perfectly
sound.

In the first place, a classroom is a technique for the achievement 3
of certain kinds of learning. It is a workable technique provided that
both the teacher and the student have the skill and, particularly, the
attitudes that are fundamental to it. Among these, from the student's
point of view, are tolerance for delayed gratification, a certain measure
of respect for and fear of authority, and a willingness to accommodate
one's individual desires to the interests of group cohesion and purpose.
These attitudes cannot be taught easily in school because they are a
necessary component of the teaching situation itself. The problem is
not unlike trying to find out how to spell a word by looking it up in
the dictionary. If you do not know how a word is spelled, it is hard
to look it up. In the same way, little can be taught in school unless
these attitudes are present. And if they are not, to teach them is difficult.

Obviously, such attitudes must be learned during the years before 4
a child starts school; that is, in the home. This is the real meaning of
the phrase "preschool education." If a child is not made ready at home
for the classroom experience, he or she usually cannot benefit from
any normal school program. Just as important, the school is defenseless
against such a child, who, typically, is a source of disorder in a situation
that requires order. I raise this issue because education reform is impossible without order in the classroom. Without the attitudes that
lead to order, the classroom is an entirely impotent technique. There-

Neil Postman, born in New York City in 1931, has taught in elementary and
secondary schools and is now a professor of communication arts and sciences
at New York University.

fore, one possible translation of Mr. O'Connor's remark is, "We have a useful technique for educating youth but too many of them have not been provided at home with the attitudes necessary for the technique to work."

In still another way Mr. O'Connor's remark makes plain sense. 5 The electronic media, with their emphasis on visual imagery, immediacy, non-linearity, and fragmentation, do not give support to the attitudes that are fundamental to the classroom; that is, Mr. O'Connor's remark can be translated as, "We would not have an inferior education if it were the nineteenth century. Our problem is that we have been getting students who are products of the twentieth century." But there is nothing nonsensical about this, either. The nineteenth century had much to recommend it, and we certainly may be permitted to allow it to exert an influence on the twentieth. The classroom is a nineteenth-century invention, and we ought to prize what it has to offer. It is one of the few social organizations left to us in which sequence, social order, hierarchy, continuity, and deferred pleasure are important.

The problem of disorder in the classroom is created largely by two 6 factors: a dissolving family structure, out of which come youngsters who are "unfit" for the presuppositions of a classroom; and a radically altered information environment, which undermines the foundation of school. The question, then, is, What should be done about the increasing tendency toward disorder in the classroom?

Liberal reformers, such as Kenneth Keniston, have answers, of a 7 sort. Keniston argues that economic reforms should be made so that the integrity and authority of the family can be restored. He believes that poverty is the main cause of family dissolution, and that by improving the economic situation of families, we may kindle a sense of order and aspiration in the lives of children. Some of the reforms he suggests in his book *All Our Children* seem practical, although they are long-range and offer no immediate response to the problem of present disorder. Some Utopians, such as Ivan Illich, have offered other solutions; for example, dissolving the schools altogether, or so completely restructuring the school environment that its traditional assumptions are rendered irrelevant. To paraphrase Karl Kraus's epigram about psychoanalysis, these proposals are the Utopian disease of which they consider themselves the cure.

One of the best answers comes from Dr. Howard Hurwitz, who 8 is neither a liberal reformer nor a Utopian. It is a good solution, I believe, because it tries to respond to the needs not only of children who are unprepared for school because of parental failure but of children of all backgrounds who are being made strangers to the assumptions of school by the biases of the electronic media.

During the eleven years Dr. Hurwitz was principal at Long Island 9
City High School, the average number of suspensions each year was three, while in many New York City high schools the average runs close to one hundred. Also, during his tenure, not one instance of an assault on a teacher was reported, and daily student attendance averaged better than 90 percent, which in the context of the New York City school scene represents a riot of devotion.

Although I consider some of Dr. Hurwitz's curriculum ideas un- 10
inspired and even wrong-headed, he understands a few things of overriding importance that many educators of more expansive imagination do not. The first is that educators must devote at least as much attention to the immediate consequences of disorder as to its abstract causes. Whatever the causes of disorder and alienation, the consequences are severe and, if not curbed, result in making the school impotent. At the risk of becoming a symbol of reaction, Hurwitz ran "a tight ship." He holds to the belief, for example, that a child's right to an education is terminated at the point where the child interferes with the right of other children to have one.

Dr. Hurwitz also understands that disorder expands proportion- 11
ately to the tolerance for it, and that children of all kinds of home backgrounds can learn, in varying degrees, to function in situations where disorder is not tolerated at all. He does not believe that it is inevitably or only the children of the poor who are disorderly. In spite of what the "revisionist" education historians may say, poor people still regard school as an avenue of social and economic advancement for their children, and do not object in the least to its being an orderly and structured experience.

All this adds up to the common sense view that the school ought 12
not to accommodate itself to disorder, or to the biases of other communication systems. The children of the poor are likely to continue to be with us. Some parents will fail to assume competent responsibility for the preschool education of their children. The media will increase the intensity of their fragmenting influence. Educators must live with these facts. But Dr. Hurwitz believes that as a technique for learning, the classroom can work if students are oriented toward its assumptions, not the other way around. William O'Connor, wherever he is, would probably agree. And so do I. The school is not an extension of the street, the movie theater, a rock concert, or a playground. And it is certainly not an extension of the psychiatric clinic. It is a special

environment that requires the enforcement of certain traditional rules of controlled group interaction. The school may be the only remaining public situation in which such rules have any meaning, and it would be a grave mistake to change those rules because some children find them hard or cannot function within them. Children who cannot ought to be removed from the environment in the interests of those who can.

Wholesale suspensions, however, are a symptom of disorder, not a cure for it. And what makes Hurwitz's school noteworthy is the small number of suspensions that have been necessary. This is not the result of his having "good" students or "bad" students. It is the result of his having created an unambiguous, rigorous, and serious attitude—a nineteenth-century attitude, if you will—toward what constitutes acceptable school behavior. In other words, Dr. Hurwitz's school turns out to be a place where children of all backgrounds—fit and unfit—can function, or can learn to function, and where the biases of our information environment are emphatically opposed. 13

At this point I should like to leave the particulars of Dr. Hurwitz's solution and, retaining their spirit, indicate some particulars of my own. 14

Let us start, for instance, with the idea of a dress code. A dress code signifies that school is a special place in which special kinds of behavior are required. The way one dresses is an indication of an attitude toward a situation. And the way one is *expected* to dress indicates what that attitude ought to be. You would not wear dungarees and a T-shirt that says "Feel Me" when attending a church wedding. That would be considered an outrage against the tone and meaning of the situation. The school has every right and reason, I believe, to expect the same sort of consideration. 15

Those who are inclined to think this is a superficial point are probably forgetting that symbols not only reflect our feelings but to some extent create them. One's kneeling in church, for example, reflects a sense of reverence but also engenders reverence. If we want school to *feel* like a special place, we can find no better way to begin than by requiring students to dress in a manner befitting the seriousness of the enterprise and the institution. I should include teachers in this requirement. I know of one high school in which the principal has put forward a dress code of sorts for teachers. (He has not, apparently, had the courage to propose one for the students.) For males the requirement is merely a jacket and tie. One of his teachers bitterly complained to me that such a regulation infringed upon his civil rights. And yet, this teacher will accept without complaint the same regulation 16 when it is enforced by an elegant restaurant. His complaint and his acquiescence tell a great deal about how he values schools and how he values restaurants.

I do not have in mind, for students, uniforms of the type some- 17 times worn in parochial schools. I am referring here to some reasonable standard of dress which would mark school as a place of dignity and seriousness. And I might add that I do not believe for one moment the argument that poor people would be unable to clothe their children properly if such a code were in force. Furthermore, I do not believe that poor people have advanced that argument. It is an argument that middle-class education critics have made on behalf of the poor.

Another argument advanced in behalf of the poor and oppressed 18 is the students' right to their own language. I have never heard this argument come from parents whose children are not competent to use Standard English. It is an argument, once again, put forward by "liberal" education critics whose children *are* competent in Standard English but who in some curious way wish to express their solidarity with and charity for those who are less capable. It is a case of pure condescension, and I do not think teachers should be taken in by it. Like the mode of dress, the mode of language in school ought to be relatively formal and exemplary, and therefore markedly different from the custom in less rigorous places. It is particularly important that teachers should avoid trying to win their students' affection by adopting the language of youth. Such teachers frequently win only the contempt of their students, who sense that the language of teachers and the language of students ought to be different; that is to say, the world of adults is different from the world of children.

In this connection, it is worth saying that the modern conception 19 of childhood is a product of the sixteenth century, as Philippe Aries has documented in his *The Centuries of Childhood*. Prior to that century, children as young as six and seven were treated in all important respects as if they were adults. Their language, their dress, their legal status, their responsibilities, their labor, were much the same as those of adults. The concept of childhood as an identifiable stage in human growth began to develop in the sixteenth century and has continued into our own times. However, with the emergence of electronic media of communication, a reversal of this trend seems to be taking place. In a culture in which the distribution of information is almost wholly undifferentiated, age categories begin to disappear. Television, in itself, may bring an end to childhood. In truth, there is no such thing as "children's programming," at least not for children over the age of eight or nine. Everyone sees and hears the same things. We have already reached a point where crimes of youth are indistinguishable from those of adults, and we may soon reach a point where the punishments will be the same.

I raise this point because the school is one of our few remaining 20 institutions based on firm distinctions between childhood and adulthood, and on the assumption that adults have something of value to teach the young. That is why teachers must avoid emulating in dress and speech the style of the young. It is also why the school ought to be a place for what we might call "manners education": the adults in school ought to be concerned with teaching youth a standard of civilized interaction.

Again those who are inclined to regard this as superficial may be 21 underestimating the power of media such as television and radio to teach how one is to conduct oneself in public. In a general sense, the media "unprepare" the young for behavior in groups. A young man who goes through the day with a radio affixed to his ear is learning to be indifferent to any shared sound. A young woman who can turn off a television program that does not suit her needs at the moment is learning impatience with any stimulus that is not responsive to her interests.

But school is not a radio station or a television program. It is a 22 social situation requiring the subordination of one's own impulses and interests to those of the group. In a word, manners. As a rule, elementary school teachers will exert considerable effort in teaching manners. I believe they refer to this effort as "socializing the child." But it is astonishing how precipitously this effort is diminished at higher levels. It is certainly neglected in the high schools, and where it is not, there is usually an excessive concern for "bad habits," such as smoking, drinking, and in some nineteenth-century schools, swearing. But, as William James noted, our virtues are as habitual as our vices. Where is the attention given to the "Good morning" habit, to the "I beg your pardon" habit, to the "Please forgive the interruption" habit?

The most civilized high school class I have ever seen was one in 23 which students and teacher said "Good morning" to each other and in which the students stood up when they had something to say. The teacher, moreover, thanked each student for any contribution made to the class, did not sit with his feet on the desk, and did not interrupt a student unless he had asked permission to do so. The students, in turn, did not interrupt each other, or chew gum, or read comic books when they were bored. To avoid being a burden to others when one is bored is the essence of civilized behavior.

Of this teacher, I might also say that he made no attempt to en- 24
tertain his students or model his classroom along the lines of a TV
program. He was concerned not only to teach his students manners
but to teach them how to attend in a classroom, which is partly a matter
of manners but also necessary to their intellectual development. One
of the more serious difficulties teachers now face in the classroom results from the fact that their students suffer media-shortened attention
spans and have become accustomed, also through intense media exposure, to novelty, variety, and entertainment. Some teachers have
made desperate attempts to keep their students "tuned in" by fashioning their classes along the lines of *Sesame Street* or the *Tonight* show.
They tell jokes. They change the pace. They show films, play records,
and avoid *anything* that would take more than eight minutes. Although
their motivation is understandable, this is what their students least
need. However difficult it may be, the teacher must try to achieve
student attention and even enthusiasm through the attraction of ideas,
not razzmatazz. Those who think I am speaking here in favor of "dull"
classes may themselves, through media exposure, have lost an understanding of the potential for excitement contained in an idea. The
media (one prays) are not so powerful that they can obliterate in the
young, particularly in the adolescent, what William James referred to
as a "theoretic instinct," a need to know reasons, causes, abstract conceptions. Such an "instinct" can be seen in its earliest stages in what
he calls the "sporadic metaphysical inquiries of children as to who
made God, and why they have five fingers. . . ."

I trust that the reader is not misled by what I have been saying. 25
As I see it, nothing in any of the above leads to the conclusion that I
favor a classroom that is authoritarian or coldhearted, or dominated
by a teacher insensitive to students and how they learn. I merely want
to affirm the importance of the classroom as a special place, aloof from
the biases of the media; a place in which the uses of the intellect are
given prominence in a setting of elevated language, civilized manners,
and respect for social symbols.

Questions

1. In paragraph 3 what does Postman mean by "tolerance for delayed
   gratification"? By the way, two paragraphs later Postman uses an
   expression that is approximately synonymous with "delayed gratification." What is this expression?
2. Postman in part blames "the electronic media," because (he says
   in paragraph 5) they emphasize "fragmentation." Does he give any

examples in his essay? Do you think you know what he means? And do you think he is right?

3. Who is Postman's audience? High school students? Parents and teachers? Professors of education? And who is Postman—that is, putting aside the biographical note on page 181, what sort of person does the author of the essay reveal himself to be? A frustrated high school teacher? A professor of education? An intelligent layperson? Does he seem to know what he is talking about?

4. In paragraph 10 we are told, with approval, that a principal named Dr. Howard Hurwitz "ran 'a tight ship.' " First, make sure that you know what the phrase means, and then write an essay of 500 words evaluating the degree of success of some instructor or administrator who ran a tight ship in your school. Your essay will, of course, have to give us a sense of what the instructor or administrator did, as well as your evaluation of the results of his or her teaching or administrating.

5. If you disagree with Postman on the value of a dress code, set forth your disagreement in a persuasive essay of 500 words.

6. Write an editorial—as an alumnus or alumna—for your high school newspaper, summarizing Postman's essay in a paragraph, and then comparing your school with Postman's idea of a good school, and, finally, evaluating your school and Postman's essay. You may, for example, conclude that, thank heavens, your school was nothing like Postman's ideal school.

Merry White

Japanese Education
How Do They Do It?

Japan has become the new reference point for the devel- 1 oping nations and the West, and comparisons with Japan cause increasing wonder and sometimes envy. Travel agents continue to profit from the curiosity of Americans, particularly businessmen, who take regular tours of Japan seeking the secrets of Japanese industry. They

Merry White is the author of *The Japanese Educational Challenge* (1987). She is also the author of a book on noodles. White, who has served as an administrator of Harvard's East Asian Studies Program, now teaches sociology at Boston University.

come back with photographs and full notebooks, convinced they have learned secrets that can be transplanted to their own companies.

Even the Japanese have entered the pop-sociological search for the secrets of their own success, their journalists suggest that they emphasize problem *prevention* while Americans make up for their lack of prescience and care through *remediation* (in the case of cars, recalls for flawed models). The explanation given by a European Economic Community report—that the Japanese are workaholics willing, masochistically, to live in "rabbit hutches" without complaint—was met with amused derision in Japan. But it seems that those who do not look for transportable "secrets" are nonetheless willing to believe that the source of Japanese success is genetic, and thus completely untransferable. There are alternatives to these positions, and an examination of Japanese education provides us with a backdrop for considering them. 2

The Social Consensus

The attention given to the decline of both American industry and American education has not yet led to an awareness here of the close relationship between the development of people and the development of society, an awareness we see everywhere in Japanese thought and institutions, and whose effects we can see in the individual achievements of Japanese children. If Americans realized how powerful the relationship is between Japanese school achievement and social and economic successes we might see the same kind of protectionist language aimed at the Japanese educational system that we see directed at their automobile industry. ("The Japanese must stop producing such able and committed students because *it isn't fair*.") 3

The Japanese understand how important it is to have not just a high level of literacy (which they have had since well before modernization), but also a high level of education in the whole population. It has been said that the Japanese high school graduate is as well educated as an American college graduate, and indeed it is impressive that any worker on the factory floor can be expected to understand statistical material, work from complex graphs and charts, and perform sophisticated mathematical operations. This consensus that education is important, however simple it may sound, is the single most important contributor to the success of Japanese schools. Across the population, among parents, at all institutional and bureaucratic levels, and highest on the list of national priorities, is the stress on excellence in education. This is not just rhetoric. If the consensus, societal mobilization, and 4 personal commitment—all focused on education—are not available to Americans, the reason is not genetic, nor are we locked in an immutable cultural pattern. We simply have not mobilized around our children.

There are clear advantages to being a Japanese child: a homogeneous population focused on perpetuating its cultural identity; an occupational system where selection and promotion are based on educational credentials; a relatively equal distribution of educational opportunities; a universal core curriculum; highly trained and rewarded teachers; and families, especially mothers, devoted to enhancing the life chances of children and working cooperatively with the educational system. Finally, there are high standards for performance in every sector, and a carefully graded series of performance expectations in the school curriculum.

It is clear from these assertions that the measurable cognitive achievements of Japanese education represent only part of the picture. The American press stresses these achievements and accounts for them in terms of government expenditures, longer school years, and early use of homework. While the International Association for the Evaluation of Educational Achievement (IEA) test scores certainly indicate that Japanese children are testing higher than any children in the world (especially in math and science), and while some researchers have even claimed that Japanese children on average score 11 points more than American children on IQ tests, the social and psychological dimensions of Japanese education are similarly impressive and are primary contributors to cognitive achievement. The support given by family and teachers to the emotional and behavioral development of the child provides a base for the child's acquisition of knowledge and problem-solving skills. But beyond this, the Japanese think a major function of education is the development of a happy, engaged, and secure child, able to work hard and cooperate with others.

Inside the Japanese School

In order to understand the context of the Japanese educational system, some basic information is necessary:

1. Education is compulsory for ages six to 15, or through lower secondary school. (Age is almost always correlated with grade level, by the way, because only rarely is a child "kept back" and almost never "put ahead.") Non-compulsory high school attendance (both public and private) is nearly universal, at 98 percent.

2. There is extensive "non-official" private education. Increasing

numbers of children attend pre-schools. Currently, about 95 percent of the five-year olds are in kindergarten or nursery school, 70 percent of the four-year olds and 10 percent of three-year olds. Many older children attend *juku* (after school classes) as well. These are private classes in a great variety of subjects, but most enhance and reinforce the material to be learned for high school or college entrance examinations. There are also *yobiko* (cram schools) for those taking an extra year between high school and college to prepare for the exams.

3. While competition for entrance to the most prestigious universities is very stiff, nearly 40 percent of the college-age group attend college or university. (The rates are slightly higher for women, since many attend two-year junior colleges.)   10

4. Japanese children attend school 240 days a year, compared to 180 in the U.S. Many children spend Sundays in study or tutoring, and vacation classes are also available. Children do not necessarily see this as oppressive, and younger children often ask their parents to send them to *juku* as a way of being with their friends after school. Homework starts in first grade, and children in Japan spend more time in home study than children in any other country except Taiwan. In Japan, 8 percent of the high school seniors spend less than five hours per week on homework, compared to 65 percent of American seniors.[1]   11

5. Primary and lower secondary schools provide what we would call a core curriculum: a required and comprehensive course of study progressing along a logical path, with attention given to children's developmental levels. In elementary and lower secondary school, language learning dominates the school curriculum, and takes up the greatest number of classroom hours, particularly from second to fourth grade. The large number of characters to be learned requires an emphasis on memorization and drill that is not exhibited in the rest of the curriculum. Arithmetic and math are next in number of class hours, followed by social studies. The curriculum includes regular physical education and morning exercise as part of a "whole-child" program. In high school all students take Japanese, English, math, science, and social studies each year, and all students have had courses in chemistry, biology, physics, and earth sciences. All high school students take calculus.   12

6. Computers and other technology do not play a large role in schools. The calculator is used, but has not replaced mental calculations or, for that matter, the abacus. There is no national program to develop   13

[1] Thomas Rohlen, *Japan's High Schools* (Berkeley: University of California Press, 1983), p. 277.

high technology skills in children. Americans spend much more money on science and technology in the schools; the Japanese spend more on teacher training and salaries.

These features should be seen in the context of a history of emphasis on education in Japan. To begin with, an interest in mass (or at least widespread) education greatly antedated the introduction of Western schools to Japan. Literacy, numeracy, and a moral education were considered important for people of all classes. When Western style universal compulsory schooling was introduced in 1872, it was after a deliberate and wide-ranging search throughout the world that resulted in a selection of features from German, French, and American educational systems that would advance Japan's modernization and complement her culture. While uniform, centralized schooling was an import, it eventually brought out Japan's already refined powers of adaptation—not the ability to adapt to a new mode as much as *the ability to adapt the foreign mode to Japanese needs and conditions.*

Also striking was the rapidity with which Japan developed a modern educational system and made it truly universal. In 1873, one year after the Education Act, there was 28 percent enrollment in primary schools, but by 1904 enrollment had already reached 98 percent—one percent less than the current rate. The rush to educate children was buttressed both by the wish to catch up with the West and by a cultural interest in schooling.

A Truly National System

Tradition, ideology, and international competition are not, however, the only motive forces in Japanese education: other factors are as significant. First, Japan has a relatively homogeneous population. Racially and economically there is little variety. Minority groups, such as Koreans and the former out-castes, exist and do suffer some discrimination, but all children have equal access to good schooling. Income is more evenly distributed in Japan than in America and most people (96 percent in a recent Prime Minister's Office poll) consider themselves middle class. There are few remaining regional differences that affect the educational system, except perhaps local accents.

Second, educational financing and planning are centralized. While American educational policy sees the responsibility for schooling as a local matter, Japanese planners can rely on a centralized source of funding, curriculum guidance, and textbook selection. In terms of educational spending as a percentage of total GNP, the U.S. and Japan are not so far apart: The U.S. devotes 6.8 percent of its GNP to education, and Japan devotes 8.6 percent. But in Japan about 50 percent of this is national funding, while in the U.S. the federal government provides only 8 percent of the total expenditure on education, most of which is applied to special education, not to core schooling. Moreover, in the U.S. there exist no national institutions to build a consensus on what and how our children are taught. The most significant outcome of centralization in Japan is the even distribution of resources and quality instruction across the country. National planners and policymakers can mobilize a highly qualified teaching force and offer incentives that make even the most remote areas attractive to good teachers.

Third (but perhaps most important in the comparison with the United States), teachers enjoy respect and high status, job security, and good pay. More than in any other country, teachers in Japan are highly qualified: Their mastery of their fields is the major job qualification, and all have at least a bachelor's degree in their specialty. Moreover, they have a high degree of professional involvement as teachers: 74 percent are said to belong to some professional teachers' association in which teaching methods and curriculum are actively discussed.[2]

Teachers are hired for life, at starting salaries equivalent to starting salaries for college graduates in the corporate world. Elementary and junior high school teachers earn $18,200 per year on the average, high school teachers $19,000. Compared to other Japanese public sector workers, who earn an average of $16,800, this is a high salary, but it is less than that of managers in large companies or bureaucrats in prestigious ministries. In comparison with American teachers, whose salaries average $17,600, it is an absolutely higher wage. The difference is especially striking when one considers that over all professions, salaries are lower in Japan than in the U.S. In fact, American teachers' salaries are near the bottom of the scale of jobs requiring a college degree. Relative status and prestige correlate with salary in both countries. Japanese teachers' pay increases, as elsewhere in Japan, are tied to a seniority ladder, and older "master teachers" are given extra pay as teacher supervisors in each subject.[3]

Japanese teachers see their work as permanent: Teaching is not a waystation on a path to other careers. Teachers work hard at improving

18

19

20

---

[2] William Cummings, *Education and Equality in Japan* (Princeton: Princeton University Press, 1980), p. 159.

[3] There is a debate in Japan today concerning rewarding good teachers with higher pay: Professor Sumiko Iwao, of Keio University, reports that when quality is measured in yen, the commitment of teachers to good teaching declines.

their skills and knowledge of their subject, and attend refresher courses
and upgrading programs provided by the Ministry of Education. While
there are tendencies, encouraged by the Teachers' Union, to downplay
the traditional image of the "devoted, selfless teacher" (since this is
seen as exploitative), and to redefine the teacher as a wage laborer
with regular hours, rather than as a member of a "sacred" profession,
teachers still regularly work overtime and see their job's sphere extending beyond classroom instruction. Classes are large: The average
is about 40 students to one teacher. Teachers feel responsible for their
students' discipline, behavior, morality, and for their general social
adjustment as well as for their cognitive development. They are "on
duty" after school hours and during vacations, and supervise vacation
play and study. They visit their students' families at home, and are
available to parents with questions and anxieties about their children.
The Teachers' Union protests strongly against this extensive role, but
both teachers and parents reinforce this role, tied as it is to the high
status of the teacher.

Fourth, there is strong ideological and institutional support for   21
education because the occupational system relies on schools to select
the right person for the right organization. Note that this is not the
same as the "right job" or "slot": A new company recruit, almost
always a recent graduate, is not expected to have a skill or special
identity, but to be appropriate in general educational background and
character for a company. The company then trains recruits in the skills
they will need, as well as in the company style. Of course, the basic
skill level of the population of high school and college graduates is
extremely high. But the important fact is that the social consensus
supports an educational system that creates a committed, productive
labor force. And although the emphasis seems to be on educational
credentials, the quality of graduates possessing these credentials is
indisputably high.

Mom

The background I have presented—of national consensus, institutional   22
centralization, and fiscal support—alone does not explain the successes of Japanese education. There are other, less tangible factors that
derive from cultural conceptions of development and learning, the valued role of maternal support, and psychological factors in Japanese
pedagogy, and which distinguish it from American schooling.

The role of mothers is especially important. The average Japanese   23 mother feels her child has the potential for success: Children are believed to be born with no distinguishing abilities (or disabilities) and can be mobilized to achieve and perform at high levels. Effort and commitment are required, and, at least at the beginning, it is the mother's job to engage the child. One way of looking at Japanese child development is to look at the words and concepts related to parental goals for their children. A "good child" has the following, frequently invoked characteristics: He is *otonashii* (mild or gentle), *sunao* (compliant, obedient, and cooperative), *akarui* (bright, alert), and *genki* (energetic and spirited). *Sunao* has frequently been translated as "obedient," but it would be more appropriate to use "open minded," "non-resistant," or "authentic in intent and cooperative in spirit." The English word "obedience" implies subordination and lack of self-determination, but *sunao* assumes that what we call compliance (with a negative connotation) is really cooperation, an act of affirmation of the self. A child who is *sunao* has not yielded his personal autonomy for the sake of cooperation; cooperation does not imply giving up the self, but in fact implies that working with others is the appropriate setting for expressing and enhancing the self.

One encourages a *sunao* child through the technique, especially 24 used by mothers and elementary school teachers, of *wakaraseru*, or "getting the child to understand." The basic principle of child rearing seems to be: Never go against the child. *Wakaraseru* is often a long-term process that ultimately engages the child in the mother's goals, and makes her goals the child's own, thus producing an authentic cooperation, as in *sunao*. The distinction between external, social expectations and the child's own personal goals becomes blurred from this point on. An American might see this manipulation of the child through what we would call "indulgence" as preventing him from having a strong will of his own, but the Japanese mother sees long term benefits of self-motivated cooperation and real commitment.

Japanese mothers are active teachers as well, and have a real cur- 25 riculum for their pre-school children: Games, teaching aids, ordinary activities are all focused on the child's development. There are counting games for very small babies, songs to help children learn new words, devices to focus the child's concentration. Parents buy an average of two or three new books every month for their preschoolers, and there are about 40 monthly activity magazines for preschoolers, very highly subscribed. The result is that most, at least most urban children, can read and write the phonetic syllabary before they enter school, and can do simple computations.

Maternal involvement becomes much more extensive and "seri- 26
ous" once she and the child enter the elementary school community.
In addition to formal involvement in frequent ceremonies and school
events, PTA meetings and visiting days, the mother spends much time
each day helping the child with homework (sometimes to the point at
which the teachers joke that they are really grading the mothers by
proxy). There are classes for mothers, called *mamajuku*, that prepare
mothers in subjects their children are studying. Homework is considered above all a means for developing a sense of responsibility in the
child, and like much in early childhood education, it is seen as a device
to train character.

The Japanese phenomenon of maternal involvement recently sur- 27
faced in Riverdale, New York, where many Japanese families have
settled. School teachers and principals there noted that each Japanese
family was purchasing two sets of textbooks. On inquiring, they found
that the second set was for the mother, who could better coach her
child if she worked during the day to keep up with his lessons. These
teachers said that children entering in September with no English ability finished in June at the top of their classes in every subject.

The effort mothers put into their children's examinations has been 28
given a high profile by the press. This is called the *kyoiku mama* syn-
drome—the mother invested in her children's progress. In contrast to
Western theories of achievement, which emphasize individual effort
and ability, the Japanese consider academic achievement to be an out-
growth of an interdependent network of cooperative effort and planning. The caricature of the mother's over-investment, however, portrays a woman who has totally identified with her child's success or
failure, and who has no separate identity of her own. The press emphasizes the negative aspects of this involvement with accounts of
maternal nervous breakdowns, reporting a murder by a mother of the
child next-door, who made too much noise while her child was studying. But the press also feeds the mother's investment by exhorting her
to prepare a good work environment for the studying child, to subscribe to special exam-preparation magazines, to hire tutors, and to
prepare a nutritious and exam-appropriate diet.

High-schoolers from outlying areas taking entrance exams in 29
Tokyo come with their mothers to stay in special rooms put aside by
hotels. They are provided with special food, study rooms, counselors,
and tension-release rooms, all meant to supply home-care away from
home. The home study-desk bought by most parents for their smaller
children symbolizes the hovering care and intensity of the mother's

involvement: All models have a high front and half-sides, cutting out distractions and enclosing the workspace in womb-like protection. There is a built-in study light, shelves, a clock, electric pencil sharpener, and built-in calculator. The most popular model includes a push-button connecting to a buzzer in the kitchen to summon mother for help or for a snack.

"How Do You Feel About Cubing?"

Not much work has been done yet to analyze the relationship between   30
the strongly supportive learning atmosphere and high achievement in Japan. In the home, mothers train small children in a disciplined, committed use of energy through what Takeo Doi has called the encouragement of "positive dependency"; in the schools as well there is a recognition that attention to the child's emotional relationship to his work, peers, and teachers is necessary for learning.

A look at a Japanese classroom yields some concrete examples of   31
this. Many Westerners believe that Japanese educational successes are due to an emphasis on rote learning and memorization, that the classroom is rigidly disciplined. This is far from reality. An American teacher walking into a fourth grade science class in Japan would be horrified: children all talking at once, leaping and calling for the teacher's attention. The typical American's response is to wonder, "who's in control of this room?" But if one understands the content of the lively chatter, it is clear that all the noise and movement is focused on the work itself—children are shouting out answers, suggesting other methods, exclaiming in excitement over results, and not gossiping, teasing, or planning games for recess. As long as it is the result of this engagement, the teacher is not concerned over the noise, which may measure a teacher's success. (It has been estimated that American teachers spend about 60 percent of class time on organizing, controlling, and disciplining the class, while Japanese teachers spend only 10 percent.)

A fifth grade math class I observed reveals some elements of this   32
pedagogy. The day I visited, the class was presented with a general statement about cubing. Before any concrete facts, formulae, or even drawings were displayed, the teacher asked the class to take out their math diaries and spend a few minutes writing down their feelings and anticipations over this new concept. It is hard for me to imagine an American math teacher beginning a lesson with an exhortation to ex-

amine one's emotional predispositions about cubing (but that may be only because my own math training was antediluvian).

After that, the teacher asked for conjectures from the children 33 about the surface and volume of a cube and asked for some ideas about formulae for calculation. The teacher asked the class to cluster into its component *han* (working groups) of four or five children each, and gave out materials for measurement and construction. One group left the room with large pieces of cardboard, to construct a model of a cubic meter. The groups worked internally on solutions to problems set by the teacher and competed with each other to finish first. After a while, the cubic meter group returned, groaning under the bulk of its model, and everyone gasped over its size. (There were many comments and guesses as to how many children could fit inside.) The teacher then set the whole class a very challenging problem, well over their heads, and gave them the rest of the class time to work on it. The class ended without a solution, but the teacher made no particular effort to get or give an answer, although she exhorted them to be energetic. (It was several days before the class got the answer—there was no deadline but the excitement did not flag.)

Several characteristics of this class deserve highlighting. First, 34 there was attention to feelings and predispositions, provision of facts, and opportunities for discovery. The teacher preferred to focus on process, engagement, commitment, and performance rather than on discipline (in our sense) and production. Second, the *han*: Assignments are made to groups, not to individuals (this is also true at the workplace) although individual progress and achievement are closely monitored. Children are supported, praised, and allowed to make mistakes through trial and error within the group. The group is also pitted against other groups, and the group's success is each person's triumph, and vice versa. Groups are made up by the teacher and are designed to include a mixture of skill levels—there is a *hancho* (leader) whose job it is to choreograph the group's work, to encourage the slower members, and to act as a reporter to the class at large.

Japanese teachers seem to recognize the emotional as well as the 35 intellectual aspects of engagement. Japanese pedagogy (and maternal socialization) are based on the belief that effort is the most important factor in achievement, and that the teacher's job is to get the child to commit himself positively and energetically to hard work. This emphasis is most explicit in elementary school, but persists later as a prerequisite for the self-discipline and effort children exhibit in high school.

American educational rhetoric does invoke "the whole child," [36] does seek "self-expression," and does promote emotional engagement in "discovery learning." But Japanese teaching style, at least in primary schools, effectively employs an engaging, challenging teaching style that surpasses most American attempts. In the cubing class, I was struck by the spontaneity, excitement, and (to American eyes) "unruly" dedication of the children to the new idea, and impressed with the teacher's ability to create this positive mood. It could be a cultural difference: We usually separate cognition and emotional affect, and then devise artificial means of reintroducing "feeling" into learning. It is rather like the way canned fruit juices are produced—first denatured by the preserving process and then topped up with chemical vitamins to replace what was lost.

The Role of Competition

The frequent accusation that Japanese education involves children in [37] hellish competition must also be examined. In the elementary school classroom, competition is negotiated by means of the *han*. The educational system tries to accommodate both the ideology of harmony and the interest in hierarchy and ranking. The introduction of graded, competitive Western modes of education into societies where minimizing differences between people is valued has often produced severe social and psychological dislocation (as in Africa and other parts of the Third World). In Japan, the importance of the modern educational system as a talent selector and the need to preserve harmony and homogeneity have produced complementary rather than conflicting forces. The regular classroom is a place where the individual does not stick out, but where individual needs are met and goals are set. Children are not held back nor advanced by ability: the cohesion of the age group is said to be more important. Teachers focus on pulling up the slower learners, rather than tracking the class to suit different abilities. For the most part, teachers and the school system refuse to engage in examination preparation hysteria. Part of the reason for this is pressure from the Teachers' Union, a very large and powerful labor union which consistently resists any moves away from the egalitarian and undifferentiating mode of learning. Turning teachers into drill instructors is said to be dehumanizing, and the process of cramming a poor substitute for education.

So where is the competitive selection principle served? In the *juku*. [38]

Juku are tough competitive classes, often with up to 500 in one lecture hall. The most prestigious are themselves very selective and there are examinations (and preparation courses for these) to enter the *juku*. Some *juku* specialize in particular universities' entrance exams, and they will boast of their rate of admission into their universities. It is estimated that one third of all primary school students and one half of all secondary school students attend *juku*, but in Tokyo the rate rises to 86 percent of junior high school students. The "king of *juku*," Furukawa Noboru, the creator of a vast chain of such classes, says that *juku* are necessary to bridge the gap of present realities in Japan. He says that public schools do not face the fact of competition, and that ignoring the reality does not help children. The Ministry of Education usually ignores this non-accredited alternative and complementary system, and permits this functional division to take the pressure off the public schools. While there is considerable grumbling by parents, and while it is clear that the *juku* introduce an inegalitarian element into the process of schooling (since they do cost money), they do, by their separation from the regular school, permit the persistence of more traditional modes of learning, while allowing for a fast track in the examinations.

It is important to note that in Japan there really is only one moment   39
of critical importance to one's career chances—the entrance examination to college. There are few opportunities to change paths or retool. Americans' belief that one can be recreated at any time in life, that the self-made person can get ahead, simply is not possible in Japan—thus the intense focus on examinations.

The Problems—in Context

This rapid tour through the Japanese educational system cannot neglect   40
the problems. However, two things must be kept in mind when considering these well-publicized difficulties: One is that although problems do exist, the statistical reality is that, compared to the West, Japan still looks very good indeed. The other is that the Japanese themselves tend to be quite critical, and educational problems are given attention. But this attention should be seen in context: Not that people are not truly concerned about real problems, but that the anxiety seems related to a sense of national insecurity. The Japanese focus on educational issues may emanate from a sense of the importance of intellectual development in a society where there are few other resources. Any educational problem seems to put the nation truly at risk.

Japanese parents are critical and watchful of the schools and are   41
not complacent about their children's successes. There was a telling
example of this in a recent comparative study of American and Japanese education. Mothers in Minneapolis and in Sendai, roughly comparable cities, were asked to evaluate their children's school experiences. The Minneapolis mothers consistently answered that the
schools were fine and that their children were doing well, while the
Sendai mothers were very critical of their schools and worried that
their children were not performing up to potential. Whose children
were, in objective tests, doing better? The Sendai group—in fact so
much better that the poorest performer in the Japanese group was well
ahead of the best in the American group. Mothers in Japan and the
U.S. have very different perspectives on performance: Japanese mothers attribute failure to lack of effort while American mothers explain
it as lack of ability. Japanese children have an external standard of
excellence to which they can aspire, while an American child normally
can only say he will "do his best."

Problems have surfaced, of course. Psychotherapists report a syn-   42
drome among children related to school and examination pressure.
School phobia, psychosomatic symptoms, and juvenile suicide are
most frequently reported. Japan does lead the world in school-related
suicides for the 15- to 19-year old age group, at about 300 per year.
Recently, the "battered teacher" and "battered parent" syndromes
have received much attention. There are cases where teenagers have
attacked or killed parents and teachers, and these have been related
to examination pressure. The numbers involved in these cases are very
small—at least in comparison with American delinquency patterns and
other juvenile pathologies. Dropouts, drug use, and violent juvenile
crimes are almost non-existent in Japan. The crimes reported in one
year among school-age children in Osaka, for example, are equal to
those reported in one day in New York.

Criticism leveled at Japanese education by Western observers fo-   43
cuses on what they regard as a suppression of genius and individuality,
and a lack of attention to the development of creativity in children.
The first may indeed be a problem—for the geniuses—because there
is little provision for tracking them to their best advantage. There has
been discussion of introducing tracking so that individual ability can
be better served, but this has not been implemented. The superbright
may indeed be disadvantaged.

On the other hand, creativity and innovation *are* encouraged, but   44
their manifestations may be different from those an American observer
would expect. We must look at our own assumptions, to see if they

are too limited. Americans see creativity in children as a fragile blossom that is stifled by rigid educational systems or adult standards. Creativity involves a necessary break with traditional content and methods, and implies the creation of a new idea or artifact. Whether creativity is in the child or in the teaching, and how it is to be measured, are questions no one has answered satisfactorily. Why we emphasize it is another question, probably related to our theories of progress and the importance we attach to unique accomplishments that push society forward. The fact is that, if anything, our schools do less to encourage creativity than do the Japanese, especially in the arts. All children in Japan learn two instruments and how to read music in elementary school, have regular drawing and painting classes, and work in small groups to create projects they themselves devise. It is true, though, that if everyone must be a soloist or composer to be considered creative, then most Japanese are not encouraged to be creative.

It is not enough to claim that the Japanese have been successful   45
in training children to take exams at the expense of a broader education. And it is not at all appropriate to say that they are unable to develop children's individuality and create the geniuses who make scientific breakthroughs. The first is untrue and the second remains to be shown as false by the Japanese themselves, who are now mobilizing to produce more scientists and technologists. In fact, the scales are tipped in favor of Japan, and to represent it otherwise would be a distortion.

The success of the Japanese model has led to its use in other rapidly   46
developing countries, including South Korea, Taiwan, and Singapore. There, education is seen as the linchpin for development, and attention to children has meant the allocation of considerable resources to schools. The results are similar to those seen in Japanese schools: highly motivated, hard-working students who like school and who have achieved very high scores on international achievement tests.

Seeing Ourselves Through Japanese Eyes

What *America* can learn from Japan is rather an open question. We can,   47
to begin with, learn more *about* Japan, and in doing so, learn more about ourselves. Japanese advancements of the past 20 years were based on American principles of productivity (such as "quality control"), not on samurai management skills and zen austerities. Looking for Japanese secrets, or worse, protesting that they are inhuman or unfair, will not get us very far. They have shown they can adjust pro-

grams and policies to the needs and resources of the times; we must do the same. We need to regain the scientific literacy we lost and reacquire the concrete skills and participatory techniques we need. We should see Japan as establishing a new standard, not as a model to be emulated. To match that standard we have to aim at general excellence, develop a long-term view, and act consistently over time with regard to our children's education.

Questions

1. In paragraph 4 White contrasts Japanese commitment to education with our own. Where in our society might one look for evidence of commitment or lack of commitment to education?

2. In paragraph 5 White lists many "clear advantages to being a Japanese child." Considering your education, or any other grounds you choose, which of these "advantages" would you like to have? Are there any you would gladly do without? Can you explain why? How many of the Japanese advantages appear to be dependent on the first that White lists, "a homogeneous population"? Are you aware of advantages to growing up in a heterogeneous population? (For an explanation of Japanese homogeneity, see paragraph 16.)

3. At the end of paragraph 6 White says that "the Japanese think a major function of education is the development of a happy, engaged, and secure child, able to work hard and cooperate with others." Complete the following sentence: "Americans think a major function of education is . . ."

4. In paragraph 11 White discusses the amount of time Japanese students spend on homework. What were your own experiences with homework? Did homework contribute significantly to your education? Were there assignments you now regard as counterproductive?

5. In paragraph 13 White says that computers do not play a large role in Japanese schools. If computers played a fairly large role in your education, what do you think you learned from them, aside from how to operate them?

6. In paragraph 18 White reports that Japanese teachers are highly qualified. Do you think that, on the whole, your high school teachers were highly qualified? If you were able to do so, what measures would you take to insure well-qualified teachers in *all* American high schools? (White's paragraph 19 may provide some ideas.)

7. In paragraph 32 White briefly describes a math class about to study cubing. Does the procedure followed in the class strike you as

being of any value? Why, or why not? And what about the procedure described in the next paragraph? (In thinking about this, consider also White's comments in paragraphs 34–35.) Looking back at a class in which you learned a good deal, what "elements of pedagogy" (White's words, paragraph 32) made the class successful?

8. In paragraph 37 White says that children in Japanese schools are almost never held back or advanced because of ability, and there is no tracking system. What do you think of this system? (Consider also paragraphs 43 and 44.)

9. In paragraph 39 White writes of the belief of Americans that "one can be recreated at any time in life, that the self-made person can get ahead." To what extent do you share these beliefs? To what extent did the schools you attended promote them?

10. Japan has produced relatively few winners of the Nobel Prize. Did White's essay help you to understand why this might be so? Do you take the lack of Nobel Prize winners to be a significant criticism of the Japanese educational system?

11. Given the great differences between our societies, what, if anything, do you think our educational system can learn from the Japanese system? (For example, we are far less homogeneous. And the mothers in our society often hold paying jobs, whereas few Japanese mothers do. Further, two thirds of our teenagers hold part-time jobs, whereas almost no Japanese teenagers hold jobs.)

Robert Coles

Student Volunteers, Academic Credit

Despite the enticements of our competitive, consumerist 1
culture, a growing number of high school, undergraduate and graduate
students are finding time to do local volunteer work. We applaud such
evidence of idealism put into daily or weekly practice in what amounts
to a national service program. As one Middle Western college dean
said, it is "exactly the kind of constructive extra-curricular activity this
school values."

I have heard many students sharply, and properly, challenge such 2
use of the phrase "extra-curricular." They object to this false distinction
between their intellectual life and their work in, say, a ghetto neighborhood. After all, isn't the mind kept busy in many important ways
when one leaves a campus to work in a neighborhood where people
live constantly in great jeopardy?

When a student crosses the ocean to study French or Spanish for 3
a year, or to assist in a social scientist's "field work," we have no
reluctance to consider such an effort intellectual and worthy of academic credit.

But when that same student spends time working with people 4
who, after all, live in a world as different in certain respects as some
of those studied by anthropologists and sociologists, they are pursuing
an "extra-curricular" activity.

Is this the right way to respond to the substantial amount of per- 5
sonal commitment involved in tutoring needy children, feeding the
homeless in soup kitchens and reaching out to vulnerable families to
provide medical or legal assistance?

When I listen to my students describe what they see and hear in 6
voluntary "extra-curricular" activities, I realize how much they are
learning.

Robert Coles received his M.D. degree in 1954 and later became a psychiatrist.
He now teaches psychiatry at Harvard, and has written several prizewinning
books on classes and cultures in the United States. He has also written about
literature.

For example, listen to an undergraduate—he has tutored and 7
played basketball in a ghetto neighborhood—trying to educate his
teacher:

> I never knew people live like that until I started going there. I'd read
> a book or two [about ghetto problems] and mostly forgotten what I
> read, but you don't forget the kids when you see them every week.
> Now I know a little of what those families are like. I know about their
> history, the story of their past: They'll talk with you and take you
> back a few generations—from the rural South to up here.

He went on: 8

> I know about the anthropology and sociology—what the people
> eat, and what they say and what they do with their time. I know
> about the psychology—what's troubling them, and what they want
> and what scares them to death. I know about the politics of that neigh-
> borhood, and the economics—where the power is, and how the peo-
> ple make their living. It's not only tutoring I'm doing, it's learning—
> the kids teach me, and their parents do, too.

He contrasted the vivid, enduring education he was getting out- 9
side of school with what occasionally takes place inside—when he sits
in class or prepares in his room for tests. "I cram stuff in, and forget
it right after the exam," he said. "I sit and take notes automatically,
and lots of times I doze off." But he was not suggesting that he deserved academic credit for the acquisition of outside learning.

A bright, able student, successful by most standards, he craves 10
intellectual and moral challenges, and has found them in the volunteer
work he has done for several years. An able writer, he found time to
contribute several articles to a local paper—descriptions of the children
he teaches, of the lives they live, of the points about life they have
made to him.

He wishes more would come of his volunteer work. He wants to 11
study carefully and discuss books by novelists, social scientists and
essayists that delineate and sort out the complexities, ironies, ambig-
uities, confusions and apprehensions he witnesses—and those in
himself as an outsider who, trying to understand and change a particular world, achieves successes but also encounters obstacles and
contends with failures.

He would like to compare his own observations, goals, hopes, 12 disappointments, discouragements, and his sense of burn-out with similar experiences described in books of the documentary tradition that have mattered over time.

Put differently, he wants to learn from what he does. He wants   13
a chance to talk and write about his volunteer work while also discussing significant books, films and collections of photographs that would give that work a broader perspective.

Surely, we who teach in universities can develop courses that will   14
respond to the challenge of student voluntarism—that connect its moral energy with the life of the mind.

Questions

1. If you speak of one of your activities, or of an activity of another student, as "extra-curricular," what do you mean by the word? What activities do you include? Do you think that Coles would agree that these activities were properly labeled extra-curricular?
2. Do you think Coles is right (paragraphs 1–2) in suggesting that it is improper to call "extra-curricular" an activity such as a student's voluntary "work in, say, a ghetto neighborhood"?
3. In paragraph 3 Coles gives examples of two kinds of activities for which schools regularly award credit. But *why* do such activities merit credit (if they do)? What are the assumptions behind giving credit to them?
4. In paragraph 4 Coles suggests that the student who volunteers to work "with people who . . . live in a world as different in certain respects as some of those studied by anthropologists and sociologists" is engaged in an activity comparable to studying a language or doing sociological fieldwork. Do you agree? Why, or why not?
5. In paragraphs 7 and 8 Coles reports a student's summary of what he or she learned by tutoring and playing basketball in a ghetto neighborhood. The student learned, for instance, "about the anthropology and sociology . . . what they say and what they do with their time." Coles goes on, quoting the student: "I know about the psychology—what's troubling them, and what they want and what scares them to death. I know about the politics of that neighborhood, and the economics—where the power is, and how the people make their living."

    Doubtless this student learned a good deal, and it is clear that Coles is enthusiastic about the student's "acquisition of outside learning" (paragraph 9). Do you imagine—judging from the whole essay—that Coles would be equally enthusiastic if the student had learned about the anthropology, sociology, and economics of persons who work on the Chicago Stock Exchange? On what do you base your answer? Would *you* be equally enthusiastic about the acquisition of such knowledge? Why, or why not?

6. How might one of the courses you are taking, or have taken, be altered to satisfy the challenge that Coles presents in his final paragraph?

John Holt

The Right to Control One's Learning

Young people should have the right to control and direct 1 their own learning, that is, to decide what they want to learn, and when, where, how, how much, how fast, and with what help they want to learn it. To be still more specific, I want them to have the right to decide if, when, how much, and by whom they want to be *taught* and the right to decide whether they want to learn in a school and if so which one and for how much of the time.

No human right, except the right to life itself, is more fundamental 2 than this. A person's freedom of learning is part of his freedom of thought, even more basic than his freedom of speech. If we take from someone his right to decide what he will be curious about, we destroy his freedom of thought. We say, in effect, you must think not about what interests and concerns *you*, but about what interests and concerns *us*.

We might call this the right of curiosity, the right to ask whatever 3 questions are most important to us. As adults, we assume that we have the right to decide what does or does not interest us, what we will look into and what we will leave alone. We take this right for granted, cannot imagine that it might be taken away from us. Indeed,

---

John Holt (1923–1985) taught in schools and colleges and wrote numerous books on education.

as far as I know, it has never been written into any body of law. Even the writers of our Constitution did not mention it. They thought it was enough to guarantee citizens the freedom of speech and the freedom to spread their ideas as widely as they wished and could. It did not occur to them that even the most tyrannical government would try to control people's minds, what they thought and knew. That idea was to come later, under the benevolent guise of compulsory universal education.

This right of each of us to control our own learning is now in   4 danger. When we put into our laws the highly authoritarian notion that someone should and could decide what all young people were to learn and beyond that, could do whatever might seem necessary (which now includes dosing them with drugs) to compel them to learn it, we took a long step down a very steep and dangerous path. The requirement that a child go to school, for about six hours a day, 180 days a year, for about ten years, whether or not he learns anything there, whether or not he already knows it or could learn it faster or better somewhere else, is such a gross violation of civil liberties that few adults would stand for it. But the child who resists is treated as a criminal. With this requirement we created an industry, an army of people whose whole work was to tell young people what they had to learn and to try to make them learn it. Some of these people, wanting to exercise even more power over others, to be even more "helpful," or simply because the industry is not growing fast enough to hold all the people who want to get into it, are now beginning to say, "If it is good for children for us to decide what they shall learn and to make them learn it, why wouldn't it be good for everyone? If compulsory education is a good thing, how can there be too much of it? Why should we allow anyone, of any age, to decide that he has had enough of it? Why should we allow older people, any more than young, not to know what we know when their ignorance may have bad consequences for all of us? Why should we not *make* them know what they *ought* to know?"

They are beginning to talk, as one man did on a nationwide TV   5 show, about "womb-to-tomb" schooling. If hours of homework every night are good for the young, why wouldn't they be good for us all— they would keep us away from the TV set and other frivolous pursuits. Some group of experts, somewhere, would be glad to decide what we all ought to know and then every so often check up on us to make sure we knew it—with, of course, appropriate penalties if we did not.

I am very serious in saying that I think this is coming unless we   6 prepare against it and take steps to prevent it. The right I ask for the young is a right that I want to preserve for the rest of us, the right *to decide what goes into our minds*. This is much more than the right to decide whether or when or how much to go to school or what school you want to go to. That right is important, but it is only part of a much larger and more fundamental right, which I might call the right to Learn, as opposed to being Educated, *i.e.*, made to learn what someone else thinks would be good for you. It is not just compulsory schooling but compulsory Education that I oppose and want to do away with.

That children might have the control of their own learning, in-   7
cluding the right to decide if, when, how much, and where they wanted to go to school, frightens and angers many people. They ask me, "Are you saying that if the parents wanted the child to go to school, and the child didn't want to go, that he wouldn't have to go? Are you saying that if the parents wanted the child to go to one school, and the child wanted to go to another, that the child would have the right to decide?" Yes, that is what I say. Some people ask, "If school wasn't compulsory, wouldn't many parents take their children out of school to exploit their labor in one way or another?" Such questions are often both snobbish and hypocritical. The questioner assumes and implies (though rarely says) that these bad parents are people poorer and less schooled than he. Also, though he appears to be defending the right of children to go to school, what he really is defending is the right of the state to compel them to go whether they want to or not. What he wants, in short, is that children should be in school, not that they should have any choice about going.

But saying that children should have the right to choose to go or   8
not to go to school does not mean that the ideas and wishes of the parents would have no weight. Unless he is estranged from his parents and rebelling against them, a child cares very much about what they think and want. Most of the time, he doesn't want to anger or worry or disappoint them. Right now, in families where the parents feel that they have some choice about their children's schooling, there is much bargaining about schools. Such parents, when their children are little, often ask them whether they want to go to nursery school or kinder-garten. Or they may take them to school for a while to try it out. Or, if they have a choice of schools, they may take them to several to see which they think they will like the best. Later, they care whether the child likes his school. If he does not, they try to do something about it, get him out of it, find a school he will like.

I know some parents who for years had a running bargain with   9
their children, "If on a given day you just can't stand the thought of

school, you don't feel well, you are afraid of something that may happen, you have something of your own that you very much want to do—well, you can stay home." Needless to say, the schools, with their supporting experts, fight it with all their might—Don't Give in to Your Child, Make Him Go to School, He's Got to Learn. Some parents, when their own plans make it possible for them to take an interesting trip, take their children with them. They don't ask the school's permission, they just go. If the child doesn't want to make the trip and would rather stay in school, they work out a way for him to do that. Some parents, when their child is frightened, unhappy, and suffering in school, as many children are, just take him out. Hal Bennett, in his excellent book *No More Public School,* talks about ways to do this.

A friend of mine told me that when her boy was in third grade, 10 he had a bad teacher, bullying, contemptuous, sarcastic, cruel. Many of the class switched to another section, but this eight-year-old, being tough, defiant, and stubborn, hung on. One day—his parents did not learn this until about two years later—having had enough of the teacher's meanness, he just got up from his desk and without saying a word, walked out of the room and went home. But for all his toughness and resiliency of spirit, the experience was hard on him. He grew more timid and quarrelsome, less outgoing and confident. He lost his ordinary good humor. Even his handwriting began to go to pieces—was much worse in the spring of the school year than in the previous fall. One spring day he sat at breakfast, eating his cereal. After a while he stopped eating and sat silently thinking about the day ahead. His eyes filled up with tears, and two big ones slowly rolled down his cheeks. His mother, who ordinarily stays out of the school life of her children, saw this and knew what it was about. "Listen," she said to him, "we don't have to go on with this. If you've had enough of that teacher, if she's making school so bad for you that you don't want to go any more, I'll be perfectly happy just to pull you right out. We can manage it. Just say the word." He was horrified and indignant. "No!" he said, "I couldn't do that." "Okay," she said, "whatever you want is fine. Just let me know." And so they left it. He had decided that he was going to tough it out, and he did. But I am sure knowing that he had the support of his mother and the chance to give it up if it got too much for him gave him the strength he needed to go on.

To say that children should have the right to control and direct 11 their own learning, to go to school or not as they chose, does not mean that the law would forbid the parents to express an opinion or wish or strong desire on the matter. It only means that if their natural authority is not strong enough the parents can't call in the cops to make the child do what they are not able to persuade him to do. And the law may say that there is a limit to the amount of pressure or coercion the parents can apply to the child to deny him a choice that he has a legal right to make.

When I urge that children should control their learning there is 12 one argument that people bring up so often that I feel I must anticipate and meet it here. It says that schools are a place where children can for a while be protected against the bad influences of the world outside, particularly from its greed, dishonesty, and commercialism. It says that in school children may have a glimpse of a higher way of life, of people acting from other and better motives than greed and fear. People say, "We know that society is bad enough as it is and that children will be exposed to it and corrupted by it soon enough. But if we let children go out into the larger world as soon as they wanted, they would be tempted and corrupted just that much sooner."

They seem to believe that schools are better, more honorable places 13 than the world outside—what a friend of mine at Harvard once called "museums of virtue." Or that people in school, both children and adults, act from higher and better motives than people outside. In this they are mistaken. There are, of course, some good schools. But on the whole, far from being the opposite of, or an antidote to, the world outside, with all its envy, fear, greed, and obsessive competitiveness, the schools are very much like it. If anything, they are worse, a terrible, abstract, simplified caricature of it. In the world outside the school, some work, at least, is done honestly and well, for its own sake, not just to get ahead of others; people are not everywhere and always being set in competition against each other; people are not (or not yet) in every minute of their lives subject to the arbitrary, irrevocable orders and judgment of others. But in most schools, a student is every minute doing what others tell him, subject to their judgment, in situations in which he can only win at the expense of other students.

This is a harsh judgment. Let me say again, as I have before, that 14 schools are worse than most of the people in them and that many of these people do many harmful things they would rather not do, and a great many other harmful things that they do not even see as harmful. The whole of school is much worse than the sum of its parts. There are very few people in the U.S. today (or perhaps anywhere, any time) in *any* occupation, who could be trusted with the kind of power that schools give most teachers over their students. Schools seem to me among the most anti-democratic, most authoritarian, most destructive, and most dangerous institutions of modern society. No other institution does more harm or more lasting harm to more people or destroys so much of their curiosity, independence, trust, dignity, and sense of identity and worth. Even quite kindly schools are inhibited and corrupted by the knowledge of children and teachers alike that they are *performing* for the judgment and approval of others—the children for the teachers; the teachers for the parents, supervisors, school board, or the state. No one is ever free from feeling that he is being judged all the time, or soon may be. Even after the best class experiences teachers must ask themselves, "Were we right to do that? Can we prove we were right? Will it get us in trouble?"

What corrupts the school, and makes it so much worse than most   15
of the people in it, or than they would like it to be, is its power—just as their powerlessness corrupts the students. The school is corrupted by the endless anxious demand of the parents to know how their child is doing—meaning is he ahead of the other kids—and their demand that he be kept ahead. Schools do not protect children from the badness of the world outside. They are at least as bad as the world outside, and the harm they do to the children in their power creates much of the badness of the world outside. The sickness of the modern world is in many ways a school-induced sickness. It is in school that most people learn to expect and accept that some expert can always place them in some sort of rank or hierarchy. It is in school that we meet, become used to, and learn to believe in the totally controlled society. We do not learn much science, but we learn to worship "scientists" and to believe that anything we might conceivably need or want can only come, and someday will come, from them. The school is the closest we have yet been able to come to Huxley's *Brave New World*, with its alphas and betas, deltas and epsilons—and now it even has its soma. Everyone, including children, should have the right to say "No!" to it.[1]

Questions

1. Holt's opening sentence pretty much dismisses the idea of compulsory education. What arguments can be offered on behalf of compulsory education? How can you defend the requirement that

[1] Aldous Huxley's *Brave New World* (1932) depicts a totalitarian society that scientifically controls the populace. Babies are created in laboratories and are conditioned; adults are given *soma* pills to prevent depression. John Holt, following Huxley, plays on the Greek letters for A, B, D, and E, suggesting that the grading system of our schools turns into a doping system. (Editors' note)

children be schooled—even if the children and their parents don't wish them to go to school?

2. In paragraph 4, Holt refers to "an industry, an army of people." To whom does he refer? What is the effect of describing them as an "industry" and an "army"?

3. Read paragraphs 12 and 13, and then write an essay of 500 words evaluating your high school in the light of Holt's comment that most schools encourage morally destructive competition.

4. If you have read Postman's essay (pages 181–187), write an essay of 500–750 words comparing and evaluating the two essays as examples of persuasive writing. Note: your topic is not "Which of the Two Essays I Subscribe to"; rather, it is an analysis and an evaluation of the essays as *persuasion.*

5. If you have read Anonymous, "Confessions of an Erstwhile Child" (pages 87–91), what ideas do you find there that are similar to Holt's? In a paragraph or two, point out the similarities, citing specific passages in each essay.

Paul Goodman

A Proposal to Abolish Grading

Let half a dozen of the prestigious Universities—Chicago, Stanford, the Ivy League—abolish grading, and use testing only and entirely for pedagogic purposes as teachers see fit.   1

Anyone who knows the frantic temper of the present schools will   2

Paul Goodman (1911–1972) received his bachelor's degree from City College in New York and his Ph.D. from the University of Chicago. He taught in several colleges and universities, and he wrote prolifically on literature, politics, and education. Goodman's view that students were victims of a corrupt society made him especially popular on campuses, even in the 1960s when students tended to distrust anyone over thirty. "A Proposal to Abolish Grading" (editors' title) is an extract from *Compulsory Miseducation and the Community of Scholars* (1966).

understand the transvaluation of values that would be effected by this modest innovation. For most of the students, the competitive grade has come to be the essence. The naïve teacher points to the beauty of the subject and the ingenuity of the research; the shrewd student asks if he is responsible for that on the final exam.

Let me at once dispose of an objection whose unanimity is quite 3 fascinating. I think that the great majority of professors agree that grading hinders teaching and creates a bad spirit, going as far as cheating and plagiarizing. I have before me the collection of essays, *Examining in Harvard College,* and this is the consensus. It is uniformly asserted, however, that the grading is inevitable; for how else will the graduate schools, the foundations the corporations *know* whom to accept, reward, hire? How will the talent scouts know whom to tap?

By testing the applicants, of course, according to the specific task- 4 requirements of the inducting institution, just as applicants for the Civil Service or for licenses in medicine, law, and architecture are tested. Why should Harvard professors do the testing *for* corporations and graduate-schools?

The objection is ludicrous. Dean Whitla, of the Harvard Office of 5 Tests, points out that the scholastic-aptitude and achievement tests used for *admission* to Harvard are a super-excellent index for all-around Harvard performance, better than high-school grades or particular Harvard course-grades. Presumably, these college-entrance tests are tailored for what Harvard and similar institutions want. By the same logic, would not an employer do far better to apply his own job-aptitude test rather than to rely on the vagaries of Harvard sectionmen. Indeed, I doubt that many employers bother to look at such grades; they are more likely to be interested merely in the fact of a Harvard diploma, whatever that connotes to them. The grades have most of their weight with the graduate schools—here, as elsewhere, the system runs mainly for its own sake.

It is really necessary to remind our academics of the ancient history 6 of Examination. In the medieval university, the whole point of the gruelling trial of the candidate was whether or not to accept him as a peer. His disputation and lecture for the Master's was just that, a master-piece to enter the guild. It was not to make comparative evaluations. It was not to weed out and select for an extra-mural licensor or employer. It was certainly not to pit one young fellow against another in an ugly competition. My philosophic impression is that the medievals thought they knew what a good job of work was and that we are competitive because we do not know. But the more status is achieved by largely irrelevant competitive evaluation, the less will we ever know.

(Of course, our American examinations never did have this purely guild orientation, just as our faculties have rarely had absolute autonomy; the examining was to satisfy Overseers, Elders, distant Regents— and they as paternal superiors have always doted on giving grades, rather than accepting peers. But I submit that this set-up itself makes it impossible for the student to *become* a master, to *have* grown up, and to commence on his own. He will always be making A or B for some overseer. And in the present atmosphere, he will always be climbing on his friend's neck.)   7

Perhaps the chief objectors to abolishing grading would be the students and their parents. The parents should be simply disregarded; their anxiety has done enough damage already. For the students, it seems to me that a primary duty of the university is to deprive them of their props, their dependence on extrinsic valuation and motivation, and to force them to confront the difficult enterprise itself and finally lose themselves in it.   8

A miserable effect of grading is to nullify the various uses of testing. Testing, for both student and teacher, is a means of structuring, and also of finding out what is blank or wrong and what has been assimilated and can be taken for granted. Review—including high-pressure review—is a means of bringing together the fragments, so that there are flashes of synoptic insight.   9

There are several good reasons for testing, and kinds of test. But if the aim is to discover weakness, what is the point of down-grading and punishing it, and thereby inviting the student to conceal his weakness, by faking and bulling, if not cheating? The natural conclusion of synthesis is the insight itself, not a grade for having had it. For the important purpose of placement, if one can establish in the student the belief that one is testing *not* to grade and make invidious comparisons but for his own advantage, the student should normally seek his own level, where he is challenged and yet capable, rather than trying to get by. If the student dares to accept himself as he is, a teacher's grade is a crude instrument compared with a student's self-awareness. But it is rare in our universities that students are encouraged to notice objectively their vast confusion. Unlike Socrates, our teachers rely on power-drives rather than shame and ingenuous idealism.   10

Many students are lazy, so teachers try to goad or threaten them by grading. In the long run this must do more harm than good. Laziness is a character-defense. It may be a way of avoiding learning, in   11 order to protect the conceit that one is already perfect (deeper, the despair that one *never* can). It may be a way of avoiding just the risk of failing and being down-graded. Sometimes it is a way of politely saying, "I won't." But since it is the authoritarian grown-up demands that have created such attitudes in the first place, why repeat the trauma? There comes a time when we must treat people as adult, laziness and all. It is one thing courageously to fire a do-nothing out of your class; it is quite another thing to evaluate him with a lordly F.

Most important of all, it is often obvious that balking in doing the work, especially among bright young people who get to great universities, means exactly what it says: The work does not suit me, not this subject, or not at this time, or not in this school, or not in school altogether. The student might not be bookish; he might be school-tired; perhaps his development ought now to take another direction. Yet unfortunately, if such a student is intelligent and is not sure of himself, he *can* be bullied into passing, and this obscures everything. My hunch is that I am describing a common situation. What a grim waste of young life and teacherly effort! Such a student will retain nothing of what he has "passed" in. Sometimes he must get mononucleosis to tell his story and be believed. 12

And ironically, the converse is also probably commonly true. A student flunks and is mechanically weeded out, who is really ready and eager to learn in a scholastic setting, but he has not quite caught on. A good teacher can recognize the situation, but the computer wreaks its will. 13

Questions

1. In his opening paragraph Goodman limits his suggestion about grading and testing to "half a dozen of the prestigious Universities." Does he offer any reason for this limitation? Can you?
2. In paragraph 3 Goodman says that "the great majority of professors agree that grading hinders teaching." What evidence does he offer to support this claim? What arguments might be made that grading assists teaching? Should Goodman have made them?
3. As a student, have grades helped you to learn, or have grades hindered you? Explain.

Mary Field Belenky, Blythe McVicker
Clinchy, Nancy Rule Goldberger, and
Jill Mattuck Tarule

Toward an Education for Women

We begin with the reminiscences of two ordinary women, 1
each recalling an hour during her first year at college. One of them,
now middle aged, remembered the first meeting of an introductory
science course. The professor marched into the lecture hall, placed
upon his desk a large jar filled with dried beans, and invited the students to guess how many beans the jar contained. After listening to
an enthusiastic chorus of wildly inaccurate estimates the professor
smiled a thin, dry smile, revealed the correct answer, and announced,
"You have just learned an important lesson about science. Never trust
the evidence of your own senses."

Thirty years later, the woman could guess what the professor had 2
in mind. He saw himself, perhaps, as inviting his students to embark
upon an exciting voyage into a mysterious underworld invisible to the
naked eye, accessible only through scientific method and scientific instruments. But the seventeen-year-old girl could not accept or even
hear the invitation. Her sense of herself as a knower was shaky, and
it was based on the belief that she could use her own firsthand experience as a source of truth. This man was saying that this belief was
fallacious. He was taking away her only tool for knowing and providing her with no substitute. "I remember feeling small and scared," the
woman says, "and I did the only thing I could do. I dropped the course
that afternoon, and I haven't gone near science since."

The second woman, in her first year at college, told a superficially 3
similar but profoundly different story about a philosophy class she had
attended just a month or two before the interview. The teacher came

---

Mary Belenky is an assistant research professor at the University of Vermont,
Blythe Clinchy is a professor of psychology at Wellesley College, Nancy Goldberger is a visiting scholar in psychology at New York University, and Jill Tarule
is an associate professor at Lesley College Graduate School. The essay printed
here is part of Chapter 9 of their book, *Women's Ways of Knowing*, a study of
how women's intellectual abilities develop. The chapter's title, which we have
borrowed, is "Toward an Education for Women."

---

into class carrying a large cardboard cube. She placed it on the desk in front of her and asked the class what it was. They said it was a cube. She asked what a cube was, and they said a cube contained six equal square sides. She asked how they knew that this object contained six equal square sides. By looking at it, they said. "But how do you know?" the teacher asked again. She pointed to the side facing her and, therefore, invisible to the students; then she lifted the cube and pointed to the side that had been face down on the desk, and, therefore, also invisible. "We can't look at all six sides of a cube at once, can we? So we can't exactly *see* a cube. And yet, you're right. You know it's a cube. But you know it not just because you have eyes but because you have intelligence. You invent the sides you cannot see. You use your intelligence to create the 'truth' about cubes."

The student said to the interviewer, 4

> It blew my mind. You'll think I'm nuts, but I ran back to the dorm and I called my boyfriend and I said, "Listen, this is just incredible," and I told him all about it. I'm not sure he could see why I was so excited. I'm not sure I understand it myself. But I really felt, for the first time, like I was really in college, like I was—I don't know—sort of *grown up*.

Both stories are about the limitations of firsthand experience as a 5 source of knowledge—we cannot simply see the truth about either the jar of beans or the cube—but there is a difference. We can know the truth about cubes. Indeed, the students did know it. As the science professor pointed out, the students were wrong about the beans; their senses had deceived them. But, as the philosophy teacher pointed out, the students were right about the cube; their minds had served them well.

The science professor was the only person in the room who knew 6 how many beans were in that jar. Theoretically, the knowledge was available to the students; they could have counted the beans. But faced with that tedious prospect, most would doubtless take the professor's word for it. He is authority. They had to rely upon his knowledge rather than their own. On the other hand, every member of the philosophy class knew that the cube had six sides. They were all colleagues.

The science professor exercised his authority in a benign fashion, 7 promising the students that he would provide them with the tools they needed to excavate invisible truths. Similarly, the philosophy teacher planned to teach her students the skills of philosophical analysis, but she was at pains to assure them that they already possessed the tools to construct some powerful truths. They had built cubes on their own, using only their own powers of inference, without the aid of elaborate procedures or fancy apparatus or even a teacher. Although a teacher might have told them once that a cube contained six equal square sides, they did not have to take the teacher's word for it; they could have easily verified it for themselves.

The lesson the science professor wanted to teach is that experience   8
is a source of error. Taught in isolation, this lesson diminished the student, rendering her dumb and dependent. The philosophy teacher's lesson was that although raw experience is insufficient, by reflecting upon it the student could arrive at truth. It was a lesson that made the student feel more powerful ("sort of grown up").

No doubt it is true that, as the professor in May Sarton's novel   9
The Small Room says, the "art" of being a student requires humility. But the woman we interviewed did not find the science lesson humbling; she found it humiliating. Arrogance was not then and is not now her natural habitat. Like most of the women in our sample she lacked confidence in herself as a thinker; and the kind of learning the science teacher demanded was not only painful but crippling.

In thinking about the education of women, Adrienne Rich writes,   10
"Suppose we were to ask ourselves, simply: What does a woman need to know?" A woman, like any other human being, does need to know that the mind makes mistakes; but our interviews have convinced us that every woman, regardless of age, social class, ethnicity, and academic achievement, needs to know that she is capable of intelligent thought, and she needs to know it right away. Perhaps men learn this lesson before going to college, or perhaps they can wait until they have proved themselves to hear it; we do not know. We do know that many of the women we interviewed had not yet learned it.

Questions

1. How is the professor in the first anecdote characterized? Look particularly at the words used in paragraphs 1 and 2 to describe him. How is the student characterized? Look back at the first sentence: Why do the writers use the word "ordinary" to describe both students? Why did they not simply say, "We begin with the reminiscences of two women"?

2. In paragraph 5 the writers say, "Both stories are about the limitations of firsthand experience as a source of knowledge." What else

do the stories have in common? What are the important differences? What particular difference is most relevant to the main point
of the essay?

3. Look again at paragraph 6. The science teacher is described as
being "authority." The students "had to rely upon his knowledge
rather than their own." Is this relationship between teacher and
students more likely in science courses than in philosophy or literature courses? Is it inevitable in sciences courses? If so, why?

4. What is the main point of the concluding paragraph? Do the two
anecdotes support this point? To what extent does your own experience confirm it, or not confirm it?

Paul Robinson

TV Can't Educate

On July 20 [1978] NBC aired a documentary on life in Marin   1
County, a bedroom community just across the Golden Gate Bridge
from San Francisco. The program was called "I Want It All Now" and
its single theme was the predominance of narcissism in Marin. The
program's host, Edwin Newman, introduced viewers, in his studied
casual manner, to a variety of "consciousness raising" groups en-
sconced in Marin and insinuated that this new narcissistic manner was
leading to a breakdown not only of the family (a divorce rate of 75
percent was mentioned three times) but also of traditional civic virtue.
The following day the *San Francisco Chronicle* carried a long, front-page
article on the outraged reaction of Marin's respectable citizenry to what
it considered a grossly distorted portrait of itself. Several residents
argued, persuasively, that Marin was in fact a highly political suburb—
that it had been a hot spot of the anti-Vietnam war movement, and
that only last year it had responded dramatically to the water crisis in
California, cutting back on water use much more than was required
by law. Television journalism appeared to be up to its old tricks: producers saw what they wanted to see, and they were not about to pass

Paul Robinson was born in San Diego in 1940. He teaches history at Stanford
University, specializing in modern European intellectual history.

up the chance to show a woman being massaged by two nude men and chirping about how delightful it was to "receive" without having to "give."

I was reminded, however improbably, of an experience in Berlin, where I had spent the previous six months teaching. The Germans are all exercised over a recent movie about Adolf Hitler (*Hitler: Eine Karriere*), which is based on a biography by the journalist Joachim Fest. The charge leveled against the film is that it glorifies Hitler (though it uses nothing but documentary footage; there are no actors), and it has been linked with a supposed resurgence of Nazism in Germany, particularly among the young. I saw only parts of the film and therefore can't speak to the justice of the charge. What I wish to report on—and what the Marin program brought to mind—is a lecture I attended by a young German historian from the Free University of Berlin, in which he took issue with the film because it had failed to treat Hitler's relations with the German industrialists, who were crucial in supporting the Nazi Party before it came to power and apparently benefited from its success.

The critics of the Newman program and my young scholar friend in Berlin were guilty of the same error. They both bought the assumption that television and movies can be a source of knowledge, that one can "learn" from them. By knowledge and learning I obviously don't mean an assortment of facts. Rather I have in mind the analytic process that locates pieces of information within a larger context of argument and meaning. Movies and TV are structurally unsuited to that process.

There is no great mystery here. It's a simple matter of time. Learning requires one kind of time, visual media are bound to another. In learning one must be able to freeze the absorption of fact or proposition at any moment in order to make mental comparisons, to test the fact or proposition against known facts and propositions, to measure it against the formal rules of logic and evidence—in short, to carry on a mental debate. Television is a matter of seconds, minutes and hours, it moves inexorably forward, and thus even with the best will in the world (a utopian assumption), it can never teach. In the last analysis there is only one way to learn: by reading. That's how you'll find out about Hitler's relations with the German industrialists, if you can find out about them at all. Such a complex, many-layered phenomenon simply cannot be reduced to a scene (which would presumably meet my scholar-friend's objection) in which Hitler has dinner with Baron

Krupp. Similarly, you will not find out about life in Marin County from an hour-long TV program or, for that matter, from a 24-hour-long one. What are the control populations? What statistical methods are being used? Is there more consciousness raising going on in Marin than in Cambridge? What is the correlation between narcissism and income level, educational background, employment, religious affiliation, marital status, sexual inclination and so forth? If these questions have answers, they are to be found in the books and articles of sociologists, not on TV.

I am prepared, indeed eager, to follow my argument to its logical 5 conclusion: the worst thing on TV is educational TV (and not just on educational stations). By comparison the gratuitous violence of most commercial shows is a mere peccadillo. Educational TV corrupts the very notion of education and renders its victims uneducable. I hear grown-ups launching conversations with, "Mike Wallace says that . . ." as if Mike Wallace actually knew something. Viewers hold forth authoritatively about South Africa, or DNA, or black holes, or whatever because they have watched a segment about them on "60 Minutes" or some such program. Complete ignorance really would be preferable, because ignorance at least preserves a mental space that might someday be filled with real knowledge, or some approximation of it.

There is a new form of slumming popular among intellectuals: 6 watching "bad" (i.e. commercial) TV and even writing books about it (as Dan Wakefield has about the afternoon soap opera "All My Children"). I would like to think that the motive behind this development is revulsion against the intellectual pretensions of "good" TV. But, as often happens with academics, the reaction has been dressed up in phony theoretical garb. "All My Children," we're supposed to believe, is the great American novel, heir to the tradition of Dickens and Trollope. Of course it's nothing of the sort. But it *is* very good entertainment. And that is precisely what TV is prepared to do: to entertain, to divert, above all to amuse. It is superbly amusing, ironically, for the same reason that it can't educate: it is tied to the clock, which has enormous comic potential. It is not accidental that one speaks of a comedian's "timing." Jack Benny would not be funny in print. He must wait just the right length of time after the robber threatens, "Your money or your life," before responding. (Imagine the situation in a novel: "The robber said, 'Your money or your life.' Jack took ten seconds trying to make up his mind.") Nor can you do a double-take in print, only on the screen. The brilliant manipulation of time made "The Honeymooners" so funny: Art Carney squandered it while Jackie Gleason, whose clock ran at double-time, burned. Audrey Meadows stood immobile, producing a magnificently sustained and silent obligato to Gleason's frantic buffo patter.

Television, then, is superbly fit to amuse. And amusement is not to be despised. At the very least it provides an escape from the world and from ourselves. It is pleasurable (by definition, one might say), and it gives us a sense of union with humanity, if only in its foibles. Herbert Marcuse might even contend that it keeps alive the image of an unrepressed existence. Television can provide all this. But it can't educate. 7

Movies are faced with the same dilemma. The desire to educate accounts, I believe, for the increasingly deliberate pace of movies. It is as if the director were trying to provide room within his time-bound narrative for the kind of reflection associated with analysis. This was brought home to me recently when, during the same week, I saw the movie *Julia* in the theater and *Jezebel* on TV. The latter, made in 1938, portrays the tragedy of a strong-willed southern girl who refuses to conform to the rules of antebellum New Orleans society. The most striking difference between the two movies is their pace. *Jezebel* moves along swiftly (there is probably more dialogue in the first 15 minutes than in all of *Julia*), treats its theme with appropriate superficiality and entertains effortlessly. *Julia,* on the other hand, is lugubrious and obviously beyond its depth. It succeeds only with the character of Julia herself, who, like Jezebel, is powerful, beautiful, virtuous and unburdened by intellectual or psychological complexity. By way of contrast, the narrative figure, Lilli, tries vainly to deal with issues that movies can't manage: the difficulty of writing, a relationship with an older man who is at once lover, mentor, and patient-to-be, the tension between literary success and political commitment. All of these are wonderfully captured in Lillian Hellman's memoir, but not even two fine actors like Jane Fonda and Jason Robards can bring such uncinematic matters to life on the screen. The "issue" of the memoir—despite all those meaningful silences—inevitably eluded the movie. 8

Let us, then, not ask more of movies and TV than they can deliver. In fact, let us discourage them from trying to "educate" us. 9

Questions

1. The first paragraph speaks of the "new narcissistic manner." What is narcissism? How is the etymology of the word (like "narcotic," it derives ultimately from the Greek *narkē*, "numbness") relevant to the meaning of narcissism?

2. In paragraph 4 Robinson argues that one can't learn from television because television doesn't allow the viewer time "to make mental comparisons, to test the fact or proposition against known facts and propositions, . . . in short, to carry on a mental debate." If this is true, does it follow that the lecture method of teaching is also inherently ineffective? Is Robinson defining teaching and learning (see especially paragraph 3) too narrowly?

Patricia Nelson Limerick

The Phenomenon of Phantom Students
Diagnosis and Treatment

On any number of occasions, students have told me that 1
I am the first and only professor they have spoken to. This was, at first, flattering. Then curiosity began to replace vanity. How had conversation between teacher and student become, for many students, a novelty? These students conducted themselves as if the University were a museum: the professors on display, the students at a distance, directing any questions to the museum's guides and guards—the graduate students.

The museum model is not University policy. No "guide for in- 2
structors" tells professors to cultivate aloofness and keep students in their place. No "guide for undergraduates" tells them to speak to graduate students, and only approach professors on extremely solemn and serious business.

This is not University policy, and it is by no means the experience 3

Patricia Nelson Limerick was born in Banning, California, in 1951, and educated at the Universities of California at Santa Cruz and Yale. She has taught history at Yale, Harvard, and the University of Colorado (her special interests are Western history, American Indian history, and environmental history), but she is also interested in the teaching of writing and in (as this essay reveals) students. "The Phenomenon of Phantom Students" was originally published in the *Harvard Gazette*, a weekly publication for the university community.

of all Harvard students. Many confidently talk to their professors; in occasional cases, introducing a measure of shyness and humility would not be altogether unfortunate. I have no notion what the actual statistics are, but it is my impression that the disengaged are no insignificant minority. Harvard has an abundance of factors creating phantoms—my term for the radically disengaged, those staying resolutely on the academic periphery, taking large lecture classes, writing survivalist papers and exams. Phantomhood—even in its milder versions—is a significant problem and deserves the University's attention.

What creates phantoms? They tell remarkably similar stories. In 4 the basic narrative, the freshman arrives with the familiar doubt: did Admissions make a mistake? Paradoxically, the doubt coexists with vanity; high school was easy, and Harvard won't be much worse for an individual of such certified achievement. Then, in the basic phantom story, a paper comes back with a devastating grade. Since a direct nerve connects the student's prose to his self-respect and dignity, and since the Expository Writing Program stands as the Ellis Island of Harvard, many of these initial injuries involve Expos.

Crucial Fork

The crucial fork in the road comes here: the paper, more than likely 5 produced in good faith, is a disaster; the student has been judged by standards he doesn't understand. The split outcome really cannot be overdramatized: one route goes direct to defeat, resignation, and cynicism; the other offers a struggle, rewriting, and very probably, the learning of new skills.

Some of those new skills involve writing, but for this subject, the 6 significant skill involves conversation—direct, productive—in which the grader of the paper says precisely and clearly how the paper went wrong, and how the author can make it better. (On the instructor's side, if there is any more intellectually demanding exercise in the academic world than this, I don't know what it is.) One successful round of this kind of dialogue has, I think, an immunizing effect; on the occasion of the next disastrous paper, the precedent set makes another collapse unlikely.

For the representative phantom, though, any number of things go 7 wrong. Even if the instructor clearly explains the paper's problems, panic keeps the phantom from hearing. Conversation with instructors becomes an unhappy experience, avoided by anyone with any sense, in which papers are picked on to no particular result.

The essential groundwork completed, the phantom can become a 8 part of a community in which groups of the radically disengaged make their unfortunate academic status a matter of pride or, alternatively, the phantom can think of himself as uniquely and distinctively cut off from the University. In either case, the crucial transition is complete: from thinking, "I *may* be the fluke in Admissions," the student has moved on to certainty: "I *am* the fluke." From here on, the prospect for positive student/faculty contact meets the unpassable obstacle: the student's own fatalism.

I draw here a portrait of extreme cases—with academic under-   9
performance part of the package. There are a substantial number of individuals doing perfectly competent academic work who still would choose a visit to the dentist over a visit to a professor. Usually, no particular unhappy event explains their shyness, and one could certainly argue that their situation is not particularly unfortunate. They are doing the reading, and writing their papers, and getting solid educations. But they are missing something. Recently, my course assistant arranged for me to have lunch with a recently graduated student who had been in my class; four years of a good academic performance, and she had never spoken to a professor. She was a remarkable person, involved over a long time in volunteer work for the homeless. I think both she and Harvard would have profited had she been comfortable talking with professors.

Student/Faculty Contact

I address myself here to the problem of student/faculty contact in the   10
case of students both with and without academic problems. Reading and writing with both ease and intensity are fundamental goals; speaking with ease and intensity should be in the package.

How are students to be persuaded to talk to professors? This en-   11
couragement should not offer false advertising. One simply cannot say that all professors are at heart accessible and friendly. Some of them are certifiably grumpy, and many of them are shy. They are still worth talking to.

With a major interest in Indian/White relations, I cannot resist   12
thinking anthropologically. White people and Indian people still confront each other through a fog of stereotypes (all Indians are noble and in touch with nature, or, alternatively, all Indians are demoralized and in touch with alcohol), and the impulse to provide a comparable analysis for student/professor relations is irresistible. Images have equal powers in both situations.

Commonly Held Student Myths about Professors

1a. *Professors Must Be Asked Specific, Better Yet, Bibliographic Questions.* 13
Professors do not converse like ordinary people. To speak their language, you must address them in this fashion: "Professor X, I was very
interested in your remarks about the unification of the Northwest Company and the Hudson's Bay Company in 1821, and I wondered if you
might direct me to further reading." If you do not have a specific question like this, then you have no business troubling a professor.

   1b. *Professors Only Like to Talk about Senior Theses.* This proposition 14
was brought home to me at a Quincy House gathering. A number of
students and I were speaking on a general, humane topic (sports?)
when they discovered my hidden identity. The truth out, they began
to tell me about their senior theses. The evening, I felt, became something of a busman's holiday.

   2. *Professors Only Want to Talk with Other Elegant, Learned and Bril-* 15
liant Conversationalists. (Numbers 1 and 2 may appear to be contradictory, but they often coexist.) Living in the intellectual equivalent of
Mt. McKinley or Mt. Whitney, professors do not like to descend the
mountain to talk to the lowlanders. They are used to sophisticated,
erudite conversation, in contrast to which normal speech sounds em-
barrassingly flat and pedestrian. Even if they seem to tolerate the
speech of mortals, professors are inwardly thinking how stupid it
sounds. They have, in their distinguished careers, heard nearly every
insight there is. If a new idea seems to occur to a student in 1983, it
can be assumed that the professor first heard that idea sometime in
the 1950s. Having a memory built on the order of a steel trap, the
professor does not need to hear it again.

   3. *If I Speak to a Professor, He Will Probably (and Maybe Rightly) Assume* 16
That I Am a Grade-grubbing Toady. (The students, of course, use a more
vivid term.) This belief actually concerns attitudes to other students:
dependent, hypocritical drudges hang around professors, asking in-
sincere questions, and seeking recommendation letters; students with
integrity keep their distance and avoid the dishonor of visibly trying
to make an impression.

   Countering these three assumptions does not require a debasing 17
of professional status; respect for achievement and authority, and excessive deference and fear are two different matters. Number 1 and
#2 are both extremely widespread, and #3 has, I think, the greatest
power over phantoms. In the further reaches of phantomhood, these
assumptions rest on considerable hostility toward the institution, a

basic act of self-defense in which the individual reasons (if that's the word): "Harvard has ignored and injured me; well, Harvard is stupid anyway." We are dealing here, in other words, with wounded dignity, a condition not known for bringing out the finest in human behavior.

In the last eight years, I have seen many phantoms emerge from hiding; I have enormous faith in their potential for recovery. Nothing encouraged me more than the Committee on College Life meeting last spring. I had promised to bring expert witnesses—verifiable phantoms. Having made the promise, I began to regret it. If these individuals barely had the courage to talk to me, how would they face a panel of five professors, two deans and five students? Would any consent to appear? The first five I called said yes—without reluctance. At the committee, they spoke with frankness and energy. To be equally frank, that amazed me—I evidently expected that I would have to act as their interpreter. They were, instead, perfectly capable of speaking for themselves.   18

There is a fairly reliable personal solution to the problem of phantomhood for faculty to follow: 19

1. *Discover the phantoms* (midterm grade sheets locate the ones with academic problems; reports from course assistants and from professorial visits to sections identify the others).   20

2. *Contact them.*   21

3. *Get an acknowledgment of the condition of phantomhood, directly and briefly.* (Don't milk it for its misery, which is often at a pretty high level.)   22

4. *Engage them in a specific project—ideally, rewriting a paper.* Here, the instructor is most productive when she uses her own enthusiasm for the subject to launch a discussion of the ideas in the paper, so that the student slides, without perceiving it, into what was hitherto unimaginable—"an intellectual conversation with a professor."   23

5. *Keep a careful eye out for achievement on the part of the student, during the conversation, and comment on it.* This is only in part "encouragement"—the primary goal is to help the individual penetrate the mysterious standards of what constitutes "insight" or a "a solid point."   24

6. *Hold out for concrete evidence of recovery—a successfully rewritten paper, for instance.* These second drafts are almost without exception much better papers—primarily because the student now has what was wholly lacking before—faith in a living, actual audience.   25

7. *Encourage a wide application of the new principles.* The student's logical next step is to say to the instructor, "I can work with you because you are different from the others." Resist this. The sports anal-   26

ogy is the best: you may need a coach at the start of learning a sport, but you do not need to coach at your elbow for the rest of your career in that sport. Professors, like most other individuals, like snowflakes, are all different. That, surely, is part of their charm.

Phantoms are not beyond understanding, and certainly not be-   27
yond recovery. But there is another, equally complex party to the basic transactions of student/faculty contact. We might now take up the question of the genesis of shyness, harriedness and grumpiness in professors.

How nice to lead a leisured life in a book-lined office, I used to   28
think, chatting, reading and (if *real* work meant actually teaching classes) working only a few hours a week. Cross the line into professorhood, and the plot thickens considerably. Those few minutes a week in class rest on hours of preparation. Reading exams and papers closely eats up time. Then, of course, there is "one's own work"— research and writing for promised articles and books. Add to this, participation in professional organizations and department and University committees, and one's leisured time in the book-lined office often comes down to checking the datebook to see where one is due next.

That is in part why professors can seem grumpy and aloof, even   29
when they are genuinely committed to teaching. Phantoms, and prospective phantoms, should be advised not to take personal injury when cut short by an individual who will have to stay up most of the night revising the next day's lecture and writing recommendation letters. Schedule a meeting for a time when the universe at least gives the illusion of being a bit more in the professor's control, and try not to resent any accidental rudeness.

More important, phantoms should be encouraged to use empathy   30
in understanding the professors. Phantoms are, after all, experts in shyness; shyness, while not universal in the professorial population, is no stranger. Consider the pattern: the individual is initially drawn to the world of books and private contemplation, communicating more often through writing than through speech. How nice, the susceptible individual thinks, that there is a profession that encourages and supports this retreat to private intellectual exertion. And that promise seems to hold for the initial years of graduate school, and then, abruptly, the treachery stands exposed. One has to walk into a classroom, cause everyone else to fall silent, and become the center of attention. It is a shy person's nightmare, and individuals evolve the best mechanisms for dealing with it that they can. Once the mechanisms are in

place, the individual holds on to them. It is undeniably more dignified to seem aloof and uncaring than to seem scared and shy.

I write as a reformed phantom myself—one, happily, in the cat- 31 egory in which academic problems did not play a part. My papers carried me through college and graduate school; I was a veritable sphinx in classes. Occupying—initially to my horror—the teacher's chair, phantomhood became a luxury I could not afford.

A few years ago, when I had just started teaching, an old professor 32 of mine from Santa Cruz came to Yale for the year. "We're so fragmented at Santa Cruz," he said, "I am really looking forward to having hard-hitting intellectual conversations again."

"Hard-hitting intellectual conversations?" I didn't seem to have 33 ever had one. It was a concept beyond the reach of an only partially recovered phantom.

Seven or eight years later, I am thoroughly addicted to the kind 34 of conversations I thought I would never have. They provide the core of vitality for the university, the only real cement that makes such a collection of disparate individuals into a community. I want the phantoms included in the community.

Questions

1. In paragraph 3 Limerick says: "This is not University policy, and it is by no means the experience of all Harvard students. Many confidently talk to their professors; in occasional cases, introducing a measure of shyness and humility would not be altogether unfortunate." Rewrite the second of these two sentences, putting the basic idea more directly. Next, compare your version with Limerick's. Which is better, and why? (By the way, the rhetorical device used in "would not be altogether unfortunate" is called *litotes*. If you don't know this word, look it up in a dictionary to see exactly what it means.)

2. Limerick mentions that after receiving an essay with a "devastating grade," a student finds that "conversation with instructors becomes an unhappy experience, avoided by anyone with any sense." If on some occasion your good sense deserted you and you therefore engaged in conversation with an instructor, was the conversation profitable? Why, or why not?

3. Let's assume that you find this essay interesting, and not simply because of the subject matter. *Why* is it interesting? What are some of the rhetorical devices that the author uses to engage your attention?

4. In paragraph 4 Limerick refers to the Expository Writing Program as "the Ellis Island of Harvard." Explain the metaphor. In the same paragraph she says: "A direct nerve connects the student's prose to his self-respect." Again, explain the metaphor and then try to explain why, for most of us, it rings true.

5. In paragraph 3 Limerick mentions, but does not define or explain, something she labels "survivalist papers and exams." In a paragraph invent a definition for this term, using both Limerick's essay and your own experience as sources.

6. Without naming or in any other way clearly identifying the instructor, write an essay of 500 words in which you explain why—at least for that instructor—you are a phantom student. Or, on the other hand, write an essay explaining why you have enjoyed conversing with an instructor. Hint: a few bits of dialogue will probably be effective.

7. Write a dialogue of an imaginary conference between a composition teacher and a phantom. (Even though this is an exercise in writing pure fiction, you may use one of your own essays as a prop.)

Wu-tsu Fa-yen

Zen and the Art of Burglary

If people ask me what Zen is like, I will say that it is like   1
learning the art of burglary. The son of a burglar saw his father growing older and thought, "If he is unable to carry on his profession, who

---

Wu-tsu Fa-yen (1025–1104) was a Chinese Zen Buddhist priest. More exactly, he was a Ch'an priest; *Zen* is Japanese for the Chinese *Ch'an*.

The practitioner of Zen (to use the more common name) seeks *satori*, "enlightenment" or "awakening." The awakening is from a world of blind strivings (including those of reason and of morality). The awakened being, free from a sense of the self in opposition to all other things, perceives the unity of all things. Wu-tsu belonged to the branch of Zen that uses "shock therapy, the purpose of which is to jolt the student out of his analytical and conceptual way of thinking and lead him back to his natural and spontaneous faculty" (Kenneth Ch'en, *Buddhism in China* [1964, rptd. 1972], p. 359).

The title of this story, from *The Sayings of Goso Hōyen*, is the editors'.

will be the breadwinner of the family, except myself? I must learn the trade." He intimated the idea to his father, who approved of it.

One night the father took the son to a big house, broke through 2 the fence, entered the house, and, opening one of the large chests, told the son to go in and pick out the clothing. As soon as the son got into it, the father dropped the lid and securely applied the lock. The father now came out to the courtyard and loudly knocked at the door, waking up the whole family; then he quietly slipped away by the hole in the fence. The residents got excited and lighted candles, but they found that the burglar had already gone.

The son, who remained all the time securely confined in the chest, 3 thought of his cruel father. He was greatly mortified, then a fine idea flashed upon him. He made a noise like the gnawing of a rat. The family told the maid to take a candle and examine the chest. When the lid was unlocked, out came the prisoner, who blew out the light, pushed away the maid, and fled. The people ran after him. Noticing a well by the road, he picked up a large stone and threw it into the water. The pursuers all gathered around the well trying to find the burglar drowning himself in the dark hole.

In the meantime he went safely back to his father's house. He 4 blamed his father deeply for his narrow escape. Said the father, "Be not offended, my son. Just tell me how you got out of it." When the son told him all about his adventures, the father remarked, "There you are, you have learned the art."

Questions

1. What assumptions about knowledge did the father make? Can you think of any of your own experiences that substantiate these assumptions?
2. Is there anything you have studied or are studying to which Zen pedagogical methods would be applicable? If so, explain by setting forth a sample lesson.

4
WORK AND PLAY

Lettuce Cutters, Salinas Valley
Dorothea Lange, 1935

Farm Security Administration Photo, Library of Congress

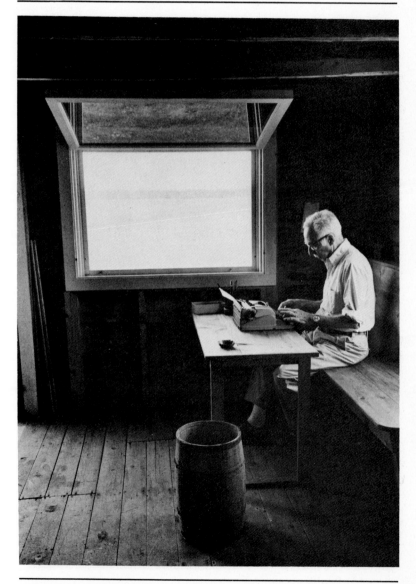

Photograph © 1976 by Jill Krementz

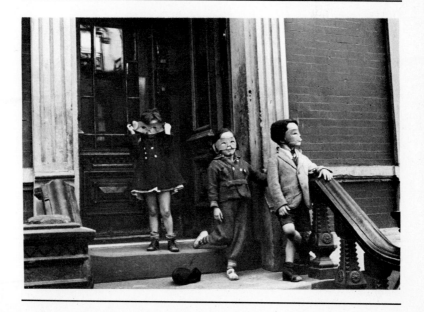

Short Views

Work and play are words used to describe the same thing under differing conditions.

Mark Twain

The Battle of Waterloo was won on the playing fields of Eton.

Attributed to the Duke of Wellington

My young men shall never work. Men who work cannot dream, and wisdom comes in dreams.

Smohalla, of the Nez Perce

Everyone who is prosperous or successful must have dreamed of something. It is not because he is a good worker that he is prosperous, but because he dreamed.

Lost Star, of the Maricopa

The possible quantity of play depends on the possible quantity of pay.

John Ruskin

It can't be just a job. It's not worth playing just for money. It's a way of life. When we were kids there was the release in playing, the sweetness in being able to move and control your body. This is what play is. Beating somebody is secondary. When I was a kid, to really *move* was my delight. I felt released because I could move around anybody. I was free.

Eric Nesterenko, Professional Hockey Player

Winning is not the most important thing; it's everything.

Vince Lombardi

Serious sport has nothing to do with fair play. It is bound up with hatred, jealousy, boastfulness, disregard of all rules and sadistic pleasure in witnessing violence: in other words, it is war minus the shooting.

George Orwell

The maturity of man—that means, to have reacquired the seriousness that one has as a child at play.
Friedrich Nietzsche

The boys throw stones at the frogs in sport, but the frogs die not in sport but in earnest.
Bion

Bertrand Russell

Work

Whether work should be placed among the causes of happiness or among the causes of unhappiness may perhaps be regarded as a doubtful question. There is certainly much work which is exceedingly irksome, and an excess of work is always very painful. I think, however, that, provided work is not excessive in amount, even the dullest work is to most people less painful than idleness. There are in work all grades, from mere relief of tedium up to the profoundest delights, according to the nature of the work and the abilities of the worker. Most of the work that most people have to do is not in itself interesting, but even such work has certain great advantages. To begin

Bertrand Russell (1872–1970) was educated at Trinity College, Cambridge. He published his first book, *The Study of German Social Democracy*, in 1896; subsequent books on mathematics and on philosophy quickly established his international reputation. His pacifist opposition to World War I cost him his appointment at Trinity College, and won him a prison sentence of six months. While serving this sentence he wrote his *Introduction to Mathematical Philosophy*. In 1940 an appointment to teach at the College of the City of New York was withdrawn because of Russell's unorthodox moral views. But he was not always treated shabbily; he won numerous awards, including (in 1950) a Nobel Prize. After World War II he devoted most of his energy to warning the world about the dangers of nuclear war.

In reading the first sentence of the essay that we reprint, you should know that the essay comes from a book called *The Conquest of Happiness*.

with, it fills a good many hours of the day without the need of deciding what one shall do. Most people, when they are left free to fill their own time according to their own choice, are at a loss to think of anything sufficiently pleasant to be worth doing. And whatever they decide on, they are troubled by the feeling that something else would have been pleasanter. To be able to fill leisure intelligently is the last product of civilization, and at present very few people have reached this level. Moreover the exercise of choice is in itself tiresome. Except to people with unusual initiative it is positively agreeable to be told what to do at each hour of the day, provided the orders are not too unpleasant. Most of the idle rich suffer unspeakable boredom as the price of their freedom from drudgery. At times, they may find relief by hunting big game in Africa, or by flying round the world, but the number of such sensations is limited, especially after youth is past. Accordingly the more intelligent rich men work nearly as hard as if they were poor, while rich women for the most part keep themselves busy with innumerable trifles of whose earth-shaking importance they are firmly persuaded.

Work therefore is desirable, first and foremost, as a preventive of 2 boredom, for the boredom that a man feels when he is doing necessary though uninteresting work is as nothing in comparison with the boredom that he feels when he has nothing to do with his days. With this advantage of work another is associated, namely that it makes holidays much more delicious when they come. Provided a man does not have to work so hard as to impair his vigor, he is likely to find far more zest in his free time than an idle man could possibly find.

The second advantage of most paid work and of some unpaid work 3 is that it gives chances of success and opportunities for ambition. In most work success is measured by income, and while our capitalistic society continues, this is inevitable. It is only where the best work is concerned that this measure ceases to be the natural one to apply. The desire that men feel to increase their income is quite as much a desire for success as for the extra comforts that a higher income can procure. However dull work may be, it becomes bearable if it is a means of building up a reputation, whether in the world at large or only in one's own circle. Continuity of purpose is one of the most essential ingredients of happiness in the long run, and for most men this comes chiefly through their work. In this respect those women whose lives are occupied with housework are much less fortunate than men, or than women who work outside the home. The domesticated wife does not receive wages, has no means of bettering herself, is taken for granted by her husband (who sees practically nothing of what she does), and is valued by him not for her housework but for quite other qualities. Of course this does not apply to those women who are sufficiently well-to-do to make beautiful houses and beautiful gardens and become the envy of their neighbors; but such women are comparatively few, and for the great majority housework cannot bring as much satisfaction as work of other kinds brings to men and to professional women.

The satisfaction of killing time and of affording some outlet, however modest, for ambition, belongs to most work, and is sufficient to make even a man whose work is dull happier on the average than a man who has no work at all. But when work is interesting, it is capable of giving satisfaction of a far higher order than mere relief from tedium. The kinds of work in which there is some interest may be arranged in a hierarchy. I shall begin with those which are only mildly interesting and end with those that are worthy to absorb the whole energies of a great man.   4

Two chief elements make work interesting; first, the exercise of skill, and second, construction.   5

Every man who has acquired some unusual skill enjoys exercising it until it has become a matter of course, or until he can no longer improve himself. This motive to activity begins in early childhood: a boy who can stand on his head becomes reluctant to stand on his feet. A great deal of work gives the same pleasure that is to be derived from games of skill. The work of a lawyer or a politician must contain in a more delectable form a great deal of the same pleasure that is to be derived from playing bridge. Here of course there is not only the exercise of skill but the outwitting of a skilled opponent. Even where this competitive element is absent, however, the performance of difficult feats is agreeable. A man who can do stunts in an aëroplane finds the pleasure so great that for the sake of it he is willing to risk his life. I imagine that an able surgeon, in spite of the painful circumstances in which his work is done, derives satisfaction from the exquisite precision of his operations. The same kind of pleasure, though in a less intense form, is to be derived from a great deal of work of a humbler kind. All skilled work can be pleasurable, provided the skill required is either variable or capable of indefinite improvement. If these conditions are absent, it will cease to be interesting when a man has acquired his maximum skill. A man who runs three-mile races will cease to find pleasure in this occupation when he passes the age at which he can beat his own previous record. Fortunately there is a very con-   6 siderable amount of work in which new circumstances call for new skill and a man can go on improving, at any rate until he has reached middle age. In some kinds of skilled work, such as politics, for example, it seems that men are at their best between sixty and seventy, the reason being that in such occupations a wide experience of other men is essential. For this reason successful politicians are apt to be happier at the age of seventy than any other men of equal age. Their only competitors in this respect are the men who are the heads of big businesses.

There is, however, another element possessed by the best work, 7 which is even more important as a source of happiness than is the exercise of skill. This is the element of constructiveness. In some work, though by no means in most, something is built up which remains as a monument when the work is completed. We may distinguish construction from destruction by the following criterion. In construction the initial state of affairs is comparatively haphazard, while the final state of affairs embodies a purpose: in destruction the reverse is the case; the initial state of affairs embodies a purpose, while the final state of affairs is haphazard, that is to say, all that is intended by the destroyer is to produce a state of affairs which does not embody a certain purpose. This criterion applies in the most literal and obvious case, namely the construction and destruction of buildings. In constructing a building a previously made plan is carried out, whereas in destroying it no one decides exactly how the materials are to lie when the demolition is complete. Destruction is of course necessary very often as a preliminary to subsequent construction; in that case it is part of a whole which is constructive. But not infrequently a man will engage in activities of which the purpose is destructive without regard to any construction that may come after. Frequently he will conceal this from himself by the belief that he is only sweeping away in order to build afresh, but it is generally possible to unmask this pretense, when it is a pretense, by asking him what the subsequent construction is to be. On this subject it will be found that he will speak vaguely and without enthusiasm, whereas on the preliminary destruction he has spoken precisely and with zest. This applies to not a few revolutionaries and militarists and other apostles of violence. They are actuated, usually without their own knowledge, by hatred: the destruction of what they hate is their real purpose, and they are comparatively indifferent to the question what is to come after it. Now I cannot deny that in the work of destruction as in the work of construction there may be joy. It is a fiercer joy, perhaps at moments more intense, but it is less profoundly satisfying, since the result is one in which little satisfaction is to be found. You kill your enemy, and when he is dead your occupation is gone, and the satisfaction that you derive from victory quickly fades. The work of construction, on the other hand, when completed is delightful to contemplate, and moreover is never so fully completed that there is nothing further to do about it. The most satisfactory purposes are those that lead on indefinitely from one success to another without ever coming to a dead end; and in this respect it will be found that construction is a greater source of happiness than destruction. Perhaps it would be more correct to say that those who find satisfaction in construction find in it greater satisfaction than the lovers of destruction can find in destruction, for if once you have become filled with hate you will not easily derive from construction the pleasure which another man would derive from it.

At the same time few things are so likely to cure the habit of hatred 8 as the opportunity to do constructive work of an important kind.

The satisfaction to be derived from success in a great constructive 9 enterprise is one of the most massive that life has to offer, although unfortunately in its highest forms it is open only to men of exceptional ability. Nothing can rob a man of the happiness of successful achievement in an important piece of work, unless it be the proof that after all his work was bad. There are many forms of such satisfaction. The man who by a scheme of irrigation has caused the wilderness to blossom like the rose enjoys it in one of its most tangible forms. The creation of an organization may be a work of supreme importance. So is the work of those few statesmen who have devoted their lives to producing order out of chaos, of whom Lenin is the supreme type in our day. The most obvious examples are artists and men of science. Shakespeare says of his verse: "So long as men can breathe, or eyes can see, so long lives this." And it cannot be doubted that the thought consoled him for misfortune. In his sonnets he maintains that the thought of his friend reconciled him to life, but I cannot help suspecting that the sonnets he wrote to his friend were even more effective for this purpose than the friend himself. Great artists and great men of science do work which is in itself delightful; while they are doing it, it secures them the respect of those whose respect is worth having, which gives them the most fundamental kind of power, namely power over men's thoughts and feelings. They have also the most solid reasons for thinking well of themselves. This combination of fortunate circumstances ought, one would think, to be enough to make any man happy. Nevertheless it is not so. Michael Angelo, for example, was a profoundly unhappy man, and maintained (not, I am sure, with truth) that he would not have troubled to produce works of art if he had not had to pay the debts of his impecunious relations. The power to produce great art is very often, though by no means always, associated with a temperamental unhappiness, so great that but for the joy which the artist derives from his work, he would be driven to suicide. We cannot, therefore, maintain that even the greatest work must make a man happy; we can only maintain that it must make him less unhappy. Men of science, however, are far less often temperamentally unhappy than artists are, and in the main the men who do great work in science are happy men, whose happiness is derived primarily from their work.

One of the causes of unhappiness among intellectuals in the   10 present day is that so many of them, especially those whose skill is literary, find no opportunity for the independent exercise of their talents, but have to hire themselves out to rich corporations directed by Philistines, who insist upon their producing what they themselves regard as pernicious nonsense. If you were to inquire among journalists in either England or America whether they believed in the policy of the newspaper for which they worked, you would find, I believe, that only a small minority do so; the rest, for the sake of a livelihood, prostitute their skill to purposes which they believe to be harmful. Such work cannot bring any real satisfaction, and in the course of reconciling himself to the doing of it, a man has to make himself so cynical that he can no longer derive whole-hearted satisfaction from anything whatever. I cannot condemn men who undertake work of this sort, since starvation is too serious an alternative, but I think that where it is possible to do work that is satisfactory to a man's constructive impulses without entirely starving, he will be well advised from the point of view of his own happiness if he chooses it in preference to work much more highly paid but not seeming to him worth doing on its own account. Without self-respect genuine happiness is scarcely possible. And the man who is ashamed of his work can hardly achieve self-respect.

The satisfaction of constructive work, though it may, as things are,   11 be the privilege of a minority, can nevertheless be the privilege of a quite large minority. Any man who is his own master in his work can feel it; so can any man whose work appears to him useful and requires considerable skill. The production of satisfactory children is a difficult constructive work capable of affording profound satisfaction. Any woman who has achieved this can feel that as a result of her labor the world contains something of value which it would not otherwise contain.

Human beings differ profoundly in regard to the tendency to re- 12
gard their lives as a whole. To some men it is natural to do so, and
essential to happiness to be able to do so with some satisfaction. To
others life is a series of detached incidents without directed movement
and without unity. I think the former sort are more likely to achieve
happiness than the latter, since they will gradually build up those
circumstances from which they can derive contentment and self-
respect, whereas the others will be blown about by the winds of
circumstances now this way, now that, without ever arriving at any
haven. The habit of viewing life as a whole is an essential part both of
wisdom and of true morality, and is one of the things which ought
to be encouraged in education. Consistent purpose is not enough to
make life happy, but it is an almost indispensable condition of a happy
life. And consistent purpose embodies itself mainly in work.

Questions

1. Russell is generally admired for his exceptionally clear prose. List
   some of the devices that make for clarity in this essay.
2. Russell is thought of as a left-winger. Aside from the casual reference to Lenin in paragraph 9, is there anything in "Work" to which
   Barry Goldwater, Ronald Reagan, or William Buckley might object?
   Of which statements might they especially approve?
3. Russell says (paragraph 3): "The desire that men feel to increase
   their income is quite as much a desire for success as for the extra
   comforts that a higher income can procure." In its context, what
   does "success" mean? In your experience, do Russell's words ring
   true? Why, or why not?

W. H. Auden

Work, Labor, and Play

So far as I know, Miss Hannah Arendt was the first person   1
to define the essential difference between work and labor. To be happy,
a man must feel, firstly, free and, secondly, important. He cannot be
really happy if he is compelled by society to do what he does not enjoy
doing, or if what he enjoys doing is ignored by society as of no value
or importance. In a society where slavery in the strict sense has been
abolished, the sign that what a man does is of social value is that he
is paid money to do it, but a laborer today can rightly be called a wage
slave. A man is a laborer if the job society offers him is of no interest
to himself but he is compelled to take it by the necessity of earning a
living and supporting his family.

The antithesis to labor is play. When we play a game, we enjoy   2
what we are doing, otherwise we should not play it, but it is a purely
private activity; society could not care less whether we play it or not.

Between labor and play stands work. A man is a worker if he is   3
personally interested in the job which society pays him to do; what
from the point of view of society is necessary labor is from his own
point of view voluntary play. Whether a job is to be classified as labor
or work depends, not on the job itself, but on the tastes of the individual who undertakes it. The difference does not, for example, coincide with the difference between a manual and a mental job; a gar-
dener or a cobbler may be a worker, a bank clerk a laborer. Which a
man is can be seen from his attitude toward leisure. To a worker,
leisure means simply the hours he needs to relax and rest in order to
work efficiently. He is therefore more likely to take too little leisure
than too much; workers die of coronaries and forget their wives' birthdays. To the laborer, on the other hand, leisure means freedom from

W[ystan] H[ugh] Auden (1907–1973) was born and educated in England. In 1939
he came to the United States and he became an American citizen. In 1972, however, he returned to England to live. Although Auden established his reputation
chiefly with his poetry, he also wrote plays, libretti, and essays, all of high quality.

One of Auden's most unusual books is *A Certain World: A Commonplace
Book.* It is an anthology of some of his favorite passages from other people's
books, along with brief reflections on his reading. The passage we print here
begins with a reference to Hannah Arendt's *The Human Condition.*

compulsion, so that it is natural for him to imagine that the fewer hours he has to spend laboring, and the more hours he is free to play, the better.

What percentage of the population in a modern technological soci- 4 ety are, like myself, in the fortunate position of being workers? At a guess I would say sixteen per cent, and I do not think that figure is likely to get bigger in the future.

Technology and the division of labor have done two things: by 5 eliminating in many fields the need for special strength or skill; they have made a very large number of paid occupations which formerly were enjoyable work into boring labor, and by increasing productivity they have reduced the number of necessary laboring hours. It is already possible to imagine a society in which the majority of the population, that is to say, its laborers, will have almost as much leisure as in earlier times was enjoyed by the aristocracy. When one recalls how aristocracies in the past actually behaved, the prospect is not cheerful. Indeed, the problem of dealing with boredom may be even more difficult for such a future mass society than it was for aristocracies. The latter, for example, ritualized their time; there was a season to shoot grouse, a season to spend in town, etc. The masses are more likely to replace an unchanging ritual by fashion which it will be in the economic interest of certain people to change as often as possible. Again, the masses cannot go in for hunting, for very soon there would be no animals left to hunt. For other aristocratic amusements like gambling, dueling, and warfare, it may be only too easy to find equivalents in dangerous driving, drug-taking, and senseless acts of violence. Workers seldom commit acts of violence, because they can put their aggression into their work, be it physical like the work of a smith, or mental like the work of a scientist or an artist. The role of aggression in mental work is aptly expressed by the phrase "getting one's teeth into a problem."

Question

Some readers have had trouble following Auden in his first three paragraphs, although by the end of the third paragraph the difficulties have disappeared. Can you summarize the first paragraph in a sentence? If you think that the development of the idea in these first three paragraphs could be clearer, insert the necessary phrases or sentences, or with arrows indicate the places to which sentences should be moved.

The Shoeshine Boy

When I got home, Ella said there had been a telephone 1
call from somebody named Shorty. He had left a message that over at
the Roseland State Ballroom, the shoeshine boy was quitting that night,
and Shorty had told him to hold the job for me.

"Malcolm, you haven't had any experience shining shoes," Ella 2
said. Her expression and tone of voice told me she wasn't happy about
my taking that job. I didn't particularly care, because I was already
speechless thinking about being somewhere close to the greatest bands
in the world. I didn't even wait to eat any dinner.

The ballroom was all lighted when I got there. A man at the front 3
door was letting in members of Benny Goodman's band. I told him I
wanted to see the shoeshine boy, Freddie.

"You're going to be the new one?" he asked. I said I thought I 4
was, and he laughed, "Well, maybe you'll hit the numbers and get a
Cadillac, too." He told me that I'd find Freddie upstairs in the men's
room on the second floor.

But downstairs before I went up, I stepped over and snatched a 5
glimpse inside the ballroom. I just couldn't believe the size of that
waxed floor! At the far end, under the soft, rose-colored lights, was
the bandstand with the Benny Goodman musicians moving around,
laughing and talking, arranging their horns and stands.

A wiry, brown-skinned, conked fellow upstairs in the men's room 6
greeted me. "You Shorty's homeboy?" I said I was, and he said he

---

Malcolm X, born Malcolm Little in Nebraska in 1925, was the son of a Baptist
minister. He completed the eighth grade, but then he got into trouble and was
sent to a reformatory. After his release he became a thief, dope peddler, and
pimp. In 1944 he was sent to jail, where he spent six and a half years. During
his years in jail he became a convert to the Black Muslim faith. Paroled in 1950,
he served as a minister and founded Muslim temples throughout the United
States. In 1964, however, he broke with Elijah Muhammad, leader of the Black
Muslims and a powerful advocate of separation of whites and blacks. Malcolm
X formed a new group, the Organization of Afro-American Unity, but a year later
he was assassinated in New York. His *Autobiography*, written with Alex Haley,
was published in 1964. Haley (b. 1921) is also the author of *Roots*, a study tracing
a black family back through seven generations.

"The Shoeshine Boy" (editors' title) is from *The Autobiography of Malcolm
X*, chapter 3.

---

was Freddie. "Good old boy," he said. "He called me, he just heard I hit the big number, and he figured right I'd be quitting." I told Freddie what the man at the front door had said about a Cadillac. He laughed and said, "Burns them white cats up when you get yourself something. Yeah, I told them I was going to get me one—just to bug them."

Freddie then said for me to pay close attention, that he was going to be busy and for me to watch but not get in the way, and he'd try to get me ready to take over at the next dance, a couple of nights later.

As Freddie busied himself setting up the shoeshine stand, he told me, "Get here early . . . your shoeshine rags and brushes by this footstand . . . your polish bottles, paste wax, suede brushes over here . . . everything in place, you get rushed, you never need to waste motion. . . ."

While you shined shoes, I learned, you also kept watch on customers inside, leaving the urinals. You darted over and offered a small white hand towel. "A lot of cats who ain't planning to wash their hands, sometimes you can run up with a towel and shame them. Your towels are really your best hustle in here. Cost you a penny apiece to launder—you always get at least a nickel tip."

The shoeshine customers, and any from the inside rest room who took a towel, you whiskbroomed a couple of licks. "A nickel or a dime tip, just give 'em that," Freddie said. "But for two bits, Uncle Tom a little—white cats especially like that. I've had them to come back two, three times a dance."

From down below, the sound of the music had begun floating up. I guess I stood transfixed. "You never seen a big dance?" asked Freddie. "Run on awhile, and watch."

There were a few couples already dancing under the rose-covered lights. But even more exciting to me was the crowd thronging in. The most glamorous-looking white women I'd ever seen—young ones, old ones, white cats buying tickets at the window, sticking big wads of green bills back into their pockets, checking the women's coats, and taking their arms and squiring them inside.

Freddie had some early customers when I got back upstairs. Between the shoeshine stand and thrusting towels to me just as they approached the wash basin, Freddie seemed to be doing four things at once. "Here, you can take over the whiskbroom," he said, "just two or three licks—but let 'em feel it."

When things slowed a little, he said, "You ain't seen nothing tonight. You wait until you see a spooks' dance! Man, our own people carry *on*!" Whenever he had a moment, he kept schooling me. "Shoelaces, this drawer here. You just starting out, I'm going to make these to you as a present. Buy them for a nickel a pair, tell cats they need laces if they do, and charge two bits."

Every Benny Goodman record I'd ever heard in my life, it seemed,   15
was filtering faintly into where we were. During another customer lull, Freddie let me slip back outside again to listen. Peggy Lee was at the mike singing. Beautiful! She had just joined the band and she was from North Dakota and had been singing with a group in Chicago when Mrs. Benny Goodman discovered her, we had heard some customers say. She finished the song and the crowd burst into applause. She was a big hit.

"It knocked me out, too, when I first broke in here," Freddie said,   16
grinning, when I went back in there. "But, look, you ever shined any shoes?" He laughed when I said I hadn't, excepting my own. "Well, let's get to work. I never had neither." Freddie got on the stand and went to work on his own shoes. Brush, liquid polish, brush, paste wax, shine rag, lacquer sole dressing . . . step by step, Freddie showed me what to do.

"But you got to get a whole lot faster. You can't waste time!"   17
Freddie showed me how fast on my own shoes. Then, because business was tapering off, he had time to give me a demonstration of how to make the shine rag pop like a firecracker. "Dig the action?" he asked. He did it in slow motion. I got down and tried it on his shoes. I had the principle of it. "Just got to do it faster," Freddie said. "It's a jive noise, that's all. Cats tip better, they figure you're knocking yourself out!"

Questions

1. In this selection Malcolm X is more concerned with Benny Goodman than with learning about shining shoes. Freddie is concerned with teaching Malcolm the trade. What are *we* concerned with in this selection?
2. How would you characterize Freddie's attitude toward his job? Compare it with Maggie Holmes's attitude (pages 262–268) toward her job.
3. In paragraph 17 Freddie demonstrates a "jive noise." Using evidence from this selection, the library, mother wit, or what you will, define "jive."
4. On what date did Malcolm begin his apprenticeship as a shoeshine boy? How did you arrive at that date?

Studs Terkel

Two Workers

I. Terry Mason, Airline Stewardess

She has been an airline stewardess for six years. She is twenty- 1
six-years old, recently married. "The majority of airline stewardesses are from
small towns. I myself am from Nebraska. It's supposed to be one of the nicest
professions for a woman—if she can't be a model or in the movies. All the
great benefits: flying around the world, meeting all those people. It is a nice
status symbol.

"I have five older sisters and they were all married before they were twenty. 2
The minute they got out of high school, they would end up getting married.
That was the thing everybody did, was get married. When I told my parents
I was going to the airlines, they got excited. They were so happy that one of
the girls could go out and see the world and spend some time being single. I
didn't get married until I was almost twenty-five. My mother especially
thought it would be great that I could have the ambition, the nerve to go to
the big city on my own and try to accomplish being a stewardess."

When people ask you what you're doing and you say stewardess, 3
you're really proud, you think it's great. It's like a stepping stone. The
first two months I started flying I had already been to London, Paris,
and Rome. And me from Broken Bow, Nebraska. But after you start
working, it's not as glamorous as you thought it was going to be.

They like girls that have a nice personality and that are pleasant 4
to look at. If a woman has a problem with blemishes, they take her
off. Until the appearance counselor thinks she's ready to go back on.
One day this girl showed up, she had a very slight black eye. They
took her off. Little things like that.

We had to go to stew school for five weeks. We'd go through a 5
whole week of makeup and poise. I didn't like this. They make you

---

Studs Terkel was born Louis Terkel in New York City in 1912. He was brought
up in Chicago and graduated from the University of Chicago. Terkel has been
an actor, playwright, columnist, and disc jockey, but he is best known as the
man who makes books out of tape recordings of people he gets to talk. These
oral histories are *Division Street: America* (1966), *Hard Times* (1970), and *Work-*
ing (1974).

"Two Workers" (editors' title) is from the last of these books.

feel like you've never been out in public. They showed you how to smoke a cigarette, when to smoke a cigarette, how to look at a man's eyes. Our teacher, she had this idea we had to be sexy. One day in class she was showing us how to accept a light for a cigarette from a man and never blow it out. When he lights it, just look in his eyes. It was really funny, all the girls laughed.

It's never proper for a woman to light her own cigarette. You hold it up and of course you're out with a guy who knows the right way to light the cigarette. You look into their eyes as they're lighting your cigarette and you're cupping his hand, but holding it just very light, so that he can feel your touch and your warmth. (Laughs.) You do not blow the match out. It used to be really great for a woman to blow the match out when she looked in his eyes, but she said now the man blows the match out.

The idea is not to be too obvious about it. They don't want you to look too forward. That's the whole thing, being a lady but still giving out that womanly appeal, like the body movement and the lips and the eyes. The guy's supposed to look in your eyes. You could be a real mean woman. You're a lady and doing all these evil things with your eyes.

She did try to promote people smoking. She said smoking can be part of your conversation. If you don't know what to say, you can always pull out a cigarette. She says it makes you more comfortable. I started smoking when I was on the airlines.

Our airline picks the girl-next-door type. At one time they wouldn't let us wear false eyelashes and false fingernails. Now it's required that you wear false eyelashes, and if you do not have the right length nails, you wear false nails. Everything is supposed to be becoming to the passenger.

That's the whole thing: meeting all these great men that either have great business backgrounds or are good looking or different. You do meet a lot of movie stars and a lot of political people, but you don't get to really visit with them that much. You never really get to go out with these men. Stewardesses are impressed only by name people. But a normal millionaire that you don't know you're not impressed about. The only thing that really thrills a stewardess is a passenger like Kennedy or movie stars or somebody political. Celebrities.

I think our average age is twenty-six. But our supervisors tell us what kind of make-up to wear, what kind of lipstick to wear, if our hair is not the right style for us, if we're not smiling enough. They even tell us how to act when you're on a pass. Like last night I met my husband. I was in plain clothes. I wanted to kiss him. But I'm not supposed to kiss anybody at the terminal. You're not supposed to walk off with a passenger, hand in hand. After you get out of the terminal, that's all yours.

The majority of passengers do make passes. The ones that do make passes are married and are business people. When I tell them I'm married, they say, "I'm married and you're married and you're away from home and so am I and nobody's gonna find out." The majority of those who make passes at you, you wouldn't accept a date if they were friends of yours at home. 12

After I was a stewardess for a year, and I was single, I came down to the near North Side of Chicago, which is the swinging place for singles. Stewardess, that was a dirty name. In a big city, it's an easy woman. I didn't like this at all. All these books—*Coffee, Tea and Me*. 13

I lived in an apartment complex where the majority there were stewardesses.[1] The other women were secretaries and teachers. They would go to our parties and they would end up being among the worst. They never had stories about these secretaries and nurses, but they sure had good ones about stewardesses. 14

I meet a lot of other wives or single women. The first minute they start talking to me, they're really cold. They think the majority of stewardesses are snobs or they may be jealous. These women think we have a great time, that we are playgirls, that we have the advantage to go out with every type of man we want. So when they first meet us, they really turn off on us. 15

When you first start flying, the majority of girls do live in apartment complexes by the airport. The men they meet are airport employees: ramp rats, cleaning airplanes and things like that, mechanics, and young pilots, not married, ones just coming in fresh. 16

After a year we get tired of that, so we move into the city to get involved with men that are usually young executives, like at Xerox or something. Young businessmen in the early thirties and late twenties, they really think stewardesses are the gals to go out with if they want to get so far. They wear their hats and their suits and in the winter their black gloves. The women are getting older, they're getting twenty-four, twenty-five. They get involved with bartenders too. Stewardesses and bartenders are a pair. (Laughs.) 17

[1] "In New York, stewardesses live five or six girls to one apartment. They think they can get by because they're in and out so much. But there's gonna be a few nights they're all gonna be home at once and a couple of 'em will have to sleep on the floor."

One time I went down into the area of swinging bars with two other girls. We just didn't want anybody to know that we were stewardesses, so we had this story made up that we were going to a women's college in Colorado. That went over. We had people that were talking to us, being nice to us, being polite. Down there, they wouldn't even be polite. They'd buy you drinks but then they'd steal your stool if you got up to go to the restroom. But when they knew you weren't stewardesses, just young ladies that were going to a women's college, they were really nice to us.

They say you can spot a stewardess by the way she wears her makeup. At that time we all had short hair and everybody had it cut in stew school exactly alike. If there's two blondes they have their hair cut very short, wearing the same shade of makeup, and they get into uniform, people say, "Oh, you look like sisters." Wonder why? (Laughs.)

The majority of us were against it because they wouldn't let you say how *you'd* like your hair cut, they wouldn't let you have your own personality, *your* makeup, *your* clothes. They'd tell you what length skirts to wear. At one time they told us we couldn't wear anything one inch above the knees. And no pants at that time. It's different now.

Wigs used to be forbidden. Now it's the style. Now it's permissible for nice women to wear wigs, eyelashes, and false fingernails. Before it was the harder looking women that wore them. Women showing up in pants, it wasn't ladylike. Hot pants are in now. Most airlines change styles every year.

She describes stewardess schools in the past as being like college dorms: it was forbidden to go out during the week; signing in and out on Friday and Saturday nights. "They've cut down stewardess school quite a bit. Cut down on how-to-serve meal classes and paperwork. A lot of girls get on aircraft these days and don't know where a magazine is, where the tray tables are for passengers. . . . Every day we used to have an examination. If you missed over two questions, that was a failure. They'd ask us ten questions. If you failed two tests out of the whole five weeks, you would have to leave. Now they don't have any exams at all. Usually we get a raise every year. We haven't been getting that lately."

We have long duty hours. We can be on duty for thirteen hours. But we're not supposed to fly over eight hours. This is in a twenty-four-hour period. During the eight hours, you could be flying from

Chicago to Flint, to Moline, short runs. You stop twenty minutes. So you get to New York finally, after five stops, let's say. You have an hour on your own. But you have to be on the plane thirty minutes before departure time. How many restaurants can serve you food in thirty minutes? So you've gone thirteen hours, off and on duty, having half-hours and no time to eat. This is the normal thing. If we have only thirty minutes and we don't have time to eat, it's our hard luck.

Pilots have the same thing too. They end up grabbing a sandwich 24 and eating in the cockpit. When I first started flying we were not supposed to eat at all on the aircraft, even though there was an extra meal left over. Now we can eat in the buffet. We have to stand there with all those dirty dishes and eat our meals—if there's one left over. We cannot eat in the public eye. We cannot bring it out if there's an extra seat. You can smoke in the cockpit, in the restrooms, but not in the public's eye.

꣠

"We have a union. It's a division of the pilot's union. It helps us out on 25 *duty time and working privileges. It makes sure that if we're in Cleveland and stuck because of weather and thirteen hours have gone by, we can go to bed. Before we had a union the stew office would call and say, 'You're working another seven.' I worked one time thirty-six hours straight."*

The other day I had fifty-five minutes to serve 101 coach passen- 26 gers, a cocktail and full-meal service. You do it fast and terrible. You're very rude. You don't mean to be rude, you just don't have time to answer questions. You smile and you just ignore it. You get three drink orders in a hurry. There's been many times when you miss the glass, pouring, and you pour it in the man's lap. You just don't say I'm sorry. You give him a cloth and you keep going. That's the bad part of the job.

Sometimes I get tired of working first class. These people think 27 they're great, paying for more, and want more. Also I get tired of coach passengers asking for something that he thinks he's a first-class passenger. We get this attitude of difference from our airlines. They're just dividing the class of people. If we're on a first-class pass, the women are to wear a dress or a nice pants suit that has a matching jacket, and the men are to dress with suit jacket and tie and white shirt. And yet so many types of first-class passengers: some have grubby clothes, jeans and moccasins and everything. They can afford to dress the way they feel. . . .

If I want to fly first class, I pay the five dollars difference. I like 28
the idea of getting free drinks, free champagne, free wine. In a coach,
you don't. A coach passenger might say, "Could I have a pillow?" So
you give him a pillow. Then he'll say, "Could you bring me a glass
of water?" A step behind him there's the water fountain. In first class,
if the guy says, "I want a glass of water," even if the water fountain
is right by his arm, you'd bring it for him. We give him all this extra
because he's first class. Which isn't fair. . . .

When you're in a coach, you feel like there's just heads and heads 29
and heads of people. That's all you can see. In first class, being less
people, you're more relaxed, you have more time. When you get on
a 727, we have one coatroom. Our airline tells us you hang up first-
class coats only. When a coach passenger says, "Could you hang up
my coat?" most of the time I'll hang it up. Why should I hang up first
class and not coach?

One girl is for first class only and there's two girls for coach. The 30
senior girl will be first class. That first-class girl gets used to working
first class. If she happens to walk through the coach, if someone asks
her for something, she'll make the other girls do it. The first stew
always stays at the door and welcomes everybody aboard and says
good-by to everybody when they leave. That's why a lot of girls don't
like to be first class.

There's an old story on the airline. The stewardess asks if he'd like 31
something to drink, him and his wife. He says, "I'd like a martini."
The stewardess asks the wife, "Would you like a drink?" She doesn't
say anything, and the husband says, "I'm sorry, she's not used to
talking to the help." (Laughs.) When I started flying, that was the first
story I heard.

I've never had the nerve to speak up to anybody that's pinched 32
me or said something dirty. Because I've always been afraid of these
onion letters. These are bad letters. If you get a certain amount of bad
letters, you're fired. When you get a bad letter you have to go in and
talk to the supervisor. Other girls now, there are many of 'em that are
coming around and telling them what they feel. The passenger reacts:
She's telling me off! He doesn't believe it. Sometimes the passenger
needs it.

One guy got his steak and he said, "This is too medium, I want 33
mine rarer." The girl said, "I'm sorry, I don't cook the food, it's pre-
cooked." He picked up the meal and threw it on the floor. She says,
"If you don't pick the meal up right now, I'll make sure the crew

members come back here and make you pick it up." (With awe) She's talking right back at him and loud, right in front of everybody. He really didn't think she would yell at him. Man, he picked up the meal. . . . The younger girls don't take that guff any more, like we used to. When the passenger is giving you a bad time, you talk back to him.

It's always: the passenger is right. When a passenger says some- 34 thing mean, we're supposed to smile and say, "I understand." We're supposed to *really* smile because stewardesses' supervisors have been getting reports that the girls have been back-talking passengers. Even when they pinch us or say dirty things, we're supposed to smile at them. That's one thing they taught us at stew school. Like he's rubbing your body somewhere, you're supposed to just put his hand down and not say anything and smile at him. That's the main thing, smile.

When I first went to class, they told me I had a crooked smile. She 35 showed me how to smile. She said, "Kinda press a little smile on"— which I did. "Oh, that's great," she said, "that's a *good* smile." But I couldn't do it. I didn't feel like I was doing it on my own. Even if we're sad, we're supposed to have a smile on our face.

I came in after a flight one day, my grandfather had died. Usually 36 they call you up or meet you at the flight and say, "We have some bad news for you." I pick up this piece of paper in my mailbox and it says, "Mother called in. Your grandfather died today." It was written like, say, two cups of sugar. Was I mad! They wouldn't give me time off for the funeral. You can only have time off for your parents or somebody you have lived with. I have never lived with my grandparents. I went anyway.

A lot of our girls are teachers, nurses, everything. They do this 37 part-time, 'cause you have enough time off for another kind of job. I personally work for conventions. I work electronic and auto shows. Companies hire me to stay in their booth and talk about products. I have this speech to tell. At others, all I do is pass out matches or candy. Nowadays every booth has a young girl in it.

People just love to drink on airplanes. They feel adventurous. So 38 you're serving drinks and meals and there's very few times that you can sit down. If she does sit down, she's forgotten how to sit down and talk to passengers. I used to play bridge with passengers. But that doesn't happen any more. We're not supposed to be sitting down, or have a magazine or read a newspaper. If it's a flight from Boston to Los Angeles, you're supposed to have a half an hour talking to passengers. But the only time we can sit down is when we go to the cockpit. You're not supposed to spend any more than five minutes up there for a cigarette.

We could be sitting down on our jump seat and if you had a su-   39
pervisor on board, she would write you up—for not mixing with the crowd. We're supposed to be told when she walks on board. Many times you don't know. They do have personnel that ride the flights that don't give their names—checking, and they don't tell you about it. Sometimes a girl gets caught smoking in the cabin. Say it's a long flight, maybe a night flight. You're playing cards with a passenger and you say, "Would it bother you if I smoke?" And he says no. She would write you up and get you fired for smoking in the airplane.

They have a limit on how far you can mix. They want you to be   40
sociable, but if he offers you a cigarette, not to take it. When you're outside, they encourage you to take cigarettes.

You give your time to everybody, you share it, not too much with   41
one passenger. Everybody else may be snoring away and there's three guys, maybe military, and they're awake 'cause they're going home and excited. So you're playing cards with 'em. If you have a supervisor on, that would be a no-no. They call a lot of things no-no's.

They call us professional people but they talk to us as very young,   42
childishly. They check us all the time on appearance. They check our weight every month. Even though you've been flying twenty years, they check you and say that's a no-no. If you're not spreading yourself around passengers enough, that's a no-no. Not hanging up first-class passenger's coats, that's a no-no, even though there's no room in the coatroom. You're supposed to somehow make room. If you're a pound over, they can take you off flight until you get under.

Accidents? I've never yet been so scared that I didn't want to get   43
in the airplane. But there've been times at take-offs, there's been something funny. Here I am thinking, What if I die today? I've got too much to do. I can't die today. I use it as a joke.

I've had emergencies where I've had to evacuate the aircraft. I was   44
coming back from Las Vegas and being a lively stewardess I stayed up all night, gambled. We had a load full of passengers. The captain tells me we're going to have an emergency landing in Chicago because we lost a pin out of the nose gear. When we land, the nose gear is gonna collapse. He wants me to prepare the whole cabin for the landing, but not for two more hours. And not to tell the other stewardesses, because they were new girls and would get all excited. So I had to keep this in me for two more hours, wondering, Am I gonna die today?

And this is Easter Sunday. And I was serving the passengers drinks and food and this guy got mad at me because his omelet was too cold. And I was gonna say, "You just wait, buddy, you're not gonna worry about that omelet." But I was nice about it, because I didn't want to have trouble with a passenger, especially when I have to prepare him for an emergency.

I told the passengers over the intercom: "The captain says it's just   45
a precaution, there's nothing to worry about." I'm just gonna explain how to get out of the airplane fast, how to be in a braced position. They can't wear glasses or high heels, purses, things out of aisles, under the seats. And make sure everybody's pretty quiet. We had a blind woman on with a dog. We had to get people to help her off and all this stuff.

They were fantastic. Nobody screamed, cried, or hollered. When   46
we got on the ground, everything was fine. The captain landed perfect. But there was a little jolt, and the passengers started screaming and hollering: They held it all back and all of a sudden we got on the ground, blah.

I was great. (Laughs.) That's what was funny. I thought, I have   47
a husband now. I don't know how he would take it, my dying on an airplane. So I thought, I can't die. When I got on the intercom, I was so calm. Also we're supposed to keep a smile on our face. Even during an emergency, you're supposed to walk through the cabin and make everybody feel comfortable with a smile. When you're on the jump seat everybody's looking at you. You're supposed to sit there, holding your ankles, in a position to get out of that airplane fast with a big fat smile on your face.

Doctors tell stewardesses two bad things about them. They're   48
gonna get wrinkles all over their face because they smile with their mouth and their eyes. And also with the pressurization on the airplane, we're not supposed to get up while we're climbing because it causes varicose veins in our legs. So they say being a stewardess ruins your looks.

A lot of stewardesses wanted to be models. The Tanya girl used   49
to be a stewardess on our airline. A stewardess is what they could get and a model is what they couldn't get. They weren't the type of person, they weren't that beautiful, they weren't that thin. So their second choice would be stewardess.

What did you want to be? I wanted to get out of Broken Bow, Nebraska.   50
(Laughs.)

POSTSCRIPT: *"Everytime I go home, they all meet me at the airplane. Not one* 51
of my sisters has been on an airplane. All their children think that Terry is
just fantastic, because their mom and dad—my sisters and their husbands—
feel so stupid. 'Look at us. I wish I could have done that.' I know they feel
bad, that they never had the chance. But they're happy I can come home and
tell them about things. I send them things from Europe. They get to tell all
their friends that their sister's a stewardess. They get real excited about that.
The first thing they come out and say, 'One of my sisters is a stewardess.'

"My father got a promotion with his company and they wrote in their 52
business news that he had a family of seven, six girls and a boy, and one girl
is a stewardess in Chicago. And went on to say what I did, and didn't say a
word about anything else."[2]

II. Maggie Holmes, Domestic

What bugs me now, since I'm on welfare, is people saying 53
they give you the money for nothin'. When I think back what we had
to come through, up from the South, comin' here. The hard work we
had to do. It really gets me, when I hear people . . . It do somethin'
to me. I think violence.

I think what we had to work for. I used to work for $1.50 a week. 54
This is five days a week, sometimes six. If you live in the servant
quarter, your time is never off, because if they decide to have a party
at night, you gotta come out. My grandmother, I remember when she
used to work, we'd get milk and a pound of butter. I mean this was
pay. I'm thinkin' about what my poor parents worked for, gettin' nothing. What do the white think about when they think? Do they ever
think about what *they* would do?

She had worked as a domestic, hotel chambermaid, and as "kitchen help in 55
cafés" for the past twenty-five years, up North and down South. She lives
with her four children.

When it come to housework, I can't do it now. I can't stand it, 56
cause it do somethin' to my mind. They want you to clean the house,
want you to wash, even the windows, want you to iron. You not
supposed to wash no dishes. You ain't supposed to make no beds up.
Lots of 'em try to sneak it in on you, think you don't know that. So
the doorbell rings and I didn't answer to. The bell's ringin' and I'm

[2]Questions on this selection appear on page 269.

still doin' my work. She ask me why I don't answer the bell, I say; "Do I come here to be a butler?" And I don't see myself to be no doormaid. I came to do some work, and I'm gonna do my work. When you end up, you's nursemaid, you's cook. They puts all this on you. If you want a job to cleanin', you ask for just cleanin'. She wants you to do in one day what she hasn't did all year.

Now this bug me: the first thing she gonna do is pull out this [57] damn rubber thing—just fittin' for your knees. Knee pads—like you're workin' in the fields, like people pickin' cotton. No mop or nothin'. That's why you find so many black women here got rheumatism in their legs, knees. When you get on that cold floor, I don't care how warm the house is, you can feel the cold on the floor, the water and stuff. I never see nobody on their knees until I come North. In the South, they had mops. Most times, if they had real heavy work, they always had a man to come in. Washin' windows, that's a man's job. They don't think nothin' about askin' you to do that here. They don't have no feeling that that's what bothers you. I think to myself; My God, if I had somebody come and do my floors, clean up for me, I'd appreciate it. They don't say nothin' about it. Act like you haven't even done anything. They has no feelin's.

I worked for one old hen on Lake Shore Drive. You remember [58] that big snow they had there?[3] Remember when you couldn't get there? When I gets to work she says: "Call the office." She complained to the lady where I got the job, said I was late to work. So I called. So I said, in the phone (Shouts), *"What do you want with me?* I got home four black, beautiful kids. Before I go to anybody's job in the morning I see that my kids are at school. I gonna see that they have warm clothes on and they fed." I'm lookin' right at the woman I'm workin' for. (Laughs.) When I get through the phone I tell this employer: "That goes for you too. The only thing I live for is my kids. There's nothin', you and nobody else." The expression on her face: What is this? (Laughs.) She thought I was gonna be like (mimics "Aunt Jemima"): "Yes ma'am, I'll try to get here a little early." But it wasn't like that. (Laughs.)

When I come in the door that day she told me pull my shoes off. [59] I said, "For what? I can wipe my feet at the door here, but I'm not gettin' out of my shoes, it's cold." She look at me like she said: Oh

---

[3]It was the week of Chicago's Big Snow-In, beginning January 25, 1967. Traffic was hopelessly snarled. Scores of thousands couldn't get to work.

my God, what I got here? (Laughs.) I'm knowin' I ain't gonna make no eight hours here. I can't take it.

She had everything in there snow white. And that means work, 60 believe me. In the dining room she had a blue set, she had sky-blue chairs. They had a bedroom with pink and blue. I look and say, "I know what this means." It means sho' 'nough—knees. I said, "I'm gonna try and make it today, *if* I can make it." Usually when they're so bad, you have to leave.

I ask her where the mop is. She say she don't have no mop. I 61 said, "Don't tell me you mop the floor on your knees. I know you don't." They usually hid these mops in the clothes closet. I go out behind all these clothes and get the mop out. (Laughs.) They don't get on their knees, but they don't think nothin' about askin' a black woman. She says, "All you—you girls. . . ." She stop. I say, "All you *niggers,* is that what you want to say?" She give me this stupid look. I say, "I'm glad you tellin' me that there's more like me." (Laughs.) I told her, "You better give me my money and let me go, 'cause I'm gettin' angry. So I made her give me my carfare and what I had worked that day.

Most when you find decent work is when you find one that work 62 themselves. They know what it's like to get up in the morning and go to work. In the suburbs they ain't got nothin' to do. They has nothin' else to think about. Their mind's just about blowed.

It's just like they're talkin' about mental health. Poor people's 63 mental health is different than the rich white. Mine could come from a job or not havin' enough money for my kids. Mine is from me being poor. That don't mean you're sick. His sickness is from money, graftin' where he want more. I don't have *any.* You live like that day to day, penny to penny.

I worked for a woman, her husband's a judge. I cleaned the whole 64 house. When it was time for me to go home, she decided she wants some ironing. She goes in the basement, she turn on the air conditioner. She said, "I think you can go down in the basement and finish your day out. It's air conditioned." I said, "I don't care what you got down there, I'm not ironing. You look at that slip, it says cleanin'. Don't say no ironin'. She wanted me to wash the walls in the bathroom. I said, "If you look at that telephone book they got all kinds of ads there under house cleanin'." She said the same thing as the other one, "All you girls—" I said same thing I said to the other one; "You mean niggers." (Laughs.)

They ever call you by your last name?   65

Oh God, they wouldn't do that. (Laughs.)   66

Do you call her by her last name?   67

Most time I don't call her, period. I don't say anything to her. I don't   68
talk nasty to nobody, but when I go to work I don't talk to people.
Most time they don't like what you're gonna say. So I keeps quiet.

Most of her jobs were "way out in the suburbs. You get a bus and you ride   69
till you get a subway. After you gets to Howard,[4] you gets the El. If you get
to the end of the line and there's no bus, they pick you up. I don't like to work
in the city, 'cause they don't pay you nothin.' And these old buildings are so
nasty. It takes so much time to clean 'em. They are not kept up so good, like
suburbs. Most of the new homes out there, it's easier to clean."

A commonly observed phenomenon: during the early evening hour, trains,   70
crowded, predominantly by young white men carrying attaché cases, pass
trains headed in the opposite direction, crowded, predominantly by middle-
aged black women carrying brown paper bags. Neither group, it appears,
glances at the other.
　　"We spend most of the time ridin'. You get caught goin' out from the   71
suburbs at nighttime, man, you're really sittin' there for hours. There's nothin'
movin'. You got a certain hour to meet trains. You get a transfer, you have
to get that train. It's a shuffle to get in and out of the job. If you miss that
train at five o'clock, what time you gonna get out that end? Sometime you
don't get home till eight o'clock. . . ."

　　You don't feel like washin' your own window when you come   72
from out there, scrubbin'. If you work in one of them houses eight
hours, you gotta come home do the same thing over . . . you don't
feel like . . . (sighs softly) . . . tired. You gotta come home, take care
of your kids, you gotta cook, you gotta wash. Most of the time, you
gotta wash for the kids for somethin' to wear to school. You gotta clean
up, 'cause you didn't have time in the morning. You gotta wash and
iron and whatever you do, nights. You be so tired, until you don't feel
like even doin' nothin'.

　　You get up at six, you fix breakfast for the kids, you get them   73
ready to go on to school. Leave home about eight. Most of the time I
make biscuits for my kids, cornbread you gotta make. I don't mean
the canned kind. This I don't call cookin', when you go in that refrig-

[4]The boundary line separating Chicago from the North Shore suburb, Evanston.

erator and get some beans and drop 'em in a pot. And TV dinners, they go stick 'em in the stove and she say she cooked. This is not cookin'.

And *she's* tired. Tired from doin' what? You got a washing dryer, 74 you got an electric sweeper, anything at fingertips. All she gotta do is unfroze 'em, dump 'em in the pot, and she's tired! I go to the store, I get my vegetables, greens, I wash 'em. I gotta pick 'em first. I don't eat none of that stuff, like in the cans. She don't do that, and she says she's tired.

When you work for them, when you get in that house in the 75 morning, boy, they got one arm in their coat and a scarf on their head. And when you open that door, she shoots by you, she's gone. Know what I mean? They want you to come there and keep the kids and let them get out. What she think about how am I gonna do? Like I gets tired of my kids too. I'd like to go out too. It bugs you to think that they don't have no feelin's about that.

Most of the time I work for them and they be out. I don't like to 76 work for 'em when they be in the house so much. They don't have no work to do. All they do is get on the telephone and talk about one another. Make you sick. I'll go and close the door. They're all the same, everybody's house is the same. You think they rehearse it . . .

When I work, only thing I be worryin' about is my kids. I just 77 don't like to leave 'em too long. When they get out of school, you wonder if they out on the street. The only thing I worry is if they had a place to play in easy. I always call two, three times. When she don't like you to call, I'm in a hurry to get out of there. (Laughs.) My mind is gettin' home, what are you gonna find to cook before the stores close.

This Nixon was sayin' he don't see nothin' wrong with people 78 doin' scrubbin'. For generations that's all we done. He should know we wants to be doctors and teachers and lawyers like him. I don't want my kids to come up and do domestic work. It's degrading. You can't see no tomorrow there. We done this for generation and generation— cooks and butlers all your life. They want their kids to be lawyers, doctors, and things. You don't want 'em in no cafés workin'. . . .

When they say about the neighborhood we live in is dirty, why 79 do they ask me to come and clean their house? We, the people in the slums, the same nasty women they have come to their house in the suburbs every day. If these women are so filthy, why you want them to clean for you? They don't go and clean for us. We go and clean for them.

I worked one day where this white person did some housework.   80
I'm lookin' at the difference how she with me and her. She had a guilt
feeling towards that lady. They feel they shouldn't ask them to do this
type of work, but they don't mind askin' me.

They want you to get in a uniform. You take me and my mother,   81
she work in what she wear. She tells you, "If that place so dirty where
I can't wear my dress, I won't do the job." You can't go to work dressed
like they do, 'cause they think you're not working—like you should
get dirty, at least. They don't say what kind of uniform, just say uniform. This is in case anybody come in, the black be workin'. They
don't want you walkin' around dressed up, lookin' like them. They
asks you sometimes, "Don't you have somethin' else to put on?" I
say, "No, 'cause I'm not gettin' on my knees."

They move with caution now, believe me. They want to know,   82
"What should I call you?" I say, "Don't call me a Negro, I'm black."
So they say, "Okay, I don't want to make you angry with me."
(Laughs.) The old-timers, a lot of 'em was real religious. "Lord'll make
a way." I say, "I'm makin' my own way." I'm not anti-Bible or anti-
God, but I just let 'em know I don't think thataway.

The younger women, they don't pay you too much attention.   83
Most of 'em work. The older women, they behind you, wiping. I don't
like nobody checkin' behind me. When you go to work, they want to
show you how to clean. That really gets me, somebody showin' me
how to clean. I been doin' it all my life. They come and get the rag
and show you how to do it. (Laughs.) I stand there, look at 'em. Lotta
times I ask her, "You finished?" I say, "If there's anything you gotta
go and do, I wish you'd go." I don't need nobody to show me how
to clean.

I had them put money down and pretend they can't find it and   84
have me look for it. I worked for one, she had dropped ten dollars on
the floor, and I was sweepin' and I'm glad I seen it, because if I had
put that sweeper on it, she coulda said I got it. I had to push the couch
back and the ten dollars was there. Oh, I had 'em, when you go to
dust, they put something . . . to test you.

I worked at a hotel. A hotel's the same thing. You makin' beds,   85
scrubbin' toilets, and things. You gotta put in linens and towels. You
still cleanin'. When people come in the room—that's what bugs me—
they give you that look: You just a maid. It do somethin' to me. It
really gets into me.

Some of the guests are nice. The only thing you try to do is to   86
hurry up and get this bed made and get outa here, 'cause they'll get

you to do somethin' else. If they take that room, they want everything they paid for. (Laughs.) They get so many towels, they can't use 'em all. But you gotta put up all those towels. They want that pillow, they want that blanket. You gotta be trottin' back and forth and gettin' all those things.

In the meantime, when they have the hotel full, we put in extra 87 beds—the little foldin' things. They say they didn't order the bed. They stand and look at you like you crazy. Now you gotta take this bed back all the way from the twelfth floor to the second. The guy at the desk, he got the wrong room. He don't say, "I made a mistake." You take the blame.

And you get some guys . . . you can't work with afightin' 'em. 88 He'll call down and say he wants some towels. When you knock, he says, "Come in." He's standing there without a stitch of clothes on, buck naked. You're not goin' in there. You only throw those towels and go back. Most of the time you wait till he got out of there.

When somethin's missin', it's always the maid took it. If we find 89 one of those type people, we tell the house lady, "You have to go in there and clean it yourself." If I crack that door, and nobody's in, I wouldn't go in there. If a girl had been in there, they would call and tell you, "Did you see something?" They won't say you got it. It's the same thing. You say no. They say, "It *musta* been in there."

Last summer I worked at a place and she missed a purse. I didn't 90 work on that floor that day. She called the office, "Did you see that lady's purse?" I said, "No, I haven't been in the room." He asked me again, Did I . . .? I had to stay till twelve o'clock. She found it. It was under some papers. I quit, 'cause they end up sayin' you stole somethin'.

You know what I wanted to do all my life? I wanted to play piano. 91 And I'd want to write songs and things, that's what I really wanted to do. If I could just get myself enough to buy a piano. . . . And I'd like to write about my life, if I could sit long enough: How I growed up in the South and my grandparents and my father—I'd like to do that. I would like to dig up more of black history, too. I would love to for my kids.

Lotta times I'm tellin' 'em about things, they'll be sayin', "Mom, 92 that's olden days." (Laughs.) They don't understand, because it's so far from what happening now. Mighty few young black women are doin' domestic work. And I'm glad. That's why I want my kids to go to school. This one lady told me, "All you people are gettin' like that." I said, "I'm glad." There's no more gettin' on their knees.

Questions

Terry Mason, Airline Stewardess
1. How satisfied is Terry Mason with her job? What are the sources of her satisfactions? Her dissatisfactions? Try to sketch her values, and to characterize her.
2. Using Mason's remarks as evidence, evaluate the training program for stewardesses (now called flight attendants). Is it intelligent? Is it immoral? Do you think that after stew school the airlines deal fairly with the stewardesses?
3. Has this selection changed your idea of the job of a stewardess? If so, in what ways?

Maggie Holmes, Domestic
1. How do you account for the difference in treatment (paragraph 57) of domestic help in the North and the South?
2. What evidence is there that Holmes is witty? resourceful? insightful?
3. How would you describe Holmes's attitude toward suburban housewives? Does it make sense?

Virginia Woolf

Professions for Women

When your secretary invited me to come here, she told   1
me that your Society is concerned with the employment of women and
she suggested that I might tell you something about my own professional experiences. It is true I am a woman; it is true I am employed,
but what professional experiences have I had? It is difficult to say. My
profession is literature; and in that profession there are fewer experiences for women than in any other, with the exception of the stage—
fewer, I mean, that are peculiar to women. For the road was cut many
years ago—by Fanny Burney, by Aphra Behn, by Harriet Martineau,
by Jane Austen, by George Eliot—many famous women, and many
more unknown and forgotten, have been before me, making the path
smooth, and regulating my steps. Thus, when I came to write, there
were very few material obstacles in my way. Writing was a reputable
and harmless occupation. The family peace was not broken by the
scratching of a pen. No demand was made upon the family purse. For
ten and sixpence one can buy paper enough to write all the plays of
Shakespeare—if one has a mind that way. Pianos and models, Paris,
Vienna and Berlin, masters and mistresses, are not needed by a writer.
The cheapness of writing paper is, of course, the reason why women
have succeeded as writers before they have succeeded in the other
professions.

But to tell you my story—it is a simple one. You have only got to   2
figure to yourselves a girl in a bedroom with a pen in her hand. She
had only to move that pen from left to right—from ten o'clock to one.
Then it occurred to her to do what is simple and cheap enough after
all—to slip a few of those pages into an envelope, fix a penny stamp
in the corner, and drop the envelope in the red box at the corner. It
was thus that I became a journalist; and my effort was rewarded on
the first day of the following month—a very glorious day it was for

Virginia Woolf (1882–1941) was born in London into an upper-middle-class literary family. In 1912 she married a writer, and with him she founded the Hogarth
Press, whose important publications included not only books by T. S. Eliot but
her own novels.

This essay was originally a talk delivered in 1931 to The Women's Service
League.

me—by a letter from an editor containing a check for one pound ten shillings and sixpence. But to show you how little I deserve to be called a professional woman, how little I know of the struggles and difficulties of such lives, I have to admit that instead of spending that sum upon bread and butter, rent, shoes and stockings, or butcher's bills, I went out and bought a cat—a beautiful cat, a Persian cat, which very soon involved me in bitter disputes with my neighbors.

What could be easier than to write articles and to buy Persian cats   3
with the profits? But wait a moment. Articles have to be about something. Mine, I seem to remember, was about a novel by a famous man. And while I was writing this review, I discovered that if I were going to review books I should need to do battle with a certain phantom. And the phantom was a woman, and when I came to know her better I called her after the heroine of a famous poem, The Angel in the House. It was she who used to come between me and my paper when I was writing reviews. It was she who bothered me and wasted my time and so tormented me that at last I killed her. You who come of a younger and happier generation may not have heard of her—you may not know what I mean by the Angel in the House. I will describe her as shortly as I can. She was intensely sympathetic. She was immensely charming. She was utterly unselfish. She excelled in the difficult arts of family life. She sacrificed herself daily. If there was chicken, she took the leg; if there was a draught she sat in it—in short she was so constituted that she never had a mind or a wish of her own, but preferred to sympathize always with the minds and wishes of others. Above all—I need not say it—she was pure. Her purity was supposed to be her chief beauty—her blushes, her great grace. In those days—the last of Queen Victoria—every house had its Angel. And when I came to write I encountered her with the very first words. The shadow of her wings fell on my page; I heard the rustling of her skirts in the room. Directly, that is to say, I took my pen in hand to review that novel by a famous man, she slipped behind me and whispered: "My dear, you are a young woman. You are writing about a book that has been written by a man. Be sympathetic; be tender; flatter; deceive; use all the arts and wiles of our sex. Never let anybody guess that you have a mind of your own. Above all, be pure." And she made as if to guide my pen. I now record the one act for which I take some credit to myself, though the credit rightly belongs to some excellent ancestors of mine who left me a certain sum of money—shall we say five hundred pounds a year?—so that it was not necessary for me to depend solely on charm for my living. I turned upon her and caught her by the throat.

I did my best to kill her. My excuse, if I were to be had up in a court of law, would be that I acted in self-defense. Had I not killed her she would have killed me. She would have plucked the heart out of my writing. For, as I found, directly I put pen to paper, you cannot review even a novel without having a mind of your own, without expressing what you think to be the truth about human relations, morality, sex. And all these questions, according to the Angel in the House, cannot be dealt with freely and openly by women; they must charm, they must conciliate, they must—to put it bluntly—tell lies if they are to succeed. Thus, whenever I felt the shadow of her wing or the radiance of her halo upon my page, I took up the inkpot and flung it at her. She died hard. Her fictitious nature was of great assistance to her. It is far harder to kill a phantom than a reality. She was always creeping back when I thought I had despatched her. Though I flatter myself that I killed her in the end, the struggle was severe; it took much time that had better have been spent upon learning Greek grammar; or in roaming the world in search of adventures. But it was a real experience; it was an experience that was bound to befall all women writers at that time. Killing the Angel in the House was part of the occupation of a woman writer.

But to continue my story. The Angel was dead; what then re-   4
mained? You may say that what remained was a simple and common object—a young woman in a bedroom with an inkpot. In other words, now that she had rid herself of falsehood, that young woman had only to be herself. Ah, but what is "herself"? I mean, what is a woman? I assure you, I do not know. I do not believe that you know. I do not believe that anybody can know until she has expressed herself in all the arts and professions open to human skill. That indeed is one of the reasons why I have come here—out of respect for you, who are in process of showing us by your experiments what a woman is, who are in process of providing us, by your failures and successes, with that extremely important piece of information.

But to continue the story of my professional experiences. I made   5
one pound ten and six by my first review; and I bought a Persian cat with the proceeds. Then I grew ambitious. A Persian cat is all very well, I said; but a Persian cat is not enough. I must have a motor car. And it was thus that I became a novelist—for it is a very strange thing that people will give you a motor car if you will tell them a story. It is a still stranger thing that there is nothing so delightful in the world as telling stories. It is far pleasanter than writing reviews of famous

novels. And yet, if I am to obey your secretary and tell you my professional experiences as a novelist, I must tell you about a very strange experience that befell me as a novelist. And to understand it you must try first to imagine a novelist's state of mind. I hope I am not giving away professional secrets if I say that a novelist's chief desire is to be as unconscious as possible. He has to induce in himself a state of perpetual lethargy. He wants life to proceed with the utmost quiet and regularity. He wants to see the same faces, to read the same books, to do the same things day after day, month after month, while he is writing, so that nothing may break the illusion in which he is living— so that nothing may disturb or disquiet the mysterious nosings about, feelings round, darts, dashes and sudden discoveries of that very shy and illusive spirit, the imagination. I suspect that this state is the same both for men and women. Be that as it may, I want you to imagine me writing a novel in a state of trance. I want you to figure to yourselves a girl sitting with a pen in her hand, which for minutes, and indeed for hours, she never dips into the inkpot. The image that comes to my mind when I think of this girl is the image of a fisherman lying sunk in dreams on the verge of a deep lake with a rod held out over the water. She was letting her imagination sweep unchecked round every rock and cranny of the world that lies submerged in the depths of our unconscious being. Now came the experience, the experience that I believe to be far commoner with women writers than with men. The line raced through the girl's fingers. Her imagination had rushed away. It had sought the pools, the depths, the dark places where the largest fish slumber. And then there was a smash. There was an explosion. There was foam and confusion. The imagination had dashed itself against something hard. The girl was roused from her dream. She was indeed in a state of the most acute and difficult distress. To speak without figure she had thought of something, something about the body, about the passions which it was unfitting for her as a woman to say. Men, her reason told her, would be shocked. The consciousness of what men will say of a woman who speaks the truth about her passions had roused her from her artist's state of unconsciousness. She could write no more. The trance was over. Her imagination could work no longer. This I believe to be a very common experience with women writers—they are impeded by the extreme conventionality of the other sex. For though men sensibly allow themselves great freedom in these respects, I doubt that they realize or can control the extreme severity with which they condemn such freedom in women.

These then were two very genuine experiences of my own. These 6
were two of the adventures of my professional life. The first—killing
the Angel in the House—I think I solved. She died. But the second,
telling the truth about my own experiences as a body, I do not think
I solved. I doubt that any woman has solved it yet. The obstacles
against her are still immensely powerful—and yet they are very difficult to define. Outwardly, what is simpler than to write books? Outwardly, what obstacles are there for a woman rather than for a man?
Inwardly, I think, the case is very different; she has still many ghosts
to fight, many prejudices to overcome. Indeed it will be a long time
still, I think, before a woman can sit down to write a book without
finding a phantom to be slain, a rock to be dashed against. And if this
is so in literature, the freest of all professions for women, how is it in
the new professions which you are now for the first time entering?

Those are the questions that I should like, had I time, to ask you. 7
And indeed, if I have laid stress upon these professional experiences
of mine, it is because I believe that they are, though in different forms,
yours also. Even when the path is nominally open—when there is
nothing to prevent a woman from being a doctor, a lawyer, a civil
servant—there are many phantoms and obstacles, as I believe, looming
in her way. To discuss and define them is I think of great value and
importance; for thus only can the labor be shared, the difficulties be
solved. But besides this, it is necessary also to discuss the ends and
the aims for which we are fighting, for which we are doing battle with
these formidable obstacles. Those aims cannot be taken for granted;
they must be perpetually questioned and examined. The whole position, as I see it—here in this hall surrounded by women practising
for the first time in history I know not how many different professions—is one of extraordinary interest and importance. You have won
rooms of your own in the house hitherto exclusively owned by men.
You are able, though not without great labor and effort, to pay the
rent. You are earning your five hundred pounds a year. But this freedom is only a beginning; the room is your own, but it is still bare. It
has to be furnished; it has to be decorated; it has to be shared. How
are you going to furnish it, how are you going to decorate it? With
whom are you going to share it, and upon what terms? These, I think,
are questions of the utmost importance and interest. For the first time
in history you are able to ask them; for the first time you are able to
decide for yourselves what the answers should be. Willingly would I
stay and discuss those questions and answers—but not tonight. My
time is up; and I must cease.

Questions

1. How would you characterize Woolf's tone, especially her attitude toward her subject and herself, in the first paragraph?
2. What do you think Woolf means when she says (paragraph 3): "It is far harder to kill a phantom than a reality"?
3. Woolf conjectures (paragraph 6) that she has not solved the problem of "telling the truth about my own experiences as a body." Is there any reason to believe that today a woman has more difficulty than a man in telling the truth about the experiences of the body?
4. In paragraph 7 Woolf suggests that phantoms as well as obstacles impede women from becoming doctors and lawyers. What might some of these phantoms be?
5. This essay is highly metaphoric. Speaking roughly (or, rather, as precisely as possible), what is the meaning of the metaphor of "rooms" in the final paragraph? What does Woolf mean when she says: "The room is your own, but it is still bare. . . . With whom are you going to share it, and upon what terms?"
6. Evaluate the last two sentences. Are they too abrupt and mechanical? Or do they provide a fitting conclusion to the speech?

Gloria Steinem

The Importance of Work

Toward the end of the 1970s, *The Wall Street Journal* de- 1
voted an eight-part, front-page series to "the working woman"—that is, the influx of women into the paid-labor force—as the greatest change in American life since the Industrial Revolution.

Gloria Steinem was born in Toledo in 1934 and educated at Smith College. An active figure in politics, civil rights affairs, and feminist issues, she was a co-founder of the Women's Action Alliance and a co-founder and editor of *Ms.* magazine. We reprint an essay from her book *Outrageous Acts and Everyday Rebellions* (1983).

Many women readers greeted both the news and the definition 2
with cynicism. After all, women have always worked. If all the productive work of human maintenance that women do in the home were
valued at its replacement cost, the gross national product of the United
States would go up by 26 percent. It's just that we are now more likely
than ever before to leave our poorly rewarded, low-security, high-risk
job of homemaking (though we're still trying to explain that it's a perfectly good one and that the problem is male society's refusal both to
do it and to give it an economic value) for more secure, independent,
and better-paid jobs outside the home.

Obviously, the real work revolution won't come until all produc- 3
tive work is rewarded—including child rearing and other jobs done
in the home—and men are integrated into so-called women's work as
well as vice versa. But the radical change being touted by the *Journal*
and other media is one part of that long integration process: the un-
precedented flood of women into salaried jobs, that is, into the labor
force as it has been male-defined and previously occupied by men. We
are already more than 41 percent of it—the highest proportion in history. Given the fact that women also make up a whopping 69 percent
of the "discouraged labor force" (that is, people who need jobs but
don't get counted in the unemployment statistics because they've
given up looking), plus an official female unemployment rate that is
substantially higher than men's, it's clear that we could expand to
become fully half of the national work force by 1990.

Faced with this determination of women to find a little independ- 4
ence and to be paid and honored for our work, experts have rushed
to ask: "Why?" It's a question rarely directed at male workers. Their
basic motivations of survival and personal satisfaction are taken for
granted. Indeed, men are regarded as "odd" and therefore subjects
for sociological study and journalistic reports only when they *don't*
have work, even if they are rich and don't need jobs or are poor and
can't find them. Nonetheless, pollsters and sociologists have gone to
great expense to prove that women work outside the home because
of dire financial need, or if we persist despite the presence of a wage-
earning male, out of some desire to buy "little extras" for our families,
or even out of good old-fashioned penis envy.

Job interviewers and even our own families may still ask salaried 5
women the big "Why?" If we have small children at home or are in
some job regarded as "men's work," the incidence of such questions
increases. Condescending or accusatory versions of "What's a nice girl
like you doing in a place like this?" have not disappeared from the
workplace.

How do we answer these assumptions that we are "working" out 6 of some pressing or peculiar need? Do we feel okay about arguing that it's as natural for us to have salaried jobs as for our husbands—whether or not we have young children at home? Can we enjoy strong career ambitions without worrying about being thought "unfeminine"? When we confront men's growing resentment of women competing in the work force (often in the form of such guilt-producing accusations as "You're taking men's jobs away" or "You're damaging your children"), do we simply state that a decent job is a basic human right for everybody?

I'm afraid the answer is often no. As individuals and as a move- 7 ment, we tend to retreat into some version of a tactically questionable defense: "Womenworkbecausewehaveto." The phrase has become one word, one key on the typewriter—an economic form of the socially "feminine" stance of passivity and self-sacrifice. Under attack, we still tend to present ourselves as creatures of economic necessity and familial devotion. "Womenworkbecausewehaveto" has become the easiest thing to say.

Like most truisms, this one is easy to prove with statistics. Eco- 8 nomic need *is* the most consistent work motive—for women as well as men. In 1976, for instance, 43 percent of all women in the paid-labor force were single, widowed, separated, or divorced, and working to support themselves and their dependents. An additional 21 percent were married to men who had earned less than ten thousand dollars in the previous year, the minimum then required to support a family of four. In fact, if you take men's pensions, stocks, real estate, and various forms of accumulated wealth into account, a good statistical case can be made that there are more women who "have" to work (that is, who have neither the accumulated wealth, nor husbands whose work or wealth can support them for the rest of their lives) than there are men with the same need. If we were going to ask one group "Do you really need this job?" we should ask men.

But the first weakness of the whole "have to work" defense is its 9 deceptiveness. Anyone who has ever experienced dehumanized life on welfare or any other confidence-shaking dependency knows that a paid job may be preferable to the dole, even when the handout is coming from a family member. Yet the will and self-confidence to work on one's own can diminish as dependency and fear increase. That may explain why—contrary to the "have to" rationale—wives of men who earn less than three thousand dollars a year are actually *less* likely to be employed than wives whose husbands make ten thousand dollars a year or more.

Furthermore, the greatest proportion of employed wives is found   10
among families with a total household income of twenty-five to fifty
thousand dollars a year. This is the statistical underpinning used by
some sociologists to prove that women's work is mainly important for
boosting families into the middle or upper middle class. Thus,
women's incomes are largely used for buying "luxuries" and "little
extras": a neat double-whammy that renders us secondary within our
families, and makes our jobs expendable in hard times. We may even
go along with this interpretation (at least, up to the point of getting
fired so a male can have our job). It preserves a husbandly ego-need
to be seen as the primary breadwinner, and still allows us a safe "feminine" excuse for working.

But there are often rewards that we're not confessing. As noted   11
in *The Two-Career Couple*, by Francine and Douglas Hall: "Women who
hold jobs by choice, even blue-collar routine jobs, are more satisfied
with their lives than are the full-time housewives."

In addition to personal satisfaction, there is also society's need for   12
all its members' talents. Suppose that jobs were given out on only a
"have to work" basis to both women and men—one job per household.
It would be unthinkable to lose the unique abilities of, for instance,
Eleanor Holmes Norton, the distinguished chair of the Equal Employment Opportunity Commission. But would we then be forced to question the important work of her husband, Edward Norton, who is also
a distinguished lawyer? Since men earn more than twice as much as
women on the average, the wife in most households would be more
likely to give up her job. Does that mean the nation could do as well
without millions of its nurses, teachers, and secretaries? Or that the
rare man who earns less than his wife should give up his job?

It was this kind of waste of human talents on a society-wide scale   13
that traumatized millions of unemployed or underemployed Americans during the Depression. Then, a one-job-per-household rule
seemed somewhat justified, yet the concept was used to displace
women workers only, create intolerable dependencies, and waste female talent that the country needed. That Depression experience, plus
the energy and example of women who were finally allowed to work
during the manpower shortage created by World War II, led Congress
to reinterpret the meaning of the country's full-employment goal in its
Economic Act of 1946. Full employment was officially defined as "the
employment of those who want to work, without regard to whether
their employment is, by some definition, necessary. This goal applies
equally to men and to women." Since bad economic times are again

creating a resentment of employed women—as well as creating more need for women to be employed—we need such a goal more than ever. Women are again being caught in a tragic double bind: We are required to be strong and then punished for our strength.

Clearly, anything less than government and popular commitment 14 to this 1946 definition of full employment will leave the less powerful groups, whoever they may be, in danger. Almost as important as the financial penalty paid by the powerless is the suffering that comes from being shut out of paid and recognized work. Without it, we lose much of our self-respect and our ability to prove that we are alive by making some difference in the world. That's just as true for the suburban woman as it is for the unemployed steel worker.

But it won't be easy to give up the passive defense of "wework- 15 becausewehaveto."

When a woman who is struggling to support her children and 16 grandchildren on welfare sees her neighbor working as a waitress, even though that neighbor's husband has a job, she may feel resentful; and the waitress (of course, not the waitress's husband) may feel guilty. Yet unless we establish the obligation to provide a job for everyone who is willing and able to work, that welfare woman may herself be penalized by policies that give out only one public-service job per household. She and her daughter will have to make a painful and divisive decision about which of them gets that precious job, and the whole household will have to survive on only one salary.

A job as a human right is a principle that applies to men as well 17 as women. But women have more cause to fight for it. The phenomenon of the "working woman" has been held responsible for everything from an increase in male impotence (which turned out, incidentally, to be attributable to medication for high blood pressure) to the rising cost of steak (which was due to high energy costs and beef import restrictions, not women's refusal to prepare the cheaper, slower-cooking cuts). Unless we see a job as part of every citizen's right to autonomy and personal fulfillment, we will continue to be vulnerable to someone else's idea of what "need" is, and whose "need" counts the most.

In many ways, women who do not have to work for simple sur- 18 vival, but who choose to do so nonetheless, are on the frontier of asserting this right for all women. Those with well-to-do husbands are dangerously easy for us to resent and put down. It's easier still to resent women from families of inherited wealth, even though men generally control and benefit from that wealth. (There is no Rockefeller Sisters

Fund, no J. P. Morgan & Daughters, and sons-in-law may be the ones who really sleep their way to power.) But to prevent a woman whose husband or father is wealthy from earning her own living, and from gaining the self-confidence that comes with that ability, is to keep her needful of that unearned power and less willing to disperse it. Moreover, it is to lose forever her unique talents.

Perhaps modern feminists have been guilty of a kind of reverse   19
snobbism that keeps us from reaching out to the wives and daughters of wealthy men; yet it was exactly such women who refused the restrictions of class and financed the first wave of feminist revolution.

For most of us, however, "womenworkbecausewehaveto" is just   20
true enough to be seductive as a personal defense.

If we use it without also staking out the larger human right to a   21
job, however, we will never achieve that right. And we will always be subject to the false argument that independence for women is a luxury affordable only in good economic times. Alternatives to layoffs will not be explored, acceptable unemployment will always be used to frighten those with jobs into accepting low wages, and we will never remedy the real cost, both to families and to the country, of dependent women and a massive loss of talent.

Worst of all, we may never learn to find productive, honored work   22
as a natural part of ourselves and as one of life's basic pleasures.

Questions

1. In a sentence or two, state Gloria Steinem's thesis.
2. In paragraph 2 Steinem characterizes homemaking as a "poorly rewarded, low-security, high-risk job." How might she justify each of these descriptions of homemaking? Do you agree that homemaking is rightly classified as a job? If so, do you agree with her description of it?
3. If you are a female reading Steinem's article, have you ever heard a version of the question, "What's a nice girl like you doing in a place like this?" If you are a male, have you ever been asked a male version of this question about a job you were doing or applying for? Describe your experience in a paragraph or two.
4. Restate in your own words Steinem's explanation (paragraph 9) of why "wives of men who earn less than three thousand dollars a year are actually *less* likely to be employed than wives whose husbands make ten thousand dollars a year or more." What is your reaction

to the fact and to this explanation of it? Surprise, disbelief, acceptance, or what?

5. To whom does Steinem appear to address her remarks? Cite evidence for your answer. In your opinion, is this audience likely to find her argument persuasive? Would a different audience find it more or less persuasive? Explain.

6. In addition to arguments, what persuasive devices does Steinem use? How, for example, does she persuade you that she speaks with authority? What other authorities does she cite? How would you characterize her diction and tone, for instance in paragraph 18? (On diction, see page 699; on tone, see page 707.)

7. Steinem suggests two reasons for working: "personal satisfaction" and "society's need for all its members' talents." Suppose that you had no financial need to work. Do you imagine that you would choose to work in order to gain "personal satisfaction"? Or, again if you had no need to work, would you assume that you are morally obligated to contribute to society by engaging in paid work?

8. Summarize, in a paragraph of about 100–150 words, Steinem's argument that it is entirely proper for wealthy women to work for pay. In the course of your paragraph you may quote briefly from the essay.

Charles Krauthammer

The Just Wage
From Bad to Worth

The latest entry on the list of sacred democratic causes is 1 comparable worth. According to that doctrine, it is demonstrable that low-paying female-dominated jobs, like nursing, are worth as much (to employers or society) as "comparable" male-dominated jobs, like plumbing, and that therefore by right and by law they should be paid the same. Comparable worth has become not only *the* women's issue

---

Charles Krauthammer holds a medical degree and has served as chief resident in psychiatry at Harvard Medical School. In 1983 he became a contributing essayist for *Time*, and in 1984 he began a weekly column for the *Washington Post*.

of the 1980s, but also the most prominent civil rights issue not specifically directed at blacks. The Democratic Party has warmly embraced it. Every one of its presidential candidates has endorsed it. In the 1984 platform, that sea of well-intended ambiguity and evasion, there are few islands of certainty. Comparable worth is one of them.

Comparable worth is advancing in the courts, too. In 1981 the Supreme Court opened the door a crack by ruling that female prison guards could sue for violation of the equal-pay provisions of the 1964 Civil Rights Act, even though they did not do precisely the same work as the better-paid male prison guards. That narrow ruling was broken open in December 1983 in a sweeping victory for comparable worth in Washington State. A federal district judge found the state guilty of massive discrimination because its female-dominated jobs were paying less than "comparable" male-dominated jobs. He ordered an immediate increase in the women's wages and restitution for past injury. The back pay alone will run into the hundreds of millions of dollars.

Comparable worth may indeed be an idea whose time has come. Where does it come from? When the plumber makes a house call and charges forty dollars an hour to fix a leak, the instinct of most people is to suspect that the plumber is overpaid—the beneficiary of some combination of scarce skills, powerful unions, and dumb luck. The instinct of comparable worth advocates is to see the plumber's wage as a standard of fairness, to conclude that the rest of us (meaning: women) are underpaid, and to identify discrimination as the source of that underpayment. But since overt discrimination on the basis of sex has been legally forbidden for twenty years, to make that charge stick nowadays requires a bit of subtlety.

One claim is that women's wages are depressed today because of a legacy of past discrimination: namely, the "crowding" of women into certain fields (like nursing, teaching, secretarial work), thus artificially depressing their wages. Did sexual stereotyping really "crowd" women into their jobs? Sexual stereotyping worked both ways: it kept women in, but it also kept men out, thus artificially excluding potential wage competition from half the population, and, more important, from about two-thirds to three-quarters of the labor force (because of the higher participation rate of men). Sex-segregation is obviously unfair, but it is hard to see how it caused downward pressure on women's wages when, at the same time, through the socially enforced exclusion of men, it sheltered "women's work" from a vast pool of competitors. Moreover, as the social barriers that kept men and women from entering each other's traditional fields have fallen during the last twenty years, there has been much more movement of women into men's fields than vice versa. "Women's work" is less crowded than ever.

If the crowding argument is weak, then one is forced to resort to 5 the "grand conspiracy" theory. "The system of wages was set up by a grand conspiracy, so to speak, that has held down the wages of women to minimize labor costs," explained the business agent of the union that in 1981 struck for and won a famous comparable-worth settlement in San Jose. But since to minimize labor costs employers try to hold down the wages of everyone, the thrust of the argument must be that there is a particular desire to do so additionally in the case of women. In other words, the market is inherently discriminatory. Women nurses are paid less than they deserve, simply because they are women. How to prove it? Comparing their wages to that of male nurses won't do, since their pay is, by law, equal. So one must compare nurses' wages to that of, say, plumbers, show that nurses make less, and claim that nurses are discriminated against because they deserve—they are worth—the same.

What is the basis of that claim? In San Jose, Washington State, 6 and other comparable worth cases, the basis is a "study." A consultant is called in to set up a committee to rank every job according to certain criteria. In Washington State, the Willis scale gives marks for "knowledge and skills," "mental demands," "accountability," and "working conditions." The committee then awards points in each category to every job, tallies them up, and declares those with equal totals to have—*voilà!*—comparable worth.

There is no need to belabor the absurdity of this system, so I'll 7 stick to the high points. It is, above all, a mandate for arbitrariness: every subjective determination, no matter how whimsically arrived at, is first enshrined in a number to give it an entirely specious solidity, then added to another number no less insubstantial, to yield a total entirely meaningless. (An exercise: compare, with numbers, the "mental demands" on a truck driver and a secretary.) Everything is arbitrary: the categories, the rankings, even the choice of judges. And even if none of this were true, even if every category were ontologically self-evident, every ranking mathematically precise, every judge Solomonic, there remains one factor wholly unaccounted for which permits the system to be skewed in any direction one wishes: the *weight* assigned to each category. In the Willis scale, points for "knowledge and skills" are worth as much as points for "working conditions." But does ten points in knowledge and skills make up for ten points in hazardous working conditions? Who is to say that a secretary's two years of college are equal in worth to—and not half or double the worth of—the trucker's risk of getting killed on the highways? Mr. Willis, that's who.

Conclusions based on such "studies" are not a whit less capricious 8 than the simple assertion, "secretaries are worth as much as truck drivers." Trotting out Willis, of course, allows you to dress up a feeling in scientific trappings. It allows H.R. 4599, Representative Mary Rose Oakar's bill legislating comparable worth in federal employment, to dispose of the arbitrariness problem in the *definitions*. "Job evaluation technique" is defined as "an objective method of determining the comparable value of different jobs." Next problem.

Some advocates of comparable worth, aware of this objectivity 9 conundrum and perhaps less confident that it can be defined out of existence, propose an alternate solution. Instead of ranking the intrinsic worth of the job (by admittedly arbitrary criteria), they propose ranking the worth of the worker. Barbara Bergmann, an economist at the University of Maryland, believes that people with similar qualifications, training and experience should be receiving the same return on their "human capital." Breaking new ground in discrimination theory, she claims that "in a nondiscriminatory setup, identical people should be paid identically." And what makes people identical? Their credentials: qualifications, training, experience. This is not just credentialism gone wild, and highly disadvantageous to non-yuppy workers with poor résumés, who need the help of the women's movement the most; it leads to the logical absurdity that people should be paid not for the actual work they do, but for the work they *could* do. We've gone from equal pay for equal work to equal pay for comparable work, to equal pay for potential work. Summarizing the Bergmann position, the Center for Philosophy in Public Policy at the University of Maryland explains helpfully that "if a nursing supervisor could do the work of a higher-paid hospital purchasing agent, then her wages should be the same as his." But why stop there? What if her credentials are the same as those of the hospital administrator, or her city councillor, or her U.S. Senator? And what about the starving actress, waiting on tables for a living? If she can act as well as Bo Derek (to set a standard anyone can meet), shouldn't she be getting a million dollars a year—that is, if the "setup" is to deserve the adjective "nondiscriminatory"?

Now, even if there were a shred of merit in any of these systems 10 for determining comparable worth, we should be wary of implementing them if only because of the sheer social chaos they would create. The only sure consequence of comparable worth one can foresee was described by the winning attorney in the Washington State case: "This decision . . . should stimulate an avalanche of private litigation on behalf of the victims of discrimination." The judicial and bureaucratic monster comparable worth will call into being—a whole new layer of judges, court-appointed "masters" (there already is one in the Washington State suit), lawyers, and consultants—will not just sit once to fix wages and then retire. The process will be endless. Fairness will require constant readjustment. There will still exist such a thing as supply and demand. Even if comparable worth advocates succeed in abolishing it for women's work (remember, Washington State was found to have broken the law for paying women market wages rather than comparable worth wages), it will still operate for men's wages, the standard by which women's (comparable worth) wages will be set. Now, what if nurses are awarded plumbers' pay, and there develops a housing slowdown and a plumber surplus, and plumbers' wages fall? Will nurses' salaries have to be ratcheted down? And if not, what is to prevent the plumbers from suing, alleging they are underpaid relative to comparably equal nurses?

Which brings us to the equity problem. Almost everyone feels he   11
or she is underpaid. Moreover, even a plumber can point to at least one person or group of persons who are getting more than they are "worth." Why can't he claim that class of people as the equitable standard, and march to court demanding restitution? If comparable worth is simple justice, as its advocates claim, why should only women be entitled to it? Why not comparable worth for everyone?

The whole search for the "just wage," which is what comparable   12
worth is all about, is, like the search for the "just price," inherently elusive in a capitalist system. It is not that justice has nothing to say about wages and prices in a market economy, but that what it does say it says negatively. For example, it declares that whatever the wage, it must be the same for people regardless of sex, race or other characterics; but it doesn't say what the wage should be. Even the minimum-wage law says merely that a wage may not be below a certain floor. (Even capitalism has a notion of exploitative labor.) Beyond that, the law is silent. The reason it is silent, the reason we decide to let the market decide, is no great mystery. It was first elaborated by Adam Smith, and amplified by the experience of the Soviet Union and other command economies. Market economies are agnostic on the question of a just wage or a just price not simply because of a philosophical

belief that the question, if it is a question, is unanswerable, but also because of the belief, and the experience, that attempts to answer it have a habit of leaving everyone worse off than before.

Finally, even granting that women in traditionally female jobs are 13 underpaid, it is not as if we live in a fixed economy which blocks off all avenues of redress. If secretaries are indeed paid less than they are "worth," they have several options. One is suggested by Coleman Young, the mayor of Detroit, a former labor leader and no conservative: "If a painter makes more than a secretary, then let more women be painters. Equal opportunity and affirmative action is how you do that." A woman entering the labor force today has no claim that she has been crowded into low-paying professions because of discrimination. She has choices.

Older women, of course, who have already invested much in their 14 professions, are more constrained. But they have the same avenues open to them—such as organizing—as other similarly constrained (predominantly male) workers who struggle for higher wages in other settings. In Denver, for example, nurses sought comparable worth wage gains in court and lost; they then went on strike and won. True, in some occupations, even strong unions can't raise wages very much. But as the president of the International Ladies Garment Workers Union (85 percent female) explained in objecting to a highfalutin AFL-CIO endorsement of comparable worth, the problem is not discrimination but the market. His workers have low wages because they compete with workers overseas who are paid thirty cents an hour. Comparable worth doctrine may declare that garment workers ought to be making as much as truck drivers. But if the theory ever became practice, garment workers would be free of more than discrimination. They would be free of their jobs.

Why is the obvious about comparable worth so rarely heard? Why 15 is it for Democrats the ultimate motherhood issue? Because here again the party of the big heart identifies a class of people who feel they aren't getting their just due, blames that condition on a single cause (discrimination), then offers a "rational" solution, on whose messy details it prefers not to dwell. But those details add up to a swamp of mindless arbitrariness and bureaucratic inefficiency, shrouded in a fine mist of pseudo-scientific objectivity. And the surest results will be unending litigation and an entirely new generation of inequities. These inequities, moreover, will be frozen in place by force of law, and thus that much more difficult to dislodge.

Comparable worth asks the question: How many nurses would it   16
take to screw in a lightbulb? The joke is that, having not the faintest
idea, it demands that a committee invent an answer, that the answer
become law and that the law supplant the market. Even Karl Marx,
who also had legitimate complaints about the equity of wages set by
the market, had a more plausible alternative.

Questions

1. Explain the pun in the title. Is it simply a joke, or is it relevant to
   Krauthammer's thesis?
2. What information is advanced in paragraph 1? What attitude? (Barbara Bergmann, whose essay on comparable worth follows, speaks
   of the "raucous, mocking tone" of critics. Do you notice that tone
   here?)
3. In paragraph 3 Krauthammer says, "Comparable worth may indeed
   be an idea whose time has come." But he does not go on, as one
   might expect, to argue in favor of comparable worth. What does he
   do in the rest of the paragraph? On the question of the plumber's
   wage that he poses in this paragraph, do you identify yourself with
   "the instinct of most people" or with "the instinct of comparable
   worth advocates"? Is it possible to take both positions simultaneously?
4. In paragraph 4 Krauthammer suggests that "sexual stereotyping
   worked both ways: it kept women in, but it also kept men out, thus
   artificially excluding potential wage competition from half the population." He mentions nursing, teaching, and secretarial work as
   female-dominated jobs, but of course other fields, such as child
   care and domestic work, could be added to his list. Do you think
   that if more men enter these fields the wages will (as Krauthammer
   implies) decline? Why, or why not?
5. In paragraph 7 Krauthammer challenges the reader to "compare,
   with numbers, the 'mental demands' on a truck driver and a secretary." Take up the challenge. Can you make this comparison? If
   so, make it; if not, explain why it cannot be made.
6. In paragraph 9 Krauthammer compares a starving actress with Bo
   Derek. Do you agree with the point he makes? If not, what argument
   can you make? (Even if you agree with his point, you may find it
   irrelevant to the argument, or so exceptional a case that perhaps
   it can be ignored.)
7. Krauthammer several times refers to the Washington State case in
   which the state was found guilty of "massive discrimination" (par-

agraph 2). In paragraph 10 he predicts that comparable worth will create ''a judicial and bureaucratic monster'' and an endless process of suits and readjustments not only of women's wages but of men's. Does he expect this monster to emerge from the Washington State case? If the judgment in the case were to inspire a multitude of suits and readjustments of wages, would that discredit the judgment or the case for comparable worth?

8. In paragraph 11 Krauthammer writes, ''Even a plumber can point to at least one person or group of persons who are getting more than they are 'worth.' Why can't he claim that class of people as the equitable standard, and march to court demanding restitution?'' How would you answer that question? Under what circumstances *could* a plumber demand equitable pay? From whom would he (or she) demand it?

9. On the basis of this article, how would you define ''comparable worth''? (If you have trouble coming up with a definition, read Barbara Bergmann's essay, which begins below, and try again.)

Barbara R. Bergmann

Pay Equity—How to Argue Back

Thanks to the pay equity campaign, state and local governments around the country are taking steps to raise the pay scales in the traditionally female occupations. The drumbeat of criticism continues, however, with that raucous, mocking tone that we are used to hearing in response to any proposal to improve women's status. Some of it comes from the same folks who oppose shelters for battered women—they are against anything that would make women more uppity. But some of the criticism is serious and needs answering.

Barbara R. Bergmann, a professor of economics at the American University, has written a book entitled *The Economic Emergence of American Women*.

The first count of the indictment is that pay equity adjustments   2
tamper with "wage scales set in the marketplace." Of course they do.
The pay that the market decrees for women's labor is badly depressed
by discrimination. Pay equity adjustments, along with affirmative action for hiring and promoting women, are attempts to get away from
the sex discrimination that most employers practice, and that now
dominates the "market." The real question is, what harm would be
done?

If women's wages are raised, then employers will want to employ   3
fewer of them, say pay equity's critics. For a response we can point
to the example of Australia, where government pay boards handed
out equity raises in the traditional women's occupations amounting to
about 30 percent. Australian economists fully expected to see women's
unemployment rates rise significantly as a result. After thorough
study, they had to report that the bad effects hadn't materialized. In
Sweden, Britain, West Germany, Holland, and Denmark, women
workers have had significant gains in pay. In terms of equity with men,
they are way ahead of American women. In none of these countries
are there reports of special unemployment problems for women. There
is no reason to think that American women will experience such problems either.

Another complaint against pay equity is that, apart from the mar-   4
ket, there is no really good way to compare men's and women's occupations, so how could we decide which ones should have comparable pay? "How can you compare a secretary to a truck driver, or a
nurse to a tree trimmer?" the opponents of pay equity ask plaintively
in mock anguish. The answer is that employers do have a method that
they rely on to make comparisons between very different occupations.
It is called "job evaluation."

Many large employers already use job evaluation techniques in   5
setting pay, and well-respected consulting firms help in the implementation. These employers use job evaluation because the idea of a
"market" that will tell them the wage for each of hundreds of job titles
is sheer fantasy. However, these firms have wanted to avoid paying
male-level salaries to women, so they never directly compared the
qualities of traditional women's jobs and traditional men's jobs. They
set up a job evaluation system for the jobs labeled "clerical" and an
entirely different one for the jobs labeled "administrative." It is as if
they were doing job evaluations on blue paper for the men and on
pink paper for the women, taking care not to compare the pink and
blue sheets. The idea of pay equity is that men's and women's jobs

should be evaluated by a unified system, and then pay scales adjusted accordingly. The basic methodology already exists, and already is in widespread use in business and in government. It just needs to be cleaned up a bit.

Another allegation about pay equity is that the costs will be huge— 6 billions of dollars. That's true, but since there are millions of women involved, billions of dollars are needed to make a dent in the problem. Where can we get the billions for pay equity? They will come out of the billions that are handed out every year as wage increases to workers. At most, for a few years, women will get larger-than-average increases, and for a few years men will get smaller-than-average increases. Nobody's pay need go down. Nor will profits or budgets be wiped out.

The silliest argument the pay equity critics have come up with is 7 that women will be so satisfied with their pay in the traditional female jobs that they will stop trying to get into the better jobs reserved for men. That argument is an insult to every secretary who has been passed over for a promotion to a job she could do better than the man who got it. Better pay has never prevented men or women from wanting promotions.

Pay equity is going forward for the women employees of state and 8 local governments because a combination of political and union pressure is being exerted behind it. For it to spread to the private sector, unions must confront the issue at the bargaining table. Where there is no union, or where the union is indifferent to women's issues, women employees must organize on their own. Whether pay equity lawsuits will be worthwhile depends on the Supreme Court.

One of the economic effects of pay equity that seldom gets mentioned 9 is its effect on poverty. A healthy boost in the pay of the traditional women's occupations is the best and may be the only way that we have of reducing poverty among women in the near future. It might rescue from poverty some of the millions of children dependent on those women. When you come to think about it, it's women's current salaries that make poor economic sense. Pay equity makes good economic sense.

Questions

1. From the title and first paragraph of this essay, would you say that Bergmann is addressing proponents or opponents of pay equity? Considering that the article was published in *Ms.*, does she strike an appropriate opening note. Does she risk alienating readers?

2. What Bergmann and many other people call "pay equity" is called, by still others, "comparable worth." If you advocate the idea, which term do you prefer? Why?

3. In paragraph 4 Bergmann mentions the opposition's belief that the only way to compare the value of a secretary with the value of a tree trimmer is to see what the market offers. Bergmann says there is an alternative, "job evaluation." In her next paragraph she offers a comment on job evaluations. If you were evaluating the two jobs she mentions in paragraph 4—secretary and tree trimmer—which job would you find deserving of higher pay? Why? What criteria would you use? Possible criteria might be the amount of education or training, or the skill level, required; the degree of responsibility; the amount of initiative (or intelligence?) required; and work conditions (e.g., congenial or uncongenial).

4. Why is the choice of criteria important in establishing pay equity? Try to explain your answer by again comparing the jobs of the secretary and the tree trimmer, this time using criteria other than those listed in question 3.

5. In paragraph 7 Bergmann speaks of certain "better jobs [that are] reserved for men." What are some examples of such jobs? What makes them "better"? Money, and nothing else?

6. In rejecting the request of Denver nurses that they be paid as much as Denver tree trimmers, a federal judge noted that such a change in pay involved "the possibility of disrupting the entire economic system in the United States." Is the possibility of such disruption a sound reason for rejecting the change? Why, or why not?

7. If you have ever been underpaid, or overpaid, because of sexual or racial discrimination, explain the circumstances and then argue the case that might have been made for pay equity.

Lester C. Thurow

Why Women Are Paid
Less Than Men

In the 40 years from 1939 to 1979 white women who work 1
full time have with monotonous regularity made slightly less than 60
percent as much as white men. Why?

Over the same time period, minorities have made substantial 2
progress in catching up with whites, with minority women making
even more progress than minority men. Black men now earn 72 percent
as much as white men (up 16 percentage points since the mid-1950's)
but black women earn 92 percent as much as white women. Hispanic
men make 71 percent of what their white counterparts do, but Hispanic
women make 82 percent as much as white women. As a result of their
faster progress, fully employed black women make 75 percent as much
as fully employed black men while Hispanic women earn 68 percent
as much as Hispanic men.

This faster progress may, however, end when minority women 3
finally catch up with white women. In the bible of the New Right,
George Gilder's *Wealth and Poverty,* the 60 percent is just one of Mother
Nature's constants like the speed of light or the force of gravity. Men
are programmed to provide for their families economically while
women are programmed to take care of their families emotionally and
physically. As a result men put more effort into their jobs than women.
The net result is a difference in work intensity that leads to that 40
percent gap in earnings. But there is no discrimination against
women—only the biological facts of life.

The problem with this assertion is just that. It is an assertion with 4
no evidence for it other than the fact that white women have made 60
percent as much as men for a long period of time.

"Discrimination against women" is an easy answer but it also has 5
its problems as an adequate explanation. Why is discrimination against
women not declining under the same social forces that are leading to

Lester C. Thurow, born in Montana in 1938, is dean of the Sloan School of
Management at the Massachusetts Institute of Technology. Among his books
are *Poverty and Discrimination* and *The Political Economy of Income Redistri-
bution Policies.*

a lessening of discrimination against minorities? In recent years women have made more use of the enforcement provisions of the Equal Employment Opportunities Commission and the courts than minorities. Why do the laws that prohibit discrimination against women and minorities work for minorities but not for women?

When men discriminate against women, they run into a problem. 6 To discriminate against women is to discriminate against your own wife and to lower your own family income. To prevent women from working is to force men to work more.

When whites discriminate against blacks, they can at least think 7 that they are raising their own incomes. When men discriminate against women they have to know that they are lowering their own family income and increasing their own work effort.

While discrimination undoubtedly explains part of the male-female 8 earnings differential, one has to believe that men are monumentally stupid or irrational to explain all of the earnings gap in terms of discrimination. There must be something else going on.

Back in 1939 it was possible to attribute the earnings gap to large 9 differences in educational attainments. But the educational gap between men and women has been eliminated since World War II. It is no longer possible to use education as an explanation for the lower earnings of women. Some observers have argued that women earn less money since they are less reliable workers who are more apt to leave the labor force. But it is difficult to maintain this position since women are less apt to quit one job to take another and as a result they tend to work as long, or longer, for any one employer. From any employer's perspective they are more reliable, not less reliable, than men.

Part of the answer is visible if you look at the lifetime earnings 10 profile of men. Suppose that you were asked to predict which men in a group of 25-year-olds would become economically successful. At age 25 it is difficult to tell who will be economically successful and your predictions are apt to be highly inaccurate. But suppose that you were asked to predict which men in a group of 35-year-olds would become economically successful. If you are successful at age 35, you are very likely to remain successful for the rest of your life. If you have not become economically successful by age 35, you are very unlikely to do so later.

The decade between 25 and 35 is when men either succeed or fail. 11 It is the decade when lawyers become partners in the good firms, when business managers make it onto the "fast track," when academics get tenure at good universities, and when blue collar workers find the job opportunities that will lead to training opportunities and the skills that will generate high earnings. If there is any one decade when it pays to work hard and to be consistently in the labor force, it is the decade between 25 and 35. For those who succeed, earnings will rise rapidly. For those who fail, earnings will remain flat for the rest of their lives.

But the decade between 25 and 35 is precisely the decade when   12
women are most apt to leave the labor force or become part-time workers to have children. When they do, the current system of promotion and skill acquisition will extract an enormous lifetime price.

This leaves essentially two avenues for equalizing male and female   13
earnings. Families where women who wish to have successful careers, compete with men, and achieve the same earnings should alter their family plans and have their children either before 25 or after 35. Or society can attempt to alter the existing promotion and skill acquisition system so that there is a longer time period in which both men and women can attempt to successfully enter the labor force. Without some combination of these two factors, a substantial fraction of the male-female earnings differentials are apt to persist for the next 40 years, even if discrimination against women is eliminated.

Questions

1. Thurow assumes that discrimination against women can't possibly be the whole explanation for their lower earnings. On what does he base this assumption? Do you agree with his assumption?
2. Evaluate Thurow's opening paragraph, explaining why you find it effective or ineffective.
3. After giving his analysis, Thurow ends the essay by suggesting two ways in which the differential in earnings may be decreased. Does he convey enthusiasm? Optimism? Is the tone of the ending consistent with the tone of the rest of the essay?
4. If you have read Bergmann's ''Pay Equity—How to Answer Back'' (page 288), set forth what you think would be Bergmann's response to Thurow's analysis of the problem and her response to his two proposals for equalizing male and female earnings.

Barbara Ehrenreich

A Step Back to the Workhouse?

The commentators are calling it a "remarkable consensus." 1
Workfare, as programs to force welfare recipients to work are known,
was once abhorred by liberals as a step back toward the 17th-century
workhouse or—worse—slavery. But today no political candidate dares
step outdoors without some plan for curing "welfare dependency" by
putting its hapless victims to work—if necessary, at the nearest Burger
King. It is as if the men who run things, or who aspire to run things
(and we are, unfortunately, talking mostly about men when we talk
about candidates), had gone off and caucused for a while and decided
on the one constituency that could be safely sacrificed in the name of
political expediency and "new ideas," and that constituency is poor
women.

Most of the arguments for workfare are simply the same indes- 2
tructible stereotypes that have been around, in one form or another,
since the first public relief program in England 400 years ago: that the
poor are poor because they are lazy and dissolute, and that they are
lazy and dissolute because they are suffering from "welfare dependency." Add a touch of modern race and gender stereotypes and you
have the image that haunts the workfare advocates: a slovenly, overweight, black woman who produces a baby a year in order to augment
her welfare checks.

But there is a new twist to this season's spurt of welfare-bashing: 3
workfare is being presented as a kind of *feminist* alternative to welfare.
As Senator Daniel Patrick Moynihan (D.-N.Y.) has put it, "A program
that was designed to pay mothers to stay at home with their children
[i.e., welfare, or Aid to Families with Dependent Children] cannot
succeed when we now observe most mothers going out to work."
Never mind the startling illogic of this argument, which is on a par
with saying that no woman should stay home with her children because other women do not, or that a laid-off male worker should not
receive unemployment compensation because most men have been

Barbara Ehrenreich, author of *The Economic Emergence of Women* (1986),
writes regularly for the *New York Times* and for *Ms.*

observed holding jobs. We are being asked to believe that pushing destitute mothers into the work force (in some versions of workfare, for no other compensation than the welfare payments they would have received anyway) is consistent with women's strivings toward self-determination.

Now I will acknowledge that most women on welfare—like most 4 unemployed women in general—would rather have jobs. And I will further acknowledge that many of the proponents of workfare, possibly including Senator Moynihan and the Democratic Presidential candidates, have mounted the bandwagon with the best of intentions. Welfare surely needs reform. But workfare is not the solution, because "dependency"—with all its implications of laziness and depravity—is not the problem. The problem is poverty, which most women enter in a uniquely devastating way—with their children in tow.

Let me introduce a real person, if only because real people, as 5 opposed to imaginative stereotypes, never seem to make an appearance in the current rhetoric on welfare. "Lynn," as I will call her, is a friend and onetime neighbor who has been on welfare for two years. She is also about as unlike the stereotypical "welfare mother" as one can get—which is to say that she is a fairly typical welfare recipient. She has only one child, which puts her among the 74 percent of welfare recipients who have only one or two children. She is white (not that that should matter), as are almost half of welfare recipients. Like most welfare recipients, she is not herself the daughter of a welfare recipient, and hence not part of anything that could be called an "intergenerational cycle of dependency." And like every woman on welfare I have ever talked to, she resents the bureaucratic hassles that are the psychic price of welfare. But, for now, there are no alternatives.

When I first met Lynn, she seemed withdrawn and disoriented. 6 She had just taken the biggest step of her 25 years; she had left an abusive husband and she was scared: scared about whether she could survive on her own and scared of her estranged husband. He owned a small restaurant; she was a high school dropout who had been a waitress when she met him. During their three years of marriage he had beaten her repeatedly. Only after he threw her down a flight of stairs had she realized that her life was in danger and moved out. I don't think I fully grasped the terror she had lived in until one summer day when he chased Lynn to the door of my house with a drawn gun.

Gradually Lynn began to put her life together. She got a divorce 7 and went on welfare; she found a pediatrician who would accept Medicaid and a supermarket that would take food stamps. She fixed up her apartment with second-hand furniture and flea market curtains. She was, by my admittedly low standards, a compulsive housekeeper and an overprotective mother; and when she wasn't waxing her floors or ironing her two-year-old's playsuits, she was studying the help-wanted ads. She spent a lot of her time struggling with details that most of us barely notice—the price of cigarettes, mittens, or of a bus ticket to the welfare office—yet, somehow, she regained her sense of humor. In fact, most of the time we spent together was probably spent laughing—over the foibles of the neighbors, the conceits of men, and the snares of welfare and the rest of "the system."

Yet for all its inadequacies, Lynn was grateful for welfare. Maybe 8 if she had been more intellectually inclined she would have found out that she was suffering from "welfare dependency," a condition that is supposed to sap the will and demolish the work ethic. But "dependency" is not an issue when it is a choice between an abusive husband and an impersonal government. Welfare had given Lynn a brief shelter in a hostile world, and as far as she was concerned, it was her ticket to *independence*.

Suppose there had been no welfare at the time when Lynn finally 9 summoned the courage to leave her husband. Suppose she had gone for help and been told she would have to "work off" her benefits in some menial government job (restocking the toilet paper in rest rooms is one such "job" assigned to New York women in a current workfare program). Or suppose, as in some versions of workfare, she had been told she would have to take the first available private sector job, which (for a non–high school graduate like Lynn) would have paid near the minimum wage, or $3.35 an hour. How would she have been able to afford child care? What would she have done for health insurance (as a welfare recipient she had Medicaid, but most low-paying jobs offer little or no coverage)? Would she have ever made the decision to leave her husband in the first place?

As Ruth Sidel points out in *Women and Children Last* (Viking), most 10 women who are or have been on welfare have stories like Lynn's. They go onto welfare in response to a crisis—divorce, illness, loss of a job, the birth of an additional child to feed—and they remain on welfare for two years or less. They are not victims of any "welfare culture," but of a society that increasingly expects women to both raise and support children—and often on wages that would barely support a woman alone. In fact, even some of the most vociferous advocates of replacing welfare with workfare admit that, in their own estimation, only about 15 percent of welfare recipients fit the stereotype associated with "welfare dependency": demoralization, long-term welfare use, lack of drive, and so on.

But workfare will not help anyone, not even the presumed 15 per- 11 cent of "bad apples" for whose sake the majority will be penalized. First, it will not help because it does not solve the problem that drives most women into poverty in the first place: how to hold a job *and* care for children. Child care in a licensed, professionally run center can easily cost as much as $100 a week per child—more than most states now pay in welfare benefits and (for two children) more than most welfare recipients could expect to earn in the work force. Any serious effort to get welfare recipients into the work force would require child-care provisions at a price that would probably end up higher than the current budget for AFDC. But none of the workfare advocates are proposing that sort of massive public commitment to child care.

Then there is the problem of jobs. So far, studies show that existing 12 state workfare programs have had virtually no success in improving their participants' incomes or employment rates. Small wonder: nearly half the new jobs generated in recent years pay poverty-level wages; and most welfare recipients will enter jobs that pay near the minimum wage, which is $6,900 a year—26 percent less than the poverty level for a family of three. A menial, low-wage job may be character-building (from a middle-class vantage point), but it will not lift anyone out of poverty.

Some of my feminist activist friends argue that it is too late to stop 13 the workfare juggernaut. The best we can do, they say, is to try to defeat the more pernicious proposals: those that are over-coercive, that do not offer funds for child care, or that would relegate workfare clients to a "subemployee" status unprotected by federal labor and civil rights legislation. Our goal, the pragmatists argue, should be to harness the current enthusiasm for workfare to push for services welfare recipients genuinely need, such as child care and job training and counseling.

I wish the pragmatists well, but for me, it would be a betrayal of 14 women like Lynn to encourage the workfare bandwagon in any way. Most women, like Lynn, do not take up welfare as a career, but as an emergency measure in a time of personal trauma and dire need. At such times, the last thing they need is to be hustled into a low-wage job, and left to piece together child care, health insurance, transportation, and all the other ingredients of survival. In fact, the main effect of workfare may be to discourage needy women from seeking any help at all—a disastrous result in a nation already suffering from a child poverty rate of nearly 25 percent. Public policy should be aimed at giving impoverished mothers (and, I would add, fathers) the help they so urgently need—not only in the form of job opportunities, but sufficient income support to live on until a job worth taking comes along.

Besides, there is an ancient feminist principle at stake. The premise 15 of all the workfare proposals—the more humane as well as the nasty— is that single mothers on welfare are *not working*. But, to quote the old feminist bumper sticker, EVERY MOTHER IS A WORKING MOTHER. And those who labor to raise their children in poverty—to feed and clothe them on meager budgets and to nurture them in an uncaring world—are working the hardest. The feminist position has never been that all women must pack off their children and enter the work force, but that all women's work—in the home or on the job—should be valued and respected.

Barbara Ehrenreich's essay stimulated a lively response from Ms. readers. The following letters were published in the February 1988 issue.

I was absolutely thrilled when I read Barbara Ehrenreich's article on 16 workfare ("A Step Back to the Workhouse?" November 1987). As a single mother who received welfare for several years (with no child support) I'm against everything that workfare stands for. I belong to an organization called Women, Work, and Welfare, a group of current and former welfare recipients trying to empower ourselves and become a part of the decisions that affect our lives as poor women. It seems as if everybody but the welfare recipient herself has a hand in the decisions that are made.

CHERI HONKALA
Minneapolis, Minn.

I arrived in Chicago in 1952 with a husband and two children from a 17 camp in Europe. I had another child in 1953, lost a newborn in 1954, had a miscarriage, a hysterectomy, and a divorce in 1955. I *never* received child support. My ex-husband was remarried within two months.

I *never* received welfare. I worked in another culture, while in very 18 bad health. I found a two-room flat, had no furniture and slept for years on the floor. I even went back to school at night and had to contend with companies like Gulf Oil Corp., which did not believe in promoting women. But I just slugged on.

By the end of the sixties, I had two daughters in college, and I 19 had bought a house. My total earnings for 1970 from three jobs came to a whopping $8,000.

A full-time minimum wage job *can* support one adult and one   20
child. One just has to learn how to do it.

URSULA SCHRAMM
Hurley, Wis.

I found myself agreeing with the problems that Barbara Ehrenreich   21
outlines in the present workfare program.

Yet deep inside a protesting rumbling exploded when I read that   22
impoverished mothers should receive sufficient income support to live
on "until a job worth taking comes along." *Bullshit!* Sure, we all should
have the right to only work a job we love, but how many of us can
afford to wait for it? That we are often forced to work at jobs that are
not fulfilling says a lot about our society in which more needs to be
changed than just the welfare system!

My mother was forced to go to work when I was nine years old.   23
Our family was in dire financial straits and at the age of 50 she took
a job in a factory. Was that job "worth taking"? Did it utilize her unique
talents? *No!* Did it bring her personal fulfillment? *No!* Did it prevent
the bank from foreclosing on our home? *Yes!* Did it give my mother
the power to overcome our financial crisis and maintain her autonomy?
Yes! You tell me if it was "worth taking." That depends on what your
self-respect is worth to you.

GAIL FREI
Newtown Square, Pa.

Barbara Ehrenreich omitted a major element in her discussion of the   24
victimization of welfare families: the inability or unwillingness of the
legal system to award *and enforce* realistic child support. Until it stops
being easier to abandon your children than to default on that car loan,
women and those who depend on them will be welfare/workfare victims.

SUSAN MARTIN RYNARD
Durham, N.C.

I went on welfare when my daughter was three, when I left my hus-   25
band. I had a high school education, but had always wanted to go to
college. I was 25.

So, with the help of the government, I got my B.S. in nursing. I   26 worked for several years as an R.N. and then returned to school for my master's degree. For graduate school, I lived on savings, loans, and grants. The loans ($19,000 for undergrad and graduate in all) will be paid off in less than a year, in time for my daughter to begin college!

KATHRYN REID
Silverado, Calif.

Although I share Barbara Ehrenreich's concerns about workfare and   27
the plight of her friend Lynn, the conclusions she draws strike me as misguided. We live in a society where the myths of the work ethic and self-help are deeply embedded in the popular culture; where resort to the dole is frowned upon unless the need is temporary or arises from disability; where the middle-class majority feels inequitably taxed, as compared to the wealthy, to support a system that directly benefits few of its members.

Feminists and other liberals should acknowledge the swelling de-   28
mand for welfare reform. Our support should be conditional upon the incorporation in any welfare reform plan of provision for *quality* child-care facilities; upon the minimization of coercion; and upon further efforts to compel ex-spouses to pay their fair share of support. Nothing in this approach rules out our going ahead simultaneously with other, parallel efforts to question the mystique of work or to expose the links between welfare and poverty, on the one hand, and capitalism and the subordination of women, on the other.

DAVID G. BECKER
Hanover, N.H.

California *is* serious about workfare, but we call it GAIN (Greater Av-   29
enues for Independence). It offers welfare recipients vocational coun-seling, up to two years of vocational training, and workshops in how to get and hold a job.

GAIN also pays for child care and transportation. No job need be   30
accepted by the recipient unless she/he will *net* at least as much as their AFCD grant, *including* child care, transportation, and medical insur-ance. And even then, they will receive funds to cover these costs for three months after they begin working to help them make the tran-sition to the work force.

JANE KIRCHMAN
Guerneville, Calif.

Questions

1. List the objections Ehrenreich makes to workfare, and pose an answer for each. Your answers may attempt to rebut her objections, on grounds either of their logic or of information she neglects to consider (for example, provisions in workfare programs you know of). Where her objections seem reasonable, propose improvements to workfare that you would like to see embodied in a program in your community. The letters answering Ehrenreich may provide some assistance. If so, quote, summarize, or paraphrase useful parts of the letters, giving appropriate acknowledgment to the writers.

2. Gloria Steinem in "The Importance of Work" (page 275) does not address the issue of welfare versus workfare, but a careful reading of her essay will suggest ideas and arguments on both sides of the question. Read her essay and report on the two or three ideas that struck you as interesting contributions to a discussion of workfare.

Marie Winn

The End of Play

Of all the changes that have altered the topography of   1
childhood, the most dramatic has been the disappearance of childhood
play. Whereas a decade or two ago children were easily distinguished
from the adult world by the very nature of their play, today children's
occupations do not differ greatly from adult diversions.

Infants and toddlers, to be sure, continue to follow certain timeless   2
patterns of manipulation and exploration; adolescents, too, have not
changed their free-time habits so very much, turning as they ever have
towards adult pastimes and amusements in their drive for autonomy,

Marie Winn, born in Czechoslovakia in 1936, came to New York when she was still a child. She later graduated from Radcliffe College and then did further academic work at Columbia University. Our selection comes from *Childhood Without Children* (1983), a book based in part on interviews with hundreds of children and parents.

self-mastery, and sexual discovery. It is among the ranks of school-age children, those six-to-twelve-year-olds who once avidly filled their free moments with childhood play, that the greatest change is evident. In the place of traditional, sometimes ancient childhood games that were still popular a generation ago, in the place of fantasy and make-believe play—"You be the mommy and I'll be the daddy"—doll play or toy-soldier play, jump-rope play, ball-bouncing play, today's children have substituted television viewing and, most recently, video games.

Many parents have misgivings about the influence of television. 3 They sense that a steady and time-consuming exposure to passive entertainment might damage the ability to play imaginatively and resourcefully, or prevent this ability from developing in the first place. A mother of two school-age children recalls: "When I was growing up, we used to go out into the vacant lots and make up week-long dramas and sagas. This was during third, fourth, fifth grades. But my own kids have never done that sort of thing, and somehow it bothers me. I wish we had cut down on the TV years ago, and maybe the kids would have learned how to play."

The testimony of parents who eliminate television for periods of 4 time strengthens the connection between children's television watching and changed play patterns. Many parents discover that when their children don't have television to fill their free time, they resort to the old kinds of imaginative, traditional "children's play." Moreover, these parents often observe that under such circumstances "they begin to seem more like children" or "they act more childlike." Clearly, a part of the definition of childhood, in adults' minds, resides in the nature of children's play.

Children themselves sometimes recognize the link between play 5 and their own special definition as children. In an interview about children's books with four ten-year-old girls, one of them said: "I read this story about a girl my age growing up twenty years ago—you know, in 1960 or so—and she seemed so much younger than me in her behavior. Like she might be playing with dolls, or playing all sorts of children's games, or jump-roping or something." The other girls all agreed that they had noticed a similar discrepancy between themselves and fictional children in books of the past: those children seemed more like children. "So what do *you* do in your spare time, if you don't play with dolls or play make-believe games or jump rope or do things kids did twenty years ago?" they were asked. They laughed and answered, "We watch TV."

But perhaps other societal factors have caused children to give up   6
play. Children's greater exposure to adult realities, their knowledge
of adult sexuality, for instance, might make them more sophisticated,
less likely to play like children. Evidence from the counterculture communes of the sixties and seventies adds weight to the argument that
it is television above all that has eliminated children's play. Studies of
children raised in a variety of such communes, all television-free,
showed the little communards continuing to fill their time with those
forms of play that have all but vanished from the lives of conventionally
reared American children. And yet these counterculture kids were cas-
ually exposed to all sorts of adult matters—drug taking, sexual intercourse. Indeed, they sometimes incorporated these matters into their
play: "We're mating," a pair of six-year-olds told a reporter to explain
their curious bumps and grinds. Nevertheless, to all observers the com-
mune children preserved a distinctly childlike and even innocent de-
meanor, an impression that was produced mainly by the fact that they
spent most of their time playing. Their play defined them as belonging
to a special world of childhood.

Not all children have lost the desire to engage in the old-style   7
childhood play. But so long as the most popular, most dominant members of the peer group, who are often the most socially precocious, are
"beyond" playing, then a common desire to conform makes it harder
for those children who still have the drive to play to go ahead and do
so. Parents often report that their children seem ashamed of previously
common forms of play and hide their involvement with such play from
their peers. "My fifth-grader still plays with dolls," a mother tells, "but
she keeps them hidden in the basement where nobody will see them."
This social check on the play instinct serves to hasten the end of childhood for even the least advanced children.

What seems to have replaced play in the lives of great numbers   8
of preadolescents these days, starting as early as fourth grade, is a
burgeoning interest in boy-girl interactions—"going out" or "going
together." These activities do not necessarily involve going anywhere
or doing anything sexual, but nevertheless are the first stage of a sexual
process that used to commence at puberty or even later. Those more
sophisticated children who are already involved in such manifestly
unchildlike interest make plain their low opinion of their peers who
still *play*. "Some of the kids in the class are real weird," a fifth-grade
boy states. "They're not interested in going out, just in trucks and
stuff, or games pretending they're monsters. Some of them don't even
try to be cool."

Video Games Versus Marbles

Is there really any great difference, one might ask, between that gang 9
of kids playing video games by the hour at their local candy store these
days and those small fry who used to hang around together spending
equal amounts of time playing marbles? It is easy to see a similarity
between the two activities: each requires a certain amount of manual
dexterity, each is almost as much fun to watch as to play, each is simple
and yet challenging enough for that middle-childhood age group for
whom time can be so oppressive if unfilled.

One significant difference between the modern pre-teen fad of 10
video games and the once popular but now almost extinct pastime of
marbles is economic: playing video games costs twenty-five cents for
approximately three minutes of play; playing marbles, after a small
initial investment, is free. The children who frequent video-game machines require a considerable outlay of quarters to subsidize their fun;
two, three, or four dollars is not an unusual expenditure for an eight-
or nine-year-old spending an hour or two with his friends playing
Asteroids or Pac-Man or Space Invaders. For most of the children the
money comes from their weekly allowance. Some augment this
amount by enterprising commercial ventures—trading and selling
comic books, or doing chores around the house for extra money.

But what difference does it make *where* the money comes from? 11
Why should that make video games any less satisfactory as an amusement for children? In fact, having to pay for the entertainment, whatever the source of the money, and having its duration limited by one's
financial resources changes the nature of the game, in a subtle way
diminishing the satisfactions it offers. Money and time become inter-
twined, as they so often are in the adult world and as, in the past,
they almost never were in the child's world. For the child playing
marbles, meanwhile, time has a far more carefree quality, bounded
only by the requirements to be home by suppertime or by dark.

But the video-game-playing child has an additional burden—a bur- 12
den of choice, of knowing that the money used for playing Pac-Man
could have been saved for Christmas, could have been used to buy
something tangible, perhaps something "worthwhile," as his parents
might say, rather than being "wasted" on video games. There is a
certain sense of adultness that spending money imparts, a feeling of
being a consumer, which distinguishes a game with a price from its
counterparts among the traditional childhood games children once
played at no cost.

There are other differences as well. Unlike child-initiated and   13
child-organized games such as marbles, video games are adult-created
mechanisms not entirely within the child's control, and thus less likely
to impart a sense of mastery and fulfillment: the coin may get jammed,
the machine may go haywire, the little blobs may stop eating the funny
little dots. Then the child must go to the storekeeper to complain, to
get his money back. He may be "ripped off" and simply lose his
quarter, much as his parents are when they buy a faulty appliance.
This possibility of disaster gives the child's play a certain weight that
marbles never imposed on its light-hearted players.

Even if a child has a video game at home requiring no coin outlay,   14
the play it provides is less than optimal. The noise level of the machine
is high—too high, usually, for the child to conduct a conversation
easily with another child. And yet, according to its enthusiasts, this
very noisiness is a part of the game's attraction. The loud whizzes,
crashes, and whirrs of the video-game machine "blow the mind" and
create an excitement that is quite apart from the excitement generated
simply by trying to win a game. A traditional childhood game such as
marbles, on the other hand, has little built-in stimulation; the excitement of playing is generated entirely by the players' own actions. And
while the pace of a game of marbles is close to the child's natural
physiological rhythms, the frenzied activities of video games serve to
"rev up" the child in an artificial way, almost in the way a stimulant
or an amphetamine might. Meanwhile the perceptual impact of a video
game is similar to that of watching television—the action, after all,
takes place on a television screen—causing the eye to defocus slightly
and creating a certain alteration in the child's natural state of consciousness.

Parents' instinctive reaction to their children's involvement with   15
video games provides another clue to the difference between this contemporary form of play and the more traditional pastimes such as marbles. While parents, indeed most adults, derive open pleasure from
watching children at play, most parents today are not delighted to
watch their kids flicking away at the Pac-Man machine. This does not
seem to them to be real play. As a mother of two school-age children
anxiously explains, "We used to do real childhood sorts of things when
I was a kid. We'd build forts and put on crazy plays and make up new
languages, and just generally we *played*. But today my kids don't play
that way at all. They like video games and of course they still go in
for sports outdoors. They go roller skating and ice skating and skiing
and all. But they don't seem to really *play*."

Some of this feeling may represent a certain nostalgia for the past 16
and the old generation's resistance to the different ways of the new.
But it is more likely that most adults have an instinctive understanding
of the importance of play in their own childhood. This feeling stokes
their fears that their children are being deprived of something irre-
placeable when they flip the levers on the video machines to manip-
ulate the electronic images rather than flick their fingers to send a
marble shooting towards another marble.

Play Deprivation

In addition to television's influence, some parents and teachers ascribe 17
children's diminished drive to play to recent changes in the school
curriculum, especially in the early grades.

"Kindergarten, traditionally a playful port of entry into formal 18
school, is becoming more academic, with children being taught specific
skills, taking tests, and occasionally even having homework," begins
a report on new directions in early childhood education. Since 1970,
according to the United States census, the proportion of three- and
four-year-olds enrolled in school has risen dramatically, from 20.5 percent to 36.7 percent in 1980, and these nursery schools have largely
joined the push towards academic acceleration in the early grades.
Moreover, middle-class nursery schools in recent years have introduced substantial doses of academic material into their daily programs,
often using those particular devices originally intended to help culturally deprived preschoolers in compensatory programs such as
Headstart to catch up with their middle-class peers. Indeed, some of
the increased focus on academic skills in nursery schools and kinder-
gartens is related to the widespread popularity among young children
and their parents of *Sesame Street*, a program originally intended to
help deprived children attain academic skills, but universally watched
by middle-class toddlers as well.

Parents of the *Sesame Street* generation often demand a "serious," 19
skill-centered program for their preschoolers in school, afraid that the
old-fashioned, play-centered curriculum will bore their alphabet-
spouting, number-chanting four- and five-year-olds. A few parents,
especially those whose children have not attended television classes
or nursery school, complain of the high-powered pace of kindergarten
these days. A father whose five-year-old daughter attends a public
kindergarten declares: "There's a lot more pressure put on little kids
these days than when we were kids, that's for sure. My daughter never

went to nursery school and never watched *Sesame,* and she had a lot of trouble when she entered kindergarten this fall. By October, just a month and a half into the program, she was already flunking. The teacher told us our daughter couldn't keep up with the other kids. And believe me, she's a bright kid! All the other kids were getting gold stars and smiley faces for their work, and every day Emily would come home in tears because she didn't get a gold star. Remember when we were in kindergarten? We were *children* then. We were allowed just to play!"

A kindergarten teacher confirms the trend towards early academic pressure. "We're expected by the dictates of the school system to push a lot of curriculum," she explains. "Kids in our kindergarten can't sit around playing with blocks any more. We've just managed to squeeze in one hour of free play a week, on Fridays." 20

The diminished emphasis on fantasy and play and imaginative activities in early childhood education and the increased focus on early academic-skill acquisition have helped to change childhood from a play-centered time of life to one more closely resembling the style of adulthood: purposeful, success-centered, competitive. The likelihood is that these preschool "workers" will not metamorphose back into players when they move on to grade school. This decline in play is surely one of the reasons why so many teachers today comment that their third- or fourth-graders act like tired businessmen instead of like children. 21

What might be the consequences of this change in children's play? Children's propensity to engage in that extraordinary series of behaviors characterized as "play" is perhaps the single great dividing line between childhood and adulthood, and has probably been so throughout history. The make-believe games anthropologists have recorded of children in primitive societies around the world attest to the universality of play and to the uniqueness of this activity to the immature members of each society. But in those societies, and probably in Western society before the middle or late eighteenth century, there was always a certain similarity between children's play and adult work. The child's imaginative play took the form of imitation of various aspects of adult life, culminating in the gradual transformation of the child's play from make-believe work to *real* work. At this point, in primitive societies or in our own society of the past, the child took her or his place in the adult work world and the distinctions between adulthood and childhood virtually vanished. But in today's technologically advanced society there is no place for the child in the adult work world. There are not enough jobs, even of the most menial kind, to go around 22 for adults, much less for children. The child must continue to be dependent on adults for many years while gaining the knowledge and skills necessary to become a working member of society.

This is not a new situation for children. For centuries children have   23
endured a prolonged period of dependence long after the helplessness of early childhood is over. But until recent years children remained childlike and playful far longer than they do today. Kept isolated from the adult world as a result of deliberate secrecy and protectiveness, they continued to find pleasure in socially sanctioned childish activities until the imperatives of adolescence led them to strike out for independence and self-sufficiency.

Today, however, with children's inclusion in the adult world both   24
through the instrument of television and as a result of a deliberately preparatory, integrative style of child rearing, the old forms of play no longer seem to provide children with enough excitement and stimulation. What then are these so-called children to do for fulfillment if their desire to play has been vitiated and yet their entry into the working world of adulthood must be delayed for many years? The answer is precisely to get involved in those areas that cause contemporary parents so much distress: addictive television viewing during the school years followed, in adolescence or even before, by a search for similar oblivion via alcohol and drugs; exploration of the world of sensuality and sexuality before achieving the emotional maturity necessary for altruistic relationships.

Psychiatrists have observed among children in recent years a   25
marked increase in the occurrence of depression, a state long considered antithetical to the nature of childhood. Perhaps this phenomenon is at least somewhat connected with the current sense of uselessness and alienation that children feel, a sense that play may once upon a time have kept in abeyance.

Questions

1. In a sentence or two sum up Winn's thesis.
2. When you were a child, what did you do in your "spare time"? Judging from your own experience, is Winn's first paragraph true, or at least roughly true?
3. Assuming that children today do indeed spend many hours watching television and playing video games, is it true that these activities "do not differ greatly from adult diversions"? To test Winn's as-

sertion, list the diversions of adults and of children that you know of from your own experience. Are the two lists indeed strikingly similar? Or do the lists reveal important differences? Explain.

4. Winn's argument is largely composed of a series of comparisons between the play of children before access to TV and after; between traditional and contemporary kindergarten; between childhood in primitive (and our own pre-industrial) society and in technologically advanced societies. List the points she makes to develop each of these comparisons. How well does each comparison support her thesis?

5. Winn obviously prefers that children in play make up stories rather than watch television. What reasons can be given to prefer making up stories, or reading stories in a book, to watching stories on television? Winn does not mention being read to by an adult as an activity of childhood. Draw your own comparison between traditional bedtime story-reading and nighttime TV-watching. Would such a comparison have strengthened or weakened Winn's argument?

6. Speaking of video games (paragraph 11), Winn argues that "having to pay for the entertainment . . . changes the nature of the game, in a subtle way diminishing the satisfactions it offers." Can one reply that having to pay helps a child to appreciate the value of money? In short, can it be argued that paying for one's pleasure is a way of becoming mature?

Black Elk

War Games

When it was summer again we were camping on the   1
Rosebud, and I did not feel so much afraid, because the Wasichus
seemed farther away and there was peace there in the valley and there

---

Black Elk, a *wichasha wakon* (holy man) of the Oglala Sioux, as a small boy witnessed the battle of the Little Bighorn (1876). He lived to see his people all but annihilated and his hopes for them extinguished. In 1931, toward the end of his life, he told his life story to the poet and scholar John G. Neihardt to preserve a sacred vision given him.

"War Games" (editors' title) is from *Black Elk Speaks*.

was plenty of meat. But all the boys from five or six years up were playing war. The little boys would gather together from the different bands of the tribe and fight each other with mud balls that they threw with willow sticks. And the big boys played the game called Throwing-Them-Off-Their-Horses, which is a battle all but the killing; and sometimes they got hurt. The horsebacks from the different bands would line up and charge upon each other, yelling; and when the ponies came together on the run, they would rear and flounder and scream in a big dust, and the riders would seize each other, wrestling until one side had lost all its men, for those who fell upon the ground were counted dead.

When I was older, I, too, often played this game. We were always 2 naked when we played it, just as warriors are when they go into battle if it is not too cold, because they are swifter without clothes. Once I fell off on my back right in the middle of a bed of prickly pears, and it took my mother a long while to pick all the stickers out of me. I was still too little to play war that summer, but I can remember watching the other boys, and I thought that when we all grew up and were big together, maybe we could kill all the Wasichus or drive them far away from our country. . . .

There was a war game that we little boys played after a big hunt. 3 We went out a little way from the village and built some grass tepees, playing we were enemies and this was our village. We had an adviser, and when it got dark he would order us to go and steal some dried meat from the big people. He would hold a stick up to us and we had to bite off a piece of it. If we bit a big piece we had to get a big piece of meat, and if we bit a little piece, we did not have to get so much. Then we started for the big people's village, crawling on our bellies, and when we got back without getting caught, we would have a big feast and a dance and make kill talks, telling of our brave deeds like warriors. Once, I remember, I had no brave deed to tell. I crawled up to a leaning tree beside a tepee and there was meat hanging on the limbs. I wanted a tongue I saw up there in the moonlight, so I climbed up. But just as I was about to reach it, the man in the tepee yelled "Ye-a-a!" He was saying this to his dog, who was stealing some meat too, but I thought the man had seen me, and I was so scared I fell out of the tree and ran away crying.

Then we used to have what we called a chapped breast dance. 4 Our adviser would look us over to see whose breast was burned most from not having it covered with the robe we wore; and the boy chosen would lead the dance while we all sang like this:

I have a chapped breast.
My breast is red.
My breast is yellow.

And we practiced endurance too. Our adviser would put dry sunflower seeds on our wrists. These were lit at the top, and we had to let them burn clear down to the skin. They hurt and made sores, but if we knocked them off or cried Owh!, we would be called women.

Questions

1. Notice the subjective passages in Black Elk's descriptions of the games he played as a child. What do they reveal about Black Elk as a child and as an adult? How appropriate are these revelations to his topic?

2. The Duke of Wellington is reported to have said that the battle of Waterloo was won on the playing fields of Eton. Try to describe a game that is a small version of an adult activity that teaches adult habits, good or bad. As an experiment, write the description as objectively as you can. Then rewrite it, allowing your description to reveal your attitudes, as a child and now, to the game, to other children, and to the adult world.

Joseph Epstein

Obsessed with Sport

I cannot remember when I was not surrounded by sports, 1 when talk of sports was not in the air, when I did not care passionately about sports. As a boy in Chicago in the late Forties, I lived in the

Joseph Epstein was born in Chicago in 1937. He is the author of several books on American culture, the editor of *American Scholar* (a quarterly review published by Phi Beta Kappa), and an occasional teacher of English at Northwestern University.

same building as the sister and brother-in-law of Barney Ross, the welterweight champion. Half a block away, down near the lake, the Sullivan High School football team worked out in the spring and autumn. Summers the same field was given over to baseball and men's softball on Sundays. A few blocks to the north was the Touhy Avenue Fieldhouse, where basketball was played, and lifeguards trained, and behind which, in a softball field frozen over in winter, crack-the-whip, hockey, and speed skating took over. To the west, a block or so up Morse Avenue, was the Morse Avenue "L" Recreations, a combined pool hall and bowling alley. Life, in short, was games.

My father had no interest in sports. He had grown up, one of the ten children of Russian Jewish immigrant parents, on tough Notre Dame Street in Montreal, where the major sports were craps, poker, and petty larceny. He left Montreal at seventeen to come to Chicago, where he worked hard and successfully so that his sons might play. Two of his boyhood friends from Notre Dame Street, who had the comic-book names of Sammy and Danny Spunt, had also come to Chicago, where they bought the Ringside Gym on Dearborn Street in the Loop. All the big names worked out at Ringside for their Chicago fights: Willie Pep, Tony Zale, Joe Louis. At eight or nine I would take the El downtown to the Ringside, be introduced around by Danny Spunt ("Tony Zale, I'd like you to meet the son of an old friend of mine. Kid, I'd like you to meet the middleweight champion of the world"), and return home with an envelope filled with autographed 8-by-10 glossies of Gus Lesnevich, Tammy Maurielo, Kid Gavilan, and the wondrous Sugar Ray.

I lived on, off, and in sports. *Sport* magazine had recently begun publication, and I gobbled up its issues cover to cover, soon becoming knowledgeable not only about the major sports—baseball, football, and basketball—but about golf, hockey, tennis, and horse racing, so that I scored reputably on the Sport Quiz, a regular department at the front of the magazine. Another regular department was the Sport Classic, which featured longish profiles of the legendary figures in the history of sports: Ty Cobb, Jim Thorpe, Bobby Jones, Big Bill Tilden, Red Grange, Man o' War. I next moved on to the sports novels of John R. Tunis—*All-American, The Iron Duke, The Kid from Tomkinsville, The Kid Comes Back, World Series*, the lot—which I read with as much excitement as any books I have read since.

The time was, as is now apparent, a splendid era in sports. Ted Williams, Joe DiMaggio, and Stan Musial were afield; first Jack Kramer, then Pancho Gonzales, dominated tennis; George Mikan led the Minneapolis Lakers, and the Harlem Globetrotters could still be taken seriously; Doc Blanchard and Glen Davis, Mr. Inside and Mr. Outside, were playing for Army, Johnny Lujack was at Notre Dame; in the pros Sammy Baugh, Bob Waterfield, and Sid Luckman were the major T-formation quarterbacks; Joe Louis and Sugar Ray Robinson fought frequently; the two Willies, Mosconi and Hoppe, put in regular appearances at Bensinger's in the Loop; Eddie Arcaro seemed to ride three, four winners a day. Giants, it truly seemed, walked the earth.

All learning of craft—which sport, like writing, most assuredly 5
is—involves imitation, especially in the early stages; and I was an ex-
cellent mimic. By the time I was ten years old I had mastery over all the big-time moves: the spit in the mitt, the fluid infield chatter, the knocking of dirt from the spikes; the rhythmic barking out of signals, hands high under the center's crotch to take the ball; the three bounces and deep breath before shooting the free throw (on this last, I regretted not being a Catholic, so that I might be able to make the sign of the cross before shooting, as was then the fashion among Catholic high-school and college players). I went in for athletic haberdashery in a big way, often going beyond mimicry to the point of flat-out phoniness—wearing, for example, a knee pad while playing basketball, though my knees were always, exasperatingly, intact.

I always looked good, which was important, because form is in- 6
trinsic to sports; but in my case it was doubly important, because the truth is that I wasn't really very good. Or at any rate not good enough. Two factors accounted for this. The first was that, without being shy about body contact, I lacked a certain indispensable aggressiveness; the second, connected closely to the first, was that, when it came right down to it, I did not care enough about winning. I would rather lose a point attempting a slashing cross-court backhand than play for an easier winner down the side; the long jump shot always had more allure for me than the safer drive to the basket. Given a choice between the two vanities of winning and looking good, I almost always preferred looking good.

I shall never forget the afternoon, sometime along about my thir- 7
teenth year, when, shooting baskets alone, I came upon the technique for shooting the hook. Although today it has nowhere near the con-
sequence of the jump shot—an innovation that has been to basketball what the jet has been to air travel—the hook is still the single most beautiful shot in the game. The rhythm and grace of it, the sway of the body off the pivot, the release of the ball behind the head and off the fingertips, the touch and instinct involved in its execution, make

the hook altogether a balletic thing, and to achieve it is to feel one of the most delectable sensations in sports. That afternoon, on a deserted side street, shooting on a rickety wooden backboard and a black rim without a net, I felt it and grew nearly drunk on the feeling. Rain came down, dirt washed in the gutters, flecks of it spattering my clothes and arms and face, but, soaked and cold though I was, I do not think I would have left that basket on that afternoon for anything. I threw up hook after hook, from every angle, from farther and farther out, off the board, without the board, and hook after hook went in. Only pitch darkness drove me home.

I do not say that not to have shot the hook is never to have lived, 8 but only that, once having done so, the pleasure it gives is not so easily forgotten. Every sport offers similar pleasures, the pleasures taken differing by temperament: the canter into the end zone to meet a floating touchdown pass, or the clean, crisp feel of a perfect block or tackle; the long straight drive or the precisely played approach shot to the green; the solid overhead; the pickup on the tricky short hop or the long ball down one of the power alleys. Different sports, different pleasures. But so keen are these pleasures—pleasures of execution, of craft completed—that, along with being unforgettable, they are also worth recapturing in any available way, and the most available way, when reflexes have slowed, when muscle no longer responds so readily to brain, is from the grandstand or, perhaps more often nowadays, from the chair before the television.

Pleasures of the Spectator

I have put in days on the bench, but years in my chair before the 9 television set. Recently it has occurred to me that over the years I have heard more hours of talk from the announcer Curt Gowdy than from my own father, who is not a reticent man. I have been thoroughly Schenkeled, Mussbergered, Summeralled, Cosselled, DeRogotissed, and Garagiolaed. How many hundreds—thousands?—of hours have I spent watching sports of all sorts, either at parks or stadiums or over television? I am glad I shall never have a precise answer. Yet neither apparently can I get enough. What is the fascination? Why is it that, with the prospect of a game to watch in the evening or on the weekend, the day seems lighter and brighter? What do I get out of it?

What I get out of it, according to one fairly prominent view, is an 10 outlet for my violent emotions. Knee-wrenching, rib-cracking, headbusting, this view has it, is what sports are really about, with sports fans being essentially sadists, and cowardly sadists at that, for they take their violence not at firsthand but at second remove. Enthusiasm for sports among Americans is little more than a reflection of the national penchant for violence. Military men talk about game plans; the long touchdown pass is called the bomb. The average pro-football fan, seeing a quarterback writhing on the ground at midfield as a result of the ministrations of Joe Green, Carl Eller, or Lyle Alzado, twitters with glee, finds his ultimate reward, and declares a little holiday in the blackest corner of his heart.

But this is a criticism that comes at sports by way of politics. To 11 believe it one has to believe that the history of the United States is chiefly one of rape, expropriation, and aggressive imperialism. To dismiss it, however, one need only know something about sports. Violence is indubitably a part of some sports; in some—hockey is an example—it sometimes comes close to being featured. But in no sport— not even boxing, that most rudimentary of sports—is it the main item, and in many other sports it plays no part at all. A distinction worth insisting on is that between violence and roughness. Roughness, a willingness to mix it up, to take if need be an elbow in the jaw, is part of rebounding in basketball, yet violence is not. Even in pro football, most maligned of modern American sports, more of roughness than of violence is involved. Roughness raises the stakes, provides the pressure, behind execution. A splendid because true phrase has come about in pro football to cover the situation in which a pass receiver, certain that he will be tackled upon the instant he makes his reception, drops a ball he should otherwise have caught easily—the phrase, best delivered in a Southern accent such as Don Meredith's, is "He heard footsteps on that one, Howard." Although a part of the attraction, it is not so much those footsteps that fill the stands and the den chairs on Sunday afternoons as it is those men who elude them: the Lynn Swanns, the Fran Tarkentons, the O. J. Simpsons. The American love of violence theory really will not wash. Dick Butkus did not get us into Vietnam.

Many who would not argue that sports reflect American violence 12 nevertheless claim that they imbue one with the competitive spirit. In some who are already amply endowed with it, sports doubtless do tend to refine (or possibly brutalize) the desire to win. Yet sports also teach a serious respect for craft. Competition, though it flourishes as always, is in bad odor nowadays; but craft, officially respected, does not flourish greatly outside the boutique.

If the love of violence or the competitive urge does not put me in   13
my chair for the countless games I watch, is it, then, nostalgia, a yearning to regain the more glowing moments of adolescence? Many argue
that this is precisely so, that American men exist in a state of perpetual
immaturity, suspended between boy- and manhood. "The difference
between men and boys," says Liberace, "is the price of their toys." (I
have paid more than $300 for two half-season tickets to the Chicago
Bulls games, parking fees not included.) Such unending enthusiasm
for games may have something to do with adolescence, but little, I
suspect, with regaining anything whatever. Instead, it has more to do
with watching men do regularly and surpassingly what, as an adolescent, one did often bumblingly though with an occasional flash of
genius. To have played these games oneself as a boy or a young man
helps immeasurably the appreciation that in watching a sport played
at professional caliber one is witnessing the extraordinary made to look
ordinary. That a game may have no consequence outside itself—no
effect on history, on one's own life, on anything really—does not make
it trivial but only makes the enjoyment of it all the purer.

The notion that men watch sports to regain their adolescence pic-   14
tures them sitting in the stands or at home watching a game and, within
their psyches, muttering, "There, but for the lack of grace of God, go
I." And it is true that a number of contemporary authors who are taken
seriously have indeed written about sports with a strong overlay of
yearning. In the men's softball games described in the fiction of Philip
Roth, center field is a place akin to Arcady. Arcadian, too, is the out-
field in Willie Morris's memoir of growing up in the South, *North Toward Home*. In the first half of *Rabbit Run* John Updike takes up the life
of a man whose days are downhill all the way after hitting his peak
as a high-school basketball star—and in the writing Updike himself
evinces a nice soft touch of undisguised longing. In *A Fan's Notes*, a
book combining yearning and self-disgust in roughly equal measure,
Frederick Exley makes plain that he would much prefer to have been
born into the skin of Frank Gifford rather than into his own.

But most men who are enraptured by sports do not think any such   15
thing. I should like to have Kareem Abdul-Jabbar's sky hook, but not,
especially for civilian life, the excessive height that is necessary to its
execution. I should like to have Jimmy Connors's ground strokes, but
no part of his mind. These are men born with certain gifts, gifts honed
by practice and determination, that I, and millions along with me,
enjoy seeing on display. But the reality principle is too deeply ingrained, at least in a man of my years, for me to even imagine ex-

changing places with them. One might as well imagine oneself in the winner's circle at Churchill Downs as the horse.

Fantasy is an element in sports when they are played in adoles- 16 cence—an alley basket becomes the glass backboard at Madison Square Garden, a concrete park district tennis court with grass creeping out of the service line becomes center court at Wimbledon—but fantasy of this kind is hard to come by. Part of this has to do with age; but as large a part has to do with the age in which we live. Sport has always been a business but never more so than currently, and nothing lends itself less to fantasy than business. Reading the sports section has become rather like reading the business section—mergers, trades, salary negotiations, contract disputes, options, and strikes fill the columns. Along with the details of business, those of the psychological and social problems of athletes have come to the fore. The old *Sport* magazine concentrated on play on the field, with only an occasional digressive reference to personal life. ("Yogi likes plenty of pizza in the off-season and spends a lot of his time at his teammate Phil Rizzuto's bowling alley" is a rough facsimile of a sentence from its pages that I recall.) But the magazine in its current version, as well as the now more popular *Sports Illustrated*, expends much space on the private lives of athletes—their divorces, hang-ups, race relations, need for approval, concern for security, potted philosophies—with the result that the grand is made to seem small.

On the other side of the ledger, there is a view that finds a shim- 17 mering significance in everything having to do with sports. Literary men in general are notoriously to be distrusted on the subject. They dig around everywhere, and can be depended upon to find much treasure where none is buried. Norman Mailer mining metaphysical ore in every jab of Muhammad Ali, an existential nugget in each of his various and profuse utterances, is a particularly horrendous example. Even the sensible William Carlos Williams was not above this sort of temptation. In a poem entitled "At the Ball Game," we find the lines "It is the Inquisition, the/Revolution." Dr. Williams could not have been much fun at the ball park.

The Real Thing ◆

If enthusiasm for sports has little to do with providing an outlet for 18 violent emotions, regaining adolescence, discovering metaphysical truths, the Inquisition or the Revolution, then what, I ask myself, am I doing past midnight, when I have to be up at 5:30 the next morning, watching on television what will turn out to be a seventeen-inning game between the New York Mets and the St. Louis Cardinals? The conversation coming out of my television set is of a very low grade, even for sports announcing. But even the dreary talk cannot put me off—the rehash of statistics, the advice to youngsters to keep their gloves low when in the field, the thin jokes. Neither the Mets nor the Cards figure to be contenders this year. The only possible effect that this game can have on my life is to make me dog-tired the next day. Yet I cannot pull myself away. I want to know how it is going to end. True, the score will be available in the morning paper. But that is not the same thing. What is going on here?

One thing that is going on is the practice of craft of a very high 19 order, which is intrinsically interesting. But something as important is involved, something rarer in contemporary life, the spectacle of which gives enormous satisfaction. To define this satisfaction negatively, it is the absence of fraudulence and fakery. No small item, this, when one stops to think that in nearly every realm of contemporary life fraud and fakery have an established—some would say a preponderant—place. Advertising, politics, business, and journalism are only the most obvious examples. Fraud seems similarly pervasive in modern art: in painters whose reputations rest on press agentry; in writers who write one way and live quite another; in composers who are taken seriously but whose work cannot be seriously listened to. At a time when *image* is one of the most frequently used words in American speech and writing, one does not too often come upon the real thing.

Sport may be the toy department of life, but one of its abiding 20 compensations is that, at least on the field, it is the real thing. Much has been done in recent years in the attempt to ruin sport—the ruthlessness of owners, the greed of players, the general exploitation of fans. But even all this cannot destroy it. On the court, down on the field, sport is fraud-free and fakeproof. With a full count, two men on, his team down by one run in the last of the eighth, a batter (as well as a pitcher) is beyond the aid of public relations. At match point at Forest Hills a player's press clippings are of no help. Last year's earnings will not sink a twelve-foot putt on the eighteenth at Augusta. Alan Page, galloping up along a quarterback's blind side, figures to be neglectful of that quarterback's image as a swinger. In all these situations, and hundreds of others, a man either comes through or he doesn't. He is alone out there, naked but for his ability, which counts for everything. Something there is that is elemental about this, and something greatly satisfying.

Another part of the satisfaction to be got from sports—from play- 21
ing them, but also from watching them being played—derives from
their special clarity. Sports offer clarity of a kind sufficient to engage
the most serious minds. That the Cambridge mathematician G. H.
Hardy closely followed cricket and avidly read cricket scores is not
altogether surprising. Numbers in sports are ubiquitous. Scores, stand-
ings, averages, times, records—comfort is found in such numbers.
ERA, RBI, FGP, pass completions, turnovers, category upon category
of statistics are kept for nearly every aspect of athletic activity. (Why,
I recently heard someone ask, are records not kept for catchers throwing out runners attempting to steal? Because, the answer is, often runners steal on pitchers, and so it would be unfair to charge these stolen
bases against catchers.) As perhaps in no other sphere, numbers in
sports tell one where things stand. No loopholes here, where figures,
for once, do not lie. Nowhere else is such specificity of result available.

Clarity about character is also available in sports. "You Americans 22
hold to the proposition that it is self-evident that all men are created
equal," I not long ago heard an Englishman say, adding, "it had better
be self-evident, for no other evidence for it exists." Sport coldly demonstrates physical inequalities—there are the larger, the faster, the
stronger, the more graceful athletes—but it also throws up human
types who have devised ways to redress these inequalities. One such
type is the hustler. In every realm but that of sports the word *hustle*
is pejorative, whereas in sports it is approbative. Two of the hustler
breed, Pete Rose of the Cincinnati Reds and Jerry Sloan of the Chicago
Bulls, are men who supplement reasonably high levels of ability with
unreasonably high levels of courage and desire. Other athletes—Joe
Morgan and Oscar Robertson come to mind—bring superior athletic
intelligence to bear upon their play. And Bill Russell, late of the Boston
Celtics, who if the truth be known was not an inherently superior
athlete, blended hustle and intelligence with what abilities he did have
and through force of character established supremacy.

Whence do hustle, intelligence, and character in sports derive, 23
especially since they apparently do not necessarily carry over into life?
Joe DiMaggio and Sugar Ray Robinson, two of the most instinctively
intelligent and physically elegant athletes, brought little of either of
these qualities over into their business or personal activities. Some
athletes can do all but one important thing well: Wilt Chamberlain at
the free-throw line, for those who recall his misery there, leaves a
permanent picture of a mental block in action. Other athletes—Connie
Hawkins, Ilie Nastase, Dick Allen—have all the physical gifts in su-
perabundance, yet, because of some insufficiency of character, some

searing flaw, never come near to fulfilling their promise. Coaches supply yet another gallery of human types, from the fanatical Vince Lombardi to the comical Casey Stengel to the measured and aptly named John Wooden. The cast of characters in sport, the variety of situations, the complexity of behavior it puts on display, the overall human exhibit it offers—together these supply an enjoyment akin to that once provided by reading interminably long but inexhaustibly rich nineteenth-century novels.

In a wider sense, sport is culture. For many American men it represents a common background, a shared interest. It has a binding power that transcends social class and education. Some years ago I found myself working in the South among men with whom I shared nothing in the way of region, religion, education, politics, or general views; we shared nothing, in fact, but sports, which was enough for us to get along and grow to become friends, in the process showing how superficial all the things that might have kept us apart in fact were. More recently, in Chicago, at a time when race relations were in a particularly jagged state, I recall emerging from an NBA game, in which the Chicago Bulls in overtime beat the Milwaukee Bucks, into a snowy night and an aura of common good feeling that, for a time, submerged the enmity between races; laughing, throwing snowballs, exuberant generally, the crowd leaving the Chicago Stadium that night was not divided by being black and white but unified by being Bull fans. Last year's Boston-Cincinnati World Series, one of the most gratifying in memory, coming hard upon a year of extreme political divisiveness, performed, however briefly, something of the same function. How much better it felt to agree about the mastery of Luis Tiant than to argue about the wretchedness of Richard Nixon. 24

In sports as in life, character does not much change. I have recently begun to play a game called racquet ball, and I find I would still rather look good than win, which is what I usually do: look good and lose. I beat the rum-dums but go down before quality players. I get compliments in defeat. Men who beat me admire the whip of my strokes, my wrist action, my anticipation, the power I get behind the ball. When this occurs I feel like a woman who is complimented for the shape of her bottom when it is her mind she craves admiration for, though of course she will take what praise she can get. 25

R. H. Tawney, the great historian of religion and capitalism, once remarked that the only progress he could note during the course of his lifetime was in the deportment of dogs. For myself, I would say that the chief progress in the course of my lifetime has been in the 26 quality and variety of athletic gear. Racquets made of metal, aluminum, wood, and fiberglass, balls of different colors, sneakers of all materials and designs, posh warm-up suits, tube socks, sweatbands for the head and wrist in various colors and pipings; only the athletic supporter, the old jockstrap, remains unornamented, but perhaps even now Vera or Peter Max is at the drawing board. In any event, with all this elegant plumage available, it is a nice time to be playing ball again.

Sports can be impervious to age. My father-in-law, a man of style, 27 seriousness, and great good humor who died a year ago in his late sixties, was born in South Bend, Indiana, and in his early manhood left the Catholic Church—two facts that conjoined to give him an intense interest in the fortunes of the teams from Notre Dame. He loved to see them lose. The torch has been passed on. I now love to see Notre Dame lose, and when it does I think of him and remember his smile.

When I was a boy I had a neighbor, a man who, after retirement, 28 had a number of strokes. An old man and a young boy, we had in common a love of sports, which, when we met on the street, was our only topic of conversation. He once inspected a new glove of mine, and instructed me to rub it down with neat's-foot-oil, place a ball firmly in the pocket, wrap string tightly around the glove, and leave it like that for the winter. I did, and it worked. After his last stroke but one, he seldom left his house. Afternoons he spent in a chair in his bedroom, a blanket over his lap, listening to Cub games over the radio. It was while listening to a ball game that he quietly died. I cannot imagine a better way.

Questions

1. In his first two paragraphs Epstein writes of the opportunities he had when growing up in Chicago in the 1940s to live "on, off, and in sports." Compare or contrast those opportunities with your own. How do you account for the differences? (Were there some similarities?)

2. In paragraph 4 Epstein writes of the 1940s: "The time was, as is now apparent, a splendid era in sports." Looking back at the decade in your life (which can be the current decade) in which you have been most engaged as a sports fan, would you characterize it also as "a splendid era"? If not, how would you characterize it—disillusioning, mediocre, uneven? Try to support your characterization concretely, as Epstein does in paragraph 4.

3. In paragraph 5 Epstein writes: "All learning of craft—which sport, like writing, most assuredly is—involves imitation, especially in the early stages." Did you learn sports by imitation? Explain. What about writing? Why, or why not?

4. In paragraph 13 Epstein points out that having played a game as a boy or young man (presumably also as a girl or young woman) helps one to appreciate the performance of professionals. Do you think the same principle holds true for literature, music, dance, art? Should all children have a chance to learn to play musical instruments, to paint, and to write, not in the expectation that they will all practice those arts as adults, but to enhance their later enjoyment and support of concerts, museums, books, and theater?

5. What makes spectator sports appealing? After dismissing violence and the spectator's nostalgia for adolescence as the source of their appeal, Epstein cites three or four reasons why spectator sports appeal to him. Why does your favorite spectator sport appeal to you?

6. If you are not a sports fan, is there an area of your experience in which you feel close to being obsessed? Music? food? clothes? dogs? sex? If you were to write about this obsession, how might outlining Epstein's essay help you to find ideas?

John Updike

A & P

In walks these three girls in nothing but bathing suits. I'm   1
in the third checkout slot, with my back to the door, so I don't see
them until they're over by the bread. The one that caught my eye first

John Updike was born in 1932 in Shillington, Pennsylvania. After graduating from college he studied art for a year in England, but he then returned to the United States and began working as a staff reporter for the *New Yorker*. He soon published stories in the magazine, and he continues to do so. He has also written novels (including *Rabbit, Run* and *The Witches of Eastwick*), essays, and light verse. The story we print here, "A & P," was published in 1961, but many readers find that except for the prices mentioned there is nothing dated about it.

was the one in the plaid green two-piece. She was a chunky kid, with a good tan and a sweet broad soft-looking can with those two crescents of white just under it, where the sun never seems to hit, at the top of the backs of her legs. I stood there with my hand on a box of HiHo crackers trying to remember if I rang it up or not. I ring it up again and the customer starts giving me hell. She's one of these cash-register-watchers, a witch about fifty with rouge on her cheekbones and no eyebrows, and I know it made her day to trip me up. She'd been watching cash registers for fifty years and probably never seen a mistake before.

By the time I got her feathers smoothed and her goodies into a 2 bag—she gives me a little snort in passing, if she'd been born at the right time they would have burned her over in Salem—by the time I get her on her way the girls had circled around the bread and were coming back, without a pushcart, back my way along the counters, in the aisle between the checkouts and the Special bins. They didn't even have shoes on. There was this chunky one, with the two-piece—it was bright green and the seams on the bra were still sharp and her belly was still pretty pale so I guessed she just got it (the suit)—there was this one, with one of those chubby berry-faces, the lips all bunched together under her nose, this one, and a tall one, with black hair that hadn't quite frizzed right, and one of these sunburns right across under the eyes, and a chin that was too long—you know, the kind of girl other girls think is very "striking" and "attractive" but never quite makes it, as they very well know, which is why they like her so much—and then the third one, that wasn't quite so tall. She was the queen. She kind of led them, the other two peeking around and making their shoulders round. She didn't look around, not this queen, she just walked straight on slowly, on these long white prima-donna legs. She came down a little hard on her heels, as if she didn't walk in her bare feet that much, putting down her heels and then letting the weight move along to her toes as if she was testing the floor with every step, putting a little deliberate extra action into it. You never know for sure how girls' minds work (do you really think it's a mind in there or just a little buzz like a bee in a glass jar?) but you got the idea she had talked the other two into coming in here with her, and now she was showing them how to do it, walk slow and hold yourself straight.

She had on a kind of dirty-pink—beige maybe, I don't know— 3 bathing suit with a little nubble all over it and, what got me, the straps were down. They were off her shoulders looped loose around the cool tops of her arms, and I guess as a result the suit had slipped a little on her, so all around the top of the cloth there was this shining rim. If it hadn't been there you wouldn't have known there could have been anything whiter than those shoulders. With the straps pushed off, there was nothing between the top of the suit and the top of her head except just *her,* this clean bare plane of the top of her chest down from the shoulder bones like a dented sheet of metal tilted in the light. I mean, it was more than pretty.

She had sort of oaky hair that the sun and salt had bleached, done   4 up in a bun that was unravelling, and a kind of prim face. Walking into the A & P with your straps down, I suppose it's the only kind of face you *can* have. She held her head so high her neck, coming up out of those white shoulders, looked kind of stretched, but I didn't mind. The longer her neck was, the more of her there was.

She must have felt in the corner of her eye me and over my shoul-   5 der Stokesie in the second slot watching, but she didn't tip. Not this queen. She kept her eyes moving across the racks, and stopped, and turned so slow it made my stomach rub the inside of my apron, and buzzed to the other two, who kind of huddled against her for relief, and then they all three of them went up the cat and dog food-breakfast cereal-macaroni-rice-raisins-seasonings-spreads-spaghetti-soft drinks-crackers-and-cookies aisle. From the third slot I look straight up this aisle to the meat counter, and I watched them all the way. The fat one with the tan sort of fumbled with the cookies, but on second thought she put the package back. The sheep pushing their carts down the aisle—the girls were walking against the usual traffic (not that we have one-way signs or anything)—were pretty hilarious. You could see them, when Queenie's white shoulders dawned on them, kind of jerk, or hop, or hiccup, but their eyes snapped back to their own baskets and on they pushed. I bet you could set off dynamite in an A & P and the people would by and large keep reaching and checking oatmeal off their lists and muttering "Let me see, there was a third thing, began with A, asparagus, no, ah, yes, applesauce!" or whatever it is they do mutter. But there was no doubt, this jiggled them. A few house slaves in pin curlers even look around after pushing their carts past to make sure what they had seen was correct.

You know, it's one thing to have a girl in a bathing suit down on   6 the beach, where what with the glare nobody can look at each other much anyway, and another thing in the cool of the A & P, under the fluorescent lights, against all those stacked packages, with her feet paddling along naked over our checker-board green-and-cream rubber-tile floor.

"Oh, Daddy," Stokesie said beside me. "I feel so faint." 7

"Darling," I said. "Hold me tight." Stokesie's married, with two 8 babies chalked up on his fuselage already, but as far as I can tell that's the only difference. He's twenty-two, and I was nineteen this April.

"Is it done?" he asks, the responsible married man finding his 9 voice. I forgot to say he thinks he's going to be manager some sunny day, maybe in 1990 when it's called the Great Alexandrov and Petrooshki Tea Company or something.

What he meant was, our town is five miles from a beach, with a 10 big summer colony out on the Point, but we're right in the middle of town, and the women generally put on a shirt or shorts or something before they get out of the car into the street. And anyway these are usually women with six children and varicose veins mapping their legs and nobody, including them, could care less. As I say, we're right in the middle of town, and if you stand at our front doors you can see two banks and the Congregational church and the newspaper store and three real estate offices and about twenty-seven old freeloaders tearing up Central Street because the sewer broke again. It's not as if we're on the Cape; we're north of Boston and there's people in this town haven't seen the ocean for twenty years.

The girls had reached the meat counter and were asking McMahon 11 something. He pointed, they pointed, and they shuffled out of sight behind a pyramid of Diet Delight peaches. All that was left for us to see was old McMahon patting his mouth and looking after them sizing up their joints. Poor kids, I began to feel sorry for them, they couldn't help it.

Now here comes the sad part of the story, at least my family says 12 it's sad, but I don't think it's so sad myself. The store's pretty empty, it being Thursday afternoon, so there was nothing much to do except lean on the register and wait for the girls to show up again. The whole store was like a pinball machine and I didn't know which tunnel they'd come out of. After a while they come around out of the far aisle, around the light bulbs, records at discount of the Caribbean Six or Tony Martin Sings or some such gunk you wonder they waste the wax on, sixpacks of candy bars, and plastic toys done up in cellophane that fall apart when a kid looks at them anyway. Around they come, Queenie still leading the way, and holding a little gray jar in her hand. Slots Three through Seven are unmanned and I could see her wondering between Stokes and me, but Stokesie with his usual luck draws an old party in baggy gray pants who stumbles up with four giant cans of pineapple juice (what do these bums *do* with all that pineapple juice? I've often asked myself) so the girls come to me. Queenie puts down the jar and I take it into my fingers icy cold. Kingfish Fancy Herring Snacks in Pure Sour Cream: 49¢. Now her hands are empty, not a ring or a bracelet, bare as God made them, and I wonder where the money's coming from. Still with that prim look she lifts a folded dollar bill out of the hollow at the center of her nubbled pink top. The jar went heavy in my hand. Really, I thought that was so cute.

Then everybody's luck begins to run out. Lengel comes in from haggling with a truck full of cabbages on the lot and is about to scuttle into the door marked MANAGER behind which he hides all day when the girls touch his eye. Lengel's pretty dreary, teaches Sunday school and the rest, but he doesn't miss that much. He comes over and says, "Girls, this isn't the beach." 13

Queenie blushes, though maybe it's just a brush of sunburn I was noticing for the first time, now that she was so close. "My mother asked me to pick up a jar of herring snacks." Her voice kind of startled me, the way voices do when you see the people first, coming out so flat and dumb yet kind of tony, too, the way it ticked over "pick up" and "snacks." All of a sudden I slid right down her voice into her living room. Her father and the other men were standing around in ice-cream coats and bow ties and the women were in sandals picking up herring snacks on toothpicks off a big glass plate and they were all holding drinks the color of water with olives and sprigs of mint in them. When my parents have somebody over they get lemonade and if it's a real racy affair Schlitz in tall glasses with "They'll Do It Every Time" cartoons stenciled on. 14

"That's all right," Lengel said. "But this isn't the beach." His repeating this struck me as funny, as if it had just occurred to him, and he had been thinking all these years the A & P was a great big dune and he was the head lifeguard. He didn't like my smiling—as I say he doesn't miss much—but he concentrates on giving the girls that sad Sunday-school-superintendent stare. 15

Queenie's blush is no sunburn now, and the plump one in plaid, that I liked better from the back—a really sweet can—pipes up, "We weren't doing any shopping. We just came in for the one thing." 16

"That makes no difference," Lengel tells her, and I could see from the way his eyes went that he hadn't noticed she was wearing a two-piece before. "We want you decently dressed when you come in here." 17

"We *are* decent," Queenie says suddenly, her lower lip pushing, getting sore now that she remembers her place, a place from which 18 the crowd that runs the A & P must look pretty crummy. Fancy Herring Snacks flashed in her very blue eyes.

"Girls, I don't want to argue with you. After this come in here 19 with your shoulders covered. It's our policy." He turns his back. That's policy for you. Policy is what the kingpins want. What the others want is juvenile delinquency.

All this while, the customers had been showing up with their carts 20 but, you know, sheep, seeing a scene, they had all bunched up on Stokesie, who shook open a paper bag as gently as peeling a peach, not wanting to miss a word. I could feel in the silence everybody getting nervous, most of all Lengel, who asks me, "Sammy, have you rung up this purchase?"

I thought and said "No" but it wasn't about that I was thinking. 21 I go through the punches, 4, 9, GROC, TOT—it's more complicated than you think and after you do it often enough, it begins to make a little song, that you hear words to, in my case "Hello (*bing*) there, you (*gung*) hap-py *peepul* (*splat*)!"—the *splat* being the drawer flying out. I uncrease the bill, tenderly as you may imagine, it just having come from between the two smoothest scoops of vanilla I had ever known were there, and pass a half and a penny into her narrow pink palm, and nestle the herrings in a bag and twist its neck and hand it over, all the time thinking.

The girls, and who'd blame them, are in a hurry to get out, so I 22 say "I quit" to Lengel quick enough for them to hear, hoping they'll stop and watch me, their unsuspected hero. They keep right on going, into the electric eye; the door flies open and they flicker across the lot to their car, Queenie and Plaid and Big Tall Goony-Goony (not that as raw material she was so bad), leaving me with Lengel and a kink in his eyebrow.

"Did you say something, Sammy?"

"I said I quit."   23

"I thought you did."   24

"You didn't have to embarrass them."   25

"It was they who were embarrassing us."   26

I started to say something that came out "Fiddle-de-doo." It's a 27 28 saying of my grandmother's, and I know she would have been pleased.

"I don't think you know what you're saying," Lengel said.   29

"I know you don't," I said. "But I do." I pull the bow at the back 30 of my apron and start shrugging it off my shoulders. A couple customers that had been heading for my slot begin to knock against each other, like scared pigs in a chute.

Lengel sighs and begins to look very patient and old and gray. He's been a friend of my parents for years. "Sammy, you don't want to do this to your Mom and Dad," he tells me. It's true, I don't. But it seems to me that once you begin a gesture it's fatal not to go through with it. I fold the apron, "Sammy" stitched in red on the pocket, and put it on the counter, and drop the bow tie on top of it. The bow tie is theirs, if you've ever wondered. "You'll feel this for the rest of your life," Lengel says, and I know that's true, too, but remembering how he made that pretty girl blush makes me so scrunchy inside I punch the No Sale tab and the machine whirs "pee-pul" and the drawer splats out. One advantage to this scene taking place in summer, I can follow this up with a clean exit, there's no fumbling around getting your coat and galoshes, I just saunter into the electric eye in my white shirt that my mother ironed the night before, and the door heaves itself open, and outside the sunshine is skating around on the asphalt.

I look around for my girls, but they're gone, of course. There wasn't anybody but some young married screaming with her children about some candy they didn't get by the door of a powder-blue Falcon station wagon. Looking back in the big windows, over the bags of peat moss and aluminum lawn furniture stacked on the pavement, I could see Lengel in my place in the slot, checking the sheep through. His face was dark gray and his back stiff, as if he'd just had an injection of iron, and my stomach kind of fell as I felt how hard the world was going to be to me hereafter.

Questions

1. Have you ever quit a job on a matter of principle? If so, explain the circumstances, and the short- and long-term consequences.
2. If you have ever thought of quitting a job on a matter of principle but then did not do so, explain the circumstances and your present analysis of your behavior.
3. Some students regard Sammy as a sexist, and say that the failure of the girls to notice his gesture is a fitting punishment for his sexism. Evaluate this view.

Theodore Roethke

Child on Top of a Greenhouse

The wind billowing out the seat of my britches,
My feet crackling splinters of glass and dried putty,
The half-grown chrysanthemums staring up like
    accusers,
Up through the streaked glass, flashing with sunlight,
A few white clouds all rushing eastward,
A line of elms plunging and tossing like horses,
And everyone, everyone pointing up and shouting!

Questions

1. What must have happened just before the scene described in the poem? What details serve as clues?
2. How does the child feel about being on top of the greenhouse? How do you know?
3. The poem is an incomplete or fragmentary sentence. By changing the present participles (from "billowing" in the first line to "shouting" in the last line) to verbs, convert the fragment to a sentence. Read the "revised" poem through, then explain what has been lost.

Theodore Roethke (1908–1963), author of eight volumes of poetry, was born in Saginaw, Michigan. Roethke's father ran a greenhouse, but the son earned his living by teaching English literature, chiefly at the University of Washington, in Seattle.

5
OPEN FOR BUSINESS

Museu Nacional de Arte Antiga, Lisbon, Portugal

Your Name _____ Date _____

Mailing address _____

May we quote you either in promotion for this book or in future publishing ventures?

Yes _____ No _____

Thank you.

	Liked best				Liked least	Didn't read
Stephen Chapman, The Prisoner's Dilemma	5	4	3	2	1	—
Joyce Carol Oates, How I Contemplated the World from the Detroit House of Correction and Began My Life Over Again	5	4	3	2	1	—
Arthur Hugh Clough, The Latest Decalogue	5	4	3	2	1	—

9. ARTICLES OF FAITH

	Liked best				Liked least	Didn't read
Genesis 1–2 (The Creation)	5	4	3	2	1	—
Genesis 3 (The Fall)	5	4	3	2	1	—
Phyllis Trible, Eve and Adam: Genesis 2–3 Reread	5	4	3	2	1	—
C. S. Lewis, What Christians Believe	5	4	3	2	1	—
William James, Religious Faith	5	4	3	2	1	—
John Steinbeck, The Sermon	5	4	3	2	1	—
Langston Hughes, Salvation	5	4	3	2	1	—
Gautama Buddha, The Sermon at Benares and Parables	5	4	3	2	1	—
Wilfred Cantwell Smith, Muslims	5	4	3	2	1	—
Idries Shah, Two Islamic Tales	5	4	3	2	1	—
Chewing Blackbones, Old Man and Old Woman	5	4	3	2	1	—
Katherine Anne Porter, The Jilting of Granny Weatherall	5	4	3	2	1	—
Gerard Manley Hopkins, God's Grandeur	5	4	3	2	1	—
Appendix A: Reading (and Writing About) Pictures	5	4	3	2	1	—
Appendix B: A Writer's Glossary	5	4	3	2	1	—

What did you think of the *Short Views*? Did you discuss them in class?

_____

_____

Did you like the idea of discussing and writing about pictures?

_____

Please add any comments or suggestions on how we might improve this book.

_____

_____

_____

	Liked best				Liked least	Didn't read
Robin Lakoff, You Are What You Say	5	4	3	2	1	—
Barbara Lawrence, Four-Letter Words Can Hurt You	5	4	3	2	1	—
Stevie Smith, Not Waving but Drowning	5	4	3	2	1	—

7. NETWORKS

	Liked best				Liked least	Didn't read
Patricia Spacks, What Have 60 Million Readers Found in Nancy Drew?	5	4	3	2	1	—
Richard Hawley, Television and Adolescents: A Teacher's View	5	4	3	2	1	—
Tipper Gore, Curbing the Sexploitation Industry	5	4	3	2	1	—
Marya Mannes, Television Advertising: The Splitting Image	5	4	3	2	1	—
Dolores Hayden, Advertisements, Pornography, and Public Space	5	4	3	2	1	—
Stephen King, Why We Crave Horror Movies	5	4	3	2	1	—
Woody Allen, The Colorization of Films Insults Artists and Society	5	4	3	2	1	—
Stanley Milgram, Confessions of a News Addict	5	4	3	2	1	—
James Thurber, The Secret Life of Walter Mitty	5	4	3	2	1	—

8. LAW AND ORDER

	Liked best				Liked least	Didn't read
Martin Luther King, Jr., Nonviolent Resistance	5	4	3	2	1	—
Plato, Crito	5	4	3	2	1	—
Luke, John, and an Anonymous Japanese, Four Short Narratives	5	4	3	2	1	—
Thomas Jefferson, The Declaration of Independence	5	4	3	2	1	—
Byron R. White, Opinion of the Supreme Court, in New Jersey v. T.L.O. [On the Right to Search Students]	5	4	3	2	1	—
John Paul Stevens, Dissent in the Case of New Jersey v. T.L.O.	5	4	3	2	1	—
Edward I. Koch, Death and Justice: How Capital Punishment Affirms Life	5	4	3	2	1	—
Henry Schwarzschild, In Opposition to Death Penalty Legislation	5	4	3	2	1	—

	Liked best				Liked least	Didn't read
Charles Krauthammer, The Just Wage: From Bad to Worth	5	4	3	2	1	—
Barbara R. Bergmann, Pay Equity— How to Argue Back	5	4	3	2	1	—
Lester C. Thurow, Why Women Are Paid Less Than Men	5	4	3	2	1	—
Barbara Ehrenreich, A Step Back to the Workhouse?	5	4	3	2	1	—
Marie Winn, The End of Play	5	4	3	2	1	—
Black Elk, War Games	5	4	3	2	1	—
Joseph Epstein, Obsessed with Sport	5	4	3	2	1	—
John Updike, A & P	5	4	3	2	1	—
Theodore Roethke, Child on Top of a Greenhouse	5	4	3	2	1	—

5. OPEN FOR BUSINESS

	Liked best				Liked least	Didn't read
W. H. Auden, The Almighty Dollar	5	4	3	2	1	—
Elbert Hubbard, A Message to Garcia	5	4	3	2	1	—
Alexandra Armstrong, Starting a Business	5	4	3	2	1	—
Robert W. Keidel, A New Game for Managers to Play	5	4	3	2	1	—
Warren Bennis, Time to Hang Up the Old Sports Clichés	5	4	3	2	1	—
Milton Friedman, The Social Responsibility of Business Is to Increase Its Profits	5	4	3	2	1	—
Barbara Ehrenreich and Annette Fuentes, Life on the Global Assembly Line	5	4	3	2	1	—
Sherwood Anderson, The Egg	5	4	3	2	1	—

6. MESSAGES

	Liked best				Liked least	Didn't read
Edward T. Hall, Proxemics in the Arab World	5	4	3	2	1	—
Keith H. Basso, "Stalking with Stories": Names, Places, and Moral Narratives Among the Western Apache	5	4	3	2	1	—
C. S. Lewis, Xmas and Christmas	5	4	3	2	1	—
Abraham Lincoln, Address at the Dedication of the Gettysburg National Cemetery	5	4	3	2	1	—
Gilbert Highet, The Gettysburg Address	5	4	3	2	1	—
George Orwell, Politics and the English Language	5	4	3	2	1	—

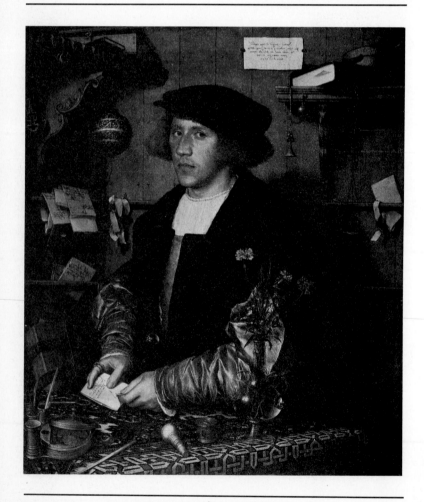

Staatlich Museum, Berlin-Dahlem. Bridgeman/Art Resource

John Pierpont Morgan
Edward Steichen, 1903

Short Views

The chief business of the American people is business.
Calvin Coolidge

The business of business is business.
Anonymous

Business underlies everything in our national life, including our spiritual life. Witness the fact that in the Lord's Prayer the first petition is for daily bread. No one can worship God or love his neighbor on an empty stomach.
Woodrow Wilson

We demand that big business give the people a square deal; in return we must insist that when anyone engaged in big business honestly endeavors to do right he shall himself be given a square deal.
Theodore Roosevelt

Entrepreneurial profit . . . is the expression of the value of what the entrepreneur contributes to production in exactly the same sense that wages are the value expression of what the worker "produces." It is not a profit of exploitation any more than are wages.
Joseph Alois Schumpeter

Every individual necessarily labors to render the annual revenue of the society as great as he can. He generally indeed neither intends to promote the public interest, nor knows how much he is promoting it.. . . . He intends only his own gain, and he is in this, as in many other cases, led by an invisible hand to promote an end which was no part of his intention. . . . By pursuing his own interest he frequently promotes that of the society more effectually than when he really intends to promote it. I have never known much good done by those who affected to trade for the public good.
Adam Smith

All systems either of preference or of restraint, therefore, being thus completely taken away, the obvious and simple system of natural liberty establishes itself of its own accord. Every man, as long as he does not violate the laws of justice, is left perfectly free to pursue his own interest in his own way, and to bring both his industry and capital into competition with those of any other man or order of men. The sovereign is completely discharged from a duty, in the attempting to perform which he must always be exposed to innumerable delusions, and for the proper performance of which no human wisdom or knowledge could ever be sufficient: the duty of superintending the industry of private people.
Adam Smith

Don't gamble. Take all your savings and buy some good stock and hold it till it goes up. If it don't go up, don't buy it.
Will Rogers

Men of business must not break their word twice.
Thomas Fuller

A corporation cannot blush.
attributed to Howel Walsh

All business sagacity reduces itself in the last analysis to a judicious use of sabotage.
Thorstein Veblen

Still we live meanly, like ants; though the fable tells us that we were long ago changed into men; like pygmies we fight with cranes; it is error upon error, and clout upon clout, and our best virtue has for its occasion a superfluous and evitable wretchedness. Our life is frittered away by detail. An honest man has hardly need to count more than his ten fingers, or in extreme cases he may add his ten toes, and lump the rest. Simplicity, simplicity, simplicity! I say, let your affairs be as two or three, and not a hundred or a thousand; instead of a million count half a dozen, and keep your accounts on your thumb nail. In the midst of this chopping sea of civilized life, such are the clouds and storms and quicksands and thousand-and-one items to be allowed for, that a man has to live, if he would not founder and go to the bottom and not make his port at all, by dead reckoning, and he must be a great calculator indeed who succeeds.

Simplify, simplify. Instead of three meals a day, if it be necessary eat but one; instead of a hundred dishes, five; and reduce other things in proportion. Our life is like a German Confederacy, made up of petty states, with its boundary forever fluctuating, so that even a German cannot tell you how it is bounded at any moment. The nation itself, with all its so-called internal improvements, which, by the way are all external and superficial, is just such an unwieldy and overgrown establishment, cluttered with furniture and tripped up by its own traps, ruined by luxury and heedless expense, by want of calculation and a worthy aim, as the million households in the land; and the only cure for it as for them is in a rigid economy, a stern and more than Spartan simplicity of life and elevation of purpose. It lives too fast. Men think that it is essential that the *Nation* have commerce, and export ice, and talk through a telegraph, and ride thirty miles an hour, without a doubt, whether *they* do or not; but whether we should live like baboons or like men, is a little uncertain. If we do not get out sleepers, and forge rails, and devote days and nights to the work, but go to tinkering upon our *lives* to improve *them*, who will build railroads? And if railroads are not built, how shall we get to heaven in season? But if we stay at home and mind our business, who will want railroads? We do not ride on the railroad; it rides upon us. Did you ever think what those sleepers are that underlie the railroad? Each one is a man, an Irishman, or a Yankee man. The rails are laid on them, and they are covered with sand, and the cars run smoothly over them. They are sound sleepers, I assure you. And every few years a new lot is laid down and run over; so that, if some have the pleasure of riding on a rail, others have the misfortune to be ridden upon. And when they run over a man that is walking in his sleep, a supernumerary sleeper in the wrong position, and wake him up, they suddenly stop the cars, and make a hue and cry about it, as if this were an exception. I am glad to know that it takes a gang of men for every five miles to keep the sleepers down and level in their beds as it is, for this is a sign that they may sometime get up again.

     Henry David Thoreau

W. H. Auden

The Almighty Dollar

Political and technological developments are rapidly ob- 1
literating all cultural differences and it is possible that, in a not remote
future, it will be impossible to distinguish human beings living on one
area of the earth's surface from those living on any other, but our
different pasts have not yet been completely erased and cultural differences are still perceptible. The most striking difference between an
American and a European is the difference in their attitudes towards
money. Every European knows, as a matter of historical fact, that in
Europe wealth could only be acquired at the expense of other human
beings, either by conquering them or by exploiting their labor in factories. Further, even after the Industrial Revolution began, the number
of persons who could rise from poverty to wealth was small; the vast
majority took it for granted that they would not be much richer nor
poorer than their fathers. In consequence, no European associates
wealth with personal merit or poverty with personal failure.

To a European, money means power, the freedom to do as he 2
likes, which also means that, consciously or unconsciously, he says:
"I want to have as much money as possible myself and others to have
as little money as possible."

In the United States, wealth was also acquired by stealing, but the 3
real exploited victim was not a human being but poor Mother Earth
and her creatures who were ruthlessly plundered. It is true that the
Indians were expropriated or exterminated, but this was not, as it had
always been in Europe, a matter of the conquerer seizing the wealth
of the conquered, for the Indian had never realized the potential riches
of his country. It is also true that, in the Southern states, men lived
on the labor of slaves, but slave labor did not make them fortunes;
what made slavery in the South all the more inexcusable was that, in
addition to being morally wicked, it didn't even pay off handsomely.

W. H. Auden (1907–1973) was born and educated in England, but in 1939 he
emigrated to the United States, and in 1946 he became a naturalized citizen.
Although Auden is known chiefly as a poet—indeed, as one of the chief poets
of the period—he also wrote plays, libretti, and essays.

Thanks to the natural resources of the country, every American, until quite recently, could reasonably look forward to making more money than his father, so that, if he made less, the fault must be his; he was either lazy or inefficient. What an American values, therefore, is not the possession of money as such, but his power to make it as proof of his manhood; once he has proved himself by making it, it has served its function and can be lost or given away. In no society in history have rich men given away so large a part of their fortunes. A poor American feels guilty at being poor, but less guilty than an American *rentier*[1] who had inherited wealth but is doing nothing to increase it; what can the latter do but take to drink and psychoanalysis?

In the Fifth Circle on the Mount of Purgatory,[2] I do not think that many Americans will be found among the Avaricious; but I suspect that the Prodigals may be almost an American colony. The great vice of Americans is not materialism but a lack of respect for matter.

Questions

1. Do you think that Auden's generalizations (in the first three paragraphs) about European versus American wealth are fundamentally accurate? If not, what are your objections?

2. In paragraph 4 Auden writes, "What an American values, therefore, is not the possession of money as such, but his power to make it as proof of his manhood. . . ." Leaving aside, for the moment, the obvious sexism of this observation, do you find any truth in it? How do you think Auden might explain why *women* want money? (Or, in your experience, do women want money to the same extent and for the same reasons men do?)

3. If you have some knowledge of an Asian, African, or Latin American country, what generalization can you offer about its citizens' attitude toward wealth?

4. Do you agree with Auden's final sentence? Why, or why not?

[1] A *rentier* (French) is one who derives income from property or investments. (Editors' note)
[2] A reference to Dante's *Divine Comedy*, part of which describes repentant souls being purged by suffering on various levels of a mountain. (Editors' note)

Elbert Hubbard

A Message to Garcia

In all this Cuban business[1] there is one man stands out on 1
my memory like Mars at perihelion.[2]

When war broke out between Spain and the United States, it was 2
very necessary to communicate quickly with the leader of the Insur-
gents. Garcia was somewhere in the mountain fastnesses of Cuba—
no one knew where. No mail nor telegraph message could reach him.
The President must secure his cooperation, and quickly.

What to do! 3

Some one said to the President, "There is a fellow by the name 4
of Rowan will find Garcia for you, if anybody can."

Rowan was sent for and given a letter to be delivered to Garcia. 5

How "the fellow by the name of Rowan" took the letter, sealed 6
it up in an oil-skin pouch, strapped it over his heart, in four days landed
by night off the coast of Cuba from an open boat, disappeared into
the jungle, and in three weeks came out on the other side of the Island,
having traversed a hostile country on foot, and delivered his letter to
Garcia, are things I have no special desire now to tell in detail. The
point I wish to make is this: McKinley gave Rowan a letter to be delivered to Garcia; Rowan took the letter and did not ask "Where is he
at?"

By the Eternal! there is a man whose form should be cast in death- 7
less bronze and the statue placed in every college of the land. It is not
book-learning young men need, nor instruction about this and that,
but a stiffening of the vertebræ which will cause them to be loyal to
a trust, to act promptly, concentrate their energies: do the thing—
"Carry a message to Garcia."

[1] Hubbard wrote the essay in 1899, hence "all this Cuban business" refers to the
Spanish-American War (1898) and to the peace settlement. Calixto Garcia y Iñigues
(1839–1898) was a Cuban revolutionary whose advice was sought by President
McKinley. Andrew S. Rowan located Garcia, who then conferred with McKinley
in Washington, D.C., where Garcia died. (Editors' note)
[2] Mars at perihelion, i.e., Mars when it is nearest to the sun. (Editors' note)

Elbert Hubbard (1856–1915), born in Bloomington, Illinois, settled in East Aurora,
New York, where he founded an artist colony and established the Roycroft Press.
The stated ideals of the press were high, but the products were rather shoddy
imitations of fine books. Hubbard also edited a magazine, *The Philistine* (1895–
1915), to which he was the chief contributor.

General Garcia is dead now, but there are other Garcias. No man 8
who has endeavored to carry out an enterprise where many hands
were needed but has been well-nigh appalled at times by the imbecility
of the average man—the inability or unwillingness to concentrate on
a thing and do it. Slip-shod assistance, foolish inattention, dowdy indifference, & half-hearted work seem the rule; and no man succeeds,
unless by hook or crook, or threat, he forces or bribes other men to
assist him; or mayhap, God in his goodness performs a miracle, and
sends him an Angel of Light for an assistant. You, reader, put this
matter to a test: You are sitting now in your office—six clerks are within
call. Summon any one and make this request: "Please look in the encyclopedia and make a brief memorandum for me concerning the life
of Correggio."

Will the clerk quietly say, "Yes sir," and go do the task?   9

On your life he will not. He will look at you out of a fishy eye and 10
ask one or more of the following questions:

Who was he?

Which encyclopedia?

Where is the encyclopedia?

Was I hired for that?

Don't you mean Bismarck?   15

What's the matter with Charlie doing it?

Is he dead?

Is there any hurry?

Shan't I bring you the book and let you look it up yourself?

What do you want to know for?   20

And I will lay you ten to one that after you have answered the
questions, & explained how to find the information, and why you want
it, the clerk will go off and get one of the other clerks to help him try
to find Garcia—and then come back and tell you there is no such man.
Of course I may lose my bet, but according to the Law of Average I
will not.

Now if you are wise you will not bother to explain to your "assistant" that Correggio is indexed under the C's, not in the K's, but
you will smile sweetly and say, "Never mind," and go look it up yourself.

And this incapacity for independent action, this moral stupidity,
this infirmity of the will, this unwillingness to cheerfully catch hold
and lift, are the things that put pure Socialism so far into the future.
If men will not act for themselves, what will they do when the benefit
of their effort is for all? A first-mate with knotted club seems necessary;
and the dread of getting 'the bounce" Saturday night, holds many a

worker to his place. Advertise for a stenographer, and nine out of ten who apply can neither spell nor punctuate—and do not think it necessary to.

Can such a one write a letter to Garcia?

"You see that book-keeper," said the foreman to me in a large   25 factory.

"Yes, what about him?"

"Well, he's a fine accountant, but if I'd send him up town on an errand, he might accomplish the errand all right, and on the other hand, might stop at four saloons on the way, and when he got to Main Street, would forget what he had been sent for."

Can such a man be entrusted to carry a message to Garcia?

We have recently been hearing much maudlin sympathy expressed for the "down-trodden denizen of the sweatshop" and the "homeless wanderer searching for honest employment," and with it all often go many hard words for the men in power.

Nothing is said about the employer who grows old before his time   30 in a vain attempt to get frowsy ne'er-do-wells to do intelligent work; and his long, patient striving with "help" that does nothing but loaf when his back is turned. In every store and factory there is a constant weeding-out process going on. The employer is constantly sending away "help" that have shown their incapacity to further the interests of the business, and others are being taken on. No matter how good times are, this sorting continues, only if times are hard and work is scarce, the sorting is done finer—but out and forever out the incompetent and unworthy go. It is the survival of the fittest. Self-interest prompts every employer to keep the best—those who can carry a message to Garcia.

I know one man of really brilliant parts who has not the ability to   31 manage a business of his own, and yet who is absolutely worthless to any one else, because he carries with him constantly the insane suspicion that his employer is oppressing, or intending to oppress him. He cannot give orders; and he will not receive them. Should a message be given him to take to Garcia, he would probably at once refer to you as a greedy, grasping Shylock, and tell you to "Take it yourself!" He regards all business men as rogues, and constantly uses the term "commercial" as an epithet. To-night this man walks the streets looking for work, the wind whistling through his thread-bare coat. No one who knows him dare employ him, for he is a regular fire-brand of discontent. He is impervious to reason, and the only thing that can impress him is the toe of a thick-soled No. 9 boot.

Of course I know that one so morally deformed is no less to be   32 pitied than a physical cripple: but in our pitying, let us drop a tear, too, for the men who are striving to carry on a great enterprise, whose working hours are not limited by the whistle, and whose hair is fast turning white through the struggle to hold in line dowdy indifference, slip-shod imbecility, and the heartless ingratitude, which, but for their enterprise, would be both hungry and homeless.

Have I put the matter too strongly? Possibly I have; but when all   33
the world has gone a-slumming I wish to speak a word of sympathy for the man who succeeds—the man who, against great odds, has directed the efforts of others, and having succeeded, finds there's nothing in it: nothing but bare board and clothes. I have carried a dinner pail and worked for day's wages, and I have also been an employer of labor, and I know there is something to be said on both sides. There is no excellence, per se, in poverty; rags are no recommendation; and all employers are not rapacious and high handed, any more than all poor men are virtuous. My heart goes out to the man who does his work when the "boss" is away, as well as when he is at home. And the man, who, when given a letter for Garcia, quietly takes the missive, without asking any idiotic questions, and with no lurking intention of chucking it into the nearest sewer, or of doing aught else but deliver it, never gets "laid off," nor has to go on a strike for higher wages. Civilization is one long anxious search for just such individuals. Anything such a man asks shall be granted. He is wanted in every city, town and village—in every office, shop, store and factory. The world cries out for such: he is needed, and is needed badly—the man who can carry a message to Garcia.

Questions

1. In paragraph 30 Hubbard invokes the phrase "survival of the fittest." Why? What does he mean?
2. In the first third of the twentieth century employers distributed to their employees millions of copies of this essay. The essay is apparently almost unknown today. Why?
3. If you did not know who Correggio was when you began this essay, did you look him up while reading the essay or immediately after finishing it? Why, or why not? If you didn't look him up, do you plan to? If you do look him up, you might think about whether Hubbard would offer him a job.
4. Under what circumstances would you go to work for Hubbard? Would you hire him to work for you? Why?

Alexandra Armstrong

Starting a Business

Marian Strong, a 33-year-old married woman with two   1
children, ages six and eight, worked at a bank until her first child was
born. Her husband, Edward, has worked for the same corporation for
the past 10 years. Paid $50,000 annually, he feels that his job is stable.
Their expenses are moderate, both mortgage on their home and the
car loan payments are low. Although they live on Edward's salary,
three years ago Marian went to work for H & R Block preparing tax
returns. While there, she managed to save $5,000 of her earnings.

In addition to enjoying the work, Marian discovered that many of   2
the company's clients needed to know how to set up and maintain
financial records. A number were willing to pay a fee to have this done
and some even wanted her to pay their monthly bills. As a result,
Marian, who recently inherited $5,000 from an aunt, would like to use
this windfall to start her own home-based business to organize and
maintain financial records for clients.

I recommended Marian prepare a business plan describing the   3
nature of her business, and why she believes there's a need for it.
Estimates of her start-up costs, as well as projected expenses and income for the first year, must also be included. I also reminded her that
people in home-based offices often find excuses not to work, and that
a wise move would be to have a separate room devoted exclusively to
business.

Having decided to give one room totally to her work, Marian   4
needed a computer, a copying machine, some furniture and stationery.
Her savings, which she estimates at $5,000, will cover these expenses.
I told her not to expect to be profitable in the first year, but to plan
for the worst case. Marian has her inheritance to fall back on, as well
as an untapped $5,000 line of credit that she shares with her husband.

Marian wasn't sure whether her business should be a sole pro-   5
prietorship, partnership, or a corporation. As a rule one should achieve

Alexandra Armstrong, president of an independent financial planning firm, has
appeared on such television programs as *Good Morning America* and *Wall Street
Week*. In 1987 *Money* magazine called her one of the "most qualified Financial
Planners in the U.S." The essay reprinted here appeared in *Ms.* magazine.

$100,000 in revenues before incorporation is worthwhile. I recommended a sole proprietorship until her revenues become substantial, because it is less encumbering than a partnership.

We then discussed her marketing strategy. She needs to make sure 6 that people find out about her business, while keeping her costs minimal. I suggested that she write letters introducing herself to estate planners and CPAs who don't want to be involved in record keeping; use personal contacts for referrals, like her former colleagues at H & R Block; and also make contact with organizations that cater to women over the age of 60, since they usually have little experience handling their own financial affairs.

It is important that Marian regularly review her situation to see 7 how her sales and profits are progressing in line with projections and whether more marketing should be done or cost reduction techniques be employed.

Last, but not least, I stressed the importance when starting a busi- 8 ness of getting good advisers: a lawyer to help determine potential liabilities that might be involved; an insurance agent to make sure of sufficient liability coverage; and a tax adviser who specializes in small businesses. This is not an area where one should try to save money, but on the other hand, one good initial conversation with a business lawyer or consultant at an hourly rate is often sufficient, and the same holds true for a tax adviser. Then one can continue to consult on a need-to-know basis.

There are also a number of organizations that Marian can turn to 9 for advice and valuable information. The National Association of Women Business Owners, 600 South Federal Street, Suite 400, Chicago, Illinois 60605, is an excellent resource for women in sole proprietorships and has many local chapters. The National Alliance of Homebased Businesswomen, P.O. Box 306, Midland Park, New Jersey 07432, and the Small Business Administration are also useful.

Questions

1. This essay is fundamentally an essay on a process—in this case, how to start a business. Reread it, and see whether (within the severe limitations of the space allowed) it covers all the main points. And does it waste space on irrelevant matters?
2. Do you think the essay is well organized? What *is* the organization?
3. What do you think of Marian Strong's idea for a business, and why?

Robert W. Keidel

A New Game for
Managers to Play

As the football season gradually gives way to basketball, 1
corporate managers would do well to consider the differences between
these games. For just as football mirrors industrial structures of the
past, basketball points the way to the corporate structure of the future.

It's the difference between the former chief executive officer of I. 2
T. T., Harold Geneen, the master football coach who dictates his players' roles and actions, and Donald Burr, the People Express Airlines
chief executive officer, who puts his players on the floor and lets them
manage themselves.

Football is, metaphorically, a way of life in work today—the cor- 3
porate sport. This is reflected in the language many managers use:

"It's taken my staff and me a sizable chunk of time, but we now 4
have a solid game plan for the XYZ job. Jack, I want you to quarterback
this thing all the way into the end zone. Of course, a lot of it will be
making the proper assignments—getting the right people to run interference and the right ones to run with the ball. But my main concern
is that we avoid mistakes. No fumbles, no interceptions, no sacks, no
penalties. I don't want us to have to play catch-up; no two-minute
drills at the end. I want the game plan executed exactly the way it's
drawn. When we're done we want to look back with pride at a win—
and not have to Monday-morning-quarterback a loss."

Does this football language represent more than just a convenient 5
shorthand? Almost certainly it does, because the metaphors we use
routinely are the means by which we structure experience. Thus, football metaphors may well reflect—and reinforce—underlying organi-
zational dynamics. But football, despite its pervasiveness, is the wrong
model for most corporations.

Consider the scenario above. Planning has been neatly separated 6
from implementation; those expected to carry out the game plan had
no part in creating it. Also, the communication flow is one-way: from

Robert W. Keidel, a graduate of Williams College and the Wharton School of the
University of Pennsylvania, directs a consulting firm. He is the author of *Game
Plans: Sports Strategies for Business* (1985) and *Corporate Players: Designs for
Working and Winning Together* (1988).

the head coach (speaker) to the quarterback (Jack)—and, presumably, from the quarterback to the other players. And the thrust of the message is risk-averse; the real name of the game is control—minimizing mistakes. But perhaps most significant is the assumption of stability—that nothing will change to invalidate the corporate game plan. "No surprises!" as Mr. Geneen likes to say.

Stability is a realistic assumption in football, even given the sport's 7 enormous complexity, because of the time available to coaches—between games and between plays. A pro football game can very nearly be programmed. Carl Peterson, formerly with the Philadelphia Eagles and now president of the United States Football League's champions, the Baltimore Stars, has estimated that managing a game is 75 percent preparation and only 25 percent adjustment.

Thus, football truly is the realm of the coach—the head coach, he 8 who calls the shots. (Most pro quarterbacks do not call their own plays.) As Bum Phillips has said in tribute to the head coach of the Miami Dolphins, Don Shula, "He can take his'n and beat your'n, or he can take your'n and beat his'n."

But football is not an appropriate model for most businesses pre- 9 cisely because instability is an overwhelming fact of life. Market competition grows ever more spastic, product life-cycles shrink unimaginably and technology courses on paths of its own.

In this milieu, corporate "players" simply cannot perform effec- 10 tively if they must wait for each play to be called for them, and remain in fixed positions—or in narrowly defined roles—like football players; increasingly, they need to deploy themselves flexibly, in novel combinations.

Thirty years ago it may have been possible to regard core business 11 functions—R&D, manufacturing and marketing—as separate worlds, with little need for interaction. R&D would design the product and then lob it over the wall to manufacturing; manufacturing would make the product and lob it over another wall to the customer.

No need to worry about problems that do not fit neatly into the 12 standard departments; these are inconsequential and infrequent. And when they do arise, they are simply bumped up the hierarchy to senior management—the head coach and his staff.

In effect, performance is roughly the sum of the functions—just 13 as a football team's performance is the sum of the performances of its platoons—offense, defense and special teams. Clearly, this view of the corporation is anachronistic. Yet it remains all too common.

Business's "season" is changing, and a new metaphor is needed. 14 While football will continue to be a useful model for pursuing machinelike efficiency and consistency—that is, for minimizing redundancies, bottlenecks and errors—this design favors stability at the expense of change. Since now more than ever businesses must continuously innovate and adapt, a more promising model is basketball.

To begin with, basketball is too dynamic a sport to permit the rigid 15 separation of planning and execution that characterizes football. Unlike football teams, basketball teams do not pause and regroup after each play. As the former star player and coach Bill Russell has noted, "Your game plan may be wiped out by what happens in the first minute of play." Success in basketball depends on the ability of the coach and players to plan and adjust while in motion. Such behavior requires all-around communication—just as basketball demands all-around passing, as opposed to football's linear sequence of "forward," one-way passing.

Basketball also puts a premium on generalist skills. Although dif- 16 ferent players will assume somewhat different roles on the court, all must be able to dribble, pass, shoot, rebound and play defense. Everyone handles the ball—a far cry from what happens on the gridiron. Indeed, basketball is much more player-oriented than football—a sport in which players tend to be viewed as interchangeable parts.

If football is a risk-averse game, basketball is risk-accepting. In 17 basketball, change is seen as normal, not exceptional; hence, change is regarded more as the source of opportunities than of threats. Mr. Geneen has claimed that "Ninety-nine percent of all surprises in business are negative."

Mr. Geneen's perspective is classic football and is tenable in stable, 18 "controllable" environments. But such environments are becoming rare. The future increasingly belongs to managers like Mr. Burr or James Treybig, the founder of Tandem Computers, who thrive on change rather than flee from it.

We need fewer head coaches and more player-coaches, less 19 scripted teamwork and more spontaneous teamwork. We need to integrate planning and doing—managing and working—far more than we have to date. Are you playing yesterday's game—or tomorrow's?

Questions

1. In his first paragraph Keidel says that "football mirrors industrial structures of the past" whereas "basketball points the way to the corporate structure of the future." He several times makes similar assertions—for instance, in paragraph 5 he says "football . . . is the

wrong model for most corporations." Does he support his view with evidence? If so, call attention to the evidence he offers. Are you convinced by his argument?

2. Keidel says (paragraph 5) that "the metaphors we use routinely are the means by which we structure experience." Consider metaphors drawn from the world of business but used in the context of education. An administrator, for instance, may say, "Last year we *produced* 1,000 majors in business administration; next year we hope to *turn out* twelve hundred; the *bottom line* is, the *supply still falls short of the demand.*" What do such metaphors tell us about the ways in which the speaker sees education (or, to use Keidel's words, the ways in which he or she "structure[s] experience")?

3. As the preceding question indicates, business itself can provide metaphors, such as "producing" or "turning out" students. In the next few days jot down examples that you encounter in newspapers, television ads, political speeches, or whatever and analyze their implications. (You may even find businesses that use metaphors drawn from business.)

4. In paragraph 2 Keidel refers to People Express Airlines. What point does he hope to make? Is People Express still in business? (If you don't know, how would you go about finding out?) Does the current status of People Express affect the status of his argument?

Warren Bennis

Time to Hang Up the Old Sports Clichés

Americans are, on the whole, simple and direct people.   1
We do not incline toward nuances or subtleties, in either our lives or our work. We opt inevitably for the concrete over the abstract. We are

Warren Bennis, born in New York City in 1925, was educated at Antioch College and the Massachusetts Institute of Technology. From 1971 to 1977 he served as the president of the University of Cincinnati. The author of several important books on management, he now teaches at the School of Business in the University of Southern California.

also extremely competitive, relishing opponents' losses as we boast of our own victories. For these reasons, sports are not only our favorite form of entertainment but the principal model and metaphor for our own lives.

At home and at work, we talk often of winning and losing, scoring touchdowns, carrying the ball, close calls, going down to the wire, batting a thousand, hitting paydirt and going into extra innings, and while we may like movie, TV and music stars, we admire sports stars. Every father wants his sons to shine on the playing fields, which is why Little League games frequently have all the carefree air of the London blitz.

Preachers and politicians, among others, see this national obsession as healthy, portray us as good people interested in good, clean fun. Universities, including mine, celebrate and reward their athletes as heroes. When the Super Bowl rolls around, the country focuses on The Game.

I am admittedly as obsessed as anyone. I seem to remember forever great plays, great players and even the scores of great games, though I sometimes cannot recall whom I sat next to at dinner three nights ago. But I am also convinced that it is time to find a new model.

Life is not a baseball game. It's never called on account of darkness, much less canceled because of inclement weather. And while major sports are big business now, business is not a sport, and never was. Indeed, thinking of business as a kind of game or sport was always simplistic. Now it's downright dangerous.

Games are of limited duration, take place on or in fixed and finite sites and are governed by openly promulgated rules that are enforced on the spot by neutral professionals. Moreover, they are performed by relatively evenly matched teams that are counseled and led through every move by seasoned hands. Scores are kept, and at the end of the game, a winner is declared.

Business is usually a little different. In fact, if there is anyone out there who can say that his business is of limited duration, takes place on a fixed site, is governed by openly promulgated rules that are enforced on the spot by neutral professionals, competes only on relatively even terms and performs in a way that can be measured in runs or points, then he is either extraordinarily lucky or seriously deluded.

The risks in thinking of business in sports terms are numerous. First, to measure a business on the basis of wins and losses is to misunderstand both the purposes of a specific business and the nature of business itself. No business—whether it sells insurance or manufactures cars—can or should be designed to win. Rather, it should be designed to grow, both quantitatively and qualitatively. In this sense, it vies more with itself than with its competition. This is not to say there are never winners or losers—in head-to-head contests, as when two ad agencies are competing for the same account, someone will win and someone will lose. It is to say, to paraphrase Vince Lombardi's legendary dictum, winning isn't everything, it's one of many things a business must accomplish.

Thus, a company designed merely to win, will probably lose in 9 the long run. For example, the John Doe Insurance Company could win the auto market overnight by offering comprehensive coverage for $100 a year. However, the company would fail when the claims began coming in.

Second, it is perilous to think of limits, rules and absolutes in 10 business. Athletes compete for a given number of hours in a given number of games over a given period of weeks or months. Businesses are in the arena for decades, sometimes centuries. Though the action may rise and subside, it never stops. It does not offer any timeouts, much less neatly defined beginnings and endings.

American business has traditionally been schizophrenic about 11 rules. When it is flourishing, it wants no rules or regulations. When it is failing, it wants a plethora of rules. For example, Detroit saw Washington as its nemesis until foreign cars flooded the market. Then, Chrysler went to the Feds for a loan, and now Detroit begs Washington to regulate imports while lobbying against Federal safety and quality controls.

Athletes perform in a static environment—the size of the field, 12 the length of the contest, even the wardrobes of the players remain the same, day after month after year. Businesses function in a volatile universe, which changes from moment to moment, and hardly ever repeats. It is affected by droughts half a world away, a new gizmo down the street, consumer attitudes and needs, a million things. Given this mercurial context, any business that is not at least as dynamic and flexible as the world in which it functions will soon be out of step or out of business.

Clearly, then, there are far more differences between sports and 13 business than similarities. But the danger is that many people will continue to imagine that success in business is like success in sports— flat-out, total victory; a world championship. But the best-run and most successful companies in America do not think in terms of victories and defeats, coming from behind, last-minute saves or shining moments, and they do not count on regulations or referees. Instead, they think in terms of staying power, dedication to quality and an endless effort to do better than they have done. They see change as the only constant, and they try to adapt to the world rather than expect the world to adapt to them. Indeed, it is a business's ability to adapt to an ever-changing world that is the basis for both its success and progress.

I should emphasize that I am not criticizing the management of 14 professional sports teams, which are themselves businesses. Some teams are poorly run but others, like the Boston Celtics or Los Angeles Lakers, operate on the same principles that other successful businesses do. They change, they plan for the long-term and they strive cease-lessly for quality. What I object to is comparing the playing field to the marketplace.

The truth is that there is no workable or appropriate metaphor for 15 business except business itself, and that should be sufficient. Like a well-played game, a well-run business is something to see, but, unlike a well-played game, it is not a diversion. Rather, it is life itself—complex, difficult, susceptible to both success and failure, sometimes un-ruly, always challenging and, often, joyful.

So let's leave the home runs to the Phillies' Mike Schmidt and the 16 touchdowns to the Bears' Walter Payton, and get down to business.

Questions

1. In paragraph 5 Bennis suggests that "it's downright dangerous" to see business in terms of metaphors drawn from the world of sports. On the other hand, presumably those who use metaphors believe that the metaphors help them see things freshly and clearly. If you have read Robert Keidel's essay (page 347), do you think that Keidel's use of metaphor clarifies your understanding of business or, on the contrary, does it lead to dangerous misapprehensions? Be as specific as possible.

2. In paragraph 8, when Bennis says that a business "should be de-signed to *grow*," he is using a metaphor, for he is comparing a business to a living organism. And in paragraph 11, when he says that American business is "schizophrenic," he uses a metaphor from psychiatry. Reread his essay closely and jot down a list of the metaphors he uses. Do you think his metaphors are useful, or are they (to quote paragraph 5) "dangerous"?

3. Evaluate Bennis's final paragraph as a final paragraph. What makes it effective or ineffective? Now look at Bennis's opening paragraph. Does his description of Americans largely exclude some groups? Are there readers his opening paragraph might unintentionally "exclude" or turn away?

Milton Friedman

The Social Responsibility of Business Is to Increase Its Profits

When I hear businessmen speak eloquently about the "social responsibilities of business in a free-enterprise system," I am reminded of the wonderful line about the Frenchman who discovered at the age of 70 that he had been speaking prose all his life. The businessmen believe that they are defending free enterprise when they declaim that business is not concerned "merely" with profit but also with promoting desirable "social" ends; that business has a "social conscience" and takes seriously its responsibilities for providing employment, eliminating discrimination, avoiding pollution and whatever else may be the catchwords of the contemporary crop of reformers. In fact they are—or would be if they or anyone else took them seriously—preaching pure and unadulterated socialism. Businessmen who talk this way are unwitting puppets of the intellectual forces that have been undermining the basis of a free society these past decades.

Milton Friedman, born in Brooklyn in 1912, is a graduate of Rutgers University, the University of Chicago, and Columbia University. Since 1946 he has taught economics at the University of Chicago. A leading conservative economist, Friedman has had considerable influence on economic thought in America, through his popular writings (he wrote a regular column in *Newsweek*), his numerous scholarly writings, and his presence on national committees.

The discussions of the "social responsibilities of business" are no- 2
table for their analytical looseness and lack of rigor. What does it mean
to say that "business" has responsibilities? Only people can have responsibilities. A corporation is an artificial person and in this sense
may have artificial responsibilities, but "business" as a whole cannot
be said to have responsibilities, even in this vague sense. The first step
toward clarity in examining the doctrine of the social responsibility of
business is to ask precisely what it implies for whom.

Presumably, the individuals who are to be responsible are busi- 3
nessmen, which means individual proprietors or corporate executives.
Most of the discussion of social responsibility is directed at corporations, so in what follows I shall mostly neglect the individual proprietors and speak of corporate executives.

In a free-enterprise, private-property system, a corporate executive 4
is an employee of the owners of the business. He has direct responsibility to his employers. That responsibility is to conduct the business
in accordance with their desires, which generally will be to make as
much money as possible while conforming to the basic rules of the
society, both those embodied in law and those embodied in ethical
custom. Of course, in some cases his employers may have a different
objective. A group of persons might establish a corporation for an
eleemosynary purpose—for example, a hospital or a school. The manager of such a corporation will not have money profit as his objectives
but the rendering of certain services.

In either case, the key point is that, in his capacity as a corporate 5
executive, the manager is the agent of the individuals who own the
corporation or establish the eleemosynary institution, and his primary
responsibility is to them.

Needless to say, this does not mean that it is easy to judge how 6
well he is performing his task. But at least the criterion of performance
is straightforward, and the persons among whom a voluntary con-
tractual arrangement exists are clearly defined.

Of course, the corporate executive is also a person in his own right. 7
As a person, he may have many other responsibilities that he recognizes or assumes voluntarily—to his family, his conscience, his feelings
of charity, his church, his clubs, his city, his country. He may feel
impelled by these responsibilities to devote part of his income to causes
he regards as worthy, to refuse to work for particular corporations,
even to leave his job, for example, to join his country's armed forces.
If we wish, we may refer to some of these responsibilities as "social
responsibilities." But in these respects he is acting as a principal, not

an agent; he is spending his own money or time or energy, not the money of his employers or the time or energy he has contracted to devote to their purposes. If these are "social responsibilities," they are the social responsibilities of individuals, not of business.

What does it mean to say that the corporate executive has a "social responsibility" in his capacity as businessman? If this statement is not pure rhetoric, it must mean that he is to act in some way that is not in the interest of his employers. For example, that he is to refrain from increasing the price of the product in order to contribute to the social objective of preventing inflation, even though a price increase would be in the best interests of the corporation. Or that he is to make expenditures on reducing pollution beyond the amount that is in the best interests of the corporation or that is required by law in order to contribute to the social objective of improving the environment. Or that, at the expense of corporate profits, he is to hire "hardcore" unemployed instead of better qualified available workmen to contribute to the social objective of reducing poverty.   8

In each of these cases, the corporate executive would be spending someone else's money for a general social interest. Insofar as his actions in accord with his "social responsibility" reduce returns to stockholders, he is spending their money. Insofar as his actions raise the price to customers, he is spending the customers' money. Insofar as his actions lower the wages of some employees, he is spending their money.   9

The stockholders or the customers or the employees could separately spend their own money on the particular action if they wished to do so. The executive is exercising a distinct "social responsibility," rather than serving as an agent of the stockholders or the customers or the employees, only if he spends the money in a different way than they would have spent it.   10

But if he does this, he is in effect imposing taxes, on the one hand, and deciding how the tax proceeds shall be spent, on the other.   11

This process raises political questions on two levels: principle and consequences. On the level of political principle, the imposition of taxes and the expenditure of tax proceeds are governmental functions. We have established elaborate constitutional, parliamentary and judicial provisions to control these functions, to assure that taxes are imposed so far as possible in accordance with the preferences and desires of the public—after all, "taxation without representation" was one of the battle cries of the American Revolution. We have a system   12 of checks and balances to separate the legislative function of imposing taxes and enacting expenditures from the executive function of collecting taxes and administering expenditure programs and from the judicial function of mediating disputes and interpreting the law.

Here the businessman—self-selected or appointed directly or indirectly by stockholders—is to be simultaneously legislator, executive and jurist. He is to decide whom to tax by how much and for what purpose, and he is to spend the proceeds—all this guided only by general exhortations from on high to restrain inflation, improve the environment, fight poverty and so on and on.   13

The whole justification for permitting the corporate executive to be selected by the stockholders is that the executive is an agent serving the interests of his principal. This justification disappears when the corporate executive imposes taxes and spends the proceeds for "social" purposes. He becomes in effect a public employee, a civil servant, even though he remains in name an employee of a private enterprise. On grounds of political principle, it is intolerable that such civil servants—insofar as their actions in the name of social responsibility are real and not just window-dressing—should be selected as they are now. If they are to be civil servants, then they must be elected through a political process. If they are to impose taxes and make expenditures to foster "social" objectives, then political machinery must be set up to make the assessment of taxes and to determine through a political process the objectives to be served.   14

This is the basic reason why the doctrine of "social responsibility" involves the acceptance of the socialist view that political mechanisms, not market mechanisms, are the appropriate way to determine the allocation of scarce resources to alternative uses.   15

On the grounds of consequences, can the corporate executive in fact discharge his alleged "social responsibilities"? On the other hand, suppose he could get away with spending the stockholders' or customers' or employees' money. How is he to know how to spend it? He is told that he must contribute to fighting inflation. How is he to know what action of his will contribute to that end? He is presumably an expert in running his company—in producing a product or selling it or financing it. But nothing about his selection makes him an expert on inflation. Will his holding down the price of his product reduce inflationary pressure? Or, by leaving more spending power in the hands of his customers, simply divert it elsewhere? Or, by forcing him to produce less because of the lower price, will it simply contribute to   16 shortages? Even if he could answer these questions, how much cost is he justified in imposing on his stockholders, customers and employees for this social purpose? What is his appropriate share and what is the appropriate share of others?

And, whether he wants to or not, can he get away with spending   17
his stockholders', customers' or employees' money? Will not the stockholders fire him? (Either the present ones or those who take over when his actions in the name of social responsibility have reduced the corporation's profits and the price of its stock.) His customers and his employees can desert him for other producers and employers less scrupulous in exercising their social responsibilities.

This facet of "social responsibility" doctrine is brought into sharp   18
relief when the doctrine is used to justify wage restraint by trade unions. The conflict of interest is naked and clear when union officials are asked to subordinate the interest of their members to some more general purpose. If the union officials try to enforce wage restraint, the consequence is likely to be wildcat strikes, rank-and-file revolts and the emergence of strong competitors for their jobs. We thus have the ironic phenomenon that union leaders—at least in the U.S.—have objected to Government interference with the market far more consistently and courageously than have business leaders.

The difficulty of exercising "social responsibility" illustrates, of   19
course, the great virtue of private competitive enterprise—it forces people to be responsible for their own actions and makes it difficult for them to "exploit" other people for either selfish or unselfish purposes. They can do good—but only at their own expense.

Many a reader who has followed the argument this far may be   20
tempted to remonstrate that it is all well and good to speak of Government's having the responsibility to impose taxes and determine expenditures for such "social" purposes as controlling pollution or training the hard-core unemployed, but that the problems are too urgent to wait on the slow course of political processes, that the exercise of social responsibility by businessmen is a quicker and surer way to solve pressing current problems.

Aside from the question of fact—I share Adam Smith's skepticism   21
about the benefits that can be expected from "those who affected to trade for the public good"—this argument must be rejected on grounds of principle. What it amounts to is an assertion that those who favor the taxes and expenditures in question have failed to persuade a majority of their fellow citizens to be of like mind and that they are seeking to attain by undemocratic procedures what they cannot attain by dem-

ocratic procedures. In a free society, it is hard for "evil" people to do "evil," especially since one man's good is another's evil.

I have, for simplicity, concentrated on the special case of the cor-   22 porate executive, except only for the brief digression on trade unions. But precisely the same argument applies to the newer phenomenon of calling upon stockholders to require corporations to exercise social responsibility (the recent G.M. crusade for example). In most of these cases, what is in effect involved is some stockholders trying to get other stockholders (or customers or employees) to contribute against their will to "social" causes favored by the activists. Insofar as they succeed, they are again imposing taxes and spending the proceeds.

The situation of the individual proprietor is somewhat different.   23 If he acts to reduce the returns of his enterprise in order to exercise his "social responsibility," he is spending his own money, not someone else's. If he wishes to spend his money on such purposes, that is his right, and I cannot see that there is any objection to his doing so. In the process, he, too, may impose costs on employees and customers. However, because he is far less likely than a large corporation or union to have monopolistic power, any such side effects will tend to be minor.

Of course, in practice the doctrine of social responsibility is fre-   24 quently a cloak for actions that are justified on other grounds rather than a reason for those actions.

To illustrate, it may well be in the long-run interest of a corporation   25 that is a major employer in a small community to devote resources to providing amenities to that community or to improving its government. That may make it easier to attract desirable employees, it may reduce the wage bill or lessen losses from pilferage and sabotage or have other worthwhile effects. Or it may be that, given the laws about the deductibility of corporate charitable contributions, the stockholders can contribute more to charities they favor by having the corporation make the gift than by doing it themselves, since they can in that way contribute an amount that would otherwise have been paid as corporate taxes.

In each of these—and many similar—cases, there is a strong temp-   26 tation to rationalize these actions as an exercise of "social responsibility." In the present climate of opinion, with its widespread aversion to "capitalism," "profits," the "soulless corporation" and so on, this is one way for a corporation to generate goodwill as a byproduct of expenditures that are entirely justified in its own self-interest.

It would be inconsistent of me to call on corporate executives to   27 refrain from this hypocritical window-dressing because it harms the foundations of a free society. That would be to call on them to exercise a "social responsibility"! If our institutions and the attitudes of the public make it in their self-interest to cloak their actions in this way, I cannot summon much indignation to denounce them. At the same time, I can express admiration for those individual proprietors or owners of closely held corporations or stockholders of more broadly held corporations who disdain such tactics as approaching fraud.

Whether blameworthy or not, the use of the cloak of social responsibility, and the nonsense spoken in its name by influential and prestigious businessmen, does clearly harm the foundations of a free society. I have been impressed time and again by the schizophrenic character of many businessmen. They are capable of being extremely far-sighted and clear-headed in matters that are internal to their businesses. They are incredibly short-sighted and muddle-headed in matters that are outside their businesses but affect the possible survival of business in general. This short-sightedness is strikingly exemplified in the calls from many businessmen for wage and price guidelines or controls or income policies. There is nothing that could do more in a brief period to destroy a market system and replace it by a centrally controlled system than effective governmental control of prices and wages. 28

The short-sightedness is also exemplified in speeches by businessmen on social responsibility. This may gain them kudos in the short run. But it helps to strengthen the already too prevalent view that the pursuit of profits is wicked and immoral and must be curbed and controlled by external forces. Once this view is adopted, the external forces that curb the market will not be the social consciences, however highly developed, of the pontificating executives; it will be the iron fist of Government bureaucrats. Here, as with price and wage controls, businessmen seem to me to reveal a suicidal impulse. 29

The political principle that underlies the market mechanism is unanimity. In an ideal free market resting on private property, no individual can coerce any other, all cooperation is voluntary, all parties to such cooperation benefit or they need not participate. There are no values, no "social" responsibilities in any sense other than the shared values and responsibilities of individuals. Society is a collection of individuals and of the various groups they voluntarily form. 30

The political principle that underlies the political mechanism is conformity. The individual must serve a more general social interest—whether that be determined by a church or a dictator or a majority. The individual may have a vote and say in what is to be done, but if 31 he is overruled, he must conform. It is appropriate for some to require others to contribute to a general social purpose whether they wish to or not.

Unfortunately, unanimity is not always feasible. There are some respects in which conformity appears unavoidable, so I do not see how one can avoid the use of the political mechanism altogether. [32]

But the doctrine of "social responsibility" taken seriously would extend the scope of the political mechanism to every human activity. It does not differ in philosophy from the most explicitly collectivist doctrine. It differs only by professing to believe that collectivist ends can be attained without collectivist means. That is why, in my book "Capitalism and Freedom," I have called it a "fundamentally subversive doctrine" in a free society, and have said that in such a society, "there is one and only one social responsibility of business—to use its resources and engage in activities designed to increase its profits so long as it stays within the rules of the game, which is to say, engages in open and free competition without deception or fraud." [33]

Questions

1. Friedman says that corporate executives who spend the corporation's money "for a general social interest" are "in effect imposing taxes . . . and deciding how the tax proceeds shall be spent . . ." (paragraphs 9 and 11). Is the use of the word "tax" effective? Is it fair? (Notice that paragraphs 12, 13, and 14, as well as some later paragraphs, also speak of taxes.)

2. "The socialist view," Friedman says in paragraph 15, is "that political mechanisms, not market mechanisms, are the appropriate way to determine the allocation of scarce resources to alternative uses." Suppose a fellow student told you that he or she found this passage puzzling. How would you clarify it?

3. Some persons in business have replied to Friedman by arguing that because the owners of today's corporations are rarely involved in running them, the corporations can properly be viewed not as private property but as social institutions able to formulate goals of their own. These people argue that the managers of a corporation are public trustees of a multipurpose organization, and their job is to use their power to promote the interests not only of stockholders but of employees and of the general public. What do you think are the strengths and the weaknesses of this reply?

4. Does Friedman argue that corporations have no responsibilities?

5. In *Religion and the Rise of Capitalism* R. H. Tawney said that "economic organization must allow for the fact that, unless industry is to be paralyzed by recurrent revolts on the part of outraged human nature, it must satisfy criteria which are not purely economic." Do you think Friedman would agree? Why, or why not?

Barbara Ehrenreich and Annette Fuentes

Life on the Global Assembly Line

In Ciudad Juárez, Mexico, Anna M. rises at 5 A.M. to feed her   1
son before starting on the two-hour bus trip to the maquiladora (factory). He will spend the day along with four other children in a neighbor's one-room home. Anna's husband, frustrated by being unable to find work for himself, left for the United States six months ago. She wonders, as she carefully applies her new lip gloss, whether she ought to consider herself still married. It might be good to take a night course, become a secretary. But she seldom gets home before eight at night, and the factory, where she stitches brassieres that will be sold in the United States through J. C. Penney, pays only $48 a week.

In Penang, Malaysia, Julie K. is up before the three other young women   2
with whom she shares a room, and starts heating the leftover rice from last night's supper. She looks good in the company's green-trimmed uniform, and she's proud to work in a modern, American-owned factory. Only not quite so proud as when she started working three years ago—she thinks as she squints out the door at a passing group of women. Her job involves peering all day through a microscope, bonding hair-thin gold wires to a silicon chip destined to end up inside a pocket calculator, and at 21, she is afraid she can no longer see very clearly.

Every morning, between four and seven, thousands of women like   3
Anna and Julie head out for the day shift. In Ciudad Juárez, they crowd into *ruteras* (rundown vans) for the trip from the slum neighborhoods

Barbara Ehrenreich writes regularly for the *New York Times* and for *Ms.* Annette Fuentes, the editor of *Sisterhood Is Global*, has also written for *Ms.*

to the industrial parks on the outskirts of the city. In Penang they squeeze, 60 or more at a time, into buses for the trip from the village to the low, modern factory buildings of the Bayan Lepas free trade zone. In Taiwan, they walk from the dormitories—where the night shift is already asleep in the still-warm beds—through the checkpoints in the high fence surrounding the factory zone.

This is the world's new industrial proletariat: young, female, Third   4
World. Viewed from the "first world," they are still faceless, genderless "cheap labor," signaling their existence only through a label or tiny imprint—"made in Hong Kong," or Taiwan, Korea, the Dominican Republic, Mexico, the Philippines. But they may be one of the most strategic blocs of womanpower in the world of the 1980s. Conservatively, there are 2 million Third World female industrial workers employed now, millions more looking for work, and their numbers are rising every year. Anyone whose image of Third World women features picturesque peasants with babies slung on their backs should be prepared to update it. Just in the last decade, Third World women have become a critical element in the global economy and a key "resource" for expanding multinational corporations.

It doesn't take more than second-grade arithmetic to understand   5
what's happening. In the United States, an assembly-line worker is likely to earn, depending on her length of employment, between $3.10 and $5 an hour. In many Third World countries, a woman doing the same work will earn $3 to $5 a *day*. According to the magazine *Business Asia*, in 1976 the average hourly wage for unskilled work (male or female) was 55 cents in Hong Kong, 52 cents in South Korea, 32 cents in the Philippines, and 17 cents in Indonesia. The logic of the situation is compelling: why pay someone in Massachusetts $5 an hour to do what someone in Manila will do for $2.50 a day? Or, as a corollary, why pay a male worker anywhere to do what a female worker will do for 40 to 60 percent less?

And so, almost everything that can be packed up is being moved   6
out to the Third World; not heavy industry, but just about anything light enough to travel—garment manufacture, textiles, toys, footwear, pharmaceuticals, wigs, appliance parts, tape decks, computer components, plastic goods. In some industries, like garment and textile, American jobs are lost in the process, and the biggest losers are women, often black and Hispanic. But what's going on is much more than a matter of runaway shops. Economists are talking about a "new international division of labor," in which the process of production is broken down and the fragments are dispersed to different parts of the

world. In general, the low-skilled jobs are farmed out to the Third World, where labor costs are minuscule, while control over the overall process and technology remains safely at company headquarters in "first world" countries like the United States and Japan.

The American electronics industry provides a classic example: circuits are printed on silicon wafers and tested in California; then the wafers are shipped to Asia for the labor-intensive process by which they are cut into tiny chips and bonded to circuit boards; final assembly into products such as calculators or military equipment usually takes place in the United States. Garment manufacture too is often broken into geographically separated steps, with the most repetitive, labor-intensive jobs going to the poor countries of the southern hemisphere. Most Third World countries welcome whatever jobs come their way in the new division of labor, and the major international development agencies—like the World Bank and the United States Agency for International Development (AID)—encourage them to take what they can get. 7

So much any economist could tell you. What is less often noted is the *gender* breakdown of the emerging international division of labor. Eighty to 90 percent of the low-skilled assembly jobs that go to the Third World are performed by women—in a remarkable switch from earlier patterns of foreign-dominated industrialization. Until now, "development" under the aegis of foreign corporations has usually meant more jobs for men and—compared to traditional agricultural society—a diminished economic status for women. But multinational corporations and Third World governments alike consider assembly-line work—whether the product is Barbie dolls or missile parts—to be "women's work." 8

One reason is that women can, in many countries, still be legally paid less than men. But the sheer tedium of the jobs adds to the multinationals' preference for women workers—a preference made clear, for example, by this ad from a Mexican newspaper: *We need female workers; older than 17, younger than 30; single and without children; minimum education primary school, maximum education one year of preparatory school [high school]: available for all shifts.* 9

It's an article of faith with management that only women can do, or will do, the monotonous, painstaking work that American business is exporting to the Third World. Bill Mitchell, whose job is to attract United States businesses to the Bermudez Industrial Park in Ciudad Juárez told us with a certain macho pride: "A man just won't stay in this tedious kind of work. He'd walk out in a couple of hours." The 10 personnel manager of a light assembly plant in Taiwan told anthropologist Linda Gail Arrigo: "Young male workers are too restless and impatient to do monotonous work with no career value. If displeased, they sabotage the machines and even threaten the foreman. But girls? At most, they cry a little."

In fact, the American businessmen we talked to claimed that Third   11
World women genuinely enjoy doing the very things that would drive a man to assault and sabotage. "You should watch these kids going into work," Bill Mitchell told us. "You don't have any sullenness here. They smile." A top-level management consultant who specializes in advising American companies on where to relocate their factories gave us this global generalization: "The [factory] girls genuinely enjoy themselves. They're away from their families. They have spending money. They can buy motorbikes, whatever. Of course it's a regulated experience too—with dormitories to live in—so it's a healthful experience."

What is the real experience of the women in the emerging Third   12
World industrial work force? The conventional Western stereotypes leap to mind: You can't really compare, the standards are so different. . . . Everything's easier in warm countries. . . . They really don't have any alternatives. . . . Commenting on the low wages his company pays its women workers in Singapore, a Hewlett-Packard vice-president said, "They live much differently here than we do. . . ." But the differences are ultimately very simple. To start with, they have less money.

The great majority of the women in the new Third World work   13
force live at or near the subsistence level for one person, whether they work for a multinational corporation or a locally owned factory. In the Philippines, for example, starting wages in U.S.-owned electronics plants are between $34 to $46 a month, compared to a cost of living of $37 a month; in Indonesia the starting wages are actually about $7 a month less than the cost of living. "Living," in these cases, should be interpreted minimally: a diet of rice, dried fish, and water—a Coke might cost a half-day's wages—lodging in a room occupied by four or more other people. Rachael Grossman, a researcher with the Southeast Asia Resource Center, found women employees of U.S. multinational firms in Malaysia and the Philippines living four to eight in a room in boardinghouses, or squeezing into tiny extensions built onto squatter huts near the factory. Where companies do provide dormitories for their employees, they are not of the "healthful," collegiate variety implied by our corporate informant. Staff from the American Friends Service Committee report that dormitory space is "likely to be

crowded, with bed rotation paralleling shift rotation—while one shift works, another sleeps, as many as twenty to a room." In one case in Thailand, they found the dormitory "filthy," with workers forced to find their own place to sleep among "splintered floorboards, rusting sheets of metal, and scraps of dirty cloth."

Wages do increase with seniority, but the money does not go to   14
pay for studio apartments or, very likely, motorbikes. A 1970 study of young women factory workers in Hong Kong found that 88 percent of them were turning more than half their earnings over to their parents. In areas that are still largely agricultural (such as parts of the Philippines and Malaysia), or places where male unemployment runs high (such as northern Mexico), a woman factory worker may be the sole source of cash income for an entire extended family.

But wages on a par with what an 11-year-old American could earn   15
on a paper route, and living conditions resembling what Engels found in nineteenth-century Manchester are only part of the story. The rest begins at the factory gate. The work that multinational corporations export to the Third World is not only the most tedious, but often the most hazardous part of the production process. The countries they go to are, for the most part, those that will guarantee no interference from health and safety inspectors, trade unions, or even free-lance reformers. As a result, most Third World factory women work under conditions that already have broken or will break their health—or their nerves—within a few years, and often before they've worked long enough to earn any more than a subsistence wage.

Consider first the electronics industry, which is generally thought   16
to be the safest and cleanest of the exported industries. The factory buildings are low and modern, like those one might find in a suburban American industrial park. Inside, rows of young women, neatly dressed in the company uniform or T-shirt, work quietly at their stations. There is air conditioning (not for the women's comfort, but to protect the delicate semiconductor parts they work with), and high-volume piped-in Bee Gees hits (not so much for entertainment, as to prevent talking).

For many Third World women, electronics is a prestige occupation,   17
at least compared to other kinds of factory work. They are unlikely to know that in the United States the National Institute on Occupational Safety and Health (NIOSH) has placed electronics on its select list of "high health-risk industries using the greatest number of toxic substances." If electronics assembly work is risky here, it is doubly so in

countries where there is no equivalent of NIOSH to even issue warnings. In many plants toxic chemicals and solvents sit in open containers, filling the work area with fumes that can literally knock you out. "We have been told of cases where ten to twelve women passed out at once," an AFSC field worker in northern Mexico told us, "and the newspapers report this as 'mass hysteria.' "

In one stage of the electronics assembly process, the workers have to dip the circuits into open vats of acid. According to Irene Johnson and Carol Bragg, who toured the National Semiconductor plant in Penang, Malaysia, the women who do the dipping "wear rubber gloves and boots, but these sometimes leak, and burns are common." Occasionally, whole fingers are lost. More commonly, what electronics workers lose is the 20/20 vision they are required to have when they are hired. Most electronics workers spend seven to nine hours a day peering through microscopes, straining to meet their quotas.

One study in South Korea found that most electronics assembly workers developed severe eye problems after only one year of employment: 88 percent had chronic conjunctivitis; 44 percent became nearsighted; and 19 percent developed astigmatism. A manager for Hewlett-Packard's Malaysia plant, in an interview with Rachael Grossman, denied that there were any eye problems: "These girls are used to working with 'scopes.' We've found no eye problems. But it sure makes me dizzy to look through those things."

Electronics, recall, is the "cleanest" of the exported industries. Conditions in the garment and textile industry rival those of any nineteenth-century sweatshop. The firms, generally local subcontractors to large American chains such as J. C. Penney and Sears, as well as smaller manufacturers, are usually even more indifferent to the health of their employees than the multinationals. Some of the worst conditions have been documented in South Korea, where the garment and textile industries have helped spark that country's "economic miracle." Workers are packed into poorly lit rooms, where summer temperatures rise above 100 degrees. Textile dust, which can cause permanent lung damage, fills the air. When there are rush orders, management may require forced overtime of as much as 48 hours at a stretch, and if that seems to go beyond the limits of human endurance, pep pills and amphetamine injections are thoughtfully provided. In her diary (originally published in a magazine now banned by the South Korean government) Min Chong Suk, 30, a sewing-machine operator, wrote of working from 7 A.M. to 11:30 P.M. in a garment factory: "When [the apprentices] shake the waste threads from the clothes, the whole room fills with dust, and it is hard to breathe. Since we've been working in such dusty air, there have been increasing numbers of people getting tuberculosis, bronchitis, and eye diseases. Since we are women, it makes us so sad when we have pale, unhealthy, wrinkled faces like dried-up spinach. . . . It seems to me that no one knows our blood dissolves into the threads and seams, with sighs and sorrow."

In all the exported industries, the most invidious, inescapable health hazard is stress. On their home ground United States corporations are not likely to sacrifice productivity for human comfort. On someone else's home ground, however, anything goes. Lunch breaks may be barely long enough for a woman to stand in line at the canteen or hawkers' stalls. Visits to the bathroom are treated as privilege; in some cases, workers must raise their hands for permission to use the toilet, and waits up to a half hour are common. Rotating shifts—the day shift one week, the night shift the next—wreak havoc with sleep patterns. Because inaccuracies or failure to meet production quotas can mean substantial pay losses, the pressures are quickly internalized; stomach ailments and nervous problems are not unusual in the multinationals' Third World female work force. In some situations, good work is as likely to be punished as slow or shoddy work. Correspondent Michael Flannery, writing for the AFL-CIO's *American Federationist*, tells the story of 23-year-old Basilia Altagracia, a seamstress who stitched collars onto ladies' blouses in the La Romana (Dominican Republic) free trade zone (a heavily guarded industrial zone owned by Gulf & Western Industries, Inc.):   21

"A nimble veteran seamstress, Miss Altagracia eventually began to earn as much as $5.75 a day. . . . 'I was exceeding my piecework quota by a lot.' . . . But then, Altagracia said, her plant supervisor, a Cuban emigré, called her into his office. 'He said I was doing a fine job, but that I and some other of the women were making too much money, and he was being forced to lower what we earned for each piece we sewed.' On the best days, she now can clear barely $3, she said. 'I was earning less, so I started working six and seven days a week. But I was tired and I could not work as fast as before.' " Within a few months, she was too ill to work at all.   22

As if poor health and the stress of factory life weren't enough to drive women into early retirement, management actually encourages a high turnover in many industries. "As you know, when seniority rises, wages rise," the management consultant to U.S. multinationals told us. He explained that it's cheaper to train a fresh supply of teen-   23 agers than to pay experienced women higher wages. "Older" women, aged 23 or 24, are likely to be laid off and not rehired.

We estimate, based on fragmentary data from several sources, that 24 the multinational corporations may already have used up (cast off) as many as 6 million Third World workers—women who are too ill, too old (30 is over the hill in most industries), or too exhausted to be useful any more. Few "retire" with any transferable skills or savings. The lucky ones find husbands.

The unlucky ones find themselves at the margins of society—as 25 bar girls, "hostesses," or prostitutes.

At 21, Julie's greatest fear is that she will never be able to find a husband. 26 *She knows that just being a "factory girl" is enough to give anyone a bad reputation. When she first started working at the electronics company, her father refused to speak to her for three months. Now every time she leaves Penang to go back to visit her home village she has to put up with a lecture on morality from her older brother—not to mention a barrage of lewd remarks from men outside her family. If they knew that she had actually gone out on a few dates, that she had been to a discotheque, that she had once kissed a young man who said he was a student . . . Julie's stomach tightens as she imagines her family's reaction. She tries to concentrate on the kind of man she would like to marry: an engineer or technician of some sort, someone who had been to California, where the company headquarters are located and where even the grandmothers wear tight pants and lipstick—someone who had a good attitude about women. But if she ends up having to wear glasses, like her cousin who worked three years at the "scopes," she might as well forget about finding anyone to marry her.*

One of the most serious occupational hazards that Julie and mil- 27 lions of women like her may face is the lifelong stigma of having been a "factory girl." Most of the cultures favored by multinational corporations in their search for cheap labor are patriarchal in the grand old style: any young woman who is not under the wing of a father, husband, or older brother must be "loose." High levels of unemployment among men, as in Mexico, contribute to male resentment of working women. (Ironically, in some places the multinationals have increased male unemployment—for example, by paving over fishing and farming villages to make way for industrial parks.) Add to all this the fact that certain companies—American electronics firms are in the lead—actively promote Western-style sexual objectification as a means of insuring employee loyalty: there are company-sponsored cosmetics classes, "guess whose legs these are" contests, and swim-suit-style beauty contests where the prize might be a free night *for two* in a fancy hotel. Corporate-promoted Westernization only heightens the hostility many men feel toward any independent working women—having a job is bad enough, wearing jeans and mascara to work is going too far.

Anthropologist Patricia Fernandez, who has worked in a *maqui-* 28 *ladora* herself, believes that the stigmatization of working women serves, indirectly, to keep them in line. "You have to think of the kind of socialization that girls experience in a very Catholic—or, for that matter, Muslim—society. The fear of having a 'reputation' is enough to make a lot of women bend over backward to be 'respectable' and ladylike, which is just what management wants." She points out that in northern Mexico, the tabloids delight in playing up stories of alleged vice in the *maquiladoras*—indiscriminate sex on the job, epidemics of venereal disease, fetuses found in factory rest rooms. "I worry about this because there are those who treat you differently as soon as they know you have a job at a *maquiladora*," one woman told Fernandez. "Maybe they think that if you have to work, there is a chance you're a whore."

And there is always a chance you'll wind up as one. Probably only 29 a small minority of Third World factory workers turn to prostitution when their working days come to an end. But it is, as for women everywhere, the employment of last resort, the only thing to do when the factories don't need you and traditional society won't—or, for economic reasons, can't—take you back. In the Philippines, the brothel business is expanding as fast as the factory system. If they can't use you one way, they can use you another.

Questions

1. Consider the title of the essay. Before you read the essay, what connotations were immediately suggested by "global assembly line"? Now that you have finished reading the essay, evaluate the title.
2. Before you read this essay, what was your image of the multinational corporation? Was it mostly positive, or negative, or neutral? To what extent has the article affected the way you think about multinational corporations? If, for example, you were offered a managerial job in a multinational, would you be inclined to ask

questions about their employment practices abroad that you might not have asked before reading this article?

3. Paragraph 1, which gives us a quick portrait of Anna, tells us that "Anna's husband, frustrated by being unable to find work for himself, left for the United States six months ago." Why do the authors bother to include this detail? Is it in any way relevant to their thesis, or is it simply for human interest?

4. According to paragraph 10, management believes "that only women can do, or will do, the monotonous, painstaking work that American business is exporting to the Third World." Do the authors of the essay believe this? Do *you* believe that women by nature— or by training—are more suited than men "to do monotonous work with no career value"?

5. Paragraph 11 reports some statements businessmen offer as reasons why Third World women supposedly enjoy their jobs. Do you think these reasons (or some of them) have any merit? Do paragraphs 12–14 and 17–21 adequately refute these reasons?

6. In paragraph 14 we learn that 88 percent of the young female workers in Hong Kong turned more than half of their wages over to their parents. What conclusions can one reasonably draw from this assertion?

7. Why do you suppose that Julie (paragraphs 2 and 26) works in a factory?

8. In paragraph 27 the author tells us that "high levels of unemployment among men, as in Mexico, contribute to male resentment of working women." Does this analysis strike you as probably true? If so, what do you think American business can do about the Mexican economy?

9. Given what you have read about the working conditions of women in Third World countries, when you buy your next sweater (or tennis racquet or calculator or whatever) will you reject products made in Third World countries?

Sherwood Anderson

The Egg

My father was, I am sure, intended by nature to be a cheerful, kindly man. Until he was thirty-four years old he worked as a farmhand for a man named Thomas Butterworth whose place lay near the town of Bidwell, Ohio. He had then a horse of his own, and on Saturday evenings drove into town to spend a few hours in social intercourse with other farmhands. In town he drank several glasses of beer and stood about in Ben Head's saloon—crowded on Saturday evenings with visiting farmhands. Songs were sung and glasses thumped on the bar. At ten o'clock father drove home along a lonely country road, made his horse comfortable for the night, and himself went to bed, quite happy in his position in life. He had at that time no notion of trying to rise in the world.

It was in the spring of his thirty-fifth year that father married my mother, then a country school-teacher, and in the following spring I came wriggling and crying into the world. Something happened to the two people. They became ambitious. The American passion for getting up in the world took possession of them.

It may have been that mother was responsible. Being a school-teacher she had no doubt read books and magazines. She had, I presume, read of how Garfield, Lincoln, and other Americans rose from poverty to fame and greatness, and as I lay beside her—in the days of her lying-in—she may have dreamed that I would some day rule men and cities. At any rate she induced father to give up his place as a farmhand, sell his horse, and embark on an independent enterprise of his own. She was a tall silent woman with a long nose and troubled gray eyes. For herself she wanted nothing. For father and myself she was incurably ambitious.

Sherwood Anderson (1876–1941) was born in Camden, Ohio. He dropped out of school at fourteen—his attendance had already been irregular—worked at odd jobs, and in 1898 served briefly in the Spanish-American War. He then turned to advertising and business, and by 1904 was a fairly prosperous manager of paint factories. In 1912, however, in the midst of dictating a business letter, he walked out of the office and disappeared for several days. Soon after he began writing poems, stories, and novels, and in 1919 he published the book still regarded as his chief work, *Winesburg, Ohio*. "The Egg" was first published in 1920.

The first venture into which the two people went turned out badly. 4
They rented ten acres of poor stony land on Grigg's road, eight miles
from Bidwell, and launched into chicken-raising. I grew into boyhood
on the place and got my first impressions of life there. From the beginning they were impressions of disaster, and if, in my turn, I am a
gloomy man inclined to see the darker side of life, I attribute it to the
fact that what should have been for me the happy joyous days of
childhood were spent on a chicken farm.

One unversed in such matters can have no notion of the many 5
and tragic things that can happen to a chicken. It is born out of an
egg, lives for a few weeks as a tiny fluffy thing such as you will see
pictured on Easter cards, then becomes hideously naked, eats quan-
tities of corn and meal bought by the sweat of your father's brow, gets
diseases called pip, cholera, and other names, stands looking with
stupid eyes at the sun, becomes sick and dies. A few hens and now
and then a rooster, intended to serve God's mysterious ends, struggle
through to maturity. The hens lay eggs out of which come other chickens and the dreadful cycle is thus made complete. It is all unbelievably
complex. Most philosophers must have been raised on chicken farms.
One hopes for so much from a chicken and is so dreadfully disillu-
sioned. Small chickens, just setting out on the journey of life, look so
bright and alert and they are in fact so dreadfully stupid. They are so
much like people they mix one up in one's judgments of life. If disease
does not kill them, they wait until your expectations are thoroughly
aroused and then walk under the wheels of a wagon—to go squashed
and dead back to their maker. Vermin infest their youth, and fortunes
must be spent for curative powders. In later life I have seen how a
literature has been built up on the subject of fortunes to be made out
of the raising of chickens. It is intended to be read by the gods who
have just eaten of the tree of the knowledge of good and evil. It is a
hopeful literature and declares that much may be done by simple ambitious people who own a few hens. Do not be led astray by it. It was
not written for you. Go hunt for gold on the frozen hills of Alaska,
put your faith in the honesty of a politician, believe if you will that
the world is daily growing better and that good will triumph over evil,
but do not read and believe the literature that is written concerning
the hen. It was not written for you.

I, however, digress. My tale does not primarily concern itself with 6
the hen. If correctly told it will center on the egg. For ten years my
father and mother struggled to make our chicken farm pay and then
they gave up their struggle and began another. They moved into the
town of Bidwell, Ohio, and embarked in the restaurant business. After

ten years of worry with incubators that did not hatch, and with tiny—and in their own way lovely—balls of fluff that passed on into semi-naked pullethood and from that into dead henhood, we threw all aside and, packing our belongings on a wagon, drove down Grigg's Road toward Bidwell, a tiny caravan of hope looking for a new place from which to start on our upward journey through life.

We must have been a sad-looking lot, not, I fancy, unlike refugees 7
fleeing from a battlefield. Mother and I walked in the road. The wagon that contained our goods had been borrowed for the day from Mr. Albert Griggs, a neighbor. Out of its side stuck the legs of cheap chairs, and at the back of the pile of beds, tables, and boxes filled with kitchen utensils was a crate of live chickens, and on top of that the baby carriage in which I had been wheeled about in my infancy. Why we stuck to the baby carriage I don't know. It was unlikely other children would be born and the wheels were broken. People who have few possessions cling tightly to those they have. That is one of the facts that make life so discouraging.

Father rode on top of the wagon. He was then a bald-headed man 8
of forty-five, a little fat, and from long association with mother and the chickens he had become habitually silent and discouraged. All during our ten years on the chicken farm he had worked as a laborer on neighboring farms and most of the money he had earned had been spent for remedies to cure chicken diseases, on Wilmer's White Wonder Cholera Cure or Professor Bidlow's Egg Producer or some other preparations that mother found advertised in the poultry papers. There were two little patches of hair on father's head just above his ears. I remember that as a child I used to sit looking at him when he had gone to sleep in a chair before the stove on Sunday afternoons in the winter. I had at that time already begun to read books and have notions of my own, and the bald path that led over the top of his head was, I fancied, something like a broad road, such a road as Caesar might have made on which to lead his legions out of Rome and into the wonders of an unknown world. The tufts of hair that grew above father's ears were, I thought, like forests. I fell into a half-sleeping, half-waking state and dreamed I was a tiny thing going along the road into a far beautiful place where there were no chicken farms and where life was a happy eggless affair.

One might write a book concerning our flight from the chicken 9
farm into town. Mother and I walked the entire eight miles—she to be sure that nothing fell from the wagon and I to see the wonders of

the world. On the seat of the wagon beside father was his greatest treasure. I will tell you of that.

On a chicken farm, where hundreds and even thousands of chickens come out of eggs, surprising things sometimes happen. Grotesques are born out of eggs as out of people. The accident does not often occur—perhaps once in a thousand births. A chicken is, you see, born that has four legs, two pairs of wings, two heads, or what not. The things do not live. They go quickly back to the hand of their maker that has for a moment trembled. The fact that the poor little things could not live was one of the tragedies of life to father. He had some sort of notion that if he could but bring into henhood or roosterhood a five-legged hen or a two-headed rooster his fortune would be made. He dreamed of taking the wonder about the county fairs and of growing rich by exhibiting it to other farmhands.

At any rate, he saved all the little monstrous things that had been born on our chicken farm. They were preserved in alcohol and put each in its own glass bottle. These he had carefully put into a box, and on our journey into town it was carried on the wagon seat beside him. He drove the horses with one hand and with the other clung to the box. When we got to our destination, the box was taken down at once and the bottles removed. All during our days as keepers of a restaurant in the town of Bidwell, Ohio, the grotesques in their little glass bottles sat on a shelf back of the counter. Mother sometimes protested, but father was a rock on the subject of his treasure. The grotesques were, he declared, valuable. People, he said, liked to look at strange and wonderful things.

Did I say that we embarked in the restaurant business in the town of Bidwell, Ohio? I exaggerated a little. The town itself lay at the foot of a low hill and on the shore of a small river. The railroad did not run through the town and the station was a mile away to the north at a place called Pickleville. There had been a cider mill and pickle factory at the station, but before the time of our coming they had both gone out of business. In the morning and in the evening busses came down to the station along a road called Turner's Pike from the hotel on the main street of Bidwell. Our going to the out-of-the-way place to embark in the restaurant business was mother's idea. She talked of it for a year and then one day went off and rented an empty store building opposite the railroad station. It was her idea that the restaurant would be profitable. Traveling men, she said, would be always waiting around to take trains out of town and town people would come to the station to await incoming trains. They would come to the restaurant to buy pieces of pie and drink coffee. Now that I am older I know that she had another motive in going. She was ambitious for me. She wanted me to rise in the world, to get into a town school and become a man of the towns.

At Pickleville father and mother worked hard, as they always had   13 done. At first there was the necessity of putting our place into shape to be a restaurant. That took a month. Father built a shelf on which he put tins of vegetables. He painted a sign on which he put his name in large red letters. Below his name was the sharp command—"EAT HERE"—that was so seldom obeyed. A showcase was bought and filled with cigars and tobacco. Mother scrubbed the floors and the walls of the room. I went to school in the town and was glad to be away from the farm, from the presence of the discouraged, sad-looking chickens. Still I was not very joyous. In the evening I walked home from school along Turner's Pike and remembered the children I had seen playing in the town school yard. A troop of little girls had gone hopping about and singing. I tried that. Down along the frozen road I went hopping solemnly on one leg. "Hippity Hop To The Barber Shop," I sang shrilly. Then I stopped and looked doubtfully about. I was afraid of being seen in my gay mood. It must have seemed to me that I was doing a thing that should not be done by one who, like myself, had been raised on a chicken farm where death was a daily visitor.

Mother decided that our restaurant should remain open at night.   14 At ten in the evening a passenger train went north past our door followed by a local freight. The freight crew had switching to do in Pickleville, and when the work was done they came to our restaurant for hot coffee and food. Sometimes one of them ordered a fried egg. In the morning at four they returned north-bound and again visited us. A little trade began to grow up. Mother slept at night and during the day tended the restaurant and fed our boarders while father slept. He slept in the same bed mother had occupied during the night and I went off to the town of Bidwell and to school. During the long nights, while mother and I slept, father cooked meats that were to go into sandwiches for the lunch baskets of our boarders. Then an idea in regard to getting up in the world came into his head. The American spirit took hold of him. He also became ambitious.

In the long nights when there was little to do, father had time to   15 think. That was his undoing. He decided that he had in the past been an unsuccessful man because he had not been cheerful enough and that in the future he would adopt a cheerful outlook on life. In the early morning he came upstairs and got into bed with mother. She woke and the two talked. From my bed in the corner I listened.

It was father's idea that both he and mother should try to entertain 16 the people who came to eat at our restaurant. I cannot now remember his words, but he gave the impression of one about to become in some obscure way a kind of public entertainer. When people, particularly young people from the town of Bidwell, came into our place, as on very rare occasions they did, bright entertaining conversation was to be made. From father's words I gathered that something of the jolly innkeeper effect was to be sought. Mother must have been doubtful from the first, but she said nothing discouraging. It was father's notion that a passion for the company of himself and mother would spring up in the breasts of the younger people of the town of Bidwell. In the evening bright happy groups would come singing down Turner's Pike. They would troop shouting with joy and laughter into our place. There would be song and festivity. I do not mean to give the impression that father spoke so elaborately of the matter. He was, as I have said, an uncommunicative man. "They want some place to go. I tell you they want some place to go," he said over and over. That was as far as he got. My own imagination has filled in the blanks.

For two or three weeks this notion of father's invaded our house. 17 We did not talk much, but in our daily lives tried earnestly to make smiles take the place of glum looks. Mother smiled at the boarders and I, catching the infection, smiled at our cat. Father became a little feverish in his anxiety to please. There was, no doubt, lurking somewhere in him, a touch of the spirit of the showman. He did not waste much of his ammunition on the railroad men he served at night, but seemed to be waiting for a young man or woman from Bidwell to come in to show what he could do. On the counter in the restaurant there was a wire basket kept always filled with eggs, and it must have been before his eyes when the idea of being entertaining was born in his brain. There was something pre-natal about the way eggs kept themselves connected with the development of his idea. At any rate, an egg ruined his new impulse in life. Late one night I was awakened by a roar of anger coming from father's throat. Both mother and I sat upright in our beds. With trembling hands she lighted a lamp that stood on a table by her head. Downstairs the front door of our restaurant went shut with a bang and in a few minutes father tramped up the stairs. He held an egg in his hand and his hand trembled as though he were having a chill. There was a half-insane light in his eyes. As he stood glaring at us I was sure he intended throwing the egg at either mother or me. Then he laid it gently on the table beside the lamp and dropped on his knees beside mother's bed. He began to cry like a boy, and I, carried away by his grief, cried with him. The two of us filled the little upstairs room with our wailing voices. It is ridiculous, but of the picture we made I can remember only the fact that mother's hand continually stroked the bald path that ran across the top of his head. I have forgotten what mother said to him and how she induced him to tell her of what had happened downstairs. His explanation also has gone out of my mind. I remember only my own grief and fright and the shiny path over father's head glowing in the lamplight as he knelt by the bed.

As to what happened downstairs. For some unexplainable reason   18 I know the story as well as though I had been a witness to my father's discomfiture. One in time gets to know many unexplainable things. On that evening young Joe Kane, son of a merchant of Bidwell, came to Pickleville to meet his father, who was expected on the ten-o'clock evening train from the South. The train was three hours late and Joe came into our place to loaf about and to wait for its arrival. The local freight train came in and the freight crew were fed. Joe was left alone in the restaurant with father.

From the moment he came into our place the Bidwell young man   19 must have been puzzled by my father's actions. It was his notion that father was angry at him for hanging around. He noticed that the res-taurant-keeper was apparently disturbed by his presence and he thought of going out. However, it began to rain and he did not fancy the long walk to town and back. He bought a five-cent cigar and or-dered a cup of coffee. He had a newspaper in his pocket and took it out and began to read. "I'm waiting for the evening train. It's late," he said apologetically.

For a long time father, whom Joe Kane had never seen before,   20 remained silently gazing at his visitor. He was no doubt suffering from an attack of stage fright. As so often happens in life he had thought so much and so often of the situation that now confronted him that he was somewhat nervous in its presence.

For one thing, he did not know what to do with his hands. He   21 thrust one of them nervously over the counter and shook hands with Joe Kane. "How-de-do," he said. Joe Kane put his newspaper down and stared at him. Father's eyes lighted on the basket of eggs that sat on the counter and he began to talk. "Well," he began hesitatingly, "well, you have heard of Christopher Columbus, eh?" He seemed to be angry. "That Christopher Columbus was a cheat," he declared emphatically. "He talked of making an egg stand on its end. He talked, he did, and then he went and broke the end of the egg."

My father seemed to his visitor to be beside himself at the duplicity   22 of Christopher Columbus. He muttered and swore. He declared it was wrong to teach children that Christopher Columbus was a great man when, after all, he cheated at the critical moment. He had declared he would make an egg stand on end and then, when his bluff had been called, he had done a trick. Still grumbling at Columbus, father took an egg from the basket on the counter and began to walk up and down. He rolled the egg between the palms of his hands. He smiled genially. He began to mumble words regarding the effect to be produced on an egg by the electricity that comes out of the human body. He declared that, without breaking its shell and by virtue of rolling it back and forth in his hands, he could stand the egg on its end. He explained that the warmth of his hands and the gentle rolling movement he gave the egg created a new center of gravity, and Joe Kane was mildly interested. "I have handled thousands of eggs," father said. "No one knows more about eggs than I do."

He stood the egg on the counter and it fell on its side. He tried   23 the trick again and again, each time rolling the egg between the palms of his hands and saying the words regarding the wonders of electricity and the laws of gravity. When after a half-hour's effort he did succeed in making the egg stand for a moment, he looked up to find that his visitor was no longer watching. By the time he had succeeded in calling Joe Kane's attention to the success of his effort, the egg had again rolled over and lay on its side.

Afire with the showman's passion and at the same time a good   24 deal disconcerted by the failure of his first effort, father now took the bottles containing the poultry monstrosities down from their place on the shelf and began to show them to his visitor. "How would you like to have seven legs and two heads like this fellow?" he asked, exhibiting the most remarkable of his treasures. A cheerful smile played over his face. He reached over the counter and tried to slap Joe Kane on the shoulder as he had seen men do in Ben Head's saloon when he was a young farmhand and drove to town on Saturday evenings. His visitor was made a little ill by the sight of the body of the terribly deformed bird floating in the alcohol in the bottle and got up to go. Coming from behind the counter, father took hold of the young man's arm and led him back to his seat. He grew a little angry and for a moment had to turn his face away and force himself to smile. Then he put the bottles back on the shelf. In an outburst of generosity he fairly compelled Joe Kane to have a fresh cup of coffee and another cigar at his expense. Then he took a pan and filling it with vinegar, taken from a jug that sat beneath the counter, he declared himself about to do a new trick. "I will heat this egg in this pan of vinegar," he said. "Then I will put it through the neck of a bottle without breaking the shell. When the egg is inside the bottle it will resume its normal shape and the shell will become hard again. Then I will give the bottle with the egg in it to you. You can take it about with you wherever you go. People will want to know how you got the egg in the bottle. Don't tell them. Keep them guessing. That is the way to have fun with this trick."

Father grinned and winked at his visitor. Joe Kane decided that the man who confronted him was mildly insane but harmless. He drank the cup of coffee that had been given him and began to read his paper again. When the egg had been heated in vinegar, father carried it on a spoon to the counter and going into a back room got an empty bottle. He was angry because his visitor did not watch him as he began to do his trick, but nevertheless went cheerfully to work. For a long time he struggled, trying to get the egg to go through the neck of the bottle. He put the pan of vinegar back on the stove, intending to reheat the egg, then picked it up and burned his fingers. After a second bath in the hot vinegar, the shell of the egg had been softened a little, but not enough for his purpose. He worked and worked and a spirit of desperate determination took possession of him. When he thought that at last the trick was about to be consummated, the delayed train came in at the station and Joe Kane started to go nonchalantly out at the door. Father made a last desperate effort to conquer the egg and make it do the thing that would establish his reputation as one who knew how to entertain guests who came into his restaurant. He worried the egg. He attempted to be somewhat rough with it. He swore and the sweat stood out on his forehead. The egg broke under his hand. When the contents spurted over his clothes, Joe Kane, who had stopped at the door, turned and laughed.   25

A roar of anger rose from my father's throat. He danced and shouted a string of inarticulate words. Grabbing another egg from the basket on the counter, he threw it, just missing the head of the young man as he dodged through the door and escaped.   26

Father came upstairs to mother and me with an egg in his hand.   27
I do not know what he intended to do. I imagine he had some idea of destroying it, of destroying all eggs, and that he intended to let mother and me see him begin. When, however, he got into the pres-

ence of mother, something happened to him. He laid the egg gently on the table and dropped on his knees by the bed as I have already explained. He later decided to close the restaurant for the night and to come upstairs and get into bed. When he did so, he blew out the light and after much muttered conversation both he and mother went to sleep. I suppose I went to sleep also, but my sleep was troubled. I awoke at dawn and for a long time looked at the egg that lay on the table. I wondered why eggs had to be and why from the egg came the hen who again laid the egg. The question got into my blood. It has stayed there, I imagine, because I am the son of my father. At any rate, the problem remains unsolved in my mind. And that, I conclude, is but another evidence of the complete and final triumph of the egg— at least as far as my family is concerned.

Questions

1. In a paragraph or two characterize the father, including in your discussion a comment on whether or not he is hypocritical. Then discuss, in an additional paragraph or two, whether his failure is based on his own inadequacies.
2. What do you make out of the narrator's statement that the story "if correctly told . . . will center on the egg"?
3. In a sentence state the theme of the story. Then in the remainder of the paragraph, offer support for your view of the theme.
4. Characterize the narrator.
5. In 250–500 words, recount a story of some businessperson you know. The story should reveal the person's character, and convey to the reader a sense of the character's view of life. Your own view— for example, admiration, amusement, or sorrow—should be implicit, but do not state this view explicitly.

6
MESSAGES

Behind the Bar, Birney, Montana
Marion Post Wolcott, 1941

Magnum Photos

Short Views

We must be as clear as our natural reticence allows us to be.
Marianne Moore

To talk too much about oneself may also be a means of concealment.
Freidrich Nietzsche

Darling Laura, sweet whiskers, do try to write me better letters. Your last, dated 19 December received today, so eagerly expected, was a bitter disappointment. Do realize that a letter need not be a bald chronicle of events; I know you lead a dull life now, my heart bleeds for it, though I believe you could make it more interesting if you had the will. But that is no reason to make your letters as dull as your life. I simply am not interested in Bridget's children. Do grasp that. A letter should be a form of conversation; write as though you were talking to me.
Evelyn Waugh

[From the dedication of Robert Louis Stevenson's *Travels with a Donkey*] Every book is, in an intimate sense, a circular letter to the friends of him who writes it. They alone take his meaning; they find private messages, assurances of love, and expressions of gratitude dropped for them in every corner. The public is but a generous patron who defrays the postage. Yet, though the letter is directed to all, we have an old and kindly custom of addressing it on the outside to one. Of what shall a man be proud, if he is not proud of his friends? And so, my dear Sidney Colvin, it is with pride that I sign myself affectionately yours,
Robert Louis Stevenson

While I am thinking about metaphor, a flock of purple finches arrives on the lawn. Since I haven't seen these birds for some years, I am only fairly sure of their being in fact purple finches, so I get down Peterson's *Field Guide* and read his description: "Male: About size of House Sparrow, rosy-red, brightest on head and rump." That checks quite well, but his next remark—"a sparrow dipped in

raspberry juice,"—is decisive: it fits. I look out the window again, and now I know that I am seeing purple finches.
Howard Nemerov

We will understand the world, and preserve ourselves and our values in it, only insofar as we have a language that is alert and responsive to it, and careful of it. I mean that literally. When we give our plows such brand names as "Sod Blaster," we are imposing on their use conceptual limits which raise the likelihood that they will be used destructively. When we speak of man's "war against nature," or of a "peace offensive," we are accepting the limitations of a metaphor that suggests, and even proposes, violent solutions. When students ask for the right of "participatory input" at the meetings of a faculty organization, they are thinking of democratic process, but they are *speaking* of a convocation of robots, and are thus devaluing the very traditions that they invoke.
Wendell Berry

A man is known by the books he reads, by the company he keeps, by the praise he gives, by his dress, by his tastes, by his distastes, by the stories he tells, by his gait, by the motion of his eye, by the look of his house, of his chamber; for nothing on earth is solitary, but everything hath affinities infinite. . . .
Ralph Waldo Emerson

Gifts from parents to children always carry the most meaningful messages. The way parents think about presents goes one step beyond the objects themselves—the ties, dolls, sleds, record players, kerchiefs, bicycles and model airplanes that wait by the Christmas tree. The gifts are, in effect, one way of telling boys and girls, "We love you even though you have been a bad boy all month" or, "We love having a daughter" or, "We treat all our children alike" or, "It is all right for girls to have some toys made for boys" or, "This alarm clock will help you get started in the morning all by yourself." Throughout all the centuries since the invention of a Santa Claus figure who represented a special recognition of children's behavior, good and bad, presents have given parents a way of telling children about their love and hopes and expectations for them.
Margaret Mead

A good painter is to paint two main things, namely, man and the working of man's mind. The first is easy, the second difficult, for it is to be represented through the gestures and movements of the limbs.

Leonardo da Vinci

If you saw a bullet hit a bird, and he told you he wasn't shot, you might weep at his courtesy, but you would certainly doubt his word.

Emily Dickinson

Edward T. Hall

Proxemics in the Arab World

In spite of over two thousand years of contact, Westerners and Arabs still do not understand each other. Proxemic research reveals some insights into this difficulty. Americans in the Middle East are immediately struck by two conflicting sensations. In public they are compressed and overwhelmed by smells, crowding, and high noise levels; in Arab homes Americans are apt to rattle around, feeling exposed and often somewhat inadequate because of too much space! (The

1

Edward T. Hall was born in Missouri in 1914. He is a professor of anthropology at Northwestern University.

Hall is especially concerned with "proxemics," a word derived from the Latin *proximus*, "nearest." Proxemics is the study of people's responses to spatial relationships—for example, their ways of marking out their territory in public places, and their responses to what they consider to be crowding. In these pages from his book *The Hidden Dimension* (1966), Hall suggests that Arabs and Westerners must understand the proxemic customs of each other's culture; without such understanding, other communications between them are likely to be misunderstood.

Arab houses and apartments of the middle and upper classes which Americans stationed abroad commonly occupy are much larger than the dwellings such Americans usually inhabit.) Both the high sensory stimulation which is experienced in public places and the basic insecurity which comes from being in a dwelling that is too large provide Americans with an introduction to the sensory world of the Arab.

Behavior in Public

Pushing and shoving in public places is characteristic of Middle Eastern 2 culture. Yet it is not entirely what Americans think it is (being pushy and rude) but stems from a different set of assumptions concerning not only the relations between people but how one experiences the body as well. Paradoxically, Arabs consider northern Europeans and Americans pushy, too. This was very puzzling to me when I started investigating these two views. How could Americans who stand aside and avoid touching be considered pushy? I used to ask Arabs to explain this paradox. None of my subjects was able to tell me specifically what particulars of American behavior were responsible, yet they all agreed that the impression was widespread among Arabs. After repeated unsuccessful attempts to gain insight into the cognitive world of the Arab on this particular point, I filed it away as a question that only time would answer. When the answer came, it was because of a seemingly inconsequential annoyance.

While waiting for a friend in a Washington, D.C., hotel lobby and 3 wanting to be both visible and alone, I had seated myself in a solitary chair outside the normal stream of traffic. In such a setting most Americans follow a rule, which is all the more binding because we seldom think about it, that can be stated as follows: as soon as a person stops or is seated in a public place, there balloons around him a small sphere of privacy which is considered inviolate. The size of the sphere varies with the degree of crowding, the age, sex, and the importance of the person, as well as the general surroundings. Anyone who enters this zone and stays there is intruding. In fact, a stranger who intrudes, even for a specific purpose, acknowledges the fact that he has intruded by beginning his request with "Pardon me, but can you tell me . . . ?"

To continue, as I waited in the deserted lobby, a stranger walked 4 up to where I was sitting and stood close enough so that not only could I easily touch him but I could even hear him breathing. In addition, the dark mass of his body filled the peripheral field of vision on my left side. If the lobby had been crowded with people, I would have understood his behavior, but in an empty lobby his presence made me exceedingly uncomfortable. Feeling annoyed by this intrusion, I moved my body in such a way as to communicate annoyance. Strangely enough, instead of moving away, my actions seemed only to encourage him, because he moved even closer. In spite of the temptation to escape the annoyance, I put aside thoughts of abandoning my post, thinking, "To hell with it. Why should I move? I was here first and I'm not going to let this fellow drive me out even if he is a boor." Fortunately, a group of people soon arrived whom my tormentor immediately joined. Their mannerisms explained his behavior, for I knew from both speech and gestures that they were Arabs. I had not been able to make this crucial identification by looking at my subject when he was alone because he wasn't talking and he was wearing American clothes.

In describing the scene later to an Arab colleague, two contrasting 5 patterns emerged. My concept and my feelings about my own circle of privacy in a "public" place immediately struck my Arab friend as strange and puzzling. He said, "After all, it's a public place, isn't it?" Pursuing this line of inquiry, I found that an Arab thought I had no rights whatsoever by virtue of occupying a given spot; neither my place nor my body was inviolate! For the Arab, there is no such thing as an intrusion in public. Public means public. With this insight, a great range of Arab behavior that had been puzzling, annoying, and sometimes even frightening began to make sense. I learned, for example, that if A is standing on a street corner and B wants his spot, B is within his rights if he does what he can to make A uncomfortable enough to move. In Beirut only the hardy sit in the last row in a movie theater, because there are usually standees who want seats and who push and shove and make such a nuisance that most people give up and leave. Seen in this light, the Arab who "intruded" on my space in the hotel lobby had apparently selected it for the very reason I had: it was a good place to watch two doors and the elevator. My show of annoyance, instead of driving him away, had only encouraged him. He thought he was about to get me to move.

Another silent source of friction between Americans and Arabs is 6 in an area that Americans treat very informally—the manners and rights of the road. In general, in the United States we tend to defer to the vehicle that is bigger, more powerful, faster, and heavily laden. While a pedestrian walking along a road may feel annoyed he will not think it unusual to step aside for a fast-moving automobile. He knows that because he is moving he does not have the right to the space around him that he has when he is standing still (as I was in the hotel lobby). It appears that the reverse is true with the Arabs who apparently *take on rights to space as they move.* For someone else to move into a space an Arab is also moving into is a violation of his rights. It is infuriating to an Arab to have someone else cut in front of him on the highway. It is the American's cavalier treatment of moving space that makes the Arab call him aggressive and pushy.

Concepts of Privacy

The experience described above and many others suggested to me that 7 Arabs might actually have a wholly contrasting set of assumptions concerning the body and the rights associated with it. Certainly the Arab tendency to shove and push each other in public and to feel and pinch women in public conveyances would not be tolerated by Westerners. It appeared to me that they must not have any concept of a private zone outside the body. This proved to be precisely the case.

In the Western world, the person is synonymous with an indi- 8 vidual inside a skin. And in northern Europe generally, the skin and even the clothes may be inviolate. You need permission to touch either if you are a stranger. This rule applies in some parts of France, where the mere touching of another person during an argument used to be legally defined as assault. For the Arab the location of the person in relation to the body is quite different. The person exists somewhere down inside the body. The ego is not completely hidden, however, because it can be reached very easily with an insult. It is protected from touch but not from words. The dissociation of the body and the ego may explain why the public amputation of a thief's hand is tolerated as standard punishment in Saudi Arabia. It also sheds light on why an Arab employer living in a modern apartment can provide his servant with a room that is a boxlike cubicle approximately 5 by 10 by 4 feet in size that is not only hung from the ceiling to conserve floor space but has an opening so that the servant can be spied on.

As one might suspect, deep orientations toward the self such as 9 the one just described are also reflected in the language. This was brought to my attention one afternoon when an Arab colleague who is the author of an Arab-English dictionary arrived in my office and threw himself into a chair in a state of obvious exhaustion. When I asked him what had been going on, he said: "I have spent the entire afternoon trying to find the Arab equivalent of the English word 'rape.' There is no such word in Arabic. All my sources, both written and spoken, can come up with no more than an approximation, such as

'He took her against her will.' There is nothing in Arabic approaching your meaning as it is expressed in that one word.''

Differing concepts of the placement of the ego in relation to the body are not easily grasped. Once an idea like this is accepted, however, it is possible to understand many other facets of Arab life that would otherwise be difficult to explain. One of these is the high population density of Arab cities like Cairo, Beirut, and Damascus. According to the animal studies described [elsewhere], the Arabs should be living in a perpetual behavioral sink. While it is probable that Arabs are suffering from population pressures, it is also just as possible that continued pressure from the desert has resulted in a cultural adaptation to high density which takes the form described above. Tucking the ego down inside the body shell not only would permit higher population densities but would explain why it is that Arab communications are stepped up as much as they are when compared to northern European communication patterns. Not only is the sheer noise level much higher, but the piercing look of the eyes, the touch of the hands, and the mutual bathing in the warm moist breath during conversation represent stepped-up sensory inputs to a level which many Europeans find unbearably intense. 10

The Arab dream is for lots of space in the home, which unfortunately many Arabs cannot afford. Yet when he has space, it is very different from what one finds in most American homes. Arab spaces inside their upper middle-class homes are tremendous by our standards. They avoid partitions because Arabs *do not like to be alone.* The form of the home is such as to hold the family together inside a single protective shell, because Arabs are deeply involved with each other. Their personalities are intermingled and take nourishment from each other like the roots and soil. If one is not with people and actively involved in some way, one is deprived of life. An old Arab saying reflects this value: "Paradise without people should not be entered because it is Hell." Therefore, Arabs in the United States often feel socially and sensorially deprived and long to be back where there is human warmth and contact. 11

Since there is no physical privacy as we know it in the Arab family, not even a word for privacy, one could expect that the Arabs might use some other means to be alone. Their way to be alone is to stop talking. Like the English, an Arab who shuts himself off in this way is not indicating that anything is wrong or that he is withdrawing, only that he wants to be alone with his own thoughts or does not want to be intruded upon. One subject said that her father would come and 12 go for days at a time without saying a word, and no one in the family thought anything of it. Yet for this very reason, an Arab exchange student visiting a Kansas farm failed to pick up the cue that his American hosts were mad at him when they gave him the "silent treatment." He only discovered something was wrong when they took him to town and tried forcibly to put him on a bus to Washington, D.C., the headquarters of the exchange program responsible for his presence in the U.S.

Arab Personal Distances

Like everyone else in the world, Arabs are unable to formulate specific rules for their informal behavior patterns. In fact, they often deny that there are any rules, and they are made anxious by suggestions that such is the case. Therefore, in order to determine how the Arab sets distances, I investigated the use of each sense separately. Gradually, definite and distinctive behavioral patterns began to emerge. 13

Olfaction occupies a prominent place in the Arab life. Not only is it one of the distance-setting mechanisms, but it is a vital part of a complex system of behavior. Arabs consistently breathe on people when they talk. However, this habit is more than a matter of different manners. To the Arab good smells are pleasing and a way of being involved with each other. To smell one's friend is not only nice but desirable, for to deny him your breath is to act ashamed. Americans, on the other hand, trained as they are not to breathe in people's faces, automatically communicate shame in trying to be polite. Who would expect that when our highest diplomats are putting on their best manners they are also communicating shame? Yet this is what occurs constantly, because diplomacy is not only "eyeball to eyeball" but breath to breath. 14

By stressing olfaction, Arabs do not try to eliminate all the body's odors, only to enhance them and use them in building human relationships. Nor are they self-conscious about telling others when they don't like the way they smell. A man leaving his house in the morning may be told by his uncle, "Habib, your stomach is sour and your breath doesn't smell too good. Better not talk too close to people today." Smell is even considered in the choice of a mate. When couples are being matched for marriage, the man's go-between will sometimes ask to smell the girl, who may be turned down if she doesn't "smell nice." Arabs recognize that smell and disposition may be linked. 15

In a word, the olfactory boundary performs two roles in Arab life.   16
It enfolds those who want to relate and separates those who don't.
The Arab finds it essential to stay inside the olfactory zone as a means
of keeping tab on changes in emotion. What is more, he may feel
crowded as soon as he smells something unpleasant. While not much
is known about "olfactory crowding," this may prove to be as significant as any other variable in the crowding complex because it is tied
directly to the body chemistry and hence to the state of health and
emotions. It is not surprising, therefore, that the olfactory boundary
constitutes for the Arabs an informal distance-setting mechanism in
contrast to the visual mechanisms of the Westerner.

Facing and Not Facing

One of my earliest discoveries in the field of intercultural communi-   17
cation was that the position of the bodies of people in conversation
varies with the culture. Even so, it is used to puzzle me that a special
Arab friend seemed unable to walk and talk at the same time. After
years in the United States, he could not bring himself to stroll along,
facing forward while talking. Our progress would be arrested while
he edged ahead, cutting slightly in front of me and turning sideways
so we could see each other. Once in this position, he would stop. His
behavior was explained when I learned that for the Arabs to view the
other person peripherally is regarded as impolite, and to sit or stand
back-to-back is considered very rude. You must be involved when in-
teracting with Arabs who are friends.

One mistaken American notion is that Arabs conduct all conver-   18
sations at close distances. This is not the case at all. On social occasions,
they may sit on opposite sides of the room and talk across the room
to each other. They are, however, apt to take offense when Americans
use what are to them ambiguous distances, such as the four- to seven-
foot social-consultative distance. They frequently complain that Americans are cold or aloof or "don't care." This was what an elderly Arab
diplomat in an American hospital thought when the American nurses
used "professional" distance. He had the feeling that he was being
ignored, that they might not take good care of him. Another Arab
subject remarked, referring to American behavior, "What's the matter?
Do I smell bad? Or are they afraid of me?"

Arabs who interact with Americans report experiencing a certain   19
flatness traceable in part to a very different use of the eyes in private
and in public as well as between friends and strangers. Even though

it is rude for a guest to walk around the Arab home eying things, Arabs look at each other in ways which seem hostile or challenging to the American. One Arab informant said that he was in constant hot water with Americans because of the way he looked at them without the slightest intention of offending. In fact, he had on several occasions barely avoided fights with American men who apparently thought their masculinity was being challenged because of the way he was looking at them. As noted earlier, Arabs look each other in the eye when talking with an intensity that makes most Americans highly uncomfortable.

Involvement

As the reader must gather by now, Arabs are involved with each other on many different levels simultaneously. Privacy in a public place is foreign to them. Business transactions in the bazaar, for example, are not just between buyer and seller, but are participated in by everyone. Anyone who is standing around may join in. If a grownup sees a boy breaking a window, he must stop him even if he doesn't know him. Involvement and participation are expressed in other ways as well. If two men are fighting, the crowd must intervene. On the political level, *to fail to intervene* when trouble is brewing is to take sides, which is what our State Department always seems to be doing. Given the fact that few people in the world today are even remotely aware of the cultural mold that forms their thoughts, it is normal for Arabs to view *our* behavior as though it stemmed from *their* own hidden set of assumptions. [20]

Feelings About Enclosed Spaces

In the course of my interviews with Arabs the term "tomb" kept cropping up in conjunction with enclosed space. In a word, Arabs don't mind being crowded by people but hate to be hemmed in by walls. They show a much greater overt sensitivity to architectural crowding than we do. Enclosed space must meet at least three requirements that I know of if it is to satisfy the Arabs: there must be plenty of unobstructed space in which to move around (possibly as much as a thousand square feet); very high ceilings—so high in fact that they do not normally impinge on the visual field; and, in addition, there must be an unobstructed view. It was spaces such as these in which the Americans referred to earlier felt so uncomfortable. One sees the Arab's need [21] for a view expressed in many ways, even negatively, for to cut off a neighbor's view is one of the most effective ways of spiting him. In Beirut one can see what is known locally as the "spite house." It is nothing more than a thick, four-story wall, built at the end of a long fight between neighbors, on a narrow strip of land, for the express purpose of denying a view of the Mediterranean to any house built on the land behind. According to one of my informants, there is also a house on a small plot of land between Beirut and Damascus which is completely surrounded by a neighbor's wall built high enough to cut off the view from all windows!

Boundaries

Proxemic patterns tell us other things about Arab culture. For example,   22
the whole concept of the boundary as an abstraction is almost impossible to pin down. In one sense, there are no boundaries. "Edges" of towns, yes, but permanent boundaries out in the country (hidden lines), no. In the course of my work with Arab subjects I had a difficult time translating our concept of a boundary into terms which could be equated with theirs. In order to clarify the distinctions between the two very different definitions, I thought it might be helpful to pinpoint acts which constituted trespass. To date, I have been unable to discover anything even remotely resembling our own legal concept of trespass.

Arab behavior in regard to their own real estate is apparently an   23
extension of, and therefore consistent with, their approach to the body. My subjects simply failed to respond whenever trespass was mentioned. They didn't seem to understand what I meant by this term. This may be explained by the fact that they organize relationships with each other according to closed social systems rather than spatially. For thousands of years Moslems, Marinites, Druses, and Jews have lived in their own villages, each with strong kin affiliations. Their hierarchy of loyalties is: first to one's self, then to kinsman, townsman, or tribesman, co-religionist and/or countryman. Anyone not in these categories is a stranger. Strangers and enemies are very closely linked, if not synonymous, in Arab thought. Trespass in this context is a matter of who you are, rather than a piece of land or a space with a boundary that can be denied to anyone and everyone, friend and foe alike.

In summary, proxemic patterns differ. By examining them it is   24
possible to reveal hidden cultural frames that determine the structure of a given people's perceptual world. Perceiving the world differently leads to differential definitions of what constitutes crowded living, dif-

ferent interpersonal relations, and a different approach to both local and international politics.

Questions

1. According to Hall, why do Arabs think Americans are pushy? And, again according to Hall, why do Arabs not consider themselves pushy?
2. Explain what Hall means by "cognitive world" (paragraph 2); by "ego" (paragraph 10); by "behavioral sink" (in the same paragraph). Then explain, for the benefit of someone who did not understand the terms, how you know what Hall means by each.
3. In paragraph 9 Hall points out that there is no Arabic equivalent of the English word "rape." Can you provide an example of a similar gap in English or in another language? Does a cultural difference account for the linguistic difference?
4. In paragraph 3 Hall says of a rule that it "is all the more binding because we seldom think about it." Is this generally true of rules? What examples or counter-examples support your view?

Keith H. Basso

"Stalking with Stories"
Names, Places, and Moral Narratives Among the Western Apache

Shortly before his death in 1960, Clyde Kluckhohn made the following observation in a course he gave at Harvard University on the history of anthropological thought: "The most interesting claims   1

Keith H. Basso has taught at the University of Arizona, Yale University, and the University of New Mexico. He has conducted linguistic and ethnographic research in the Western Apache community at Cibecue, in Arizona, since 1959.

Figure 1. *Map showing location of the community of Cibecue on the Fort Apache Indian Reservation, Arizona.*

people make are those they make about themselves. Cultural anthropologists should keep this in mind, especially when they are doing fieldwork." This essay focuses on a small set of spoken texts in which members of a contemporary American Indian society express claims about themselves, their language, and the lands on which they live. Specifically, I shall be concerned here with a set of statements that were made by men and women from the Western Apache community at Cibecue, a dispersed settlement of 1100 people that has been inhabited by Apaches for centuries and is located near the center of Fort Apache Indian Reservation in east-central Arizona (see Figure 1). The statements that interest me, which could be supplemented by a large number of others, are the following.

1. The land is always stalking people. The land makes people live right. The land looks after us. The land looks after people. [Mrs. Annie Peaches, age 77, 1977]
2. Our children are losing the land. It doesn't go to work on them anymore. They don't know the stories about what happened at

these places. That's why some get into trouble. [Mr. Ronnie Lupe, age 42; Chairman, White Mountain Apache Tribe, 1978]

3. We used to survive only off the land. Now it's no longer that way. Now we live only with money, so we need jobs. But the land still looks after us. We know the names of the places where everything happened. So we stay away from badness. [Mr. Nick Thompson, age 64, 1980]

4. I think of that mountain called "white rocks lie above in a compact cluster" as if it were my maternal grandmother. I recall stories of how it once was at that mountain. The stories told to me were like arrows. Elsewhere, hearing that mountain's name, I see it. Its name is like a picture. Stories go to work on you like arrows. Stories make you live right. Stories make you replace yourself. [Mr. Benson Lewis, age 64, 1979]

5. One time I went to L.A., training for mechanic. It was no good, sure no good. I start drinking, hang around bars all the time. I start getting into trouble with my wife, fight sometimes with her. It was *bad*. I forget about this country here around Cibecue. I forget all the names and stories. I don't hear them in my mind anymore. I forget how to live right, forget how to be strong. [Mr. Wilson Lavender, age 52, 1975]

If the texts of these statements resist quick and easy interpretation, it is not because the people who made them are confused or cloudy thinkers. Neither is it because, as one unfortunate commentator would have us believe, the Western Apache are "mystically inclined and correspondingly inarticulate." The problem we face is a semiotic* one, a barrier to constructing appropriate sense and significance. It arises from the obvious circumstance that all views articulated by Apache people are informed by their experience in a culturally constituted world of objects and events with which most of us are unfamiliar. What sort of world is it? Or, to draw the question into somewhat sharper focus, what is the cultural context in which Apache statements such as those presented above find acceptance as valid claims about reality?

More specifically, what is required to interpret Annie Peaches's claim that the land occupied by the Western Apache is "always stalking people" and that because of this they know how to "live right"? And how should we understand Chairman Lupe's assertion that Apache children sometimes misbehave because the land "doesn't go to work

---

* "Semiotics" is the science of signs—not merely of language (verbal signs), traffic signals, and semaphor but also of other things that make "statements," such as gestures, clothing, posture, houses. (Editors' note)

on them anymore"? Why does Nick Thompson claim that his knowledge of place-names and historical events enables him to "stay away
from badness"? And why does Benson Lewis liken place-names to
pictures, stories to arrows, and a mountain near the community of
Cibecue to his maternal grandmother? What should we make of Wilson
Lavender's recollection of an unhappy time in California when forgetting place-names and stories caused him to forget "how to be
strong"? Are these claims structured in metaphorical terms, or, given
Western Apache assumptions about the physical universe and the
place of people within it, are they somehow to be interpreted literally?
In any case, what is the reasoning that lies behind the claims, the
informal logic of which they are simultaneously products and expressions? Above all, what makes the claims make sense?

I address these and other questions through an investigation of   4
how Western Apaches talk about the natural landscape and the importance they attach to named locations within it. Accordingly, my
discussion focuses on elements of language and patterns of speech,
my purpose being to discover from these elements and patterns something of how Apache people construe their land and render it intel-
ligible. Whenever Apaches describe the land—or, as happens more
frequently, whenever they tell stories about incidents that have occurred at particular points upon it—they take steps to constitute it in
relation to themselves. Which is simply to say that in acts of speech,
mundane and otherwise, Apaches negotiate images and understand-
ings of the land which are accepted as credible accounts of what it
actually is, why it is significant, and how it impinges on the daily lives
of men and women.

"Learn the Names"

Nick Thompson is, by his own admission, an old man. It is possible,   5
he told me once, that he was born in 1918. Beneath snow-white hair
cut short, his face is round and compact, his features small and sharply
molded. His large, black, and very bright eyes move quickly, and when
he smiles he acquires an expression that is at once mischievous and
intimidating. I have known him for more than 20 years, and he has
instructed me often on matters pertaining to Western Apache language
and culture. A man who delights in play, he has also teased me un-
mercifully, concocted humorous stories about me that are thoroughly
apocryphal, and embarrassed me before large numbers of incredulous
Apaches by inquiring publicly into the most intimate details of my

private life. Described by many people in Cibecue as a true "Slim Coyote" (*ma' ts'ósé*), Nick Thompson is outspoken, incorrigible, and unabashed.[1] He is also generous, thoughtful, and highly intelligent. I value his friendship immensely.

As I bring my Jeep to a halt on the road beside the old man's camp, I hear Nick complaining loudly to his wife about the changing character of life in Cibecue and its regrettable effects on younger members of the community. I have heard these complaints before and I know they are deeply felt. But still, on this sunny morning in June 1977, it is hard to suppress a smile, for the image Nick presents, a striking example of what can be achieved with sartorial *bricolage,* is hardly what one would expect of a staunch tribal conservative. Crippled since childhood and partially paralyzed by a recent stroke, the old man is seated in the shade of a cottonwood tree a few yards from the modest wooden cabin where he lives with his wife and two small grandchildren. He is smoking a mentholated Salem cigarette and is studying with undisguised approval the shoes on his feet—a new pair of bright blue Nike running shoes trimmed in incandescent orange. He is also wearing a pair of faded green trousers, a battered brown cowboy hat, and a white T-shirt with "Disneyland" printed in large red letters across the front. Within easy reach of his chair, resting on the base of an upended washtub, is a copy of the *National Enquirer,* a mug of hot coffee, and an open box of chocolate-covered doughnuts. If Nick Thompson is an opponent of social change, it is certainly not evident from his appearance. But appearances can be deceiving, and Nick, who is an accomplished singer and a medicine man of substantial reputation, would be the first to point this out.

The old man greets me with his eyes. Nothing is said for a minute or two, but then we begin to talk, exchanging bits of local news until enough time has passed for me to politely announce the purpose of my visit. I explain that I am puzzled by certain statements that Apaches have made about the country surrounding Cibecue and that I am anxious to know how to interpret them. To my surprise, Nick does not ask what I have been told or by whom. He responds instead by swinging out his arm in a wide arc. "Learn the names," he says. "Learn the names of all these places." Unprepared for such a firm and unequivocal

<small>6</small>

<small>7</small>

---

[1] A prominent figure in Western Apache oral literature, Slim Coyote is appreciated by Apache people for his keen and crafty intelligence, his complex and unpredictable personality, and his penchant for getting himself into difficult situations from which he always manages to extract himself, usually with humorous and embarrassing results.

suggestion (it sounds to me like nothing less than an order), I retreat into silence. "Start with the names," the old man continues. "I will teach you like before. Come back tomorrow morning." Nodding in agreement, I thank Nick for his willingness to help and tell him what I will be able to pay him. He says the wage is fair.

A few moments later, as I stand to take my leave, Nick's face breaks 8 suddenly into a broad smile and his eyes begin to dance. I know that look very well and brace myself for the farewell joke that almost always accompanies it. The old man wastes no time. He says I look lonely. He urges me to have prolonged and abundant sex with very old women. He says it prevents nosebleeds. He says that someday I can write a book about it. Flustered and at a loss for words, I smile weakly and shake my head. Delighted with this reaction, Nick laughs heartily and reaches for his coffee and a chocolate-covered doughnut. Our encounter has come to an end.

I return to the old man's camp the following day and start to learn 9 Western Apache place-names. My lessons, which are interrupted by mapping trips with more mobile Apache consultants, continue for the next ten weeks. In late August, shortly before I must leave Cibecue, Nick asks to see the maps. He is not impressed. "White men need paper maps," he observes. "We have maps in our minds."

Located in a narrow valley at an elevation of 1507 m, the settlement 10 at Cibecue (from *deeschii' bikoh*, "valley with elongated red bluffs") is bisected by a shallow stream emanating from springs that rise in low-lying mountains to the north. Apache homes, separated by horse pastures, agricultural plots, and ceremonial dancegrounds, are located on both sides of the stream for a distance of approximately 8 km. The valley itself, which is bounded on the east and west by a broken series of red sandstone bluffs, displays marked topographic diversity in the form of heavily dissected canyons and arroyos, broad alluvial flood plains, and several clusters of prominent peaks. Vegetation ranges from a mixed Ponderosa Pine–Douglas Fir association near the headwaters of Cibecue Creek to a chaparral community, consisting of scrub oak, cat's-claw, agave, and a variety of cactus species, at the confluence of the creek with the Salt River. In between, numerous other floral associations occur, including dense riparian communities and heavy stands of cottonwood, oak, walnut, and pine.

Together with Michael W. Graves, I have mapped nearly 104 km^2 11 in and around the community at Cibecue and within this area have recorded the Western Apache names of 296 locations; it is, to say the least, a region densely packed with place-names. But large numbers alone do not account for the high frequency with which place-names typically appear in Western Apache discourse. In part, this pattern of regular and recurrent use results from the fact that Apaches, who travel a great deal to and from their homes, habitually call on each other to describe their trips in detail. Almost invariably, and in sharp contrast to comparable reports delivered by Anglos living at Cibecue, these descriptions focus as much on *where* events occurred as on the nature and consequences of the events themselves. This practice has been observed in other Apachean groups as well, including, as Harry Hoijer (personal communication, 1973) notes, the Navajo: "Even the most minute occurrences are described by Navajos in close conjunction with their physical settings, suggesting that unless narrated events are *spatially anchored* their significance is somehow reduced and cannot be properly assessed." Hoijer could just as well be speaking of the Western Apache.

Something else contributes to the common use of place-names in Western Apache communities, however, and that, quite simply, is that Apaches enjoy using them. For example, several years ago, when I was stringing a barbed-wire fence with two Apache cowboys from Cibecue, I noticed that one of them was talking quietly to himself. When I listened carefully, I discovered that he was reciting a list of place-names—a long list, punctuated only by spurts of tobacco juice, that went on for nearly ten minutes. Later, when I ventured to ask him about it, he said he frequently "talked names" to himself. Why? "I like to," he said. "I ride that way in my mind." And on dozens of other occasions when I have been working or traveling with Apaches, they have taken satisfaction in pointing out particular locations and pronouncing their names—once, twice, three times or more. Why? "Because we like to," or "Because those names are good to say." More often, however, Apaches account for their enthusiastic use of place-names by commenting on the precision with which the names depict their referents. "That place looks just like its name," someone will explain, or "That name makes me see that place like it really is." Or, as Benson Lewis (example 4) states so succinctly, "Its name is like a picture."

Statements such as these may be interpreted in light of certain facts about the linguistic structure of Western Apache place-names. To begin with, it is essential to understand that all but a very few Apache place-names take the form of complete sentences. This is made possible by one of the most prominent components of the Western Apache

language: an elaborate system of prefixes that operates most extensively and productively to modify the stems of verbs. Thus, well-
formed sentences can be constructed that are extremely compact yet
semantically very rich. It is this combination of brevity and expres-
siveness, I believe, that appeals to Apaches and makes the mere pro-
nunciation of place-names a satisfying experience.

"All These Places Have Stories"

When I return to Cibecue in the spring of 1978, Nick Thompson is   14
recovering from a bad case of the flu. He is weak, despondent, and
uncomfortable. We speak very little and no mention is made of place-
names. His wife is worried about him and so am I. Within a week,
however, Nick's eldest son comes to my camp with a message: I am
to visit his father and bring with me two packs of Salem cigarettes and
a dozen chocolate-covered doughnuts. This is good news.

When I arrive at the old man's camp, he is sitting under the cot-   15
tonwood tree by his house. A blanket is draped across his knees and
he is wearing a heavy plaid jacket and a red vinyl cap with white fur-
lined earflaps. There is color in his cheeks and the sparkle is back in
his eyes. Shortly after we start to converse, and apropos of nothing I
can discern, Nick announces that in 1931 he had sexual intercourse
eight times in one night. He wants to know if I have ever been so
fortunate. His wife, who has brought us each a cup of coffee, hears
this remark and tells him that he is a crazy old man. Nick laughs loudly.
Plainly, he is feeling better.

Eventually, I ask Nick if he is ready to resume our work together.   16
"Yes," he says, "but no more on names." What then? "Stories," is his
reply. "All these places have stories. We shoot each other with them,
like arrows. Come back tomorrow morning." Puzzled once again, but
suspecting that the old man has a plan he wants to follow, I tell him
I will return. We then discuss Nick's wages. He insists that I pay him
more than the year before as it is necessary to keep up with inflation.
I agree and we settle on a larger sum. Then comes the predictable
farewell joke: a fine piece of nonsense in which Nick, speaking English
and imitating certain mannerisms he has come to associate with Anglo
physicians, diagnoses my badly sunburned nose as an advanced case
of venereal disease.[2] This time it is Nick's wife who laughs loudest.

---

[2] Jokes of this type are intended to poke fun at the butt of the joke and, at the same
time, to comment negatively on the interactional practices of Anglo-Americans.

The next day Nick begins to instruct me on aspects of Western 17
Apache storytelling. Consulting on a regular basis with other Apaches
from Cibecue as well, I pursue this topic throughout the summer of
1978.

Western Apache Historical Tales

If place-names appear frequently in ordinary forms of Western Apache 18
discourse, their use is equally conspicuous in oral narratives. It is here,
in conjunction with stories Apaches tell, that we can move closer to
an interpretation of native claims about the symbolic importance of
geographical features and the personalized relationships that individuals may have with them. The people of Cibecue classify "speech"
(*yat'i'*) into three major forms: "ordinary talk" (*yat'i*), "prayer"
(*'okąąhí*), and "narratives" or "stories" (*nagoldi'é*). Narratives are further classified into four major and two minor genres. The major genres
include "myths" (*godiyįhgo nagoldi'*; literally, "to tell the holiness"),
"historical tales" (*'ágod-zaahí* or *'ágodzaahí nagoldi'*; literally, "that which
has happened" or "to tell of that which has happened"), "sagas"
(*nlt'éégo nagoldi'*; literally, "to tell of pleasantness"), and stories that
arise in the context of "gossip" (*ch'idii*). The minor genres, which do
not concern us here, are "Coyote stories" (*ma' highaalyú' nagoldi'*;
literally "to tell of Coyote's travels") and "seduction tales" (*biníima'
nagoldi'*; literally, "to tell of sexual desires").

Western Apaches distinguish among the major narrative genres 19
on two basic semantic dimensions: time and purpose. Values on the
temporal dimension identify in general terms when the events recounted in narratives took place, while values on the purposive dimension describe the objectives that Apache narrators typically have
in recounting them (see Figure 2). Accordingly, "myths" deal with
events that occurred "in the beginning" (*'godiyaaná*), a time when the
universe and all things within it were achieving their present form and
location. Performed only by the medicine men and medicine women,
myths are presented for the primary purpose of enlightenment and
instruction: to explain and reaffirm the complex processes by which
the known world came into existence. "Historical tales" recount events
that took place "long ago" (*doo 'ánííná*) when the Western Apache
people, having emerged from below the surface of the earth, were
developing their own distinctive ways and customs. Most historical
tales describe incidents that occurred prior to the coming of the white
man, but some of these stories are set in postreservation times, which

Narrative Category	Temporal Locus of Events	Purposes
godiyįhgo nagoldi' ("myth")	*godiyaaná'* ("in the beginning")	to enlighten; to instruct
'ágodzaahí ("historical tale")	*doo 'ánííná'* ("long ago")	to criticize; to warn; to "shoot"
nlt'éégo nagoldi' ("saga")	*dííjįigo* ("modern times")	to entertain; to engross
ch'idii ("gossip")	*k'ad* ("now")	to inform; to malign

Figure 2. *Major categories of Western Apache narrative distinguished by temporal locus of events and primary purposes for narration.*

began for the Western Apache in 1872. Like myths, historical tales are intended to edify, but their main purpose is to alarm and criticize social delinquents (or, as the Apache say, to "shoot" them), thereby impressing such individuals with the undesirability of improper behavior and alerting them to the punitive consequences of further misconduct.

Although sagas deal with historical themes, these narratives are 20 chiefly concerned with events that have taken place in "modern times" (*dííjįigo*), usually within the last 60 or 70 years. In contrast to historical tales, which always focus on serious and disturbing matters, sagas are largely devoid of them. Rather than serving as vehicles of personal criticism, the primary purpose of sagas is to provide their listeners with relaxation and entertainment. Stories of the kind associated with gossip consist of reports in which persons relate and interpret events involving other members of the Western Apache community. These stories, which embrace incidents that have occurred "now" or "at present" (*k'ad*), are often told for no other reason than to keep people informed of local developments. Not uncommonly, however, narratives in gossip are also used to ridicule and malign the character of their subjects.

Nowhere do place-names serve more important communicative 21 functions than in the context of historical tales. As if to accentuate this fact, stories of the *'ágodzaahí* genre are stylistically quite simple. Historical tales require no specialized lexicon, display no unusual syntactical constructions, and involve no irregular morphophonemic alternations; neither are they characterized by unique patterns of stress, pitch, volume, or intonation. In these ways *'agodzaahí* narratives contrast sharply with myths and sagas, which entail the use of a variety of genre-specific stylistic devices. Historical tales also differ from myths and sagas by virtue of their brevity. Whereas myths and sagas may take hours to complete, historical tales can usually be delivered in less than five minutes. Western Apache storytellers point out that this is both fitting and effective, because *'ágodzaahí* stories, like the "arrows" (*k'aa*) they are commonly said to represent, work best when they move swiftly. Finally, and most significant of all, historical tales are distinguished from all other forms of Apache narrative by an opening and closing line that identifies with a place-name where the events in the narrative occurred. These lines frame the narrative, mark it unmistakably as belonging to the *'agodzaahí* genre, and evoke a particular physical setting in which listeners can imaginatively situate everything that happens. It is hardly surprising, then, that while Apache storytellers agree that historical tales are "about" the events recounted in the tales, they also emphasize that the tales are "about" the sites at which the events took place.

If the style of Western Apache historical tales is relatively unremarkable, their content is just the opposite. Without exception, and usually in very graphic terms, historical tales focus on persons who suffer misfortune as the consequence of actions that violate Apache standards for acceptable social behavior. More specifically, *'ágodzaahí* stories tell of persons who have acted unthinkingly and impulsively in open disregard for "Apache custom" (*ndee bi 'at'ee'*) and who pay for their transgressions by being humiliated, ostracized, or killed. Stories of the *'agodzaahí* variety are morality tales pure and simple. When viewed as such by the Apaches—as compact commentaries on what should be avoided so as to deal successfully and effectively with other people—they are highly informative. For what these narratives assert—tacitly, perhaps, but with dozens of compelling examples—is that immoral behavior is irrevocably a community affair and that persons who behave badly will be punished sooner or later. Thus, just as *'ágodzaahí* stories are "about" historical events and their geographical locations, they are also "about" the system of rules and values according to which Apaches expect each other to organize and regulate their lives. In an even more fundamental sense, then, historical tales are "about" what it means to *be* a Western Apache, or, to make the point less dramatically, what it is that being an Apache should normally and properly entail.

To see how this is so, let us consider the texts of three historical tales and examine the manner in which they have been interpreted by their Apache narrators.

1.   It happened at "big cottonwood trees stand spreading here and there."

Long ago, the Pimas and Apaches were fighting. The Pimas were carrying long clubs made from mesquite wood; they were also heavy and hard. Before dawn the Pimas arrived at Cibecue and attacked the Apaches there. The Pimas attacked while the Apaches were still asleep. The Pimas killed the Apaches with their clubs. An old woman woke up; she heard the Apaches crying out. The old woman thought it was her son-in-law because he often picked on her daughter. The old woman cried out: "You pick on my child a lot. You should act pleasantly toward her." Because the old woman cried out, the Pimas learned where she was. The Pimas came running to the old woman's camp and killed her with their clubs. A young girl ran away from there and hid beneath some bushes. She alone survived.

It happened at "big cottonwood trees stand spreading here and there."

Narrated by Mrs. Annie Peaches, this historical tale deals with the harmful consequences that may come to persons who overstep traditional role boundaries. During the first year of marriage it is customary for young Apache couples to live in the camp of the bride's parents. At this time, the bride's mother may request that her son-in-law perform different tasks and she may also instruct and criticize him. Later, however, when the couple establishes a separate residence, the bride's mother forfeits this right and may properly interfere in her son-in-law's affairs only at the request of her daughter. Mrs. Peaches explains that women who do not abide by this arrangement imply that their sons-in-law are immature and irresponsible, which is a source of acute embarrassment for the young men and their wives. Thus, even when meddling might seem to serve a useful purpose, it should be scrupulously avoided. The woman on whom this story centers failed to remember this—and was instantly killed. 24

2.   It happened at "coarse-textured rocks lie above in a compact cluster."

Long ago, a man became sexually attracted to his stepdaughter. He was living below "coarse-textured rocks lie above in a compact cluster" with his stepdaughter and her mother. Waiting until no one else was present, and sitting alone with her, he started to molest her. The girl's maternal uncle happened to come by and he killed the man with a rock. The man's skull was cracked open. It was raining. The girl's maternal uncle dragged the man's body up above to "coarse-textured rocks lie above in a compact cluster" and placed it there in a storage pit. The girl's mother came home and was told by her daughter of all that had happened. The people who owned the storage pit removed the man's body and put it somewhere else. The people never had a wake for the dead man's body.

It happened at "coarse-textured rocks lie above in a compact cluster."

Narrated by Mr. Benson Lewis, this historical tale deals with the 25 theme of incest, for sexual contact with stepchildren is considered by Western Apaches to be an incestuous act. According to Mr. Lewis, the key line in the story is the penultimate one in which he observes, "The people never had a wake for the dead man's body." We may assume, Mr. Lewis says, that because the dead man's camp was located near the storage pit in which his body was placed, the people who owned the pit were also his relatives. This makes the neglect with which his corpse was treated all the more profound, since kinsmen are bound by the strongest of obligations to care for each other when they die. That the dead man's relatives chose to dispense with customary mortuary ritual shows with devastating clarity that they wished to disown him completely.

3. It happened at "men stand above here and there."

Long ago, a man killed a cow off the reservation. The cow belonged to a Whiteman. The man was arrested by a policeman living at Cibecue at "men stand above here and there." The policeman was an Apache. The policeman took the man to the head Army officer at Fort Apache. There, at Fort Apache, the head Army officer questioned him. "What do you want?" he said. The policeman said, "I need cartridges and food." The policeman said nothing about the man who had killed the Whiteman's cow. That night some people spoke to the policeman. "It is best to report on him," they said to him. The next day the policeman returned to the head Army officer. "Now what do you want?" he said. The policeman said, "Yesterday I was going to say HELLO and GOOD-BYE but I forgot to do it." Again he said nothing about the man he arrested. Someone was working with words on his mind. The policeman returned with the man to Cibecue. He released him at "men stand above here and there."

It happened at "men stand above here and there."

This story, narrated by Nick Thompson, describes what happened 26 to a man who acted too much like a white man. Between 1872 and 1895, when the Western Apache were strictly confined to their reservations by U.S. military forces, disease and malnutrition took the lives of many people. Consequently, Apaches who listen to this historical tale find it perfectly acceptable that the man who lived at "men stand above here and there" should have killed and butchered a white man's cow. What is not acceptable is that the policeman, another Apache from the same settlement, should have arrested the rustler and contemplated taking him to jail. But the policeman's plans were thwarted. Someone used witchcraft on him and made him stupid and forgetful. He never informed the military officer at Fort Apache of the real purpose of his visit, and his second encounter with the officer—in which he apologized for neglecting to say "hello" and "good-bye" the previous day—revealed him to be an absurd and laughable figure. Although Western Apaches find portions of this story amusing, Nick Thompson explains that they understand it first and foremost as a harsh indictment of persons who join with outsiders against members of their own community and who, as if to flaunt their lack of allegiance, parade the attitudes and mannerisms of white men.

Thus far, my remarks on what Western Apache historical tales are "about" have centered on features of textual content. This is a familiar strategy and certainly a necessary one, but it is also incomplete. In addition to everything else—places, events, moral standards, conceptions of cultural identity—every historical tale is also "about" the person at whom it is directed. This is because the telling of a historical tale is always prompted by an individual having committed one or more social offenses to which the act of narration, together with the tale itself, is intended as a critical and remedial response. Thus, on those occasions when 'agodzaahí stories are actually told—by real Apache storytellers, in real interpersonal contexts, to real social offenders—these narratives are understood to be accompanied by an unstated message from the storyteller that may be phrased something like this: "I know that you have acted in a way similar or analogous to the way in which someone acted in the story I am telling you. If you continue to act in this way, something similar or analogous to what happened to the character in the story might also happen to you." This metacommunicative message is just as important as any conveyed by the text of the storyteller's tale. For Apaches contend that if the message is taken to heart by the person at whom the tale is aimed—and if, in conjunction with lessons drawn from the tale itself, he or she resolves to improve his or her behavior—a lasting bond will have been created between that individual and the site or sites at which events in the tale took place. The cultural premises that inform this powerful idea will be made explicit presently; but first, in order to understand more clearly what the idea involves, let us examine the circumstances that led to the telling of a historical tale at Cibecue and see how this narrative affected the person for whom it was told.

In early June 1977, a 17-year-old Apache woman attended a girls' puberty ceremonial at Cibecue with her hair rolled up in a set of over-sized pink plastic curlers. She had returned home two days before from a boarding school in Utah where this sort of ornamentation was considered fashionable by her peers. Something so mundane would have gone unnoticed by others were it not for the fact that Western Apache women of all ages are expected to appear at puberty ceremonials with their hair worn loose. This is one of several ways that women have of showing respect for the ceremonial and also, by implication, for the people who have staged it. The practice of presenting oneself with free-flowing hair is also understood to contribute to the ceremonial's effectiveness, for Apaches hold that the ritual's most basic objectives, which are to invest the pubescent girl with qualities necessary for life as an adult, cannot be achieved unless standard forms of respect are faithfully observed. On this occasion at Cibecue, everyone was following custom except the young woman who arrived wearing curlers. She soon became an object of attention and quiet expressions of disapproval, but no one spoke to her about the large cylindrical objects in her hair.

Two weeks later, the same young woman made a large stack of tortillas and brought them to the camp of her maternal grandmother, a widow in her mid-60s who had organized a small party to celebrate the birthday of her eldest grandson. Eighteen people were on hand, myself included, and all of us were treated to hot coffee and a dinner of boiled beef and potatoes. When the meal was over casual conversation began to flow, and the young woman seated herself on the ground next to her younger sister. And then—quietly, deftly, and totally without warning—her grandmother narrated a version of the historical tale about the forgetful Apache policeman who behaved too much like a white man. Shortly after the story was finished, the young woman stood up, turned away wordlessly, and walked off in the direction of her home. Uncertain of what had happened, I asked her grandmother why she had departed. Had the young woman suddenly become ill? "No," her grandmother replied. "I shot her with an arrow."

Approximately two years after this incident occurred, I found myself again in the company of the young woman with the taste for distinctive hairstyles. She had purchased a large carton of groceries at the trading post at Cibecue, and when I offered to drive her home with them she accepted. I inquired on the way if she remembered the time that her grandmother had told us the story about the forgetful police-man. She said she did and then went on, speaking in English, to de-scribe her reactions to it. "I think maybe my grandmother was getting after me, but then I think maybe not, maybe she's working on some-body else. Then I think back on that dance and I know it's me for sure. I sure don't like how she's talking about me, so I quit looking like that. I threw those curlers away." In order to reach the young woman's camp, we had to pass within a few hundred yards of *ndee dah naazį́į́h* ("men stand above here and there"), the place where the man had lived who was arrested in the story for rustling. I pointed it out to my companion. She said nothing for several moments. Then she smiled and spoke softly in her own language: "I know that place. It stalks me every day."

The comments of this Western Apache woman on her experience   31
as the target of a historical tale are instructive in several respects. To begin with, her statement enables us to imagine something of the siz-able psychological impact that historical tales may have on the persons to whom they are presented. Then, too, we can see how *'ágodzaahí* stories may produce quick and palpable effects on the behavior of such individuals, causing them to modify their social conduct in quite spe-cific ways. Lastly, and most revealing of all, the young woman's re-marks provide a clear illustration of what Apaches have in mind when they assert that historical tales may establish highly meaningful rela-tionships between individuals and features of the natural landscape.

To appreciate fully the significance of these relationships, as well   32
as their influence on the lives of Western Apache people, we must explore more thoroughly the manner in which the relationships are conceptualized. This can be accomplished through a closer examina-tion of Apache ideas about the activity of storytelling and the acknowl-edged power of oral narratives, especially historical tales, to promote beneficial changes in people's attitudes toward their responsibilities as members of a moral community. These ideas, which combine to form a native model of how oral narratives work to achieve their intended effects, are expressed in terms of a single dominant metaphor. By now it should come as no surprise to learn that the metaphor draws heavily on the imagery of hunting.

"Stalking with Stories"

Nick Thompson is tired. We have been talking about hunting with   33
stories for two days now and the old man has not had an easy time

of it. Yesterday, my uneven control of the Western Apache language prevented him from speaking as rapidly and eloquently as he would have liked, and on too many occasions I was forced to interrupt him with questions. At one point, bored and annoyed with my queries, he told me that I reminded him of a horsefly buzzing around his head. Later, however, when he seemed satisfied that I could follow at least the outline of his thoughts, he recorded on tape a lengthy statement which he said contained everything he wanted me to know. "Take it with you and listen to it," he said. "Tomorrow we put it in English." For the last six hours that is what we have been trying to do. We are finished now and weary of talking. In the weeks to come I will worry about the depth and force of our translation, and twice more I will return to Nick's camp with other questions. But the hardest work is over and both of us know it. Nick has taught me already that hunting with stories is not a simple matter, and as I prepare to leave I say so. "We know," he says, and that is all. Here is Nick Thompson's statement:

> This is what we know about our stories. They go to work on your mind and make you think about your life. Maybe you've not been acting right. Maybe you've been stingy. Maybe you've been chasing after women. Maybe you've been trying to act like a Whiteman. People don't *like* it! So someone goes hunting for you—maybe your grandmother, your grandfather, your uncle. It doesn't matter. Anyone can do it.
>
> So someone stalks you and tells a story about what happened long ago. It doesn't matter if other people are around—you're going to know he's aiming that story at you. All of a sudden it *hits* you! It's like an arrow, they say. Sometimes it just bounces off—it's too soft and you don't think about anything. But when it's strong it goes in *deep* and starts working on your mind right away. No one says anything to you, only that story is all, but now you know that people have been watching you and talking about you. They don't like how you've been acting. So you have to think about your life.
>
> Then you feel weak, real weak, like you are sick. You don't want to eat or talk to anyone. That story is working on you now. You keep thinking about it. That story is changing you now, making you want to live right. That story is making you want to replace yourself. You think only of what you did that was wrong and you don't like it. So you want to live better. After a while, you don't like to think of what you did wrong. So you try to forget that story. You try to pull that arrow out. You think it won't hurt anymore because now you want to live right.

It's hard to keep on living right. Many things jump up at you and block your way. But you won't forget that story. You're going to see the place where it happened, maybe every day if it's nearby and close to Cibecue. If you don't see it, you're going to hear its name and see it in your mind. It doesn't matter if you get old—that place will keep on stalking you like the one who shot you with the story. Maybe that person will die. Even so, that place will keep on stalking you. It's like that person is still alive.

Even if we go far away from here to some big city, places around here keep stalking us. If you live wrong, you will hear the names and see the places in your mind. They keep on stalking you, even if you go across oceans. The names of all these places are good. They make you remember how to live right, so you want to replace yourself again.

After stories and storytellers have served this beneficial purpose, 34 features of the physical landscape take over and perpetuate it. Mountains and arroyos step in symbolically for grandmothers and uncles. Just as the latter have "stalked" delinquent individuals in the past, so too particular locations continue to "stalk" them in the present. Such surveillance is essential, Apaches maintain, because "living right" requires constant care and attention, and there is always a possibility that old stories and their initial impact, like old arrows and their wounds, will fade and disappear. In other words, there is always a chance that persons who have "replaced themselves" once—or twice, or three times—will relax their guard against "badness" and slip back into undesirable forms of social conduct. Consequently, Apaches explain, individuals need to be continuously reminded of why they were "shot" in the first place and how they reacted to it at the time. Geographical sites, together with the crisp mental "pictures" of them presented by their names, serve admirably in this capacity, inviting people to recall their earlier failings and encouraging them to resolve, once again, to avoid them in the future. Grandmothers and uncles must perish but the landscape endures, and for this the Apache people are deeply grateful. "The land," Nick Thompson observes, "looks after us. The land keeps badness away."

It should now be possible for the reader to interpret the Western 35 Apache texts at the beginning of this essay in a manner roughly compatible with the Apache ideas that have shaped them. Moreover, we should be able to appreciate that the claims put forward in the texts are reasonable and appropriate, culturally credible and "correct," the principled expressions of an underlying logic that invests them with internal consistency and coherent conceptual structure. As we have seen, this structure is supplied in large part by the hunting metaphor for Western Apache storytelling. It is chiefly in accordance with this metaphor—or, more exactly, in accordance with the symbolic associations it orders and makes explicit—that the claims presented earlier finally make sense.

Thus, the claim of Annie Peaches—that the land occupied by the 36 Western Apache "makes the people live right"—becomes understandable as a proposition about the moral significance of geographical locations as this has been established by historical tales with which the locations are associated. Similarly, Wilson Lavender's claim—that Apaches who fail to remember place-names "forget how to be strong"—rests on an association of place-names with a belief in the power of historical tales to discourage forms of socially unacceptable behavior. Places and their names are also associated by Apaches with the narrators of historical tales, and Benson Lewis's claim—that a certain mountain near Cibecue is his maternal grandmother—can only be interpreted in light of this assumption. The hunting metaphor for storytelling also informs Ronnie Lupe's claim that Western Apache children who are not exposed to historical tales tend to have interpersonal difficulties. As he puts it, "They don't know the stories of what happened at these places. That's why some of them get into trouble." What Mr. Lupe is claiming, of course, is that children who do not learn to associate places and their names with historical tales cannot appreciate the utility of these narratives as guidelines for dealing responsibly and amicably with other people. Consequently, he believes, such individuals are more likely than others to act in ways that run counter to Apache social norms, a sure sign that they are "losing the land." Losing the land is something the Western Apache can ill afford to do, for geographical features have served the people for centuries as indispensable mnemonic pegs on which to hang the moral teachings of their history.

The Apache landscape is full of named locations where time and 37 space have fused and where, through the agency of historical tales, their intersection is made visible for human contemplation. It is also apparent that such locations, charged as they are with personal and social significance, work in important ways to shape the images that Apaches have—or should have—of themselves. Speaking to people like Nick Thompson and Ronnie Lupe, to Annie Peaches and Benson Lewis, one forms the impression that Apaches view the landscape as a repository of distilled wisdom, a stern but benevolent keeper of tradition, an ever-vigilant ally in the efforts of individuals and whole communities to put into practice a set of standards for social living that are uniquely and distinctively their own. In the world that the Western Apache have constituted for themselves, features of the landscape have become symbols of and for this way of living, the symbols of a culture and the enduring moral character of its people.

We may assume that this relationship with the land has been pervasive throughout Western Apache history; but in today's climate of accelerating social change, its importance for Apache people may well be deepening. Communities such as Cibecue, formerly isolated and very much turned inward, were opened up by paved roads less than 20 years ago, and the consequences of improved access and freer travel—including, most noticeably, greatly increased contact with Anglo-Americans—have been pronounced. Younger Apaches, who today complain frequently about the tedium of village life, have started to develop new tastes and ambitions, and some of them are eager to explore the outside world. To the extent that the landscape remains not merely a physical presence but an omnipresent moral force, young Apaches are not likely to forget that the "Whiteman's way" belongs to a different world.

A number of American Indian authors, among them Vine Deloria, Jr. (Sioux), Simon Ortiz (Acoma), Joy Harjo (Creek), and the cultural anthropologist Alfonso Ortiz (San Juan), have written with skill and insight about the moral dimensions of Native American conceptions of the land. No one, however, has addressed the subject with greater sensitivity than N. Scott Momaday (Kiowa). The following passages, taken from his short essay entitled "Native American Attitudes to the Environment" (1974), show clearly what is involved, not only for the Western Apache but for other tribes as well.

> You cannot understand how the Indian thinks of himself in relation to the world around him unless you understand his conception of what is appropriate; particularly what is morally appropriate within the context of that relationship. [1974:82]

> The native American ethic with respect to the physical world is a matter of reciprocal appropriation: apropriations in which man invests himself in the landscape, and at the same time incorporates the landscape into his own most fundamental experience. . . . This appropriation is primarily a matter of imagination which is moral in kind. I mean to say that we are all, I suppose, what we imagine ourselves to be. And that is certainly true of the American Indian. . . . [The

Indian] is someone who thinks of himself in a particular way and his idea comprehends his relationship to the physical world. He imagines himself in terms of that relationship and others. And it is that act of imagination, that moral act of imagination, which constitutes his understanding of the physical world. [1974:80]

The summer of 1980 is almost gone and soon I must leave Cibecue.   40
I have walked to Nick's camp to tell him good-bye. This is never easy for me, and we spend most of the time talking about other things. Eventually, I move to thank him for his generosity, his patience, and the things he has taught me. Nick responds by pointing with his lips to a low ridge that runs behind his home in an easterly direction away from Cibecue Creek. "That is a good place," he says. "These are all good places. Goodness is all around."

Postscript

If the thoughts presented here have a measure of theoretical interest,   41
recent experience has persuaded me that they can have practical value as well. During the last six years, I have authored a number of documents for use in litigation concerning the settlement of Western Apache water rights in the state of Arizona. Until a final decision is reached in the case, I am not permitted to describe the contents of these documents in detail, but one of my assignments has been to write a report dealing with Apache conceptions of the physical environment. That report contains sections on Western Apache place-names, oral narratives, and certain metaphors that Apache people use to formulate aspects of their relationship with the land.

Preliminary hearings resulted in a judgment favorable to Apache   42
interests, and apparently my report was useful, mainly because it helped pave the way for testimony by native witnesses. One of these witnesses was Nick Thompson; and according to attorneys on both sides, the old man's appearance had a decisive impact. After Nick had taken his place on the stand, he was asked by an attorney why he considered water to be important to his people. A man of eminent good sense, Nick replied, "Because we drink it!" And then, without missing a beat, he launched into a historical tale about a large spring not far from Cibecue—tú nchaa halíí' ("much water flows up and out")—where long ago a man drowned mysteriously after badly mistreating his wife. When Nick finished the story he went on to say: "We know it happened, so we know not to act like that man who died. It's

good we have that water. We need it to live. It's good we have that spring. We need it to live right." Then the old man smiled to himself and his eyes began to dance.

Questions

1. Basso suggests in paragraph 2 that the five statements by Native Americans in paragraph 1 "resist quick and easy interpretation." When you first read the essay were you puzzled by these statements? Which, if any, did you find especially moving? Why?

2. In paragraphs 5 through 8 (as well as in later paragraphs) Basso tells us a good deal about Nick Thompson's appearance and personality. What function do you think these descriptions serve?

3. Judging from this essay, what do cultural anthropologists do? What personal (as distinguished from professional) qualifications should they have, or what "claims" might they make about themselves?

4. The stories Basso records describe what has happened and also teach moral lessons. Does the lesson taught by the third story (paragraphs 25 and 26) conflict with your own morality? Or do you also find the theft of the cow "perfectly acceptable" under the circumstances?

5. In paragraph 38 Basso says that in a "climate of accelerating social change" the importance of the Western Apache's relationship with the land "may well be deepening." What evidence does he offer that it is deepening? Might it be argued from the same evidence that it is probably weakening?

6. If you come from a culture in which landscape is more than inert matter, explain the role of landscape in that culture. ("Landscape" need not be limited to *natural* landscape; it can be urban landscape. Substitute a neighborhood or city block, if appropriate, but the landscape must be a place and not simply individuals associated with it.)

7. If you come from a culture in which stories are widely regarded as more than casual entertainment, explain the role of stories in that culture.

C. S. Lewis

Xmas and Christmas
A Lost Chapter from Herodotus

And beyond this there lies in the ocean, turned towards 1
the west and north, the island of Niatirb which Hecataeus indeed declares to be the same size and shape as Sicily, but it is larger, though
in calling it triangular a man would not miss the mark. It is densely
inhabited by men who wear clothes not very different from the other
barbarians who occupy the north-western parts of Europe though they
do not agree with them in language. These islanders, surpassing all
the men of whom we know in patience and endurance, use the following customs.

In the middle of winter when fogs and rains most abound they 2
have a great festival which they call Exmas, and for fifty days they
prepare for it in the fashion I shall describe. First of all, every citizen
is obliged to send to each of his friends and relations a square piece
of hard paper stamped with a picture, which in their speech is called
an Exmas-card. But the pictures represent birds sitting on branches,
or trees with dark green prickly leaf, or else men in such garments as
the Niatirbians believe that their ancestors wore two hundred years
ago riding in coaches such as their ancestors used, or houses with snow
on their roofs. And the Niatirbians are unwilling to say what these
pictures have to do with the festival, guarding (as I suppose) some
sacred mystery. And because all men must send these cards the market-place is filled with the crowd of those buying them, so that there
is great labour and weariness.

But having bought as many as they suppose to be sufficient, they 3
return to their houses and find there the like cards which others have
sent to them. And when they find cards from any to whom they also
have sent cards, they throw them away and give thanks to the gods
that this labour at least is over for another year. But when they find

C[live] S[taples] Lewis (1898–1963) taught medieval and Renaissance literature
at Oxford and later at Cambridge. He wrote about literature, and he wrote fiction
(including children's books), poetry, and numerous essays and books on Christianity, from the point of view of a believer.

cards from any to whom they have not sent, then they beat their breasts and wail and utter curses against the sender; and, having sufficiently lamented their misfortune, they put on their boots again and go out into the fog and rain and buy a card for him also. And let this account suffice about Exmas-cards.

They also send gifts to one another, suffering the same things 4 about the gifts as about the cards, or even worse. For every citizen has to guess the value of the gift which every friend will send to him so that he may send one of equal value, whether he can afford it or not. And they buy as gifts for one another such things as no man ever bought for himself. For the sellers, understanding the custom, put forth all kinds of trumpery, and whatever, being useless and ridiculous, they have been unable to sell throughout the year they now sell as an Exmas gift. And though the Niatirbians profess themselves to lack sufficient necessary things, such as metal, leather, wood and paper, yet an incredible quantity of these things is wasted every year, being made into the gifts.

But during these fifty days the oldest, poorest and most miserable 5 of the citizens put on false beards and red robes and walk about the market-place; being disguised (in my opinion) as *Cronos*. And the sellers of gifts no less than the purchasers become pale and weary, because of the crowds and the fog, so that any man who came into a Niatirbian city at this season would think some great public calamity had fallen on Niatirb. This fifty days of preparation is called in their barbarian speech the Exmas *Rush*.

But when the day of the festival comes, then most of the citizens, 6 being exhausted with the *Rush*, lie in bed till noon. But in the evening they eat five times as much supper as on other days and, crowning themselves with crowns of paper, they become intoxicated. And on the day after Exmas they are very grave, being internally disordered by the supper and the drinking and reckoning how much they have spent on gifts and on the wine. For wine is so dear among the Niatirbians that a man must swallow the worth of a talent before he is well intoxicated.

Such, then, are their customs about the Exmas. But the few among 7 the Niatirbians have also a festival, separate and to themselves, called Crissmas, which is on the same day as Exmas. And those who keep Crissmas, doing the opposite to the majority of the Niatirbians, rise early on that day with shining faces and go before sunrise to certain temples where they partake of a sacred feast. And in most of the temples they set out images of a fair woman with a new-born Child on her knees and certain animals and shepherds adoring the Child. (The reason of these images is given in a certain sacred story which I know but do not repeat.)

But I myself conversed with a priest in one of these temples and asked him why they kept Crissmas on the same day as Exmas; for it appeared to me inconvenient. But the priest replied, It is not lawful, O Stranger, for us to change the date of Crissmas, but would that Zeus would put it into the minds of the Niatirbians to keep Exmas at some other time or not to keep it at all. For Exmas and the *Rush* distract the minds even of the few from sacred things. And we indeed are glad that men should make merry at Crissmas; but in Exmas there is no merriment left. And when I asked him why they endured the *Rush*, he replied, It is, O Stranger, a *racket*; using (as I suppose) the words of some oracle and speaking unintelligibly to me (for a *racket* is an instrument which the barbarians use in a game called *tennis*).

But what Hecataeus says, that Exmas and Crissmas are the same, is not credible. For first, the pictures which are stamped on the Exmas-cards have nothing to do with the sacred story which the priests tell about Crissmas. And secondly, the most part of the Niatirbians, not believing the religion of the few, nevertheless send the gifts and cards and participate in the *Rush* and drink, wearing paper caps. But it is not likely that men, even being barbarians, should suffer so many and great things in honour of a god they do not believe in. And now, enough about Niatirb.

Questions

1. An encyclopedia, or even a dictionary, will give you some information about Herodotus. Check your library for a copy of Herodotus's *History*, read a few pages in it, and then point to two or three places where Lewis has captured something of the flavor of Herodotus.

2. In this semicomic piece, Lewis is making a serious point. What is it?

3. Lewis, an Englishman (let's say a citizen of Great Britain), wrote about Niatirb. Write another lost chapter from Herodotus, describing a custom celebrated in Acirema (or your college, dormitory, or wherever).

4. In an essay of 500 words, respond to Lewis, either explaining why you believe his satire is unfair, or (if in general you approve of his position) setting forth your reasons for agreeing, and perhaps adding additional evidence.

Abraham Lincoln

Address at the Dedication of the Gettysburg National Cemetery

Four score and seven years ago our fathers brought forth 1 on this continent, a new nation, conceived in Liberty, and dedicated to the proposition that all men are created equal.

Now we are engaged in a great civil war; testing whether that 2 nation, or any nation so conceived and so dedicated, can long endure. We are met on a great battlefield of that war. We have come to dedicate a portion of that field as a final resting-place for those who here gave their lives that that nation might live. It is altogether fitting and proper that we should do this.

But, in a larger sense, we cannot dedicate—we cannot conse- 3 crate—we cannot hallow—this ground. The brave men, living and dead, who struggled here have consecrated it, far above our poor power to add or detract. The world will little note, nor long remember, what we say here, but it can never forget what they did here. It is for us the living, rather, to be dedicated here to the unfinished work which they who fought here have thus far so nobly advanced. It is rather for

Abraham Lincoln (1809–1865), sixteenth president of the United States, is not usually thought of as a writer, but his published speeches and writings comprise about 1,078,000 words, the equivalent of about 4,000 pages of double-spaced typing. They were all composed without the assistance of a speech writer.

us to be here dedicated to the great task remaining before us—that from these honored dead we take increased devotion to that cause for which they gave the last full measure of devotion; that we here highly resolve that these dead shall not have died in vain; that this nation, under God, shall have a new birth of freedom; and that government of the people, by the people, for the people, shall not perish from the earth.

Gilbert Highet

The Gettysburg Address

Fourscore and seven years ago. . . .   1

These five words stand at the entrance to the best-known mon- 2 ument of American prose, one of the finest utterances in the entire language, and surely one of the greatest speeches in all history. Greatness is like granite: it is molded in fire, and it lasts for many centuries.

Fourscore and seven years ago. . . . It is strange to think that Pres- 3 ident Lincoln was looking back to the 4th of July 1776, and that he and his speech are now further removed from us than he himself was from George Washington and the Declaration of Independence. Fourscore and seven years before the Gettysburg Address, a small group of patriots signed the Declaration. Fourscore and seven years after the Gettysburg Address, it was the year 1950, and that date is already receding rapidly into our troubled, adventurous, and valiant past.

Inadequately prepared and at first scarcely realized in its full im- 4 portance, the dedication of the graveyard at Gettysburg was one of the supreme moments of American history. The battle itself had been

Gilbert Highet (1906–1978) was born in Glasgow, Scotland, and was educated at Glasgow University and at Oxford University. In 1937 he came to the United States, and in 1951 he was naturalized. Until his retirement in 1972 he taught Latin, Greek, and comparative literature at Columbia University. In addition to writing scholarly studies of classical authors he wrote several general and more popular books.

a turning point of the war. On the 4th of July 1863, General Meade repelled Lee's invasion of Pennsylvania. Although he did not follow up his victory, he had broken one of the most formidable aggressive enterprises of the Confederate armies. Losses were heavy on both sides. Thousands of dead were left on the field, and thousands of wounded died in the hot days following the battle. At first, their burial was more or less haphazard; but thoughtful men gradually came to feel that an adequate burying place and memorial were required. These were established by an interstate commission that autumn, and the finest speaker in the North was invited to dedicate them. This was the scholar and statesman Edward Everett of Harvard. He made a good speech—which is still extant: not at all academic, it is full of close strategic analysis and deep historical understanding.

Lincoln was not invited to speak, at first. Although people knew   5 him as an effective debater, they were not sure whether he was capable of making a serious speech on such a solemn occasion. But one of the impressive things about Lincoln's career is that he constantly strove to *grow*. He was anxious to appear on that occasion and to say something worthy of it. (Also, it has been suggested, he was anxious to remove the impression that he did not know how to behave properly—an impression which had been strengthened by a shocking story about his clowning on the battlefield of Antietam the previous year.) Therefore when he was invited he took considerable care with his speech. He drafted rather more than half of it in the White House before leaving, finished it in the hotel at Gettysburg the night before the ceremony (not in the train, as sometimes reported), and wrote a fair copy next morning.

There are many accounts of the day itself, 19 November 1863.   6 There are many descriptions of Lincoln, all showing the same curious blend of grandeur and awkwardness, or lack of dignity, or—it would be best to call it humility. In the procession he rode horseback: a tall lean man in a high plug hat, straddling a short horse, with his feet too near the ground. He arrived before the chief speaker, and had to wait patiently for half an hour or more. His own speech came right at the end of a long and exhausting ceremony, lasted less than three minutes, and made little impression on the audience. In part this was because they were tired, in part because (as eyewitnesses said) he ended almost before they knew he had begun, and in part because he did not speak the Address, but read it, very slowly, in a thin high voice, with a marked Kentucky accent, pronouncing "to" as "toe" and dropping his final R's.

Some people of course were alert enough to be impressed. Everett   7
congratulated him at once. But most of the newspapers paid little attention to the speech, and some sneered at it. The *Patriot and Union*
of Harrisburg wrote, "We pass over the silly remarks of the President;
for the credit of the nation we are willing . . . that they shall no more
be repeated or thought of"; and the London *Times* said, "The ceremony
was rendered ludicrous by some of the sallies of that poor President
Lincoln," calling his remarks "dull and commonplace." The first com-
mendation of the Address came in a single sentence of the Chicago
Tribune, and the first discriminating and detailed praise of it appeared
in the Springfield *Republican*, the Providence *Journal*, and the Philadelphia *Bulletin.* However, three weeks after the ceremony and then
again the following spring, the editor of *Harper's Weekly* published a
sincere and thorough eulogy of the Address, and soon it was attaining
recognition as a masterpiece.

At the time, Lincoln could not care much about the reception of   8
his words. He was exhausted and ill. In the train back to Washington,
he lay down with a wet towel on his head. He had caught smallpox.
At that moment he was incubating it, and he was stricken down soon
after he re-entered the White House. Fortunately it was a mild attack,
and it evoked one of his best jokes: he told his visitors, "At last I have
something I can give to everybody."

He had more than that to give to everybody. He was a unique   9
person, far greater than most people realize until they read his life
with care. The wisdom of his policy, the sources of his statesmanship—
these were things too complex to be discussed in a brief essay. But we
can say something about the Gettysburg Address as a work of art.[1]

A work of art. Yes: for Lincoln was a literary artist, trained both   10
by others and by himself. The textbooks he used as a boy were full of
difficult exercises and skillful devices in formal rhetoric, stressing the
qualities he practiced in his own speaking: antithesis, parallelism, and
verbal harmony. Then he read and reread many admirable models of
thought and expression: the King James Bible, the essays of Bacon,
the best plays of Shakespeare. His favorites were *Hamlet, Lear, Macbeth,
Richard III,* and *Henry VIII,* which he had read dozens of times. He
loved reading aloud, too, and spent hours reading poetry to his friends.
(He told his partner Herndon that he preferred getting the sense of

---

[1] For further reference, see W. E. Barton, *Lincoln at Gettysburg* (Bobbs-Merrill, 1930);
R. P. Basler, "Abraham Lincoln's Rhetoric," *American Literature* 11 (1939–40), 167–
182; and L. E. Robinson, *Abraham Lincoln as a Man of Letters* (Chicago, 1918).

any document by reading it aloud.) Therefore his serious speeches are important parts of the long and noble classical tradition of oratory which begins in Greece, runs through Rome to the modern world, and is still capable (if we do not neglect it) of producing masterpieces.

The first proof of this is that the Gettysburg Address is full of 11 quotations—or rather of adaptations—which give it strength. It is partly religious, partly (in the highest sense) political: therefore it is interwoven with memories of the Bible and memories of American history. The first and the last words are Biblical cadences. Normally Lincoln did not say "fourscore" when he meant eighty; but on this solemn occasion he recalled the important dates in the Bible—such as the age of Abraham when his first son was born to him, and he was "fourscore and six years old." Similarly, he did not say there was a chance that democracy might die out: he recalled the somber phrasing in the Book of Job—where Bildad speaks of the destruction of one who shall vanish without a trace, and says that "his branch shall be cut off; his remembrance shall perish from the earth." Then again, the famous description of our State as "government of the people, by the people, for the people" was adumbrated by Daniel Webster in 1830 (he spoke of "the people's government, made for the people, made by the people, and answerable to the people") and then elaborated in 1854 by the abolitionist Theodore Parker (as "government of all the people, by all the people, for all the people"). There is good reason to think that Lincoln took the important phrase "under God" (which he interpolated at the last moment) from Weems, the biographer of Washington; and we know that it had been used at least once by Washington himself.

Analyzing the Address further, we find that it is based on a highly 12 imaginative theme, or group of themes. The subject is—how can we put it so as not to disfigure it?—the subject is the kinship of life and death, that mysterious linkage which we see sometimes as the physical succession of birth and death in our world, sometimes as the contrast, which is perhaps a unity, between death and immortality. The first sentence is concerned with birth:

Our *fathers brought forth a new* nation, *conceived* in liberty.

The final phrase but one expresses the hope that

this nation, under God, shall have a *new birth* of freedom.

And that last phrase of all speaks of continuing life as the triumph over death. Again and again throughout the speech, this mystical contrast and kinship reappear: "those who *gave their lives* that that nation might *live*," "the brave men *living* and *dead*," and so in the central assertion that the dead have already consecrated their own burial place, while "it is for us, the *living*, rather to be dedicated . . . to the great task remaining." The Gettysburg Address is a prose poem; it belongs to the same world as the great elegies, and the adagios of Beethoven.

Its structure, however, is that of a skillfully contrived speech. The [13] oratorical pattern is perfectly clear. Lincoln describes the occasion, dedicates the ground, and then draws a larger conclusion by calling on his hearers to dedicate themselves to the preservation of the Union. But within that, we can trace his constant use of at least two important rhetorical devices.

The first of these is *antithesis:* opposition, contrast. The speech is [14] full of it. Listen:

> The world will little   *note*
>   nor long   *remember*   what   *we say* here
>   but   it can never   *forget*   what   *they did* here

And so in nearly every sentence: "brave men, *living* and *dead*"; "to *add* or *detract*." There is the antithesis of the Founding Fathers and men of Lincoln's own time:

> Our *fathers brought forth* a new nation . . .
> now *we* are testing whether that nation . . . can *long endure.*

And there is the more terrible antithesis of those who have already died and those who still live to do their duty. Now, antithesis is the figure of contrast and conflict. Lincoln was speaking in the midst of a great civil war.

The other important pattern is different. It is technically called [15] *tricolon*—the division of an idea into three harmonious parts, usually of increasing power. The most famous phrase of the Address is a tricolon:

> government of the people
>   by the people
>   for the people.

The most solemn sentence is a tricolon:

> we cannot dedicate
> we cannot consecrate
> we cannot hallow   this ground.

And above all, the last sentence (which has sometimes been criticized as too complex) is essentially two parallel phrases, with a tricolon growing out of the second and then producing another tricolon: a trunk, three branches, and a cluster of flowers. Lincoln says that it is for his hearers to be dedicated to the great task remaining before them. Then he goes on.

> that from these honored dead

—apparently he means "in such a way that from these honored dead"—

> we take increased devotion to that cause.

Next, he restates this more briefly:

> that we here highly resolve. . . .

And now the actual resolution follows, in three parts of growing intensity:

> that these dead shall not have died in vain
> that this nation, under God, shall have a new birth
>   of freedom

and that (one more tricolon)

> government of the people
>   by the people
>   for the people
> shall not perish from the earth.

Now, the tricolon is the figure which, through division, emphasizes basic harmony and unity. Lincoln used antithesis because he was speaking to a people at war. He used the tricolon because he was hoping, planning, praying for peace.

No one thinks that when he was drafting the Gettysburg Address, 16
Lincoln deliberately looked up these quotations and consciously chose
these particular patterns of thought. No, he chose the theme. From its
development and from the emotional tone of the entire occasion, all
the rest followed, or grew—by that marvelous process of choice and
rejection which is essential to artistic creation. It does not spoil such
a work of art to analyze it as closely as we have done; it is altogether
fitting and proper that we should do this: for it helps us to penetrate
more deeply into the rich meaning of the Gettysburg Address, and it
allows us the very rare privilege of watching the workings of a great
man's mind.

Questions

1. At the start of his essay, after quoting the opening words of Lincoln's speech, Highet uses a metaphor and a simile: he says that
the words "stand at the entrance to the best-known monument,"
and that "greatness is like granite: it is molded in fire, and it lasts
for many centuries." Are these figures of speech effective? Why or
why not? How are the two figures related to each other?

2. Analyze the structure of Highet's essay.

3. This essay was a talk given on the radio, presumably to a large
general public. Find passages in the essay that suggest oral delivery
to an unspecialized audience. How would you describe Highet's
tone?

4. It has been suggested that "government of the people, by the people" is redundant; a government *of* the people, it is argued, must
be the same as a government *by* the people. Did Lincoln repeat
himself merely to get a triad: "of the people, by the people, for the
people"? If so, is this a fault? Or can it be argued that "government
of the people" really means "government over the people"? If so,
what does the entire expression mean?

George Orwell

Politics and the English Language

Most people who bother with the matter at all would admit that the English language is in a bad way, but it is generally assumed that we cannot by conscious action do anything about it. Our civilization is decadent and our language—so the argument runs—must inevitably share in the general collapse. It follows that any struggle against the abuse of language is a sentimental archaism, like preferring candles to electric light or hansom cabs to aeroplanes. Underneath this lies the half-conscious belief that language is a natural growth and not an instrument which we shape for our own purposes.

Now, it is clear that the decline of a language must ultimately have political and economic causes: it is not due simply to the bad influence of this or that individual writer. But an effect can become a cause, reinforcing the original cause and producing the same effect in an intensified form, and so on indefinitely. A man may take to drink because he feels himself to be a failure, and then fail all the more completely because he drinks. It is rather the same thing that is happening to the English language. It becomes ugly and inaccurate because our thoughts are foolish, but the slovenliness of our language makes it easier for us to have foolish thoughts. The point is that the process is reversible. Modern English, especially written English, is full of bad habits which spread by imitation and which can be avoided if one is willing to take the necessary trouble. If one gets rid of these habits one can think more clearly, and to think clearly is a necessary first step towards political regeneration: so that the fight against bad English is not frivolous and is not the exclusive concern of professional writers. I will come back to this presently, and I hope that by that time the meaning of what I

George Orwell (1903–1950) was the pen name adopted by Eric Blair, an Englishman born in India. Orwell was educated at Eton, in England, but in 1921 he went back to the East and served for five years as a police officer in Burma. He then returned to Europe, doing odd jobs while writing novels and stories. In 1936 he fought in the Spanish Civil War on the side of the Republicans, an experience reported in *Homage to Catalonia* (1938). His last years were spent writing in England.

have said here will have become clearer. Meanwhile, here are five specimens of the English language as it is now habitually written.

These five passages have not been picked out because they are 3 especially bad—I could have quoted far worse if I had chosen—but because they illustrate various of the mental vices from which we now suffer. They are a little below the average, but are fairly representative samples. I number them so that I can refer back to them when necessary:

1. I am not, indeed, sure whether it is not true to say that the Milton who once seemed not unlike a seventeenth-century Shelley had not become, out of an experience ever more bitter in each year, more alien [*sic*] to the founder of that Jesuit sect which nothing could induce him to tolerate.

    Professor Harold Laski (Essay in *Freedom of Expression*)

2. Above all, we cannot play ducks and drakes with a native battery of idioms which prescribes such egregious collocations of vocables as the Basic *put up with* for *tolerate* or *put at a loss* for *bewilder*.

    Professor Lancelot Hogben (*Interglossa*)

3. On the one side we have the free personality: by definition it is not neurotic, for it has neither conflict nor dream. Its desires, such as they are, are transparent, for they are just what institutional approval keeps in the forefront of consciousness; another institutional pattern would alter their number and intensity; there is little in them that is natural, irreducible, or culturally dangerous. But *on the other side*, the social bond itself is noticing but the mutual reflection of these self-secure integrities. Recall the definition of love. Is not this the very picture of a small academic? Where is there a place in this hall of mirrors for either personality or fraternity?

    Essay on Psychology in *Politics* (New York)

4. All the "best people" from the gentlemen's clubs, and all the frantic fascist captains, united in common hatred of Socialism and bestial horror of the rising tide of the mass revolutionary movement, have turned to acts of provocation, to foul incendiarism, to medieval legends of poisoned wells, to legalize their own destruction of proletarian organizations, and rouse the agitated petty-bourgeoisie to chauvinistic fervor on behalf of the fight against the revolutionary way out of the crisis.

    Communist Pamphlet

5.   If a new spirit *is* to be infused into this old country, there is one thorny and contentious reform which must be tackled, and that is the humanization and galvanization of the B.B.C. Timidity here will bespeak canker and atrophy of the soul. The heart of Britain may be sound and of strong beat, for instance, but the British lion's roar at present is like that of Bottom in Shakespeare's *Midsummer Night's Dream*—as gentle as any sucking dove. A virile new Britain cannot continue indefinitely to be traduced in the eyes or rather ears, of the world by the effete languors of Langham Place, brazenly masquerading as "standard English." When the voice of Britain is heard at nine o'clock, better far and infinitely less ludicrous to hear aitches honestly dropped than the present priggish, inflated, inhibited, school-ma'amish arch braying of blameless bashful mewing maidens!

Letter in *Tribune*

Each of these passages has faults of its own, but, quite apart from 4
avoidable ugliness, two qualities are common to all of them. The first is staleness of imagery; the other is lack of precision. The writer either has a meaning and cannot express it, or he inadvertently says something else, or he is almost indifferent as to whether his words mean anything or not. This mixture of vagueness and sheer incompetence is the most marked characteristic of modern English prose, and especially of any kind of political writing. As soon as certain topics are raised, the concrete melts into the abstract and no one seems able to think of turns of speech that are not hackneyed: prose consists less and less of *words* chosen for the sake of their meaning, and more and more of *phrases* tacked together like the sections of a prefabricated henhouse. I list below, with notes and examples, various of the tricks by means of which the work of prose-construction is habitually dodged:

Dying Metaphors

A newly invented metaphor assists thought by evoking a visual image, 5
while on the other hand a metaphor which is technically "dead" (e.g., *iron resolution*) has in effect reverted to being an ordinary word and can generally be used without loss of vividness. But in between these two classes there is a huge dump of worn-out metaphors which have lost all evocative power and are merely used because they save people the trouble of inventing phrases for themselves. Examples are: *Ring the changes on, take up the cudgels for, toe the line, ride roughshod over, stand shoulder to shoulder with, play into the hands of, no axe to grind, grist to the*

mill, fishing in troubled waters, on the order of the day, Achilles' heel, swan song, hotbed. Many of these are used without knowledge of their meaning (what is a "rift," for instance?), and incompatible metaphors are frequently mixed, a sure sign that the writer is not interested in what he is saying. Some metaphors now current have been twisted out of their original meaning without those who use them even being aware of the fact. For example, *toe the line* is sometimes written *tow the line.* Another example is *the hammer and the anvil,* now always used with the implication that the anvil gets the worst of it. In real life it is always the anvil that breaks the hammer, never the other way about: a writer who stopped to think what he was saying would be aware of this, and would avoid perverting the original phrase.

Operators or Verbal False Limbs

These save the trouble of picking out appropriate verbs and nouns, and at the same time pad each sentence with extra syllables which give it an appearance of symmetry. Characteristic phrases are *render inoperative, militate against, make contact with, be subjected to, give rise to, give grounds for, have the effect of, play a leading part (role) in, make itself felt, take effect, exhibit a tendency to, serve the purpose of, etc., etc.* The keynote is the elimination of simple verbs. Instead of being a single word, such as *break, stop, spoil, mend, kill,* a verb becomes *a phrase,* made up of a noun or adjective tacked on to some general-purpose verb such as *prove, serve, form, play, render.* In addition, the passive voice is wherever possible used in preference to the active, and noun constructions are used instead of gerunds (*by examination of* instead of *by examining*). The range of verbs is further cut down by means of the *-ize* and *de-* formations, and the banal statements are given an appearance of profundity by means of the *not un-* formation. Simple conjunctions and prepositions are replaced by such phrases as *with respect to, having regard to, the fact that, by dint of, in view of, in the interests of, on the hypothesis that;* and the ends of sentences are saved from anticlimax by such resounding common-places as *greatly to be desired, cannot be left out of account, a development to be expected in the near future, deserving of serious consideration, brought to a satisfactory conclusion,* and so on and so forth.

Pretentious Diction

Words like *phenomenon, element, individual* (as noun), *objective, categorical, effective, virtual, basic, primary, promote, constitute, exhibit, exploit, utilize, eliminate, liquidate,* are used to dress up simple statements and give an air of scientific impartiality to biased judgments. Adjectives like *epoch-making, epic, historic, unforgettable, triumphant, age-old, inevitable, inexorable, veritable,* are used to dignify the sordid processes of international politics, while writing that aims at glorifying war usually takes on an archaic color, its characteristic words being: *realm, throne, chariot, mailed fist, trident, sword, shield, buckler, banner, jackboot, clarion.* Foreign words and expressions such as *cul de sac, ancien régime, deus ex machina, mutatis mutandis, status quo, gleichschaltung, weltanschauung,* are used to give an air of culture and elegance. Except for the useful abbreviations *i.e., e.g.,* and *etc.,* there is no real need for any of the hundreds of foreign phrases now current in English. Bad writers, and especially scientific, political and sociological writers, are nearly always haunted by the notion that Latin or Greek words are grander than Saxon ones, and unnecessary words like *expedite, ameliorate, predict, extraneous, deracinated, clandestine, subaqueous* and hundreds of others constantly gain ground from their Anglo-Saxon opposite numbers.[1] The jargon peculiar to Marxist writing (*hyena, hangman, cannibal, petty bourgeois, these gentry, lacquey, flunkey, mad dog, White Guard,* etc.) consists largely of words and phrases translated from Russian, German or French; but the normal way of coining a new word is to use a Latin or Greek root with the appropriate affix and, where necessary, the *-ize* formation. It is often easier to make up words of this kind (*deregionalize, impermissible, extramarital, nonfragmentary* and so forth) than to think up the English words that will cover one's meaning. The result, in general, is an increase in slovenliness and vagueness.

Meaningless Words

In certain kinds of writing, particularly in art criticism and literary criticism, it is normal to come across long passages which are almost completely lacking in meaning.[2] Words like *romantic, plastic, values, human,*   8

[1] An interesting illustration of this is the way in which the English flower names which were in use till very recently are being ousted by Greek ones, *snapdragon* becoming *antirrhinum, forget-me-not* becoming *myosotis,* etc. It is hard to see any practical reason for this change of fashion: it is probably due to an instinctive turning-away from the more homely word and a vague feeling that the Greek word is scientific.

[2] Example: "Comfort's catholicity of perception and image, strangely Whitman-esque in range, almost the exact opposite in aesthetic compulsion, continues to evoke that trembling atmospheric accumulative hinting at a cruel, an inexorably serene timelessness. . . . Wrey Gardiner scores by aiming at simple bull's-eyes with precision. Only they are not simple, and through this contented sadness runs more than the surface bitter-sweet of resignation." (*Poetry Quarterly.*)

dead, sentimental, natural, vitality, as used in art criticism, are strictly meaningless, in the sense that they not only do not point to any discoverable object, but are hardly ever expected to do so by the reader. When one critic writes, "The outstanding feature of Mr. X's work is its living quality," while another writes, "the immediately striking thing about Mr. X's work is its peculiar deadness," the reader accepts this as a simple difference of opinion. If words like *black* and *white* were involved, instead of the jargon words *dead* and *living,* he would see at once that language was being used in an improper way. Many political words are similarly abused. The word *Fascism* has now no meaning except in so far as it signifies "something not desirable." The words *democracy, socialism, freedom, patriotic, realistic, justice,* have each of them several different meanings which cannot be reconciled with one another. In the case of a word like *democracy,* not only is there no agreed definition, but the attempt to make one is resisted from all sides. It is almost universally felt that when we call a country democratic we are praising it: consequently the defenders of every kind of régime claim that it is a democracy, and fear that they might have to stop using the word if it were tied down to any one meaning. Words of this kind are often used in a consciously dishonest way. That is, the person who uses them has his own private definition, but allows his hearer to think he means something quite different. Statements like *Marshal Pétain was a true patriot, The Soviet Press is the freest in the world, The Catholic Church is opposed to persecution,* are almost always made with intent to deceive. Other words used in variable meanings, in most cases more or less dishonestly, are: *class, totalitarian, science, progressive, reactionary, bourgeois, equality.*

Now that I have made this catalogue of swindles and perversions,   9
let me give another example of the kind of writing that they lead to. This time it must of its nature be an imaginary one. I am going to translate a passage of good English into modern English of the worst sort. Here is a well-known verse from *Ecclesiastes:*

> I returned and saw under the sun, that the race is not to the swift, nor the battle to the strong, neither yet bread to the wise, nor yet riches to men of understanding, nor yet favour to men of skill; but time and chance happeneth to them all.

Here it is in modern English: 10

> Objective consideration of contemporary phenomena compels the conclusion that success or failure in competitive activities exhibits no

tendency to be commensurate with innate capacity, but that a considerable element of the unpredictable must invariably be taken into account.

This is a parody, but not a very gross one. Exhibit (3), above, for instance, contains several patches of the same kind of English. It will be seen that I have not made a full translation. The beginning and ending of the sentence follow the original meaning fairly closely, but in the middle the concrete illustrations—race, battle, bread—dissolve into the vague phrase "success or failure in competitive activities." This had to be so, because no modern writer of the kind I am discussing—no one capable of using phrases like "objective consideration of contemporary phenomena"—would ever tabulate his thoughts in that precise and detailed way. The whole tendency of modern prose is away from concreteness. Now analyze these two sentences a little more closely. The first contains forty-nine words but only sixty syllables, and all its words are those of everyday life. The second contains thirty-eight words of ninety syllables: eighteen of its words are from Latin roots, and one from Greek. The first sentence contains six vivid images, and only one phrase ("time and chance") that could be called vague. The second contains not a single fresh, arresting phrase, and in spite of its ninety syllables it gives only a shortened version of the meaning contained in the first. Yet without a doubt it is the second kind of sentence that is gaining ground in modern English. I do not want to exaggerate. This kind of writing is not yet universal, and outcrops of simplicity will occur here and there in the worst-written page. Still, if you or I were told to write a few lines on the uncertainty of human fortunes, we should probably come much nearer to my imaginary sentence than to the one from *Ecclesiastes.*

As I have tried to show, modern writing at its worst does not consist in picking out words for the sake of their meaning and inventing images in order to make the meaning clearer. It consists in gumming together long strips of words which have already been set in order by someone else, and making the results presentable by sheer humbug. The attraction of this way of writing is that it is easy. It is easier—even quicker, once you have the habit—to say *In my opinion it is not an unjustifiable assumption that* than to say *I think.* If you use ready-made phrases, you not only don't have to hunt about for words; you also don't have to bother with the rhythms of your sentences, since these phrases are generally so arranged as to be more or less euphonious. When you are composing in a hurry—when you are dictating to a stenographer, for instance, or making a public speech—it is natural to fall into a pretentious, Latinized style. Tags like *a consideration which we should do well to bear in mind* or *a conclusion to which all of us would readily assent* will save many a sentence from coming down with a bump. By using stale metaphors, similes and idioms, you save much mental effort, at the cost of leaving your meaning vague, not only for your reader but for yourself. This is the significance of mixed metaphors. The sole aim of a metaphor is to call up a visual image. When these images clash—as in *The Fascist octopus has sung its swan song, the jackboot is thrown into the melting pot*—it can be taken as certain that the writer is not seeing a mental image of the objects he is naming; in other words he is not really thinking. Look again at the examples I gave at the beginning of this essay. Professor Laski (1) uses five negatives in fifty-three words. One of these is superfluous, making nonsense of the whole passage, and in addition there is the slip *alien* for *akin*, making further nonsense, and several avoidable pieces of clumsiness which increase the general vagueness. Professor Hogben (2) plays ducks and drakes with a battery which is able to write prescriptions, and while, disapproving of the everyday phrase *put up with*, is unwilling to look *egregious* up in the dictionary and see what it means; (3), if one takes an uncharitable attitude towards it, is simply meaningless: probably one could work out its intended meaning by reading the whole of the article in which it occurs. In (4), the writer knows more or less what he wants to say, but an accumulation of stale phrases chokes him like tea leaves blocking a sink. In (5), words and meaning have almost parted company. People who write in this manner usually have a general emotional meaning—they dislike one thing and want to express solidarity with another—but they are not interested in the detail of what they are saying. A scrupulous writer, in every sentence that he writes, will ask himself at least four questions, thus: What am I trying to say? What words will express it? What image or idiom will make it clearer? Is this image fresh enough to have an effect? And he will probably ask himself two more: Could I put it more shortly? Have I said anything that is avoidably ugly? But you are not obliged to go to all this trouble. You can shirk it by simply throwing your mind open and letting the ready-made phrases come crowding in. They will construct your sentences for you—even think your thoughts for you, to a certain extent—and at need they will perform the important service of partially concealing your meaning even from yourself. It is at this point that the special connection between politics and the debasement of language becomes clear.

In our time it is broadly true that political writing is bad writing.   13
Where it is not true, it will generally be found that the writer is some
kind of rebel, expressing his private opinions and not a "party line."
Orthodoxy, of whatever color, seems to demand a lifeless, imitative
style. The political dialects to be found in pamphlets, leading articles,
manifestos, White Papers and the speeches of undersecretaries do, of
course, vary from party to party, but they are all alike in that one almost
never finds in them a fresh, vivid, home-made turn of speech. When
one watches some tired hack on the platform mechanically repeating
the familiar phrases—*bestial atrocities, iron heel, bloodstained tyranny, free
peoples of the world, stand shoulder to shoulder*—one often has a curious
feeling that one is not watching a live human being but some kind of
dummy: a feeling which suddenly becomes stronger at moments when
the light catches the speaker's spectacles and turns them into blank
discs which seem to have no eyes behind them. And this is not altogether fanciful. A speaker who uses that kind of phraseology has
gone some distance towards turning himself into a machine. The appropriate noises are coming out of his larynx, but his brain is not involved as it would be if he were choosing his words for himself. If the
speech he is making is one that he is accustomed to make over and
over again, he may be almost unconscious of what he is saying, as one
is when one utters the responses in church. And this reduced state of
consciousness, if not indispensable, is at any rate favorable to political
conformity.

In our time, political speech and writing are largely the defense   14
of the indefensible. Things like the continuance of British rule in India,
the Russian purges and deportations, the dropping of the atom bombs
on Japan, can indeed be defended, but only by arguments which are
too brutal for most people to face, and which do not square with the
professed aims of political parties. Thus political language has to consist largely of euphemism, question-begging and sheer cloudy vagueness. Defenseless villages are bombarded from the air, the inhabitants
driven out into the countryside, the cattle machine-gunned, the huts
set on fire with incendiary bullets: this is called *pacification.* Millions of
peasants are robbed of their farms and sent trudging along the roads
with no more than they can carry: this is called *transfer of population* or
rectification of frontiers. People are imprisoned for years without trial,
or shot in the back of the neck or sent to die of scurvy in Arctic lumber
camps: this is called *elimination of unreliable elements.* Such phraseology
is needed if one wants to name things without calling up mental pictures of them. Consider for instance some comfortable English pro-

fessor defending Russian totalitarianism. He cannot say outright, "I believe in killing off your opponents when you can get good results by doing so." Probably, therefore, he will say something like this:

> While freely conceding that the Soviet regime exhibits certain features which the humanitarian may be inclined to deplore, we must, I think, agree that a certain curtailment of the right to political opposition is an unavoidable concomitant of transitional periods, and that the rigors which the Russian people have been called upon to undergo have been amply justified in the sphere of concrete achievement.

The inflated style is itself a kind of euphemism. A mass of Latin words falls upon the facts like soft snow, blurring the outlines and covering up all the details. The great enemy of clear language is insincerity. When there is a gap between one's real and one's declared aims, one turns as it were instinctively to long words and exhausted idioms, like a cuttlefish squirting out ink. In our age there is no such thing as "keeping out of politics." All issues are political issues, and politics itself is a mass of lies, evasions, folly, hatred and schizophrenia. When the general atmosphere is bad, language must suffer. I should expect to find—this is a guess which I have not sufficient knowledge to verify—that the German, Russian and Italian languages have all deteriorated in the last ten to fifteen years, as a result of dictatorship. 15

But if thought corrupts language, language can also corrupt thought. A bad usage can spread by tradition and imitation, even among people who should and do know better. The debased language that I have been discussing is in some ways very convenient. Phrases like *a not unjustifiable assumption, leaves much to be desired, would serve no good purpose, a consideration which we should do well to bear in mind,* are a continuous temptation, a packet of aspirins always at one's elbow. Look back through this essay, and for certain you will find that I have again and again committed the very faults I am protesting against. By this morning's post I have received a pamphlet dealing with conditions in Germany. The author tells me that he "felt impelled" to write it. I open it at random, and here is almost the first sentence that I see: "[The Allies] have an opportunity not only of achieving a radical transformation of Germany's social and political structure in such a way as to avoid a nationalistic reaction in Germany itself, but at the same time of laying the foundations of cooperative and unified Europe." You see, he "feels impelled" to write—feels, presumably, that he has something new to say—and yet his words, like cavalry horses answering the 16 bugle, group themselves automatically into the familiar dreary pattern. This invasion of one's mind by ready-made phrases (*lay the foundations, achieve a radical transformation*) can only be prevented if one is constantly on guard against them, and every such phrase anaesthetizes a portion of one's brain.

I said earlier that the decadence of our language is probably cur-   17
able. Those who deny this would argue, if they produced an argument at all, that language merely reflects existing social conditions, and that we cannot influence its development by any direct tinkering with words and constructions. So far as the general tone or spirit of a language goes, this may be true, but it is not true in detail. Silly words and expressions have often disappeared, not through any evolutionary process but owing to the conscious action of a minority. Two recent examples were *explore every avenue* and *leave no stone unturned*, which were killed by the jeers of a few journalists. There is a long list of flyblown metaphors which could similarly be got rid of if enough people would interest themselves in the job; and it should also be possible to laugh the *not un-* formation out of existence,[3] to reduce the amount of Latin and Greek in the average sentence, to drive out foreign phrases and strayed scientific words, and, in general, to make pretentiousness unfashionable. But all these are minor points. The defense of the English language implies more than this, and perhaps it is best to start by saying what it does *not* imply.

To begin with it has nothing to do with archaism, with the sal-   18
vaging of obsolete words and turns of speech, or with the setting up of a "standard English" which must never be departed from. On the contrary, it is especially concerned with the scrapping of every word or idiom which has outworn its usefulness. It has nothing to do with correct grammar and syntax, which are of no importance so long as one makes one's meaning clear, or with the avoidance of Americanisms, or with having what is called a "good prose style." On the other hand it is not concerned with fake simplicity and the attempt to make written English colloquial. Nor does it even imply in every case preferring the Saxon word to the Latin one, though it does imply using the fewest and shortest words that will cover one's meaning. What is above all needed is to let the meaning choose the word, and not the other way about. In prose, the worst thing one can do with words is to surrender to them. When you think of a concrete object, you think

---

[3] One can cure oneself of the *not un-* formation by memorizing this sentence: *A not unblack dog was chasing a not unsmall rabbit across a not ungreen field.*

wordlessly, and then, if you want to describe the thing you have been visualizing you probably hunt about till you find the exact words that seem to fit in. When you think of something abstract you are more inclined to use words from the start, and unless you make a conscious effort to prevent it, the existing dialect will come rushing in and do the job for you, at the expense of blurring or even changing your meaning. Probably it is better to put off using words as long as possible and get one's meaning as clear as one can through pictures or sensations. Afterwards one can choose—not simply *accept*—the phrases that will best cover the meaning, and then switch round and decide what impression one's words are likely to make on another person. This last effort of the mind cuts out all stale or mixed images, all prefabricated phrases, needless repetitions, and humbug and vagueness generally. But one can often be in doubt about the effect of a word or a phrase, and one needs rules that one can rely on when instinct fails. I think the following rules will cover most cases:

  (i)   Never use a metaphor, simile or other figure of speech which you are used to seeing in print.
 (ii)   Never use a long word where a short one will do.
(iii)   If it is possible to cut a word out, always cut it out.
 (iv)   Never use the passive where you can use the active.
  (v)   Never use a foreign phrase, a scientific word or a jargon word if you can think of an everyday English equivalent.
 (vi)   Break any of these rules sooner than say anything outright barbarous.

These rules sound elementary, and so they are, but they demand a deep change of attitude in anyone who has grown used to writing in the style now fashionable. One could keep all of them and still write bad English, but one could not write the kind of stuff that I quoted in those five specimens at the beginning of this article.

I have not here been considering the literary use of language, but merely language as an instrument for expressing and not for concealing or preventing thought. Stuart Chase and others have come near to claiming that all abstract words are meaningless, and have used this as a pretext for advocating a kind of political quietism. Since you don't know what Fascism is, how can you struggle against Fascism? One need not swallow such absurdities as this, but one ought to recognize that the present political chaos is connected with the decay of language, and that one can probably bring about some improvement by starting at the verbal end. If you simplify your English, you are freed from the worst follies of orthodoxy. You cannot speak any of the necessary dialects, and when you make a stupid remark its stupidity will be obvious, even to yourself. Political language—and with variations this is true of all political parties, from Conservatives to Anarchists—is designed to make lies sound truthful and murder respectable, and to give an appearance of solidity to pure wind. One cannot change this all in a moment, but one can at least change one's own habits, and from time to time, one can even, if one jeers loudly enough, send some worn-out and useless phrase—some *jackboot, Achilles' heel, hotbed, melting pot, acid test, veritable inferno* or other lump of verbal refuse—into the dustbin where it belongs.

Questions

1. Revise one or two of Orwell's examples of bad writing.
2. Examine Orwell's metaphors. Do they fulfill his requirements for good writing?
3. Look again Orwell's grotesque revision (paragraph 10) of a passage from the Bible. Write a similar version of another passage from the Bible.
4. Can you recall any occasion when you have used words, in writing or speaking, in a consciously dishonest way? If so, can you explain why, or go further and justify your behavior?
5. In paragraph 2 Orwell says, "Written English is full of bad habits which spread by imitation." Are you aware of having acquired any bad writing habits by imitation? If so, imitation of what or whom?

Robin Lakoff

You Are What You Say

Women's language is that pleasant (dainty?), euphemistic 1
never-aggressive way of talking we learned as little girls. Cultural bias
was built into the language we were allowed to speak, the subjects we
were allowed to speak about, and the ways we were spoken of. Having
learned our linguistic lesson well, we go out in the world, only to
discover that we are communicative cripples—damned if we do, and
damned if we don't.

If we refuse to talk "like a lady," we are ridiculed and criticized 2
for being unfeminine. ("She thinks like a man" is, at best, a left-handed
compliment.) If we do learn all the fuzzy-headed, unassertive language
of our sex, we are ridiculed for being unable to think clearly, unable
to take part in a serious discussion, and therefore unfit to hold a position of power.

It doesn't take much of this for a woman to begin feeling she de- 3
serves such treatment because of inadequacies in her own intelligence
and education.

"Women's language" shows up in all levels of English. For ex- 4
ample, women are encouraged and allowed to make far more precise
discriminations in naming colors than men do. Words like *mauve, beige,
ecru, aquamarine, lavender,* and so on, are unremarkable in a woman's
active vocabulary, but largely absent from that of most men. I know
of no evidence suggesting that women actually *see* a wider range of
colors than men do. It is simply that fine discriminations of this sort
are relevant to women's vocabularies, but not to men's; to men, who
control most of the interesting affairs of the world, such distinctions
are trivial—irrelevant.

In the area of syntax, we find similar gender-related peculiarities 5
of speech. There is one construction, in particular, that women use
conversationally far more than men: the tag question. A tag is midway

Robin Lakoff was born in 1943, and educated at Radcliffe College and Harvard
University. A professor of linguistics at the University of California at Berkeley,
she has been especially interested in the language that women use. The essay
that we give here was first published in *Ms.* magazine in 1974.

between an outright statement and a yes-no question; it is less assertive than the former, but more confident than the latter.

A *flat statement* indicates confidence in the speaker's knowledge 6 and is fairly certain to be believed; a *question* indicates a lack of knowledge on some point and implies that the gap in the speaker's knowledge can and will be remedied by an answer. For example, if, at a Little League game, I have had my glasses off, I can legitimately ask someone else: "Was the player out at third?" A *tag question*, being intermediate between statement and question, is used when the speaker is stating a claim, but lacks full confidence in the truth of that claim. So if I say, "Is Joan here?" I will probably not be surprised if my respondent answers "no"; but if I say, "Joan is here, isn't she?" instead, chances are I am already biased in favor of a positive answer, wanting only confirmation. I still want a response, but I have enough knowledge (or think I have) to predict that response. A tag question, then, might be thought of as a statement that doesn't demand to be believed by anyone but the speaker, a way of giving leeway, of not forcing the addressee to go along with the views of the speaker.

Another common use of the tag question is in small talk when the 7 speaker is trying to elicit conversation: "Sure is hot here, isn't it?"

But in discussing personal feelings or opinions, only the speaker 8 normally has any way of knowing the correct answer. Sentences such as "I have a headache, don't I?" are clearly ridiculous. But there are other examples where it is the speaker's opinions, rather than perceptions, for which corroboration is sought, as in "The situation in Southeast Asia is terrible, isn't it?"

While there are, of course, other possible interpretations of a sen- 9 tence like this, one possibility is that the speaker has a particular answer in mind—"yes" or "no"—but is reluctant to state it badly. This sort of tag question is much more apt to be used by women than by men in conversation. Why is this the case?

The tag question allows a speaker to avoid commitment, and 10 thereby avoid conflict with the addressee. The problem is that, by so doing, speakers may also give the impression of not really being sure of themselves, or looking to the addressee for confirmation of their views. This uncertainty is reinforced in more subliminal ways, too. There is a peculiar sentence-intonation pattern, used almost exclusively by women, as far as I know, which changes a declarative answer into a question. The effect of using the rising inflection typical of a yes-no question is to imply that the speaker is seeking confirmation, even though the speaker is clearly the only one who has the requisite information, which is why the question was put to her in the first place:

(Q)   When will dinner be ready?
(A)   Oh . . . around six o'clock . . .?

It is as though the second speaker was saying, "Six o'clock—if that's okay with you, if you agree." The person being addressed is put in the position of having to provide confirmation. One likely consequence of this sort of speech pattern in a woman is that, often unbeknownst to herself, the speaker builds a reputation of tentativeness, and others will refrain from taking her seriously or trusting her with any real responsibilities, since she "can't make up her mind," and "isn't sure of herself."

Such idiosyncrasies may explain why women's language sounds much more "polite" than men's. It is polite to leave a decision open, not impose your mind, or views, or claims, or anyone else. So a tag question is a kind of polite statement, in that it does not force agreement or belief on the addressee. In the same way a request is a polite command, in that it does not force obedience on the addressee, but rather suggests something be done as a favor to the speaker. A clearly stated order implies a threat of certain consequences if it is not followed, and—even more impolite—implies that the speaker is in a superior position and able to enforce the order. By couching wishes in the form of a request, on the other hand, a speaker implies that if the request is not carried out, only the speaker will suffer; noncompliance cannot harm the addressee. So the decision is really left up to the addressee. The distinction becomes clear in these examples: 11

Close the door.
Please close the door.
Will you close the door?
Will you please close the door?
Won't you close the door?

In the same ways as words and speech patterns used *by* women undermine her image, those used to *describe* women make matters even worse. Often a word may be used of both men and women (and perhaps of things as well); but when it is applied to women, it assumes a special meaning that, by implication rather than outright assertion, is derogatory to women as a group.   12

The use of euphemisms has this effect. A euphemism is a substitute for a word that has acquired a bad connotation by association with something unpleasant or embarrassing. But almost as soon as the new word comes into common usage, it takes on the same old bad connotations, since feelings about the things or people referred to are not   13 altered by a change of name; thus new euphemisms must be constantly found.

There is one euphemism for *woman* still very much alive. The word, 14 of course, is *lady*. *Lady* has a masculine counterpart, namely *gentleman*, occasionally shortened to *gent*. But for some reason *lady* is very much commoner than *gent(leman)*.

The decision to use *lady* rather than *woman*, or vice versa, may 15 considerably alter the sense of a sentence, as the following examples show:

(a)   A woman (lady) I know is a dean at Berkeley.
(b)   A woman (lady) I know makes amazing things out of shoelaces and old boxes.

The use of *lady* in (a) imparts a frivolous, or nonserious, tone to 16 the sentence: the matter under discussion is not one of great moment. Similarly, in (b), using *lady* here would suggest that the speaker considered the "amazing things" not to be serious art, but merely a hobby or an aberration. If *woman* is used, she might be a serious sculptor. To say *lady doctor* is very condescending, since no one ever says *gentleman doctor* or even *man doctor*. For example, mention in the San Francisco *Chronicle* of January 31, 1972, of Madalyn Murray O'Hair as the *lady atheist* reduces her position to that of scatterbrained eccentric. Even *woman atheist* is scarcely defensible: sex is irrelevant to her philosophical position.

Many women argue that, on the other hand, *lady* carries with it 17 overtones recalling the age of chivalry: conferring exalted stature on the person so referred to. This makes the term seem polite at first, but we must also remember that these implications are perilous: they suggest that a "lady" is helpless, and cannot do things by herself.

Lady can also be used to infer frivolousness, as in titles of orga- 18 nizations. Those that have a serious purpose (not merely that of enabling "the ladies" to spend time with one another) cannot use the word *lady* in their titles, but less serious ones may. Compare the *Ladies' Auxiliary* of a men's group, or the *Thursday Evening Ladies' Browning and Garden Society* with *Ladies' Liberation* or *Ladies' Strike for Peace*.

What is curious about this split is that *lady* is in origin a euphe- 19 mism—a substitute that puts a better face on something people find uncomfortable—for *woman*. What kind of euphemism is it that subtly denigrates the people to whom it refers? Perhaps *lady* functions as a euphemism for *woman* because it does not contain the sexual implications present in *woman*: it is not "embarrassing" in that way. If this is so, we may expect that, in the future, *lady* will replace woman as the primary word for the human female, since *woman* will have become too blatantly sexual. That this distinction is already made in some contexts at least is shown in the following examples, where you can try replacing *woman* with *lady:*

(a)   She's only twelve, but she's already a woman.
(b)   After ten years in jail, Harry wanted to find a woman.
(c)   She's my woman, see, so don't mess around with her.

Another common substitute for *woman* is *girl*. One seldom hears   20
a man past the age of adolescence referred to as a boy, save in expressions like "going out with the boys," which are meant to suggest an air of adolescent frivolity and irresponsibility. But women of all ages are "girls": one can have a man—not a boy—Friday, but only a girl—never a woman or even a lady—Friday; women have girlfriends, but men do not—in a nonsexual sense—have boyfriends. It may be that this use of *girl* is euphemistic in the same way the use of *lady* is: in stressing the idea of immaturity, it removes the sexual connotations lurking in *woman*. *Girl* brings to mind irresponsibility: you don't send a girl to do a woman's errand (or even, for that matter, a boy's errand). She is a person who is both too immature and too far from real life to be entrusted with responsibilities or with decisions of any serious or important nature.

Now let's take a pair of words which, in terms of the possible   21
relationships in an earlier society, were simple male-female equivalents, analogous to *bull: cow*. Suppose we find that, for independent reasons, society has changed in such a way that the original meanings now are irrelevant. Yet the words have not been discarded, but have acquired new meanings, metaphorically related to their original senses. But suppose these new metaphorical uses are no longer parallel to each other. By seeing where the parallelism breaks down, we discover something about the different roles played by men and women in this culture. One good example of such a divergence through time is found in the pair, *master: mistress*. Once used with reference to one's power over servants, these words have become unusable today in their original master-servant sense as the relationship has become less prevalent in our society. But the words are still common.

Unless used with reference to animals, *master* now generally refers   22
to a man who has acquired consummate ability in some field, normally nonsexual. But its feminine counterpart cannot be used this way. It is practically restricted to its sexual sense of "paramour." We start out

with two terms, both roughly paraphrasable as "one who has power over another." But the masculine form, once one person is no longer able to have absolute power over another, becomes usable metaphorically in the sense of "having power over *something.*" *Master* requires as its object only the name of some activity, something inanimate and abstract. But *mistress* requires a masculine noun in the possessive to precede it. One cannot say: "Rhonda is a mistress." One must be *someone's* mistress. A man is defined by what he does, a woman by her sexuality, that is, in terms of one particular aspect of her relationship to men. It is one thing to be an *old master* like Hans Holbein,[1] and another to be an *old mistress.*

The same is true of the words *spinster* and *bachelor*—gender words 23 for "one who is not married." The resemblance ends with the definition. While *bachelor* is a neuter term, often used as a compliment, *spinster* normally is used pejoratively, with connotations of prissiness, fussiness, and so on. To be a bachelor implies that one has a choice of marrying or not, and this is what makes the idea of a bachelor existence attractive, in the popular literature. He has been pursued and has successfully eluded his pursuers. But a spinster is one who has not been pursued, or at least not seriously. She is old, unwanted goods. The metaphorical connotations of *bachelor* generally suggest sexual freedom; of *spinster*, puritanism or celibacy.

These examples could be multiplied. It is generally considered a 24 *faux pas*, in society, to congratulate a woman on her engagement, while it is correct to congratulate her fiancé. Why is this? The reason seems to be that it is impolite to remind people of things that may be uncomfortable to them. To congratulate a woman on her engagement is really to say, "Thank goodness! You had a close call!" For the man, on the other hand, there was no such danger. His choosing to marry is viewed as a good thing, but not something essential.

The linguistic double standards holds throughout the life of the 25 relationship. After marriage, bachelor and spinster become man and wife, not man and woman. The woman whose husband dies remains "John's widow"; John, however, is never "Mary's widower."

Finally, why is it that salesclerks and others are so quick to call 26 women customers "dear," "honey," and other terms of endearment they really have no business using? A male customer would never put up with it. But women, like children, are supposed to enjoy these endearments, rather than being offended by them.

In more ways than one, it's time to speak up.   27

---

[1] A German painter of the sixteenth century. (Editors' note)

Questions

1. Lakoff's first example of "women's language" (paragraph 4) has to do with colors. She says that women are more likely than men to use such words as *mauve, beige,* and *lavender* not because women see a wider range of colors but because men, "who control most of the interesting affairs of the world," regard distinctions of color as trivial and presumably leave them to the women. How adequate does this explanation seem to you?

2. For a day or so try to notice if Lakoff is correct in suggesting that women are more inclined than men to use "tag questions" and to use a "rising inflection" with a declarative sentence. Jot down examples you hear, and write an essay of about 500 words, either supporting or refuting Lakoff.

3. While you are eavesdropping, you might notice, too, whether or not in mixed company women talk more than men. Many men assume that "women talk a lot," but is it true? If, for instance, you spend an evening with an adult couple, try to form an impression about which of the two does more of the talking. Of course this is too small a sample to allow for a generalization; still, it is worth thinking about. If you are at a meeting—perhaps a meeting of a committee with men and women—again try to see whether the males or the females do most of the talking. Try also to see whether one sex interrupts the other more often than the other way around. And try to make some sense out of your findings.

4. In paragraph 11 Lakoff says, "Women's language sounds much more 'polite' than men's," and she implies that this politeness is a way of seeming weak. Do you associate politeness with weakness?

5. The essay originally appeared in *Ms.,* a feminist magazine, rather than in an academic journal devoted to language or to sociology. Why do you suppose she chose *Ms.?* What would you say Lakoff's purpose was in writing and publishing the essay?

Barbara Lawrence

Four-Letter Words Can Hurt You

Why should any words be called obscene? Don't they all 1
describe natural human functions? Am I trying to tell them, my students demand, that the "strong, earthy, gut-honest"—or, if they are
fans of Norman Mailer, the "rich, liberating, existential"—language
they use to describe sexual activity isn't preferable to "phony-sound-
ing, middle-class words like 'intercourse' and 'copulate'?" "Cop You
Late!" they say with fancy inflections and gagging grimaces. "Now,
what is *that* supposed to mean?"

Well, what is it supposed to mean? And why indeed should one 2
group of words describing human functions and human organs be
acceptable in ordinary conversation and another, describing presumably the same organs and functions, be tabooed—so much so, in fact,
that some of these words still cannot appear in print in many parts of
the English-speaking world?

The argument that these taboos exist only because of "sexual han- 3
gups" (middle-class, middle-age, feminist), or even that they are a
result of class oppression (the contempt of the Norman conquerors for
the language of their Anglo-Saxon serfs), ignores a much more likely
explanation, it seems to me, and that is the sources and functions of
the words themselves.

The best known of the tabooed sexual verbs, for example, comes 4
from the German *ficken,* meaning "to strike"; combined, according to
Partridge's etymological dictionary *Origins,* with the Latin sexual verb
futuere; associated in turn with the Latin *fustis,* "a staff or cudgel"; the
Celtic *buc,* "a point, hence to pierce"; the Irish *bot,* "the male member";
the Latin *battuere,* "to beat"; the Gaelic *batair,* "a cudgeller"; the Early
Irish *bualaim,* "I strike"; and so forth. It is one of what etymologists
sometimes call "the sadistic group of words for the man's part in cop-
ulation."

Barbara Lawrence was born in Hanover, New Hampshire, and she was educated
at Connecticut College and at New York University. She teaches at the State
University of New York, at Old Westbury. This essay first appeared in *Ms.* magazine.

The brutality of this word, then, and its equivalents ("screw," "bang," etc.), is not an illusion of the middle class or a crotchet of Women's Liberation. In their origins and imagery these words carry undeniably painful, if not sadistic, implications, the object of which is almost always female. Consider, for example, what a "screw" actually does to the wood it penetrates; what a painful, even mutilating, activity this kind of analogy suggests. "Screw" is particularly interesting in this context, since the noun, according to Partridge, comes from words meaning "groove," "nut," "ditch," "breeding sow," "scrofula" and "swelling," while the verb, besides its explicit imagery, has antecedent associations to "write on," "scratch," "scarify," and so forth—a revealing fusion of a mechanical or painful action with an obviously denigrated object.

Not all obscene words, of course, are as implicitly sadistic or denigrating to women as these, but all that I know seem to serve a similar purpose: to reduce the human organism (especially the female organism) and human functions (especially sexual and procreative) to their least organic, most mechanical dimension; to substitute a trivializing or deforming resemblance for the complex human reality of what is being described.

Tabooed male descriptives, when they are not openly denigrating to women, often serve to divorce a male organ or function from any significant interaction with the female. Take the word "testes," for example, suggesting "witnesses" (from the Latin *testis*) to the sexual and procreative strengths of the male organ; and the obscene counterpart of this word, which suggests little more than a mechanical shape. Or compare almost any of the "rich," "liberating" sexual verbs, so fashionable today among male writers, with that much-derided Latin word "copulate" ("to bind or join together") or even that Anglo-Saxon phrase (which seems to have had no trouble surviving the Norman Conquest) "make love."

How arrogantly self-involved the tabooed words seem in comparison to either of the other terms, and how contemptuous of the female partner. Understandably so, of course, if she is only a "skirt," a "broad," a "chick," a "pussycat" or a "piece." If she is, in other words, no more than her skirt, or what her skirt conceals; no more than a breeder, or the broadest part of her; no more than a piece of a human being or a "piece of tail."

The most severely tabooed of all the female descriptives, incidentally, are those like a "piece of tail," which suggest (either explicitly or through antecedents) that there is no significant difference between the female channel through which we are all conceived and born and the anal outlet common to both sexes—a distinction that pornographers have always enjoyed obscuring.

This effort to deny women their biological identity, their individuality, their humanness, is such an important aspect of obscene language that one can only marvel at how seldom, in an era preoccupied with definitions of obscenity, this fact is brought to our attention. One problem, of course, is that many of the people in the best position to do this (critics, teachers, writers) are so reluctant today to admit that they are angered or shocked by obscenity. Bored, maybe, unimpressed, aesthetically, displeased, but—no matter how brutal or denigrating the material—never angered, never shocked. 10

And yet how eloquently angered, how piously shocked many of these same people become if denigrating language is used about any minority group other than women; if the obscenities are racial or ethnic, that is, rather than sexual. Words like "coon," "kike," "spic," "wop," after all, deform identity, deny individuality and humanness in almost exactly the same way that sexual vulgarisms and obscenities do. 11

No one that I know, least of all my students, would fail to question the values of a society whose literature and entertainment rested heavily on racial or ethnic pejoratives. Are the values of a society whose literature and entertainment rest as heavily as ours on sexual pejoratives any less questionable? 12

Question

In addition to giving evidence to support her view, what persuasive devices (such as irony, analogy) does Lawrence use? (On irony, see pages 702–703; on analogy, see page 697.)

Stevie Smith

Not Waving but Drowning

Nobody heard him, the dead man,
But still he lay moaning:
I was much further out than you thought
And not waving but drowning.   4

Poor chap, he always loved larking
And now he's dead
must have been too cold for him his heart gave way,
They said   8

Oh, no no no, it was too cold always
(Still the dead one lay moaning)
I was much too far out all my life
And not waving but drowning.   12

Questions

1. The first line, "Nobody heard him, the dead man," is, of course, literally true. Dead men do not speak. In what other ways is it true?
2. Who are "they" whose voices we hear in the second stanza? What does the punctuation—or lack of it—in line 7 tell us of their feelings for the dead man? What effect is produced by the brevity of line 6? of line 8?
3. In the last stanza, does the man reproach himself, or others, or simply bemoan his fate? What was the cause of his death?

Stevie Smith (1902–1971) was born Florence Margaret Smith in England. Her first book was a novel, published in 1936, but she is best known for her several volumes of poetry.

7
NETWORKS

Restaurant—US 1 Leaving Columbia, South Carolina
Robert Frank, 1955

Punch and Judy Show at Ilfracombe
Paul Martin, 1894

By courtesy of the Board of Trustees of the Victoria and Albert Museum

Just what is it that makes today's homes so different, so appealing?
Richard Hamilton, 1956

Short Views

Ballads, *bon mots,* anecdotes, give us better insight into the depths of past centuries than grave and voluminous chronicles. "A Straw," says Selden, "thrown up into the air will show how the wind sits, which cannot be learned by casting up a stone."
Ralph Waldo Emerson

For a while everybody was laughing at Marvel because we were going after the college crowd. But I've always felt comics were a very valid form of entertainment. There's no reason to look down on telling a good story in the comic book medium. It's just dialogue and illustrations, after all, like film, except that it's a little harder than film because our action is frozen. If Ernest Hemingway had written comic books, they would have been just as good as his novels.
Stan Lee, of *Marvel Comics*

The medium is the message.
Marshall McLuhan

I beheld the wretch—the miserable monster whom I had created.
Mary Shelley, *Frankenstein*

Patricia Meyer Spacks

What Have 60 Million Readers Found in Nancy Drew?

I had quite a lot of trouble managing to reread Nancy Drew. 1
First I went to the New Haven Public Library. They didn't have any
Nancy Drew books; the librarian said that kind of reading wasn't good
for children. Then I asked my secretary if *she* owned any Nancy Drew.
She said she had had all eighty volumes, she'd read them and her
children read them, but she'd sold them three weeks before at a garage
sale. She lives in a small town outside New Haven; she thought her
public library might be able to supply me with some books. The next
day she brought me a pile, with copyrights ranging from 1935 to 1985.
Every book in the stack had been taken out consistently about once a
month. If Nancy Drew isn't good for children, it's clear that the children don't realize that.

I started asking people at random whether they'd ever read Nancy 2
Drew. Each woman in my arbitrary sample of highly intellectual types
said yes; all remembered their childhood experience of Nancy with
great pleasure. More surprisingly, several men had also enjoyed Nancy
Drew. More surprising still, one of my colleagues reported that his six
year old daughter's favorite bedtime reading-aloud books at the moment are Nancy Drew mysteries. And a colleague from another institution revealed that he teaches Nancy Drew in his course on mystery
novels.

In this context of official disapproval and unofficial enthusiasm, I 3
began my own rereading, feeling rather dutiful about it, expecting to
be bored. Not at all: the more I read, the more interested I became in

Patricia Meyer Spacks, a teacher of English literature at Yale University, is a
specialist in eighteenth-century literature, but she has written widely on other
subjects. Among her books are *Gossip* and *The Female Imagination.*
    This essay was originally delivered as a talk in conjunction with an exhibition
of the Nancy Drew books at the Wellesley College Library. Harriet Stratemeyer
Adams (mentioned in the final paragraph) used the pseudonym Carolyn Keene
for more than fifty Nancy Drew books.

how these reiterative, simple plots and sketchily defined characters worked on their readers. For what it's worth, I concluded that Nancy Drew—the old-fashioned, "out-of-date" version of Nancy Drew—is probably rather good for children.

Some of you may remember Bruno Bettelheim's book on fairytales. *The Use of Enchantment.* Analyzing the effect of fairytales on child readers, Bettelheim concludes that such stories provide developmental models. His accounts of individual tales make clear that they offer little boys patterns of mastery. For girls, on the other hand, the most familiar stories reinforce images of passivity and dependence. Sleeping Beauty must await in a state of literal unconsciousness the coming of her prince. Goodness is rewarded in girls—think of Cinderella's domestic virtues!—while courage, independence, and adventurousness (as well as generosity and compassion) win success for boys. Girls are constantly warned (in "Snow White," for instance) of the dangers of their own sexuality. The fairytales, in other words, reinforce cultural stereotypes about male and female roles. Bettelheim doesn't put it this way, but feminist critics after him have repeatedly made the point, often suggesting in what ways women's fairytales might be different. Usually their proposals for useful tales emphasize expression of rage at male domination and of attachment among females.

The Nancy Drew stories aren't fairytales or versions of fairytales. Nor do they provide developmental models. On the contrary, Nancy remains staggeringly the same—eighteen years old, "titian-haired," driving her convertible—through one book after another. And no one reads *one* Nancy Drew book: it would be like eating one peanut. (An academic father told me that his eight year old currently has a list of fifty-two more Nancy Drew books she's determined to read.) In an utterly unthreatening way, though, these books generate imaginative power by creating images of female mastery that clearly and directly address little girls' wishes and fears without encouraging their rage. Let me remind you in some detail of the characters who inhabit these books, the kinds of situations they confront, and the typical outcomes of those situations; then I'll try to say more about how these elements may work to instruct and reassure child readers.

Nancy, the perpetual eighteen year old, lives with her father, a prosperous and generous lawyer who has great respect for her abilities and who interferes not at all with her plans. Indeed, if someone steals Nancy's car, her father will promptly provide her with a new and better one (*The Haunted Showboat*, 1957). Her mother having died when Nancy was three, there is no one to come between her and her father; no mother makes restrictive rules or keeps a penetrating eye on Nancy's activities. Nor does she have a cruel stepmother. Instead, a kindly housekeeper (often described as "motherly") exclaims at the girl's cleverness and provides her and her friends with hot cocoa and apple pie. As much of the last two centuries' literature testifies, this is a little girl's dream situation.

Nancy has two female allies her own age: Bess, always characterized either as "a little plump" or as "slightly overweight," with blonde hair and occasional feminine fears; and George, Bess's "spunky cousin, an attractive brunette, who liked athletics and was proud of her boy's name" (*The Clue in the Crumbling Wall*, 1945). Although Nancy originates the most useful tactics for solving mysteries, all solutions result from the combined efforts of the three girls. There is also a boyfriend, Ned Nickerson, who often inhabits the remote peripheries of the narratives. Occasionally someone in the stories will suggest romantic feeling between Nancy and Ned; on such occasions, Ned blushes, and Nancy says "Don't be silly." 7

Always competent, Nancy possesses a surprising range of knowledge. If a car starts making ominous noises, Nancy will look underneath and announce "the whole rear housing has given way!" (*The Haunted Showboat*). On the basis of artistic style, she can decide (correctly) that the creator of a given painting was female (*The Strange Message in the Parchment*, 1977). She makes her own travel arrangements, checks into hotels by herself with aplomb (*The Eskimo's Secret*, 1985), goes off on airplane trips alone. If one path is blocked, literally or metaphorically, she can always figure out another. 8

Whether she is asked to solve a mystery or simply finds herself in the middle of one, she invariably discovers and analyzes the evidence that leads to the solution. Along the way to that solution, she often acquires new funds of knowledge: about the nature of sheep-raising, for instance, including the realities of slaughter, unsentimentally treated; or about how buttons are made; or how you tell good from bad mink pelts. (The reader, of course, learns the same facts.) 9

Each mystery conforms to a single pattern, with variations. Someone appeals to Nancy for help: an inheritance will be forfeited if the missing heir doesn't show up within a month; a New Orleans family wants to tow an old showboat from a bayou for Mardi Gras, but mysterious forces prevent the boat's being moved. Alternatively, something happens to Nancy herself: two rosebushes disappear from her yard; a sheepskin coat is stolen from her living room. In either case, she sets out, with paternal approval, to solve the problem, which typi- 10 cally becomes increasingly complicated as she investigates it. Soon she finds a clue, most often a scrap of paper with a cryptic, usually fragmentary message on it. It takes some time to decipher these messages, but all eventually yield to Nancy's common sense and acumen, with a little help from her friends. And to her dogged persistence. As the housekeeper remarks on one occasion, "I can see why you're a good detective. If you don't find hidden gold under one stone, you turn up another" (*Nancy's Mysterious Letter*, 1968).

Each book has its "scary parts," but no threatening situation lasts very long—sometimes only from one sentence to the next. The most common form of menace consists in something being thrown at Nancy. Stones, concrete blocks, bottles come whizzing through the air, from no immediately comprehensible source. Sometimes Nancy is locked up somewhere, but soon she gets away. Sometimes a bridge collapses, or a ladder, or a car tries to run her down. Occasionally cars are tampered with or boats sink; once in a while the heroine faces less definable forms of danger, like the strange sounds that come from the haunted showboat. In the end, always, Nancy discovers the source of every threat and arranges the capture of all threateners. And each book concludes with the promise of its successor, in a formulation of this sort: "Nancy was thoughtful for a moment [sometimes, more forthrightly, she is *sad*] as she realized this mystery was solved. Little did she know that she would soon become involved in the exciting *Mystery of Crocodile Island*" (*The Strange Message in the Parchment*). 11

All mysteries provide the satisfaction of problems solved and allow their readers vicarious participation in the process of solution. At this level, one can readily explain the appeal of the Nancy Drew books to a young audience. They are just scary enough, just difficult enough, to supply titillation and stimulation without making excessive demands on intelligence or endurance. Reading one Nancy Drew book educates the reader in how to approach the next. Soon a child grows into awareness of the pattern and can almost expect without quite knowing what's going to happen. The combination of familiarity and novelty generates a potent source of pleasure. 12

But the pleasure goes deeper than this, and the meaning of mysteries stated and resolved has special weight for youthful readers. The Nancy Drew stories, over and over, insist that growing up provides no unmanageable difficulties, that adolescence is even for girls a time of freedom and power, not a time of dangerous sexuality, and that young people can play a meaningful part in society. The reassurance of these messages, I suspect, accounts for the enduring popularity of this series—and for the fact that boys as well as girls read them. 13

At no time in the series' history, I suspect, have eighteen year olds 14 read Nancy Drew. The form of identification invited by these books depends on more remote varieties of fantasy than that produced by interaction between a fictional and a literal teen-ager. For eight year olds, on the other hand, the fantasy is utterly satisfying: keeping your loving, approving father all to yourself; not having to endure obscure, troubling rivalries with a mother, yet retaining the forms of maternal comfort; living in conflict-free egalitarian relationship to boys without suspicion or rivalry or teasing from other girls. Lots of love, no overt sex—an ideal situation.

The near sexlessness of these narratives must contribute to their 15 appeal for some boys as well. Gender is almost never an explicit issue here. The narrator assumes that girls take care of themselves as boys do, that girls and boys alike face problems and solve them. The freedom of a world in which gender is suppressed as a category manifestly extends to boys as well as girls.

So the fables of mastery can apply to both sexes. Over and over, 16 these stories tell child-readers the same thing: if you persist, you can figure it out—"it" being not only the individual mystery that concerns Nancy at any given moment, but the larger mystery of grown-up existence. Nancy never needs to be aggressive and she feels angry only at injustices, but she can rarely be scared. No one succeeds in bullying her. Although she's by no means remarkably articulate, she knows what she thinks and she has a solid sense of self-confidence, presumably based on her repeated successes.

The notion of "growing up" that Nancy and her friends epitomize 17 offers all kinds of reassurance to a child. It's a kind of up-to-date version of *Peter Pan*: instead of remaining forever a child, to be taken care of by big dogs and charming female fairies, one can imagine retaining the innocence of childhood, the father who pays the bills, the housekeeper who worries about you just enough and offers warm cookies when they're needed—but also fulfilling, without undue pain, the responsibilities of adulthood and enjoying some of adulthood's privileges. Indeed, Nancy excels most of the literal adults around her. The police, for instance, in these fables turn out to be kindly and helpful, but *they* never solve the crime or find the heiress. Over and over, apparent complexity becomes simple as Nancy works at it. What could be more comforting?

Children see around them, and hear about, dangers and difficul- 18 ties of adolescence. In the Nancy Drew stories, they can read about adolescence in which all danger is externalized and objectified. If someone sneaks into your house while you're giving the poor old mailman a cup of hot cocoa and steals a mailbag containing letters of value, that someone can be found and punished. It's a far easier problem to locate and punish him than it is to deal with internal conflicts or external demands for conformity with troubling norms. Even if the mail-thief interests young readers because at some level they recognize in themselves fleeting impulses to make off with someone else's letters, such impulses are usually less worrisome to little boys and girls than, say, their fantasies about sex. After all, they already know that they're not supposed to steal mail, so it's satisfying to them to learn that the person who breaks the prohibition gets his comeuppance.

The adult reader of Nancy Drew notices a striking contrast in these   19
books between the sparseness of realistic detail and the elaboration of plot. The narrator seems more interested in button-making and mink-raising than in the appearance of people or of the physical world, or in details of what people say, wear, and do in day-to-day contact. But she also has a rather intricate conception of plot. Although no single episode takes long to develop and be resolved, a dizzying sequence of events occurs in virtually all Nancy Drew stories. In the first eight pages of *The Clue in the Crumbling Wall,* a policewoman asks Nancy to find a dancer who has disappeared, two rosebushes vanish from the front yard, a clamseller shows up. Nancy finds a pearl, she goes to the jeweler to sell it, encounters an "unpleasant man," and has her purse snatched. (And one of those eight pages is occupied by an illustration; and some space is taken up by explanations of Nancy's situation, with housekeeper and father, and her history of successful mystery-solving.) Eventually all these happenings will interlock: for the moment, several seem to promise different directions. And Nancy's life continues at a comparable pace. The stories make considerable demands on a child-reader's attention, moving from one episode to another at breakneck speed and connecting episodes in complicated ways. Although the large outlines of plot, as I've already suggested, remain constant from one book to another, it would be difficult to summarize in adequate detail the intricacies of any individual plot.

Perhaps it's my training as an eighteenth-century scholar that   20
makes this conjunction of generalized scene and highly specified plot so interesting to me: it's a very eighteenth-century combination. Dr. Johnson, you may remember, suggested through a fictional character that the poet should not try to describe the streaks on the tulip; he should, instead, evoke the type of the tulip, reminding every reader of his or her own direct knowledge of the flower. I have a hunch that that's how the Nancy Drew books work for children. The sketches of

scene, character, and conversation create vague outlines for the reader to fill in from personal experience. Dark hair, blonde hair, titian hair: most readers can identify quite straightforwardly with one or another of the girls, given the lack of detail in their characterizations. The father, the housekeeper, the boyfriend, the houses and gardens, the clothes: they could be *anyone's* father or clothes or whatever. On the other hand, details about sheepshearing or the feeding of minks provide a sense of solid information, imaginably useful in the real world.

Those complicated plots also involve the process of working things out; they declare that no matter how fast or how crazily things happen, they always turn out to make sense, given persistent effort to fathom them. When you know that everything *will* eventually make sense, it becomes delightful to indulge in the vicarious experience of utter confusion. 21

It might be argued—I'm sure it has been argued—that the unrealistic aspects of this fiction make it useless if not dangerous for children. After all, if I'm right, these books suggest what is neither psychologically nor literally true. Adolescents do not have so much effectual power as Nancy and her friends wield: they do not lead lives free of familial and of internal conflict; they are not always readily able to figure things out; they often feel troubled by their own and other people's sexuality; they sometimes fight with their friends, they sometimes feel depressed, they rarely get to have their fathers all to themselves (if there's no mother, there's usually a girlfriend). Many recent stories for children are predicated on the assumption that useful fictions provide realistic accounts of dangers to be faced in the world. You tell the little girl about drug dealers and divorce, the theory goes, and she'll be better prepared to deal with them when she confronts them herself. 22

Maybe so; I don't know. I wouldn't want children to read *only* about the idealized white middle-class harmonies depicted in the Nancy Drew books. But I suspect that it's useful for a white middle-class eight year old—and such, obviously, is the intended audience of the series—to be reassured about what lies ahead, to be told that she can solve problems by using available resources, that cooperative models of accomplishment are meaningful, and that she doesn't have to grow up until she wants to. Nancy Drew as she exists on the page resembles an eight year old's idealized self-image more than a realistic portrayal of an eighteen year old. But it's eight year olds who like to read about her, and I strongly suspect that a more up-to-date, "realistic" version of the character will enjoy less popular success than her 23 implausible predecessor. Harriet Stratemeyer Adams took pride in having created an early version of the independent woman. Her achievement—the degree to which she causes young readers to feel deeply involved with that figure of the independent woman—may depend partly on exactly the aspects of her fictions that make them seem unrealistic and uncompelling to adults.

Questions

1. Spacks offers an explanation of why the Nancy Drew books interest children. If you read such books when you were a child, do you now agree with Spacks's analysis of their appeal?

2. If as a child you read some other sort of book designed for children—for example, the kind Spacks refers to in the last two sentences of paragraph 22—what were its appeals?

3. In paragraph 20 Spacks says that "most readers can identify . . . with" Nancy or one of her friends. But in paragraph 23 she refers to the "white middle-class eight year old" as the "intended audience of the series." Does Spacks contradict herself? Or, though she doesn't address the question directly, does her analysis suggest reasons that the books might also appeal to eight-year-olds of other races and classes?

4. In her first paragraph, and in the next-to-last paragraph, Spacks suggests that some people find the Nancy Drew books not good for children, or even dangerous for them. She clearly disagrees. Whether or not you are convinced by her argument, imagine some books that might be, in your opinion, "not good" or "dangerous" for children to read. What would they be like? What would you do about them? Would you try to keep them out of children's libraries (as the Nancy Drew books have been kept out of the New Haven library)? Or put pressure on publishers not to publish them? Or what?

5. Spacks does not discuss the illustrations in the Nancy Drew books. Consider (in these books or in some others with which you are familiar) the episodes illustrated and also the style of the illustrations. (You may find it helpful to compare the style with other styles used in other books designed for children.)

Richard A. Hawley

Television and Adolescents
A Teacher's View

Ever since its novelty wore off in the fifties, we have all 1
known, really, that television in its commercial form wasn't up to much
good. This isn't to say that millions of people don't still depend on it,
but dependency is hardly a sign of virtue. Except for Marshall Mc-
Luhan's grab-bag theoretics, few claims have been advanced for the
improving effects of television. In fact, recently there has been a flurry
of publishing activity, most notably Marie Winn's *The Plug-in Drug*,
about television as a cause of downright mental erosion. But what I
think Marie Winn and others need is a concrete, closely observed, and
intensely felt illustration of the larger thesis. That's what I offer here.

Television has a way of intruding into our lives, and last year it 2
intruded into my life and into the life of the school where I work in a
way that many of us there will never forget. We had all taken our seats
for morning assembly. The usual announcements were read, after
which the morning's senior speaker was introduced. Like many independent schools, ours requires each senior to address the student
body in some manner before he graduates. Since public speaking is
not a widely distributed gift these days, the senior speeches are infrequently a source of much interest or intentional amusement.

As the curtains parted, we could see that the speaker had opted 3
for a skit. On the stage were a covered table and a number of cooking
implements. Out stepped the speaker wearing an apron and chef's
hat, which very quickly established that he was going to satirize one
of my colleagues who has a national reputation as a gourmet chef.
Since this colleague is also a man who can take a joke, the prospects
for the skit seemed bright. But not for long.

At first, I think almost all of us pretended that we didn't hear, that 4
we were making too much of certain, possibly accidental, double en-
tendres. But then came the direct statements and a few blatant physical

Richard A. Hawley is dean of students at University School in Hunting Valley,
Ohio.

gestures. Then it was clear! This boy was standing before five hundred of us making fun of what he suggested at some length was the deviant sexual nature of one of his teachers. The response to this was at first stupefaction, then some outbursts of laughter (the groaning kind of laughter that says, "I don't believe you said that"), then a quieting, as the speech progressed, to periodic oohs (the kind that say, "You *did* say that, and you're in for it").

When he had finished, there was a nearly nauseating level of ten- 5 sion afloat. As the students filed off to class, I made my way backstage to find the speaker. It had by now dawned on him that he had done something wrong, even seriously wrong. We met in my office.

He expressed remorse at having offended a teacher whom he said 6 he particularly liked. (Before the conference I had checked briefly with the teacher and found him badly flustered and deeply hurt.) The remorse was, I felt, genuine. But something was decidedly missing in the boy's explanation of how he came to think that such a presentation might, under any circumstances, have been appropriate. He hadn't, he admitted, really thought about it, and some of his friends thought the idea was funny, and, well, he didn't know. When it occurred to him that serious school action was in the offing, he protested that in no way had he intended the sexual references to be taken seriously— they were, you know, a joke.

I pointed out to him that the objects of such jokes have no way 7 to respond: To ignore the insinuation might affirm its validity; on the other hand, to object vigorously would draw additional attention to the offense and sustain the embarrassment connected with it. I pointed out further that sometimes innocent parties *never* regain their stature after being offended in this manner, and that the injured party was, at the very least, in for a terrible day of school.

The boy became reflective and said, "Was it *that* bad? You can see 8 worse on 'Saturday Night Live'." I told him I doubted this, but if it were true, and were I in a position to judge, I would be in favor of expelling "Saturday Night Live" from the air. He left the office, and subsequently endured the appropriate consequences.

For my part, I resolved to turn on "Saturday Night Live," and 9 when I did, I realized the student had spoken truly. The show's quick-succession, absurdist comedy spots depended for their appeal on establishing an almost dangerous sense of inappropriateness: exactly that sense created by our senior speaker. To me, for some years a lapsed viewer, it seemed that both the variety and specificity of sexual innuendo had developed considerably since, say, the once daring Smothers Brothers show of the sixties. What struck me more, however, was how many punch lines and visual gags depended on suddenly introducing the idea of injury or violent death.

I happened to tune in the night a funny caption was put over the documentary shot of Middle Eastern political partisans being dragged to death behind an automobile. Was this funny? I asked my students. They said it was "sick" and laughed. Does this kind of fun trivialize crisis? Trivialize cruelty? Inure us to both? Or is it, you know, a joke? 10

The right things were said, I think, to our students about the boy's speech. But I can't say the situation improved. Not more than a couple of weeks later, a speaker garbed in a woman's tennis dress took the podium and began to talk humorously about the transsexual tennis player Renee Richards. I can't think of a subject harder for an adolescent to discuss before an adolescent audience. Rarely noted for their confidence and breadth of vision in matters of human sexuality, adolescents are unlikely to be objective, sympathetic, or (let me tell you) funny about so disturbing a phenomenon as sex change. This particular boy, whose inflection is very flat and whose normal countenance is especially stony, managed to convey almost a sense of bitterness in making his string of insulting and, in his reference to genitals and to menstruation, awfully tasteless cracks. 11

So there it was again: the inappropriateness, the tension. This time the injured party was remote from our particular world, so the hastily arranged conference with the boy turned on general considerations of taste and judgment. This time, however, the speaker was recalcitrant: We could disapprove of his speech and discipline him if we chose, but we ought to know that we could hear the same thing on television. 12

At that moment something clicked for me. Not only did my brief exposure to "Saturday Night Live" convince me that, yes, I would hear the same thing on television, but I was suddenly struck with the realization that he was using television as an arbiter of taste—that is, *as an arbiter of good taste.* I began to see in this premise a common ground upon which he and I could at least argue. Both of us were in agreement that what is broadcast over television ought to be acceptable; our point of disagreement was his feeling that broadcasting something over television *made* it acceptable. Alarming as such a feeling is to me, it is not hard to see how it has developed over the past few decades. 13

Until the middle sixties, with the exception of the very earthiest plays and novels, the values of home and school and the values of the popular culture were fairly continuous; if anything, radio, television, 14 and motion pictures were more staid than real life. Of course, all this would change very quickly—not because change was requested or even consented to, but because it wasn't, perhaps couldn't be, resisted. And suddenly there it all was at once: the most embarrassing expletives as common speech; every imaginable kind of sexual coupling depicted in ever increasing candor; obsessively specific wounds, mutilations.

These formerly unacceptable kinds of stimulation made their way   15
more easily into the relatively insulated world of print and film than they did into the more communal world of the television set. Television is typically viewed in homes, and what is communally seen and heard must be communally integrated, or there will be friction. Since American households—set-holds?—share this communal experience for an estimated two to seven hours per day, the potential for friction is considerable. This is why, on grounds of taste, criticism of television programming tends to be more bitter and more relentless than criticism of books and films.

Television foes and partisans alike continue to advise, with some   16
reason, that those who object to certain programs ought not to watch them. But given the impossibility of monitoring the set at all hours, control over the amount and quality of viewing is difficult to maintain even in principled, surveillant households. Too, some viewers will insist on being their brother's keeper. Not everyone who is convinced that what is beaming over the national airwaves is inhumane, unscrupulous, or scurrilous is going to fight to the death for the networks' right to be so.

For many people, television is no longer on the polite side of real   17
life. This is an obvious observation about a novel development, one whose consequences are only just dawning on us. A realist or an existentialist may argue that the unflappably suburban world of "Father Knows Best" revealed none of the complex, ambivalent, and often irrational forces at work in real families: But it is hard to argue that "Father Knows Best" in any way *contributed* to those dark forces. On the contrary, it is possible to argue—although one hesitates to carry it too far—that the theme of Father Knowing Best serves as a psychologically soothing backdrop to the prickly dynamics of real family life. And while today's most highly rated shows suggest that the prevailing seventies' theme is Nobody Knows Anything, there are still apparently enough viewers who like Father Knowing Best to support series like "The Waltons" and "Little House on the Prairie."

Sometimes the theme is compromised in a typical seventies' man-   18
ner, of which "James at 16" provides a good example: The parents are cast very much in the Robert Young-Jane Wyatt mold, but their son

James is, to borrow a phrase, kind of now. By far the most interesting thing he did was to lose his virginity on prime time. The fifteen-going-on-sixteen-year-old boys I work with, many of them at least as sophisticated as James, typically hold on to their virginity a bit longer, until the disposition of their sexual feelings is under surer control. The best clinical evidence maintains that the process of bringing newly emergent sexuality under control is *inherently* delicate and troublesome. James' television plunge planted the anxiety-provoking notion in the mind of the adolescent viewer that he was sexually lagging behind not only the precocious kid down the block, but the Average American Boy character of James. (One was allowed to be less anxious when Father Knew Best.)

Why shouldn't television make people anxious? say the producers   19
of programs that make people anxious. After all, the *world* is anxious. (An awfully self-serving position: Programs that arouse anxiety are relevant; those that don't are enjoyable.) Before long, this line of argument begins to lay claim that programs which bring up irritating subjects in an irritating manner are performing a valuable social mission. Norman Lear, the producer of comedies such as "All in the Family" and "Maude," makes such a claim. According to the Lear formula, a controversial topic will be raised, tossed around for laughs, then either discarded or resolved. Resolution occurs when one of the characters tolerates or forgives the controversial person or practice, while some other character, usually a combination of lovable old coot and ass, does not.

As many critics have pointed out, this is only apparent resolution.   20
Nothing much really happens to a racial or sexual conflict when it is laughed at (a device that is supposed to soften outright slurring and stereotyping), discarded, tolerated, or forgiven. The idea that "if we can joke about it this way, we have taken a humanitarian stride" is mistaken. There is plenty of evidence, particularly among the student population, that, for one thing, race relations are more strained today than they were a decade ago. No one would want to claim that racism among youth disappeared during the politically active sixties; however, a claim can be made that when a student was confronted then with having made a racial slur, he seemed to be aware of having violated a standard.

Who is to say that Archie Bunker hath no sting? More and more   21
television comedians, in the manner of Don Rickles, seek *only* to sting. It is really an empirical question, not a matter of taste, whether or not it is harmless, much less healing, to denigrate everybody, including oneself. A hit song by Randy Newman insults small people: this is no

parody of unkindness or bigotry, but the real thing. My students understand it perfectly and parrot it enthusiastically. Rebuked, they grimace in exasperation. Nothing in their youthful experience tells them that bigotry is a sign of cultural regression ("It isn't bigotry; it's, you know, a joke"). They prefer to see whatever wicked delights crop up in the media as a progressive casting off of prudish inhibitions. According to such a view, progress is whatever happens next.

Toleration of the intolerable is always worrying, but it is especially   22
so when it takes place among the young, in whom we want to invest so much hope. Tolerating the intolerable is part of a dynamic, not a static, process; the intolerable, when it is nurtured, grows.

Which brings me back to the senior speeches. Two so thoroughly   23
inappropriate presentations in a single year represented a high count for us, so we were not ready, at least I wasn't, for the third.

This time the talk was about a summer spent working on a ranch,   24
and the format was that of a commentary with slides. No apparent harm in this, but there were a number of factors working against the speech's success. The first was that the speaker was renowned for being a card, a reputation the welcoming ovation insisted he live up to. Second, he had not adequately rehearsed the projection of the slides, so that they tended to appear out of order and askew, the effect of which was to provide a subtextual comedy of visual non sequiturs. Third, he chose to capitalize on the audience's nearly unrestrained hilarity by playing up certain questionable references.

The speaker made a fairly good, not too inappropriate crack about   25
a slide which depicted a bull mounting a cow—"Sometimes the corrals get so crowded we have to stack the cattle on top of one another." But he chose to exploit his references to the gelding of bulls. There were, in all, four jokey and brutal evocations of this process which served to keep the image of bull genitalia before our minds for quite a few minutes. Since laughter had already been spent, the castration jokes were met with a kind of nervous applause. Bolstered by this, the speaker closed with a coda to the effect that he would be available after assembly to anybody who wanted tips on "cutting meat."

Since I happened to be in charge that day, I sent him home. It   26
seemed to me, in light of the various reprisals and forewarnings connected with the previous speeches, that this particular performance, though perhaps less offensive in its specific references than the other two, ought to be the last straw. The speaker had clearly exceeded

anything required by either schoolboy or cowboy saltiness. He had created an anything-goes atmosphere, and then he had let it go—for which he was applauded. "That was great!" said the boy next to me on the way out of the auditorium.

That morning and afterward scores of students, most, but not all, 27 of them civil, hastened to let me know that they felt it was unfair to have sent the speaker home. Not one of them failed to remind me that I could see worse on television. Had I never seen "Saturday Night Live"? That afternoon an opinion poll went up requesting signatures from those who disapproved of the action I had taken and, in an opposing column, those who approved. Within the hour, hundreds expressed disapproval, only one approved.

For a day or two at school there was an animated atmosphere of 28 martyrdom (the speaker's, not mine), but it dissipated rapidly, possibly because the right to make castration jokes from the stage was not, as a cause, very catalytic. The banished speaker, a very likable boy, returned, was received warmly, and apologized not at all cringingly.

In the calm that has followed, my colleagues and I have taken 29 pains to stress to our students, especially at the commencement of the new school year, that whenever somebody addresses an assembly, it is a special occasion. Speakers are expected to observe definite standards when they speak or perform; audiences are expected to be courteous and restrained. Humor at someone else's expense is out, unless it is prearranged with the party lampooned, and even then it ought not to be inhumane. Excretory and copulatory humor is out; it's too easy. Preparation is important. Being persuasive is important. Being controversial is important. Being funny is a delight to all, though it is harder than it looks.

Perhaps these expectations are high. However, schools, especially 30 parochial and independent schools, are gloriously unencumbered in setting such standards: Schools are often *chosen* for the standards they set, the difference they represent. One of the things schools have an opportunity to be different from is television, for although we are all wired into it and it feels public, like the law, it is actually private, like a door-to-door salesman. We don't have to buy the goods.

Since children who watch a fair amount of television will quite 31 naturally assume they are being told and shown the truth, it seems to me crucial that they are exposed to models who view it selectively and critically, who judge it by criteria other than its potential to engage. My own experience has been that students are surprised, but not hostile, when television programming is harshly judged. I think they may even come to like the idea that they themselves, at their discriminating best, are in the process of becoming people television ought to measure up to.

Questions

1. The three speeches that disturbed Hawley all had to do with sex, yet (aside from a few casual references, such as the one to the Smothers Brothers) his references to television are to violence, including verbal violence. Is Hawley muddling things?
2. Hawley begins paragraph 19 by asking: "Why shouldn't television make people anxious?" and he goes on to repeat the word "anxious." What is the meaning of "anxious" in this context?
3. Judging from this essay, what sort of person is Hawley? In a paragraph, try to characterize him. (Don't attempt to summarize his argument; confine your remarks to his personality.)

Tipper Gore

Curbing the Sexploitation Industry

I can't even count the times in the last three years, since 1
I began to express my concern about violence and sexuality in rock music, that I have been called a prude, a censor, a music hater, even a book burner. So let me be perfectly clear: I detest censorship. I'm not advocating censorship but rather a candid and vigorous debate about the dangers posed for our children by what I call the "sexploitation industry."

Tipper Gore, co-founder of the Parents' Music Resource Center, is the author of a book about violence and obscenity in the arts. Her husband is a United States senator from Tennessee.

We don't need to put a childproof cap on the world, but we do   2
need to remind the nation that children live in it, too, and deserve
respect and sensitive treatment.

When I launched this campaign in 1985 . . . I went to the source   3
of the problem, sharing my concerns and proposals with the entertainment industry. Many producers were sympathetic. Some coop-
erated with my efforts. But others have been overtly hostile, accusing
me of censorship and suggesting, unfairly, that my motives are political. This resistance and hostility has convinced me of the need for a
two-pronged campaign, with equal effort from the entertainment industry and concerned parents. Entertainment producers must take the
first step, by labeling sexually explicit material.

But the industry cannot be expected to solve the problem on its   4
own. Parents should encourage producers to cooperate and praise
them when they do. Producers need to know that parents are aware
of the issue and are reading their advisory labels. Above all, they need
to know that somebody out there cares, that the community at large
is not apathetic about the deep and lasting damage being done to our
children.

What's at issue is not the occasional sexy rock lyric. What trou-   5
bles—indeed, outrages—me is far more vicious: a celebration of the
most gruesome violence, coupled with the explicit message that sado-
masochism is the essence of sex. We're surrounded by examples—in
rock lyrics, on television, at the movies and in rental videos. One major
TV network recently aired a preview of a soap opera rape scene during
a morning game show.

The newest craze in horror movies is something called the "teen   6
slasher" film, and it typically depicts the killing, torture and sexual
mutilation of women in sickening detail. Several rock groups now
simulate sexual torture and murder during live performances. Others
titillate youthful audiences with strippers confined in cages on stage
and with half-naked dancers, who often act out sex with band members. Sexual brutality has become the common currency of America's
youth culture and with it the pervasive degradation of women.

Why is this graphic violence dangerous? It's especially damaging   7
for young children because they lack the moral judgment of adults.
Many children are only dimly aware of the consequences of their actions, and, as parents know, they are excellent mimics. They often
imitate violence they see on TV, without necessarily understanding
what they are doing or what the consequences might be. One 5-year-
old boy from Boston recently got up from watching a teen-slasher film

and stabbed a 2-year-old girl with a butcher knife. He didn't mean to kill her (and luckily he did not). He was just imitating the man in the video.

Nor does the danger end as children grow older. National health 8 officials tell us that children younger than teen-agers are apt to react to excessive violence with suicide, satanism, drug and alcohol abuse. Even grown-ups are not immune. One series of studies by researchers at the University of Wisconsin found that men exposed to films in which women are beaten, butchered, maimed and raped were significantly desensitized to the violence. Not only did they express less sympathy for the victims, they even approved of lesser penalties in hypothetical rape trials.

Sado-masochistic pornography is a kind of poison. Like most poi- 9 sons, it probably cannot be totally eliminated, but it certainly could be labeled for what it is and be kept away from those who are most vulnerable. The largest record companies have agreed to this—in principle at least. In November 1985, the Recording Industry Association of America adopted my proposal to alert parents by having producers either put warning labels on records with explicitly sexual lyrics or display the lyrics on the outside of the record jackets. Since then, some companies have complied in good faith, although others have not complied at all.

This is where we parents must step in. We must let the industry 10 know we're angry. We must press for uniform voluntary compliance with labeling guidelines. And we must take an active interest at home in what our children are watching and listening to. After all, we can hardly expect that the labels or printed lyrics alone will discourage young consumers.

Some parents may want to write to the record companies. Others 11 can give their support to groups like the Parent Teacher Association, which have endorsed the labeling idea. All of us can use our purchasing power. We have more power than we think, and we must use it. For the sake of our children, we simply can't afford to slip back into apathy.

My concern for the health and welfare of children has nothing to 12 do with politics: It is addressed to conservatives and liberals alike. Some civil libertarians believe it is wrong even to raise these questions—just as some conservatives believe that the Government should police popular American culture. I reject both these views. I have no desire to restrain artists or cast a "chill" over popular culture. But I believe parents have First Amendment rights, too.

The fate of the family, the dignity of women, the mental health   13
of children—these concerns belong to everyone. We must protect our
children with choice, not censorship. Let's start working in our communities to forge a moral consensus for the 1990's. Children need our
help, and we must summon the courage to examine the culture that
shapes their lives.

Questions

1. Analyze and evaluate Gore's opening paragraph.
2. Gore says she is not advocating censorship. In a sentence or two
   state what she *is* advocating. If you agree with her position, what
   can you add to it? If you disagree, what are the grounds for your
   disagreement?
3. Consider the songs of some prominent singer, perhaps Madonna,
   Sade, Michael Jackson, or Bruce Springsteen. Do you find them
   offensive in any way? If so, explain. If not, explain why parents
   should not be distressed by the music of the person you have selected.
4. Gore concentrates on rock lyrics, movies, and soap operas. Where
   else in our society are we given images of violence and of the degradation of women? Do you think that parents can protect their
   children from such images? If so, how?

Marya Mannes

Television Advertising
The Splitting Image

$\mathbf{A}$ bride who looks scarcely fourteen whispers, "Oh, Mom,   1
I'm so *happy!*" while a doting family adjust her gown and veil and a
male voice croons softly, "A woman is a harder thing to be than a
man. She has more feelings to feel." The mitigation of these excesses,

Marya Mannes has published in many journals, from *TV Guide* to *The New Republic.*

it appears, is a feminine deodorant called Secret, which allows our bride to approach the altar with security as well as emotion.

Eddie Albert, a successful actor turned pitchman, bestows his at- 2 tention on a lady with two suitcases, which prompt him to ask her whether she has been on a journey. "No," she says, or words to that effect, as she opens the suitcases. "My two boys bring back their soiled clothes every weekend from college for me to wash." And she goes into the familiar litany of grease, chocolate, mud, coffee, and fruitjuice stains, which presumably record the life of the average American male from two to fifty. Mr. Albert compliments her on this happy device to bring her boys home every week and hands her a box of Biz, because "Biz *is* better."

Two women with stony faces meet cart to cart in a supermarket 3 as one takes a jar of peanut butter off a shelf. When the other asks her in a voice of nitric acid why she takes that brand, the first snaps, "Because I'm choosy for my family!" The two then break into delighted smiles as Number Two makes Number One taste Jif for "mothers who are choosy."

If you have not come across these dramatic interludes, it is because 4 you are not home during the day and do not watch daytime television. It also means that your intestinal tract is spared from severe assaults, your credibility unstrained. Or, for that matter, you may look at commercials like these every day and manage either to ignore them or find nothing—given the fact of advertising—wrong with them. In that case, you are either so brainwashed or so innocent that you remain unaware of what this daily infusion may have done and is doing to an entire people as the long-accepted adjunct of free enterprise and support of "free" television.

"Given the fact" and "long-accepted" are the key words here. 5 Only socialists, communists, idealists (or the BBC) fail to realize that a mass television system cannot exist without the support of sponsors, that the massive cost of maintaining it as a free service cannot be met without the massive income from selling products. You have only to read of the unending struggle to provide financial support for public, noncommercial television for further evidence.

Besides, aren't commercials in the public interest? Don't they help 6 you choose what to buy? Don't they provide needed breaks from programming? Aren't many of them brilliantly done, and some of them funny? And now, with the new sexual freedom, all those gorgeous chicks with their shining hair and gleaming smiles? And if you didn't have commercials taking up a good part of each hour, how on earth would you find enough program material to fill the endless space/time void?

Tick off the yesses and what have you left? You have, I venture 7 to submit, these intangible but possibly high costs: the diminution of human worth, the infusion and hardening of social attitudes no longer valid or desirable, pervasive discontent, and psychic fragmentation.

Should anyone wonder why deception is not an included detri- 8 ment, I suggest that our public is so conditioned to promotion as a way of life, whether in art or politics or products, that elements of exaggeration or distortion are taken for granted. Nobody really believes that a certain shampoo will get a certain swain, or that an unclogged sinus can make a man a swinger. People are merely prepared to hope it will.

But the diminution of human worth is much more subtle and just 9 as pervasive. In the guise of what they consider comedy, the producers of television commercials have created a loathsome gallery of men and women patterned, presumably, on Mr. and Mrs. America. Women liberationists have a major target in the commercial image of woman flashed hourly and daily to the vast majority. There are, indeed, only four kinds of females in this relentless sales procession: the gorgeous teen-age swinger with bouncing locks; the young mother teaching her baby girl the right soap for skin care; the middle-aged housewife with a voice like a power saw; and the old lady with dentures and irregularity. All these women, to be sure, exist. But between the swinging sex object and the constipated granny there are millions of females never shown in commercials. These are—married or single—intelligent, sensitive women who bring charm to their homes, who work at jobs as well as lend grace to their marriage, who support themselves, who have talents or hobbies or commitments, or who are skilled at their professions.

To my knowledge, as a frequent if reluctant observer, I know of 10 only one woman on a commercial who has a job; a comic plumber pushing Comet. Funny, heh? Think of a dame with a plunger.

With this one representative of our labor force, which is well over 11 thirty million women, we are left with nothing but the full-time housewife in all her whining glory: obsessed with whiter wash, moister cakes, shinier floors, cleaner children, softer diapers, and greaseless fried chicken. In the rare instances when these ladies are not in the kitchen, at the washing machine, or waiting on hubby, they are buying beauty soaps (fantasy, see?) to take home so that their hair will have more body. Or out at the supermarket being choosy.

If they were attractive in their obsessions, they might be bearable. 12
But they are not. They are pushy, loud-mouthed, stupid, and—of all
things now—bereft of sexuality. Presumably, the argument in the tenets of advertising is that once a woman marries she changes overnight
from plaything to floor-waxer.

To be fair, men make an equivalent transition in commercials. The 13
swinging male with the mod hair and the beautiful chick turns inevitably into the paunchy slob who chokes on his wife's cake. You will
notice, however, that the voice urging the viewer to buy the product
is nearly always male: gentle, wise, helpful, seductive. And the visible
presence telling the housewife how to get shinier floors and whiter
wash and lovelier hair is almost invariably a man: the Svengali in modern dress, the Trilby (if only she were!), his willing object.[1]

Woman, in short, is consumer first and human being fourth. A 14
wife and mother who stays home all day buys a lot more than a woman
who lives alone or who—married or single—has a job. The young girl
hell-bent on marriage is the next most susceptible consumer. It is entirely understandable, then, that the potential buyers of detergents,
foods, polishes, toothpastes, pills, and housewares are the housewives, and that the sex object spends more of *her* money on cosmetics,
hair lotions, soaps, mouthwashes, and soft drinks.

Here we come, of course, to the youngest class of consumers, the 15
swinging teen-agers so beloved by advertisers keen on telling them
(and us) that they've "got a lot to live, and Pepsi's got a lot to give."
This affords a chance to show a squirming, leaping, jiggling group of
beautiful kids having a very loud high on rock and—of all things—
soda pop. One of commercial TV's most dubious achievements, in fact,
is the reinforcement of the self-adulation characteristic of the young
as a group.

As for the aging female citizen, the less shown of her the better. 16
She is useful for ailments, but since she buys very little of anything,
not having a husband or any children to feed or house to keep, nor—
of course—sex appeal to burnish, society and commercials have little
place for her. The same is true, to be sure, of older men, who are
handy for Bosses with Bad Breath or Doctors with Remedies. Yet, on
the whole, men hold up better than women at any age—in life or on
television. Lines on their faces are marks of distinction, while on
women they are signatures of decay.

---

[1] In George Du Maurier's novel, *Trilby* (1894), Svengali mesmerizes Trilby and
causes her to become a famous singer; when Svengali dies, Trilby loses her voice,
dwindles, and soon dies. (Editors' note)

There is no question, in any case, that television commercials (and 17
many of the entertainment programs, notably the soap serials that are
part of the selling package) reinforce, like an insistent drill, the assumption that a woman's only valid function is that of wife, mother,
and servant of men: the inevitable sequel to her earlier function as sex
object and swinger.

At a time when more and more women are at long last learning 18
to reject these assumptions as archaic and demeaning, and to grow
into individual human beings with a wide option of lives to live, the
sellers of the nation are bent upon reinforcing the ancient pattern. They
know only too well that by beaming their message to the Consumer
Queen they can justify her existence as the housebound Mrs. America:
dumber than dumb, whiter than white.

The conditioning starts very early: with the girl child who wants 19
the skin Ivory soap has reputedly given her mother, with the nine-
year-old who brings back a cake of Camay instead of the male deodorant her father wanted. (When she confesses that she bought it so
she could be "feminine," her father hugs her, and, with the voice of
a child-molester, whispers, "My little girl is growing up on me, huh.")
And then, before long, comes the teen-aged bride who "has feelings
to feel." It is the little boys who dream of wings, in an airplane commercial; who grow up (with fewer cavities) into the doers. Their little
sisters turn into *Cosmopolitan* girls, who in turn become housewives
furious that their neighbors' wash is cleaner than theirs.

There is good reason to suspect that this manic obsession with 20
cleanliness, fostered, quite naturally, by the giant soap and detergent
interests, may bear some responsibility for the cultivated sloppiness
of so many of the young in their clothing as well as in their chosen
hideouts. The compulsive housewife who spends more time washing
and vacuuming and polishing her possessions than communicating to,
or stimulating her children creates a kind of sterility that the young
would instinctively reject. The impeccably tidy home, the impeccably
tidy lawn are—in a very real sense—unnatural and confining. Yet the
commercials confront us with broods of happy children, some of
whom—believe it or not—notice the new fresh smell their clean, white
sweatshirts exhale thanks to Mom's new "softener."

Some major advertisers, for that matter, can even cast a benign 21
eye on the population explosion. In another Biz commercial, the genial
Eddie Albert surveys with surprise a long row of dirty clothes heaped
before him by a young matron. She answers his natural query by telling
him gaily they are the products of her brood of eleven "with one more
to come!" she adds as the twelfth turns up. "That's great!" says Mr.

Albert, curdling the soul of Planned Parenthood and the future of this planet.

Who are, one cannot help but ask, the writers who manage to 22 combine the sales of products with the selling-out of human dreams and dignity? Who people this cosmos of commercials with dolts and fools and shrews and narcissists? Who know so much about quirks and mannerisms and ailments and so little about life? So much about presumed wants and so little about crying needs?

Can women advertisers so demean their own sex? Or are there no 23 women in positions of decision high enough to see that their real selves stand up? Do they not know, these extremely clever creators of commercials, what they could do for their audience even while they exploit and entertain them? How they could raise the levels of manners and attitudes while they sell their wares? Or do they really share the worm's-eye view of mass communication that sees, and addresses, only the lowest common denominator?

It can be argued that commercials are taken too seriously, that their 24 function is merely to amuse, engage, and sell, and that they do this brilliantly. If that were all to this wheedling of millions, well and good. But it is not. There are two more fallouts from this chronic sales explosion that cannot be measured but that at least can be expected. One has to do with the continual celebration of youth at the expense of maturity. In commercials only the young have access to beauty, sex, and joy in life. What do older women feel, day after day, when love is the exclusive possession of a teen-age girl with a bobbing mantle of hair? What older man would not covet her in restless impotence?

The constant reminder of what is inaccessible must inevitably pro- 25 duce a subterranean but real discontent, just as the continual sight of things and places beyond reach has eaten deeply into the ghetto soul. If we are constantly presented with what we are not or cannot have, the dislocation deepens, contentment vanishes, and frustration reigns. Even for the substantially secure, there is always a better thing, a better way, to buy. That none of these things makes a better life may be consciously acknowledged, but still the desire lodges in the spirit, nagging and pulling.

This kind of fragmentation works in potent ways above and be- 26 yond the mere fact of program interruption, which is much of the time more of a blessing than a curse, especially in those rare instances when the commercial is deft and funny: the soft and subtle sell. Its overall curse, due to the large number of commercials in each hour, is that it reduces the attention span of a people already so conditioned to constant change and distraction that they cannot tolerate continuity in print or on the air.

Specifically, commercial interruption is most damaging during that 27 10 per cent of programing (a charitable estimate) most important to the mind and spirit of a people: news and public affairs, and drama. To many (and among these are network news producers), commercials have no place or business during the vital process of informing the public. There is something obscene about a newscaster pausing to introduce a deodorant or shampoo commercial between an airplane crash and a body count. It is more than an interruption; it tends to reduce news to a form of running entertainment, to smudge the edges of reality by treating death or disaster or diplomacy on the same level as household appliances or a new gasoline.

The answer to this would presumably be to lump the commercials 28 before and after the news or public affairs broadcasts—an answer unpalatable, needless to say, to the sponsors who support them.

The same is doubly true of that most unprofitable sector of tele- 29 vision, the original play. Essential to any creative composition, whether drama, music or dance, are mood and continuity, both inseparable from form and meaning. They are shattered by the periodic intrusion of commercials, which have become intolerable to the serious artists who have deserted commercial television in droves because the system allows them no real freedom or autonomy. The selling comes first, the creation must accommodate itself. It is the rare and admirable sponsor who restricts or fashions his commercials so as to provide a minimum of intrusion or damaging inappropriateness.

If all these assumptions and imponderables are true, as many sus- 30 pect, what is the answer or alleviation?

One is in the course of difficult emergence: the establishment of 31 a public television system sufficiently funded so that it can give a maximum number of people an alternate diet of pleasure, enlightenment, and stimulation free from commercial fragmentation. So far, for lack of funds to buy talent and equipment, this effort has been in terms of public attention a distinctly minor operation. Even if public television should greatly increase its scope and impact, it cannot in the nature of things and through long public conditioning equal the impact and reach the size of audience now tuned to commercial television.

Enormous amounts of time, money, and talent go into commer- 32 cials. Technically they are often brilliant and innovative, the product not only of the new skills and devices but of imaginative minds. A few of them are both funny and endearing. Who, for instance, will forget the miserable young man with the appalling cold, or the kids taught to use—as an initiation into manhood—a fork instead of a spoon with a certain spaghetti? Among the enlightened sponsors, moreover, are some who manage to combine an image of their corporation and their products with accuracy and restraint.

What has to happen to mass medium advertisers as a whole, and especially on TV, is a totally new approach to their function not only as sellers but as social influencers. They have the same obligation as the broadcast medium itself: not only to entertain but to reflect, not only to reflect but to enlarge public consciousness and human stature.   33

This may be a tall order, but it is a vital one at a time when Americans have ceased to know who they are and where they are going, and when all the multiple forces acting upon them are daily diminishing their sense of their own value and purpose in life, when social upheaval and social fragmentation have destroyed old patterns, and when survival depends on new ones.   34

If we continue to see ourselves as the advertisers see us, we have no place to go. Nor, I might add, has commercial broadcasting itself.   35

Questions

1. Spend an hour or two looking at daytime television and see if Mannes's observations about the advertisements are accurate.
2. Compare the image of women in daytime advertisements with the image of women in evening advertisements. Are there differences?
3. Mannes says (paragraph 17) that advertisements assume that "a woman's only valid function is that of wife, mother, and servant of men." What do television advertisers assume about a man's "valid function"?
4. In paragraph 20 Mannes suggests: "There is good reason to suspect that this manic obsession with cleanliness, fostered, quite naturally, by the giant soap and detergent interests, may bear some responsibility for the cultivated sloppiness of so many of the young in their clothing as well as in their chosen hideouts." Is there really good reason to suspect this connection? Does Mannes sometimes make doubtful assumptions? If so, point them out.
5. Examine some of Mannes's metaphors, such as "There are two more fallouts from this chronic sales explosion" (paragraph 24), and evaluate them. Are they effective or strained?

Dolores Hayden

Advertisements, Pornography, and Public Space

Americans need to look more consciously at the ways in   1
which the public domain is misused for spatial displays of gender
stereotypes: These appear in outdoor advertising, and to a lesser extent
in commercial displays, architectural decoration, and public sculpture.
While the commercial tone and violence of the American city is often
criticized, there is little analysis of the routine way that crude stereotypes appear in public, urban spaces as the staple themes of commercial art. Most Americans are accustomed to seeing giant females
in various states of undress smiling and carressing products such as
whiskey, food, and records. Male models also sell goods, but they are
usually active and clothed—recent ad campaigns aimed at gay men
seem to be the first major exception. Several geographers have established that men are most often shown doing active things, posed in
the great outdoors; women are shown in reflective postures responding to male demands in interior spaces. As the nineteenth-century
sexual double standard is preserved by the urban advertising, many
twentieth-century urban men behave as if good women are at home
while bad ones adorn the billboards and travel on their own in urban
space; at the same time, many urban women are encouraged to think
of emotionless, war-mongering, and sexual inexhaustibility as natural
to the Marlboro cowboy, war heroes' statues, and every other male
adult.

This double standard is the result of advertising practices, graphic   2
design, and urban design. Sanctioned by the zoning laws, billboards
are approved by the same urban planning boards who will not permit
child care centers or mother-in-law apartments in many residential

Dolores Hayden was born in New York City in 1945. She did her undergraduate
work at Mount Holyoke, and she earned a master's degree in architecture at
Harvard. Hayden has taught architecture at the University of California (Berkeley)
and at Massachusetts Institute of Technology. She is especially concerned with
the political and social implications of public spaces.

districts. But the problem with billboards is not only aesthetic degradation. By presenting gender stereotypes in the form of nonverbal body language, fifty feet long and thirty feet high, billboards turn the public space of the city into a stage set for a drama starring enticing women and stern men.

Let us observe outdoor advertising and other urban design phenomena with similar effects, as they are experienced by two women on an urban commuting trip along the Sunset Strip in Los Angeles in June 1981. Standing on a street corner, the two women are waiting for a bus to go to work. The bus arrives, bearing a placard on the side advertising a local night club. It shows strippers doing their act, their headless bodies naked from neck to crotch except for a few blue sequins. The two women get on the bus and find seats for the ride along Sunset Boulevard. They look out the windows. As the bus pulls away, their heads appear incongruously above the voluptuous cardboard female bodies displayed on the side. They ride through a district of record company headquarters and film offices, one of the most prosperous in L.A.

Their first views reveal rows of billboards. Silent Marlboro man rides the range; husky, khaki-clad Camel man stares at green hills; gigantic, uniformed professional athletes catch passes and hit home runs on behalf of booze. These are the male images. Then, on a billboard for whiskey, a horizontal blonde in a backless black velvet dress, slit to the thigh, invites men to "Try on a little Black Velvet." Next, a billboard shows a well-known actress, reclining with legs spread, who notes that avocadoes are only sixteen calories a slice. "Would this body lie to you?" she asks coyly, emphasizing that the body language which communicates blatant sexual availability is only meant to bring attention to her thin figure. Bo Derek offers a pastoral contrast garbed in nothing but a few bits of fur and leather, as she swings on a vine of green leaves, promoting *Tarzan, the Ape Man.*

Next the bus riders pass a club called the Body Shop that advertises "live, nude girls." Two reclining, realistic nudes, one in blue tones in front of a moonlight cityscape, one in orange sunshine tones, stretch their thirty-foot bodies along the sidewalk. This is the same neighborhood where a billboard advertising a Rolling Stones' record album called "Black and Blue" made news ten years ago. A manacled, spread-legged woman with torn clothes proclaimed "I'm Black and Blue from the Rolling Stones—and I love it!" Members of a group called Women Against Violence Against Women (WAVAW) arrived with cans of spray paint and climbed the scaffolding to make small, uneven letters of protest: "This is a crime against women." Demonstrations and boy-cotts eventually succeeded in achieving the removal of that image, but not in eliminating the graphic design problem. "Black and Blue" has been replaced by James Bond in a tuxedo, pistol in hand, viewed through the spread legs and buttocks of a giant woman in a bathing suit and improbably high heels, captioned "For Your Eyes Only."

When the two women get off the bus in Hollywood, they expe-   6
rience more gender stereotypes as pedestrians. First, they walk past a department store. In the windows mannequins suggest the prevail-ing ideals of sartorial elegance. The male torsos lean forward, as if they are about to clinch a deal. The female torsos, pin-headed, tip backward and sideways, at odd angles, as if they are about to be pushed over onto a bed. The themes of gender advertisements are trumpeted here in the mannequins' body language as well as on billboards. Next, the women pass an apartment building. Two neoclassical caryatids sup-port the entablature over the front door. Their breasts are bared, their heads carry the load. They recall the architecture of the Erechtheum on the Acropolis in Athens, dating from the 5th century B.C., where the sculptured stone forms of female slaves were used as support for a porch in place of traditional columns and capitals. This is an ancient image of servitude.

After the neo-classical apartment house, the commuters approach   7
a construction site. Here they are subject to an activity traditionally called "running the gauntlet," but referred to as "girl watching" by urban sociologist William H. Whyte. Twelve workers stop whatever they are doing, whistle, and yell: "Hey, baby!" The women put their heads down, and walk faster, tense with anger. The construction work-ers take delight in causing exactly this response: "You're cute when you're mad!" Whyte regards this type of behavior as charming, pe-destrian fun in "Street Life," where he even takes pleasure in tracing its historic antecedents, but he has never been whistled at, hooted at, and had the dimensions of his body parts analyzed out loud on a public street.[1]

Finally, these women get to the office building where they work.   8
It has two statues out front of women. Their bronze breasts culminate in erect nipples. After they pass this last erotic public display of

---

[1] William H. Whyte, "Street Life," *Urban Open Spaces* (Summer 1980), 2. For a more detailed critique of hassling: Lindsy Van Gelder, "The International Language of Street Hassling," *Ms.* 9 (May 1981), 15–20, and letters about this article, *Ms.* (Sept. 1981); and Cheryl Benard and Edith Schlaffer, "The Man in the Street: Why He Harasses," *Ms.* 9 (May 1981), 18–19.

women's flesh, sanctioned as fine art, they walk in the door to begin the day's work. Their journey has taken them through an urban landscape filled with images of men as sexual aggressors and women as submissive sexual objects.

The transient quality of male and female interaction in public   9
streets makes the behavior provoked by billboards and their public design images particularly difficult to attack. Psychologist Erving Goffman has analyzed both print ads and billboards as *Gender Advertisements* because art directors use exaggerated body language to suggest that consumers buy not products but images of masculinity or femininity.[2] If passers-by are driving at fifty miles per hour, these gender cues cannot be subtle. In *Ways of Seeing,* art historian John Berger describes the cumulative problem that gender stereotypes in advertising create for woman as "split consciousness."[3] While many women guard themselves, some men assume that ogling is part of normal public life. Women are always wary, watching men watch them, and wondering if and when something is going to happen to them.

Urban residents also encounter even more explicit sexual images   10
in urban space. Tawdry strip clubs, X-rated films, "adult" bookstores and sex shops are not uncommon sights. Pornographic video arcades are the next wave to come. Pornography is a bigger, more profitable industry in the United States than all legitimate film and record business combined.[4] It spills over into soft-porn, quasi-porn, and tasteless public imagery everywhere. In the midst of this sex-exploitation, if one sees a real prostitute, there is mild surprise. Yet soliciting is still a crime. Of course, the male customer of an adult prostitute is almost never arrested, but the graphic designer, the urban designer, and the urban planner never come under suspicion for their contributions to a commercial public landscape that preserves the sexual double standard in a brutal and vulgar way.

Feminist Laura Shapiro calls our society a "rape culture."[5] Ad-   11
rienne Rich has written of "a world masculinity made unfit for women

[2] Erving Goffman, *Gender Advertisements* (New York: Harper Colphon, 1976), 24–27; Nancy Henley, *Body Politics: Power, Sex, and Nonverbal Communication* (Englewood Cliffs, N.J.: Prentice-Hall, 1977), 30; Marianne Wex, *Let's Take Back Our Space* (Berlin: Movimento Druck, 1979).

[3] John Berger, et al., *Ways of Seeing* (Harmondsworth, England: BBC and Penguin, 1972), 45–64.

[4] Tom Hayden, *The American Future: New Visions Beyond Old Frontiers* (Boston: South End Press, 1980), 15.

[5] Laura Shapiro, "Violence: The Most Obscene Fantasy," in Freeman, ed., *Women: A Feminist Perspective,* 469–73.

or men."[6] But surely most Americans do not consciously, deliberately accept public space given over to commercial exploitation, violence and harassment of women. Indeed, the success of the "Moral Majority" displays how a few activists were able to tap public concern effectively about commercialized sexuality, albeit in a narrow, antihumanist way. In contrast, the example of the Women's Christian Temperance Union under Frances Willard's leadership, and the parks movement under Olmsted's,[7] show religious idealism, love of nature, and concern for female safety can be activated into dynamic urban reform movements that enlarge domestic values into urban values, instead of diminishing them into domestic pieties.

Questions

1. What is Hayden's thesis? Where is it stated? How does she support it?
2. How does Hayden organize her material? Note, in particular, the narrative of two women traveling to work. What does this device add to the essay?
3. Does Hayden suggest that displays of gender stereotypes contribute to violence against women? Do you believe that they do?
4. In an essay of two or three pages, describe and analyze two billboards, one featuring a man and one featuring a woman. How do they present the "gender stereotypes" that Hayden talks about? Your essay should respond to this question with a clearly formulated thesis sentence (see pages 24 and 707).
5. In paragraph 6, Hayden speaks of two "neo-classical caryatids" (architectural pillars in the form of women) flanking a door. She sees these as "an ancient image of servitude." Consult a book such as Spiro Kostof's *History of Architecture* for information about caryatids and then consider whether or not Hayden's interpretation is sound. Formulate a thesis and defend it in a brief essay (a page or a page-and-a-half). Include a citation to the book you have consulted, and, if possible, a photocopy of a picture of a caryatid.
6. If you are familiar with a sculpture of a female figure in a public space in your neighborhood (perhaps in a plaza or in a public building), in a paragraph set forth what the image "says." Or, compare

[6] *Ibid.*, 469.
[7] Frederick Law Olmsted (1822–1903) was an American landscape architect. Among his noble works are Central Park in Manhattan and Prospect Park in Brooklyn.

two sculptures, one of a female and one of a male, and explain what each says.

7. In a paragraph or two, describe and analyze a magazine advertisement that promotes gender stereotypes or one that is aimed at gay men. (See Hayden's first paragraph.)

Stephen King

Why We Crave Horror Movies

I think that we're all mentally ill; those of us outside the   1
asylums only hide it a little better—and maybe not all that much better, after all. We've all known people who talk to themselves, people who sometimes squinch their faces into horrible grimaces when they believe no one is watching, people who have some hysterical fear—of snakes, the dark, the tight place, the long drop . . . and, of course, those final worms and grubs that are waiting so patiently underground.

When we pay our four or five bucks and seat ourselves at tenth-   2
row center in a theater showing a horror movie, we are daring the nightmare.

Why? Some of the reasons are simple and obvious. To show that   3
we can, that we are not afraid, that we can ride this roller coaster. Which is not to say that a really good horror movie may not surprise a scream out of us at some point, the way we may scream when the roller coaster twists through a complete 360 or plows through a lake at the bottom of the drop. And horror movies, like roller coasters, have always been the special province of the young; by the time one turns 40 or 50, one's appetite for double twists or 360-degree loops may be considerably depleted.

Stephen King, with 50 millions copies of his books in print, is one of America's most popular authors. King was born in Portland, Maine, in 1947. After graduating from the University of Maine he taught English in high school until he was able to devote himself full-time to writing. In addition to writing stories and novels—some of which have been made into films—he has written *Danse Macabre*, a book that, like the essay we reprint here, discusses the appeal of horror.

We also go to re-establish our feelings of essential normality; the   4
horror movie is innately conservative, even reactionary. Freda Jackson
as the horrible melting woman in *Die, Monster, Die!* confirms for us
that no matter how far we may be removed from the beauty of a Robert
Redford or a Diana Ross, we are still light-years from true ugliness.

And we go to have fun.   5

Ah, but this is where the ground starts to slope away, isn't it?   6
Because this is a very peculiar sort of fun, indeed. The fun comes from
seeing others menaced—sometimes killed. One critic has suggested
that if pro football has become the voyeur's version of combat, then
the horror film has become the modern version of the public lynching.

It is true that the mythic, "fairy-tale" horror film intends to take   7
away the shades of gray. . . . It urges us to put away our more civilized
and adult penchant for analysis and to become children again, seeing
things in pure blacks and whites. It may be that horror movies provide
psychic relief on this level because this invitation to lapse into simplicity, irrationality and even outright madness is extended so rarely.
We are told we may allow our emotions a free rein . . . or no rein at
all.

If we are all insane, then sanity becomes a matter of degree. If   8
your insanity leads you to carve up women like Jack the Ripper or the
Cleveland Torso Murderer, we clap you away in the funny farm (but
neither of those two amateur-night surgeons was ever caught, heh-
heh-heh); if, on the other hand, your insanity leads you only to talk
to yourself when you're under stress or to pick your nose on your
morning bus, then you are left alone to go about your business . . .
though it is doubtful that you will ever be invited to the best parties.

The potential lyncher is in almost all of us (excluding saints, past   9
and present; but then, most saints have been crazy in their own ways),
and every now and then, he has to be let loose to scream and roll
around in the grass. Our emotions and our fears form their own body,
and we recognize that it demands its own exercise to maintain proper
muscle tone. Certain of these emotional muscles are accepted—even
exalted—in civilized society; they are, of course, the emotions that tend
to maintain the status quo of civilization itself. Love, friendship, loyalty, kindness—these are all the emotions that we applaud, emotions
that have been immortalized in the couplets of Hallmark cards and in
the verses (I don't dare call it poetry) of Leonard Nimoy.

When we exhibit these emotions, society showers us with positive   10
reinforcement; we learn this even before we get out of diapers. When,
as children, we hug our rotten little puke of a sister and give her a
kiss, all the aunts and uncles smile and twit and cry, "Isn't he the

sweetest little thing?" Such coveted treats as chocolate-covered graham crackers often follow. But if we deliberately slam the rotten little puke of a sister's fingers in the door, sanctions follow—angry remonstrance from parents, aunts and uncles; instead of a chocolate-covered graham cracker, a spanking.

But anticivilization emotions don't go away, and they demand periodic exercise. We have such "sick" jokes as, "What's the difference between a truckload of bowling balls and a truckload of dead babies?" (You can't unload a truckload of bowling balls with a pitchfork . . . a joke, by the way, that I heard originally from a ten-year-old). Such a joke may surprise a laugh or a grin out of us even as we recoil, a possibility that confirms the thesis: If we share a brotherhood of man, then we also share an insanity of man. None of which is intended as a defense of either the sick joke or insanity but merely as an explanation of why the best horror films, like the best fairy tales, manage to be reactionary, anarchistic, and revolutionary all at the same time.   11

The mythic horror movie, like the sick joke, has a dirty job to do.   12
It deliberately appeals to all that is worst in us. It is morbidity unchained, our most base instincts let free, our nastiest fantasies realized . . . and it all happens, fittingly enough, in the dark. For those reasons, good liberals often shy away from horror films. For myself, I like to see the most aggressive of them—*Dawn of the Dead*, for instance—as lifting a trap door in the civilized forebrain and throwing a basket of raw meat to the hungry alligators swimming around in that subterranean river beneath.

Why bother? Because it keeps them from getting out, man. It keeps   13
them down there and me up here. It was Lennon and McCartney who said that all you need is love, and I would agree with that.

As long as you keep the gators fed.   14

Questions

1. In paragraph 6 King, paraphrasing an unnamed critic, suggests that "the horror film has become the modern version of the public lynching." In your opinion, why did some people find excitement in a lynching? Does the horror film offer somewhat similar excitement(s)?

2. King suggests, in paragraph 11, that we have within us a stock of "anticivilization emotions [that] don't go away, and they demand periodic exercise." What evidence, if any, are you aware of that supports this view?

3. In paragraph 11 King tells a joke about dead babies. He suggests that jokes of this sort "may surprise a laugh or a grin out of us even as we recoil." Analyze your own response to the joke, or to similar jokes. Did you laugh, or grin? Or was your response utterly different? If so, what was it?

4. In paragraphs 12 and 13 King says that horror movies serve a valuable social purpose. Do you think he has proved his point? What are the strengths (if any) and the weaknesses (if any) of his argument?

5. Read Tipper Gore's essay (page 478). Then respond to King's argument as you think she might.

Woody Allen

The Colorization of Films Insults Artists and Society

In the world of potent self-annihilation, famine and AIDS, terrorists and dishonest public servants and quack evangelists and contras and Sandinistas and cancer, does it really matter if some kid snaps on his TV and happens to see *The Maltese Falcon* in color? Especially if he can simply dial the color out and choose to view it in its original black and white?

I think it does make a difference and the ramifications of what's called colorization are not wonderful to contemplate. Simply put, the owners of thousands of classic American black and white films believe that there would be a larger public for the movies, and consequently more money, if they were reissued in color. Since they have computers

Woody Allen, born in Brooklyn in 1935, began writing comic monologues while he was in high school. He soon wrote for Sid Caesar and Art Carney, and then developed a nightclub act of his own. Although he still publishes an occasional story in *The New Yorker*, he is now engaged chiefly in writing and directing films and in acting in them.

that can change such masterpieces as *Citizen Kane* and *City Lights* and *It's A Wonderful Life* into color, it has become a serious problem for anyone who cares about these movies and has feelings about our image of ourselves as a culture.

I won't comment about the quality of the color. It's not good, but ³ probably it will get better. Right now it's like elevator music. It has no soul. All faces are rendered with the same deadening pleasance. The choices of what colors people should be wearing or what colors rooms should be (all crucial artistic decisions in making a film) are left to caprices and speculations by computer technicians who are not qualified to make those choices.

Probably false, but not worth debating here, is the claim that young ⁴ people won't watch black and white. I would think they would, judging from the amount of stylish music videos and MTV ads that are done in black and white, undoubtedly after market research. The fact that audiences of all ages have been watching Charlie Chaplin, Humphrey Bogart, Jimmy Stewart, Fred Astaire—in fact, all the stars and films of the so-called Golden Age of Hollywood—in black and white for decades with no diminution of joy also makes me wonder about these high claims for color. Another point the coloroids make is that one can always view the original if one prefers. The truth is, however, that in practical terms, what will happen is that the color versions will be aired while token copies of the original black and white will lie around preserved in a vault, unpromoted and unseen.

Another aspect of the problem that one should mention (although ⁵ it is not the crucial ground on which I will make my stand) is that American films are a landmark heritage that do our nation proud all over the world, and should be seen as they were intended to be. One would wince at defacing great buildings or paintings, and, in the case of movies, what began as a popular entertainment has, like jazz music, developed into a serious art form. Now, someone might ask: "Is an old Abbott and Costello movie art? Should it be viewed in the same way as *Citizen Kane?*" The answer is that it should be protected, because all movies are entitled to their personal integrity and, after all, who knows what future generations will regard as art works of our epoch?

Yet another question: "Why were directors not up in arms about ⁶ cutting films for television or breaking them up for commercials, insulting them with any number of technical alterations to accommodate the television format?" The answer is that directors always hated these assaults on their work but were powerless to stop them. As in life, one lives with the first few wounds, because to do battle is an overwhelmingly time-consuming and pessimistic prospect.

Still, when the assaults come too often, there is a revolution. The 7
outrage of seeing one's work transformed into color is so dramatically
appalling, so "obvious"—as against stopping sporadically for commercials—that this time all the directors, writers and actors chose to
fight.

But let me get to the real heart of the matter and to why I think 8
the issue is not merely one that affronts the parties directly involved
but has a larger meaning. What's at stake is a moral issue and how
our culture chooses to define itself. No one should be able to alter an
artist's work in any way whatsoever, for any reason, without the artist's consent. It's really as simple as that.

John Huston has made it clear that he doesn't want *The Maltese* 9
Falcon seen in color. This is his right as an artist and certainly must be
his choice alone. Nor would I want to see my film *Manhattan* in color.
Not if it would bring in 10 times the revenue. Not if all the audiences
in the world begged or demanded to see it that way.

I believe the people who are coloring movies have contempt for 10
the audience by claiming, in effect, that viewers are too stupid and
too insensitive to appreciate black and white photography—that they
must be given, like infants or monkeys, bright colors to keep them
amused. They have contempt for the artsit, caring little for the moral
right these directors have over their own creations. And, finally, they
have contempt for society because they help define it as one that
chooses to milk every last dollar out of its artists' work, even if it means
mutilating the work and humiliating the culture's creative talent.

This is how we are viewed around the world and how we will be 11
viewed by future generations. Most civilized governments abroad, realizing that their society is at least as much shaped and identified by
its artists as by its businessmen, have laws to protect such things from
happening. In our society, merchants are willing to degrade anything
or anyone so long as it brings in a financial profit. Allowing the colorization of films is a good example of our country's regard for its
artists, and why I think the issue of moral rights requires legislative
help and protection.

The recent Federal copyright decision says that if a human being 12
uses a certain minimum amount of creativity in coloring a black and
white film, the new color version is a separate work that can be copyrighted. In short, if a man colors *Citizen Kane,* it becomes a new movie
that can be copyrighted. This must be changed. How? By making sure
that Representative Richard A. Gephardt's film integrity bill is passed.
It would legalize the moral rights of film artists and, in the process,
make colorization without consent illegal.

It is, after all, a very short step to removing the score from *Gone*   13
With the Wind and replacing it with a rock score under the mistaken
notion that it will render it more enjoyable to young people.

Questions

1. We find Allen's argumentative strategy worth analyzing. But first,
    restate in a sentence or two the point he is arguing and the occasion
    that prompted it. (Note that Allen reports the occasion in his next-
    to-last paragraph.)
    Now look at Allen's opening paragraph. What does it assume about
    his audience? What does Allen imply about himself in relation to
    his audience?
2. In paragraph 2 Allen contrasts two groups. How does he make sure
    that you will identify yourself with one group and not with the other?
3. In paragraph 3, what words or phrases strike you as particularly
    lively or persuasive?
4. In paragraph 4 Allen says that "the claim that young people won't
    watch black and white" is "not worth debating." What does the rest
    of the paragraph do? Again, what particularly effective words or
    phrases underscore the point?
5. To what emotions does Allen appeal in paragraph 5?
6. Now consider the substance of his argument. In paragraph 8 Allen
    says, "No one should be able to alter an artist's work in any way
    whatsoever, for any reason, without the artist's consent. It's really
    as simple as that." Do you agree? If so, would you agree to the
    following propositions? Why or why not?

    a. Producers should be prohibited from showing on television films in-
        tended for the theater, unless the producers have the consent of the
        film director.
    b. Similarly, filmmakers should be prohibted from filming a novel, play,
        opera, or ballet without the consent of the author or composer. If the
        author or composer is dead, well, that's unfortunate, but the work can-
        not be adapted to a film.

    What parallel strictures might govern the display of objects in mu-
    seums, reproductions of works of art, and the translation of classic
    works of literature?
7. Finally, consider some black and white film that you admire. What
    do you think would be lost (or gained) by colorization? (If you have
    seen the original black and white film and also a colorized version,

of course you are in a good position to make comparisons. But in any case you can make a "thought-experiment." You might, for example, imagine a colorized version of Woody Allen's *Manhattan*.)

Stanley Milgram

Confessions of a News Addict

Let me begin with a confession. I am a news addict. Upon 1 awakening I flip on the *Today* show to learn what events transpired during the night. On the commuter train which takes me to work, I scour *The New York Times,* and find myself absorbed in tales of earthquakes, diplomacy, and economics. I read the newspaper as religiously as my grandparents read their prayerbooks. The sacramental character of the news extends into the evening. The length of my workday is determined precisely by my need to get home in time for Walter Cronkite. My children understand that my communion with Cronkite is something serious and cannot be interrupted for light and transient causes.

But what is it, precisely, that is happening when I and millions of 2 others scour our newspapers, stare at the tube, and pour over the news magazines that surround us? Does it make sense? What is news, and why does it occupy a place of special significance for so many people?

Let us proceed from a simple definition: news is information about 3 events that are going on outside immediate experience. In this sense, news has always been a part of the human situation. In its earliest form, it took the shape of an account brought by a traveler, or a member of the group who wandered further than the rest and found water, game, or signs of a nearby enemy. The utility of such information is self-evident. News is a social mechanism that extends our own eyes

Stanley Milgram, at the time of his death in 1984, was a professor of social psychology at the Graduate Center of the City University of New York. His best-known work is a book entitled *Obedience to Authority*.

and ears to embrace an ever wider domain of events. A knowledge of remote events allows us to prepare for them and take whatever steps are needed to deal with them. This is the classic function of news.

News is the consciousness of Society. It is the means whereby 4 events in the body politic are brought into awareness. And it is curious that regimes which we call *repressive* tend to exhibit the same characteristic of repressed personalities; they are unable, or unwilling, to allow conflictive material into awareness. The disability stems from deep insecurities. The censoring of the repressed material does not eliminate it, but forces it to fester without anyone's rationally coming to grips with it.

Inevitably news comes to be controlled by the dominant political 5 forces of a society. In a totalitarian regime the government attempts to create the image of a world, and of events, that reflects most favorably on those in power. The democratization of news, which goes hand in hand with the diffusion of political power among those governed, is a relatively recent development whose permanence cannot be assured. Democracies are far better able to cope with the reality of events than are totalitarian regimes. Such regimes promulgate a myth of their omnipotence, and are threatened even by events outside the control of the political process. Thus, typically, the Soviet press does not report air crashes, and even natural disasters such as earthquakes are suppressed, out of the notion—rooted in political insecurity—that the event in some manner reflects badly on the regime.

The question for any society is not whether there shall be news, 6 but rather who shall have access to it. Every political system may be characterized by the proportion of information it has which is shared with the people and the proportion withheld. That is why the growth of secret news-gathering agencies, such as the C.I.A., is a troubling one for a democracy. It appears our government wants to keep some news to itself.

At a deeper historical level we can see that news in its present 7 form is closely tied to the rise of the economy, and specifically to the exploitative and risk elements of capitalism. For the nineteenth-century merchant, news meant reports of his ship, of resources to exploit, and the means of minimizing the risk element inherent in entrepreneurship by gaining as much information as possible before his competitors. News services, such as Reuters, developed to serve business and investment interests, who discovered that getting the news quickly was the first step to financial gain.

In a civilization in which all activities tend toward commercial 8 expression—for example, our own—news becomes a product to manufacture and dispense to the consumer. Thus a large-scale industry for the production and consumption of news has evolved. We ingest it with the same insatiable appetite that moves us to purchase the manifold products of our commercial civilization.

News under such circumstances tends toward decadent use. It no   9 longer serves first the classic function of giving us information on which to act, or even to help us construct a mental model of the larger world. It serves mainly as entertainment. The tales of earthquakes, political assassinations, and bitterly fought elections are the heady stuff of which drama or melodrama is made. Happily, we are able to indulge our taste for thriller, romance, or murder mystery under the guise of a patently respectable pursuit. All enlightened people are supposed to know what is going on in the world. If what is going on also happens to be thrilling and exciting, so much the better.

Another feature of the decadent use of news is its increasing rit-   10 ualization. The information becomes subservient to the form in which it is delivered. News is broadcast every evening, whether or not there is vital information to be conveyed. Indeed, the problem for the news networks is to generate sufficient news to fill a given time period. The time period becomes the fundamental fact, the framework into which events must be fitted. As in any ritual, the form persists even when a meaningful content is missing.

Those groups whose survival and well-being are most affected by   11 remote events will be most persistently attuned to them. For example, Israelis, who view the survival of their state as a day-to-day contingency, are among the most news-oriented people in the world. During periods of crisis, portable radios blare in buses and in the market place. Jews, in general, have felt the need to develop antennae for remote events because of a communal insecurity. Any event, no matter how remote—even a farcical *putsch* in Munich led by a paper hanger—may grow into a formidable threat. Thus, constant monitoring of events is strongly reinforced.

Although I am a news addict, my addiction is strongest for news   12 that in many respects seems most remote from my own life and experience. International news receives top priority, followed by national domestic news, and finally—and of least interest—local news. I feel more concerned reading about a student strike in Paris than a murder in my own neighborhood. I am especially uninterested in those news programs that provide a constant litany of fires and local crimes as their standard fare. Yet there is a paradox in this. Surely a criminal loose in my city is of greater personal consequence than an election outcome in Uruguay. Indeed, I sometimes ask what difference it makes to the actual conduct of my life to know about a fracas in Zaire, or a train wreck in Sweden. The total inconsequences of the news for my life is most strikingly brought home when we return from a vacation of several weeks where we have been without any news. I normally scan the accumulated pile of newspapers, but cannot help noticing how little difference it all made to me. And least consequential of all were those remote international events that so rivet my attention in the normal course of the week.

Why this interest in things far away, with a lesser interest in events 13 close at home? Perhaps it is essentially a romantic impulse in the projection of meaning into remote countries, places, and people. Such a romantic impulse stems from a dissatisfaction with the mundane reality of everyday life. The events and places described in the news are remote, and thus we can more readily fix our imaginative sentiments to them. Moreover, an interest in news reinforces the "cosmopolitan" attitude which characterizes modern life, a desire to focus not only on the immediate community, but on the larger world. It is thus the opposite of the "provincialism" which characterized an earlier rural existence.

Living in the modern world, I cannot help but be shaped by it, 14 suckered by the influence and impact of our great institutions. *The New York Times, CBS,* and *Newsweek* have made me into a news addict. In daily life I have come to accept the supposition that if *The New York Times* places a story on the front page, it deserves my attention. I feel obligated to know what is going on. But sometimes, in quieter moments, another voice asks: If the news went away, would the world be any worse for it?

Questions

1. Why does Milgram describe himself as an "addict" and call his essay "confessions"? How seriously is he using the term? (Consider the connotations of "addict" compared with "reader," "consumer," and "fan.")
2. What reasons does Milgram give for being more interested in "things far away" than in "events close at home"? Do you find his reasons adequate? In answering this question reflect on the three or four items of news that have been of absorbing interest to you. What did those items have in common? Why did they interest you?

James Thurber

The Secret Life of
Walter Mitty

We're going through!" The Commander's voice was like   1
thin ice breaking. He wore his full-dress uniform, with the heavily
braided white cap pulled down rakishly over one cold gray eye. "We
can't make it, sir. It's spoiling for a hurricane, if you ask me." "I'm
not asking you, Lieutenant Berg," said the Commander. "Throw on
the power lights! Rev her up to 8,500! We're going through!" The
pounding of the cylinders increased; ta-pocketa-pocketa-pocketa-*pock-
eta-pocketa*. The Commander stared at the ice forming on the pilot window. He walked over and twisted a row of complicated dials. "Switch
on No. 8 auxiliary!" he shouted. "Switch on No. 8 auxiliary!" repeated
Lieutenant Berg. "Full strength in No. 3 turret!" shouted the Commander. "Full strength in No. 3 turret!" The crew, bending to their
various tasks in the huge, hurtling eight-engined Navy hydroplane,
looked at each other and grinned. "The Old Man'll get us through,"
they said to one another. "The Old Man ain't afraid of Hell!" . . .

"Not so fast! You're driving too fast!" said Mrs. Mitty. "What are   2
you driving so fast for?"

"Hmm?" said Walter Mitty. He looked at his wife, in the seat   3
beside him, with shocked astonishment. She seemed grossly unfamiliar, like a strange woman who had yelled at him in a crowd. "You
were up to fifty-five," she said. "You know I don't like to go more
than forty. You were up to fifty-five." Walter Mitty drove on toward
Waterbury in silence, the roaring of the SN202 through the worst storm
in twenty years of Navy flying fading in the remote, intimate airways
of his mind. "You're tensed up again," said Mrs. Mitty. "It's one of
your days. I wish you'd let Dr. Renshaw look you over."

Walter Mitty stopped the car in front of the building where his   4
wife went to have her hair done. "Remember to get those overshoes
while I'm having my hair done," she said. "I don't need overshoes,"
said Mitty. She put her mirror back into her bag. "We've been all

James Thurber (1894–1961) published most of his essays, stories, and cartoons
in *The New Yorker*.

through that," she said, getting out of the car. "You're not a young man any longer." He raced the engine a little. "Why don't you wear your gloves? Have you lost your gloves?" Walter Mitty reached in a pocket and brought out the gloves. He put them on, but after she had turned and gone into the building and he had driven on to a red light, he took them off again. "Pick it up, brother," snapped a cop as the light changed, and Mitty hastily pulled on his gloves and lurched ahead. He drove around the streets aimlessly for a time, and then he drove past the hospital on his way to the parking lot.

. . . "It's the millionaire banker, Wellington McMillan," said the 5 pretty nurse. "Yes?" said Walter Mitty, removing his gloves slowly. "Who has the case?" "Dr. Renshaw and Dr. Benbow, but there are two specialists here, Dr. Remington from New York and Dr. Pritchard-Mitford from London. He flew over." A door opened down a long, cool corridor and Dr. Renshaw came out. He looked distraught and haggard. "Hello, Mitty," he said. "We're having the devil's own time with McMillan, the millionaire banker and close personal friend of Roosevelt. Obstreosis of the ductal tract. Tertiary. Wish you'd take a look at him." "Glad to," said Mitty.

In the operating room there were whispered introductions: "Dr. 6 Remington, Dr. Mitty. Dr. Pritchard-Mitford, Dr. Mitty." "I've read your book on streptothricosis," said Pritchard-Mitford, shaking hands. "A brilliant performance, sir." "Thank you," said Walter Mitty. "Didn't know you were in the States, Mitty," grumbled Remington. "Coals to Newcastle, bringing Mitford and me up here for a tertiary." "You are very kind," said Mitty. A huge, complicated machine, connected to the operating table, with many tubes and wires, began at this moment to go pocketa-pocketa-pocketa. "The new anaesthetizer is giving away!" shouted an interne. "There is no one in the East who knows how to fix it!" "Quiet, man!" said Mitty, in a low, cool voice. He sprang to the machine, which was now going pocketa-pocketa-queep-pocketa-queep. He began fingering delicately a row of glistening dials. "Give me a fountain pen!" he snapped. Someone handed him a fountain pen. He pulled a faulty piston out of the machine and inserted the pen in its place. "That will hold for ten minutes," he said. "Get on with the operation." A nurse hurried over and whispered to Renshaw, and Mitty saw the man turn pale. "Coreopsis has set in," said Renshaw nervously. "If you would take over, Mitty?" Mitty looked at him and at the craven figure of Benbow, who drank, and at the grave, uncertain faces of the two great specialists. "If you wish," he said. They slipped a white gown on him; he adjusted a mask and drew on thin gloves; nurses handed him shining . . .

"Back it up, Mac! Look out for that Buick!" Walter Mitty jammed   7
on the brakes. "Wrong lane, Mac," said the parking-lot attendant,
looking at Mitty closely. "Gee. Yeh," muttered Mitty. He began cautiously to back out of the lane marked "Exit Only." "Leave her sit
there," said the attendant. "I'll put her away." Mitty got out of the
car. "Hey, better leave the key." "Oh," said Mitty, handing the man
the ignition key. The attendant vaulted into the car, backed it up with
insolent skill, and put it where it belonged.

They're so damn cocky, thought Walter Mitty, walking along Main   8
Street; they think they know everything. Once he had tried to take his
chains off, outside New Milford, and he had got them wound around
the axles. A man had had to come out in a wrecking car and unwind
them, a young, grinning garage man. Since then Mrs. Mitty always
made him drive to a garage to have the chains taken off. The next time,
he thought, I'll wear my right arm in a sling; they won't grin at me
then. I'll have my right arm in a sling and they'll see I couldn't possibly
take the chains off myself. He kicked at the slush on the sidewalk.
"Overshoes," he said to himself, and he began looking for a shoe store.

When he came out into the street again, with the overshoes in a   9
box under his arm, Walter Mitty began to wonder what the other thing
was his wife had told him to get. She had told him, twice before they
set out from their house for Waterbury. In a way he hated these weekly
trips to town—he was always getting something wrong. Kleenex, he
thought, Squibb's, razor blades? No. Toothpaste, toothbrush, bicar-
bonate, carborundum, initiative and referendum? He gave it up. But
she would remember it. "Where's the what's-its-name?" She would
ask. "Don't tell me you forgot the what's-its-name." A newsboy went
by shouting something about the Waterbury trial.

. . . "Perhaps this will refresh your memory." The District Attor-   10
ney suddenly thrust a heavy automatic at the quiet figure on the witness stand. "Have you ever seen this before?" Walter Mitty took the
gun and examined it expertly. "This is my Webley-Vickers 50-80," he
said calmly. An excited buzz ran around the courtroom. The judge
rapped for order. "You are a crack shot with any sort of firearms, I
believe?" said the District Attorney, insinuatingly. "Objection!"
shouted Mitty's attorney. "We have shown that the defendant could
not have fired the shot. We have shown that he wore his right arm in
a sling on the night of the fourteenth of July." Walter Mitty raised his
hand briefly and the bickering attorneys were stilled. "With any known
make of gun," he said evenly, "I could have killed Gregory Fitzhurst
at three hundred feet *with my left hand*." Pandemonium broke loose in
the courtroom. A woman's scream rose above the bedlam and sud-

denly a lovely, dark-haired girl was in Walter Mitty's arms. The District
Attorney struck at her savagely. Without rising from his chair. Mitty
let the man have it on the point of the chin. "You miserable cur!"

"Puppy biscuit," said Walter Mitty. He stopped walking and the   11
buildings of Waterbury rose up out of the misty courtroom and surrounded him again. A woman who was passing laughed. "He said
'Puppy biscuit'," she said to her companion. "That man said 'Puppy
biscuit' to himself." Walter Mitty hurried on. He went into an A. &
P., not the first one he came to but a smaller one farther up the street.
"I want some biscuit for small, young dogs," he said to the clerk. "Any
special brand, sir?" The greatest pistol shot in the world thought a
moment. "It says 'Puppies Bark for It' on the box," said Walter Mitty.

His wife would be through at the hairdresser's in fifteen minutes,   12
Mitty saw in looking at his watch, unless they had trouble drying it;
sometimes they had trouble drying it. She didn't like to get to the hotel
first; she would want him to be there waiting for her as usual. He
found a big leather chair in the lobby, facing a window, and he put
the overshoes and the puppy biscuit on the floor beside it. He picked
up an old copy of *Liberty* and sank down into the chair. "Can Germany
Conquer the World through the Air?" Walter Mitty looked at the pictures of bombing planes and of ruined streets.

. . . "The cannonading has got the wind up in young Raleigh, sir,"   13
said the sergeant. Captain Mitty looked up at him through tousled
hair. "Get him to bed," he said wearily, "with the others. I'll fly alone."
"But you can't, sir," said the sergeant anxiously. "It takes two men
to handle that bomber and the Archies are pounding hell out of the
air. Von Richtman's circus is between here and Saulier." "Somebody's
got to get the ammunition dump," said Mitty. "I'm going over. Spot
of brandy?" He poured a drink for the sergeant and one for himself.
War thundered and whined around the dugout and battered at the
door. There was a rending of wood and splinters flew through the
room. "A bit of a near thing," said Captain Mitty carelessly. "The box
barrage is closing in," said the sergeant. "We only live once, sergeant,"
said Mitty, with his faint, fleeting smile. "Or do we?" He poured another brandy and tossed it off. "I never see a man could hold his brandy
like you, sir," said the sergeant. "Begging your pardon, sir." Captain
Mitty stood up and strapped on his huge Webley-Vickers automatic.
"It's forty kilometers through hell, sir," said the sergeant. Mitty finished one last brandy. "After all," he said softly, "what isn't?" The
pounding of the cannon increased; there was the rat-tat-tatting of machine guns, and from somewhere came the menacing pocketa-pocketa-

pocketa of the new flame-throwers. Walter Mitty walked to the door of the dugout humming "Après de Ma Blonde." He turned and waved to the sergeant. "Cheerio!" he said. . . .

Something struck his shoulder. "I've been looking all over this 14 hotel for you," said Mrs. Mitty. "Why do you have to hide in this old chair? How did you expect me to find you?" "Things close in," said Walter Mitty vaguely. "What?" Mrs. Mitty said. "Did you get the what's-its-name? The puppy biscuit? What's in that box?" "Overshoes," said Mitty. "Couldn't you have put them on in the store?" "I was thinking," said Walter Mitty. "Does it ever occur to you that I am sometimes thinking?" She looked at him. "I'm going to take your temperature when I get you home," she said.

They went out through the revolving doors that made a faintly 15 derisive whistling sound when you pushed them. It was two blocks to the parking lot. At the drugstore on the corner she said, "Wait here for me. I forgot something. I won't be a minute." She was more than a minute. Walter Mitty lighted a cigarette. It began to rain, rain with sleet in it. He stood up against the wall of the drugstore, smoking. . . . He put his shoulders back and his heels together. "To hell with the handkerchief," said Walter Mitty scornfully. He took one last drag on his cigarette and snapped it away. Then, with that faint, fleeting smile playing about his lips, he faced the firing squad; erect and motionless, proud and disdainful, Walter Mitty the Undefeated, inscrutable to the last.

Questions

1. Why does Mitty have daydreams? From what sources has he derived the substance of his daydreams?
2. We may sympathize with Mitty, but we laugh at him, too. Why do we find the story primarily comic instead of pathetic? If it were intended to move us deeply, rather than to amuse us, what kinds of changes would have to be made in Mitty's daydreams? What other changes would have to be made in the characterization of Mitty and of his wife?
3. In the last sentence Mitty imagines himself facing a firing squad, "Mitty the Undefeated, inscrutable to the last." To what degree can it be argued that he is undefeated and inscrutable?

8
LAW AND ORDER

Flower Power
Bernie Boston, 1967

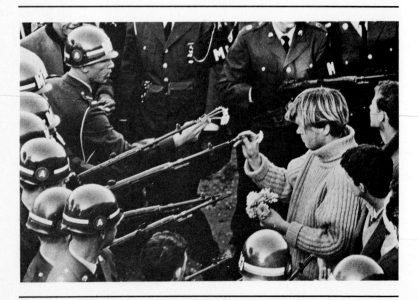

The Problem We All Live With
Norman Rockwell, 1964

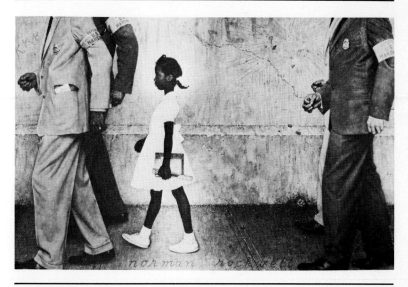

The Death of Socrates
Jacques-Louis David, 1787

Short Views

The trouble for the thief is not how to steal the bugle, but where to blow it.

African proverb

And God spake all these words, saying, "I am the LORD thy God, which have brought thee out of the land of Egypt, out of the house of bondage.

"Thou shalt have no other gods before me.

"Thou shalt not make unto thee any graven image, or any likeness of any thing that is in heaven above, or that is in the earth beneath, or that is in the water under the earth: thou shalt not bow down thyself to them, nor serve them: for I the LORD thy God am a jealous God, visiting the iniquity of the fathers upon the children unto the third and fourth generation of them that hate me; and showing mercy unto thousands of them that love me, and keep my commandments.

"Thou shalt not take the name of the LORD thy God in vain; for the LORD will not hold him guiltless that taketh his name in vain.

"Remember the sabbath day, to keep it holy. Six days shalt thou labor, and do all thy work: but the seventh day is the sabbath of the LORD thy God: in it thou shalt not do any work, thou, nor thy son, nor thy daughter, thy manservant, nor thy maidservant, nor thy cattle, nor thy stranger that is within thy gates: for in six days the LORD made heaven and earth, the sea, and all that in them is, and rested the seventh day: wherefore the LORD blessed the sabbath day, and hallowed it.

"Honor thy father and thy mother: that thy days may be long upon the land which the LORD thy God giveth thee.

"Thou shalt not kill.

"Thou shalt not commit adultery.

"Thou shalt not steal.

"Thou shalt not bear false witness against thy neighbor.

"Thou shalt not covet thy neighbor's house, thou shalt not covet thy neighbor's wife, nor his manservant, nor his maidservant, nor his ox, nor his ass, nor any thing that is thy neighbor's."

Exodus 20:1–17

It is questionable whether, when we break a murderer on the wheel, we aren't lapsing into precisely the mistake of the child who hits the chair he bumps into.
        G. C. Lichtenberg

If a man were permitted to make all the ballads, he need not care who should make the laws of a nation.
        Andrew Fletcher

Nature has given women so much power that the law has very wisely given them very little.
        Samuel Johnson

I asked him whether, as a moralist, he did not think that the practice of the law, in some degree, hurt the nice feeling of honesty. JOHNSON. "Why no, Sir, if you act properly. You are not to deceive your clients with false representations of your opinion: you are not to tell lies to a judge." BOSWELL. "But what do you think of supporting a cause which you know to be bad?" JOHNSON. "Sir, you do not know it to be good or bad till the Judge determines it. I have said that you are to state facts fairly; so that your thinking, or what you call knowing, a cause to be bad, must be from reasoning, must be from your supposing your arguments to be weak and inconclusive. But, Sir, that is not enough. An argument which does not convince yourself, may convince the Judge to whom you urge it; and if it does convince him, why, then, Sir, you are wrong, and he is right. It is his business to judge; and you are not to be confident in your own opinion that a cause is bad, but to say all you can for your client, and then hear the Judge's opinion." BOSWELL. "But, Sir, does not affecting a warmth when you have no warmth, and appearing to be clearly of one opinion when you are in reality of another opinion, does not such dissimulation impair one's honesty? Is there not some danger that a lawyer may put on the same mask in common life, in the intercourse with his friends?" JOHNSON. "Why no, Sir. Everybody knows you are paid for affecting warmth for your client; and it is, therefore, properly no dissimulation: the moment you come from the bar you resume your usual behaviour. Sir, a man will no more carry the artifice of the bar into the common intercourse of society, than a man who is paid for

tumbling upon his hands will continue to tumble upon his hands
when he should walk on his feet."
        James Boswell

One law for the ox and the ass is oppression.
        William Blake

The law, in its majestic equality, forbids the rich as well as the poor
to sleep under bridges, to beg in the streets, and to steal bread.
        Anatole France

Decency, security and liberty alike demand that government officials
shall be subjected to the same rules of conduct that are commands
to the citizen. In a government of laws, existence of the government
will be imperilled if it fails to observe the law scrupulously. Our
Government is the potent, the omnipresent teacher. For good or for
ill, it teaches the whole people by its example. Crime is contagious.
If the Government becomes a lawbreaker, it breeds contempt for
law; it invites every man to become a law unto himself; it invites
anarchy. To declare that in the administration of the criminal law
the end justifies the means—to declare that the Government may
commit crimes in order to secure the conviction of a private
criminal—would bring terrible retribution. Against that pernicious
doctrine this Court should resolutely set its face.
        Louis D. Brandeis

The trouble about fighting for human freedom is that you have to
spend much of your life defending sons of bitches; for oppressive
laws are always aimed at them originally, and oppression must be
stopped in the beginning if it is to be stopped at all.
        H. L. Mencken

Censorship upholds the dignity of the profession, know what I
mean?
        Mae West

Martin Luther King, Jr.

Nonviolent Resistance

Oppressed people deal with their oppression in three characteristic ways. One way is acquiescence: the oppressed resign themselves to their doom. They tacitly adjust themselves to oppression, and thereby become conditioned to it. In every movement toward freedom some of the oppressed prefer to remain oppressed. Almost 2800 years ago Moses set out to lead the children of Israel from the slavery of Egypt to the freedom of the promised land. He soon discovered that slaves do not always welcome their deliverers. They become accustomed to being slaves. They would rather bear those ills they have, as Shakespeare pointed out, than flee to others that they know not of. They prefer the "fleshpots of Egypt" to the ordeals of emancipation. 1

There is such a thing as the freedom of exhaustion. Some people are so worn down by the yoke of oppression that they give up. A few years ago in the slum areas of Atlanta, a Negro guitarist used to sing almost daily: "Ben down so long that down don't bother me." This is the type of negative freedom and resignation that often engulfs the life of the oppressed. 2

But this is not the way out. To accept passively an unjust system is to coöperate with that system; thereby the oppressed become as evil as the oppressor. Noncoöperation with evil is as much a moral obligation as is coöperation with good. The oppressed must never allow the conscience of the oppressor to slumber. Religion reminds every man that he is his brother's keeper. To accept injustice or segregation passively is to say to the oppressor that his actions are morally right. It is a way of allowing his conscience to fall asleep. At this moment the oppressed fails to be his brother's keeper. So acquiescence—while often the easier way—is not the moral way. It is the way of the coward. The Negro cannot win the respect of his oppressor by acquiescing; he 3

Martin Luther King, Jr. (1929–1968), clergyman and civil rights leader, achieved national fame in 1955–1956 when he led the boycott against segregated bus lines in Montgomery, Alabama. His policy of passive resistance succeeded in Montgomery, and King then organized the Southern Christian Leadership Conference in order to extend his efforts. In 1964 he was awarded the Nobel Peace Prize, but he continued to encounter strong opposition. On April 4, 1968, while in Memphis to support striking sanitation workers, he was shot and killed.

merely increases the oppressor's arrogance and contempt. Acquiescence is interpreted as proof of the Negro's inferiority. The Negro cannot win the respect of the white people of the South or the peoples of the world if he is willing to sell the future of his children for his personal and immediate comfort and safety.

A second way that oppressed people sometimes deal with oppression is to resort to physical violence and corroding hatred. Violence often brings about momentary results. Nations have frequently won their independence in battle. But in spite of temporary victories, violence never brings permanent peace. It solves no social problem; it merely creates new and more complicated ones. 4

Violence as a way of achieving racial justice is both impractical and immoral. It is impractical because it is a descending spiral ending in destruction for all. The old law of an eye for an eye leaves everybody blind. It is immoral because it seeks to humiliate the opponent rather than win his understanding; it seeks to annihilate rather than to convert. Violence is immoral because it thrives on hatred rather than love. It destroys community and makes brotherhood impossible. It leaves society in monologue rather than dialogue. Violence ends by defeating itself. It creates bitterness in the survivors and brutality in the destroyers. A voice echoes through time saying to every potential Peter, "Put up your sword." History is cluttered with the wreckage of nations that failed to follow his command. 5

If the American Negro and other victims of oppression succumb to the temptation of using violence in the struggle for freedom, future generations will be the recipients of a desolate night of bitterness, and our chief legacy to them will be an endless reign of meaningless chaos. Violence is not the way. 6

The third way open to oppressed people in their quest for freedom is the way of nonviolent resistance. Like the synthesis in Hegelian philosophy, the principle of nonviolent resistance seeks to reconcile the truths of two opposites—acquiescence and violence—while avoiding the extremes and immoralities of both. The nonviolent resister agrees with the person who acquiesces that one should not be physically aggressive toward his opponent; but he balances the equation by agreeing with the person of violence that evil must be resisted. He avoids the nonresistance of the former and the violent resistance of the latter. With nonviolent resistance, no individual or group need submit to any wrong, nor need anyone resort to violence in order to right a wrong. 7

It seems to me that this is the method that must guide the actions 8
of the Negro in the present crisis in race relations. Through nonviolent
resistance the Negro will be able to rise to the noble height of opposing
the unjust system while loving the perpetrators of the system. The
Negro must work passionately and unrelentingly for full stature as a
citizen, but he must not use inferior methods to gain it. He must never
come to terms with falsehood, malice, hate, or destruction.

Nonviolent resistance makes it possible for the Negro to remain 9
in the South and struggle for his rights. The Negro's problem will not
be solved by running away. He cannot listen to the glib suggestion of
those who would urge him to migrate en masse to other sections of
the country. By grasping his great opportunity in the South he can
make a lasting contribution to the moral strength of the nation and set
a sublime example of courage for generations yet unborn.

By nonviolent resistance, the Negro can also enlist all men of good 10
will in his struggle for equality. The problem is not a purely racial one,
with Negroes set against whites. In the end, it is not a struggle between
people at all, but a tension between justice and injustice. Nonviolent
resistance is not aimed against oppressors but against oppression.
Under its banner consciences, not racial groups, are enlisted.

If the Negro is to achieve the goal of integration, he must organize 11
himself into a militant and nonviolent mass movement. All three elements are indispensable. The movement for equality and justice can
only be a success if it has both a mass and militant character; the barriers to be overcome require both. Nonviolence is an imperative in
order to bring about ultimate community.

A mass movement of militant quality that is not at the same time 12
committed to nonviolence tends to generate conflict, which in turn
breeds anarchy. The support of the participants and the sympathy of
the uncommitted are both inhibited by the threat that bloodshed will
engulf the community. This reaction in turn encourages the opposition
to threaten and resort to force. When, however, the mass movement
repudiates violence while moving resolutely toward its goal, its opponents are revealed as the instigators and practitioners of violence if
it occurs. Then public support is magnetically attracted to the advocates
of nonviolence, while those who employ violence are literally disarmed
by overwhelming sentiment against their stand.

Only through a nonviolent approach can the fears of the white 13
community be mitigated. A guilt-ridden white minority lives in fear
that if the Negro should ever attain power, he would act without re-

straint or pity to revenge the injustices and brutality of the years. It is something like a parent who continually mistreats a son. One day that parent raises his hand to strike the son, only to discover that the son is now as tall as he is. The parent is suddenly afraid—fearful that the son will use his new physical power to repay his parent for all the blows of the past.

The Negro, once a helpless child, has now grown up politically, 14 culturally, and economically. Many white men fear retaliation. The job of the Negro is to show them that they have nothing to fear, that the Negro understands and forgives and is ready to forget the past. He must convince the white man that all he seeks is justice, *for both himself and the white man*. A mass movement exercising nonviolence is an object lesson in power under discipline, a demonstration to the white community that if such a movement attained a degree of strength, it would use its power creatively and not vengefully.

Nonviolence can touch men where the law cannot reach them. 15 When the law regulates behavior it plays an indirect part in molding public sentiment. The enforcement of the law is itself a form of peaceful persuasion. But the law needs help. The courts can order desegregation of the public schools. But what can be done to mitigate the fears, to disperse the hatred, violence, and irrationality gathered around school integration, to take the initiative out of the hands of racial demagogues, to release respect for the law? In the end, for laws to be obeyed, men must believe they are right.

Here nonviolence comes in as the ultimate form of persuasion. It 16 is the method which seeks to implement the just law by appealing to the conscience of the great decent majority who through blindness, fear, pride, or irrationality have allowed their consciences to sleep.

The nonviolent resisters can summarize their message in the fol- 17 lowing simple terms: We will take direct action against injustice without waiting for other agencies to act. We will not obey unjust laws or submit to unjust practices. We will do this peacefully, openly, cheerfully because our aim is to persuade. We adopt the means of nonviolence because our end is a community at peace with itself. We will try to persuade with our words, but if our words fail, we will try to persuade with our acts. We will always be willing to talk and seek fair compromise, but we are ready to suffer when necessary and even risk our lives to become witnesses to the truth as we see it.

The way of nonviolence means a willingness to suffer and sacrifice. 18 It may mean going to jail. If such is the case the resister must be willing to fill the jail houses of the South. It may even mean physical death.

But if physical death is the price that a man must pay to free his children and his white brethren from a permanent death of the spirit, then nothing could be more redemptive.

Questions

1. In the first paragraph, the passage about Moses and the children of Israel is not strictly necessary; the essential idea of the paragraph is stated in the previous sentence. Why, then, does King add this material? And why the quotation from Shakespeare?
2. Pick out two or three sentences that seem to you to be especially effective and analyze the sources of their power. You can choose either isolated sentences or (because King often effectively links sentences with repetition of words or of constructions) consecutive ones.
3. In a paragraph set forth your understanding of what nonviolent resistance is. Use whatever examples from your own experience or reading you find useful. In a second paragraph, explain how Maya Angelou's "Graduation" (page 158) offers an example of nonviolent resistance.

Plato

Crito

Persons of the Dialogue: Socrates and Crito

Scene: The Prison of Socrates

Socrates. Why have you come at this hour, Crito? It must be quite early?

Crito. Yes, certainly.

Soc. What is the exact time?

Cr. The dawn is breaking.

Soc. I wonder that the keeper of the prison would let you in. 5

Cr. He knows me, because I often come, Socrates; moreover, I have done him a kindness.

Soc. And are you only just arrived?

Cr. No, I came some time ago.

Soc. Then why did you sit and say nothing, instead of at once awakening me?

Cr. I should not have liked myself, Socrates, to be in such great 10 trouble and unrest as you are—indeed I should not: I have been watching with amazement your peaceful slumbers; and for that reason I did not awake you, because I wished to minimize the pain. I have always thought you to be of a happy disposition; but never did I see anything like the easy, tranquil manner in which you bear this calamity.

Plato (427–347 B.C.) in his dialogues often uses the Athenian philosopher Socrates as a mouthpiece for ideas that scholars believe are Platonic, but in the dialogue called *Crito* he probably was fairly careful to represent Socrates' own ideas.

In 399 B.C. Socrates was convicted of impiety and was sentenced to death. Behind the charge of impiety was another, that Socrates had "corrupted the young." It seems clear, however, that the trial was a way of getting rid of a man considered by some to be a troublesome questioner of conventional opinions.

About a month intervened between the trial and Socrates' death because the law prohibited execution until a sacred ship had returned to Athens. Socrates could easily have escaped from prison but made no effort to leave, as we see in this dialogue reporting his decision to abide by the unjust decision of a duly constituted group of jurors.

Soc. Why, Crito, when a man has reached my age he ought not to be repining at the approach of death.

Cr. And yet other old men find themselves in similar misfortunes, and age does not prevent them from repining.

Soc. That is true. But you have not told me why you come at this early hour.

Cr. I come to bring you a message which is sad and painful; not, as I believe, to yourself, but to all of us who are your friends, and saddest of all to me.

Soc. What? Has the ship come from Delos, on the arrival of which   15
I am to die?

Cr. No, the ship has not actually arrived, but she will probably be here today, as persons who have come from Sunium tell me that they left her there; and therefore tomorrow, Socrates, will be the last day of your life.

Soc. Very well, Crito; if such is the will of God, I am willing; but my belief is that there will be a delay of a day.

Cr. Why do you think so?

Soc. I will tell you, I am to die on the day after the arrival of the ship.

Cr. Yes; that is what the authorities say.   20

Soc. But I do not think that the ship will be here until tomorrow; this I infer from a vision which I had last night, or rather only just now, when you fortunately allowed me to sleep.

Cr. And what was the nature of the vision?

Soc. There appeared to me the likeness of a woman, fair and comely, clothed in bright raiment, who called to me and said: O Socrates,

The third day hence to fertile Phthia shalt thou go.[1]

Cr. What a singular dream, Socrates!

Soc. There can be no doubt about the meaning, Crito, I think.   25

Cr. Yes; the meaning is only too clear. But, oh! my beloved Socrates, let me entreat you once more to take my advice and escape. For if you die I shall not only lose a friend who can never be replaced, but there is another evil: people who do not know you and me will believe that I might have saved you if I had been willing to give money, but that I did not care. Now, can there be a worse disgrace than this—that I should be thought to value money more than the life of a friend?

---

[1] Homer, *Iliad*, ix. 363.

For the many will not be persuaded that I wanted you to escape, and that you refused.

Soc. But why, my dear Crito, should we care about the opinion of the many? Good men, and they are the only persons who are worth considering, will think of these things truly as they occurred.

Cr. But you see, Socrates, that the opinion of the many must be regarded, for what is now happening shows that they can do the greatest evil to any one who has lost their good opinion.

Soc. I only wish it were so, Crito; and that the many could do the greatest evil; for then they would also be able to do the greatest good— and what a fine thing this would be! But in reality they can do neither; for they cannot make a man either wise or foolish; and whatever they do is the result of chance.

Cr. Well, I will not dispute with you; but please to tell me, Socrates, 30 whether you are not acting out of regard to me and your other friends: are you not afraid that if you escape from prison we may get into trouble with the informers for having stolen you away, and lose either the whole or a great part of our property; or that even a worse evil may happen to us? Now, if you fear on our account, be at ease; for in order to save you, we ought surely to run this, or even a greater risk; be persuaded, then, and do as I say.

Soc. Yes, Crito, that is one fear which you mention, but by no means the only one.

Cr. Fear not—there are persons who are willing to get you out of 32 prison at no great cost; and as for the informers, they are far from being exorbitant in their demands—a little money will satisfy them. My means, which are certainly ample, are at your service, and if you have a scruple about spending all mine, here are strangers who will give you the use of theirs; and one of them, Simmias the Theban, has brought a large sum of money for this very purpose; and Cebes and many others are prepared to spend their money in helping you to escape. I say, therefore, do not hesitate on our account, and do not say, as you did in the court, that you will have a difficulty in knowing what to do with yourself anywhere else. For men will love you in other places to which you may go, and not in Athens only; there are friends of mine in Thessaly, if you like to go to them, who will value and protect you, and no Thessalian will give you any trouble. Nor can I think that you are at all justified, Socrates, in betraying your own life when you might be saved; in acting thus you are playing into the hands of your enemies, who are hurrying on your destruction. And further I should say that you are deserting your own children; for you might bring them up and educate them; instead of which you go away and leave them, and they will have to take their chance; and if they do not meet with the usual fate of orphans, there will be small thanks to you. No man should bring children into the world who is unwilling to persevere to the end in their nurture and education. But you appear to be choosing the easier part, not the better and manlier, which would have been more becoming in one who professes to care for virtue in all his actions, like yourself. And indeed, I am ashamed not only of you, but of us who are your friends, when I reflect that the whole business will be attributed entirely to our want of courage. The trial need never have come on, or might have been managed differently; and this last act, or crowning folly, will seem to have occurred through our negligence and cowardice, who might have saved you, if we had been good for anything; and you might have saved yourself, for there was no difficulty at all. See now, Socrates, how sad and discreditable are the consequences, both to us and you. Make up your mind then, or rather have your mind already made up, for the time of deliberation is over, and there is only one thing to be done, which must be done this very night, and if we delay at all will be no longer practicable or possible; I beseech you therefore, Socrates, be persuaded by me, and do as I say.

Soc. Dear Crito, your zeal is invaluable, if a right one; but if wrong, 33 the greater the zeal the greater the danger; and therefore we ought to consider whether I shall or shall not do as you say. For I am and always have been one of those natures who must be guided by reason, whatever the reason may be which upon reflection appears to me to be the best; and now that this chance has befallen me, I cannot repudiate my own words: the principles which I have hitherto honored and revered I still honor, and unless we can at once find other and better principles, I am certain not to agree with you; no, not even if the power of the multitude could inflict many more imprisonments, confiscations, deaths, frightening us like children with hobgoblin terrors. What will be the fairest way of considering the question? Shall I return to your old argument about the opinions of men?—we were saying that some of them are to be regarded, and others not. Now were we right in maintaining this before I was condemned? And has the argument which was once good now proved to be talk for the sake of talking— mere childish nonsense? That is what I want to consider with your help, Crito:—whether, under my present circumstances, the argument appears to be in any way different or not; and is to be allowed by me or disallowed. That argument, which, as I believe, is maintained by many persons of authority, was to the effect, as I was saying, that the opinions of some men are to be regarded, and of other men not to be regarded. Now you, Crito, are not going to die tomorrow—at least, there is no human probability of this—and therefore you are disinterested and not liable to be deceived by the circumstances in which you are placed. Tell me then, whether I am right in saying that some opinions, and the opinions of some men only, are to be valued, and that other opinions, and the opinions of other men, are not to be valued. I ask you whether I was right in maintaining this?

Cr. Certainly.

Soc. The good are to be regarded, and not the bad?   35

Cr. Yes.

Soc. And the opinions of the wise are good, and the opinions of the unwise are evil?

Cr. Certainly.

Soc. And what was said about another matter? Is the pupil who devotes himself to the practice of gymnastics supposed to attend to the praise and blame and opinion of every man, or of one man only— his physician or trainer, whoever he may be?

Cr. Of one man only.   40

Soc. And he ought to fear the censure and welcome the praise of that one only, and not of the many?

Cr. Clearly so.

Soc. And he ought to act and train, and eat and drink in the way which seems good to his single master who has understanding, rather than according to the opinion of all other men put together?

Cr. True.

Soc. And if he disobeys and disregards the opinion and approval   45 of the one, and regards the opinion of the many who have no understanding, will he not suffer evil?

Cr. Certainly he will.

Soc. And what will the evil be, whither tending and what affecting, in the disobedient person?

Cr. Clearly, affecting the body; that is what is destroyed by the evil.

Soc. Very good; and is not this true, Crito, of other things which we need not separately enumerate? In questions of just and unjust, fair and foul, good and evil, which are the subjects of our present consultation, ought we to allow the opinion of the many and to fear them; or the opinion of the one man who has understanding? ought we not to fear and reverence him more than all the rest of the world:

and if we desert him shall we not destroy and injure that principle in us which may be assumed to be improved by justice and deteriorated by injustice;—there is such a principle?

Cr. Certainly there is, Socrates.

Soc. Take a parallel instance—if, acting under the advice of those who have no understanding, we destroy that which is improved by health and is deteriorated by disease, would life be worth having? And that which has been destroyed is—the body?

Cr. Yes.

Soc. Could we live, having an evil and corrupted body?

Cr. Certainly not.

Soc. And will life be worth having, if that higher part of man be destroyed, which is improved by justice and depraved by injustice? Do we suppose that principle, whatever it may be in man, which has to do with justice and injustice, to be inferior to the body?

Cr. Certainly not.

Soc. More honorable than the body?

Cr. Far more.

Soc. Then, my friend, we must not regard what the many say of us: but what he, the one man who has understanding of just and unjust, will say, and what the truth will say. And therefore you begin in error when you advise that we should regard the opinion of the many about just and unjust, good and evil, honorable and dishonorable—"Well," some one will say, "but the many can kill us."

Cr. Yes, Socrates; that will clearly be the answer.

Soc. And it is true: but still I find with surprise that the old argument is unshaken as ever. And I should like to know whether I may say the same of another proposition—that not life, but a good life, is to be chiefly valued?

Cr. Yes, that also remains unshaken.

Soc. And a good life is equivalent to a just, honorable one—that holds also?

Cr. Yes, it does.

Soc. From these premises I proceed to argue the question whether I ought or ought not to try and escape without the consent of the Athenians: and if I am clearly right in escaping, then I will make the attempt; but if not, I will abstain. The other considerations which you mention, of money and loss of character and duty of educating one's children, are, I fear, only the doctrines of the multitude, who would be as ready to restore people to life, if they were able, as they are to put them to death—and with as little reason. But now, since the argument has thus far prevailed, the only question which remains to be considered is, whether we shall do rightly either in escaping or in suffering others to aid in our escape and paying them in money and thanks, or whether in reality we shall not do rightly; and if the latter, then death or any other calamity which may ensue on my remaining here must not be allowed to enter into the calculation.

Cr. I think that you are right, Socrates; how then shall we proceed?

Soc. Let us consider the matter together, and do you either refute me if you can, and I will be convinced; or else cease, my dear friend, from repeating to me that I ought to escape against the wishes of the Athenians: for I highly value your attempts to persuade me to do so, but I may not be persuaded against my own better judgment. And now please to consider my first position, and try how you can best answer me.

Cr. I will.

Soc. Are we to say that we are never intentionally to do wrong, or that in one way we ought and in another we ought not to do wrong, or is doing wrong always evil and dishonorable, as I was just now saying, and as has been already acknowledged by us? Are all our former admissions which were made within a few days to be thrown away? And have we, at our age, been earnestly discoursing with one another all our life long only to discover that we are no better than children? Or, in spite of the opinion of the many, and in spite of consequences whether better or worse, shall we insist on the truth of what was then said, that injustice is always an evil and dishonor to him who acts unjustly? Shall we say so or not?

Cr. Yes.   70

Soc. Then we must do no wrong?

Cr. Certainly not.

Soc. Nor when injured injure in return, as the many imagine; for we must injure no one at all?

Cr. Clearly not.   75

Soc. Again, Crito, may we do evil?

Cr. Surely not, Socrates.

Soc. And what of doing evil in return for evil, which is the morality of the many—is that just or not?

Cr. Not just.

Soc. For doing evil to another is the same as injuring him?

Cr. Very true.   80

Soc. Then we ought not to retaliate or render evil for evil to any one, whatever evil we may have suffered from him. But I would have you consider, Crito, whether you really mean what you are saying.

For this opinion has never been held, and never will be held, by any considerable number of persons; and those who are agreed and those who are not agreed upon this point have no common ground, and can only despise one another when they see how widely they differ. Tell me, then, whether you agree with and assent to my first principle, that neither injury nor retaliation nor warding off evil by evil is ever right. And shall that be the premise of our argument? Or do you decline and dissent from this? For so I have ever thought, and continue to think; but, if you are of another opinion, let me hear what you have to say. If, however, you remain of the same mind as formerly, I will proceed to the next step.

Cr. You may proceed, for I have not changed my mind.

Soc. Then I will go on to the next point, which may be put in the form of a question:—Ought a man to do what he admits to be right, or ought he to betray the right?

Cr. He ought to do what he thinks right.

Soc. But if this is true, what is the application? In leaving the prison against the will of the Athenians, do I wrong any? or rather do I not wrong those whom I ought least to wrong? Do I not desert the principles which were acknowledged by us to be just—what do you say?

Cr. I cannot tell, Socrates; for I do not know.

Soc. Then consider the matter in this way:—Imagine that I am about to play truant (you may call the proceeding by any name which you like), and the laws and the government come and interrogate me: "Tell us, Socrates," they say; "what are you about? are you not going by an act of yours to overturn us—the laws, and the whole state, as far as in you lies? Do you imagine that a state can subsist and not be overthrown, in which the decisions of law have no power, but are set aside and trampled upon by individuals?" What will be our answer, Crito, to these and the like words? Any one, and especially a rhetorician, will have a good deal to say on behalf of the law which requires a sentence to be carried out. He will argue that this law should not be set aside; and shall we reply, "Yes; but the state has injured us and given an unjust sentence." Suppose I say that?

Cr. Very good, Socrates.

Soc. "And was that our agreement with you?" the law would answer; "or were you to abide by the sentence of the state?" And if I were to express my astonishment at their words, the law would probably add: "Answer, Socrates, instead of opening your eyes—you are in the habit of asking and answering questions. Tell us—What complaint have you to make against us which justifies you in attempting to destroy us and the state? In the first place did we not bring you into existence? Your father married your mother by our aid and begat you. Say whether you have any objection to urge against those of us who regulate marriage?" None, I should reply. "Or against those of us who after birth regulate the nurture and education of children, in which you also were trained? Were not the laws, which have the charge of education, right in commanding your father to train you in music and gymnastic?" Right, I should reply. "Well then, since you were brought into the world and nurtured and educated by us, can you deny in the first place that you are our child and slave, as your fathers were before you? And if this is true you are not on equal terms with us; nor can you think that you have a right to do to us what we are doing to you. Would you have any right to strike or revile or do any other evil to your father or your master, if you had one, because you have been struck or reviled by him, or received some other evil at his hands?— you would not say this? And because we think right to destroy you, do you think that you have any right to destroy us in return, and your country as far as in you lies? Will you, O professor of true virtue, pretend that you are justified in this? Has a philosopher like you failed to discover that our country is more to be valued and higher and holier far than mother or father or any ancestor, and more to be regarded in the eyes of the gods and of men of understanding? also to be soothed, and gently and reverently entreated when angry, even more than a father, and either to be persuaded, or if not persuaded, to be obeyed? And when we are punished by her, whether with imprisonment or stripes, the punishment is to be endured in silence; and if she leads us to wounds or death in battle, thither we follow as is right; neither may any one yield or retreat or leave his rank, but whether in battle or in a court of law, or in any other place, he must do what his city and his country order him; or he must change their view of what is just: and if he may do no violence to his father or mother, much less may he do violence to his country." What answer shall we make to this, Crito? Do the laws speak truly, or do they not?

Cr. I think that they do.

Soc. Then the laws will say, "Consider, Socrates, if we are speaking   truly that in your present attempt you are going to do us an injury. For, having brought you into the world, and nurtured and educated you, and given you and every other citizen a share in every good which we had to give, we further proclaim to any Athenian by the liberty which we allow him, that if he does not like us when he has become of age and has seen the ways of the city, and made our acquaintance, he may go where he pleases and take his goods with him. None of us laws will forbid him or interfere with him. Any one who does not like us and the city, and who wants to emigrate to a colony or to any other city, may go where he likes, retaining his property. But he who has experience of the manner in which we order justice and administer the state, and still remains, has entered into an implied contract that he will do as we command him. And he who disobeys us is, as we maintain, thrice wrong; first, because in disobeying us he is disobeying his parents; secondly, because we are the authors of his education; thirdly, because he has made an agreement with us that he will duly obey our commands; and he neither obeys them nor convinces us that our commands are unjust; and we do not rudely impose them, but give him the alternative of obeying or convincing us;—that is what we offer, and he does neither.

"These are the sort of accusations to which, as we were saying, 92 you, Socrates, will be exposed if you accomplish your intentions; you, above all other Athenians." Suppose now I ask, why I rather than anybody else? they will justly retort upon me that I above all other men have acknowledged the agreement. "There is clear proof," they will say, "Socrates, that we and the city were not displeasing to you. Of all Athenians you have been the most constant resident in the city, which, as you never leave, you may be supposed to love. For you never went out of the city either to see the games, except once when you went to the Isthmus, or to any other place unless when you were on military service; nor did you travel as other men do. Nor had you any curiosity to know other states or their laws: your affections did not go beyond us and our state; we were your special favorites, and you acquiesced in our government of you; and here in this city you begat your children, which is a proof of your satisfaction. Moreover, you might in the course of the trial, if you had liked, have fixed the penalty at banishment; the state which refuses to let you go now would have let you go then. But you pretended that you preferred death to exile, and that you were not unwilling to die. And now you have forgotten these fine sentiments, and pay no respect to us the laws, of whom you are the destroyer; and are doing what only a miserable slave would do, running away and turning your back upon the compacts and agreements which you made as a citizen. And first of all answer this very question: Are we right in saying that you agreed to be governed according to us in deed, and not in word only? Is that true or not?" How shall we answer, Crito? Must we not assent?

Cr. We cannot help it, Socrates. 93

Soc. Then will they not say: "You, Socrates, are breaking the cov- 94 enants and agreements which you made with us at your leisure, not in any haste or under any compulsion or deception, but after you have had seventy years to think of them, during which time you were at liberty to leave the city, if we were not to your mind, or if our covenants appeared to you to be unfair. You had your choice, and might have gone either to Lacedaemon or Crete, both which states are often praised by you for their good government, or to some other Hellenic or foreign state. Whereas you, above all other Athenians, seemed to be so fond of the state, or, in other words, of us her laws (and who would care about a state which has no laws?), that you never stirred out of her; the halt, the blind, the maimed were not more stationary in her than you were. And now you run away and forsake your agreements. Not so, Socrates, if you will take our advice; do not make yourself ridiculous by escaping out of the city.

"For just consider, if you transgress and err in this sort of way, 95 what good will you do either to yourself or to your friends? That your friends will be driven into exile and deprived of citizenship, or will lose their property, is tolerably certain; and you yourself, if you fly to one of the neighboring cities, as, for example, Thebes or Megara, both of which are well governed, will come to them as an enemy, Socrates, and their government will be against you, and all patriotic citizens will cast an evil eye upon you as a subverter of the laws, and you will confirm in the minds of the judges the justice of their own condemnation of you. For he who is a corrupter of the laws is more than likely to be a corrupter of the young and foolish portion of mankind. Will you then flee from well-ordered cities and virtuous men? and is existence worth having on these terms? Or will you go to them without shame, and talk to them, Socrates? And what will you say to them? What you say here about virtue and justice and institutions and laws being the best things among men? Would that be decent of you? Surely not. But if you go away from well-governed states to Crito's friends in Thessaly, where there is great disorder and license, they will be charmed to hear the tale of your escape from prison, set off with ludicrous particulars of the manner in which you were wrapped in a goatskin or some other disguise, and metamorphosed as the manner is of runaways; but will there be no one to remind you that in your old age you were not ashamed to violate the most sacred laws for a miserable desire of a little more life? Perhaps not, if you keep them in a good temper; but if they are out of temper you will hear many degrading things; you will live, but how?—as the flatterer of all men, and the servant of all men; and doing what?—eating and drinking in Thessaly, having gone abroad in order that you may get a dinner. And where will be your fine sentiments about justice and virtue? Say that you wish to live for the sake of your children—you want to bring them up and educate them—will you take them into Thessaly and deprive them of Athenian citizenship? Is this the benefit which you will confer upon them? Or are you under the impression that they will be better cared for and educated here if you are still alive, although absent from them; for your friends will take care of them? Do you fancy that if you are an inhabitant of Thessaly they will take care of them, and if you are an inhabitant of the other world that they will not take care of them? Nay; but if they who call themselves friends are good for anything, they will—to be sure they will.

"Listen, then, Socrates, to us who have brought you up. Think 96 not of life and children first, and of justice afterward, but of justice first, that you may be justified before the princes of the world below. For neither will you nor any that belong to you be happier or holier or juster in this life, or happier in another, if you do as Crito bids. Now you depart in innocence, a sufferer and not a doer of evil; a victim, not of the laws but of men. But if you go forth, returning evil for evil, and injury for injury, breaking the covenants and agreements which you have made with us, and wronging those whom you ought least of all to wrong, that is to say, yourself, your friends, your country, and us, we shall be angry with you while you live, and our brethren, the laws in the world below, will receive you as an enemy; for they will know that you have done your best to destroy us. Listen, then, to us and not to Crito."

This, dear Crito, is the voice which I seem to hear murmuring in 97 my ears, like the sound of the flute in the ears of the mystic; that voice, I say, is humming in my ears, and prevents me from hearing any other. And I know that anything more which you may say will be vain. Yet speak, if you have anything to say.

Cr. I have nothing to say, Socrates.   98

Soc. Leave me then, Crito, to fulfill the will of God, and to follow 99 whither he leads.

Questions

1. Socrates argues that because throughout his life he lived in Athens, in effect he established a compact with the city to live by its laws and must therefore now accept the judgment—however mistaken—of a duly constituted court. How convincing is this argu-

ment? Suppose this argument were omitted. Would Socrates' conclusion be affected?

2. Socrates argues that just as in matters of caring for the body we heed only experts and not the multitude, so in moral matters we should heed the expert, not the multitude. How convincing is this analogy between bodily health and moral goodness? Socrates sometimes compared himself to an athletic coach, saying he trained people to think. Judging from the dialogue, how did he train a student to think?

3. The personified figure of the laws does not add much to the essential argument. Why, then, is the passage included?

4. The ancient Chinese teacher Confucius asked one of his pupils, "Do you think of me as a man who knows about things as the result of wide study?" When the pupil replied "Yes," Confucius disagreed: "I have one thing, and upon it all the rest is rooted." Exactly what did Confucius mean? If Socrates had been asked the question, would he have given Confucius's answer?

Luke, John, and an Anonymous Japanese

Four Short Narratives

1. Luke *Parable of the Prodigal Son*

Then drew near unto [Jesus] all the publicans and sinners for to hear him. And the Pharisees and scribes murmured, saying "This man receiveth sinners, and eateth with them." And he said, "A certain man had two sons: and the younger of them said to his father, 'Father,

Luke, the author of the third of the four Gospels, was a second-generation Christian. He probably was a Roman, though some early accounts refer to him as a Syrian; in any case, he wrote in Greek. John, the author of the fourth Gospel, is traditionally said to be John, son of Zebedee, one of the twelve apostles of Jesus. Tradition also holds that John is the author of three epistles and of Revelation, though much modern scholarship doubts that the same man could have written these works, which differ in matters of style and doctrine. Our two selections from Luke and our one selection from John are all from the King James Version (1611).

The author of the Japanese anecdote called "Muddy Road" is not known.

give me the portion of goods that falleth to me.' And he divided unto them their living. And not many days after, the younger son gathered all together, and took his journey into a far country, and there wasted his substance with riotous living. And when he had spent all, there arose a mighty famine in that land, and he began to be in want. And he went and joined himself to a citizen of that country, and he sent him into his fields to feed swine. And he would fain have filled his belly with the husks that the swine did eat: and no man gave unto him. And when he came to himself, he said, 'How many hired servants of my father's have bread enough and to spare, and I perish with hunger? I will arise and go to my father, and will say unto him, "Father, I have sinned against heaven, and before thee. And am no more worthy to be called thy son: make me as one of thy hired servants." ' And he arose, and came to his father. But when he was yet a great way off, his father saw him, and had compassion, and ran, and fell on his neck, and kissed him. And the son said unto him, 'Father, I have sinned against heaven, and in thy sight, and am no more worthy to be called thy son.' But the father said to his servants, 'Bring forth the best robe, and put it on him, and put a ring on his hand, and shoes on his feet. And bring hither the fatted calf, and kill it, and let us eat, and be merry. For this my son was dead, and is alive again; he was lost, and is found.' And they began to be merry.

Now his elder son was in the field, and as he came and drew nigh to the house, he heard music and dancing. And he called one of the servants, and asked what these things meant. And he said unto him, 'Thy brother is come, and thy father hath killed the fatted calf, because he hath received him safe and sound.' And he was angry, and would not go in: therefore came his father out, and entreated him. And he answering said to his father, 'Lo, these many years do I serve thee, neither transgressed I at any time thy commandment, and yet thou never gavest me a kid, that I might make merry with my friends: but as soon as this thy son was come, which hath devoured thy living with harlots, thou hast killed for him the fatted calf.' And he said unto him, 'Son, thou art ever with me, and all that I have is thine. It was meet that we should make merry, and be glad: for this thy brother was dead, and is alive again: and was lost, and is found.' ''

2. Luke *Parable of the Good Samaritan*

But [a certain lawyer], willing to justify himself, said unto Jesus, and who is my neighbor?

And Jesus answering said, "A certain man went down from Jerusalem to Jericho, and fell among thieves, which stripped him of his raiment, and wounded him, and departed, leaving him half dead. And by chance there came down a certain priest that way: and when he saw him, he passed by on the other side. And likewise a Levite,[1] when he was at the place, came and looked on him, and passed by on the other side. But a certain Samaritan, as he journeyed, came where he was: and when he saw him, he had compassion on him, and went to him, and bound up his wounds, pouring in oil and wine, and set him on his own beast, and brought him to an inn, and took care of him. And on the morrow when he departed, he took out two pence, and gave them to the host, and said unto him, 'Take care of him; and whatsoever thou spendest more, when I come again, I will repay thee.' Which now of these three, thinkest thou, was neighbor unto him that fell among the thieves?"

And he said, "He that shewed mercy on him."

Then said Jesus unto him, "Go, and do thou likewise."

3. John *The Woman Taken in Adultery*

Jesus went unto the Mount of Olives. And early in the morning he came again into the temple, and all the people came unto him; and he sat down, and taught them.

And the scribes and Pharisees brought unto him a woman taken in adultery; and when they had set her in the midst, they said unto him, "Master, this woman was taken in adultery, in the very act. Now Moses in the law commanded us that such should be stoned: but what sayest thou?" This they said, tempting him, that they might have to accuse him. But Jesus stooped down, and with his finger wrote on the ground, as though he heard them not. So when they continued asking him, he lifted up himself, and said unto them, "He that is without sin among you, let him first cast a stone at her." And again he stooped down, and wrote on the ground. And they which heard it, being convicted by their own conscience, went out one by one, beginning at the eldest, even unto the last: and Jesus was left alone, and the woman standing in the midst.

---

[1] The Levites were assistants to the temple priests. The Samaritans (referred to in the next sentence) claimed to be Israelites but were regarded by the Jews as transplanted Assyrians. (Editors' note)

When Jesus had lifted up himself, and saw none but the woman, he said unto her, "Woman, where are those thine accusers? Hath no man condemned thee?" She said, "No man, Lord." And Jesus said unto her, "Neither do I condemn thee; go, and sin no more."

4. Anonymous Japanese *Muddy Road*

Tanzan and Ekido were once traveling together down a muddy road. A heavy rain was still falling.

Coming around a bend, they met a lovely girl in a silk kimono and sash, unable to cross the intersection.

"Come on, girl," said Tanzan at once. Lifting her in his arms, he carried her over the mud.

Ekido did not speak again until that night when they reached a lodging temple. Then he no longer could restrain himself. "We monks don't go near females," he told Tanzan, "especially not young and lovely ones. It is dangerous. Why did you do that?"

"I left the girl there," said Tanzan. "Are you still carrying her?"

Questions

1. What is the function of the older brother in the Parable of the Prodigal Son? Characterize him, and compare him with the younger brother.
2. Is the father foolish and sentimental? Do we approve or disapprove of his behavior at the end? Explain.
3. The biblical command is to love one's neighbor. The question put to Jesus, before he recounts the Parable of the Good Samaritan, is, "Who is my neighbor?" In the parable, what is Jesus' interpretation of the question and of the commandment?
4. Do you interpret the episode of the Woman Taken in Adultery to say that crime should go unpunished? Or that a judge cannot punish a crime if he himself is guilty of it? Or what?
5. What is the moral of the Japanese story? Does it bear any resemblance to the moral of the Parable of the Good Samaritan? Explain.

Thomas Jefferson

The Declaration of Independence

In CONGRESS, July 4, 1776. 1

The Unanimous Declaration of the Thirteen United States of America.

When in the Course of human events, it becomes nec- 2
essary for one people to dissolve the political bands which have connected them with another, and to assume among the powers of the
earth, the separate and equal station to which the Laws of Nature and
of Nature's God entitle them, a decent respect to the opinions of mankind requires that they should declare the causes which impel them
to the separation.

We hold these truths to be self-evident, that all men are created 3
equal, that they are endowed by their Creator with certain unalienable
Rights, that among these are Life, Liberty and the pursuit of Happiness.

That to secure these rights, Governments are instituted among 4
Men, deriving their just powers from the consent of the governed.

That whenever any Form of Government becomes destructive of 5
these ends, it is the Right of the People to alter or to abolish it, and
to institute new Government, laying its foundation on such principles
and organizing its powers in such form, as to them shall seem most
likely to effect their Safety and Happiness. Prudence, indeed, will dictate that Governments long established should not be changed for light
and transient causes; and accordingly all experience hath shewn, that
mankind are more disposed to suffer, while evils are sufferable, than
to right themselves by abolishing the forms to which they are accustomed. But when a long train of abuses and usurpations, pursuing
invariably the same Object evinces a design to reduce them under
absolute Despotism, it is their right, it is their duty, to throw off such
Government, and to provide new Guards for their future security.

Thomas Jefferson (1743–1826), governor of Virginia and the third president of
the United States, devoted most of his adult life, until his retirement, to the service
of Virginia and of the nation. The spirit and the wording of the Declaration are
almost entirely Jefferson's.

Such has been the patient sufferance of these Colonies; and such is now the necessity which constrains them to alter their former Systems of Government. The history of the present King of Great Britain is a history of repeated injuries and usurpations, all having in direct object the establishment of an absolute Tyranny over these States. To prove this, let Facts be submitted to a candid world.

He has refused his Assent to Laws, the most wholesome and necessary for the public good.

He has forbidden his Governors to pass Laws of immediate and pressing importance, unless suspended in their operation till his Assent should be obtained; and when so suspended, he has utterly neglected to attend to them.

He has refused to pass other Laws for the accommodation of large districts of people, unless those people would relinquish the right of Representation in the Legislature, a right inestimable to them and formidable to tyrants only.

He has called together legislative bodies at places unusual, uncomfortable, and distant from the depository of their public Records, for the sole purpose of fatiguing them into compliance with his measures.   10

He has dissolved Representative Houses repeatedly, for opposing with manly firmness his invasions on the rights of people.

He has refused for a long time, after such dissolutions, to cause others to be elected; whereby the Legislative powers, incapable of Annihilation, have returned to the People at large for their exercise; the State remaining in the mean time exposed to all the dangers of invasion from without, and convulsions within.

He has endeavoured to prevent the population of these States; for that purpose obstructing the Laws for Naturalization of Foreigners; refusing to pass others to encourage their migrations hither, and raising the conditions of new Appropriations of Lands.

He has obstructed the Administration of Justice, by refusing his Assent to Laws for establishing Judiciary powers.

He has made Judges dependent on his Will alone, for the tenure   15 of their offices, and the amount and payment of their salaries.

He has erected a multitude of New Offices, and sent hither swarms of Officers to harass our people, and eat out their substance.

He has kept among us, in times of peace, Standing Armies without the Consent of our legislatures.

He has affected to render the Military independent of and superior to the Civil power.

He has combined with others to subject us to a jurisdiction foreign to our constitution, and unacknowledged by our laws; giving his Assent to their Acts of pretended Legislation:

For Quartering large bodies of armed troops among us: 20

For Protecting them, by a mock Trial, from punishment for any Murders which they should commit on the Inhabitants of these States:

For cutting off our Trade with all parts of the world:

For imposing Taxes on us without our Consent:

For depriving us in many cases, of the benefits of Trial by Jury:

For transporting us beyond Seas to be tried for pretended offences: 25

For abolishing the free System of English Laws in a neighbouring Province, establishing therein an Arbitrary government, and enlarging its Boundaries so as to render it at once an example and fit instrument for introducing the same absolute rule into these Colonies:

For taking away our Charters, abolishing our most valuable Laws, and altering fundamentally the Forms of our Governments:

For suspending our own Legislatures, and declaring themselves invested with power to legislate for us in all cases whatsoever.

He has abdicated Government here, by declaring us out of his Protection and waging War against us:

He has plundered our seas, ravaged our Coasts, burnt our towns,   30 and destroyed the lives of our people.

He is at this time transporting large Armies of foreign Mercenaries   31 to compleat the works of death, desolation and tyranny, already begun with circumstances of Cruelty & perfidy scarcely paralleled in the most barbarous ages, and totally unworthy the Head of a civilized nation.

He has constrained our fellow Citizens taken Captive on the high   32 Seas to bear Arms against their Country, to become the executioners of their friends and Brethren, or to fall themselves by their Hands.

He has excited domestic insurrections amongst us, and has en-   33 deavoured to bring on the inhabitants of our frontiers, the merciless Indian Savages, whose known rule of warfare, is an undistinguished destruction of all ages, sexes and conditions. In every stage of these Oppressions We have Petitioned for Redress in the most humble terms: Our repeated Petitions have been answered only by repeated injury. A Prince, whose character is thus marked by every act which may define a Tyrant, is unfit to be the ruler of a free people. Nor have We been wanting in attentions to our British brethren. We have warned them from time to time of attempts by their legislature to extend an unwarrantable jurisdiction over us. We have reminded them of the circumstances of our emigration and settlement here. We have appealed to their native justice and magnanimity, and we have conjured them by the ties of our common kindred to disavow these usurpations, which, would inevitably interrupt our connections and correspondence. They too have been deaf to the voice of justice and of consanguinity. We must, therefore, acquiesce in the necessity, which denounces our Separation, and hold them, as we hold the rest of mankind, Enemies in War, in Peace Friends.

We, THEREFORE, the Representatives of the UNITED STATES OF AMER-   34
ICA, in General Congress Assembled, appealing to the Supreme Judge of the world for the rectitude of our intentions, do, in the Name and by Authority of the good People of these Colonies, solemnly publish and declare, That these United Colonies are, and of Right ought to be FREE AND INDEPENDENT STATES; that they are Absolved from all Allegiance to the British Crown, and that all political connection between them and the State of Great Britain, is and ought to be totally dissolved; and that as Free and Independent States, they have full Power to levy War, conclude Peace, contract Alliances, establish Commerce, and to do all other Acts and Things which Independent States may of right do.

And for the support of this Declaration, with a firm reliance on   35
the protection of divine Providence, we mutually pledge to each other our Lives, our Fortunes and our sacred Honor.

Questions

1. What assumptions lie behind the numerous specific reasons that are given to justify the rebellion? Set forth the gist of that argument of the Declaration using the form of reasoning known as a syllogism, which consists of a major premise (such as "All men are mortal"), a minor premise ("Socrates is a man"), and a conclusion ("Therefore, Socrates is mortal"). For a brief discussion of syllogisms, see pages 698–699 (*deduction*).
2. What audience is being addressed in the Declaration of Independence? Cite passages in the text that support your answer.
3. The Library of Congress has the original manuscript of the rough draft of the Declaration. This manuscript itself includes revisions that are indicated below, but it was later further revised. We print the first part of the second paragraph of the draft, and after it the corresponding part of the final version. Try to account for the changes within the draft, and from the revised draft to the final version.

self-evident

We hold these truths to be, ~~sacred & undeniable~~, that all men are

they are endowed by their Creator

created equal ~~& independent~~, that, ~~from that equal creation they~~

with

~~derive equal rights some of which are~~   ~~in rights~~

rights; that   these

inherent & inalienable, among ~~which~~ are the ~~preservation~~

~~of~~ life, ~~&~~ liberty, & the pursuit of happiness.

We hold these Truths to be self-evident, that all Men are created equal, that they are endowed by their Creator with certain unalienable Rights, that among these are Life, Liberty, and the Pursuit of Happiness.

In a paragraph evaluate the changes. Try to put yourself into Jefferson's mind and see if you can sense why Jefferson made the changes.

4. In a paragraph define *happiness*, and then in a second paragraph explain why, in your opinion, Jefferson spoke of "the pursuit of happiness" rather than of "happiness."

5. In a paragraph argue that the assertion that "all Men are created equal" is nonsense, or, on the other hand, that it makes sense.

6. If every person has an unalienable right to life, how can capital punishment be reconciled with the Declaration of Independence? (You need not in fact be a supporter of capital punishment; simply offer the best defense you can think of, in an effort to make it harmonious with the Declaration.)

Byron R. White

Opinion of the Supreme Court, in *New Jersey* v. *T.L.O.* [On the Right to Search Students]

In determining whether the search at issue in this case vi- 1
olated the Fourth Amendment, we are faced initially with the question
whether that amendment's prohibition on unreasonable searches and
seizures applies to searches conducted by public school officials. We
hold that it does.

It is now beyond dispute that "the Federal Constitution, by virtue 2
of the 14th Amendment, prohibits unreasonable searches and seizures
by state officers." Equally indisputable is the proposition that the 14th
Amendment protects the rights of students against encroachment by
public school officials.

On reargument, however, the State of New Jersey has argued that 3
the history of the Fourth Amendment indicates that the amendment

---

In January 1985, a majority of the United States Supreme Court, in a case called
New Jersey v. *T.L.O.* (a student's initials), ruled 6–3 that a school official's search
of a student who is suspected of disobeying a school regulation does not violate
the Fourth Amendment's protection against unreasonable searches and seizures.

The case originated thus: an assistant principal in a New Jersey high school
opened the purse of a fourteen-year-old girl who had been caught violating
school rules by smoking in the lavatory. The girl denied that she ever smoked,
and the assistant principal thought that the contents of her purse would show
whether or not she was lying. The purse was found to contain cigarettes, marijuana, and some notes that seemed to indicate that she sold marijuana to other
students. The school then called the police.

The case went through three lower courts; almost five years after the event
occurred, the case reached the Supreme Court. Associate Justice Byron R. White
wrote the majority opinion, joined by Chief Justice Warren E. Burger and by
Associate Justices Lewis F. Powell, Jr., William H. Rehnquist, and Sandra Day
O'Connor. Associate Justice Harry A. Blackmun concurred in a separate opinion.
Associate Justices William J. Brennan, Jr., John Paul Stevens, and Thurgood
Marshall dissented in part.

was intended to regulate only searches and seizures carried out by law enforcement officers; accordingly, although public school officials are concededly state agents for purposes of the 14th Amendment, the Fourth Amendment creates no rights enforceable against them.

But this Court has never limited the amendment's prohibition on unreasonable searches and seizures to operations conducted by the police. Rather, the Court has long spoken of the Fourth Amendment's strictures as restraints imposed upon "governmental action"—that is, "upon the activities of sovereign authority." Accordingly, we have held the Fourth Amendment applicable to the activities of civil as well as criminal authorities: building inspectors, OSHA inspectors, and even firemen entering privately owned premises to battle a fire, are all subject to the restraints imposed by the Fourth Amendment.   4

Notwithstanding the general applicability of the Fourth Amendment to the activities of civil authorities, a few courts have concluded that school officials are exempt from the dictates of the Fourth Amendment by virtue of the special nature of their authority over schoolchildren. Teachers and school administrators, it is said, act *in loco parentis* [i.e., in place of a parent] in their dealings with students: their authority is that of the parent, not the State, and is therefore not subject to the limits of the Fourth Amendment.   5

Such reasoning is in tension with contemporary reality and the teachings of this Court. We have held school officials subject to the commands of the First Amendment, and the Due Process Clause of the 14th Amendment. If school authorities are state actors for purposes of the constitutional guarantees of freedom of expression and due process, it is difficult to understand why they should be deemed to be exercising parental rather than public authority when conducting searches of their students.   6

In carrying out searches and other disciplinary functions pursuant to such policies, school officials act as representatives of the State, not merely as surrogates for the parents, and they cannot claim the parents' immunity from the strictures of the Fourth Amendment.   7

To hold that the Fourth Amendment applies to searches conducted by school authorities is only to begin the inquiry into the standards governing such searches. Although the underlying command of the Fourth Amendment is always that searches and seizures be reasonable, what is reasonable depends on the context within which a search takes place.   8

[*Standard of Reasonableness*]

The determination of the standard of reasonableness governing any 9
specific class of searches requires balancing the need to search against
the invasion which the search entails. On one side of the balance are
arrayed the individual's legitimate expectations of privacy and personal security; on the other, the government's need for effective methods to deal with breaches of public order.

We have recognized that even a limited search of the person is a 10
substantial invasion of privacy. A search of a child's person or of a
closed purse or other bag carried on her person, no less than a similar
search carried out on an adult, is undoubtedly a severe violation of
subjective expectations of privacy.

Of course, the Fourth Amendment does not protect subjective ex- 11
pectations of privacy that are unreasonable or otherwise "illegitimate."
The State of New Jersey has argued that because of the pervasive su-
pervision to which children in the schools are necessarily subject, a
child has virtually no legitimate expectation of privacy in articles of
personal property "unnecessarily" carried into a school. This argument
has two factual premises: (1) the fundamental incompatibility of expectations of privacy with the maintenance of a sound educational
environment; and (2) the minimal interest of the child in bringing any
items of personal property into the school. Both premises are severely
flawed.

Although this Court may take notice of the difficulty of maintain- 12
ing discipline in the public schools today, the situation is not so dire
that students in the schools may claim no legitimate expectations of
privacy.

[*Privacy and Discipline*]

Against the child's interest in privacy must be set the substantial in- 13
terest of teachers and administrators in maintaining discipline in the
classroom and on school grounds. Maintaining order in the classroom
has never been easy, but in recent years, school disorder has often
taken particularly ugly forms; drug use and violent crime in the schools
have become major social problems. Accordingly, we have recognized
that maintaining security and order in the schools requires a certain
degree of flexibility in school disciplinary procedures, and we have

respected the value of preserving the informality of the student-teacher relationship.

How, then, should we strike the balance between the school-   14
child's legitimate expectations of privacy and the school's equally legitimate need to maintain an environment in which learning can take place? It is evident that the school setting requires some easing of the restrictions to which searches by public authorities are ordinarily subject. The warrant requirement, in particular, is unsuited to the school environment; requiring a teacher to obtain a warrant before searching a child suspected of an infraction of school rules (or of the criminal law) would unduly interfere with the maintenance of the swift and informal disciplinary procedures needed in the schools. We hold today that school officials need not obtain a warrant before searching a student who is under their authority.

The school setting also requires some modification of the level of   15
suspicion of illicit activity needed to justify a search. Ordinarily, a search—even one that may permissibly be carried out without a warrant—must be based upon "probable cause" to believe that a violation of the law has occurred. However, "probable cause" is not an irreducible requirement of a valid search.

[Balancing of Interests]

The fundamental command of the Fourth Amendment is that searches   16
and seizures be reasonable, and although "both the concept of probable cause and the requirement of a warrant bear on the reasonableness of a search, . . . in certain limited circumstances neither is required." Thus, we have in a number of cases recognized the legality of searches and seizures based on suspicions that, although "reasonable," do not rise to the level of probable cause. Where a careful balancing of governmental and private interests suggests that the public interest is best served by a Fourth Amendment standard of reasonableness that stops short of probable cause, we have not hesitated to adopt such a standard.

We join the majority of courts that have examined this issue in   17
concluding that the accommodation of the privacy interests of school-children with the substantial need of teachers and administrators for freedom to maintain order in the schools does not require strict adherence to the requirement that searches be based on probable cause

to believe that the subject of the search has violated or is violating the law.

Rather, the legality of a search of a student should depend simply   18
on the reasonableness, under all the circumstances, of the search. Determining the reasonableness of any search involves a twofold inquiry; first, one must consider "whether the . . . action was justified at its inception," second, one must determine whether the search as actually conducted "was reasonably related in scope to the circumstances which justified the interference in the first place."

Under ordinary circumstances, a search of a student by a teacher   19
or other school official will be "justified at its inception" when there are reasonable grounds for suspecting that the search will turn up evidence that the student has violated or is violating either the law or the rules of the school. Such a search will be permissible in its scope when the measures adopted are reasonably related to the objectives of the search and not excessively intrusive in light of the age and sex of the student and the nature of the infraction.

This standard will, we trust, neither unduly burden the efforts of   20
school authorities to maintain order in their schools nor authorize unrestrained intrusions upon the privacy of schoolchildren. By focusing attention on the question of reasonableness, the standard will spare teachers and school administrators the necessity of schooling themselves in the niceties of probable cause and permit them to regulate their conduct according to the dictates of reason and common sense. At the same time, the reasonableness standard should insure that the interests of students will be invaded no more than is necessary to achieve the legitimate end of preserving order in the schools.

There remains the question of the legality of the search in this   21
case. We recognize that the "reasonable grounds" standard applied by the New Jersey Supreme Court in its consideration of this question is not substantially different from the standard that we have adopted today. Nonetheless, we believe that the New Jersey court's application of that standard to strike down the search of T.L.O.'s purse reflects a somewhat crabbed notion of reasonableness. Our review of the facts surrounding the search leads us to conclude that the search was in no sense unreasonable for Fourth Amendment purposes. [End of majority opinion][1]

----

[1] Questions on this selection appear on pages 550–552.

John Paul Stevens

Dissent in the Case of
New Jersey v. *T.L.O.*

The majority holds that "a search of a student by a teacher 1
or other school official will be 'justified at its inception' when there are
reasonable grounds for suspecting that the search will turn up evidence
*that the student has violated or is violating either the law or the rules of the
school."*

This standard will permit teachers and school administrators to 2
search students when they suspect that the search will reveal evidence
of [violation of] even the most trivial school regulation or precatory
guideline for students' behavior. For the Court, a search for curlers
and sunglasses in order to enforce the school dress code is apparently
just as important as a search for evidence of heroin addiction or violent
gang activity.

A standard better attuned to this concern would permit teachers 3
and school administrators to search a student when they have reason
to believe that the search will uncover *evidence that the student is violating
the law or engaging in conduct that is seriously disruptive of school order, or
the educational process.*

A standard that varies the extent of the permissible intrusion with 4
the gravity of the suspected offense is also more consistent with com-
mon-law experience and this Court's precedent. Criminal law has traditionally recognized a distinction between essentially regulatory offenses and serious violations of the peace, and graduated the response
of the criminal justice system depending on the character of the violation.

Questions

1. The Fourth Amendment specifies that a search may not be "unreasonable," and it indicates that authorities may obtain a search
   warrant only for "probable cause" that something illegal will be
   found. The Fourteenth Amendment extends this protection, saying
   (in part) that "No State shall make or enforce any law which shall
   abridge the privileges or immunities of citizens." (Parents are ex-

empted from these strictures, and school authorities have sometimes argued that they serve *in loco parentis,* but the Court has not
accepted this argument.) In a case decided in 1969, sixteen years
before the case we are looking at, Associate Justice Abe Fortas
stated for the majority of the Supreme Court that neither "students
[nor] teachers shed their constitutional rights at the schoolhouse
gate." But in *New Jersey* v. *T.L.O.* the Court says that any public
school student may be searched by school officials, without a warrant, merely because there are "reasonable grounds for suspecting
that the search will turn up evidence that the student has violated
or is violating either the law or the rules of the school." Remember,
in this case the student was searched not because she was suspected of possessing marijuana—a crime—but merely because she
was suspected of violating a school rule by smoking a cigarette. A
related point: Even if a student is suspected of violating a school
prohibition against smoking, does such a suspicion justify searching her purse for cigarettes? After all, a student might bring in her
purse cigarettes which she will smoke on her way home from school
rather than in school. Moreover, the discovery of cigarettes in T. L.
O.'s purse could scarcely be taken as proof that she had indeed
been smoking in the lavatory. It could not even be taken as proof
that she lied when she said she was a nonsmoker.

   In the majority opinion Justice White says that it is "evident
that the school setting requires some easing of the restrictions to
which searches by public authorities are ordinarily subject." Does
White offer evidence supporting what he says is "evident"? List the
evidence, if you can find it in White, or if you can think of any. Does
this evidence seem to you to be sufficiently compelling to refute
Fortas's view?

2. Let's admit that maintaining order in schools may be extremely dif-
    ficult. In your opinion does the difficulty justify diminishing the
    rights of citizens? Smoking is not an illegal activity, yet in this in-
    stance a student suspected of smoking—that is, merely of violating
    a school rule—was searched. A student reasonably suspected of
    concealing a gun in her purse might conceivably be searched on
    the grounds that she posed a danger to the school, but can it be
    held that T. L. O.'s alleged infraction of a school rule posed a serious
    danger to the school? Admittedly there were strong reasons for
    thinking she had been smoking and thus violating the school's rule,
    but does the maintenance of school discipline in such a matter
    justify a search?

3. Could a search undertaken on the principle enunciated by the
    Court's majority mean that whenever authorities perceive what they
    choose to call "disorder"—perhaps in the activity of an assembly

of protesters in the streets of a big city—they may justify unlawful searches and seizures?

4. Some forty years before this case, Justice Robert H. Jackson argued that the schools have a special responsibility for adhering to the Constitution: "That they are educating the young for citizenship is reason for scrupulous protection of constitutional freedoms of the individual, if we are not to strangle the free mind at its source and teach youth to discount important principles of our government as mere platitudes." Similarly, in 1967 in an analogous case involving another female pupil, Justice Brennan argued that "The lesson the school authorities taught her that day will undoubtedly make a greater impression than the one her teacher had hoped to convey. . . . Schools cannot expect their students to learn the lessons of good citizenship when the school authorities themselves disregard the fundamental principles underpinning our constitutional freedoms." Do you find these arguments compelling? Why, or why not?

Edward I. Koch

Death and Justice: How Capital Punishment Affirms Life

Last December a man named Robert Lee Willie, who had   1 been convicted of raping and murdering an 18-year-old woman, was executed in the Louisiana state prison. In a statement issued several minutes before his death, Mr. Willie said: "Killing people is wrong. . . . It makes no difference whether it's citizens, countries, or governments. Killing is wrong." Two weeks later in South Carolina, an admitted killer named Joseph Carl Shaw was put to death for mur-

Edward I. Koch, born in 1924 in New York City, was educated at City College and at New York University Law School. Active in Democratic politics, Mr. Koch has served as mayor of New York.

dering two teenagers. In an appeal to the governor for clemency, Mr. Shaw wrote: "Killing is wrong when I did it. Killing is wrong when you do it. I hope you have the courage and moral strength to stop the killing."

It is a curiosity of modern life that we find ourselves being lectured 2 on morality by cold-blooded killers. Mr. Willie previously had been convicted of aggravated rape, aggravated kidnapping, and the murders of a Louisiana deputy and a man from Missouri. Mr. Shaw committed another murder a week before the two for which he was executed, and admitted mutilating the body of the 14-year-old girl he killed. I can't help wondering what prompted these murderers to speak out against killing as they entered the death-house door. Did their newfound reverence for life stem from the realization that they were about to lose their own?

Life is indeed precious, and I believe the death penalty helps to 3 affirm this fact. Had the death penalty been a real possibility in the minds of these murderers, they might well have stayed their hand. They might have shown moral awareness before their victims died, and not after. Consider the tragic death of Rosa Velez, who happened to be home when a man named Luis Vera burglarized her apartment in Brooklyn. "Yeah, I shot her," Vera admitted. "She knew me, and I knew I wouldn't go to the chair."

During my 22 years in public service, I have heard the pros and 4 cons of capital punishment expressed with special intensity. As a district leader, councilman, congressman, and mayor, I have represented constituencies generally thought of as liberal. Because I support the death penalty for heinous crimes of murder, I have sometimes been the subject of emotional and outraged attacks by voters who find my position reprehensible or worse. I have listened to their ideas. I have weighed their objections carefully. I still support the death penalty. The reasons I maintain my position can be best understood by examining the arguments most frequently heard in opposition.

1. *The death penalty is "barbaric."* Sometimes opponents of capital 5 punishment horrify with tales of lingering death on the gallows, of faulty electric chairs, or of agony in the gas chamber. Partly in response to such protests, several states such as North Carolina and Texas switched to execution by lethal injection. The condemned person is put to death painlessly, without ropes, voltage, bullets, or gas. Did this answer the objections of death penalty opponents? Of course not. On June 22, 1984, *The New York Times* published an editorial that sarcastically attacked the new "hygienic" method of death by injection,

and stated that "execution can never be made humane through science." So it's not the method that really troubles opponents. It's the death itself they consider barbaric.

Admittedly, capital punishment is not a pleasant topic. However, 6 one does not have to like the death penalty in order to support it any more than one must like radical surgery, radiation, or chemotherapy in order to find necessary these attempts at curing cancer. Ultimately we may learn how to cure cancer with a simple pill. Unfortunately, that day has not yet arrived. Today we are faced with the choice of letting the cancer spread or trying to cure it with the methods available, methods that one day will almost certainly be considered barbaric. But to give up and do nothing would be far more barbaric and would certainly delay the discovery of an eventual cure. The analogy between cancer and murder is imperfect, because murder is not the "disease" we are trying to cure. The disease is injustice. We may not like the death penalty, but it must be available to punish crimes of cold-blooded murder, cases in which any other form of punishment would be inadequate and, therefore, unjust. If we create a society in which injustice is not tolerated, incidents of murder—the most flagrant form of injustice—will diminish.

2. *No other major democracy uses the death penalty.* No other major 7 democracy—in fact, few other countries of any description—are plagued by a murder rate such as that in the United States. Fewer and fewer Americans can remember the days when unlocked doors were the norm and murder was a rare and terrible offense. In America the murder rate climbed 122 percent between 1963 and 1980. During that same period, the murder rate in New York City increased by almost 400 percent, and the statistics are even worse in many other cities. A study at M.I.T. showed that based on 1970 homicide rates a person who lived in a large American city ran a greater risk of being murdered than an American soldier in World War II ran of being killed in combat. It is not surprising that the laws of each country differ according to differing conditions and traditions. If other countries had our murder problem, the cry for capital punishment would be just as loud as it is here. And I daresay that any other major democracy where 75 percent of the people supported the death penalty would soon enact it into law.

3. *An innocent person might be executed by mistake.* Consider the work 8 of Hugo Adam Bedau, one of the most implacable foes of capital punishment in this country. According to Mr. Bedau, it is "false senti-

mentality to argue that the death penalty should be abolished because of the abstract possibility that an innocent person might be executed." He cites a study of the 7,000 executions in this country from 1893 to 1971, and concludes that the record fails to show that such cases occur. The main point, however, is this. If government functioned only when the possibility of error didn't exist, government wouldn't function at all. Human life deserves special protection, and one of the best ways to guarantee that protection is to assure that convicted murderers do not kill again. Only the death penalty can accomplish this end. In a recent case in New Jersey, a man named Richard Biegenwald was freed from prison after serving 18 years for murder; since his release he has been convicted of committing four murders. A prisoner named Lemuel Smith, who while serving four life sentences for murder (plus two life sentences for kidnapping and robbery) in New York's Green Haven Prison, lured a woman corrections officer into the chaplain's office and strangled her. He then mutilated and dismembered her body. An additional life sentence for Smith is meaningless. Because New York has no death penalty statute, Smith has effectively been given a license to kill.

But the problem of multiple murder is not confined to the nation's   9
penitentiaries. In 1981, 91 police officers were killed in the line of duty in this country. Seven percent of those arrested in the cases that have been solved had a previous arrest for murder. In New York City in 1976 and 1977, 85 persons arrested for homicide had a previous arrest for murder. Six of these individuals had two previous arrests for murder, and one had four previous murder arrests. During those two years the New York police were arresting for murder persons with a previous arrest for murder on the average of one every 8.5 days. This is not surprising when we learn that in 1975, for example, the median time served in Massachusetts for homicide was less than two-and-a-half years. In 1976 a study sponsored by the Twentieth Century Fund found that the average time served in the United States for first-degree murder is ten years. The median time served may be considerably lower.

4. *Capital punishment cheapens the value of human life.* On the con-   10
trary, it can be easily demonstrated that the death penalty strengthens the value of human life. If the penalty for rape were lowered, clearly it would signal a lessened regard for the victims' suffering, humiliation, and personal integrity. It would cheapen their horrible experience, and expose them to an increased danger of recurrence. When we lower the penalty for murder, it signals a lessened regard for the value of the

victim's life. Some critics of capital punishment, such as columnist Jimmy Breslin, have suggested that a life sentence is actually a harsher penalty for murder than death. This is sophistic nonsense. A few killers may decide not to appeal a death sentence, but the overwhelming majority make every effort to stay alive. It is by exacting the highest penalty for the taking of human life that we affirm the highest value of human life.

5. *The death penalty is applied in a discriminatory manner.* This factor   11
no longer seems to be the problem it once was. The appeals process for a condemned prisoner is lengthy and painstaking. Every effort is made to see that the verdict and sentence were fairly arrived at. However, assertions of discrimination are not an argument for ending the death penalty but for extending it. It is not justice to exclude everyone from the penalty of the law if a few are found to be so favored. Justice requires that the law be applied equally to all.

6. *Thou Shalt Not Kill.* The Bible is our greatest source of moral   12
inspiration. Opponents of the death penalty frequently cite the sixth of the Ten Commandments in an attempt to prove that capital punishment is divinely proscribed. In the original Hebrew, however, the Sixth Commandment reads, "Thou Shalt Not Commit Murder," and the Torah specifies capital punishment for a variety of offenses. The biblical viewpoint has been upheld by philosophers throughout history. The greatest thinkers of the 19th century—Kant, Locke, Hobbes, Rousseau, Montesquieu, and Mill—agreed that natural law properly authorizes the sovereign to take life in order to vindicate justice. Only Jeremy Bentham was ambivalent. Washington, Jefferson, and Franklin endorsed it. Abraham Lincoln authorized executions for deserters in wartime. Alexis de Tocqueville, who expressed profound respect for American institutions, believed that the death penalty was indispensable to the support of social order. The United States Constitution, widely admired as one of the seminal achievements in the history of humanity, condemns cruel and inhuman punishment, but does not condemn capital punishment.

7. *The death penalty is state-sanctioned murder.* This is the defense   13
with which Messrs. Willie and Shaw hoped to soften the resolve of those who sentenced them to death. By saying in effect, "You're no better than I am," the murderer seeks to bring his accusers down to his own level. It is also a popular argument among opponents of capital punishment, but a transparently false one. Simply put, the state has rights that the private individual does not. In a democracy, those rights are given to the state by the electorate. The execution of a lawfully

condemned killer is no more an act of murder than is legal imprisonment an act of kidnapping. If an individual forces a neighbor to pay him money under threat of punishment, it's called extortion. If the state does it, it's called taxation. Rights and responsibilities surrendered by the individual are what give the state its power to govern. This contract is the foundation of civilization itself.

Everyone wants his or her rights, and will defend them jealously.   14
Not everyone, however, wants responsibilities, especially the painful responsibilities that come with law enforcement. Twenty-one years ago a woman named Kitty Genovese was assaulted and murdered on a street in New York. Dozens of neighbors heard her cries for help but did nothing to assist her. They didn't even call the police. In such a climate the criminal understandably grows bolder. In the presence of moral cowardice, he lectures us on our supposed failings and tries to equate his crimes with our quest for justice.

The death of anyone—even a convicted killer—diminishes us all.   15
But we are diminished even more by a justice system that fails to function. It is an illusion to let ourselves believe that doing away with capital punishment removes the murderer's deed from our conscience. The rights of society are paramount. When we protect guilty lives, we give up innocent lives in exchange. When opponents of capital punishment say to the state: "I will not let you kill in my name," they are also saying to murderers: "You can kill in your *own* name as long as I have an excuse for not getting involved."

It is hard to imagine anything worse than being murdered while   16
neighbors do nothing. But something worse exists. When those same neighbors shrink back from justly punishing the murderer, the victim dies twice.

Questions

1. Koch is, of course, writing an argument. He wants to persuade his readers. Beginning with paragraph 5, he states the opposition's arguments and tries to refute them. But why did he include his first four paragraphs? What, as persuasion, does each contribute?

2. In paragraph 6, Koch compares our use of capital punishment to our use of "radical surgery, radiation, or chemotherapy." Do you find this analogy impressive—or not—and why? (Note that in this paragraph Koch goes on to say that "the analogy between cancer and murder is imperfect." Should he, then, not have used it?)

3. At the end of paragraph 6, Koch says: "If we create a society in which injustice is not tolerated, incidents of murder—the most flagrant form of injustice—will diminish." Has the earlier part of the paragraph prepared us for this statement?
4. Why, or why not, are you persuaded by Koch's second argument, about the likelihood that if other countries had high rates of murder they too would enact the death penalty?
5. In paragraph 9, Koch speaks of "murder" and then of "homicide." Are these two the same? If not, *why* is Koch bringing in statistics about homicide?
6. In paragraph 12, Koch lists authorities who supported the death penalty. Some of these, for instance Washington and Jefferson, also supported slavery. What can be said in behalf of, and what can be said against, Koch's use of these authorities?
7. In paragraph 15, Koch puts a sentence into the mouths of his opponents. *Is* this what his opponents are in effect saying or thinking?
8. If you have read Schwarzschild's remarks opposing capital punishment, below, write an essay indicating which essay you think is a better piece of persuasive writing. Note that it is not a matter of which position you subscribe to; in your essay you are concerned only with the essays as examples of persuasive writing.

Henry Schwarzschild

In Opposition to Death Penalty Legislation

You know the classic arguments about the merits of the   1
death penalty:

Its dubious and unproved value as a deterrent to violent crime;
The arbitrariness and mistakes inevitable in any system of justice instituted and administered by fallible human beings;

Henry Schwarzschild is the director of the National Coalition Against the Death Penalty. The material that we print is an excerpt from his statement submitted at the hearing in 1978 before the Subcommittee on Criminal Justice of the Committee on the Judiciary, House of Representatives, 95th Congress, 2nd Session.

The persistent and ineradicable discrimination on grounds of race, class, and sex in its administration in our country's history (including the present time);

The degrading and hurtful impulse toward retribution and revenge that it expresses;

The barbarousness of its process (whether by burning at the stake, by hanging from the gallows, by frying in the electric chair, by suffocating in the gas chamber, by shooting at the hands of a firing squad, or by lethal injection with a technology designed to heal and save lives);

Even the deeply distorting and costly effect the death penalty has upon the administration of the courts, upon law enforcement, and upon the penal institutions of the country.

Let me therefore concentrate my remarks upon a few selected issues about which much unclarity exists in the public mind, in the media, and even in many legislative chambers. 2

I want to discuss these issues in the context of the evident support of public opinion for the reintroduction of capital punishment in the country. Let me be candid: For the past few years, public opinion polls, whether national or regional, have tended to reflect a substantial majority of the American people affirming their support for the death penalty, to the level of between 65 percent and 75 percent—enough to make many an elected official surrender his or her religious or moral principles against capital punishment. As little as twenty years ago, the polls reflected almost precisely the opposite distribution of views in the country. It is not hard to infer what has turned the American people back toward support of so atavistic and demonstrably useless a criminal sanction. The causes are (a) the rising rate of violent crime in the past two decades, (b) the increasing panic about the rising crime rate, together with a justified (as well as exaggerated) fear for the safety of lives and property, (c) the understandable reaction to a terrible series of assassinations and attempted assassinations of our national leaders and other prominent personalities (President John Kennedy, Senator Robert Kennedy, the Rev. Dr. Martin Luther King Jr., Governor George Wallace, Malcolm X, Medgar Evers, and others), (d) the rise of international terrorism, including aircraft hijackings and the murder of prominent political and business leaders as well as the random political killings of innocent victims, (e) many years of the effective discontinuation of capital punishment and the remoteness from actual experience of its horrors, and finally (f) a largely subliminal but some- 3 times almost articulated racism that attributes most violent criminality to the minority community, that knows quite well that the poor and the black are most often the subjects of the death penalty, and that thinks that's just the way it ought to be.

What, then, are the rational answers to this series of partly un-　4 derstandable and partly impermissible misconceptions in the American public?

True, violent crime has risen sharply in the past two decades, but　5 to begin with it has been abundantly demonstrated by social research that the availability of the death penalty has no effect whatsoever upon the rate of violent crime; to the contrary, there is some scientific evidence that death sentences imposed and carried out may, for peculiar reasons of social and psychic pathology, be an incentive to further acts of violence in the society. Furthermore, while the rates of most major, violent felonies have been rising—most probably by reason of increased urbanization, social mobility, economic distress, and the like— the rate of non-negligent homicide has been rising at a rate *slower* than the other major felonies, and non-negligent homicide is, of course, the only crime for which the death penalty has been declared constitutionally permissible by the Supreme Court. The crisis in violent crime, such as it is, has therefore been least acute in the area of homicide. Indeed, in the past three years, the murder rate in this country has actually been declining. Thirdly, there is an appalling number of about 20,000 non-negligent homicides in this country per year. But we would have to return to the condition of the mid-1950s to execute as many as one hundred persons per year, and even that would constitute only one in every two hundred murderers. In other words, we have always picked quite arbitrarily a tiny handful of people among those convicted of murder to be executed, not those who have committed the most heinous, the most revolting, the most destructive murders, but always the poor, the black, the friendless, the life's losers, those without competent, private attorneys, the illiterate, those despised or ignored by the community for reasons having nothing to do with their crime. Ninety-nine and one-half percent of all murderers were never executed—and the deterrent value (which very likely does not exist at all in any case) is reduced to invisibility by the overwhelming likelihood that one will not be caught, or not be prosecuted, or not be tried on a capital charge, or not be convicted, or not be sentenced to death, or have the conviction or sentence reversed on appeal, or have one's sentence commuted.

And if we took the other course and eliminated those high chances　6 of not being executed, but rather carried out the death penalty for every murder, then we should be executing 400 persons per week, every week of the month, every month of the year—and that, Mr. Chairman, should strike even the most ardent supporters of the death penalty as a bloodbath, not as a civilized system of criminal justice.

Assassinations and terrorism are well known to be undeterrable 7 by the threat of the death penalty. They are acts of political desperation or political insanity, always committed by people who are at least willing, if not eager, to be martyrs to their cause. Nor would executing terrorists be a preventive against the subsequent taking of hostages for the purpose of setting political assassins or terrorists free. There would of course be a considerable interval of time between arrest and execution, at least for the purpose of trial and the accompanying processes of law, and during that time their fellow activists would have a far more urgent incentive for taking hostages, since not only the freedom but the very lives of their arrested and sentenced colleagues would be at stake. Let me only respectfully add that distinguished fellow citizens of ours such as Senator Edward Kennedy and Ms. Coretta King, who have suffered terrible sadness in their lives at the hands of assassins, are committed opponents of the death penalty.

There has been only one execution in the United States since 1967, 8 that of Gary Mark Gilmore, by a volunteer firing squad in Utah on January 17, 1977. Gilmore's execution troubled the public conscience less than it might have otherwise because of his own determination to die. The public and perhaps the legislators of our states and in the Congress have forgotten in a decade that was virtually without executions what sort of demoralizing and brutalizing spectacle executions are. There are now enough people on death row in the country to stage one execution each and every single day for more than a year, to say nothing of the other people who are liable to be sentenced to death during that time. We will again know the details of men crazed with fear, screaming like wounded animals, being dragged from the cell, against their desperate resistance, strapped into the electric chair, voiding their bowels and bladder, being burned alive, almost breaking the restraints from the impact of the high voltage, with their eyeballs popping out of their sockets, the smell of their burning flesh in the nostrils of the witnesses. The ghastly experience of men being hanged, their heads half torn off their bodies, or of the slow strangulation in the gas chamber, or of the press sticking their fingers into the bloody bullet holes of the chair in which Gilmore sat to be executed by rifles, or the use of forcible injection by a paralyzing agent—these reports will not ennoble the image of the United States of America that wants to be the defender of human rights and decency in a world that has largely given up the death penalty as archaic.

No one in this Committee surely is guilty of that shoddiest of all 9 impulses toward capital punishment, namely the sense that white, middle-class people, irrespective of their crime, in fact hardly ever get sentenced to death and in such an extremely rare case are virtually never executed. You, Mr. Chairman and Members, and I and probably everyone in this hearing room are in fact absolutely immune, no matter what ghastly crime we might commit, from the likelihood of being executed for it. The penalty of death is imposed almost entirely upon members of what the distinguished social psychologist Kenneth B. Clark has referred to as "the lower status elements of American society."

Blacks have always constituted a dramatically disproportionate 10 number of persons executed in the United States, far beyond their share of capital crimes, and even as we sit here today they represent half of the more than 500 persons on the death rows of our state pris-ons. Indeed, not only the race of the criminal is directly proportional to the likelihood of his being sentenced to death and executed but the race of the victim of the crime as well. The large majority of criminal homicides are still disasters between people who have some previous connection with each other (as husband and wife, parent and child, lovers, business associates, and the like), and murder is therefore still largely an intra-racial event, i.e. black on black or white on white. Yet while half the people under sentence of death right now are black (showing egregious discrimination on the grounds of the race of the murderer), about 85 percent of their victims were white.

In other words, it is far more likely to get the murderer into the 11 electric chair or the gas chamber if he has killed a white person than if he had killed a black person, quite irrespective of his own race. (I say "he" in this context for good reason: the death penalty is also highly discriminatory on grounds of sex. Of the 380 death-row inmates in the country today, only two are women, and even they are far more likely objects of executive commutation of their death sentences than their male counterparts.)

Let me add here that, to the extent to which fear of crime and 12 greater exposure to it, combined with inadequate police protection and more callous jurisprudence, has made the minority communities also voice increasing support for the death penalty, they have not yet fully realized that the death penalty will not protect them from what they (and all of us) rightly fear but that their support of capital punishment will only put their brothers and husbands and sons in jeopardy of being killed by the same state that has been unable properly to protect their lives, their rights, or their property to begin with.

In sum: The public is deeply uninformed about the real social facts   13
of the death penalty and is responding to the seemingly insoluble problem of crime by a retreat to the hope that an even more severe criminal penalty will stem the tide of violence. But it will not. We do not know what will. Judges and lawyers do not know, philosophers and criminologists don't, not even civil libertarians or legislators know the answer—if any of us did, we would have long since accomplished our purpose of reducing crime to the irreducible minimum. But legislators are not therefore entitled to suborn illusory solutions merely because they would garner widespread though uninformed public approval, in order to signal to the electorate that they are "tough on crime." Capital punishment does not deal with crime in any useful fashion and in fact deludes the public into an entirely false sense of greater security about that complex social problem. The death penalty is a legislative way of avoiding rather than dealing with the problem of crime, and the American public will come to learn this very dramatically and tragically if the Congress should unwisely enact the bill before you today.

Two final words about public support for the death penalty.   14

There are strong indications that the public in great numbers an-   15
swers in the affirmative when asked whether they support capital punishment because they want a death penalty law on the books in the hope that this threat will deter criminals from committing violent crimes. Many, perhaps most, of the people who support the enactment of the death penalty do not want executions and would be horrified at being asked to sentence a living human being to a premeditated, ceremonial, legally sanctioned killing. They want deterrence, not electrocutions; prevention, not lethal injections; safety, not firing squads. But a re-enactment by this Congress of a federal death penalty statute will give them at best only electrocutions or lethal injections or firing squads, but neither deterrence nor crime prevention nor safety from violence.

The last stand of supporters for the death penalty, when all the   16
other arguments have been rebutted or met, is that of retribution or revenge, the proposition that a murderer has forfeited his life and that we should kill him as an act of abstract equity, irrespective of whether executions serve any social purpose whatsoever. We do not need to

preach to each other here this morning, but it is important to have it said once more that civilized societies have instituted systems of justice precisely in order to overcome private acts of retribution and revenge and that they have done so with the understanding that social necessity and social usefulness will be the guideposts of their punishments. Since there has never been and cannot be a showing of social useful-ness or social necessity for capital punishment, the virtually unani-mous voices of the religious community of our land, our leading think-ers and social analysts, in unison with enlightened opinion for hundreds, perhaps thousands, of years should guide your actions on this matter. Whatever the understandable, bitter, vengeful impulses might be of any of us who suffer the disastrous tragedy of having someone we love or respect murdered by pathological or cruel killers, the society's laws are written not to gratify those impulses but to chan-nel them into helpful, healing, and life-sustaining directions. Gratify-ing the impulse for revenge is not the business of a government that espouses the humane and liberating ideas expressed in our Declaration of Independence and Constitution. It would be rather a return to the darkest instincts of mankind. It would be arrogating unto the state, unto government, either the god-like wisdom to judge who shall live and who shall die or else the totalitarian arrogance to make that judg-ment. We, as a nation, have foresworn that idolatry of the state that would justify either of these grounds for the legally sanctioned killing of our fellow citizens, of any human being, except perhaps in personal or national self-defense.

Mr. Chairman: The question before the country and before the [17] Congress ultimately is whether it is the right of the state, with pre-meditation, with the long foreknowledge of the victim, under color of law, in the name of all of us, with great ceremony, and to the approval of many angry people in our land, to kill a fellow citizen, a fellow human being, to do that which we utterly condemn, which we utterly abhor in him for having done. What does the penalty, after all, say to the American people and to our children? That killing is all right if the right people do it and think they have a good enough reason for doing it! That is the rationale of every pathological murderer walking the street: he thinks he is the right person to do it and has a good reason for doing his destructive deed. How can a thoughtful and sensible person justify killing people who kill people to teach that killing is wrong? How can you avert your eyes from the obvious: that the death penalty and that executions in all their bloody and terrible reality only aggravate the deplorable atmosphere of violence, the disrespect for life, and brutalization of ourselves that we need to overcome?

If the death penalty were shown, or even could be shown, to be 18 socially necessary or even useful, I would personally still have a deep objection to it. But those who argue for its re-enactment have not and cannot meet the burden of proving its necessity or usefulness. At the very least, before you kill a human being under law, do you not have to be absolutely certain that you are doing the right thing? But how can you be sure that the criminal justice system has worked with absolute accuracy in designating this single person to be the guilty one, that this single person is the one that should be killed, that killing him is the absolutely right thing to do? You cannot be sure, because human judgment and human institutions are demonstrably fallible. And you cannot kill a man when you are not absolutely sure. You can (indeed sometimes you must) make sure that he is incapacitated from repeating his crime, and we obviously accomplish that by ways other than killing him. And while there is fallibility there also, death is different: it is final, irreversible, barbarous, brutalizing to all who come into contact with it. That it is a very hurtful model for the United States to play in the world, it is a very hurtful model for a democratic and free government to play for its people.

Questions

1. In the first paragraph, what is Schwarzschild getting at when he says that administration of the death penalty has been discriminatory?

2. In paragraph 5 Schwarzschild points out that even when capital punishment was relatively common, "ninety-nine and one-half percent of all murderers were never executed." Assuming the truth of this statement, is it inherently unjust to execute the remaining half of one percent? Would it be adequate to reply thus, by way of analogy: Most of the people who steal are not caught, but those who *are* caught should be punished; the law cannot excuse known wrongdoers simply on the ground that other wrongdoers escape undetected?

3. In paragraph 8, Schwarzschild briefly describes some of the horrible physical responses of persons about to be executed. If one believes that the death penalty serves a useful purpose as a deterrent, should one argue (against Schwarzschild) that executions ought to be televised, so that they would have a maximum effect as deterrents?

4. Can it be argued that in paragraph 16, Schwarzschild distorts an important point: Capital punishment partly satisfies society's sense

of justice; that is, certain crimes are so outrageous that a moral society must exact capital punishment—for instance, to satisfy the legitimate outrage of the friends and family of the murderer's victim?

5. What is Schwarzschild's strategy in his next-to-last paragraph?
6. Evaluate Schwarzschild's final paragraph as a piece of persuasion.
7. If you have read Koch's essay (page 552) supporting the death penalty, indicate which of Koch's arguments, if any, Schwarzschild does not face.

Stephen Chapman

The Prisoner's Dilemma

If the punitive laws of Islam were applied for only one year, all the devastating injustices would be uprooted. Misdeeds must be punished by the law of retaliation: cut off the hands of the thief; kill the murderers; flog the adulterous woman or man. Your concerns, your "humanitarian" scruples are more childish than reasonable. Under the terms of Koranic law, any judge fulfilling the seven requirements (that he have reached puberty, be a believer, know the Koranic laws perfectly, be just, and not be affected by amnesia, or be a bastard, or be of the female sex) is qualified to be a judge in any type of case. He can thus judge and dispose of twenty trials in a single day, whereas the Occidental justice might take years to argue them out.

From *Sayings of the Ayatollah Khomeini* (Bantam Books)

One of the amusements of life in the modern West is the opportunity to observe the barbaric rituals of countries that are attached to the customs of the dark ages. Take Pakistan, for example, our newest ally and client state in Asia. Last October President Zia, in harmony with the Islamic fervor that is sweeping his part of the world, revived the traditional Moslem practice of flogging lawbreakers in public. In Pak- 1

Stephen Chapman was on the staff of *New Republic*, where this essay was first published.

istan, this qualified as mass entertainment, and no fewer than 10,000 law-abiding Pakistanis turned out to see justice done to 26 convicts. To Western sensibilities the spectacle seemed barbaric—both in the sense of cruel and in the sense of pre-civilized. In keeping with Islamic custom each of the unfortunates—who had been caught in prostitution raids the previous night and summarily convicted and sentenced— was stripped down to a pair of white shorts, which were painted with a red stripe across the buttocks (the target). Then he was shackled against an easel, with pads thoughtfully placed over the kidneys to prevent injury. The floggers were muscular, fierce-looking sorts—con-victed murderers, as it happens—who paraded around the flogging platform in colorful loincloths. When the time for the ceremony began, one of the floggers took a running start and brought a five-foot stave down across the first victim's buttocks, eliciting screams from the con-vict and murmurs from the audience. Each of the 26 received from five to 15 lashes. One had to be carried from the stage unconscious.

Flogging is one of the punishments stipulated by Koranic law, which has made it a popular penological device in several Moslem countries, including Pakistan, Saudi Arabia, and, most recently, the ayatollah's Iran. Flogging, or *ta'zir*, is the general punishment pre-scribed for offenses that don't carry an explicit Koranic penalty. Some crimes carry automatic *hadd* punishment—stoning or scourging (a se-vere whipping) for illicit sex, scourging for drinking alcoholic bever-ages, amputation of the hands for theft. Other crimes—as varied as murder and abandoning Islam—carry the death penalty (usually car-ried out in public). Colorful practices like these have given the Islamic world an image in the West, as described by historian G. H. Jansen, "of blood dripping from the stumps of amputated hands and from the striped backs of malefactors, and piles of stones barely concealing the battered bodies of adulterous couples." Jansen, whose book *Militant Islam* is generally effusive in its praise of Islamic practices, grows squeamish when considering devices like flogging, amputation, and stoning. But they are given enthusiastic endorsement by the Koran itself.

Such traditions, we all must agree, are no sign of an advanced civilization. In the West, we have replaced these various punishments (including the death penalty in most cases) with a single device. Our custom is to confine criminals in prison for varying lengths of time. In Illinois, a reasonably typical state, grand theft carries a punishment of three to five years; armed robbery can get you from six to 30. The lowest form of felony theft is punishable by one to three years in prison.

Most states impose longer sentences on habitual offenders. In Kentucky, for example, habitual offenders can be sentenced to life in prison. Other states are less brazen, preferring the more genteel sounding "indeterminate sentence," which allows parole boards to keep inmates locked up for as long as life. It was under an indeterminate sentence of one to 14 years that George Jackson served 12 years in California prisons for committing a $70 armed robbery. Under a Texas law imposing an automatic life sentence for a third felony conviction, a man was sent to jail for life last year because of three thefts adding up to less than $300 in property value. Texas also is famous for occasionally imposing extravagantly long sentences, often running into hundreds or thousands of years. This gives Texas a leg up on Maryland, which used to sentence some criminals to life plus a day—a distinctive if superfluous flourish.

The punishment *intended* by Western societies in sending their 4
criminals to prison is the loss of freedom. But, as everyone knows, the actual punishment in most American prisons is of a wholly different order. The February 2 riot at New Mexico's state prison in Santa Fe, one of several bloody prison riots in the nine years since the Attica bloodbath, once again dramatized the conditions of life in an American prison. Four hundred prisoners seized control of the prison before dawn. By sunset the next day 33 inmates had died at the hands of other convicts and another 40 people (including five guards) had been seriously hurt. Macabre stories came out of prisoners being hanged, murdered with blow-torches, decapitated, tortured, and mutilated in a variety of gruesome ways by drug-crazed rioters.

The Santa Fe penitentiary was typical of most maximum-security 5
facilities, with prisoners subject to overcrowding, filthy conditions, and routine violence. It also housed first-time, non-violent offenders, like check forgers and drug dealers, with murderers serving life sentences. In a recent lawsuit, the American Civil Liberties Union called the prison "totally unfit for human habitation." But the ACLU says New Mexico's penitentiary is far from the nation's worst.

That American prisons are a disgrace is taken for granted by ex- 6
perts of every ideological stripe. Conservative James Q. Wilson has criticized our "[c]rowded, antiquated prisons that require men and women to live in fear of one another and to suffer not only deprivation of liberty but a brutalizing regimen." Leftist Jessica Mitford has called our prisons "the ultimate expression of injustice and inhumanity." In 1973 a national commission concluded that "the American correctional

system today appears to offer minimum protection to the public and maximum harm to the offender." Federal courts have ruled that confinement in prisons in 16 different states violates the constitutional ban on "cruel and unusual punishment."

What are the advantages of being a convicted criminal in an advanced culture? First there is the overcrowding in prisons. One Tennessee prison, for example, has a capacity of 806, according to accepted space standards, but it houses 2300 inmates. One Louisiana facility has confined four and five prisoners in a single six-foot-by-six-foot cell. Then there is the disease caused by overcrowding, unsanitary conditions, and poor or inadequate medical care. A federal appeals court noted that the Tennessee prison had suffered frequent outbreaks of infectious diseases like hepatitis and tuberculosis. But the most distinctive element of American prison life is its constant violence. In his book *Criminal Violence, Criminal Justice,* Charles Silberman noted that in one Louisiana prison, there were 211 stabbings in only three years, 11 of them fatal. There were 15 slayings in a prison in Massachusetts between 1972 and 1975. According to a federal court, in Alabama's penitentiaries (as in many others), "robbery, rape, extortion, theft and assault are everyday occurrences." 7

At least in regard to cruelty, it's not at all clear that the system of punishment that has evolved in the West is less barbaric than the grotesque practices of Islam. Skeptical? Ask yourself: would you rather be subjected to a few minutes of intense pain and considerable public humiliation, or to be locked away for two or three years in a prison cell crowded with ill-tempered sociopaths? Would you rather lose a hand or spend 10 years or more in a typical state prison? I have taken my own survey on this matter. I have found no one who does not find the Islamic system hideous. And I have found no one who, given the choices mentioned above, would not prefer its penalties to our own. 8

The great divergence between Western and Islamic fashions in punishment is relatively recent. Until roughly the end of the 18th century, criminals in Western countries rarely were sent to prison. Instead they were subjected to an ingenious assortment of penalties. Many perpetrators of a variety of crimes simply were executed, usually by some imaginative and extremely unpleasant method involving prolonged torture, such as breaking on the wheel, burning at the stake, or drawing and quartering. Michel Foucault's book *Discipline and Punish: The Birth of the Prison* notes one form of capital punishment in which the condemned man's "belly was opened up, his entrails quickly ripped out, so that he had time to see them, with his own eyes, being 9 thrown on the fire; in which he was finally decapitated and his body quartered." Some criminals were forced to serve on slave galleys. But in most cases various corporal measures such as pillorying, flogging, and branding sufficed.

In time, however, public sentiment recoiled against these mea- 10
sures. They were replaced by imprisonment, which was thought to have two advantages. First, it was considered to be more humane. Second, and more important, prison was supposed to hold out the possibility of rehabilitation—purging the criminal of his criminality— something that less civilized punishments did not even aspire to. An 1854 report by inspectors of the Pennsylvania prison system illustrates the hopes nurtured by humanitarian reformers:

> Depraved tendencies, characteristic of the convict, have been re-
> strained by the absence of vicious association, and in the mild teaching
> of Christianity, the unhappy criminal finds a solace for an involuntary
> exile from the comforts of social life. If hungry, he is fed; if naked,
> he is clothed; if destitute of the first rudiments of education, he is
> taught to read and write; and if he has never been blessed with a
> means of livelihood, he is schooled in a mechanical art, which in after
> life may be to him the source of profit and respectability. Employment
> is not his toil nor labor, weariness. He embraces them with alacrity,
> as contributing to his moral and mental elevation.

Imprisonment is now the universal method of punishing criminals 11
in the United States. It is thought to perform five functions, each of which has been given a label by criminologists. First, there is simple *retribution:* punishing the lawbreaker to serve society's sense of justice and to satisfy the victims' desire for revenge. Second, there is *specific deterrence:* discouraging the offender from misbehaving in the future. Third, *general deterrence:* using the offender as an example to discourage others from turning to crime. Fourth, *prevention:* at least during the time he is kept off the streets, the criminal cannot victimize other members of society. Finally, and most important, there is *rehabilitation:* re-forming the criminal so that when he returns to society he will be inclined to obey the laws and able to make an honest living.

How satisfactorily do American prisons perform by these criteria? 12
Well, of course, they do punish. But on the other scores they don't do so well. Their effect in discouraging future criminality by the prisoner or others is the subject of much debate, but the soaring rates of the last 20 years suggest that prisons are not a dramatically effective de-terrent to criminal behavior. Prisons do isolate convicted criminals, but

only to divert crime from ordinary citizens to prison guards and fellow inmates. Almost no one contends anymore that prisons rehabilitate their inmates. If anything, they probably impede rehabilitation by forcing inmates into prolonged and almost exclusive association with other criminals. And prisons cost a lot of money. Housing a typical prisoner in a typical prison costs far more than a stint at a top university. This cost would be justified if prisons did the job they were intended for. But it is clear to all that prisons fail on the very grounds—humanity and hope of rehabilitation—that caused them to replace earlier, cheaper forms of punishment.

The universal acknowledgment that prisons do not rehabilitate   13 criminals has produced two responses. The first is to retain the hope of rehabilitation but do away with imprisonment as much as possible and replace it with various forms of "alternative treatment," such as psychotherapy, supervised probation, and vocational training. Psychiatrist Karl Menninger, one of the principal critics of American penology, has suggested even more unconventional approaches, such as "a new job opportunity or a vacation trip, a course of reducing exercises, a cosmetic surgical operation or a herniotomy, some night school courses, a wedding in the family (even one for the patient!), an inspiring sermon." This starry-eyed approach naturally has produced a backlash from critics on the right, who think that it's time to abandon the goal of rehabilitation. They argue that prisons perform an important service just by keeping criminals off the streets, and thus should be used with that purpose alone in mind.

So the debate continues to rage in all the same old ruts. No one,   14 of course, would think of copying the medieval practices of Islamic nations and experimenting with punishments such as flogging and amputation. But let us consider them anyway. How do they compare with our American prison system in achieving the ostensible objectives of punishment? First, do they punish? Obviously they do, and in a uniquely painful and memorable way. Of course any sensible person, given the choice, would prefer suffering these punishments to years of incarceration in a typical American prison. But presumably no Western penologist would criticize Islamic punishments on the grounds that they are not barbaric enough. Do they deter crime? Yes, and probably more effectively than sending convicts off to prison. Now we read about a prison sentence in the newspaper, then think no more about the criminal's payment for his crimes until, perhaps, years later we read a small item reporting his release. By contrast, one can easily imagine the vivid impression it would leave to be wandering through a local shopping center and to stumble onto the scene of some poor wretch being lustily flogged. And the occasional sight of an habitual offender walking around with a bloody stump at the end of his arm no doubt also would serve as a forceful reminder that crime does not pay.

Do flogging and amputation discourage recidivism? No one knows   15
whether the scars on his back would dissuade a criminal from risking another crime, but it is hard to imagine that corporal measures could stimulate a higher rate of recidivism than already exists. Islamic forms of punishment do not serve the favorite new right goal of simply iso-lating criminals from the rest of society, but they may achieve the same purpose of making further crimes impossible. In the movie *Bonnie and Clyde*, Warren Beatty successfully robs a bank with his arm in a sling, but this must be dismissed as artistic license. It must be extraordinarily difficult, at the very least, to perform much violent crime with only one hand.

Do these medieval forms of punishment rehabilitate the criminal?   16
Plainly not. But long prison terms do not rehabilitate either. And it is just as plain that typical Islamic punishments are no crueler to the convict than incarceration in the typical American state prison.

Of course there are other reasons besides its bizarre forms of pun-   17
ishment that the Islamic system of justice seems uncivilized to the Western mind. One is the absence of due process. Another is the long list of offenses—such as drinking, adultery, blasphemy, "profiteer-ing," and so on—that can bring on conviction and punishment. A third is all the ritualistic mumbo-jumbo in pronouncements of Islamic law (like that talk about puberty and amnesia in the ayatollah's quotation at the beginning of this article). Even in these matters, however, a little cultural modesty is called for. The vast majority of American criminals are convicted and sentenced as a result of plea bargaining, in which due process plays almost no role. It has been only half a century since a wave of religious fundamentalism stirred this country to outlaw the consumption of alcoholic beverages. Most states also still have laws imposing austere constraints on sexual conduct. Only two weeks ago the *Washington Post* reported that the FBI had spent two and a half years and untold amounts of money to break up a nationwide por-nography ring. Flogging the clients of prostitutes, as the Pakistanis did, does seem silly. But only a few months ago Mayor Koch of New York was proposing that clients caught in his own city have their names broadcast by radio stations. We are not so far advanced on such matters as we often like to think. Finally, my lawyer friends assure me that

the rules of jurisdiction for American courts contain plenty of petty requirements and bizarre distinctions that would sound silly enough to foreign ears.

Perhaps it sounds barbaric to talk of flogging and amputation, and 18 perhaps it is. But our system of punishment also is barbaric, and probably more so. Only cultural smugness about their system and willful ignorance about our own make it easy to regard the one as cruel and the other as civilized. We inflict our cruelties away from public view, while nations like Pakistan stage them in front of 10,000 onlookers. Their outrages are visible; ours are not. Most Americans can live their lives for years without having their peace of mind disturbed by the knowledge of what goes on in our prisons. To choose imprisonment over flogging and amputation is not to choose human kindness over cruelty, but merely to prefer that our cruelties be kept out of sight, and out of mind.

Public flogging and amputation may be more barbaric forms of 19 punishment than imprisonment, even if they are not more cruel. Society may pay a higher price for them, even if the particular criminal does not. Revulsion against officially sanctioned violence and infliction of pain derives from something deeply ingrained in the Western conscience, and clearly it is something admirable. Grotesque displays of the sort that occur in Islamic countries probably breed a greater tolerance for physical cruelty, for example, which prisons do not do precisely because they conceal their cruelties. In fact it is our admirable intolerance for calculated violence that makes it necessary for us to conceal what we have not been able to do away with. In a way this is a good thing, since it holds out the hope that we may eventually find a way to do away with it. But in another way it is a bad thing, since it permits us to congratulate ourselves on our civilized humanitarianism while violating its norms in this one area of our national life.

Questions

1. What is the effect of juxtaposing the epigraph (the quotation at the top of the essay) with the first paragraph? By the time we finish the first paragraph, do we feel confident that the Ayatollah has been put into his place? Having read the entire essay, how would you explain Chapman's strategy in beginning the way he begins?
2. Consider the two systems of punishment, and make a list of the pros and cons for each, drawing on Chapman's essay but adding any other points that you can think of.

3. Despite apparent disclaimers, implied for example by using the word "barbaric" when speaking of Islamic punishments, is Chapman in fact arguing that we adopt a system of punishment more or less similar to the Islamic system? If not, what *is* he arguing? What do you think is the chief message that he wishes to convey?

4. In paragraph 8, Chapman says that the persons whom he surveyed preferred the Islamic punishments to our own. Ask a dozen or so people to read Chapman's essay, at least up to this point, and find out their preferences. In 500 words report the result of your survey, including some effective quotations.

Joyce Carol Oates

How I Contemplated the World from the Detroit House of Correction and Began My Life Over Again

Notes *for an essay for an English class at Baldwin Country Day*   1
School; poking around in debris; disgust and curiosity; a revelation of the
meaning of life; a happy ending. . . .

I. Events

1. The girl (myself) is walking through Branden's, that excellent store.   2
Suburb of a large famous city that is a symbol for large famous Amer-

Joyce Carol Oates was born in 1938 in Millerport, New York. She won a scholarship to Syracuse University, from which she graduated (Phi Beta Kappa and valedictorian) in 1960. She went on to do graduate work in English, first at the University of Wisconsin and then at Rice University, but she withdrew from Rice in order to devote more time to writing. Her first collection of stories, *By the North Gate,* was published in 1963. Since then she has published steadily—stories, poems, essays, and some twenty novels.

ican cities. The event sneaks up on the girl, who believes she is herding it along with a small fixed smile, a girl of fifteen, innocently experienced. She dawdles in a certain style by a counter of costume jewelry. Rings, earrings, necklaces. Prices from $5 to $50, all within reach. All ugly. She eases over to the glove counter, where everything is ugly too. In her close-fitted coat with its black fur collar she contemplates the luxury of Branden's, which she has known for many years: its many mild pale lights, easy on the eye and the soul, its elaborate tinkly decorations, its women shoppers with their excellent shoes and coats and hairdos, all dawdling gracefully, in no hurry.

Who was ever in a hurry here?   3

2. The girl seated at home. A small library, paneled walls of oak.   4
Someone is talking to me. An earnest husky female voice drives itself against my ears, nervous, frightened, groping around my heart, saying, "If you wanted gloves why didn't you say so? Why didn't you ask for them?" That store, Branden's, is owned by Raymond Forrest who lives on DuMaurier Drive. We live on Sioux Drive. Raymond Forrest. A handsome man? An ugly man? A man of fifty or sixty, with gray hair, or a man of forty with earnest courteous eyes, a good golf game, who is Raymond Forrest, this man who is my salvation? Father has been talking to him. Father is not his physician; Dr. Berg is his physician. Father and Dr. Berg refer patients to each other. There is a connection. Mother plays bridge with. . . . On Mondays and Wednesdays our maid Billie works at. . . . The strings draw together in a cat's cradle, making a net to save you when you fall. . . .

3. *Harriet Arnold's*. A small shop, better than Branden's. Mother   5
in her black coat, I in my close-fitted blue coat. Shopping. Now look at this, isn't this cute, do you want this, why don't you want this, try this on, take this with you to the fitting room, take this also, what's wrong with you, what can I do for you, why are you so strange . . . ? "I wanted to steal but not to buy," I don't tell her. The girl droops along in her coat and gloves and leather boots, her eyes scan the horizon which is pastel pink and decorated like Branden's, tasteful walls and modern ceilings with graceful glimmering lights.

4. Weeks later, the girl at a bus-stop. Two o'clock in the afternoon, 6
a Tuesday, obviously she has walked out of school.

5. The girl stepping down from a bus. Afternoon, weather chang-   7
ing to colder. Detroit. Pavement and closed-up stores; grillwork over the windows of a pawnshop. What is a pawnshop, exactly?

II. Characters

1. The girl stands five feet five inches tall. An ordinary height. Baldwin   8
Country Day School draws them up to that height. She dreams along
the corridors and presses her face against the Thermoplex glass. No
frost or steam can ever form on that glass. A smudge of grease from
her forehead . . . could she be boiled down to grease? She wears her
hair loose and long and straight in suburban teenage style, 1968. Eyes
smudged with pencil, dark brown. Brown hair. Vague green eyes. A
pretty girl? An ugly girl? She sings to herself under her breath, idling
in the corridor, thinking of her many secrets (the thirty dollars she
once took from the purse of a friend's mother, just for fun, the basement window she smashed in her own house just for fun) and thinking
of her brother who is at Susquehanna Boys' Academy, an excellent
preparatory school in Maine, remembering him unclearly . . . he has
long manic hair and a squeaking voice and he looks like one of the
popular teenage singers of 1968, one of those in a group, *The Certain
Forces, The Way Out, The Maniacs Responsible.* The girl in her turn looks
like one of those fieldsful of girls who listen to the boys' singing,
dreaming and mooning restlessly, breaking into high sullen laughter,
innocently experienced.

2. The mother. A midwestern woman of Detroit and suburbs. Be-   9
longs to the Detroit Athletic Club. Also the Detroit Golf Club. Also
the Bloomfield Hills Country Club. The Village Women's Club at which
lectures are given each winter on Genet and Sartre and James Baldwin,
by the Director of the Adult Education Program at Wayne State University. . . . The Bloomfield Art Association. Also the Founders Society
of the Detroit Institute of Arts. Also. . . . Oh, she is in perpetual motion, this lady, hair like blown-up gold and finer than gold, hair and
fingers and body of inestimable grace. Heavy weighs the gold on the
back of her hairbrush and hand mirror. Heavy heavy the candlesticks
in the dining room. Very heavy is the big car, a Lincoln, long and
black, that on one cool autumn day split a squirrel's body in two unequal parts.

3. The father, Dr. _____. He belongs to the same club as #2. A   10
player of squash and golf; he has a golfer's umbrella of stripes. Candy
stripes. In his mouth nothing turns to sugar, however, saliva works
no miracles here. His doctoring is of the slightly sick. The sick are sent
elsewhere (to Dr. Berg?), the deathly sick are sent back for more tests
and their bills are sent to their homes, the unsick are sent to Dr. Coronet (Isabel, a lady), an excellent psychiatrist for unsick people who

angrily believe they are sick and want to do something about it. If they demand a male psychiatrist, the unsick are sent by Dr. _____(my father) to Dr. Lowenstein, a male psychiatrist, excellent and expensive, with a limited practice.

4. Clarita. She is twenty, twenty-five, she is thirty or more? Pretty, 11 ugly, what? She is a woman lounging by the side of a road, in jeans and a sweater, hitch-hiking, or she is slouched on a stool at a counter in some roadside diner. A hard line of jaw. Curious eyes. Amused eyes. Behind her eyes processions move, funeral pageants, cartoons. She says, "I never can figure out why girls like you bum around down here. What are you looking for anyway?" An odor of tobacco about her. Unwashed underclothes, or no underclothes, unwashed skin, gritty toes, hair long and falling into strands, not recently washed.

5. Simon. In this city the weather changes abruptly, so Simon's 12 weather changes abruptly. He sleeps through the afternoon. He sleeps through the morning. Rising he gropes around for something to get him going, for a cigarette or a pill to drive him out to the street, where the temperature is hovering around 35°. Why doesn't it drop? Why, why doesn't the cold clean air come down from Canada, will he have to go up into Canada to get it, will he have to leave the Country of his Birth and sink into Canada's frosty fields . . . ? Will the F.B.I. (which he dreams about constantly) chase him over the Canadian border on foot, hounded out in a blizzard of broken glass and horns . . . ?

"Once I was Huckleberry Finn," Simon says, "but now I am Rod- 13 erick Usher." Beset by frenzies and fears, this man who makes my spine go cold, he takes green pills, yellow pills, pills of white and capsules of dark blue and green . . . he takes other things I may not mention, for what if Simon seeks me out and climbs into my girl's bedroom here in Bloomfield Hills and strangles me, what then . . . ? (As I write this I begin to shiver. Why do I shiver? I am now sixteen and sixteen is not an age for shivering.) It comes from Simon, who is always cold.

III. World Events

Nothing.   14

IV. People & Circumstances Contributing to This Delinquency

Nothing.   15

V. Sioux Drive

George, Clyde G. 240 Sioux. A manufacturer's representative; children,   16
a dog; a wife. Georgian with the usual columns. You think of the White
House, then of Thomas Jefferson, then your mind goes blank on the
white pillars and you think of nothing. Norris, Ralph W. 246 Sioux.
Public relations. Colonial. Bay window, brick, stone, concrete, wood,
green shutters, sidewalk, lantern, grass, trees, blacktop drive, two children, one of them my classmate Esther (Esther Norris) at Baldwin.
Wife, cars. Ramsey, Michael D. 250 Sioux. Colonial. Big living room,
thirty by twenty-five, fireplaces in living room, library, recreation
room, paneled walls wet bar five bathrooms five bedrooms two lav-
atories central air conditioning automatic sprinkler automatic garage
door three children one wife two cars a breakfast room a patio a large
fenced lot fourteen trees a front door with a brass knocker never
knocked. Next is our house. Classic contemporary. Traditional modern. Attached garage, attached Florida room, attached patio, attached
pool and cabana, attached roof. A front door mailslot through which
pour *Time Magazine, Fortune, Life, Business Week, The Wall Street Journal,
The New York Times, The New Yorker, The Saturday Review, M.D., Modern
Medicine, Disease of the Month* . . . and also. . . . And in addition to all
this, a quiet sealed letter from Baldwin saying: *Your daughter is not doing
work compatible with her performance on the Stanford-Binet.* . . . And your
son is not doing well, not well at all, very sad. Where is your son
anyway? Once he stole trick-and-treat candy from some six-year-old
kids, he himself being a robust ten. The beginning. Now your daughter
steals. In the Village Pharmacy she made off with, yes she did, don't
deny it, she made off with a copy of *Pageant Magazine* for no reason,
she swiped a roll of lifesavers in a green wrapper and was in no need
of saving her life or even in need of sucking candy; when she was no
more than eight years old she stole, don't blush, she stole a package
of *Tums* only because it was out on the counter and available, and the
nice lady behind the counter (now dead) said nothing. . . . Sioux
Drive. Maples, oaks, elms. Diseased elms cut down. Sioux Drive runs
into Roosevelt Drive. Slow turning lanes, not streets, all drives and
lanes and ways and passes. A private police force. Quiet private police,
in unmarked cars. Cruising on Saturday evenings with paternal smiles
for the residents who are streaming in and out of houses, going to and
from parties, a thousand parties, slightly staggering, the women in
their furs alighting from automobiles bought of Ford and General Mo-
tors and Chrysler, very heavy automobiles. No foreign cars. Detroit.

In 275 Sioux, down the block, in that magnificent French Normandy mansion, lives _____himself, who has the C _____account itself, imagine that! Look at where he lives and look at the enormous trees and chimneys, imagine his many fireplaces, imagine his wife and children, imagine his wife's hair, imagine her fingernails, imagine her bathtub of smooth clean glowing pink, imagine their embraces, his trouser pockets filled with odd coins and keys and dust and peanuts, imagine their ecstasy on Sioux Drive, imagine their income tax returns, imagine their little boy's pride in his experimental car, a scaled-down C _____, as he roars around the neighborhood on the sidewalks frightening dogs and Negro maids, oh imagine all these things, imagine everything, let your mind roar out all over Sioux Drive and DuMaurier Drive and Roosevelt Drive and Ticonderoga Pass and Burning Bush Way and Lincolnshire Pass and Lois Lane.

When spring comes, its winds blow nothing to Sioux Drive, no   17
odors of hollyhocks or forsythia, nothing Sioux Drive doesn't already possess, everything is planted and performing. The weather vanes, had they weather vanes, don't have to turn with the wind, don't have to contend with the weather. There is no weather.

VI. Detroit

There is always weather in Detroit. Detroit's temperature is always 32°.   18
Fast falling temperatures. Slow rising temperatures. Wind from the north-northeast four to forty miles an hour, small craft warnings, partly cloudy today and Wednesday changing to partly sunny through Thursday . . . small warnings of frost, soot warnings, traffic warnings, hazardous lake conditions for small craft and swimmers, restless Negro gangs, restless cloud formations, restless temperatures aching to fall out the very bottom of the thermometer or shoot up over the top and boil everything over in red mercury.

Detroit's temperature is 32°. Fast falling temperatures. Slow rising   19
temperatures. Wind from the north-northeast four to forty miles an hour. . . .

VII. Events

1. The girl's heart is pounding. In her pocket is a pair of gloves! In a   20
plastic bag! Airproof breathproof plastic bag, gloves selling for twenty-five dollars on Branden's counter! In her pocket! Shoplifted! . . . In her purse is a blue comb, not very clean. In her purse is a leather billfold

(a birthday present from her grandmother in Philadelphia) with snap-shots of the family in clean plastic windows, in the billfold are bills, she doesn't know how many bills. . . . In her purse is an ominous note from her friend Tykie *What's this about Joe H. and the kids hanging around at Louise's Sat. night? You heard anything? . . .* passed in French class. In her purse is a lot of dirty yellow Kleenex, her mother's heart would break to see such dirty Kleenex, and at the bottom of her purse are brown hairpins and safety pins and a broken pencil and a ballpoint pen (blue) stolen from somewhere forgotten and a purse-size compact of Cover Girl Make-Up, Ivory Rose. . . . Her lipstick is Broken Heart, a corrupt pink; her fingers are trembling like crazy; her teeth are be-ginning to chatter; her insides are alive; her eyes glow in her head; she is saying to her mother's astonished face *I want to steal but not to buy.*

2. At Clarita's. Day or night? What room is this? A bed, a regular   21
bed, and a mattress on the floor nearby. Wallpaper hanging in strips. Clarita says she tore it like that with her teeth. She was fighting a barbaric tribe that night, high from some pills she was battling for her life with men wearing helmets of heavy iron and their faces no more than Christian crosses to breathe through, every one of those bastards looking like her lover Simon, who seems to breathe with great difficulty through the slits of mouth and nostrils in his face. Clarita has never heard of Sioux Drive. Raymond Forrest cuts no ice with her, nor does the C _____account and its millions; Harvard Business School could be at the corner of Vernor and 12th Street for all she cares, and Vietnam might have sunk by now into the Dead Sea under its tons of debris, for all the amazement she could show . . . her face is overworked, overwrought, at the age of twenty (thirty?) it is already exhausted but fanciful and ready for a laugh. Clarita says mournfully to me *Honey somebody is going to turn you out let me give you warning.* In a movie shown on late television Clarita is not a mess like this but a nurse, with short neat hair and a dedicated look, in love with her doctor and her doctor's patients and their diseases, enamored of needles and sponges and rubbing alcohol. . . . Or no: she is a private secretary. Robert Cummings is her boss. She helps him with fantastic plots, the canned audience laughs, no, the audience doesn't laugh because noth-ing is funny, instead her boss is Robert Taylor and they are not boss and secretary but husband and wife, she is threatened by a young starlet, she is grim, handsome, wifely, a good companion for a good man. . . . She is Claudette Colbert. Her sister too is Claudette Colbert. They are twins, identical. Her husband Charles Boyer is a very rich

handsome man and her sister, Claudette Colbert, is plotting her death in order to take her place as the rich man's wife, no one will know because they are *twins*. . . . All these marvelous lives Clarita might have lived, but she fell out the bottom at the age of thirteen. At the age when I was packing my overnight case for a slumber party at Toni Deshield's she was tearing filthy sheets off a bed and scratching up a rash on her arms. . . . Thirteen is uncommonly young for a white girl in Detroit, Miss Brook of the Detroit House of Correction said in a sad newspaper interview for the *Detroit News;* fifteen and sixteen are more likely. Eleven, twelve, thirteen are not surprising in colored . . . they are more precocious. What can we do? Taxes are rising and the tax base is falling. The temperature rises slowly but falls rapidly. Everything is falling out the bottom, Woodward Avenue is filthy, Livernois Avenue is filthy! Scraps of paper flutter in the air like pigeons, dirt flies up and hits you right in the eye, oh Detroit is breaking up into dangerous bits of newspaper and dirt, watch out. . . .

Clarita's apartment is over a restaurant. Simon her lover emerges   22
from the cracks at dark. Mrs. Olesko, a neighbor of Clarita's an aged white wisp of a woman, doesn't complain but sniffs with contentment at Clarita's noisy life and doesn't tell the cops, hating cops, when the cops arrive. I should give fake names, more blanks, instead of telling all these secrets. I myself am a secret; I am a minor.

3. My father reads a paper at a medical convention in Los Angeles.   23
There he is, on the edge of the North American continent, when the unmarked detective put his hand so gently on my arm in the aisle of Branden's and said, "Miss, would you like to step over here for a minute?"

And where was he when Clarita put her hand on my arm, that   24
wintry dark sulphurous aching day in Detroit, in the company of closed-down barber shops, closed-down diners, closed-down movie houses, homes, windows, basements, faces . . . she put her hand on my arm and said, "Honey, are you looking for somebody down here?"

And was he home worrying about me, gone for two weeks solid,   25
when they carried me off . . . ? It took three of them to get me in the police cruiser, so they said, and they put more than their hands on my arm.

4. I work on this lesson. My English teacher is Mr. Forest, who   26
is from Michigan State. Not handsome, Mr. Forest, and his name is plain unlike Raymond Forrest's, but he is sweet and rodent-like, he has conferred with the principal and my parents, and everything is fixed . . . treat her as if nothing has happened, a new start, begin again,

only sixteen years old, what a shame, how did it happen?—nothing happened, nothing could have happened, a slight physiological modification known only to a gynecologist or to Dr. Coronet. I work on my lesson. I sit in my pink room. I look around the room with my sad pink eyes. I sigh, I dawdle, I pause, I eat up time, I am limp and happy to be home, I am sixteen years old suddenly, my head hangs heavy as a pumpkin on my shoulders, and my hair has just been cut by Mr. Faye at the Crystal Salon and is said to be very becoming.

(Simon too put his hand on my arm and said, "Honey, you have 27 got to come with me," and in his six-by-six room we got to know each other. Would I go back to Simon again? Would I lie down with him in all that filth and craziness? Over and over again.

a Clarita is being 28 betrayed as in front of a Cunningham Drug Store she is nervously eyeing a colored man who may or may not have money, or a nervous white boy of twenty with sideburns and an Appalachian look, who may or may not have a knife hidden in his jacket pocket, or a husky red-faced man of friendly countenance who may or may not be a member of the Vice Squad out for an early twilight walk.)

I work on my lesson for Mr. Forest. I have filled up eleven pages. 29 Words pour out of me and won't stop. I want to tell everything . . . what was the song Simon was always humming, and who was Simon's friend in a very new trench coat with an old high school graduation ring on his finger . . . ? Simon's bearded friend? When I was down too low for him Simon kicked me out and gave me to him for three days, I think, on Fourteenth Street in Detroit, an airy room of cold cruel drafts with newspapers on the floor. . . . Do I really remember that or am I piecing it together from what they told me? Did they tell the truth? Did they know much of the truth?

VIII. Characters

1. Wednesdays after school, at four; Saturday mornings at ten. Mother 30 drives me to Dr. Coronet. Ferns in the office, plastic or real, they look the same. Dr. Coronet is queenly, an elegant nicotine-stained lady who would have studied with Freud had circumstances not prevented it, a bit of a Catholic, ready to offer you some mystery if your teeth will ache too much without it. Highly recommended by Father! Forty dollars an hour, Father's forty dollars! Progress! Looking up! Looking better! That new haircut is so becoming, says Dr. Coronet herself, showing

how normal she is for a woman with an I.Q. of 180 and many advanced degrees.

2. Mother. A lady in a brown suede coat. Boots of shiny black 31 material, black gloves, a black fur hat. She would be humiliated could she know that of all the people in the world it is my ex-lover Simon who walks most like her . . . self-conscious and unreal, listening to distant music, a little bowlegged with craftiness. . . .

3. Father. Tying a necktie. In a hurry. On my first evening home 32 he put his hand on my arm and said, "Honey, we're going to forget all about this."

4. Simon. Outside a plane is crossing the sky, in here we're in a 33 hurry. Morning. It must be morning. The girl is half out of her mind, whimpering and vague. Simon her dear friend is wretched this morning . . . he is wretched with morning itself . . . he forces her to give him an injection with that needle she knows is filthy, she has a dread of needles and surgical instruments and the odor of things that are to be sent into the blood, thinking somehow of her father. . . . This is a bad morning, Simon says that his mind is being twisted out of shape, and so he submits to the needle which he usually scorns and bites his lip with his yellowish teeth, his face going very pale. *Ah baby!* he says in his soft mocking voice, which with all women is a mockery of love, *do it like this—Slowly—*And the girl, terrified, almost drops the precious needle but manages to turn it up to the light from the window . . . it is an extension of herself then? She can give him this gift then? *I wish you wouldn't do this to me,* she says, wise in her terror, because it seems to her that Simon's danger—in a few minutes he may be dead—is a way of pressing her against him that is more powerful than any other embrace. She has to work over his arm, the knotted corded veins of his arm, her forehead wet with perspiration as she pushes and releases the needle, staring at that mixture of liquid now stained with Simon's bright blood. . . . When the drug hits him she can feel it herself, she feels that magic that is more than any woman can give him, striking the back of his head and making his face stretch as if with the impact of a terrible sun. . . . She tries to embrace him but he pushes her aside and stumbles to his feet. *Jesus Christ,* he says. . . .

5. Princess, a Negro girl of eighteen. What is her charge? She is 34 closemouthed about it, shrewd and silent, you know that no one had to wrestle her to the sidewalk to get her in here; she came with dignity. In the recreation room she sits reading *Nancy Drew and the Jewel Box Mystery,* which inspires in her face tiny wrinkles of alarm and interest: what a face! Light brown skin, heavy shaded eyes, heavy eyelashes,

a serious sinister dark brow, graceful fingers, graceful wristbones, graceful legs, lips, tongue, a sugar-sweet voice, a leggy stride more masculine than Simon's and my mother's, decked out in a dirty white blouse and dirty white slacks; vaguely nautical is Princess's style. . . . At breakfast she is in charge of clearing the table and leans over me, saying, *Honey you sure you ate enough?*

6. The girl lies sleepless, wondering. Why here, why not there? Why Bloomfield Hills and not jail? Why jail and not her pink room? Why downtown Detroit and not Sioux Drive? What is the difference? Is Simon all the difference? The girl's head is a parade of wonders. She is nearly sixteen, her breath is marvelous with wonders, not long ago she was coloring with crayons and now she is smearing the landscape with paints that won't come off and won't come off her fingers either. She says to the matron *I am not talking about anything,* not because everyone has warned her not to talk but because, because she will not talk, because she won't say anything about Simon who is her secret. And she says to the matron *I won't go home* up until that night in the lavatory when everything was changed. . . . "No, I won't go home I want to stay here," she says, listening to her own words with amazement, thinking that weeds might climb everywhere over that marvelous $180,000 house and dinosaurs might return to muddy the beige carpeting, but never never will she reconcile four o'clock in the morning in Detroit with eight o'clock breakfasts in Bloomfield Hills . . . oh, she aches still for Simon's hands and his caressing breath, though he gave her little pleasure, he took everything from her (five-dollar bills, ten-dollar bills, passed into her numb hands by men and taken out of her hands by Simon) until she herself was passed into the hands of other men, police, when Simon evidently got tired of her and her hysteria. . . . *No, I won't go home, I don't want to be bailed out,* the girl thinks as a *Stubborn and Wayward Child* (one of several charges lodged against her) and the matron understands her crazy white-rimmed eyes that are seeking out some new violence that will keep her in jail, should someone threaten to let her out. Such children try to strangle the matrons, the attendants, or one another . . . they want the locks locked forever, the doors nailed shut . . . and this girl is no different up until that night her mind is changed for her. . . .

IX. *That Night*

Princess and Dolly, a little white girl of maybe fifteen, hardy however as a sergeant and in the House of Correction for armed robbery, corner her in the lavatory at the farthest sink and the other girls look away and file out to bed, leaving her. God how she is beaten up! Why is she beaten up? Why do they pound her, why such hatred? Princess vents all the hatred of a thousand silent Detroit winters on her body, this girl whose body belongs to me, fiercely she rides across the midwestern plains on this girl's tender bruised body . . . revenge on the oppressed minorities of America! revenge on the slaughtered Indians! revenge on the female sex, on the male sex, revenge on Bloomfield Hills, revenge revenge. . . .

X. Detroit

In Detroit weather weighs heavily upon everyone. The sky looms large. 37
The horizon shimmers in smoke. Downtown the buildings are imprecise in the haze. Perpetual haze. Perpetual motion inside the haze. Across the choppy river is the city of Windsor, in Canada. Part of the continent has bunched up here and is bulging outward, at the tip of Detroit; a cold hard rain is forever falling on the expressways . . . shoppers shop grimly, their cars are not parked in safe places, their windshields may be smashed and graceful ebony hands may drag them out through their shatterproof smashed windshields crying *Revenge for the Indians!* Ah, they all fear leaving Hudson's and being dragged to the very tip of the city and thrown off the parking roof of Cobo Hall, that expensive tomb, into the river. . . .

XI. Characters We Are Forever Entwined with

1. Simon drew me into his tender rotting arms and breathed gravity 38
into me. Then I came to earth, weighted down. He said *You are such a little girl,* and he weighed me down with his delight. In the palms of his hands were teeth marks from his previous life experiences. He was thirty-five, they said. Imagine Simon in this room, in my pink room: he is about six feet tall and stoops slightly, in a feline cautious way, always thinking, always on guard, with his scuffed light suede shoes and his clothes which are anyone's clothes, slightly rumpled ordinary clothes that ordinary men might wear to not-bad jobs. Simon has fair, long hair, curly hair, spent languid curls that are like . . . exactly like the curls of wood shavings to the touch, I am trying to be exact . . . and he smells of unheated mornings and coffee and too many pills coating his tongue with a faint green-white scum. . . . Dear Simon, who would be panicked in this room and in this house (right now Billie is vacuuming next door in my parents' room; a vacuum cleaner's roar is a sign of all good things), Simon who is said to have

come from a home not much different from this, years ago, fleeing all the carpeting and the polished banisters . . . Simon has a deathly face, only desperate people fall in love with it. His face is bony and cautious, the bones of his cheeks prominent as if with the rigidity of his ceaseless thinking, plotting, for he has to make money out of girls to whom money means nothing, they're so far gone they can hardly count it, and in a sense money means nothing to him either except as a way of keeping on with his life. *Each Day's Proud Struggle,* the title of a novel we could read at jail. . . . Each day he needs a certain amount of money. He devours it. It wasn't love he uncoiled in me with his hollowed-out eyes and his courteous smile, that remnant of a prosperous past, but a dark terror that needed to press itself flat against him, or against another man . . . but he was the first, he came over to me and took my arm, a claim. We struggled on the stairs and I said, *Let me loose, you're hurting my neck, my face,* it was such a surprise that my skin hurt where he rubbed it, and afterward we lay face to face and he breathed everything into me. In the end I think he turned me in.

2. Raymond Forrest. I just read this morning that Raymond Forrest's father, the chairman of the board at _____, died of a heart attack on a plane bound for London. I would like to write Raymond Forrest a note of sympathy. I would like to thank him for not pressing charges against me one hundred years ago, saving me, being so generous . . . well, men like Raymond Forrest are generous men, not like Simon. I would like to write him a letter telling of my love, or of some other emotion that is positive and healthy. Not like Simon and his poetry, which he scrawled down when he was high and never changed a word . . . but when I try to think of something to say, it is Simon's language that comes back to me, caught in my head like a bad song, it is always Simon's language:

> There is no reality only dreams
> Your neck may get snapped when you wake
> My love is drawn to some violent end
> She keeps wanting to get away
> My love is heading downward
> And I am heading upward
> She is going to crash on the sidewalk
> And I am going to dissolve into the clouds

XII. Events

1. Out of the hospital, bruised and saddened and converted, with Princess's grunts still tangled in my hair . . . and Father in his overcoat

looking like a Prince himself, come to carry me off. Up the expressway and out north to home. Jesus Christ, but the air is thinner and cleaner here. Monumental houses. Heartbreaking sidewalks, so clean.

2. Weeping in the living room. The ceiling is two storeys high and two chandeliers hang from it. Weeping, weeping, though Billie the maid is *probably listening*. I will never leave home again. Never. Never leave home. Never leave this home again, never.   41

3. Sugar doughnuts for breakfast. The toaster is very shiny and my face is distorted in it. Is that my face?   42

4. The car is turning in the driveway. Father brings me home. Mother embraces me. Sunlight breaks in movieland patches on the roof of our traditional-contemporary home, which was designed for the famous automotive stylist whose identity, if I told you the name of the famous car he designed, you would all know, so I can't tell you because my teeth chatter at the thought of being sued . . . or having someone climb into my bedroom window with a rope to strangle me. . . . The car turns up the blacktop drive. The house opens to me like a doll's house, so lovely in the sunlight, the big living room beckons to me with its walls falling away in a delirium of joy at my return, Billie the maid is *no doubt* listening from the kitchen as I burst into tears and the hysteria Simon got so sick of. Convulsed in Father's arms, I say I will never leave again, never, why did I leave, where did I go, what happened, my mind is gone wrong, my body is one big bruise, my backbone was sucked dry, it wasn't the men who hurt me and Simon never hurt me but only those girls . . . my God, how they hurt me . . . I will never leave home again. . . . The car is perpetually turning up the drive and I am perpetually breaking down in the living room and we are perpetually taking the right exit from the expressway (Lahser Road) and the wall of the restroom is perpetually banging against my head and perpetually are Simon's hands moving across my body and adding everything up and so too are Father's hands on my shaking bruised back, far from the surface of my skin on the surface of my good blue cashmere coat (dry-cleaned for my release). . . . I weep for all the money here, for God in gold and beige carpeting, for the beauty of chandeliers and the miracle of a clean polished gleaming toaster and faucets that run both hot and cold water, and I tell them *I will never leave home, this is my home, I love everything here, I am in love with everything here.* . . .   43

I am home.   44

Questions

1. In the title the narrator tells us that the story will be about how she "began [her] life over again." What do you imagine her later life is like?
2. The introductory paragraph says that the story is "a revelation of the meaning of life." Is it?
3. The introductory paragraph announces that there is "a happy ending." The last words of the story are, "I am home." Is there a happy ending? Why, or why not?
4. Why do the girls beat up the narrator? What is the effect of the beating?
5. Oates's story takes the fairly unusual form of "notes for an essay for an English class." What does the form convey about the girl aside from what it says explicitly?

Arthur Hugh Clough

The Latest Decalogue

Thou shalt have one God only; who
Would be at the expense of two?
No graven images may be
Worshiped, except the currency.
Swear not at all; for, for thy curse   5
Thine enemy is none the worse.
At church on Sunday to attend
Will serve to keep the world thy friend.
Honor thy parents; that is, all
From whom advancement may befall.   10

Arthur Hugh Clough (1819–1861), whose name rhymes with "rough," was born into a family of English cotton merchants. He spent 5 years of his early childhood in South Carolina, but was educated in England, where his teachers and friends, recognizing him as a gifted student and a talented poet, expected him to go on to a promising career. But Clough, deeply troubled both by doubts about the authenticity of the teachings of the Christian church and by the materialism of his age, never fulfilled those expectations.

Thou shalt not kill; but need'st not strive
Officiously to keep alive.
Do not adultery commit;
Advantage rarely comes of it.
Thou shalt not steal; an empty feat.   15
When it's so lucrative to cheat.
Bear not false witness; let the lie
Have time on its own wings to fly.
Thou shalt not covet, but tradition
Approves all forms of competition.   20

The sum of all is, thou shalt love,
If anybody, God above:
At any rate shall never labor
More than thyself to love thy neighbor.

Questions

1. Explain the title.
2. The commandments in this poem (e.g., "Thou shalt have one God only," "Thou shalt not kill") are ancient (see page 516) and they are widely accepted as a guide to our moral life. What is new in the poem?
3. The poem was written in 1849. On the basis of this poem, how would you characterize the period? Does the poem speak to our own period also?

9
ARTICLES OF FAITH

The Creation of Adam
Michelangelo

Short Views

A little philosophy inclineth man's mind to atheism, but depth in philosophy bringeth men's minds about to religion.
Francis Bacon

Religion is the opium of the people.
Karl Marx

If one wishes to form a true estimate of the full grandeur of religion, one must keep in mind what it undertakes to do for men. It gives them information about the source and origin of the universe, it assures them of protection and final happiness amid the changing vicissitudes of life, and it guides their thoughts and motions by means of precepts which are backed by the whole force of its authority.
Sigmund Freud

Religion is an attempt to get control over the sensory world, in which we are placed, by means of the wish-world, which we have developed inside us as a result of biological and psychological necessities.
Sigmund Freud

The language of "sonship," "brotherhood," "fellowship," "good Christian men," which pervades liturgy, prayerbooks and hymnbooks, . . . alienates women in their specific identity as women. Many women and most men are not aware of the alienation which is produced by the structures of English grammar. In pronouns and many other words, the male specific and the generic coincide. Thus when a word which is both male specific and generic is used, men naturally identify, whereas women can only identify by denying their specific identity as female.

To be sure, the image of woman is not entirely excluded from the language of Christian liturgy and theology. The church has been portrayed as a woman, referred to as "She," and discussed in feminine categories. But language applied to the church embodies sexual stereotypes and reflects and reinforces the secondary status

of women. "She" receives life, sustenance and power from "her" relation to a male Christ and is clearly subordinated to him. Women's identification with the church has not led to an elevation of their status, but rather has set the seal on their subordination.
Carol Christ and Marilyn Collins

To stand on one leg and prove God's existence is a very different thing from going down on one's knees and thanking him for it.
Sören Kierkegaard

Ethiopians have gods with snub noses and black hair; Thracians have gods with gray eyes and red hair.
Xenophanes of Colophon

God offers to every mind its choice between truth and repose. Take which you please; you can never have both. Between these, as a pendulum, man oscillates. He in whom the love of repose predominates will accept the first creed, the first philosophy, the first political party he meets—most likely his father's. He gets rest, commodity, reputation; but he shuts the door of truth. He in whom the love of truth predominates will keep himself aloof from all the moorings, afloat. He will abstain from dogmatism, and recognize all the opposite negations between which, as walls, his being is swung. He submits to the inconvenience of suspense and imperfect opinions, but he is a candidate for truth, as the other is not, and respects the highest law of his being.
Ralph Waldo Emerson

We cannot know whether we love God, although there may be strong reasons for thinking so, but there can be no doubt about whether we love our neighbor or no.
Saint Theresa

To the [Hebrew] biblical mind, man is above all a commanded being, a being of whom demands may be made. The central problem is not, What is being? but rather, What is required of me?
Abraham Heschel

The Sabbath lays down a judgment on the fundamental issues of our civilization and, specifically, demands restraint, dignity, reticence, and silent rest—not commonplace virtues. . . . The

Sabbath . . . calls into question the foundations of the life of one dimension only, asking how people can imagine that all there is is what they see just now.

Jacob Neusner

"What," it will be questioned, "When the sun rises do you not see a round disk of fire somewhat like a guinea?" O no no, I see an Innumerable Company of the Heavenly Host crying, "Holy holy holy is the Lord God Almighty." I question not my corporeal or vegetative eye any more than I would question a window concerning sight. I look through it and not with it.

William Blake

A Note on Genesis

Genesis, the first book of the Hebrew Bible, gives an account of the creation of the universe and of the earth's early history. Most scholars agree that the book contains material from three traditions, which are conventionally called J, E, and P. It should be emphasized at the outset that J, E, and P are not so much three individual writers as three bodies of tradition or three composite works, even though one tends to say such things as "the J writer," or "J says."

J comes from JHVA (Jahveh), the German form of YHWH (Yahweh); J, known also as the Yahwist writer, used Yahweh as the name for God. The Yahwist material was probably compiled chiefly in the tenth century B.C., but parts of it may have been compiled earlier and other parts later. E stands for the Elohist—the writer (probably in the ninth century B.C.) who used Elohim as the word for God. P stands for the priestly writer, that is, the priest or priests who in the sixth century B.C., after the fall of Jerusalem and the destruction of the Jerusalem temple, reworked the accounts of J and E, and added material from documents preserved by priests. P was especially concerned with genealogies, precise dates, and description of rituals.

There is, of course, some disagreement about exactly which portions of the text are properly attributed to each of the three traditions, but scholars are in general agreement that, for example, P was responsible for Genesis 1:1–31 and for 2:1–4, and that J was responsible for the second half of 2:4 to 2:25. E apparently did not influence the early chapters.

Genesis

The Creation

Chapter 1

1 In the beginning God created the heaven and the earth.

2 And the earth was without form, and void; and darkness was upon the face of the deep. And the Spirit of God moved upon the face of the waters.

3 And God said, Let there be light, and there was light.

4 And God saw the light, that *it was* good: and God divided the light from the darkness.

5 And God called the light Day, and the darkness he called Night. And the evening and the morning were the first day.

6 ¶And God said, Let there be a firmament in the midst of the waters, and let it divide the waters from the waters.

7 And God made the firmament, and divided the waters which *were* under the firmament from the waters which *were* above the firmament: and it was so.

8 And God called the firmament Heaven. And the evening and the morning were the second day.

9 ¶And God said, Let the waters under the heaven be gathered together unto one place, and let the dry *land* appear: and it was so.

10 And God called the dry *land* Earth; and the gathering together of the waters called he Seas: and God saw that *it was* good.

11 And God said, Let the earth bring forth grass, the herb yielding seed, *and* the fruit tree yielding fruit after his kind, whose seed *is* in itself, upon the earth: and it was so.

12 And the earth brought forth grass, *and* herb yielding seed after his kind, and the tree yielding fruit, whose seed *was* in itself, after his kind: and God saw that *it was* good.

13 And the evening and the morning were the third day.

14 ¶And God said, Let there be lights in the firmament of the heaven to divide the day from the night; and let them be for signs, and for seasons, and for days, and years:

15 And let them be for lights in the firmament of the heaven to give light upon the earth: and it was so.

16 And God made two great lights; the greater light to rule the day, and the lesser light to rule the night: *he made* the stars also.

17 And God set them in the firmament of the heaven to give light upon the earth.

18 And to rule over the day and over the night, and to divide the light from the darkness: and God saw that *it was* good.

19 And the evening and the morning were the fourth day.

20 And God said, Let the waters bring forth abundantly the moving creature that hath life, and fowl *that* may fly above the earth in the open firmament of heaven.

21 And God created great whales, and every living creature that moveth, which the waters brought forth abundantly, after their kind, and every winged fowl after his kind: and God saw that *it was* good.

22 And God blessed them, saying, Be fruitful, and multiply, and fill the waters in the seas, and let fowl multiply in the earth.

23 And the evening and the morning were the fifth day.

24 ¶And God said, Let the earth bring forth the living creature after his kind, cattle, and creeping thing, and beast of the earth after his kind: and it was so.

25 And God made the beast of the earth after his kind, and cattle after their kind, and every thing that creepeth upon the earth after his kind: and God saw that *it was* good.

26 ¶And God said, Let us make man in our image, after our likeness: and let them have dominion over the fish of the sea, and over the fowl of the air, and over the cattle, and over all the earth, and over every creeping thing that creepeth upon the earth.

27 So God created man in his *own* image, in the image of God created he him; male and female created he them.

28 And God blessed them, and God said unto them, Be fruitful, and multiply, and replenish the earth, and subdue it: and have dominion over the fish of the sea, and over the fowl of the air, and over every living thing that moveth upon the earth.

29 ¶And God said, Behold, I have given you every herb bearing seed, which *is* upon the face of all the earth, and every tree, in the which *is* the fruit of a tree yielding seed; to you it shall be for meat.

30 And to every beast of the earth, and to every fowl of the air, and to every thing that creepeth upon the earth, wherein *there is* life, *I have given* every green herb for meat: and it was so.

31 And God saw every thing that he had made, and, behold, *it was* very good. And the evening and the morning were the sixth day.

Chapter 2

1 Thus the heavens and the earth were finished, and all the host of them.

2 And on the seventh day God ended his work which he had made; and he rested on the seventh day from all his work which he had made.

3 And God blessed the seventh day, and sanctified it: because that in it he had rested from all his work which God created and made.

4 ¶These *are* the generations of the heavens and of the earth when they were created, in the day that the LORD God made the earth and the heavens,

5 And every plant of the field before it was in the earth, and every herb of the field before it grew: for the LORD God had not caused it to rain upon the earth, and *there was* not a man to till the ground.

6 But there went up a mist from the earth, and watered the whole face of the ground.

7 And the LORD God formed man *of* the dust of the ground, and breathed into his nostrils the breath of life; and man became a living soul.

8 ¶And the LORD God planted a garden eastward in Eden; and there he put the man whom he had formed.

9 And out of the ground made the LORD God to grow every tree that is pleasant to the sight, and good for food; the tree of life also in the midst of the garden, and the tree of knowledge of good and evil.

10 And a river went out of Eden to water the garden; and from thence it was parted, and became into four heads.

11 The name of the first *is* Pison: that *is* it which compasseth the whole land of Havilah, where *there is* gold;

12 And the gold of that land *is* good: there *is* bdellium and the onyx stone.

13 And the name of the second river *is* Gihon: the same *is* it that compasseth the whole land of Ethiopia.

14 And the name of the third river *is* Hiddekel: that *is* it which goeth toward the east of Assyria. And the fourth river *is* Euphrates.

15 And the LORD God took the man, and put him into the garden of Eden to dress it and to keep it.

16 And the LORD God commanded the man, saying, Of every tree of the garden thou mayest freely eat:

17 But of the tree of the knowledge of good and evil, thou shalt not eat of it: for in the day that thou eatest thereof thou shalt surely die.

18 ¶And the LORD God said, *It is* not good that the man should be alone; I will make him an help meet for him.

19 And out of the ground the LORD God formed every beast of the field, and every fowl of the air; and brought *them* unto Adam to see what he would call them: and whatsoever Adam called every living creature, that *was* the name thereof.

20 And Adam gave names to all cattle, and to the fowl of the air, and to every beast of the field; but for Adam there was not found an help meet for him.

21 And the LORD God caused a deep sleep to fall upon Adam, and he slept: and he took one of his ribs, and closed up the flesh instead thereof;

22 And the rib, which the LORD God had taken from man, made he a woman, and brought her unto the man.

23 And Adam said, This *is* now bone of my bones, and flesh of my flesh: she shall be called Woman, because she was taken out of Man.

24 Therefore shall a man leave his father and his mother, and shall cleave unto his wife: and they shall be one flesh.

25 And they were both naked, the man and his wife, and were not ashamed.

Questions

1. In 1:6–9 God creates a "firmament," a sort of inverted bowl or other solid covering over the earth, thereby protecting the earth from water above heaven. How might belief in this kind of creation (and creator) differ in emotion or "feel," so to speak, from belief in a creation that consisted only of an airy heaven above a solid earth?

2. In 1:1–8 God creates form, light, and darkness, and He separates heaven from earth. Speaking broadly, or generally, what besides *things* does he create?

3. Many readers find that the account of the creation in 2:5–25 differs from the account in Chapter 1. Do you think, for instance, that in one account God seems somewhat more human and less tran-

scendent than in the other? On what evidence do you base your view? Do you find some differences in the details concerning the creation? If so, what are they?

The Fall

Chapter 3

1 Now the serpent was more subtil than any beast of the field which the LORD God had made. And he said unto the woman, Yea, hath God said, Ye shall not eat of every tree of the garden?

2 And the woman said unto the serpent, We may eat of the fruit of the trees of the garden:

3 But of the fruit of the tree which *is* in the midst of the garden, God hath said, Ye shall not eat of it, neither shall ye touch it, lest ye die.

4 And the serpent said unto the woman, Ye shall not surely die:

5 For God doth know that in the day ye eat thereof, then your eyes shall be opened, and ye shall be as gods, knowing good and evil.

6 And when the woman saw that the tree *was* good for food, and that it *was* pleasant to the eyes, and a tree to be desired to make *one* wise, she took of the fruit thereof, and did eat, and gave also unto her husband with her; and he did eat.

7 And the eyes of them both were opened, and they knew that they *were* naked; and they sewed fig leaves together, and made themselves aprons.

8 And they heard the voice of the LORD God walking in the garden in the cool of the day: and Adam and his wife hid themselves from the presence of the LORD God amongst the trees of the garden.

9 And the LORD God called unto Adam, and said unto him, Where *art* thou?

10 And he said, I heard thy voice in the garden, and I was afraid, because I *was* naked; and I hid myself.

11 And he said, Who told thee that thou *wast* naked? Hast thou eaten of the tree, whereof I commanded thee that thou shouldest not eat?

12 And the man said, The woman whom thou gavest *to be* with me, she gave me of the tree, and I did eat.

13 And the LORD God said unto the woman, What *is* this *that* thou hast done? And the woman said, The serpent beguiled me, and I did eat.

14 And the Lord God said unto the serpent, Because thou hast done this, thou *art* cursed above all cattle, and above every beast of the field; upon thy belly shalt thou go, and dust shalt thou eat all the days of thy life:

15 And I will put enmity between thee and the woman, and between thy seed and her seed; it shall bruise thy head, and thou shalt bruise his heel.

16 Unto the woman he said, I will greatly multiply thy sorrow and thy conception; in sorrow thou shalt bring forth children; and thy desire *shall be* to thy husband, and he shall rule over thee.

17 And unto Adam he said, Because thou hast hearkened unto the voice of thy wife, and hast eaten of the tree, of which I commanded thee, saying, Thou shalt not eat of it: cursed *is* the ground for thy sake; in sorrow shalt thou eat *of* it all the days of thy life;

18 Thorns also and thistles shall it bring forth to thee; and thou shalt eat the herb of the field;

19 In the sweat of thy face shalt thou eat bread, till thou return unto the ground; for out of it wast thou taken: for dust thou *art*, and unto dust shalt thou return.

20 And Adam called his wife's name Eve; because she was the mother of all living.

21 Unto Adam also and to his wife did the Lord God make coats of skins, and clothed them.

22 ¶And the Lord God said, Behold, the man is become as one of us, to know good and evil: and now, lest he put forth his hand, and take also of the tree of life, and eat, and live for ever:

23 Therefore the Lord God sent him forth from the garden of Eden, to till the ground from whence he was taken.

24 So he drove out the man; and he placed at the east of the garden of Eden Cherubims, and a flaming sword which turned every way, to keep the way of the tree of life.

Questions

1. The serpent tempts the woman, but exactly why (according to 3:6) does she eat the forbidden fruit? (We are not given the reasons why the man ate, but presumably they were similar to the woman's reasons.) What is the author implying about the nature of sin?

2. In 3:5 the serpent promises the man and the woman knowledge of "good and evil." Judging from 3:7, do they gain knowledge? If so,

is it the sort of knowledge they had anticipated? If not, what can be said about this knowledge?

3. The consequences of eating the forbidden fruit were, most obviously, pain (in sustaining oneself and in bearing children), expulsion from Eden, and death. But in terms of human emotions and relationships, what were the consequences?

4. The disobedience of the man and woman, leading to their expulsion from Eden, is usually called "the Fall," a term which implies loss or diminution. Can one, however, argue that the Fall might also have had positive qualities—for instance, that it led to a creative activity impossible in Eden?

Phyllis Trible

Eve and Adam

Genesis 2–3 Reread

On the whole, the Women's Liberation Movement is hostile to the Bible, even as it claims that the Bible is hostile to women. The Yahwist account of creation and fall in Genesis 2–3 provides a strong proof text for that claim. Accepting centuries of (male) exegesis, many feminists interpret this story as legitimating male supremacy and female subordination.[1] They read to reject. My suggestion is that we reread to understand and to appropriate. Ambiguity characterizes the meaning of 'adham in Genesis 2–3. On the one hand, man is the first creature formed (2:7). The Lord God puts him in the garden "to till it and keep it," a job identified with the male (cf. 3:17–19). On the other

[1] *See inter alia*, Kate Millett, *Sexual Politics* (New York: Doubleday, 1970), pp. 51–54; Eva Figes, *Patriarchal Attitudes* (Greenwich, Conn.: Fawcett, 1970), pp. 38f; Mary Daly, "The Courage to See," *The Christian Century*, September 22, 1971, p. 1110; Sheila D. Collins, "Toward a Feminist Theology," *The Christian Century*, August 2, 1972, p. 798; Lilly Rivlin, "Lilith: The First Woman," *Ms.*, December 1972, pp. 93, 114.

Phyllis Trible, a member of the faculty of Union Theological Seminary in New York City, received her Ph.D. from Union Theological Seminary and Columbia University. Trible is the author of two books, *God and the Rhetoric of Sexuality* and *Texts of Terror: Literary-Feminist Readings of Biblical Narratives*. The essay we reprint, originally published in 1973, has come to be regarded as a landmark in feminist analysis of the Bible.

hand, 'adham is a generic term for humankind. In commanding 'adham not to eat of the tree of the knowledge of good and evil, the Deity is speaking to both the man and the woman (2:16–17). Until the differentiation of female and male (2:21–23), 'adham is basically androgynous: one creature incorporating two sexes.

Concern for sexuality, specifically for the creation of woman, comes last in the story, after the making of the garden, the trees, and the animals. Some commentators allege female subordination based on this order of events.[2] They contrast it with Genesis 1:27 where God creates 'adham as male and female in one act.[3] Thereby they infer that whereas the Priests recognized the equality of the sexes, the Yahwist made woman a second, subordinate, inferior sex.[4] But the last may be first, as both the biblical theologian and the literary critic know. Thus the Yahwist account moves to its climax, not its decline, in the creation of woman.[5] She is not an afterthought; she is the culmination. Genesis 1 itself supports this interpretation, for there male and female are indeed the last and truly the crown of all creatures. The last is also first where beginnings and endings are parallel. In Hebrew literature, the central concerns of a unit often appear at the beginning and the end as an *inclusio** device.[6] Genesis 2 evinces this structure. The creation of man first and of woman last constitutes a ring composition whereby

---

[2] Cf. E. Jacob, *Theology of the Old Testament* (New York: Harper & Bros., 1958), pp. 172f; S. H. Hooke, "Genesis," *Peake's Commentary on the Bible* (London: Thomas Nelson, 1962), p. 179.

[3] E.g., Elizabeth Cady Stanton observed that Genesis 1:26–28 "dignifies woman as an important factor in the creation, equal in power and glory with man," while Genesis 2 "makes her a mere afterthought" (*The Woman's Bible*, Part I [New York: European Publishing Company, 1895], p. 20). See also Elsie Adams and Mary Louise Briscoe, *Up Against the Wall, Mother . . .* (Beverly Hills: Glencoe Press, 1971), p. 4.

[4] Cf. Eugene H. Maly, "Genesis," *The Jerome Biblical Commentary* (Englewood Cliffs, N.J.: Prentice-Hall, 1968), p. 12: "But woman's existence, psychologically and in the social order, is dependent on man."

[5] See John L. McKenzie, "The Literary Characteristics of Gen. 2–3," *Theological Studies*, Vol. 15 (1954), p. 559; John A. Bailey, "Initiation and the Primal Woman in Gilgamesh and Genesis 2–3," *Journal of Biblical Literature*, June 1970, p. 143. Bailey writes emphatically of the remarkable importance and position of the woman in Genesis 2–3, "all the more extraordinary when one realizes that this is the only account of the creation of woman as such in ancient Near Eastern literature." He hedges, however, in seeing the themes of helper and naming (Genesis 2:18–23) as indicative of a "certain subordination" of woman to man. These reservations are unnecessary; see below. Cf. also Claus Westermann, *Genesis, Biblischer Kommentar* 1/4 (Neukerchener-Vluyn: Newkirchener Verlag, 1970), p. 312.

* *Inclusio*: a paragraph or other unit marked by the same words at the beginning and the end. (Editors' note)

[6] James Muilenburg, "Form Criticism and Beyond," *Journal of Biblical Literature*, March 1969, pp. 9f; Mitchell Dahood, "Psalm I," *The Anchor Bible* (New York: Doubleday, 1966), *passim* and esp. p. 5.

the two creatures are parallel. In no way does the order disparage woman. Content and context augment this reading.

The context for the advent of woman is a divine judgment: "It is   3 not good that 'adham should be alone; I will make him a helper fit for him" (2:18). The phrase needing explication is "helper fit for him." In the Old Testament the word *helper* (*'ezer*) has many usages. It can be a proper name for a male.[7] In our story, it describes the animals and the woman. In some passages, it characterizes Deity. God is the helper of Israel. As helper Yahweh creates and saves.[8] Thus *'ezer* is a relational term; it designates a beneficial relationship; and it pertains to God, people, and animals. By itself, the word does not specify positions within relationships; more particularly, it does not imply inferiority. Position results from additional content or from context. Accordingly, what kind of relationship does *'ezer* entail in Genesis 2:18, 20? Our answer comes in two ways: (1) The word *neged*, which joins *'ezer*, connotes equality: a helper who is a counterpart.[9] (2) The animals are helpers, but they fail to fit 'adham. There is physical, perhaps psychic, rapport between 'adham and the animals, for Yahweh forms (*yasar*) them both out of the ground (*'adhamah*). Yet their similarity is not equality. 'Adham names them and thereby exercises power over them. No fit helper is among them. And thus the narrative moves to woman. . . . God is the helper superior to man; the animals are helpers inferior to man; woman is the helper equal to man.

Let us pursue the issue by examining the account of the creation   4 of woman ([verses] 21–22). This episode concludes the story even as the creation of man commences it. . . . The ring composition suggests an interpretation of woman and man as equals. To establish this meaning, structure and content must mesh. They do. In both episodes, Yahweh alone creates. For the last creation the Lord God "caused a deep sleep (*tardemah*) to fall upon the man." Man has no part in making woman; he is out of it. He exercises no control over her existence. He is neither participant nor spectator nor consultant at her birth. Like man, woman owes her life solely to God. For both of them, the origin of life is a divine mystery. Another parallel of equality is creation out of raw materials: dust for man and a rib for woman. Yahweh chooses these fragile materials and in both cases processes them before human

---

[7] See 1 Chronicles 4:4; 12:9; Nehemiah 3:19.

[8] See Psalm 121:2, 124:8; 146:5; 33:20; 115:9–11; Exodus 18:4; Deuteronomy 33:7, 26, 29.

[9] L. Koehler and W. Baumgartner, *Lexicon in Veteris Testamenti Libros* (Leiden: E. J. Brill, 1958), pp. 591f.

beings happen. As Yahweh shapes dust and then breathes into it to form man, so Yahweh takes out the rib and then builds it into woman.[10] To call woman "Adam's rib" is to misread the text, which states carefully and clearly that the extracted bone required divine labor to become female, a datum scarcely designed to bolster the male ego. Moreover, to claim that the rib means inferiority or subordination is to assign the man qualities over the woman which are not in the narrative itself. Superiority, strength, aggressiveness, dominance, and power do not characterize man in Genesis 2. By contrast, he is formed from dirt; his life hangs by a breath which he does not control; and he himself remains silent and passive while the Deity plans and interprets his existence.

The rib means solidarity and equality. 'Adham recognizes this   5 meaning in a poem:[11]

> This at last is bone of bones
> and flesh of my flesh.
> She shall be called 'ishshah [woman]
> because she was taken out of 'ish [man].(2:23)

The pun proclaims both the similarity and the differentiation of female and male. Before this episode the Yahwist has used only the generic term 'adham. No exclusively male reference has appeared. Only with the specific creation of woman ('ishshah) occurs the first specific terms for man as male ('ish). In other words, sexuality is simultaneous for woman and man. The sexes are interrelated and interdependent. Man as male does not precede woman as female but happens concurrently with her. Hence, the first act in Genesis 2 is the creation of androgyny (2:7), and the last is the creation of sexuality (2:23).[12] Male embodies female, and female embodies male. The two are neither dichotomies nor duplicates. The birth of woman corresponds to the birth of man but does not copy it. Only in responding to the female does the man

---

[10] The verb *bnh* (to build) suggests considerable labor. It is used of towns, towers, altars, and fortifications, as well as of the primeval woman (Koehler-Baumgartner, op. cit., p. 134). In Genesis 2:22, it may mean the fashioning of clay around the rib (Ruth Amiran, "Myths of the Creation of Man and the Jericho Statues," *BASOR*, No. 167 [October 1962], p. 24).

[11] See Walter Brueggemann, "Of the Same Flesh and Bone (Gen. 2:23a)," *Catholic Biblical Quarterly*, October 1970, pp. 532–42.

[12] In proposing as primary an androgynous interpretation of 'adham, I find virtually no support from (male) biblical scholars. But my view stands as documented from the text, and I take refuge among a remnant of ancient (male) rabbis (see George Foot Moore, *Judaism* [Cambridge, Mass.: Harvard University Press, 1927]), I, 453; also Joseph Campbell, *The Hero with a Thousand Faces* (Meridian Books, The World Publishing Company, 1970), pp. 152ff., 279f.

discover himself as male. No longer a passive creature, *'ish* comes alive in meeting *'ishshah*.

Some read into the poem a naming motif. The man names the woman and thereby has power and authority over her.[13] But again . . . reread. Neither the verb nor the noun *name* is in the poem. We find instead the verb *gara'*, to call: "She shall be called woman." Now, in the Yahwist primeval history this verb does not function as a synonym or parallel or substitute for *name*. The typical formula for naming is the verb *to call* plus the explicit object *name*. This formula applies to Deity, people, places, and animals. For example, in Genesis 4 we read:

> Cain built a city and *called* the *name* of the city after the *name* of his son Enoch. (v. 17)
> And Adam knew his wife again, and she bore a son and *called* his *name* Seth. (v. 25)
> To Seth also a son was born and he *called* his *name* Enoch. (v. 26a)
> At that time men began to *call* upon the *name* of the Lord. (v. 26b)

Genesis 2:23 has the verb *call* but does not have the object *name*. Its absence signifies the absence of a naming motif in the poem. The presence of both the verb *call* and the noun *name* in the episode of the animals strengthens the point:

> So out of the ground the Lord God formed every beast of the field and every bird of the air, and brought them to the man to see what he would *call* them; and whatever the man *called* every living creature, that was its *name*. The man gave *names* to all cattle, and to the birds of the air, and to every beast of the field. (2:19–20)

In calling the animals by name, *'adham* establishes supremacy over them and fails to find a fit helper. In calling woman, *'adham* does not name her and does find in her a counterpart. Female and male are equal sexes. Neither has authority over the other.[14]

A further observation secures the argument: *Woman* itself is not a name. It is a common noun; it is not a proper noun. It designates gender; it does not specify person. *'Adham* recognizes sexuality by the words *'ishshah* and *'ish*. This recognition is not an act of naming to assert the power of male over female. Quite the contrary. But the true

[13] See e.g., G. von Rad, *Genesis* (Philadelphia: Westminster Press, 1961), pp. 80–82; John H. Marks, "Genesis," *The Interpreter's One-Volume Commentary on the Bible* (Nashville: Abingdon Press, 1971), p. 5; Bailey, op. cit., p. 143.
[14] Cf. Westermann, op. cit., pp. 316ff.

skeptic is already asking: What about Genesis 3:20, where "the man called his wife's name Eve"? We must wait to consider that question. Meanwhile, the words of the ancient poem as well as their context proclaim sexuality originating in the unity of 'adham. From this one (androgynous) creature come two (female and male). The two return to their original unity as 'ish and 'ishshah become one flesh (2:24):[15] another instance of the ring composition.

Next the differences which spell harmony and equality yield to the differences of disobedience and disaster. The serpent speaks to the woman. Why to the woman and not to the man? The simplest answer is that we do not know. The Yahwist does not tell us anymore than he explains why the tree of the knowledge of good and evil was in the garden. But the silence of the text stimulates speculations, many of which only confirm the patriarchal mentality which conceived them. Cassuto identifies serpent and woman, maintaining that the cunning of the serpent is "in reality" the cunning of the woman.[16] He impugns her further by declaring that "for the very reason that a woman's imagination surpasses a man's, it was the woman who was enticed first." Though more gentle in his assessment, von Rad avers that "in the history of Yahweh religion, it has always been the women who have shown an inclination for obscure astrological cults" (a claim which he does not document).[17] Consequently, he holds that the woman "confronts the obscure allurements and mysteries that beset our limited life more directly than the man does," and then he calls her a "temptress." Paul Ricoeur says that woman "represents the point of weakness," as the entire story "gives evidence of a very masculine resentment."[18] McKenzie links the "moral weakness" of the woman with

8

---

[15] Verse 24 probably mirrors a matriarchal society (so Von Rad, op. cit., p. 83). If the myth were designed to support patriarchy, it is difficult to explain how this verse survived without proper alteration. Westermann contends, however, that an emphasis on matriarchy misunderstands the point of the verse, which is the total communion of woman and man (ibid., p. 317).

[16] U. Cassuto, *A Commentary on the Book of Genesis,* Part I (Jerusalem: Magnes Press, n.d.), pp. 142f.

[17] Von Rad, op. cit., pp. 87f.

[18] Ricoeur departs from the traditional interpretation of the woman when he writes: "*Eve n'est donc pas la femme en tant que 'deuxieme sexe'; toute femme et tout homme sont Adam; tout homme et toute femme sont Eve.*" But the fourth clause of his sentence obscures this complete identity of Adam and Eve: "*toute femme peche 'en Adam, tout homme est seduit 'en Eve.*" By switching from an active to a passive verb, Ricoeur makes only the woman directly responsible for both sinning and seducing. (Paul Ricoeur, Finitude et Culpabilite, II. *La Symbolique du Mal,* Aubier, Editions Montaigne [Paris: 1960]. Cf. Paul Ricoeur, *The Symbolism of Evil* [Boston: Beacon Press, 1969], p. 255).

her "sexual attraction" and holds that the latter ruined both the woman and the man.[19]

But the narrative does not say any of these things. It does not 9 sustain the judgment that woman is weaker or more cunning or more sexual than man. Both have the same Creator, who explicitly uses the word *good* to introduce the creation of woman (2:18). Both are equal in birth. There is complete rapport, physical, psychological, sociological, and theological, between them: bone of bone and flesh of flesh. If there be moral frailty in one, it is moral frailty in two. Further, they are equal in responsibility and in judgment, in shame and in guilt, in redemption and in grace. What the narrative says about the nature of woman it also says about the nature of man.

Why does the serpent speak to the woman and not to the man? 10 Let a female speculate. If the serpent is "more subtle" than its fellow creatures, the woman is more appealing than her husband. Throughout the myth, she is the more intelligent one, the more aggressive one, and the one with greater sensibilities.[20] Perhaps the woman elevates the animal world by conversing theologically with the serpent. At any rate, she understands the hermeneutical task. In quoting God, she interprets the prohibition ("neither shall you touch it"). The woman is both theologian and translator. She contemplates the tree, taking into account all the possibilities. The tree is good for food; it satisfies the physical drives. It pleases the eyes; it is esthetically and emotionally desirable. Above all, it is coveted as the source of wisdom (*haskîl*). Thus the woman is fully aware when she acts, her vision encompassing the gamut of life. She takes the fruit, and she eats. The initiative and the decision are hers alone. There is no consultation with her husband. She seeks neither his advice nor his permission. She acts independently.

By contrast, the man is a silent, passive, and bland recipient: "She 11 also gave some to her husband, and he ate." The narrator makes no attempt to depict the husband as reluctant or hesitating. The man does not theologize; he does not contemplate; he does not envision the full possibilities of the occasion. His one act is belly oriented, and it is an act of quiescence, not of initiative. The man is not dominant; he is not aggressive; he is not a decision maker. Even though the prohibition not to eat of the tree appears before the female was specifically created, she knows that it applies to her. She has interpreted it, and now she

[19] McKenzie, op. cit., p. 570.
[20] See Bailey, op. cit., p. 148.

struggles with the temptation to disobey. But not the man, to whom the prohibition came directly (2:16). He follows his wife without question or comment, thereby denying his own individuality. If the woman be intelligent, sensitive, and ingenious, the man is passive, brutish, and inept. These character portrayals are truly extraordinary in a culture dominated by men. I stress their contrast not to promote female chauvinism but to undercut patriarchal interpretations alien to the text.

The contrast between woman and man fades after their acts of disobedience. They are one in the new knowledge of their nakedness (3:7). They are one in hearing and in hiding. They flee from the sound of the Lord God in the Garden (3:8). First to the man come questions of responsibility (3:9, 11), but the man fails to be responsible: "The woman whom Thou gavest to be with me, she gave me fruit of the tree, and I ate" (3:12). Here the man does not blame the woman; he does not say that the woman seduced him,[21] he blames the Deity. The verb which he uses for both the Deity and the woman is *ntn* (cf. 3:6). . . . This verb neither means nor implies seduction in this context or in the lexicon. Again, if the Yahwist intended to make woman the temptress, he missed a choice opportunity. The woman's response supports the point. "The serpent beguiled me, and I ate" (3:13). Only here occurs the strong verb *nsh'*, meaning to deceive, to seduce. God accepts this subject-verb combination when, immediately following the woman's accusation, Yahweh says to the serpent, "Because you have done this, cursed are you above all animals" (3:14).

Though the tempter (the serpent) is cursed,[22] the woman and the man are not. But they are judged, and the judgments are commentaries on the disastrous effects of their shared disobedience. They show how terrible human life has become as it stands between creation and grace. We misread if we assume that these judgments are mandates. They describe; they do not prescribe. They protest; they do not condone. Of special concern are the words telling the woman that her husband shall rule over her (3:16). This statement is not license for male supremacy, but rather it is condemnation of that very pattern.[23] Subju-

12
13

[21] See Westermann, op. cit., p. 340.

[22] For a discussion of the serpent, see Ricoeur, *The Symbolism of Evil*, op. cit., pp. 255–60.

[23] Cf. Edwin M. Good, *Irony in the Old Testament* (Philadelphia: Westminster Press, 1965), p. 84, note 4: "Is it not surprising that, in a culture where the subordination of woman to man was a virtually unquestioned social principle, the etiology of the subordination should be in the context of man's primal sin? Perhaps woman's subordination was not unquestioned in Israel." Cf. also Henricus Renckens, *Israel's Concept of the Beginning* (New York: Herder & Herder, 1964), pp. 127f.

gation and supremacy are perversions of creation. Through disobedience, the woman has become slave. Her initiative and her freedom
vanish. The man is corrupted also, for he has become master, ruling
over the one who is his God-given equal. The subordination of female
to male signifies their shared sin.[24] This sin vitiates all relationships:
between animals and human beings (3:15); mothers and children (3:16);
husbands and wives (3:16); people and the soil (3:17–18); humanity
and its work (3:19). Whereas in creation man and woman know harmony and equality, in sin they know alienation and discord. Grace
makes possible a new beginning.

A further observation about these judgments: they are culturally
conditioned. Husband and work (childbearing) define the woman; wife
and work (farming) define the man. A literal reading of the story limits
both creatures and limits the story. To be faithful translators, we must
recognize that women as well as men move beyond these culturally
defined roles, even as the intentionality and function of the myth move
beyond its original setting. Whatever forms stereotyping takes in our
own culture, they are judgments upon our common sin and disobedience. The suffering and oppression we women and men know now
are marks of our fall, not of our creation.

At this place of sin and judgment, "the man calls his wife's name
Eve" (3:20), thereby asserting his rule over her. The naming itself faults
the man for corrupting a relationship of mutuality and equality. And
so Yahweh evicts the primeval couple from the Garden, yet with signals of grace.[25] Interestingly, the conclusion of the story does not specify the sexes in flight. Instead the narrator resumes use of the generic
and androgynous term 'adham with which the story began and thereby
completes an overall ring composition (3:22–24).

Visiting the Garden of Eden in the days of the Women's Movement, we need no longer accept the traditional exegesis of Genesis 2–
3. Rather than legitimating the patriarchal culture from which it comes,
the myth places that culture under judgment. And thus it functions
to liberate, not to enslave. This function we can recover and appropriate. The Yahwist narrative tells us who we are (creatures of equality
and mutuality); it tells us who we have become (creatures of oppression); and so it opens possibilities for change, for a return to our true
liberation under God. In other words, the story calls female and male
to repent.

[24] *Contra* Westermann, op. cit., p. 357.
[25] Von Rad, op. cit., pp. 94, 148.

Questions

1. Trible says (paragraph 2) of Genesis 2:1–23 that the story "moves to its climax, not its decline, in the creation of woman. She is not an afterthought; she is the culmination." Do you agree with her interpretation? If not, on what do you base your disagreement with Trible?

2. Trible admits (paragraph 8) that "we do not know" why the serpent speaks to the woman and not to the man, but in the next two paragraphs she offers a speculation. Do you find her speculation persuasive? Why, or why not?

3. This essay is fairly technical, drawing as it does on the Hebrew text rather than simply on an English translation. Did you find the writing clear? If so, what are some of the devices by which Trible eased the reader's task? If you found the writing obscure, what are some of the sources of obscurity? For instance, does Trible fail to organize her material lucidly, or fail to define key terms, or make unexplained leaps in her argument?

C. S. Lewis

What Christians Believe

---

1. The Rival Conceptions of God

I have been asked to tell you what Christians believe, and I am going   1
to begin by telling you one thing that Christians do not need to believe. If you are a Christian you do not have to believe that all the other religions are simply wrong all through. If you are an atheist you do have to believe that the main point in all the religions of the whole world is simply one huge mistake. If you are a Christian, you are free

---

Clive Staples Lewis (1898–1963) taught medieval and renaissance literature at Oxford and later at Cambridge. He wrote about literature, and he wrote fiction (including children's books), poetry, and numerous essays and books on Christianity, from the point of view of a believer.

The material reprinted here was originally delivered to the British public in the early 1940s, in a series of radio addresses.

---

to think that all these religions, even the queerest ones, contain at least some hint of the truth. When I was an atheist I had to try to persuade myself that most of the human race have always been wrong about the question that mattered to them most: when I became a Christian I was able to take a more liberal view. But, of course, being a Christian does mean thinking that where Christianity differs from other religions, Christianity is right and they are wrong. As in arithmetic—there is only one right answer to a sum, and all other answers are wrong: but some of the wrong answers are much nearer being right than others.

The first big division of humanity is into the majority, who believe 2 in some kind of God or gods, and the minority who do not. On this point, Christianity lines up with the majority—lines up with ancient Greeks and Romans, modern savages, Stoics, Platonists, Hindus, Mohammedans, etc., against the modern Western European materialist.

Now I go on to the next big division. People who all believe in 3 God can be divided according to the sort of God they believe in. There are two very different ideas on this subject. One of them is the idea that He is beyond good and evil. We humans call one thing good and another thing bad. But according to some people that is merely our human point of view. These people would say that the wiser you become the less you would want to call anything good or bad, and the more clearly you would see that everything is good in one way and bad in another, and that nothing could have been different. Consequently, these people think that long before you got anywhere near the divine point of view the distinction would have disappeared altogether. We call a cancer bad, they would say, because it kills a man; but you might just as well call a successful surgeon bad because he kills a cancer. It all depends on the point of view. The other and opposite idea is that God is quite definitely "good" or "righteous," a God who takes sides, who loves love and hates hatred, who wants us to behave in one way and not in another. The first of these views—the one that thinks God beyond good and evil—is called Pantheism. It was held by the great Prussian philosopher Hegel and, as far as I can understand them, by the Hindus. The other view is held by Jews, Mohammedans and Christians.

And with this big difference between Pantheism and the Christian 4 idea of God, there usually goes another. Pantheists usually believe that God, so to speak, animates the universe as you animate your body: that the universe almost *is* God, so that if it did not exist He would not exist either, and anything you find in the universe is a part of God.

The Christian idea is quite different. They think God invented and made the universe—like a man making a picture or composing a tune. A painter is not a picture, and he does not die if his picture is destroyed. You may say, "He's put a lot of himself into it," but you only mean that all its beauty and interest has come out of his head. His skill is not in the picture in the same way that it is in his head, or even in his hands. I expect you see how this difference between Pantheists and Christians hangs together with the other one. If you do not take the distinction between good and bad very seriously, then it is easy to say that anything you find in this world is a part of God. But, of course, if you think some things really bad, and God really good, then you cannot talk like that. You must believe that God is separate from the world and that some of the things we see in it are contrary to His will. Confronted with a cancer or a slum the Pantheist can say, "If you could only see it from the divine point of view, you would realize that this also is God." The Christian replies, "Don't talk damned nonsense."[1] For Christianity is a fighting religion. It thinks God made the world— that space and time, heat and cold, and all the colors and tastes, and all the animals and vegetables, are things that God "made up out of His head" as a man makes up a story. But it also thinks that a great many things have gone wrong with the world that God made and that God insists, and insists very loudly, on our putting them right again.

And, of course, that raises a very big question. If a good God made 5 the world why has it gone wrong? And for many years I simply refused to listen to the Christian answers to this question, because I kept on feeling "whatever you say, and however clever your arguments are, isn't it much simpler and easier to say that the world was not made by any intelligent power? Aren't all your arguments simply a complicated attempt to avoid the obvious?" But then that threw me back into another difficulty.

My argument against God was that the universe seemed so cruel 6 and unjust. But how had I got this idea of *just* and *unjust*? A man does not call a line crooked unless he has some idea of a straight line. What was I comparing this universe with when I called it unjust? If the whole show was bad and senseless from A to Z, so to speak, why did I, who was supposed to be part of the show, find myself in such violent reaction against it? A man feels wet when he falls into water, because

---

[1] One listener complained of the word *damned* as frivolous swearing. But I mean exactly what I say—nonsense that is *damned* is under God's curse, and will (apart from God's grace) lead those who believe it to eternal death.

man is not a water animal: a fish would not feel wet. Of course I could have given up my idea of justice by saying it was nothing but a private idea of my own. But if I did that, then my argument against God collapsed too—for the argument depended on saying that the world was really unjust, not simply that it did not happen to please my private fancies. Thus in the very act of trying to prove that God did not exist—in other words, that the whole of reality was senseless—I found I was forced to assume that one part of reality—namely my idea of justice—was full of sense. Consequently atheism turns out to be too simple. If the whole universe has no meaning, we should never have found out that it has no meaning: just as, if there were no light in the universe and therefore no creatures with eyes, we should never know it was dark. *Dark* would be without meaning.

2. The Invasion

Very well then, atheism is too simple. And I will tell you another view that is also too simple. It is the view I call Christianity-and-water, the view which simply says there is a good God in Heaven and everything is all right—leaving out all the difficult and terrible doctrines about sin and hell and the devil, and the redemption. Both these are boys' philosophies. 7

It is no good asking for a simple religion. After all, real things are not simple. They look simple, but they are not. The table I am sitting at looks simple: but ask a scientist to tell you what it is really made of—all about the atoms and how the light waves rebound from them and hit my eye and what they do to the optic nerve and what it does to my brain—and, of course, you find that what we call "seeing a table" lands you in mysteries and complications which you can hardly get to the end of. A child saying a child's prayer looks simple. And if you are content to stop there, well and good. But if you are not—and the modern world usually is not—if you want to go on and ask what is really happening—then you must be prepared for something difficult. If we ask for something more than simplicity, it is silly then to complain that the something more is not simple. 8

Very often, however, this silly procedure is adopted by people who are not silly, but who, consciously or unconsciously, want to destroy Christianity. Such people put up a version of Christianity suitable for a child of six and make that the object of their attack. When you try to explain the Christian doctrine as it is really held by an instructed adult, they then complain that you are making their heads 9 turn round and that it is all too complicated and that if there really were a God they are sure He would have made "religion" simple, because simplicity is so beautiful, etc. You must be on your guard against these people for they will change their ground every minute and only waste your time. Notice, too, their idea of God "making religion simple": as if "religion" were something God invented, and not His statement to us of certain quite unalterable facts about His own nature.

Besides being complicated, reality, in my experience, is usually 10 odd. It is not neat, not obvious, not what you expect. For instance, when you have grasped that the earth and the other planets all go round the sun, you would naturally expect that all the planets were made to match—all at equal distances from each other, say, or distances that regularly increased, or all the same size, or else getting bigger or smaller as you go farther from the sun. In fact, you find no rhyme or reason (that we can see) about either the sizes or the distances; and some of them have one moon, one has four, one has two, some have none, and one has a ring.

Reality, in fact, is usually something you could not have guessed. 11 That is one of the reasons I believe Christianity. It is a religion you could not have guessed. If it offered us just the kind of universe we had always expected, I should feel we were making it up. But, in fact, it is not the sort of thing anyone would have made up. It has just that queer twist about it that real things have. So let us leave behind all these boys' philosophies—these oversimple answers. The problem is not simple and the answer is not going to be simpler either.

What is the problem? ∴ universe that contains much that is ob- 12 viously bad and apparently meaningless, but containing creatures like ourselves who know that it is bad and meaningless. There are only two views that face all the facts. One is the Christian view that this is a good world that has gone wrong, but still retains the memory of what it ought to have been. The other is the view called Dualism. Dualism means the belief that there are two equal and independent powers at the back of everything, one of them good and the other bad, and that this universe is the battlefield in which they fight out an endless war. I personally think that next to Christianity Dualism is the manliest and most sensible creed on the market. But it has a catch in it.

The two powers, or spirits, or gods—the good one and the bad 13 one—are supposed to be quite independent. They both existed from all eternity. Neither of them made the other, neither of them has any more right than the other to call itself God. Each presumably thinks it is good and thinks the other bad. One of them likes hatred and cruelty, the other likes love and mercy, and each backs its own view. Now what do we mean when we call one of them the Good Power and the other the Bad Power? Either we are merely saying that we happen to prefer the one to the other—like preferring beer to cider—or else we are saying that, whatever the two powers think about it, and whichever we humans, at the moment, happen to like, one of them is actually wrong, actually mistaken, in regarding itself as good. Now if we mean merely that we happen to prefer the first, then we must give up talking about good and evil at all. For good means what you ought to prefer quite regardless of what you happen to like at any given moment. If "being good" meant simply joining the side you happened to fancy, for no real reason, then good would not deserve to be called good. So we must mean that one of the two powers is actually wrong and the other actually right.

But the moment you say that, you are putting into the universe a   14
third thing in addition to the two Powers: some law or standard or rule of good which one of the powers conforms to and the other fails to conform to. But since the two powers are judged by this standard, then this standard, or the Being who made this standard, is farther back and higher up than either of them, and He will be the real God. In fact, what we meant by calling them good and bad turns out to be that one of them is in a right relation to the real ultimate God and the other in a wrong relation to Him.

The same point can be made in a different way. If Dualism is true,   15
then the bad Power must be a being who likes badness for its own sake. But in reality we have no experience of anyone liking badness just because it is bad. The nearest we can get to it is in cruelty. But in real life people are cruel for one of two reasons—either because they are sadists, that is, because they have a sexual perversion which makes cruelty a cause of sensual pleasure to them, or else for the sake of something they are going to get out of it—money, or power, or safety. But pleasure, money, power, and safety are all, as far as they go, good things. The badness consists in pursuing them by the wrong method, or in the wrong way, or too much. I do not mean, of course, that the people who do this are not desperately wicked. I do mean that wickedness, when you examine it, turns out to be the pursuit of some good in the wrong way. You can be good for the mere sake of goodness: you cannot be bad for the mere sake of badness. You can do a kind action when you are not feeling kind and when it gives you no plea-

sure, simply because kindness is right; but no one ever did a cruel action simply because cruelty is wrong—only because cruelty was pleasant or useful to him. In other words badness cannot succeed even in being bad in the same way in which goodness is good. Goodness is, so to speak, itself: badness is only spoiled goodness. And there must be something good first before it can be spoiled. We called sadism a sexual perversion; but you must first have the idea of a normal sexuality before you can talk of its being perverted: and you can see which is the perversion, because you can explain the perverted from the normal, and cannot explain the normal from the perverted. It follows that this Bad Power, who is supposed to be on an equal footing with the Good Power, and to love badness in the same way as the Good Power loves goodness, is a mere bogy. In order to be bad he must have good things to want and then to pursue in the wrong way: he must have impulses which were originally good in order to be able to pervert them. But if he is bad he cannot supply himself either with good things to desire or with good impulses to pervert. He must be getting both from the Good Power. And if so, then he is not independent. He is part of the Good Power's world: he was made either by the Good Power or by some power above them both.

Put it more simply still. To be bad, he must exist and have intel- 16
ligence and will. But existence, intelligence and will are in themselves good. Therefore he must be getting them from the Good Power: even to be bad he must borrow or steal from his opponent. And do you now begin to see why Christianity has always said that the devil is a fallen angel? That is not a mere story for the children. It is a real recognition of the fact that evil is a parasite, not an original thing. The powers which enable evil to carry on are powers given it by goodness. All the things which enable a bad man to be effectively bad are in themselves good things—resolution, cleverness, good looks, existence itself. That is why Dualism, in a strict sense, will not work.

But I freely admit that real Christianity (as distinct from Christi- 17
anity-and-water) goes much nearer to Dualism than people think. One of the things that surprised me when I first read the New Testament seriously was that it talked so much about a Dark Power in the universe—a mighty evil spirit who was held to be the Power behind death and disease, and sin. The difference is that Christianity thinks this Dark Power was created by God, and was good when he was created, and went wrong. Christianity agrees with Dualism that this universe is at war. But it does not think this is a war between independent powers. It thinks it is a civil war, a rebellion, and that we are living in a part of the universe occupied by the rebel.

Enemy-occupied territory—that is what this world is. Christianity 18
is the story of how the rightful king has landed, you might say landed
in disguise, and is calling us all to take part in a great campaign of
sabotage. When you go to church you are really listening in to the
secret wireless from our friends: that is why the enemy is so anxious
to prevent us from going. He does it by playing on our conceit and
laziness and intellectual snobbery. I know someone will ask me, "Do
you really mean, at this time of day, to reintroduce our old friend the
devil—hoofs and horns and all?" Well, what the time of day has to
do with it I do not know. And I am not particular about the hoofs and
horns. But in other respects my answer is "Yes, I do." I do not claim
to know anything about his personal appearance. If anybody really
wants to know him better I would say to that person, "Don't worry.
If you really want to, you will. Whether you'll like it when you do is
another question."

3. *The Shocking Alternative*

Christians, then, believe that an evil power has made himself for the 19
present the Prince of this World. And, of course, that raises problems.
Is this state of affairs in accordance with God's will or not? If it is, He
is a strange God, you will say: and if it is not, how can anything happen
contrary to the will of a being with absolute power?

But anyone who has been in authority knows how a thing can be 20
in accordance with your will in one way and not in another. It may
be quite sensible for a mother to say to the children, "I'm not going
to go and make you tidy the schoolroom every night. You've got to
learn to keep it tidy on your own." Then she goes up one night and
finds the Teddy bear and the ink and the French Grammar all lying
in the grate. That is against her will. She would prefer the children to
be tidy. But on the other hand, it is her will which has left the children
free to be untidy. The same thing arises in any regiment, or trade
union, or school. You make a thing voluntary and then half the people
do not do it. That is not what you willed, but your will has made it
possible.

It is probably the same in the universe. God created things which 21
had free will. That means creatures which can go either wrong or right.
Some people think they can imagine a creature which was free but had
no possibility of going wrong; I cannot. If a thing is free to be good it
is also free to be bad. And free will is what has made evil possible.
Why, then, did God give them free will? Because free will, though it
makes evil possible, is also the only thing that makes possible any love

or goodness or joy worth having. A world of automata—of creatures that worked like machines—would hardly be worth creating. The happiness which God designs for His higher creatures is the happiness of being freely, voluntarily united to Him and to each other in an ecstasy of love and delight compared with which the most rapturous love between a man and a woman on this earth is mere milk and water. And for that they must be free.

Of course God knew what would happen if they used their freedom the wrong way: apparently He thought it worth the risk. Perhaps we feel inclined to disagree with Him. But there is a difficulty about disagreeing with God. He is the source from which all your reasoning power comes: you could not be right and He wrong any more than a stream can rise higher than its own source. When you are arguing against Him you are arguing against the very power that makes you able to argue at all: it is like cutting off the branch you are sitting on. If God thinks this state of war in the universe a price worth paying for free will—that is, for making a live world in which creatures can do real good or harm and something of real importance can happen, instead of a toy world which only moves when He pulls the strings— then we may take it it is worth paying. 22

When we have understood about free will, we shall see how silly it is to ask, as somebody once asked me: "Why did God make a creature of such rotten stuff that it went wrong?" The better stuff a creature is made of—the cleverer and stronger and freer it is—then the better it will be if it goes right, but also the worse it will be if it goes wrong. A cow cannot be very good or very bad; a dog can be both better and worse; a child better and worse still; an ordinary man, still more so; a man of genius, still more so; a superhuman spirit best—or worst— of all. 23

How did the Dark Power go wrong? Here, no doubt, we ask a question to which human beings cannot give an answer with any certainty. A reasonable (and traditional) guess, based on our own experiences of going wrong, can, however, be offered. The moment you have a self at all, there is a possibility of putting yourself first—wanting to be the center—wanting to be God, in fact. That was the sin of Satan: and that was the sin he taught the human race. Some people think the fall of man had something to do with sex, but that is a mistake. (The story in the Book of Genesis rather suggests that some corruption in our sexual nature followed the fall and was its result, not its cause.) What Satan put into the heads of our remote ancestors was the idea that they could "be like gods"—could set up on their own as if they 24 had created themselves—be their own masters—invent some sort of happiness for themselves outside God, apart from God. And out of that hopeless attempt has come nearly all that we call human history—money, poverty, ambition, war, prostitution, classes, empires, slavery—the long terrible story of man trying to find something other than God which will make him happy.

The reason why it can never succeed is this. God made us: invented us as a man invents an engine. A car is made to run on gasoline, and it would not run properly on anything else. Now God designed the human machine to run on Himself. He Himself is the fuel our spirits were designed to burn, or the food our spirits were designed to feed on. There is no other. That is why it is just no good asking God to make us happy in our own way without bothering about religion. God cannot give us a happiness and peace apart from Himself, because it is not there. There is no such thing. **25**

That is the key to history. Terrific energy is expended—civilizations are built up—excellent institutions devised; but each time something goes wrong. Some fatal flaw always brings the selfish and cruel people to the top and it all slides back into misery and ruin. In fact, the machine conks. It seems to start up all right and runs a few yards, and then it breaks down. They are trying to run it on the wrong juice. That is what Satan has done to us humans. **26**

And what did God do? First of all He left us conscience, the sense of right and wrong: and all through history there have been people trying (some of them very hard) to obey it. None of them ever quite succeeded. Secondly, He sent the human race what I call good dreams: I mean those queer stories scattered all through the heathen religions about a god who dies and comes to life again and, by his death, has somehow given new life to men. Thirdly, He selected one particular people and spent several centuries hammering into their heads the sort of God He was—that there was only one of Him and that He cared about right conduct. Those people were the Jews, and the Old Testament gives an account of the hammering process. **27**

Then comes the real shock. Among these Jews there suddenly turns up a man who goes about talking as if He was God. He claims to forgive sins. He says He has always existed. He says He is coming to judge the world at the end of time. Now let us get this clear. Among Pantheists, like the Indians, anyone might say that he was a part of God, or one with God: there would be nothing very odd about it. But this man, since He was a Jew, could not mean that kind of God. God, in their language, meant the Being outside the world Who had made **28** it and was infinitely different from anything else. And when you have grasped that, you will see that what this man said was, quite simply, the most shocking thing that has ever been uttered by human lips.

One part of the claim tends to slip past us unnoticed because we have heard it so often that we no longer see what it amounts to. I mean the claim to forgive sins: any sins. Now unless the speaker is God, this is really so preposterous as to be comic. We can all understand how a man forgives offenses against himself. You tread on my toe and I forgive you, you steal my money and I forgive you. But what should we make of a man, himself unrobbed and untrodden on, who announced that he forgave you for treading on other men's toes and stealing other men's money? Asinine fatuity is the kindest description we should give of his conduct. Yet this is what Jesus did. He told people that their sins were forgiven, and never waited to consult all the other people whom their sins had undoubtedly injured. He unhesitatingly behaved as if He was the party chiefly concerned, the person chiefly offended in all offenses. This makes sense only if He really was the God whose laws are broken and whose love is wounded in every sin. In the mouth of any speaker who is not God, these words would imply what I can only regard as a silliness and conceit unrivalled by any other character in history.

Yet (and this is the strange, significant thing) even His enemies, when they read the Gospels, do not usually get the impression of silliness and conceit. Still less do unprejudiced readers. Christ says that He is "humble and meek" and we believe Him; not noticing that, if He were merely a man, humility and meekness are the very last characteristics we could attribute to some of His sayings.

I am trying here to prevent anyone saying the really foolish thing that people often say about Him: "I'm ready to accept Jesus as a great moral teacher, but I don't accept His claim to be God." That is the one thing we must not say. A man who was merely a man and said the sort of things Jesus said would not be a great moral teacher. He would either be a lunatic—on a level with the man who says he is a poached egg—or else he would be the Devil of Hell. You must make your choice. Either this man was, and is, the Son of God: or else a madman or something worse. You can shut Him up for a fool, you can spit at Him and kill Him as a demon; or you can fall at His feet and call Him Lord and God. But let us not come with any patronizing nonsense about His being a great human teacher. He has not left that open to us. He did not intend to.

4. *The Perfect Penitent*

We are faced, then, with a frightening alternative. This man we are   32
talking about either was (and is) just what He said or else a lunatic,
or something worse. Now it seems to me obvious that He was neither
a lunatic nor a fiend: and consequently, however strange or terrifying
or unlikely it may seem, I have to accept the view that He was and is
God. God has landed on this enemy-occupied world in human form.

And now, what was the purpose of it all? What did He come to   33
do? Well, to teach, of course; but as soon as you look into the New
Testament or any other Christian writing you will find they are constantly talking about something different—about His death and His
coming to life again. It is obvious that Christians think the chief point
of the story lies here. They think the main thing He came to earth to
do was to suffer and be killed.

Now before I became a Christian I was under the impression that   34
the first thing Christians had to believe was one particular theory as
to what the point of this dying was. According to that theory God
wanted to punish men for having deserted and joined the Great Rebel,
but Christ volunteered to be punished instead, and so God let us off.
Now I admit that even this theory does not seem to me quite so immoral and so silly as it used to; but that is not the point I want to make.
What I came to see later on was that neither this theory nor any other
is Christianity. The central Christian belief is that Christ's death has
somehow put us right with God and given us a fresh start. Theories
as to how it did this are another matter. A good many different theories
have been held as to how it works: what all Christians are agreed on
is that it does work. I will tell you what I think it is like. All sensible
people know that if you are tired and hungry a meal will do you good.
But the modern theory of nourishment—all about the vitamins and
proteins—is a different thing. People ate their dinners and felt better
long before the theory of vitamins was ever heard of: and if the theory
of vitamins is some day abandoned they will go on eating their dinners
just the same. Theories about Christ's death are not Christianity: they
are explanations about how it works. Christians would not all agree
as to how important these theories are. My own church—the Church
of England—does not lay down any one of them as the right one. The
Church of Rome goes a bit further. But I think they will all agree that
the thing itself is infinitely more important than any explanations that
theologians have produced. I think they would probably admit that

no explanation will ever be quite adequate to the reality. But . . . I am only a layman, and at this point we are getting into deep water. I can only tell you, for what it is worth, how I, personally, look at the matter.

On my view the theories are not themselves the thing you are 35 asked to accept. Many of you no doubt have read Jeans or Eddington. What they do when they want to explain the atom, or something of that sort, is to give you a description out of which you can make a mental picture. But then they warn you that this picture is not what the scientists actually believe. What the scientists believe is a mathematical formula. The pictures are there only to help you to understand the formula. They are not really true in the way the formula is; they do not give you the real thing but only something more or less like it. They are only meant to help, and if they do not help you can drop them. The thing itself cannot be pictured, it can only be expressed mathematically. We are in the same boat here. We believe that the death of Christ is just that point in history at which something absolutely unimaginable from outside shows through into our own world. And if we cannot picture even the atoms of which our own world is built, of course we are not going to be able to picture this. Indeed, if we found that we could fully understand it, that very fact would show it was not what it professes to be—the inconceivable, the uncreated, the thing from beyond nature, striking down into nature like lightning. You may ask what good will it be to us if we do not understand it. But that is easily answered. A man can eat his dinner without understanding exactly how food nourishes him. A man can accept what Christ has done without knowing how it works; indeed, he certainly would not know how it works until he has accepted it.

We are told that Christ was killed for us, that His death has washed 36 out our sins, and that by dying He disabled death itself. That is the formula. That is Christianity. That is what has to be believed. Any theories we build up as to how Christ's death did all this are, in my view, quite secondary: mere plans or diagrams to be left alone if they do not help us, and, even if they do help us, not to be confused with the thing itself. All the same, some of these theories are worth looking at.

The one most people have heard is the one I mentioned before— 37 the one about our being let off because Christ had volunteered to bear a punishment instead of us. Now on the face of it that is a very silly theory. If God was prepared to let us off, why on earth did He not do so? And what possible point could there be in punishing an innocent person instead? None at all that I can see, if you are thinking of punishment in the police-court sense. On the other hand, if you think of a debt, there is plenty of point in a person who has some assets paying it on behalf of someone who has not. Or if you take "paying the penalty," not in the sense of being punished, but in the more general sense of "standing the racket" or "footing the bill," then, of course, it is a matter of common experience that, when one person has got himself into a hole, the trouble of getting him out usually falls on a kind friend.

Now what was the sort of "hole" man had got himself into? He 37 had tried to set up on his own, to behave as if he belonged to himself. In other words, fallen man is not simply an imperfect creature who needs improvement: he is a rebel who must lay down his arms. Laying down your arms, surrendering, saying you are sorry, realizing that you have been on the wrong track and getting ready to start life over again from the ground floor—that is the only way out of a "hole." This process of surrender—this movement full speed astern—is what Christians call repentance. Now repentance is no fun at all. It is something much harder than merely eating humble pie. It means unlearning all the self-conceit and self-will that we have been training ourselves into for thousands of years. It means killing part of yourself, undergoing a kind of death. In fact, it needs a good man to repent. And here comes the catch. Only a bad person needs to repent: only a good person can repent perfectly. The worse you are the more you need it and the less you can do it. The only person who could do it perfectly would be a perfect person—and he would not need it.

Remember, this repentance, this willing submission to humiliation 38 and a kind of death, is not something God demands of you before He will take you back and which He could let you off if He chose: it is simply a description of what going back to Him is like. If you ask God to take you back without it, you are really asking Him to let you go back without going back. It cannot happen. Very well, then, we must go through with it. But the same badness which makes us need it, makes us unable to do it. Can we do it if God helps us? Yes, but what do we mean when we talk of God helping us? We mean God putting into us a bit of Himself, so to speak. He lends us a little of His reasoning powers and that is how we think: He puts a little of His love into us and that is how we love one another. When you teach a child writing, you hold its hand while it forms the letters: that is, it forms the letters because you are forming them. We love and reason because God loves and reasons and holds our hand while we do it. Now if we had not fallen, that would be all plain sailing. But unfortunately we now need

God's help in order to do something which God, in His own nature, never does at all—to surrender, to suffer, to submit, to die. Nothing in God's nature corresponds to this process at all. So that the one road for which we now need God's leadership most of all is a road God, in His own nature, has never walked. God can share only what He has: this thing, in His own nature, He has not.

But supposing God became a man—suppose our human nature   39
which can suffer and die was amalgamated with God's nature in one person—then that person could help us. He could surrender His will, and suffer and die, because He was man; and He could do it perfectly because He was God. You and I can go through this process only if God does it in us; but God can do it only if He becomes man. Our attempts at this dying will succeed only if we men share in God's dying, just as our thinking can succeed only because it is a drop out of the ocean of His intelligence: but we cannot share God's dying unless God dies; and He cannot die except by being a man. That is the sense in which He pays our debt, and suffers for us what He Himself need not suffer at all.

I have heard some people complain that if Jesus was God as well   40
as man, then His sufferings and death lose all value in their eyes, "because it must have been so easy for him." Others may (very rightly) rebuke the ingratitude and ungraciousness of this objection; what staggers me is the misunderstanding it betrays. In one sense, of course, those who make it are right. They have even understated their own case. The perfect submission, the perfect suffering, the perfect death were not only easier to Jesus because He was God, but were possible only because He was God. But surely that is a very odd reason for not accepting them. The teacher is able to form the letters for the child because the teacher is grown-up and knows how to write. That, of course, makes it easier for the teacher; and only because it is easier for him can he help the child. If it rejected him because "it's easy for grown-ups" and waited to learn writing from another child who could not write itself (and so had no "unfair" advantage), it would not get on very quickly. If I am drowning in a rapid river, a man who still has one foot on the bank may give me a hand which saves my life. Ought I to shout back (between my gasps), "No, it's not fair! You have an advantage! You're keeping one foot on the bank"? That advantage— call it "unfair" if you like—is the only reason why he can be of any use to me. To what will you look for help if you will not look to that which is stronger than yourself?

Such is my own way of looking at what Christians call the Atone-   41
ment. But remember this is only one more picture. Do not mistake it
for the thing itself: and if it does not help you, drop it.

5. *The Practical Conclusion*

The perfect surrender and humiliation were undergone by Christ: per-   42
fect because He was God, surrender and humiliation because He was
man. Now the Christian belief is that if we somehow share the humility
and suffering of Christ we shall also share in His conquest of death
and find a new life after we have died and in it become perfect, and
perfectly happy, creatures. This means something much more than
our trying to follow His teaching. People often ask when the next step
in evolution—the step to something beyond man—will happen. But
in the Christian view, it has happened already. In Christ a new kind
of man appeared: and the new kind of life which began in Him is to
be put into us.

How is this to be done? Now, please remember how we acquired   43
the old, ordinary kind of life. We derived it from others, from our
father and mother and all our ancestors, without our consent—and
by a very curious process, involving pleasure, pain, and danger. A
process you would never have guessed. Most of us spend a good many
years in childhood trying to guess it: and some children, when they
are first told, do not believe it—and I am not sure that I blame them,
for it is very odd. Now the God who arranged that process is the same
God who arranges how the new kind of life—the Christ life—is to be
spread. We must be prepared for it being odd too. He did not consult
us when He invented sex: He has not consulted us either when He
invented this.

There are three things that spread the Christ life to us: baptism,   44
belief, and that mysterious action which different Christians call by
different names—Holy Communion, the Mass, the Lord's Supper. At
least, those are the three ordinary methods. I am not saying there may
not be special cases where it is spread without one or more of these.
I have not time to go into special cases, and I do not know enough.
If you are trying in a few minutes to tell a man how to get to Edinburgh
you will tell him the trains: he can, it is true, get there by boat or by
a plane, but you will hardly bring that in. And I am not saying anything
about which of these three things is the most essential. My Methodist
friend would like me to say more about belief and less (in proportion)

about the other two. But I am not going into that. Anyone who professes to teach you Christian doctrine will, in fact, tell you to use all three, and that is enough for our present purpose.

I cannot myself see why these things should be the conductors of 45 the new kind of life. But then, if one did not happen to know, I should never have seen any connection between a particular physical pleasure and the appearance of a new human being in the world. We have to take reality as it comes to us: there is no good jabbering about what it ought to be like or what we should have expected it to be like. But though I cannot see why it should be so, I can tell you why I believe it is so. I have explained why I have to believe that Jesus was (and is) God. And it seems plain as a matter of history that He taught His followers that the new life was communicated in this way. In other words, I believe it on His authority. Do not be scared by the word authority. Believing things on authority only means believing them because you have been told them by someone you think trustworthy. Ninety-nine percent of the things you believe are believed on authority. I believe there is such a place as New York. I have not seen it myself. I could not prove by abstract reasoning that there must be such a place. I believe it because reliable people have told me so. The ordinary man believes in the Solar System, atoms, evolution, and the circulation of the blood on authority—because the scientists say so. Every historical statement in the world is believed on authority. None of us has seen the Norman Conquest or the defeat of the Armada. None of us could prove them by pure logic as you prove a thing in mathematics. We believe them simply because people who did see them have left writings that tell us about them: in fact, on authority. A man who jibbed at authority in other things as some people do in religion would have to be content to know nothing all his life.

Do not think I am setting up baptism and belief and the Holy 46 Communion as things that will do instead of your own attempts to copy Christ. Your natural life is derived from your parents; that does not mean it will stay there if you do nothing about it. You can lose it by neglect, or you can drive it away by committing suicide. You have to feed it and look after it: but always remember you are not making it, you are only keeping up a life you got from someone else. In the same way a Christian can lose the Christ-life which has been put into him, and he has to make efforts to keep it. But even the best Christian that ever lived is not acting on his own steam—he is only nourishing or protecting a life he could never have acquired by his own efforts. And that has practical consequences. As long as the natural life is in your body, it will do a lot towards repairing that body. Cut it, and up to a point it will heal, as a dead body would not. A live body is not one that never gets hurt, but one that can to some extent repair itself. In the same way a Christian is not a man who never goes wrong, but a man who is enabled to repent and pick himself up and begin over again after each stumble—because the Christ-life is inside him, repairing him all the time, enabling him to repeat (in some degree) the kind of voluntary death which Christ Himself carried out.

That is why the Christian is in a different position from other people who are trying to be good. They hope, by being good, to please God if there is one; or—if they think there is not—at least they hope to deserve approval from good men. But the Christian thinks any good he does comes from the Christ-life inside him. He does not think God will love us because we are good, but that God will make us good because He loves us; just as the roof of a greenhouse does not attract the sun because it is bright, but becomes bright because the sun shines on it.

And let me make it quite clear that when Christians say the Christ-life is in them, they do not mean simply something mental or moral. When they speak of being "in Christ" or of Christ being "in them," this is not simply a way of saying that they are thinking about Christ or copying Him. They mean that Christ is actually operating through them; that the whole mass of Christians are the physical organism through which Christ acts—that we are His fingers and muscles, the cells of His body. And perhaps that explains one or two things. It explains why this new life is spread not only by purely mental acts like belief, but by bodily acts like baptism and Holy Communion. It is not merely the spreading of an idea; it is more like evolution—a biological or super-biological fact. There is no good trying to be more spiritual than God. God never meant man to be a purely spiritual creature. That is why He uses material things like bread and wine to put the new life into us. We may think this rather crude and unspiritual. God does not: He invented eating. He likes matter. He invented it.

Here is another thing that used to puzzle me. Is it not frightfully unfair that this new life should be confined to people who have heard of Christ and been able to believe in Him? But the truth is God has not told us what His arrangements about the other people are. We do know that no man can be saved except through Christ; we do not know that only those who know Him can be saved through Him. But in the meantime, if you are worried about the people outside, the most unreasonable thing you can do is to remain outside yourself. Christians are Christ's body, the organism through which He works. Every addition to that body enables Him to do more. If you want to help those outside you must add your own little cell to the body of Christ who alone can help them. Cutting off a man's fingers would be an odd way of getting him to do more work.

Another possible objection is this. Why is God landing in this 50 enemy-occupied world in disguise and starting a sort of secret society to undermine the devil? Why is He not landing in force, invading it? Is it that He is not strong enough? Well, Christians think He is going to land in force; we do not know when. But we can guess why He is delaying. He wants to give us the chance of joining His side freely. I do not suppose you and I would have thought much of a Frenchman who waited till the Allies were marching into Germany and then announced he was on our side. God will invade. But I wonder whether people who ask God to interfere openly and directly in our world quite realize what it will be like when He does. When that happens, it is the end of the world. When the author walks on to the stage the play is over. God is going to invade, all right: but what is the good of saying you are on His side then, when you see the whole natural universe melting away like a dream and something else—something it never entered your head to conceive—comes crashing in; something so beautiful to some of us and so terrible to others that none of us will have any choice left? For this time it will be God without disguise; something so overwhelming that it will strike either irresistible love or irresistible horror into every creature. It will be too late then to choose your side. There is no use saying you choose to lie down when it has become impossible to stand up. That will not be the time for choosing: it will be the time when we discover which side we really have chosen, whether we realized it before or not. Now, today, this moment, is our chance to choose the right side. God is holding back to give us that chance. It will not last for ever. We must take it or leave it.

Questions

1. In paragraphs 1 and 2 Lewis argues that Christianity is a more reasonable position than atheism. How does he make this argument?
2. What is Lewis's purpose in this essay? Is it comparable to a minister's purpose in preaching a sermon? In what ways does his essay differ from a sermon?
3. Lewis says that Christians believe in an evil power, and he suggests that our world is in the midst of a civil war. "Enemy-occupied ter-

ritory—that is what this world is," he says in paragraph 18. Does Lewis ask us to accept this idea literally, or metaphorically? In considering your answer to this question read the definition of "metaphor" in the Glossary, and look also at paragraph 35 in Lewis's essay. Is it relevant that the talks on which this essay is based were given in the 1940s?

4. As a writer Lewis strives to be clear, and he uses examples frequently. Would you agree that he uses examples effectively? Without looking back at the essay, which example do you remember most vividly? What point was he trying to make by it? (It's OK to look back as you answer the last part of this question.)

5. Where does Lewis introduce the example of sex? Why does he introduce it at that point in the essay, rather than earlier?

6. Lewis says (paragraph 11) that one reason for believing Christianity is that "it is a religion you could not have guessed." Why does he think that's a good reason? Do you agree that it is?

William James

Religious Faith[1]

Religion has meant many things in human history; but when from now onward I use the word I mean to use it in the supernaturalist sense, as declaring that the so-called order of nature, which constitutes this world's experience, is only one portion of the total universe, and that there stretches beyond this visible world an unseen world of which we now know nothing positive, but in its re-

[1] From *The Will to Believe*. (Editors' note)

William James (1842–1910), the older brother of the novelist Henry James, was one of the founders of the discipline of psychology in the United States. As he once remarked, the first lectures he ever heard on the subject were the ones he delivered in the 1870s.

James studied philosophy, science, and then medicine at Harvard University during the Civil War. In 1869–1870 he suffered extreme depression and experienced a nervous collapse, but he emerged from it with the conviction that only a belief in freedom of the will gives life meaning. This essay comes from a collection of James's essays called *The Will to Believe* (1897).

lation to which the true significance of our present mundane life consists. A man's religious faith (whatever more special items of doctrine it may involve) means for me essentially his faith in the existence of an unseen order of some kind in which the riddles of the natural order may be found explained. In the more developed religions the natural world has always been regarded as the mere scaffolding or vestibule of a truer, more eternal world, and affirmed to be a sphere of education, trial, or redemption. In these religions, one must in some fashion die to the natural life before one can enter into life eternal. The notion that this physical world of wind and water, when the sun rises and the moon sets, is absolutely and ultimately the divinely aimed-at and established thing, is one which we find only in very early religions. . . . It is this natural religion (primitive still, in spite of the fact that poets and men of science whose good-will exceeds their perspicacity keep publishing it in new editions tuned to our contemporary ears) that, as I said a while ago, has suffered definitive bankruptcy in the opinion of a circle of persons, among whom I must count myself, and who are growing more numerous every day. For such persons the physical order of nature, taken simply as science knows it, cannot be held to reveal any one harmonious spiritual intent. It is mere *weather*, as Chauncey Wright called it, doing and undoing without end.

Now, I wish to make you feel, if I can in the short remainder of   2 this hour, that we have a right to believe the physical order to be only a partial order; that we have a right to supplement it by an unseen spiritual order which we assume on trust, if only thereby life may seem to us better worth living again. But as such a trust will seem to some of you sadly mystical and execrably unscientific, I must first say a word or two to weaken the veto which you may consider that science opposes to our act.

There is included in human nature an ingrained naturalism and   3 materialism of mind which can only admit facts that are actually tangible. Of this sort of mind the entity called "science" is the idol. Fondness for the word "scientist" is one of the notes by which you may know its votaries; and its short way of killing any opinion that it disbelieves in is to call it "unscientific." It must be granted that there is no slight excuse for this. Science has made such glorious leaps in the last three hundred years, and extended our knowledge of nature so enormously both in general and in detail; men of science, moreover, have as a class displayed such admirable virtues—that it is no wonder if the worshippers of science lose their head. In this very University, accordingly, I have heard more than one teacher say that all the fundamental conceptions of truth have already been found by science, and that the future has only the details of the picture to fill in. But the slightest reflection on the real conditions will suffice to show how barbaric such notions are. They show such a lack of scientific imagination, that it is hard to see how one who is actively advancing any part of science can make a mistake so crude. Think how many absolutely new scientific conceptions have arisen in our own generation, how many new problems have been formulated that were never thought of before, and then cast an eye upon the brevity of science's career. It began with Galileo, not three hundred years ago. Four thinkers since Galileo, each informing his successor of what discoveries his own lifetime had seen achieved, might have passed the torch of science into our hands as we sit here in this room. Indeed, for the matter of that, an audience much smaller than the present one, an audience of some five or six score people, if each person in it could speak for his own generation, would carry us away to the black unknown of the human species, to days without a document or monument to tell their tale. Is it credible that such a mushroom knowledge, such a growth overnight as this, *can* represent more than the minutest glimpse of what the universe will really prove to be when adequately understood? No! our science is a drop, our ignorance a sea. Whatever else be certain, this at least is certain—that the world of our present natural knowledge *is* enveloped in a larger world of *some* sort of whose residual properties we at present can frame no positive idea.

    Agnostic positivism,[2] of course, admits this principle theoretically   4 in the most cordial terms, but insists that we must not turn it to any practical use. We have no right, this doctrine tells us, to dream dreams, or suppose anything about the unseen part of the universe, merely because to do so may be for what we are pleased to call our highest interests. We must always wait for sensible evidence for our beliefs; and where such evidence is inaccessible we must frame no hypotheses whatever. Of course this is a safe enough position *in abstracto*. If a thinker had no stake in the unknown, no vital needs, to live or languish according to what the unseen world contained, a philosophic neutrality and refusal to believe either one way or the other would be his wisest cue. But, unfortunately, neutrality is not only inwardly difficult, it is also outwardly unrealizable, where our relations to an alternative are practical and vital. This is because, as the psychologists tell us, belief

[2] A belief that human knowledge must be based on sense perceptions. (Editors' note)

and doubt are living attitudes, and involve conduct on our part. Our only way, for example, of doubting, or refusing to believe, that a certain thing *is,* is continuing to act as if it were *not.* If, for instance, I refuse to believe that the room is getting cold, I leave the windows open and light no fire just as if it still were warm. If I doubt that you are worthy of my confidence, I keep you uninformed of all my secrets just as if you were *un*worthy of the same. If I doubt the need of insuring my house, I leave it uninsured as much as if I believed there were no need. And so if I must not believe that the world is divine, I can only express that refusal by declining ever to act distinctively as if it were so, which can only mean acting on certain critical occasions as if it were *not* so, or in an irreligious way. There are, you see, inevitable occasions in life when inaction is a kind of action, and must count as action, and when not to be for is to be practically against; and in all such cases strict and consistent neutrality is an unattainable thing.

And, after all, is not this duty of neutrality where only our inner   5 interests would lead us to believe the most ridiculous of commands? Is it not sheer dogmatic folly to say that our inner interests can have no real connection with the forces that the hidden world may contain? In other cases divinations based on inner interests have proved prophetic enough. Take science itself! Without an imperious inner demand on our part for ideal logical and mathematical harmonies, we should never have attained to proving that such harmonies lie hidden between all the chinks and interstices of the crude natural world. Hardly a law has been established in science, hardly a fact ascertained, which was not first sought after, often with sweat and blood, to gratify an inner need. Whence such needs come from we do not know: we find them in us, and biological psychology so far only classes them with Darwin's "accidental variations." But the inner need of believing that this world of nature is a sign of something more spiritual and eternal than itself is just as strong and authoritative in those who feel it, as the inner need of uniform laws of causation ever can be in a professionally scientific head. The toil of many generations has proved the latter need prophetic. Why *may* not the former one be prophetic, too? And if needs of ours outrun the visible universe, why *may* not that be a sign that an invisible universe is there? What, in short, has authority to debar us from trusting our religious demands? Science as such assuredly has no authority, for she can only say what is, not what is not; and the agnostic "thou shalt not believe without coercive sensible evidence" is simply an expression (free to any one to make) of private personal appetite for evidence of a certain peculiar kind.

Now, when I speak of trusting our religious demands, just what 6
do I mean by "trusting"? Is the word to carry with it license to define
in detail an invisible world, and to anathematize and excommunicate
those whose trust is different? Certainly not! Our faculties of belief
were not primarily given us to make orthodoxies and heresies withal;
they were given us to live by. And to trust our religious demands
means first of all to live in the light of them, and to act as if the invisible
world which they suggest were real. It is a fact of human nature, that
men can live and die by the help of a sort of faith that goes without
a single dogma or definition. The bare assurance that this natural order
is not ultimate but a mere sign or vision, the external staging of a many-
storied universe, in which spiritual forces have the last word and are
eternal—this bare assurance is to such men enough to make life seem
worth living in spite of every contrary presumption suggested by its
circumstances on the natural plane. Destroy this inner assurance, however, vague as it is, and all the light and radiance of existence is extinguished for these persons at a stroke. Often enough the wild-eyed
look at life—the suicidal mood—will then set in.

And now the application comes directly home to you and me. 7
Probably to almost every one of us here the most adverse life would
seem well worth living, if we only could be *certain* that our bravery
and patience with it were terminating and eventuating and bearing
fruit somewhere in an unseen spiritual world. But granting we are not
certain, does it then follow that a bare trust in such a world is a fool's
paradise and lubberland, or rather that it is a living attitude in which
we are free to indulge? Well, we are free to trust at our own risks
anything that is not impossible, and that can bring analogies to bear
in its behalf. That the world of physics is probably not absolute, all
the converging multitude of arguments that make in favor of idealism
tend to prove; and that our whole physical life may lie soaking in a
spiritual atmosphere, a dimension of being that we at present have no
organ for apprehending, is vividly suggested to us by the analogy of
the life of our domestic animals. Our dogs, for example, are in our
human life but not of it. They witness hourly the outward body of
events whose inner meaning cannot, by any possible operation, be
revealed to their intelligence—events in which they themselves often
play the cardinal part. My terrier bites a teasing boy, for example, and
the father demands damages. The dog may be present at every step
of the negotiations, and see the money paid, without an inkling of
what it all means, without a suspicion that it has anything to do with
him; and he never *can* know in his natural dog's life. Or take another

case which used greatly to impress me in my medical-student days. Consider a poor dog whom they are vivisecting in a laboratory. He lies strapped on a board and shrieking at his executioners, and to his own dark consciousness is literally in a sort of hell. He cannot see a single redeeming ray in the whole business; and yet all these diabolical-seeming events are often controlled by human intentions with which, if his poor benighted mind could only be made to catch a glimpse of them, all that is heroic in him would religiously acquiesce. Healing truth, relief to future sufferings of beast and man, are to be bought by them. It may be genuinely a process of redemption. Lying on his back on the board there he may be performing a function incalculably higher than any that prosperous canine life admits of; and yet, of the whole performance, this function is the one portion that must remain absolutely beyond his ken.

Now turn from this to the life of man. In the dog's life we see the   8
world invisible to him because we live in both worlds. In human life, although we only see our world, and his within it, yet encompassing both these worlds a still wider world may be there, as unseen by us as our world is by him; and to believe in that world *may* be the most essential function that our lives in this world have to perform. But "*may* be! *may* be!" one now hears the positivist contemptuously exclaim; "what use can a scientific life have for maybes?" Well, I reply, the "scientific" life itself has much to do with maybes, and human life at large has everything to do with them. So far as man stands for anything, and is productive or originative at all, his entire vital function may be said to have to deal with maybes. Not a victory is gained, not a deed of faithfulness or courage is done, except upon a maybe; not a service, not a sally of generosity, not a scientific exploration or experiment or textbook, that may not be a mistake. It is only by risking our persons from one hour to another that we live at all. And often enough our faith beforehand in an uncertified result *is the only thing that makes the result come true.* Suppose, for instance, that you are climbing a mountain, and have worked yourself into a position from which the only escape is by a terrible leap. Have faith that you can successfully make it, and your feet are nerved to its accomplishment. But mistrust yourself, and think of all the sweet things you have heard the scientists say of *maybes,* and you will hesitate so long that, at last, all unstrung and trembling, and launching yourself in a moment of despair, you roll in the abyss. In such a case (and it belongs to an enormous class), the part of wisdom as well as of courage is to *believe what is in the line of your needs,* for only by such belief is the need fulfilled. Refuse to believe, and you shall indeed be right, for you shall irretrievably perish.

But believe, and again you shall be right, for you shall save yourself. You make one or the other of two possible universes true by your trust or mistrust—both universes having been only *maybes*, in this particular, before you contributed your act.

Now, it appears to me that the question whether life is worth living 9 is subject to conditions logically much like these. It does, indeed, depend on you *the liver.* If you surrender to the nightmare view and crown the evil edifice by your own suicide, you have indeed made a picture totally black. Pessimism, completed by your act, is true beyond a doubt, so far as your world goes. Your mistrust of life has removed whatever worth your own enduring existence might have given to it; and now, throughout the whole sphere of possible influence of that existence, the mistrust has proved itself to have had divining power. But suppose, on the other hand, that instead of giving way to the nightmare view you cling to it that this world is not the *ultimatum.* Suppose you find yourself a very well-spring, as Wordsworth says, of—

> Zeal, and the virtue to exist by faith
> As soldiers live by courage; as, by strength
> Of heart, the sailor fights with roaring seas.

Suppose, however thickly evils crowd upon you, that your unconquerable subjectivity proves to be their match, and that you find a more wonderful joy than any passive pleasure can bring in trusting ever in the larger whole. Have you not now made life worth living on these terms? What sort of a thing would life really be, with your qualities ready for a tussle with it, if it only brought fair weather and gave these higher faculties of yours no scope? Please remember that optimism and pessimism are definitions of the world, and that our own reactions on the world, small as they are in bulk, are integral parts of the whole thing, and necessarily help to determine the definition. They may even be the decisive elements in determining the definition. A large mass can have its unstable equilibrium overturned by the addition of a feather's weight; a long phrase may have its sense reversed by the addition of the three letters *n-o-t.* This life *is* worth living, we can say, *since it is what we make it, from the moral point of view;* and we are determined to make it from that point of view, so far as we have anything to do with it, a success.

Now, in this description of faiths that verify themselves I have 10 assumed that our faith in an invisible order is what inspires those efforts and that patience which make this visible order good for moral men. Our faith in the seen world's goodness (goodness now meaning fitness for successful moral and religious life) has verified itself by leaning on our faith in the unseen world. But will our faith in the unseen world similarly verify itself? Who knows?

Once more it is a case of *maybe*; and once more *maybes* are the essence of the situation. I confess that I do not see why the very existence of an invisible world may not in part depend on the personal response which any one of us may make to the religious appeal. God himself, in short, may draw vital strength and increase of very being from our fidelity. For my own part, I do not know what the sweat and blood and tragedy of this life mean, if they mean anything short of this. If this life be not a real fight, in which something is eternally gained for the universe by success, it is no better than a game of private theatricals from which one may withdraw at will. But it *feels* like a real fight—as if there were something really wild in the universe which we, with all our idealities and faithfulnesses, are needed to redeem; and first of all to redeem our own hearts from atheisms and fears. For such a half-wild, half-saved universe our nature is adapted. The deepest thing in our nature is this *Binnenleben*[3] (as a German doctor lately has called it), this dumb region of the heart in which we dwell alone with our willingnesses and unwillingnesses, our faiths and fears. As through the cracks and crannies of caverns those waters exude from the earth's bosom which then form the fountainheads of springs, so in these crepuscular depths of personality the sources of all our outer deeds and decisions take their rise. Here is our deepest organ of communication with the nature of things; and compared with these concrete movements of our soul all abstract statements and scientific arguments—the veto, for example, which the strict positivist pronounces upon our faith—sound to us like mere chatterings of the teeth. For here possibilities, not finished facts, are the realities with which we have actively to deal; and to quote my friend William Salter, of the Philadelphia Ethical Society, "as the essence of courage is to stake one's life on a possibility, so the essence of faith is to believe that the possibility exists."

These, then, are my last words to you: Be not afraid of life. Believe that life *is* worth living, and your belief will help create the fact. The "scientific proof" that you are right may not be clear before the day of judgment (or some stage of being which that expression may serve to symbolize) is reached. But the faithful fighters of this hour, or the

3 Interior life. (Editors' note)

beings that then and there will represent them, may then turn to the faint-hearted, who here decline to go on, with words like those with which Henry IV[4] greeted the tardy Crillon after a great victory had been gained: "Hang yourself, brave Crillon! We fought at Arques, and you were not there."

Questions

1. From the first two paragraphs what can you infer about James's audience? How would you characterize his relationship to the audience and the tone he establishes? Is his tone formal, or informal? Are he and his listeners on an equal footing. Does he expect that they will share most of his opinions and beliefs, or only some, or none?

2. James mentions the words "science" and "scientist" several times in his opening paragraphs, especially in paragraph 3. What is his attitude toward science? Is it mostly favorable, or critical, or mixed? How is science related to "natural religion," which he discussed in paragraph 1? And in paragraph 3, what argument (which he will further develop in paragraph 5) is suggested by the phrase "worshippers of science"?

3. In paragraph 4, what is James's argument against agnosticism? What is the *tone* of his remarks in this paragraph?

4. James frequently uses comparisons in building his argument. Read the entry on "analogy" in the Glossary, and then note the comparisons James makes that qualify as analogies. Do you find these analogies effective, or perhaps even persuasive? Is there anything about his subject matter that particularly lends itself to the use of analogy?

[4] Henry IV of France put down a rebellion at the battle of Arques, 1589. (Editors' note)

John Steinbeck

The Sermon

Sunday morning, in a Vermont town, my last day in New   1
England, I shaved, dressed in a suit, polished my shoes, whited my
sepulcher,[1] and looked for a church to attend. Several I eliminated for
reasons I do not now remember, but on seeing a John Knox church I
drove into a side street and parked Rocinante out of sight, gave Charley
his instructions about watching the truck, and took my way with dignity to a church of blindingly white ship lap. I took my seat in the rear
of the spotless, polished place of worship. The prayers were to the
point, directing the attention of the Almighty to certain weaknesses
and undivine tendencies I know to be mine and could only suppose
were shared by others gathered there.

The service did my heart and I hope my soul some good. It had   2
been long since I had heard such an approach. It is our practice now,
at least in the large cities, to find from our psychiatric priesthood that
our sins aren't really sins at all but accidents that are set in motion by
forces beyond our control. There was no such nonsense in this church.
The minister, a man of iron with tool-steel eyes and a delivery like a
pneumatic drill, opened up with prayer and reassured us that we were
a pretty sorry lot. And he was right. We didn't amount to much to
start with, and due to our own tawdry efforts we had been slipping

[1] In the Gospel according to St. Matthew 23:27 Jesus denounces hypocritical scribes
and Pharisees, comparing them to "whited sepulchers [i.e., tombs], which indeed
appear beautiful outward, but are within full of dead men's bones, and of all un-
cleanness." Steinbeck's next sentence refers to Rocinante, his genial name for his
truck. Rocinante was the name of Don Quixote's horse. Literally it means "formerly
a nag."

John Steinbeck (1902–1968) was born in Salinas, California, and much of his
writing concerns the Salinas Valley. In 1919 he entered Stanford University but
he left without a degree. He was determined to become a writer, yet for some
ten years he had little success and supported himself by odd jobs. Between 1935
and 1939, however, he achieved fame with several important books, including
Tortilla Flat (1935), *In Dubious Battle* (1936), *Of Mice and Men* (1937), and *The
Grapes of Wrath* (1939).

In addition to writing novels and short stories, Steinbeck wrote some non-
fiction, notably *Travels with Charley* (1962), a record of his automobile tour—
with his poodle, Charley—of forty states. The passage we print here comes from
Travels; the title of the selection is our own.

ever since. Then, having softened us up, he went into a glorious sermon, a fire-and-brimstone sermon. Having proved that we, or perhaps only I, were no damn good, he painted with cool certainty what was likely to happen to us if we didn't make some basic reorganizations for which he didn't hold out much hope. He spoke of hell as an expert, not the mush-mush hell of these soft days, but a well-stoked, white-hot hell served by technicians of the first order. This reverend brought it to a point where we could understand it, a good hard coal fire, plenty of draft, and a squad of open-hearth devils who put their hearts into their work, and their work was me. I began to feel good all over. For some years now God has been a pal to us, practicing togetherness, and that causes the same emptiness a father does playing softball with his son. But this Vermont God cared enough about me to go to a lot of trouble kicking the hell out of me. He put my sins in a new perspective. Whereas they had been small and mean and nasty and best forgotten, this minister gave them some size and bloom and dignity. I hadn't been thinking very well of myself for some years, but if my sins had this dimension there was some pride left. I wasn't a naughty child but a first rate sinner, and I was going to catch it.

I felt so revived in spirit that I put five dollars in the plate, and afterward, in front of the church, shook hands warmly with the minister and as many of the congregation as I could. It gave me a lovely sense of evil-doing that lasted clear through till Tuesday. I even considered beating Charley to give him some satisfaction too, because Charley is only a little less sinful than I am. All across the country I went to church on Sundays, a different denomination every week, but nowhere did I find the quality of that Vermont preacher. He forged a religion designed to last, not predigested obsolescence.

Questions

1. In his first sentence Steinbeck says: "Sunday morning, in a Vermont town, my last day in New England, I shaved, dressed in a suit, polished my shoes, whited my sepulcher, and looked for a church to attend." In a footnote we explain that Jesus, in the Gospel according to St. Matthew, applies the term "whited sepulchers" to hypocrites. But what is Steinbeck's tone here? Pretentious? Playful? Reverential? Savage? Or what? How does this reference prepare us for what comes later in the selection?

2. In paragraph 2 Steinbeck says, "The service did my heart . . . good." Do you think he means exactly what he says? If yes, what good *did*

it do? And do you think he means, in the final paragraph, that he really considered beating his dog? If he does mean—at least to some degree—that the service did his heart good, why not beat the dog?

3. How seriously do you think Steinbeck takes religion?

Langston Hughes

Salvation

I was saved from sin when I was going on thirteen. But 1 not really saved. It happened like this. There was a big revival at my Auntie Reed's church. Every night for weeks there had been much preaching, singing, praying, and shouting, and some very hardened sinners had been brought to Christ, and the membership of the church had grown by leaps and bounds. Then just before the revival ended, they held a special meeting for children, "to bring the young lambs to the fold." My aunt spoke of it for days ahead. That night I was escorted to the front row and placed on the mourners' bench with all the other young sinners, who had not yet been brought to Jesus.

My aunt told me that when you were saved you saw a light, and 2 something happened to you inside! And Jesus came into your life! And God was with you from then on! She said you could see and hear and feel Jesus in your soul. I believed her. I had heard a great many old people say the same thing and it seemed to me they ought to know. So I sat there calmly in the hot, crowded church, waiting for Jesus to come to me.

The preacher preached a wonderful rhythmical sermon, all moans 3 and shouts and lonely cries and dire pictures of hell, and then he sang a song about the ninety and nine safe in the fold, but one little lamb was left out in the cold. Then he said: "Won't you come? Won't you

Langston Hughes (1902–1967) was the first black American writer to establish an international reputation. Enormously versatile, he wrote poems, plays, stories, novels, children's books, filmscripts, autobiographies, and essays. Hughes also exerted a great influence on American literature by organizing poetry readings for black writers, and by founding three theater groups.

come to Jesus? Young lambs, won't you come?" And he held out his arms to all us young sinners there on the mourners' bench. And the little girls cried. And some of them jumped up and went to Jesus right away. But most of us just sat there.

A great many old people came and knelt around us and prayed, 4 old women with jet-black faces and braided hair, old men with work-gnarled hands. And the church sang a song about the lower lights are burning, some poor sinners to be saved. And the whole building rocked with prayer and song.

Still I kept waiting to *see* Jesus.   5

Finally all the young people had gone to the altar and were saved, 6 but one boy and me. He was a rounder's son named Westley. Westley and I were surrounded by sisters and deacons praying. It was very hot in the church, and getting late now. Finally Westley said to me in a whisper: "God damn! I'm tired o' sitting here. Let's get up and be saved." So he got up and was saved.

Then I was left all alone on the mourners' bench. My aunt came 7 and knelt at my knees and cried, while prayers and songs swirled all around me in the little church. The whole congregation prayed for me alone, in a mighty wail of moans and voices. And I kept waiting se-renely for Jesus, waiting, waiting—but he didn't come. I wanted to see him, but nothing happened to me. Nothing! I wanted something to happen to me, but nothing happened.

I heard the songs and the minister saying: "Why don't you come? 8 My dear child, why don't you come to Jesus? Jesus is waiting for you. He wants you. Why don't you come? Sister Reed, what is this child's name?"

"Langston," my aunt sobbed.   9

"Langston, why don't you come? Why don't you come and be 10 saved? Oh, Lamb of God! Why don't you come?"

Now it was really getting late. I began to be ashamed of myself, 11 holding everything up so long. I began to wonder what God thought about Westley, who certainly hadn't seen Jesus either, but who was now sitting proudly on the platform, swinging his knickerbockered legs and grinning down at me, surrounded by deacons and old women on their knees praying. God had not struck Westley dead for taking his name in vain or for lying in the temple. So I decided that maybe to save further trouble, I'd better lie, too, and say that Jesus had come, and get up and be saved.

So I got up.   12

Suddenly the whole room broke into a sea of shouting, as they 13 saw me rise. Waves of rejoicing swept the place. Women leaped in the air. My aunt threw her arms around me. The minister took me by the hand and led me to the platform.

When things quieted down, in a hushed silence, punctuated by a 14 few ecstatic "Amens," all the new young lambs were blessed in the name of God. Then joyous singing filled the room.

That night, for the last time in my life but one—for I was a big 15 boy twelve years old—I cried. I cried, in bed alone, and couldn't stop. I buried my head under the quilts, but my aunt heard me. She woke up and told my uncle I was crying because the Holy Ghost had come into my life, and because I had seen Jesus. But I was really crying because I couldn't bear to tell her that I had lied, that I had deceived everybody in the church, and I hadn't seen Jesus, and that now I didn't believe there was a Jesus any more, since he didn't come to help me.

Questions

1. Is this piece amusing, or serious, or both? Explain.
2. How would you characterize the style or voice of the first three sentences? Childlike? Sophisticated? How would you characterize the final sentence? How can you explain the change in style or tone?
3. Why does Hughes bother to tell us, in paragraph 11, that Westley was "swinging his knickerbockered legs and grinning"? Do you think that Westley, too, may have cried that night? Give your reasons.
4. Is the episode told from the point of view of someone "going on thirteen," or from the point of view of a mature man? Consult the entry on "persona" in the Glossary. One way to answer this question about point of view is to describe Hughes's persona in this essay. Does the essay strike you as in some ways "a performance"? If so, who is the audience—or who might be the ideal audience for this performance?

A Note on Buddhism

Buddhism was founded by Siddhartha (c. 563 B.C.–c. 483 B.C.) of the princely Gautama family. This family, which lived in the part of northeast India that is now Nepal, belonged to the Shakya clan, and so Siddhartha is also called Shakyamuni, the "Wise Man of the

Shakya Clan.'' He is also called Buddha, although ''Buddha''—meaning ''enlightened'' or ''awakened''—is a description of a condition, not a name. Anyone and everyone can become a Buddha, and much Buddhist thought holds that we are all Buddhas even though we do not know it.

At the age of twenty-nine Siddhartha vowed to save not only himself but all humanity from suffering. He left his father's palace, changed his princely robes for rags, and lived a life of asceticism, hoping to perceive a way of escaping from repeated rebirths in the cycle of existence. (Traditional Indian religion held that all actions produce fruit, good or evil. The deeds and their results are one's *karma*, and they determine the nature of the next rebirth.)

After six years, however, Siddhartha concluded that asceticism—like luxury—was not the way to perception. He abandoned a group of five monks with whom he had lived, and he wandered to Benares, where he achieved enlightenment (Sanskrit: *sambodhi;* Japanese: *satori*) or, as some prefer to call it, an ''awakening'' or an opening of the mind. This release of inner light or intuitive knowledge was not attained by self-castigation (e.g., by long fasts) or by scrupulous observations of rituals prescribed in sacred texts, but by meditation. Exactly what ''meditation'' is, however, is a topic much discussed by Buddhist sects.

The Buddha saw that the path to peace is the extinction of desires, the extinction of selfishness or of selfhood. The achievement of enlightenment is the attainment of *nirvana,* or release from the cycle of endless rebirth because all physical and psychic ties to the world are broken. Nirvana, which means something like ''where no wind blows'' or ''without motion,'' is for Buddhism the real world; the illusory world that the unenlightened mistakenly believe is real is called *samsara.*

Some months after Shakyamuni became enlightened he revealed his doctrine in a sermon preached in the Deer Park near Benares. The gist of this sermon, later called ''Setting in Motion the Wheel of Righteousness,'' is this:

1. all existence is suffering;
2. suffering is caused by craving for existence;
3. suffering can be suppressed;
4. the way to suppress suffering is to follow the eightfold path, which consists of right views, right intentions, right speech, right action, right livelihood, right effort, right mindfulness, and right concentration.

Early Buddhism, it should be noted, dispensed with the idea of divinity. Odd though it sounds, Buddhism was an atheistic religion.

Among Buddhist teachings are these:

that the phenomenal world is impermanent;
there is no permanent self, no soul (belief in a permanent self breeds attachment egotism, and a craving for existence);
good intentions are not enough;
sin is not a violation of a divine law, but is rather an act harmful to oneself or to another.

A few additional technical words in the Sermon at Benares need explanation. The Buddha is also called the *Tathagata*, which means "Thus Gone," i.e., he is one who has attained enlightenment. The *Vedas* are ancient sacred Hindu writings; a *deva* is a good spirit; the *wheel* is a common Buddhist symbol for the teachings of the Buddha. In ancient India the wheel symbolized empire, so in Buddhist thinking "to set the wheel in motion" is to engage in an expedition on behalf of the Kingdom of Righteousness.

Gautama Buddha

The Sermon at Benares and Parables

The five [monks] saw their old teacher approach and   1
agreed among themselves not to salute him, nor to address him as a
master, but by his name only. "For," so they said, "he has broken his
vow and has abandoned holiness. He is no [monk] but Gautama, and
Gautama has become a man who lives in abundance and indulges in
the pleasures of worldliness."

But when the Blessed One approached in a dignified manner, they
involuntarily rose from their seats and greeted him in spite of their
resolution. Still they called him by his name and addressed him as
"friend."

When they had thus received the Blessed One, he said: "Do not call the Tathagata by his name nor address him 'friend,' for he is Buddha, the Holy One. Buddha looks equally with a kind heart on all living beings and they therefore call him 'Father.' To disrespect a father is wrong; to despise him, is sin.

"The Tathagata," Buddha continued, "does not seek salvation in austerities, but for that reason you must not think that he indulges in worldly pleasures, nor does he live in abundance. The Tathagata has found the middle path.

"Neither abstinence from fish or flesh, nor going naked, nor shaving the head, nor wearing matted hair, nor dressing in a rough garment, nor covering oneself with dirt, nor sacrificing to Agni, will cleanse a man who is not free from delusions.

"Reading the Vedas, making offerings to priests, or sacrifices to the gods, self-mortification by heat or cold, and many such penances performed for the sake of immortality, these do not cleanse the man who is not free from delusions.

"Anger, drunkenness, obstinacy, bigotry, deception, envy, self-praise, disparaging others, superciliousness, and evil intentions are rooted in delusion.

"Let me teach you, O [monks], the middle path, which keeps aloof from both extremes. By suffering, the emaciated devotee produces confusion and sickly thoughts in his mind. Mortification is not conducive even to worldly knowledge; how much less to a triumph over the senses!

"He who fills his lamp with water will not dispel the darkness, and he who tries to light a fire with rotten wood will fail.

"Mortifications are painful, vain, and profitless. And how can any one be free from self by leading a wretched life if he does not succeed in quenching the fires of lust.

"All mortification is vain so long as self remains, so long as self continues to lust after either worldly or heavenly pleasures. But he in whom self has become extinct is free from lust; he will desire neither worldly nor heavenly pleasures, and the satisfaction of his natural wants will not defile him. Let him eat and drink according to the needs of the body.

"Water surrounds the lotus-flower, but does not wet its petals.

"On the other hand, sensuality of all kind is enervating. The sensual man is a slave of his passions, and pleasure-seeking is degrading and vulgar.

"But to satisfy the necessities of life is not evil. To keep the body in good health is a duty, for otherwise we shall not be able to trim the lamp of wisdom, and keep our mind strong and clear.

"This is the middle path, O [monks], that keeps aloof from both 15 extremes."

And the Blessed One spoke kindly to his disciples, pitying them for their errors, and pointing out the uselessness of their endeavors, and the ice of ill-will that chilled their hearts melted away under the gentle warmth of the Master's persuasion.

Now the Blessed One set the wheel of the most excellent law a-rolling, and he began to preach to the five [monks], opening to them the gate of immortality, and showing them the bliss of Nirvana.

And when the Blessed One began his sermon, a rapture thrilled through all the universes.

The devas left their heavenly abodes to listen to the sweetness of the truth; the saints that had parted from life crowded around the great teacher to receive the glad tidings; even the animals of the earth felt the bliss that rested upon the words of the Tathagata: and all the creatures of the host of sentient beings, gods, men, and beasts, hearing the message of deliverance, received and understood it in their own language.

Buddha said: 20

"The spokes of the wheel are the rules of pure conduct; justice is the uniformity of their length; wisdom is the tire; modesty and thoughtfulness are the hub in which the immovable axle of truth is fixed.

"He who recognizes the existence of suffering, its cause, its remedy, and its cessation has fathomed the four noble truths. He will walk in the right path.

"Right views will be the torch to light his way. Right aims will be his guide. Right words will be his dwelling-place on the road. His gait will be straight, for it is right behavior. His refreshments will be the right way of earning his livelihood. Right efforts will be his steps: right thoughts his breath; and peace will follow in his footprints."

And the Blessed One explained the instability of the ego.

"Whatsoever is originated will be dissolved again. All worry about 25 the self is vain; the ego is like a mirage, and all the tribulations that touch it will pass away. They will vanish like a nightmare when the sleeper awakes.

"He who has awakened is freed from fear; he has become Buddha; he knows the vanity of all his cares, his ambitions, and also of his pains.

"It easily happens that a man, when taking a bath, steps upon a wet rope and imagines that it is a snake. Horror will overcome him, and he will shake from fear, anticipating in his mind all the agonies caused by the serpent's venomous bite. What a relief does this man experience when he sees that the rope is no snake. The cause of his fright lies in his error, his ignorance, his illusion. If the true nature of the rope is recognized, his tranquillity of mind will come back to him; he will feel relieved; he will be joyful and happy.

"This is the state of mind of one who has recognized that there is no self, that the cause of all his troubles, cares, and vanities is a mirage, a shadow, a dream.

"Happy is he who has overcome all selfishness; happy is he who has attained peace; happy is he who has found the truth.

"The truth is noble and sweet; the truth can deliver you from evil. There is no saviour in the world except the truth.

"Have confidence in the truth, although you may not be able to comprehend it, although you may suppose its sweetness to be bitter, although you may shrink from it at first. Trust in the truth.

"The truth is best as it is. No one can alter it; neither can any one improve it. Have faith in the truth and live it.

"Errors lead astray; illusions beget miseries. They intoxicate like strong drinks; but they fade away soon and leave you sick and disgusted.

"Self is a fever; self is a transient vision, a dream; but truth is wholesome, truth is sublime, truth is everlasting. There is no immortality except in truth. For truth alone abideth forever."

And when the doctrine was propounded, the venerable Kaundinya, the oldest one among the five [monks], discerned the truth with his mental eye, and he said: "Truly, O Buddha, our Lord, thou hast found the truth."

And the devas and saints and all the good spirits of the departed generations that had listened to the sermon of the Tathagata joyfully received the doctrine and shouted: "Truly, the Blessed One has founded the kingdom of righteousness. The Blessed One has moved the earth; he has set the wheel of Truth rolling, which by no one in the universe, be he god or man, can ever be turned back. The kingdom of Truth will be preached upon earth; it will spread; and righteousness, good-will, and peace will reign among mankind. . . ."

A foolish man, learning that the Buddha observed the principle of great love which commends the return of good for evil, came and abused him. The Buddha was silent, pitying his folly.

When the man had finished his abuse, the Buddha asked him, saying: "Son, if a man declined to accept a present made to him, to whom would it belong?" And he answered: "In that case, it would belong to the man who offered it."

"My son," said the Buddha, "thou hast railed at me, but I decline to accept thy abuse, and request thee to keep it thyself. Will it not be a source of misery to thee? As the echo belongs to the sound, and the shadow to the substance, so misery will overtake the evil-doer without fail."

The abuser made no reply, and Buddha continued: "A wicked man 40 who reproaches a virtuous one is like one who looks up and spits at heaven; the spittle soils not the heaven, but comes back and defiles his own person. The slanderer is like one who flings dust at another when the wind is contrary; the dust does but return on him who threw it. The virtuous man cannot be hurt and the misery that the other would inflict comes back on himself."

The abuser went away ashamed, but he came again and took refuge in the Buddha, the Law of Righteousness, and the Monastic Order.

And Buddha said: "All that we are is the result of what we have thought: it is founded on our thoughts, it is made up of our thoughts. If a man speaks or acts with an evil thought, pain follows him, as the wheel follows the foot of the ox that draws the carriage: If a man speaks or acts with a pure thought, happiness follows him, like a shadow that never leaves him.

"He abused me, he beat me, he defeated me, he robbed me"—in those who harbor such thoughts, hatred will never cease; in those who do not harbor such thoughts, hatred will cease. For hatred does not cease by hatred at any time: hatred ceases by love—that is an old rule.

He who lives looking for pleasures only, his senses uncontrolled, immoderate in his food, idle and weak, will certainly be overthrown by temptation, as the wind throws down a weak tree. He who lives without looking for pleasures, his senses well controlled, moderate in his food, faithful and strong, will certainly not be overthrown, any more than the wind throws down a rocky mountain. . . .

The thoughtless man, even if he can recite a large portion of the 45 law, but is not a doer of it, has no share in the priesthood, but is like a cowherd counting the cows of others. The follower of the law, even if he can recite only a small portion of the law, but, having forsaken passion and hatred and foolishness, possesses true knowledge and serenity of mind, he, caring for nothing in this world or that to come, has indeed a share in the priesthood. . . .

As a fletcher makes straight his arrow, a wise man makes straight his trembling and unsteady thought, which is difficult to guard, difficult to hold back. It is good to tame the mind, which is difficult to hold in and flighty, rushing wherever it listeth; a tamed mind brings happiness. Let the wise man guard his thoughts, for they are difficult to perceive, very artful, and they rush wherever they list. . . .

And Punna, wishing to preach the path to enlightenment, sought the Buddha, and the Buddha said, "But, O Punna, the men of that country are violent, cruel and savage. When they become angry at you and do you harm, what will you think then?"

"I shall think them truly good and kind folk, for whilst they speak angry and insolent words, they refrain from striking or stoning me."

"They are very violent folk, Punna. What if they strike or stone you?"

"I shall think them kind and good not to smite me with their staff and sword." 50

"And what if they do so?"

"I shall think them kind and good indeed who free me from this vile body with so little pain."

"Well said, Punna, well said. With your gift of patience, you may indeed essay this task. Go, Punna, yourself saved, save others."

Questions

1. In paragraph 2, why do you suppose the monks partly violated the resolution they had formed earlier? And why only partly?
2. In paragraphs 3 and 4 the Buddha speaks of himself in the third person. What do you make of this?
3. Why, in paragraph 7, are "anger, drunkenness," and other vices called "delusions."
4. The Buddha uses many metaphors, for example in paragraphs 9, 12, and 21. Do you think these passages are effective? If you were abridging this sermon, would you delete them? And would you omit paragraph 27 (the passage about the man who imagines that he has stepped on a snake)? Why, or why not would you omit such material?
5. In paragraph 39, in speaking of a "foolish man" who abused him, the Buddha says that if someone declines to accept the abuse of another person, the abuse "will . . . be a source of misery" to the abuser. Does this strike you as psychologically sound? Does your own experience confirm or contradict the point?
6. In paragraphs 47–51, *why* does the Buddha question Punna as he does?

Wilfred Cantwell Smith

Muslims

Almost any visitor to India interested in the religious life 1
of its people will note a striking difference architecturally between a
Hindu temple and a Muslim mosque. The temple is apt to be ornate,
even florid. Its involute complexity suggests that truth is much more
elaborate than one had supposed, and denies nothing, not even incongruity. Very different is the stark simplicity of the Muslim place of
worship. The mighty Imperial Mosque in Delhi, for example, is a structure whose artistic impressiveness and power come from the use of
straight lines and simple curves, splendidly graceful and yet austerely
disciplined. Certainly it is brilliantly conceived and its impact is immediate: one grasps at once the balance and dignity, the spacious reverence, the serenity of its straightforward affirmation. Its architect's
vision of the glory of God, and of man's service due to Him, is evidently
an ordered vision.

Such a point is confirmed if one has the privilege of witnessing a 2
service in such a mosque, especially at one of the great festival prayers,
where perhaps a hundred thousand people array themselves in neat
lines and bow in precise unison as token of their personal and corporate
submission to the will of God, which is definite and sure.

A similar contrast can be seen in the realm of doctrine. For a Hindu, 3
there are various systems of ideas, involute, elaborate, and always
tentative, from among which he may choose. In contrast, the Muslim
community symbolizes its belief in probably the simplest, tidiest creed
in all the world. I am sure that you have all heard it: "There is no god
but God, and Muhammad is God's apostle." The Muslims themselves
refer to this simply as "the two words," or even "the word." And
while this may be carrying compression just a trifle far, still its two
pithy clauses are, certainly, as succinct and clean as one could hope
to find.

Wilfred Cantwell Smith was born in Toronto in 1916, and educated at the University of Toronto and at Princeton University. After working from 1941 to 1949
with Muslims in India, he returned to Canada where he taught Islamic studies
at McGill University from 1949 to 1963. Since 1964 he has taught religion at
Harvard University.

Because of its centrality, and its neatness, this simple creed may   4
well provide us with the item for our consideration of the Muslims.
As with other religious communities, so with the Islamic, we choose
one element from out of the formal pattern of their faith, in the hope
that, exploring it, we may find that it can lead us, if not to the heart
of their religious life, at least into its precincts, and can suggest something of the richness of what lies behind. What better emblem of the
Muslim's faith, for our purposes, than this crystallized creed, which
the Muslims themselves have chosen to sum up their belief? To repeat
this creed is, formally, to become a Muslim; perhaps to understand it
is to understand a Muslim. Or let me put the point more realistically:
to begin to understand it may be to go some distance, at least, towards
understanding the position of those whose faith it typifies.

In suggesting the coherence and simplicity of the Muslim confes-   5
sion of faith, I do not wish to suggest that it is limited or lacks profundity. A mosque may be very intricately decorated—fine interlacing
arabesques and the endlessly delicate complexities of an elaborate calligraphy usually embroider the arches and the walls—yet these decorations, however ornate in themselves, are regularly held in strict
subordination to an over-all pattern that is essentially simple, so that
detail is organized into a coherent unity. Similarly in the realm of doctrine. The Muslim world has produced its philosophers and theologians, constructing elaborate systems of ideas—the names of Avicenna
and Averroes are probably the best known in the West, but there are
many others also who worked out in careful detail considerable structures of thought. And there were also meticulously elaborate systems
of law, comprehensive and ramified. But again, these were subordinate
to the higher truth, the simpler truth, of the creed.

As one gets closer to truth, one gets closer to God; and God is   6
one. He is majestic, mighty, awesome, merciful, and many other
things, but above all, for the Muslim, He is one. Every other sin, the
theologians affirm, may be forgiven man, but not that of *shirk*, polytheism, the failure to recognize that the final truth and power of the
universe is one.

Before we turn to questions of meaning, which are of course our   7
chief concern, let us note a few points about the formula as a formula.
I suppose that every effective religious symbol is not only inexhaustibly
meaningful in what it stands for, but is also in some ways intrinsically
interesting in itself. This one certainly is. We have already remarked
that it is short. It is also pungent and crisp. In the original Arabic—
the language in which it is always used, no matter what the actual

language of the people concerned, from Indonesian to African Swahili, from South Indian Malayalam to Turkish—in Arabic it is resonant and rolling, packing quite a punch. It so happens that of the fifteen syllables, about half begin with an *l* sound, or end with it, or both. This liquid alliteration, added to the rhyme, and to a very marked rhythm, is quite forceful. *Lā-'i-lā-ha-'il-lal-lāh; Mu-ham-ma-dur-ra-sū-lul-lāh.*

Then there is a calligraphic point. In the Arabic alphabet, which   8
is anyway highly decorative, it so happens that this particular set of words when written out is strikingly patterned, and lends itself to very picturesque presentation.

The formula is certainly in constant service. For example, it is whis-   9
pered in the ears of the newborn baby, so that its affirmation may be the first words that a Muslim shall hear on entering this world. And between then and its use at his funeral, he will hear it, and pronounce it, often and often and often. And apart from its ceremonial and—as it were—sacred use, it can be found in everyday affairs also. I remember a scene in India some years ago when my wife and I were one summer at a mountain resort in the Himalayas, and were out for a hike in the hills; we came upon a work-gang busy in the construction of a rude mountain road. It was, of course, all hand labor; they had crushed the stones with hammers, and were now rolling them with a large and very heavy roller. Rather in the fashion of sailors working to a sea shanty, they were rhythmically pulling this heavy roller in spurts of concerted effort: the foreman would sing out *Lā ilāha illa 'llāh*, and the rest of the gang, then, would put their shoulders to the ropes and with a heave would respond *Muhammadur rasūlu 'llāh*. This went on and on, as they continued to work, with a will and with good strong heaves. *Lā ilāha illa 'llāh* he would chant; *Muhammadur rasūlu 'llāh* would come the vigorous response. Such a scene represents, of course, a kind of living in which a split into religious and secular has not come—or has not yet come—to segment life. At a different level, of course, are the formal ceremonies in the weekly service of some of the Islamic Sufi orders, in which the initiate devotees will induce a mystic ecstasy or trance by the solemn and rhythmic repetition or incantation of the formula.

Between these two comes a religious use such as that by the   10
mu'azzin in his call to prayer five times a day, whose sonorous recitative from the minaret punctuates village or town life and summons the faithful to turn for a moment from their routine affairs to the life of the spirit.

I have called this creed a symbol; and in some ways it plays in   11
Muslim life a role similar to that played, for instance, for Christians
by the cross. Nonetheless it is not a pictorial sign but a verbal one,
and this itself is significant and appropriate. The role of linguistic form,
of words, in Islamic religious life is quite special. I have already spoken
of the written word—calligraphy—as a typical Muslim art form. This
community has carried the decorative use of writing probably further
than has any other people. And take revelation itself. In the Christian
case this takes the form of a person, whereas for the Muslim it too is
verbal. In the Qur'an, God makes himself and His purpose known to
man in the form of words. It is altogether appropriate, then, that the
chief symbol of Islam should also be verbal.

So far, I have allowed myself to follow the usual Western practice   12
of calling this two-phrase synopsis of the Muslim's faith a "creed."
For to do this is not altogether misleading, though you will have seen
that its place in Muslim life is only partly correlative with that of the
creed for us. It is time now, however, to modify this still further. We
need to see more carefully ways in which the faith of other people is
expressed in patterns that do not quite correspond to our own—or
even to what we expect of them.

In some ways, then, the "two words" of the Islamic assertion do   13
constitute a creed, a statement of belief, but in other ways they do not;
and the Muslims do not themselves call this formula a creed. They call
it, rather, a "witness." Regularly the statement is preceded by the
words "I bear witness that" there is no god . . . and so on. And even
when these actual terms are not employed, an idea of witnessing is
involved, and can be quite basic. The Islamic has been one of the three
great missionary communities in human history (along with the
Buddhist and the Christian); and the idea of bearing witness to his
faith is quite central to a Muslim's attitudes. His assertion is not so
much an affirmation of belief, as a proclamation—of conviction. And
in a subtle fashion, there is involved here a point that I rather imagine
is more basic in all religious life perhaps than is usually recognized.
It is this: that it is not so much that the Muslim *believes* that God is
one, and Muhammad is His prophet, as it is that he takes this for
granted. He presupposes it, and goes on from there. From his own
point of view, one might almost say that, so far as he is concerned,
he *knows* that these things are so, and what he is doing is simply announcing them, bearing witness to them.

The same kind of thing is true, I think, of all religious life. One   14 distorts a Christian's faith, for example, by saying simply that he believes Jesus Christ to be divine, to be the son of God. He would rather say that he recognizes this—these are the facts, and he has been fortunate enough to see them. In the Christian case the matter has been somewhat complicated by the use in Western languages of a single verb, *credo*, "I believe," and so on, both for intellectual belief (belief that) and for religious faith (belief in)—though men of faith have insisted that the two things are different. Anyway, I feel that true faith has already begun to crumble a bit, if it has not actually gone, as soon as people have reduced what used to be the data, the presuppositions, of their world view to a set of true-or-false propositions—I mean, when what was once the presupposed context or intellectual background for a transcending religious faith becomes rather the foreground of intellectual belief. This is one of the fundamental troubles in the modern world, and one of the fundamental problems arising from a recognition of religious diversity—that what used to be unconscious premises become, rather, scrutinized intellectualizations. At this new level the believer himself begins to wonder if he really "believes," in this new sense (and often enough finds that he àctually does not).

In the Islamic case, as in the Jewish, the word of God is, fundamentally, an imperative. And even the proclamation of God's oneness is in some ways more a command, to worship Him alone, than merely an invitation to believe that He is there alone. Faith differs from belief in many ways, and goes beyond it; one way is that faith in God's oneness is a recognition of His unique and exclusive authority, and an active giving of oneself to it. Like the Christian, the classical Muslim theologian has seen faith as a commitment. He would understand at once St. James in the New Testament writing, "You believe that God is one? You do well: the devils also believe—and tremble." To a truly religious man, the question is not one merely of belief, but of doing something about it. [15]

Having said that, however, we on the outside may still ask what the presuppositions are; what belief is presumed, for those who do go on to commitment. [16]

We find ourselves having come round, then, to the question that we earlier postponed, the question of the meaning of the "two words." What does it mean to say "There is no god but God, and Muhammad is His apostle"? What does it mean, that is, to a Muslim—to someone to whom these two clauses are not merely true, but profoundly and cosmically true, are the two most important and final truths in the world, and the most crucial for man and his destiny? [17]

Let us look at each in turn.   18

To say that there is one God, and that He alone is to be wor-   19
shipped, means at its most immediate, as it meant in pagan Arabia
when it was first proclaimed, a rejection of polytheism and idolatry.
When Muhammad captured Mecca in A.D. 630, and set up Islam in
triumph, he gave a general amnesty to the human beings there who
had resisted his cause and were now defeated, but he smashed without
quarter the idols—three hundred and sixty of them, it is said—in the
shrine of the Ka'bah, the figures of the pagans' gods. From that day
to this, Islam has been uncompromising in its doctrine of monotheism,
and its insistence on transcendence: God the Creator and Judge is Lord
of all the universe, is high above all his creatures and beyond them,
and beyond all their imaginings—and certainly beyond all their representations. Other deities, it asserts, are but the figments of men's
wayward imagination, are unadulterated fiction; they just do not exist.
Man must not bow down to them nor worship them, or look to them
for help, or think about them. God is God alone; on this point Islam
is emphatic, positive, and clear.

Historically, as the Islamic movement has spread, across the cen-   20
turies, from Arabia through the Near East and into Central Asia and
has penetrated China, into India and South-East Asia, across Africa
and still today is spreading down into Africa, it has met polytheism
in many forms, has attacked it and replaced it. Like the Church in the
Roman Empire and Northern Europe, and later in the Americas, so
Islam in large parts of the world has superseded polytheistic practice
and thought with monotheistic.

At a subtler level, for those capable of seeing it, the doctrine has   21
meant also at times, and certainly ought to mean, a rejection of human
tyranny. God alone is to be worshipped, to be served. For the man
for whom this faith is sufficiently vivid, this can mean that no earthly
power, no human figure, deserves or can legitimately claim man's allegiance; and any attempt to impose a purely human yoke on man's
neck is an infringement not only of human dignity but of cosmic order,
and to submit to it would be sin. Admittedly there has been, especially
in periods of decline, an alternative interpretation whereby God's gov-
ernance of affairs is taken as determining not what ought to be but
what is. This view has led to fatalism—a passive acceptance of whatever happens. Perhaps you will feel that I am intruding my own pre-
dilections here in siding with those Muslims who have taken rather
the activist line, asserting God's will as something to be striven for,
as was done more widely in Islam's earlier centuries, and is beginning

to be done again in our own day. You will agree, in any case, that it is legitimate and proper, in interpreting other men's faith as in one's own, to try to see it at its best and highest. That at least is what I am trying to do throughout these talks.

There is still a third level of meaning, which was stressed partic-   22 ularly by the Sufi mystics in the medieval period, and is beginning to get wide support today. According to this view, to worship God alone is to turn aside from false gods not only in the concrete sense of idols and religious polytheism, but also in the subtler sense of turning aside from a moral polytheism, from false values—the false gods of the heart. To pursue merely earthly goals, to value them, to give them one's allegiance and in a sense to worship them—goals such as wealth, prestige, sex, national aggrandizement, comfort, or all the other distractions and foibles of human life—this, says the sensitive Muslim conscience, like the sensitive Christian or Jewish one, is to infringe the principle of monotheism. Similarly, to look for help to purely mundane forces, to rely upon armies or clever stratagems, to trust anything that is not intrinsically good—this is to have more than one god. The affirmation that God alone is to be worshipped means, for the man of true piety and rigorous sincerity, that no other objective must claim man's effort or loyalty; he must fear no other power, honor no other prize, pursue no other goal.

I would mention, finally, one other interpretation of the "no god   23 but God" phrase, one that again has been put forward by some of the mystics. This one has not been widespread, even among these; yet I mention it because I personally find it attractive, and it shows the kind of thing that can be done. This particular view is in line with the general position taken by the mystics that the religious life is a process, a movement in faith. According to this interpretation, then, the statement that "there is no god but God" is to be taken in stages. No man, this reading suggests, can legitimately and truly say "God" who has not previously said, and meant, "no god." To arrive at true faith, one must first pass through a stage of unbelief. "There is no god": this comes first, and must be lived through in all sincerity, and all terror. A person brought up in a religious tradition must have seen through that tradition, its forms and fancies, its shams and shibboleths; he must have learned the bleakness of atheism, and have experienced its meaninglessness and eventually its dread. Only such a person is able to go on, perhaps only years later, to a faith that is without superficiality and without merely cheap and secondhand glibness. If one has said "there is no god" with the anguish of a genuine despair, one may then, with

God's grace, go on to say ". . . but God," and say it with the ecstasy of genuine insight.

Let us turn, next, to the second proposition: "Muhammad is the 24 apostle of God." The first thing to grasp here is that this is a statement not about Muhammad's status but about his function. The Islamic concept of apostle, or prophet, is quite special; and one is misled if one too readily assumes that this corresponds to ideas familiar to us in the West. The underlying notion here, and it is tacitly presupposed by the formulation, is that God has something to say to mankind, and has from time to time chosen certain persons in various communities through whom to say it; the assertion here is that Muhammad was one of those persons. It too, then, is in significant degree, and even primarily, a statement about God. As the theologians worked it out, it involves the conviction that God is not essentially passive, inscrutable, content to remain transcendent; rather than from all eternity, and as part of His very nature, He is the kind of God who has something to say to mankind. What He has to say is what we would call the moral law. When He created the universe and when He created man, He did not exactly create the moral law, for this comes closer to being, rather, a part of Himself—but anyway He ordained it, or set it forth, and He created man to receive it, free and responsible to carry it out.

This is the first affirmation. The second is that He communicated 25 this moral law to mankind. He did not leave man to grope about in the dark, to discover for himself, by his own efforts, what he could. No; God Himself acted, and spoke—spoke through the mouth of the prophets and apostles, beginning with Adam, that is, from the very beginning of history. Religion is nowadays sometimes spoken of as man's search for God. On this, the Islamic position is like the Jewish and the Christian, rejecting such a view emphatically, and asserting rather that God takes the initiative. As Micah put it, in our Judeo-Christian tradition, "He hath *shown* thee, O man, what is good. . . ." Man's business in the religious life is not a quest but a response.

Thirdly, in the message that God communicated is to be found, 26 in the Muslim view, not what is true so much, though of course they do hold this, but what is *right*. The position differs from the Christian in that it is a revelation *from* God, more than *of* God. The apostle or prophet is one who conveys to men the message that God wants them to know; namely, how they should live. Accordingly, out of the message theoreticians and systematizers have extracted and constructed a law, finally elaborated in all detail and ultimately turned into a static system.

One last point, and with this I close. I said a moment ago that the 27 phrase "Muhammad is the apostle of God" is a statement not about Muhammad's status so much as about his function. Let me elaborate this just a little. The position stands over against the quite different Christian orientation, which sees the person of Christ as central and ultimate, pre-existent and divine. Muslims also posit a central and ultimate truth, pre-existent and divine, namely the Qur'an—not a person but a book, or better, what the book says. Muhammad plays in the Islamic scheme the role played in the Christian system by St. Paul or St. Peter; namely, that of an apostle who proclaims among men God's gift to them, which in the Islamic case is the scripture. In contrast to the Christian conviction, you might almost say that the Muslims' affirmation about their prophet is not a statement about Muhammad's person at all, but about the Qur'an and "what Muhammad brought." To say that he is an apostle, sent by God, is to affirm these things that we have noted, about God, and about the kind of universe that we live in, and about the human situation, and morality; and then within that framework it is to assert further that the message purveyed by Muhammad is authentic. If you believe this, then you are accepting as incumbent upon you in an ultimate moral sense the practical duties that flow from this tradition. For you are recognizing the obligation to perform them as not of human origin but of divine. Those of us for whom the content of morality is not defined in this historical source should nonetheless not allow this to obscure from us the cosmic things that those inspired from this source are saying about morality, about man, and about God.

Questions

1. Consider the first three paragraphs as a piece of writing. Are they clear? If so, by what means did the author achieve clarity? If they are not clear, what are the causes of the obscurity?
2. In paragraph 14 Smith distinguishes between "belief in" and "belief that." Suppose a friend did not quite get Smith's point. Clarify it for this friend.
3. In paragraph 15 Smith says, "To a truly religious man, the question is not one merely of belief, but of doing something about it." (Presumably "doing something" means more than making an occa-

sional monetary contribution to the church, and more than attending church sporadically or even regularly.) Do you think Smith is going too far here? Do you know many people who, by this standard, are "truly religious"? If so—and of course you yourself may be such a person—what do they do?

4. In the West, Muslims (or followers of Islam) are often called Muhammadans (or Mohammedans). Why is the term "Muhammadan" offensive to Muslims? Why is the term *not* comparable to "Christian"? (Notice that Smith touches on this point in paragraph 27.)

5. Taking the criteria set forth in the first paragraph, where a Hindu temple is contrasted with a Muslim mosque, what does a Gothic cathedral suggest, contasted with a New England Protestant church or with a southwest adobe Roman Catholic church? (You can find pictures of temples and mosques in Hugh Honour and John Fleming, *The Visual Arts;* for Hindu temples, see also Sherman E. Lee, *A History of Far Eastern Art;* for mosques, see Bernard Lewis, ed., *Islam and the Arab World;* and for Gothic cathedrals, see H. W. Janson, *History of Art.*)

Idries Shah

Two Islamic Tales

1. The Three Perceptives

There were once three Sufis, so observant and experienced in life that they were known as The Three Perceptives.

One day during their travels they encountered a camelman, who said: 'Have you seen my camel? I have lost it.'

'Was it blind in one eye?' asked the first Perceptive.

'Yes,' said the cameldriver.

'Has it one tooth missing in front?' asked the second Perceptive.

'Yes, yes,' said the cameldriver.

'Is it lame in one foot?' asked the third Perceptive.

'Yes, yes, yes,' said the cameldriver.

Idries Shah, born in 1924, is a leading authority on Sufi thought.

The three Perceptives then told the man to go back along the way they had come, and that he might hope to find it. Thinking that they had seen it, the man hurried on his way.

But the man did not find his camel, and he hastened to catch up with the Perceptives, hoping that they would tell him what to do.

He found them that evening, at a resting-place.

'Has your camel honey on one side and a load of corn on the other?' asked the first Perceptive.

'Yes,' said the man.

'Is there a pregnant woman mounted upon it?' asked the second Perspective.

'Yes, yes,' said the man.

'We do not know where it is,' said the third Perceptive.

The cameldriver was now convinced that the Perceptives had stolen his camel, passenger and all, and he took them to the judge, accusing them of the theft.

The Judge thought that he had made out a case, and detained the three men in custody on suspicion of theft.

A little later, the man found his camel wandering in some fields, and returning to the court, arranged for the Perceptives to be released.

The judge, who had not given them a chance to explain themselves before, asked how it was that they knew so much about the camel, since they had apparently not even seen it.

'We saw the footprints of a camel on the road,' said the first Perceptive.

'One of the tracks was faint: it must have been lame,' said the second Perceptive.

'It had stripped the bushes at only one side of the road, so it must have been blind in one eye,' said the third Perceptive.

'The leaves were shredded, which indicated the loss of a tooth,' continued the first Perceptive.

'Bees and ants, on different sides of the road, were swarming over something deposited; we saw that this was honey and corn,' said the second Perceptive.

'We found long human hair where someone had stopped and dismounted, it was a woman's,' said the third Perceptive.

'Where the person had sat down there were palm-prints, we thought from the use of the hands that the woman was probably very pregnant and had to stand up in that way,' said the first Perceptive.

'Why did you not apply for your side of the case to be heard so that you could explain yourselves?' asked the judge.

'Because we reckoned that the cameldriver would continue looking for his camel and might find it soon,' said the first Perceptive.

'He would feel generous in releasing us through his discovery,' said the second Perceptive.

'The curiosity of the Judge would prompt an enquiry,' said the third Perceptive.

'Discovering the truth by his own enquiries would be better for all than for us to claim that we had been impatiently handled,' said the first Perceptive.

'It is our experience that it is generally better for people to arrive at truth through what they take to be their own volition,' said the second Perceptive.

'It is time for us to move on, for there is work to be done,' said the third Perceptive.

And the Sufi thinkers went on their way. They are still to be found at work on the highways of the earth.

2. The Man, the Snake, and the Stone

One day a man who had not a care in the world was walking along a road. An unusual object to one side of him caught his eye. 'I must find out what this is,' he said to himself.

As he came up to it, he saw that it was a large, very flat stone.

'I must find out what is underneath this,' he told himself. And he lifted the stone.

No sooner had he done so than he heard a loud, hissing sound, and a huge snake came gliding out from a hole under the stone. The man dropped the stone in alarm. The snake wound itself into a coil, and said to him:

'Now I am going to kill you, for I am a venomous snake.'

'But I have released you,' said the man, 'how can you repay good with evil? Such an action would not accord with reasonable behaviour.'

'In the first place,' said the snake, 'you lifted the stone from curiosity and in ignorance of the possible consequences. How can this now suddenly become "I have released you"?'

'We must always try to return to reasonable behaviour, when we stop to think,' murmured the man.

'Return to it when you think invoking it might suit your interests,' said the snake.

'Yes,' said the man, 'I was a fool to expect reasonable behaviour from a snake.'

'From a snake, expect snake-behaviour,' said the snake. 'To a snake, snake-behaviour is what can be regarded as reasonable.'

'Now I am going to kill you,' it continued.

'Please do not kill me,' said the man, 'give me another chance. You have taught me about curiosity, reasonable behaviour and snake-behaviour. Now you would kill me before I can put this knowledge into action.'

'Very well,' said the snake, 'I shall give you another chance. I shall come along with you on your journey. We will ask the next creature whom we meet, who shall be neither a man nor a snake, to adjudicate between us.'

The man agreed, and they started on their way.

Before long they came to a flock of sheep in a field. The snake stopped, and the man cried to the sheep:

'Sheep, sheep, please save me! This snake intends to kill me. If you tell him not to do so he will spare me. Give a verdict in my favour, for I am a man, the friend of sheep.'

One of the sheep answered:

'We have been put out into this field after serving a man for many years. We have given him wool year after year, and now that we are old, tomorrow he will kill us for mutton. That is the measure of the generosity of men. Snake, kill that man!'

The snake reared up and his green eyes glittered as he said to the man: 'This is how your friends see you. I shudder to think what your enemies are like!'

'Give me one more chance,' cried the man in desperation. 'Please let us find someone else to give an opinion, so that my life may be spared.'

'I do not want to be as unreasonable as you think I am,' said the snake, 'and I will therefore continue in accordance with your pattern, and not with mine. Let us ask the next individual whom we may meet—being neither a man nor a snake—what your fate is to be.'

The man thanked the snake, and they continued on their journey.

Presently they came upon a lone horse, standing hobbled in a field. The snake addressed him:

'Horse, horse, why are you hobbled like that?'

The horse said:

'For many years I served a man. He gave me food, for which I had not asked, and he taught me to serve him. He said that this was in exchange for the food and stable. Now that I am too infirm to work, he has decided to sell me soon for horse-meat. I am hobbled because the man thinks that if I roam over this field I will eat too much of his grass.'

'Do not make this horse my judge, for God's sake!' exclaimed the man.

'According to our compact,' said the snake inexorably, 'this man and I have agreed to have our case judged by you.'

He outlined the matter, and the horse said:

'Snake, it is beyond my capabilities and not in my nature to kill a man. But I feel that you, as a snake, have no alternative but to do so if a man is in your power.'

'If you will give me just one more chance,' begged the man, 'I am sure that something will come to my aid. I have been unlucky on this journey so far, and have only come across creatures who have a grudge. Let us therefore choose some animal which has no such knowledge and hence no generalised animosity towards my kind.'

'People do not know snakes,' said the snake, 'and yet they seem to have a generalised animosity towards them. But I am willing to give you just one more chance.'

They continued their journey.

Soon they saw a fox, lying asleep under a bush beside the road. The man woke the fox gently, and said:

'Fear nothing, brother fox. My case is such-and-such, and my future depends upon your decision. The snake will give me no further chance, so only your generosity or altruism can help me.'

The fox thought for a moment, and then he said:

'I am not sure that only generosity or altruism can operate here. But I will engage myself in this matter. In order to come to a decision I must rely upon something more than hearsay. We must demonstrate as well. Come, let us return to the beginning of your journey, and examine the facts on the spot.'

They returned to where the first encounter had taken place.

'Now we will reconstruct the situation,' said the fox; 'snake, be so good as to take your place once more, in your hole under that flat stone.'

The man lifted the stone, and the snake coiled itself up in the hollow beneath it. The man let the stone fall.

The snake was now trapped again, and the fox, turning to the man, said: 'We have returned to the beginning. The snake cannot get out unless you release him. He leaves our story at this point.'

'Thank you, thank you,' said the man, his eyes full of tears.

'Thanks are not enough, brother,' said the fox; 'In addition to generosity and altruism there is the matter of my payment.'

'How can you enforce payment?' asked the man.

'Anyone who can solve the problem which I have just concluded,' said the fox, 'is well able to take care of such a detail as that. I again invite you to recompense me, from fear if not from any sense of justice. Shall we call it, in your words, being "reasonable"?'

The man said:

'Very well, come to my house and I will give you a chicken.'

They went to the man's house. The man went into his chicken-coop, and came back in a moment with a bulging sack. The fox seized it and was about to open it when the man said:

'Friend fox, do not open the sack here. I have human neighbours and they should not know that I am co-operating with a fox. They might kill you, as well as censuring me.'

'That is a reasonable thought,' said the fox; 'what do you suggest I do?'

'Do you see that clump of trees yonder?' said the man, pointing. 'Yes,' said the fox.

'You run with the sack into that cover, and you will be able to enjoy your meal unmolested.'

The fox ran off.

As soon as he reached the trees a party of hunters, whom the man knew would be there, caught him. He leaves our story here.

And the man? His future is yet to come.

Questions

The Three Perceptives

1. Early in the story the first Perceptive asks if the camel is blind, but later it is the third Perceptive who explains how they knew it was blind. Similarly, the second asks if the camel lacks a tooth, but it is the first who explains how they knew this; and it is the third who asks if the camel is lame, but it is the second who cites the evidence. Why not have the first give the evidence that explains his conjecture, the second give the evidence for *his* conjecture, and the third give the evidence for *his*? Would such an arrangement in any way change the meaning of the story?

2. Near the end of the story the third Perceptive says, "It is time for us to move on, for there is work to be done." What kind of work do you suppose he has in mind?

3. We are told that the three Perceptives are Sufis—that is, Muslim mystics. But we do not see them in ecstatic states, or in trances. What, perhaps, is the teller of the tale implying about Sufis? Or about wisdom?
4. What, in your opinion, is the chief point (or what are the chief points) of the story?

The Man, the Snake, and the Stone
1. At the outset we are told that the man "had not a care in the world." What, if anything, does this detail add to the story?
2. When the man addresses the sheep he says, "Sheep, sheep," and when he addresses the horse he says, "Horse, horse," but when he addresses the fox the pattern is varied to "Fear nothing, brother fox." As you know, folk tales use a good deal of repetition, for instance, the thrice-said "Someone has eaten my porridge" in "Goldilocks and the Three Bears." Why, then, is the line varied here?
3. The last line reads: "And the man? His future is yet to come." What future do you suppose the teller of the tale has in mind?

Chewing Blackbones

Old Man and Old Woman
A Blackfoot Indian Myth Retold

Long, long ago, there were only two persons in the world: Old Man and Old Woman. One time when they were traveling about the earth, Old Woman said to Old Man, "Now let us come to an agreement of some kind. Let us decide how the people shall live when they shall be on the earth."

"Well," replied Old Man, "I am to have the first say in everything."

Nothing is known about Chewing Blackbones except that he was a Blackfoot Indian described in 1953 as "an elderly grandfather . . . [who] could tell the old tales only in the old Blackfoot language." Ella E. Clark collected this tale in 1953, and published it in her 1966 collection, *Indian Legends from the Northern Rockies*.

"I agree with you," said Old Woman. "That is—if I may have the second say."

Then Old Man began his plans. "The women will have the duty of tanning the hides. They will rub animals' brains on the hides to make them soft and scrape them with scraping tools. All this they will do very quickly, for it will not be hard work."

"No," said Old Woman, "I will not agree to this. They must tan hides in the way you say; but it must be very hard work, so that the good workers may be found out."

"Well," said Old Man, "we will let the people have eyes and mouths, straight up and down in their faces."

"No," replied Old Woman, "let us not have them that way. We will have the eyes and mouths in the faces, as you say, but they shall be set crosswise."

"Well," said Old Man, "the people shall have ten fingers on each hand."

"Oh, no!" replied Old Woman. "That will be too many. They will be in the way. There will be four fingers and one thumb on each hand."

So the two went on until they had provided for everything in the lives of the people who were to be.

"What shall we do about life and death?" asked Old Woman. "Should the people live forever, or should they die?"

Old Woman and Old Man had difficulty agreeing about this. Finally Old Man said, "I will tell you what we will do. I will throw a buffalo chip into the water. If it floats, the people will die for four days and then come to life again; if it sinks, they will die forever."

So he threw a buffalo chip into the water, and it floated.

"No," said Old Woman, "we will not decide in that way. I will throw this rock into the water. If it floats, the people will die for four days; if it sinks, they will die forever."

Then Old Woman threw the rock into the water, and it sank to the bottom.

"There," said she. "It is better for the people to die forever. If they did not, they would not feel sorry for each other, and there would be no sympathy in the world."

"Well," said Old Man, "let it be that way."

After a time, Old Woman had a daughter, who soon became sick and died. The mother was very sorry then that they had agreed that people should die forever. "Let us have our say over again," she said.

"No," replied Old Man. "Let us not change what we have agreed upon."

And so people have died ever since.

Questions

1. Do we think of Old Man and Old Woman as people or as gods? Explain.
2. Though briefly sketched, Old Man and Old Woman are distinct characters. What are the important differences between them?
3. The dialogue helps to characterize Old Man and Old Woman. What other function does it serve?
4. If the story ended six sentences earlier (after Old Man says: "Well . . . let it be that way"), the myth would still provide an explanation of why people die. What would be lost?

Katherine Anne Porter

The Jilting of Granny Weatherall

She flicked her wrist neatly out of Doctor Harry's pudgy careful fingers and pulled the sheet up to her chin. The brat ought to be in knee breeches. Doctoring around the country with spectacles on his nose! "Get along now, take your schoolbooks and go. There's nothing wrong with me."

Katherine Anne Porter (1890–1980) had the curious habit of inventing details in her life, but it is true that she was born in a log cabin in Indian Creek, Texas, that she was originally named Callie Russell Porter, that her mother died when the child was two years old, and that Callie was brought up by her maternal grandmother in Kyle, Texas. Apparently, the family was conscious of former wealth and position in Louisiana and Kentucky, for Callie was sent to convent schools, where, in her words, she received a "strangely useless and ornamental education." When she was sixteen she left school, married (and soon divorced), and worked as a reporter, first in Texas and later in Denver and Chicago. She moved around a good deal, both within the United States and abroad: she lived for a while in Mexico, Belgium, Switzerland, France, and Germany.

Even as a child she was interested in writing, but she did not publish her first story until she was thirty-three. She wrote essays and one novel (*Ship of Fools*), but she is best known for her stories. Porter's *Collected Stories* won the Pulitzer Prize and the National Book Award in 1965.

Doctor Harry spread a warm paw like a cushion on her forehead where the forked green vein danced and made her eyelids twitch. "Now, now, be a good girl, and we'll have you up in no time."

"That's no way to speak to a woman nearly eighty years old just because she's down. I'd have you respect your elders, young man."

"Well, Missy, excuse me." Doctor Harry patted her cheek. "But I've got to warn you, haven't I? You're a marvel, but you must be careful or you're going to be good and sorry."

"Don't tell me what I'm going to be. I'm on my feet now, morally speaking. It's Cornelia. I had to go to bed to get rid of her."

Her bones felt loose, and floated around in her skin, and Doctor Harry floated like a balloon around the foot of the bed. He floated and pulled down his waistcoat and swung his glasses on a cord. "Well, stay where you are, it certainly can't hurt you."

"Get along and doctor your sick," said Granny Weatherall. "Leave a well woman alone. I'll call for you when I want you. . . . Where were you forty years ago when I pulled through milk-leg and double pneumonia? You weren't even born. Don't let Cornelia lead you on," she shouted, because Doctor Harry appeared to float up to the ceiling and out. "I pay my own bills, and I don't throw my money away on nonsense!"

She meant to wave good-by, but it was too much trouble. Her eyes closed of themselves, it was like a dark curtain drawn around the bed. The pillow rose and floated under her, pleasant as a hammock in a light wind. She listened to the leaves rustling outside the window. No, somebody was swishing newspapers: no, Cornelia and Doctor Harry were whispering together. She leaped broad awake, thinking they whispered in her ear.

"She was never like this, *never* like this!" "Well, what can we expect?" "Yes, eighty years old. . . ."

Well, and what if she was? She still had ears. It was like Cornelia to whisper around doors. She always kept things secret in such a public way. She was always being tactful and kind. Cornelia was dutiful; that was the trouble with her. Dutiful and good: "So good and dutiful," said Granny, "and I'd like to spank her." She saw herself spanking Cornelia and making a fine job of it.

"What'd you say, Mother?"

Granny felt her face tying up in hard knots.

"Can't a body think, I'd like to know?"

"I thought you might want something."

"I do. I want a lot of things. First off, go away and don't whisper."

She lay and drowsed, hoping in her sleep that the children would keep out and let her rest a minute. It had been a long day. Not that she was tired. It was always pleasant to snatch a minute now and then. There was always so much to be done, let me see: tomorrow.

Tomorrow was far away and there was nothing to trouble about. Things were finished somehow when the time came; thank God there was always a little margin over for peace: then a person could spread out the plan of life and tuck in the edges orderly. It was good to have everything clean and folded away, with the hair brushes and tonic bottles sitting straight on the white embroidered linen: the day started without fuss and the pantry shelves laid out with rows of jelly glasses and brown jugs and white stone-china jars with blue whirligigs and words painted on them: coffee, tea, sugar, ginger, cinnamon, allspice: and the bronze clock with the lion on top nicely dusted off. The dust that lion could collect in twenty-four hours! The box in the attic with all those letters tied up, she'd have to go through that tomorrow. All those letters—George's letters and John's letters and her letters to them both—lying around for the children to find afterwards made her uneasy. Yes, that would be tomorrow's business. No use to let them know how silly she had been once.

While she was rummaging around she found death in her mind and it felt clammy and unfamiliar. She had spent so much time preparing for death there was no need for bringing it up again. Let it take care of itself now. When she was sixty she had felt very old, finished, and went around making farewell trips to see her children and grandchildren, with a secret in her mind: This is the very last of your mother, children! Then she made her will and came down with a long fever. That was all just a notion like a lot of other things, but it was lucky too, for she had once for all got over the idea of dying for a long time. Now she couldn't be worried. She hoped she had better sense now. Her father had lived to be one hundred and two years old and had drunk a noggin of strong hot toddy on his last birthday. He told the reporters it was his daily habit, and he owed his long life to that. He had made quite a scandal and was very pleased about it. She believed she'd just plague Cornelia a little.

"Cornelia! Cornelia!" No footsteps, but a sudden hand on her cheek. "Bless you, where have you been?"

"Here, Mother."

"Well, Cornelia, I want a noggin of hot toddy."

"Are you cold, darling?"

"I'm chilly, Cornelia. Lying in bed stops the circulation. I must have told you that a thousand times."

Well, she could just hear Cornelia telling her husband that Mother was getting a little childish and they'd have to humor her. The thing that most annoyed her was that Cornelia thought she was deaf, dumb, and blind. Little hasty glances and tiny gestures tossed around her and over her head saying, "Don't cross her, let her have her way, she's eighty years old," and she sitting there as if she lived in a thin glass cage. Sometimes Granny almost made up her mind to pack up and move back to her own house where nobody could remind her every minute that she was old. Wait, wait, Cornelia, till your own children whisper behind your back!

In her day she had kept a better house and had got more work done. She wasn't too old yet for Lydia to be driving eighty miles for advice when one of the children jumped the track, and Jimmy still dropped in and talked things over: "Now, Mammy, you've a good business head, I want to know what you think of this? . . ." Old. Cornelia couldn't change the furniture around without asking. Little things, little things! They had been so sweet when they were little. Granny wished the old days were back again with the children young and everything to be done over. It had been a hard pull, but not too much for her. When she thought of all the food she had cooked, and all the clothes she had cut and sewed, and all the gardens she had made—well, the children showed it. There they were, made out of her, and they couldn't get away from that. Sometimes she wanted to see John again and point to them and say, Well, I didn't do so badly, did I? But that would have to wait. That was for tomorrow. She used to think of him as a man, but now all the children were older than their father, and he would be a child beside her if she saw him now. It seemed strange and there was something wrong in the idea. Why, he couldn't possibly recognize her. She had fenced in a hundred acres once, digging the post holes herself and clamping the wires with just a negro boy to help. That changed a woman. John would be looking for a young woman with the peaked Spanish comb in her hair and the painted fan. Digging post holes changed a woman. Riding country roads in the winter when women had their babies was another thing: sitting up nights with sick horses and sick negroes and sick children and hardly ever losing one. John, I hardly ever lost one of them! John would see that in a minute, that would be something he could understand, she wouldn't have to explain anything!

It made her feel like rolling up her sleeves and putting the whole place to rights again. No matter if Cornelia was determined to be everywhere at once, there were a great many things left undone on this place. She would start tomorrow and do them. It was good to be strong enough for everything, even if all you made melted and changed and slipped under your hands, so that by the time you finished you almost forgot what you were working for. What was it I set out to do? she asked herself intently, but she could not remember. A fog rose over the valley, she saw it marching across the creek swallowing the trees and moving up the hill like an army of ghosts. Soon it would be at the near edge of the orchard, and then it was time to go in and light the lamps. Come in, children, don't stay out in the night air.

Lighting the lamps had been beautiful. The children huddled up to her and breathed like little calves waiting at the bars in the twilight. Their eyes followed the match and watched the flame rise and settle in a blue curve, then they moved away from her. The lamp was lit, they didn't have to be scared and hang on to mother any more. Never, never, never more. God, for all my life I thank Thee. Without Thee, my God, I could never have done it. Hail, Mary, full of grace.

I want you to pick all the fruit this year and see that nothing is wasted. There's always someone who can use it. Don't let good things rot for want of using. You waste life when you waste good food. Don't let things get lost. It's bitter to lose things. Now, don't let me get to thinking, not when I am tired and taking a little nap before supper. . . .

The pillow rose about her shoulders and pressed against her heart and the memory was being squeezed out of it: oh, push down the pillow, somebody: it would smother her if she tried to hold it. Such a fresh breeze blowing and such a green day with no threats in it. But he had not come, just the same. What does a woman do when she has put on the white veil and set out the white cake for a man and he doesn't come? She tried to remember. No, I swear he never harmed me but in that. He never harmed me but in that . . . and what if he did? There was the day, the day, but a whirl of dark smoke rose and covered it, crept up and over into the bright field where everything was planted so carefully in orderly rows. That was hell, she knew hell when she saw it. For sixty years she had prayed against remembering him and against losing her soul in the deep pit of hell, and now the two things were mingled in one and the thought of him was a smoky cloud from hell that moved and crept in her head when she had just got rid of Doctor Harry and was trying to rest a minute. Wounded vanity, Ellen, said a sharp voice in the top of her mind. Don't let your wounded vanity get the upper hand of you. Plenty of girls get jilted. You were jilted, weren't you? Then stand up to it. Her eyelids wavered and let in streamers of blue-gray light like tissue paper over her eyes.

She must get up and pull the shades down or she'd never sleep. She was in bed again and the shades were not down. How could that happen? Better turn over, hide from the light, sleeping in the light gave you nightmares. "Mother, how do you feel now?" and a stinging wetness on her forehead. But I don't like having my face washed in cold water!

Hapsy? George? Lydia? Jimmy? No, Cornelia, and her features were swollen and full of little puddles. "They're coming, darling, they'll all be here soon." Go wash your face, child, you look funny.

Instead of obeying, Cornelia knelt down and put her head on the pillow. She seemed to be talking but there was no sound. "Well, are you tongue-tied? Whose birthday is it? Are you going to give a party?"

Cornelia's mouth moved urgently in strange shapes. "Don't do that, you bother me, daughter."

"Oh, no, Mother. Oh, no. . . ."

Nonsense. It was strange about children. They disputed your every word. "No what, Cornelia?"

"Here's Doctor Harry."

"I won't see that boy again. He just left five minutes ago."

"That was this morning, Mother. It's night now. Here's the nurse."

"This is Doctor Harry, Mrs. Weatherall. I never saw you look so young and happy!"

"Ah, I'll never be young again—but I'd be happy if they'd let me lie in peace and get rested."

She thought she spoke up loudly, but no one answered. A warm weight on her forehead, a warm bracelet on her wrist, and a breeze went on whispering, trying to tell her something. A shuffle of leaves in the everlasting hand of God. He blew on them and they danced and rattled. "Mother, don't mind, we're going to give you a little hypodermic." "Look here, daughter, how do ants get in this bed? I saw sugar ants yesterday." Did you send for Hapsy too?

It was Hapsy she really wanted. She had to go a long way back through a great many rooms to find Hapsy standing with a baby on her arm. She seemed to herself to be Hapsy also, and the baby on Hapsy's arm was Hapsy and himself and herself, all at once, and there was no surprise in the meeting. Then Hapsy melted from within and turned flimsy as gray gauze and the baby was a gauzy shadow, and Hapsy came up close and said, "I thought you'd never come," and looked at her very searchingly and said, "You haven't changed a bit!"

They leaned forward to kiss, when Cornelia began whispering from a long way off, "Oh, is there anything you want to tell me? Is there anything I can do for you?"

Yes, she had changed her mind after sixty years and she would like to see George. I want you to find George. Find him and be sure to tell him I forgot him. I want him to know I had my husband just the same and my children and my house like any other woman. A good house too and a good husband that I loved and fine children out of him. Better than I hoped for even. Tell him I was given back everything he took away and more. Oh, no, oh, God, no, there was something else besides the house and the man and the children. Oh, surely they were not all? What was it? Something not given back. . . . Her breath crowded down under her ribs and grew into a monstrous frightening shape with cutting edges; it bored up into her head, and the agony was unbelievable: Yes, John, get the doctor now, no more talk, my time has come.

When this one was born it should be the last. The last. It should have been born first, for it was the one she had truly wanted. Everything came in good time. Nothing left out, left over. She was strong, in three days she would be as well as ever. Better. A woman needed milk in her to have her full health.

"Mother, do you hear me?"

"I've been telling you—"

"Mother, Father Connolly's here."

"I went to Holy Communion only last week. Tell him I'm not so sinful as all that."

"Father just wants to speak to you."

He could speak as much as he pleased. It was like him to drop in and inquire about her soul as if it were a teething baby, and then stay on for a cup of tea and a round of cards and gossip. He always had a funny story of some sort, usually about an Irishman who made his little mistakes and confessed them, and the point lay in some absurd thing he would blurt out in the confessional showing his struggles between native piety and original sin. Granny felt easy about her soul. Cornelia, where are your manners? Give Father Connolly a chair. She had her secret comfortable understanding with a few favorite saints who cleared a straight road to God for her. All as surely signed and sealed as the papers for the new Forty Acres. Forever . . . heirs and assigns forever. Since the day the wedding cake was not cut, but thrown out and wasted. The whole bottom dropped out of the world, and there she was blind and sweating with nothing under her feet and the walls falling away. His hand had caught her under the breast, she had not fallen, there was the freshly polished floor with the green rug on it, just as before. He had cursed like a sailor's parrot and said, "I'll kill him for you." Don't lay a hand on him, for my sake leave something to God. "Now, Ellen, you must believe what I tell you. . . ."

So there was nothing, nothing to worry about any more, except sometimes in the night one of the children screamed in a nightmare, and they both hustled out shaking and hunting for the matches and calling, "There, wait a minute, here we are!" John, get the doctor now, Hapsy's time has come. But there was Hapsy standing by the bed in a white cap. "Cornelia, tell Hapsy to take off her cap. I can't see her plain."

Her eyes opened very wide and the room stood out like a picture she had seen somewhere. Dark colors with the shadows rising towards the ceiling in long angles. The tall black dresser gleamed with nothing on it but John's picture, enlarged from a little one, with John's eyes very black when they should have been blue. You never saw him, so how do you know how he looked? But the man insisted the copy was perfect, it was very rich and handsome. For a picture, yes, but it's not my husband. The table by the bed had a linen cover and a candle and a crucifix. The light was blue from Cornelia's silk lampshades. No sort of light at all, just frippery. You had to live forty years with kerosene lamps to appreciate honest electricity. She felt very strong and she saw Doctor Harry with a rosy nimbus around him.

"You look like a saint, Doctor Harry, and I vow that's as near as you'll ever come to it."

"She's saying something."

"I heard you, Cornelia. What's all this carrying on?"

"Father Connolly's saying—"

Cornelia's voice staggered and bumped like a cart in a bad road. It rounded corners and turned back again and arrived nowhere. Granny stepped up in the cart very lightly and reached for the reins, but a man sat beside her and she knew him by his hands, driving the cart. She did not look in his face, for she knew without seeing, but looked instead down the road where the trees leaned over and bowed to each other and a thousand birds were singing a Mass. She felt like singing too, but she put her hand in the bosom of her dress and pulled out a rosary, and Father Connolly murmured Latin in a very solemn voice and tickled her feet. My God, will you stop that nonsense? I'm a married woman. What if he did run away and leave me to face the priest by myself? I found another a whole world better. I wouldn't have exchanged my husband for anybody except St. Michael himself, and you may tell him that for me with a thank you in the bargain.

Light flashed on her closed eyelids, and a deep roaring shook her. Cornelia, is that lightning? I hear thunder. There's going to be a storm. Close all the windows. Call the children in. . . . "Mother, here we are, all of us." "Is that you, Hapsy?" "Oh, no, I'm Lydia. We drove as fast as we could." Their faces drifted above her, drifted away. The rosary fell out of her hands and Lydia put it back. Jimmy tried to help, their hands fumbled together, and Granny closed two fingers around Jimmy's thumb. Beads wouldn't do, it must be something alive. She was so amazed her thoughts ran round and round. So, my dear Lord, this is my death and I wasn't even thinking about it. My children have come to see me die. But I can't, it's not time. Oh, I always hated surprises. I wanted to give Cornelia the amethyst set—Cornelia, you're to have the amethyst set, but Hapsy's to wear it when she wants, and, Doctor Harry, do shut up. Nobody sent for you. Oh, my dear Lord, do wait a minute. I meant to do something about the Forty Acres, Jimmy doesn't need it and Lydia will later on, with that worthless husband of hers. I meant to finish the altar cloth and send six bottles of wine to Sister Borgia for her dyspepsia. I want to send six bottles of wine to Sister Borgia, Father Connolly, now don't let me forget.

Cornelia's voice made short turns and tilted over and crashed. "Oh, Mother, oh, Mother, oh, Mother. . . ."

"I'm not going, Cornelia. I'm taken by surprise. I can't go."

You'll see Hapsy again. What about her? "I thought you'd never come." Granny made a long journey outward, looking for Hapsy. What if I don't find her? What then? Her heart sank down and down, there was no bottom to death, she couldn't come to the end of it. The blue light from Cornelia's lampshade drew into a tiny point in the center of her brain, it flickered and winked like an eye, quietly it fluttered and dwindled. Granny lay curled down within herself, amazed and watchful, staring at the point of light that was herself; her body was now only a deeper mass of shadow in an endless darkness and this darkness would curl around the light and swallow it up, God, give a sign!

For the second time there was no sign. Again no bridegroom and the priest in the house. She could not remember any other sorrow because this grief wiped them all away. Oh, no, there's nothing more cruel than this—I'll never forgive it. She stretched herself with a deep breath and blew out the light.

Questions

1. Who is Hapsy? What do we know about her? *How* do we know these things?
2. How would you describe Granny Weatherall? In what ways does her name suit her?
3. The final paragraph begins: "For the second time there was no sign." What happened the first time? What is happening now? How are the two events linked? (The paragraph alludes to Christ's parable of the bridegroom, in Matthew 25:1–13. If you are unfamiliar with the parable, read it in the Gospel according to St. Matthew.)
4. What do you think happens in the last line of the story?

Gerard Manley Hopkins

God's Grandeur

The world is charged with the grandeur of God.
  It will flame out, like shining from shook foil;
  It gathers to a greatness, like the ooze of oil
Crushed. Why do men then now not reck[1] his rod?   4
Generations have trod, have trod, have trod;
  And all is seared with trade; bleared, smeared with toil;
  And wears man's smudge and shares man's smell: the soil
Is bare now, nor can foot feel, being shod.   8

---

[1] Heed. (Editors' note)

Gerard Manley Hopkins (1844–1889) was born in London of a prosperous family. He was educated at Oxford, where he became increasingly interested in the High Church wing of the Anglican Church and then in Roman Catholicism. In 1866 Hopkins converted to Roman Catholicism, and in 1868 he became a Jesuit priest. For the rest of his life he served as a parish priest (chiefly in the slums of London) and as a teacher. He wrote poetry and showed it to a few friends, but his work did not become widely known until 1918, twenty-nine years after his death, when his literary executor gave the material to a publisher.

And for all this, nature is never spent;
    There lives the dearest freshness deep down things;
And though the last lights off the black West went
    Oh, morning, at the brown brink eastward, springs—   12
Because the Holy Ghost over the bent
    World broods with warm breast and with ah! bright wings.

Questions

1. Hopkins, a Roman Catholic priest, lived in England during the last
    decades of the nineteenth century—that is, in an industrialized
    society. Where in the poem do you find him commenting on his
    setting? Circle the words in the poem that can refer both to Eng-
    land's physical appearance and to the sinful condition of human
    beings.
2. What is the speaker's tone in the first three and a half lines (through
    "Crushed")? In the rest of line 4? In lines 5–8? Is the second part
    of the sonnet (the next six lines) more unified in tone or less?

APPENDIX A

Reading (and Writing About) Pictures

Let's begin by talking about pictures that most of us would agree are "art"—paintings and drawings rather than photographs, though we shall go on to argue that most of what we say from the outset is also true of photography.

Until the twentieth century most pictures were representational, showing gods and goddesses and kings and saints and landscapes and dishes of fruit; but they were also expressive, revealing the artist's feelings toward the subject, the artist's (or society's) particular vision. An object is seen, but not only with the eye; the mind interprets it, and when the object ends up on canvas, it has been shaped by an idea. As the painter Degas said, "The artist does not draw what he sees, but what he must make others see." Van Gogh put it thus, when he heard that a painter complained that his figures were distorted:

> I don't want them to be "correct." Real artists paint things not as they are, in a dry analytical way, but as *they* feel them. I adore Michelangelo's figures, though the legs are too long and the hips and backsides too large. What I most want to do is to make these incorrectnesses, deviations, remodelings, or adjustments of reality something that may be "untrue" but is at the same time more true than literal truth.

The proportion of (on the one hand) accurate optical representation to (on the other hand) distortion introduced by the expression of an idea of course varies from age to age and from painter to painter, but even in periods when individuality was not highly valued we may speak of an expressive content; the expression is that of the age. After all, it is entirely possible that innumerable nameless and almost indistinguishable twelfth-century painters expressed their religious ideals while working comfortably within the established traditions of medieval art. In twelfth-century art Christ is regularly shown seated on the heavens with the earth as a footstool; he holds the Bible in his left hand and gives a benediction with his right hand. The pose and setting, and even the rendering of stylized details, are traditional; the difference between one rendition and another is chiefly a matter of the painter's technical competence. But all the renditions, similar though they are, may express what the artists wanted to express about Christ. Don't we often express ourselves in thoroughly traditional ways? We applaud at the end of a performance that has impressed us; we feel no need to find a personal way (throwing white mice into the air?) of expressing our pleasure and approval. We are content to express ourselves in the traditional way.

The artist of course often works within bounds that severely limit personal expression. If a court painter, obliged to represent the splendor of his king, did not share the king's opinions, he might very well have had to suppress his feelings. Then again, he might have been able to smuggle something subversive into his painting, so that the royal sitter might see the painting as the image of kingliness, though the painter and the perceptive viewer saw it as the image of arrogance. A painter might even, with a splendid painting and a sitter endowed with taste, persuade the king that arrogance was more interesting and attractive than kingliness.

Even artists working under tight control, then, may—and do— endow their paintings with a life beyond optical representation of the apparent subject. In ordinary language we recognize that a painting is not simply *of* something but *by* someone; we may say, "That's a painting of a Dutch merchant," but more often we say, "That's a painting by Rembrandt," or, more tellingly, "Look at that Rembrandt." For when we look at the picture we experience Rembrandt—his way of seeing—quite as much as a merchant-sitter.

Although many of the world's greatest artists have had to please their royal or ecclesiastical or bourgeois patrons by representing certain subjects in certain ways, we know that often another subject lies on the canvas: the paintings give visible form to the artist's mind. A picture, then, is a sort of utterance, an "outterance," a sending out of attitudes, an outer report of feelings. The picture conveys meaning (as well as phenomena) in visual form, and it may intensify or newly shape the spectator's perception of any aspect of life.

Speaking metaphorically, we can say that this meaning is conveyed in the *language* of painting. Just as a succession of short sentences "says" something different from a succession of long ones (probably if it doesn't convey mere childishness it tells of tight-lipped assurance, authority, or at least self-restraint), so too a picture with short, choppy, angular lines will "say" something different from a picture with gentle curves, even though the object represented (let's say a woman sitting at a table) is about the same. Similarly, a painting with a rough surface built up with vigorous or agitated brushstrokes will not say the same thing as a painting with a smooth polished surface that gives no evidence of the brush. And a soft pencil drawing on pale gray paper will say something different from a pen drawing made with a broad nib on bright white paper; at the very least, the medium and the subdued contrast of one are "quieter" or "less active" than the other.

What are some of the basic things to look for in understanding the language of pictures? One can begin almost anywhere, but let's begin with the relationship among the parts:

Do the figures share the space evenly, or does one figure overpower another, taking most of the space or the light?

Are the figures harmoniously related, perhaps by a similar stance or shared action, or are they opposed, perhaps by diagonals thrusting at each other? (Speaking generally, diagonals may suggest instability, except when they form a triangle resting on its base. Horizontal lines suggest stability, as do vertical lines when connected by a horizontal line. Circular lines are often associated with motion, and sometimes—especially by men—with the female body and with fertility. These simple formulas, however, must be applied cautiously, for they are not always appropriate.)

In a landscape, what is the relation between humans and nature? Are the figures at ease in nature, or are they dwarfed by it? Are they earthbound, beneath the horizon, or (because the viewpoint is low) do they stand out against the horizon and perhaps seem in touch with the heavens, or at least with open air? If there are woods, are these woods threatening or are they an inviting place of refuge? If there is a clearing, is the clearing a vulnerable place or is it a place of refuge from threatening woods? Do the natural objects in the landscape somehow reflect the emotions of the figures in it?

If the picture is a portrait, how do the furnishings and the background and the angle of the head or the posture of the head and body (as well, of course, as the facial expression) contribute to our sense of the person portrayed?

What is the effect of light in the picture? Does it produce sharp contrasts, brightly illuminating some parts and throwing others into darkness, or does it, by means of gentle gradations, unify most or all of the parts? Does the light seem theatrical or natural, disturbing or comforting? If the picture is in color, is the color realistic or is it expressive, or both?

We believe that you can stimulate responses by asking yourself two kinds of questions:

1. *What is this doing?* Why is this figure here and not there, why is this tree so brightly illuminated, why are shadows omitted, why is this seated figure leaning forward like that?
2. *Why do I have this response?* Why do I find this figure pathetic, this landscape oppressive, this child revoltingly sentimental but that child fascinating?

The first of these questions, "What is this doing?," requires you to identify yourself with the artist, wondering perhaps whether pen is better than pencil for this drawing, or watercolor better than oil paint for this painting. The second question, "Why do I have this response?," requires you to trust your feelings. If you are amused or repelled or unnerved or soothed, assume that these responses are appropriate and follow them up, at least until further study of the work provides other responses.

Let's turn to a specific painting, Velázquez's *The Water Seller*, painted about 1620. Velázquez painted it while he lived in Seville, but the precise locale and the time are unimportant, because even if we didn't realize until now that in the seventeenth century people required the services of a water carrier, the picture tells us so. Velázquez reproduces appearances with careful fidelity to nature. But what is Velázquez saying, and how does he say it?

We'll begin with the largest figure, the old man who, in full light, dominates the center of the picture and who seems to stand closest to us, his hand on the great jar that appears easily within our reach. His clothes are tattered, but he has immense dignity, partly because he seems almost a central pillar, partly because his hand rests assuredly on the big globular vessel of life-sustaining water, partly because his facial expression is serious, and partly because we see his face in profile. If we think of the profile of Lincoln on a penny, of Jefferson on a nickel, of Roosevelt on a dime, of Washington on a quarter or in the painting *Washington Crossing the Delaware,* we notice that a face in profile is in no immediate relation to us. It stares off, ignoring us, looking at something that exists only in the flat world of the picture plane. Because a profile avoids contact with the space or world between the picture and the viewer, it usually strikes us as independent, even aloof. If a profile has a personality or inner life, it is probably not jovial or confiding or anguished; it is probably solemn, poised, self-sufficient. And there is another important thing about a profile: it can be very interesting, for we are attracted to, say, that high forehead, long nose, downturned mouth. The line that defines the profile is sharply arresting, in a way that the lines of a frontal view usually are not.

In any case, if we ask ourselves which figure in Velázquez's painting is the center of interest, the answer must be evident. But the other
figures are not mere contrasts to set off the water carrier. The old water
seller is giving a glass to a boy, and we notice that between the two
figures, to the rear, is a third person, apparently older than the boy
and younger than the old man. And so we have the ages of man: youth,
maturity, old age. The man in the middle, whose glass is tipped in
front of his face, has already drunk substantially—even in this frozen
action he is in mid-career, so to speak—but the boy is about to receive
a full glass, for his life is all ahead of him. The figure in the middle,
mostly obscured, although the least important, is not unimportant; he
is represented because Velázquez wants more than the obvious contrast of youth and age. The painter, however, concentrates his vision
on the old man passing the life-sustaining water to the young man.
We see the renewal of life.

And what of the vessels, so prominent in the picture? Of course
they belong in the picture; a water seller must have a jar of water, and
his customers must have jars or glasses to receive the water. These
vessels are handsome ones, interesting shapes beautifully painted.
Still, realism would have been satisfied with a glass and perhaps the
top of the large pot. The painter must have had not only a perceptive
eye for things of the real world, but an idea for a picture. (This is not
to say that an artist's idea precedes visual stimulus. Quite the reverse:
almost surely the artist first sees something, something he feels he
wants to capture and to show to others, and this initial perception
stimulates whatever idea he develops. Velázquez perhaps was first
moved by the face of the water carrier, or by the way the old man
poured water into a glass, or even by the gleaming droplets on the
shoulder of a great earthenware jar; this, he may have felt, glows with
such an inner life that it must be recorded for others to see, forever.
Perhaps with some such thought the picture began, but it did not stop
there.) Velázquez's utensils, beautiful though they are in themselves,
contribute to the whole picture and take their fullest life from the whole
picture. What do they contribute?

For one thing, although the three figures are closely bound by
their physical positions and (even more important) by participating in
a unified action, the vessels help to bring them still closer to one another, for our eye makes a sort of wheeling motion as it goes from one
bright patch to another, from the water carrier's face to his shoulder
and arm, perhaps then to the large vessel and then to the smaller one,
then to the boy's illuminated hand and up along the glass to the boy's

face, and finally to the shadowy face of the man in the middle. But there may be more. What is the effect of that great bulging jar at the bottom of the canvas? Why should earthenware receive so much space and be painted so much more illusionistically than the rather flat face of the mature man drinking from the glass?

Our own response—and the picture has long exerted a spell on us—is that this vessel, the thing nearest to us, almost bulging into the space we occupy, and made of the substance to which we return, is given prominence and exerts it appeal because it contains not only the stuff that sustains life but the stuff out of which life came. First, water; then, nourished by water, life. In fact, impressive though the figures are, it seems to us that it is to this pregnant jar with unseen precious contents that the eye (or at least the mind's eye) returns after it surveys the figures.

After we have admired the astounding technical skill that can render people and objects so convincingly and interestingly, what can we say about the meaning of the picture? The painter, in pictorial language, perhaps is saying something like this. Our lives may seem poor battered things, as the water carrier's torn smock and wrinkled face indicate, but a source whose bottom we cannot see has given us the gift of life, and we can live with dignity and nourish succeeding generations.

Of course Velázquez probably never said anything like this in words, but he did say it in paint. Our summary is crudely put and takes no account of the sheer sensuous appeal of the lines and colors (mostly earthy colors), but anything that we say about a great picture is crude compared with the richness of the picture itself. We realize too that our commentary has come close to turning the picture into an allegory. We hope that we have not quite said that the three men stand for three parts of a life span, that the water stands for life, that the rip in the carrier's sleeve stands for the hardships of this world. When we look at this painting, we never forget that it is a representation of men engaged in a specific commonplace action. Still, the more we respond to this representation, the more we feel that it adds up to something; and the more we feel that the whole is greater than the sum of its parts, the more we want to account for its mysterious appeal. By asking ourselves questions and trying to answer them, we may heighten our understanding of the picture and of life.

We have banged this picture around a good deal, but it can withstand anything we do to it, and we want to spend another minute on it, setting forth what we might write if we were asked to write a paragraph about it, perhaps as a caption in a picture-book or a label on a museum wall. Up to now we have tried to show, in some detail, how we came to our understanding of the picture, but of course in writing, a finished piece one does not reproduce all the byways of thought. Here is what we would say.

> Velázquez's *The Water Seller* was painted in Seville, and doubtless it represents a common enough sight, people receiving the carrier's services. But we sense more than mere realism here, more than an optically convincing report of what happened at a particular moment. Velázquez has turned the disorder of daily experience into a pattern and a meaning. We see three people closely joined; an old man of enormous gravity (despite his tattered appearance) hands a glassful of water to a youth; between them, and between them in years, too, a mature man drinks a glass, and so we see a cycle of life, a cycle reinforced as our eyes move from the great water jar in the foreground up to the glass, to the boy's attentive face, across the adult's face to the water seller's solemn profile, and down again to the jar that is the source of nourishment for all ages.

In 1839, more than two hundred years after Velázquez painted *The Water Seller*, Louis Jacques Mandé Daguerre made public the daguerreotype, an early photographic process. "From this moment," the painter Paul Delaroche is supposed to have said, "painting is dead." This remark implies, of course, that painting seeks to render external appearances and that it cannot compete with a camera. But another and far greater painter of the period took a different view. Honoré Daumier said that photography describes everything and explains nothing. The implication is that photography offers optical realism but cannot offer the idea, the vision, which a work of art embodies. Daumier's statement, it turned out, was as inadequate as Delaroche's, as we shall try to show in a capsule historical analysis of photography.

In the middle of the nineteenth century, after a few years of intoxication with machines that could produce a permanent image that was neither drawn nor painted, photographers began to divide into two schools, which we can call *pictorialists* and *reporters*. (Of course we are simplifying; the labels are overstatements, and some photographers occupied a middle ground, or shifted allegiance from one school to the other.) The pictorialists had artistic ambitions. They posed their subjects carefully into compositions resembling those of the old master painters, and they often used religious or literary motifs, as painting had done. Julia Margaret Cameron (1815–1879) pressed her friends and servants to dress up like King Arthur's knights so that she might photograph scenes from Tennyson's *Idylls of the King,* or she arranged a woman and children into a composition that she called "Madonna with Children." She also did portrait photography, and although it might at first be thought that this at least was tied to reportage, her subjects were such notables as Tennyson, Browning, Longfellow, and Darwin, and she did not at all wish to present them as ordinary men caught in some trivial act of daily living:

> When I have had such men before my camera my whole soul has endeavored to do its duty towards them in recording faithfully the greatness of the inner as well as the features of the outer man. The photograph thus taken has been almost the embodiment of a prayer.

Moreover, because early photography required a long exposure during which the subject could not move, almost all the pictures of people—even of ordinary people, say a man supposedly sawing wood or a middle-class family dining—have a studied, posed, pictorial effect.

In Julia Cameron's time, however, other photographers (we are calling them reporters) specialized in a technique that was supposed to be the mere reproduction of anything the eye might see. Many of these concentrated on exotic sights—the Nile, American Indians, Greek architecture. The idea was that the folks back home could see exactly what these strange places and people looked like. These photographs were documents, it was claimed, showing what you would see if you were able to take the long, expensive, arduous trip. Supposedly, the photograph offered the facts—not the Ideal Truth of the pictorialists but the truth of the fleeting moment. This tradition of recording the passing scene was fostered by technical developments that greatly decreased the time required for the exposure, allowing shots of moving objects; the development of easily portable cameras, too, was essential to the documentary or reportorial tradition. The result was photo-journalism, which implicitly offers the facts without comment, and also the run-of-the-mill snapshot, which tells us what Aunt Julie looks like, standing on the porch of her new house.

Still speaking broadly, we can say that the pictorialists usually emphasize an obviously studied composition; they often use a soft focus to suppress details, they alter the negative by underdeveloping or by overdeveloping it, and they print their pictures (often retouched) on warm, soft, matte (dully finished) paper. On the other hand, the reporters value pictures with seemingly unplanned compositions (a figure cut at the side, or the top of a head cut off); they also prefer a sharp focus and prints on cold, hard, glossy paper. The effect, they might claim, is that of the moment, not that of the ages; truth, not beauty.

Now, a newspaper photograph or an amateur's snapshot does not in fact record the object-as-it-really-is. It records what you would see if you had only one eye and stood at a particular place at a particular time of day, and if what you saw was printed on a particular kind of paper. Besides, except for a few pictures taken in desperation—a picture of a parade taken by a photographer who, unable to see over the heads of a crowd, simply holds the camera as high as he can and snaps at random—the pictures of the reporters (and we include the amateur who takes snapshots) are, like those of the pictorialists, at least somewhat composed. After all, one backs up a little, shifts the lens to the right a bit, bends the knees, waits for someone to get out of the way, or, conversely, waits for a dog to come along and sniff the garbage. A Victorian reportorial photographer went up in a balloon so that he could get an interesting shot of the entrance to a cave in India, and today there is scarcely a serious photographer who has not gone to great pains to get a shot that seems "natural," "inevitable," "spontaneous." There is, of course, a visible difference between pictures at either extreme, but most of the reporters as well as the pictorialists will have to say with the late Minor White, "I don't take pictures, I make them."

What we said about reading paintings, then, applies to reading photographs too, whether they are conspicuously pictorial or allegedly reportorial. The relationships between one object and another (of one figure to another, or figures to background) are revealing, and so too is the angle of vision. And the focus—soft, or precise and hard—and the degree of contrast—gentle gradations suggesting harmony, or unity, or sharp contrasts of black and white suggesting dislocations or conflict or at least harshness—contribute to the meaning of a photograph. Because photographers make these and many other choices, they might agree with the painter Cézanne, who said that pictures are "the means of making the public feel what we feel ourselves."

Let's look at a photograph from Robert Frank's book, *The Americans* (1969), "Drugstore—Detroit." If he had to choose from our categories, Frank would unhesitatingly call himself a reporter, so his photograph will be a severe but fair test of a method of analysis derived from studying painting.

©Robert Frank, from *The Americans*, 1958. Courtesy Pace MacGill Gallery

As we look at Frank's photograph, here are some of the things we see. (We see them partly because we have asked ourselves questions, as suggested on pages 685–686.)

1. A line of crowded people. Possibly the seating really is ample, but the angle from which the picture was taken gives us the impression that the eaters are crowded.
2. Most of these people, though in an eating place, are in fact waiting, not eating. Each is waiting by himself. Although there is a crowd, no one seems to be conversing with a neighbor. It's a lonely crowd. Those who are not staring blankly are looking curiously at the photographer, but even the unusual experience of seeing a photographer taking a picture at a lunch counter does not seem to break through to most of the men here.
3. The counter serves a useful purpose in the eatery, but in the picture it gives the effect of a barrier, separating all the customers (white males) from the women (apparently black) who serve them. Moreover, the angle from which the picture was taken (relatively high) produces a swift foreshortening; the rear of the picture seems eerily tilted up, giving a slightly surrealistic effect.
4. A good deal of machinery (apparently mini-jukeboxes) is evident along the counter, further dehumanizing the place.
5. Advertisements for Orange Whip, Orange Whip, Orange Whip, hang over the heads of the customers, almost threateningly. If the man in the foreground is indeed drinking Orange Whip, he shows no sign of enjoying it.

If we were to write a short paragraph on this picture, then, trying to report not only what it says but also *how* it says it, we might write:

Robert Frank's photograph shows us people at mealtime, but this occasion is not a time of relaxed and friendly renewal of body or of spirit. The picture shows clutter, machine after machine, boredom, and isolation. Men sit, for the most part not dining but staring into space, each avoiding eye-contact with his neighbor, and separated by a counter from the women who serve them. Apparently not even two of the dozen or so are friends with a word to exchange. In the foreground, perhaps submitting to the aggressive advertisements for Orange Whip that dangle overhead, a man sips a beverage. He shows no sign of pleasure. The steep perspective unsettles us as we look at this picture of people who seem almost as dehumanized as the counter they sit at.

The Chinese aphorism says that a picture is worth a thousand words; but sometimes it takes that many words (well, a couple of dozen, anyway) to bring the picture home to us.

APPENDIX B

A Writer's Glossary

analogy. An analogy (from the Greek *analogos*, proportionate, resembling) is a kind of comparison. Normally an analogy compares substantially different kinds of things and reports several points of resemblance. A comparison of one city with another ("New York is like Chicago in several ways") does not involve an analogy because the two things are not substantially different. And a comparison giving only one resemblance is usually not considered an analogy ("Some people, like olives, are an acquired taste"). But if we claim that a state is like a human body, and we find in the state equivalents for the brain, heart, and limbs, we are offering an analogy. Similarly, one might construct an analogy between feeding the body with food and supplying the mind with ideas: the diet must be balanced, taken at approximately regular intervals, in proper amounts, and digested. An analogy may be useful in explaining the unfamiliar by comparing it to the familiar ("The heart is like a pump . . ."), but of course the things compared are different, and the points of resemblance can go only so far. For this reason, analogies cannot prove anything, though they are sometimes offered as proof.

analysis. Examination of the parts and their relation to the whole. For a brief example, see the paragraph on page 688 analyzing Velázquez's painting, *The Water Seller*.

argument. Discourse in which some statements are offered as *reasons* for other statements. Argument, then, like emotional appeal and wit, is a form of persuasion, but argument seeks to persuade by appealing to reason. (See *deduction*, pages 698–699.)

audience. The writer's imagined readers. An essay on inflation written for the general public—say, for readers of *Newsweek*—will assume less specialized knowledge than will an essay written for professional economists—say, the readers of *Journal of Economic History*. In general, the imagined audience in a composition course is *not* the instructor (though in fact the instructor may be the only reader of the essay); the imagined audience usually is the class, or, to put it a little differently, someone rather like the writer but without the writer's specialized knowledge of the topic.

cliché.   Literally, a *cliché* was originally (in French) a stereotype or an electrotype plate for printing; in English the word has come to mean an oft-repeated expression such as "a sight for sore eyes," "a heart-warming experience," "the acid test," "a meaningful relationship," "last but not least." Because these expressions implicitly claim to be impressive or forceful, they can be distinguished from such unpretentious common expressions as "good morning," "thank you," and "see you tomorrow." Clichés in fact are not impressive or forceful; they strike the hearer as tired, vague, and unimaginative.

compare/contrast.   Strictly speaking, to compare is to examine in order to show similarities. (It comes from the Latin *comparare*, "to pair," "to match.") To contrast is to set into opposition in order to show differences. (It comes from the Latin *contra*, "against," and *stare*, "to stand.") But in ordinary usage a comparison may include not only similarities but also differences. (For a particular kind of comparison, emphasizing similarities, see *analogy*.) In comparing and contrasting, a writer usually means not simply to list similarities or differences but to reveal something clearly, by calling attention either to its resemblances to something we might not think it resembles, or to its differences from something we might think it does resemble.

connotation.   The associations that cluster around a word. "Mother" has connotations that "female parent" does not have, yet both words have the same denotation or explicit meaning.

convention.   An agreed-on usage. Beginning each sentence with a capital letter is a convention.

deduction.   Deduction is the process of reasoning from premises to a logical conclusion. Here is the classic example: "All men are mortal" (the major premise); "Socrates is a man" (the minor premise); "therefore Socrates is mortal" (the conclusion). Such an argument, which takes two truths and joins them to produce a third truth, is called a syllogism (from Greek for "a reckoning together"). Deduction (Latin for "lead down from") moves from a general statement to a specific application; it is, therefore, the opposite of *induction* (page 702), which moves from specific instances to a general conclusion.

Notice that if a premise of a syllogism is not true, one can reason logically yet can come to a false conclusion. Example: "All teachers are members of a union"; "Jones is a teacher"; "therefore Jones is a member of a union." Although the process of reasoning is correct here, the major premise is false and so the conclusion is worthless—Jones may or may not be a member of the union.

Another point: some arguments superficially appear logical but are not. Let's take this attempt at a syllogism: "All teachers of Spanish know that in Spanish *hoy* means 'today' " (major premise); "John knows that in Spanish *hoy* means 'today' " (minor premise); "therefore John is a teacher of Spanish" (conclusion). Both of the premises are correct, but the conclusion does not follow. What's wrong? Valid deduction requires that the subject or condition of the major premise (in this case, teachers of Spanish) appear also in the minor premise, but here it does not. The minor premise should be "John is a teacher of Spanish," and the valid conclusion, of course, would be "therefore John knows that *hoy* means 'today.' "

denotation.   The explicit meaning of a word, as given in a dictionary, without its associations. "Daytime serial" and "soap opera" have the same denotation, though "daytime serial" probably has a more favorable connotation (see *connotation*).

description.   Discourse that aims chiefly at producing a sensory response (usually a mental image) to, for example, a person, object, scene, taste, smell, and so on. A descriptive essay, or passage in an essay, uses concrete words (words that denote observable qualities such as "hair" and "stickiness") and it uses specific language (words such as "basketball" rather than "game," and "steak, potatoes, and salad" rather than "hearty meal").

diction.   Choice of words. Examples: between "car," "auto," and "automobile," between "lie" and "falsehood," between "can't" and "cannot."

euphemism.   An expression such as "passed away" for "died," used to avoid realities that the writer finds unpleasant. Thus, oppressive governments "relocate people" (instead of putting them in concentration camps).

evaluation.   Whereas an interpretation seeks to explain the meaning, an evaluation judges worth. After we interpret a difficult piece of writing we may evaluate it as not worth the effort.

explication.   An attempt to reveal the meaning by calling attention to implications, such as the connotations of words and the tone conveyed by the brevity or length of a sentence. Unlike a paraphrase, which is a rewording or rephrasing in order to set forth the gist of the meaning, an explication is a commentary that makes explicit what is implicit. If we paraphrased the beginning of the Gettysburg Address (page 424), we might turn "Four score and seven years ago our fathers brought forth" into "Eighty-seven years ago our ancestors established," or some such statement. In an explication, however, we would mention that "four score" evokes the language of the Bible, and that the biblical echo helps to establish the solemnity and holiness of the occasion. In an explication we would also mention that "fathers" initiates a chain of images of birth, continued in "conceived in liberty," "any nation so conceived," and "a new birth." (See Highet's explication of the Gettysburg Address, page 425.)

exposition.   An expository essay is chiefly concerned with giving information—how to register for classes, the causes of the French Revolution, or the tenets of Zen Buddhism. The writer of exposition must, of course, have a point of view (an attitude or a thesis), but because exposition—unlike persuasion—does not assume that the reader's opinion differs from the writer's, the point of view in exposition often is implicit rather than explicit.

general and **specific** (or **particular**).   A general word refers to a class or group; a specific (particular) word refers to a member of the class or group. Example: "vehicle" is general compared with "automobile" or with "motorcycle." But "general" and "specific" are relative. "Vehicle" is general when compared to "automobile," but "vehicle" is specific when compared to "machine," for "machine" refers to a class or group that includes not only vehicles but clocks, typewriters, and dynamos. Similarly, although "automobile" is specific in comparison with "vehicle," "automobile" is general in comparison with "Volkswagen" or "sportscar."

generalization.   A statement relating to every member of a class or category, or, more loosely, to most members of a class or category. Example: "Students from Medford High are well prepared." Compare: (1) "Janet Kuo is well prepared" (a report of a specific condition); (2) "Students from Medford High are well prepared" (a low-level generalization, because it is limited to one school); (3) "Students today are well prepared" (a high-level generalization, covering many people in many places).

imagery and **symbolism.**   When we read "rose," we may more or less call to mind a picture of a rose, or perhaps we are reminded of the odor or texture of a rose. Whatever in a piece of writing appeals to any of our senses (including sensations of heat and pressure as well as of sight, smell, taste, touch, sound) is an image. In short, images are the sensory content of a work, whether literal (the roses discussed in an essay on rose-growing) or figurative (a comparison, in a poem, of a girl to a rose). It is usually easy to notice images in literature, particularly in poems, which often include comparisons such as "I wandered lonely as a cloud," "a fiery eye," and "seems he a dove? His feathers are but borrowed." In literature, imagery (again, literal as well as figurative) plays a large part in communicating the meaning of the work. For instance, in *Romeo and Juliet* abundant imagery of light and dark reenforces the conflict between life and death. Juliet especially is associated with light (Romeo says, "What light through yonder window breaks? It is the east and Juliet is the sun"), and at the end of the play, when the lovers have died, we are told that the morning is dark: "The sun for sorrow will not show his head."

If we turn from imaginative literature to the essay, we find, of course, that descriptive essays are rich in images. But other kinds of essays, too, may make use of imagery—and not only by literal references to real people or things. Such essays may use figures of speech, as Thoreau does when he says that the imagination as well as the body should "both sit down at the same table." The imagination, after all, does not literally sit down at a table—but Thoreau personifies the imagination, seeing it as no less concrete than the body.

The distinction between an image and a symbol is partly a matter of emphasis and partly a matter of a view of reality. If an image is so insisted on that we feel that the writer sees it as highly significant in itself and also as a way of representing something else, we can call it a symbol. In Henry James's words, symbolism is the presentation "of objects casting . . . far behind them a shadow more curious . . . than the apparent figure." A symbol is what it is, and yet it is also much more. We may feel that a passage about the railroad, emphasizing its steel tracks and its steel cars, its speed and its noise, may be not only about the railroad but also about industrialism and, even further, about an entire way of life—a way of thinking and feeling—that came into being in the nineteenth century.

A symbol, then, is an image so loaded with significance that it is not simply literal, and it does not simply stand as a figure for something else; it is both itself *and* something else that it richly suggests, a kind of manifestation of something too complex or too elusive to be otherwise revealed. In a symbol, Thomas Carlyle wrote, "the Infinite is made to blend with the Finite, to stand visible, and as it were, attainable there." Still, having said all of this, one must add that the distinction between image and symbol is not sharp, and usage allows us even to say such things as, "The imagery of light symbolizes love," meaning that the imagery stands for or represents or is in part about love.

induction.   Reasoning from the particular to the general, or drawing a conclusion about all members of a class from a study of some members of the class. Every elephant I have seen is grayish, so by induction (from Latin, "lead into," "lead up to") I conclude that all elephants are grayish. Another example: I have met ten graduates of Vassar College and all are females, so I conclude that all Vassar graduates are females. This conclusion, however, happens to be incorrect; a few years ago Vassar began to admit males, and so although male graduates are few they do exist. Induction is valid only if the sample is representative.

Because one can rarely be certain that it *is* representative, induced conclusions are usually open to doubt. Still, we live our lives largely by induction; we have dinner with a friend, we walk the dog, we write home for money—all because these actions have produced certain results in the past and we assume that actions of the same sort will produce results consistent with our earlier findings. Nelson Algren's excellent advice must have been arrived at inductively: "Never eat at a place called Mom's, and never play cards with a man called Doc."

interpretation.   An explanation of the meaning. If we see someone clench his fist and tighten his mouth, we may interpret these signs as revealing anger. When we say that in the New Testament the passage alluding to the separation of sheep from goats is to be understood as referring to the saved and the damned, we are offering an interpretation.

irony.   In *verbal irony*, the meaning of the words intentionally contradicts the literal meaning, as in "that's not a very good idea," where the intended meaning is "that's a terrible idea."

Irony, in distinction from sarcasm, employs at least some degree of wit or wryness. Sarcasm reveals contempt obviously and heavily, usually by asserting the opposite of what is meant: "You're a great guy" (if said sarcastically) means "It's awful of you to do this to me." Notice that the example of irony we began with was at least a trifle more ingenious than this sarcastic remark, for the sarcasm here simply is the opposite of what is meant, whereas our example of verbal irony is not quite the opposite. The opposite of "that's not a very good idea" is "that is a very good idea," but clearly (in our example) the speaker's meaning is something else. Put it this way: sarcasm is irony at its crudest, and finer irony commonly uses overstatement or especially understatement, rather than a simple opposite. (For a brief discussion of the use of irony in satire, see the entry on satire, pages 705–706.)

If the speaker's words have an *un*intentional double meaning, the irony may be called *dramatic irony:* a character, about to go to bed, says, "I think I'll have a sound sleep," and dies in her sleep. Similarly, an action can turn dramatically ironic: a character seeks to help a friend and unintentionally harms her. Finally, a situation can be ironic: thirsty sailors are surrounded by water that cannot be drunk.

All these meanings of irony are held together, then, by the sense of a somewhat bitter contrast.

jargon.   Technical language used inappropriately or inexactly. "Viable" means "able to survive." To speak of "a viable building" is to use jargon. "A primary factor in my participation in the dance" is jargon if what is meant is "I dance because. . . ."

metaphor.   Words have literal meanings: a lemon is a yellow, egg-shaped citrus fruit; to drown is to suffocate in water or other fluid. But words can also have metaphoric meanings: we can call an unsatisfactory automobile a lemon, and we can say that we are drowning in paperwork. Metaphoric language is literally absurd; if we heed only the denotation it is clearly untrue, for an automobile cannot be a kind of citrus fruit, and we cannot drown in paperwork. (Even if the paper literally suffocated someone, the death could not be called a drowning.) Metaphor, then, uses not the denotation of the word but the associations, the connotations. Because we know that the speaker is not crazy, we turn from the literal meaning (which is clearly untrue) to the association.

myth.   (1) A traditional story dealing with supernatural beings or with heroes, often accounting for why things are as they are. Myths tell of the creation of the world, the creation of man, the changes of the season, the achievements of heroes. A Zulu myth, for example, explains that rain is the tears of a god weeping for a beloved slain bird. *Mythology* is a system or group of such stories, and so we speak of Zulu mythology, or Greek mythology, or Norse mythology. (2) Mark Schorer, in *William Blake,* defines myth as "a large controlling image that gives philosophic meaning to the facts of ordinary life. . . . All real convictions involve a mythology. . . . Wars may be described as the clash of mythologies." In this sense, then, a myth is not a traditional story we do not believe, but any idea, true or false, to which people subscribe. Thus, one can speak of the "myth" of democracy or of communism.

narration.   Discourse that recounts a real or a fictional happening. An anecdote is a narrative, and so is a history of the decline and fall of the Roman Empire. Narration may, of course, include substantial exposition ("four possible motives must be considered") and description ("the horse was an old gray mare"), but the emphasis is on a sequence of happenings ("and then she says to me, . . .").

parable.   A parable is a short narrative from which a moral or a lesson can be drawn. Christ's tale of the prodigal son (page 536) is told in order to reveal the blindness of the Pharisees who blame Christ for receiving sinners. A parable may, but need not, be an allegory wherein, say, each character stands for an abstraction that otherwise would be hard to grasp. Usually the parable lacks the *detailed* correspondence of an allegory.

paradox.   An apparent self-contradiction, such as "He was happiest when miserable."

paraphrase.   A rewording of a passage, usually in order to clarify the meaning. A paraphrase is a sort of translating within the same language; it can help to make clear the gist of the passage. But one must recognize the truth of Robert Frost's charge that when one paraphrases a line of good writing one puts it "in other and worse English." Paraphrase should not be confused with *explication,* pages 699–700.

parody.   A parody (from the Greek "counter song") seeks to amuse by imitating the style—the diction, the sentence structure—of another work, but normally the parody substitutes a very different subject. Thus, it might use tough-guy Hemingway talk to describe not a bullfighter but a butterfly catcher. Often a parody of a writer's style is a good-natured criticism of it.

persona.   The writer or speaker in a role adopted for a specific audience. When Abraham Lincoln wrote or spoke, he sometimes did so in the persona of commander in chief of the Union army, but at other times he did so in the persona of the simple man from Springfield, Illinois. The persona is a mask put on for a performance (*persona* is the Latin word for mask). If mask suggests insincerity, we should remember that whenever we speak or write we do so in a specific role—as friend, or parent, or teacher, or applicant for a job, or whatever. Although Lincoln was a husband, a father, a politician, a president, and many other things, when he wrote a letter or speech he might write solely as one of these; in a letter to his son, the persona (or, we might say, personality) is that of father, not that of commander in chief. The distinction between the writer (who necessarily fills many roles) and the persona who writes or speaks a work is especially useful in talking about satire, because the satirist often invents a mouthpiece very different from himself. The satirist—say, Jonathan Swift—may be strongly opposed to a view, but his persona (his invented essayist) may favor the view; the reader must perceive that the real writer is ridiculing the invented essayist.

persuasion.   Discourse that seeks to change a reader's mind. Persuasion usually assumes that the writer and the reader do not agree, or do not fully agree, at the outset. Persuasion may use logical argument (appeal to reason), but it may also try to win the reader over by other means—by appeal to the emotions, by wit, by geniality.

rhetoric.   Although in much contemporary usage the word's meaning has sadly decayed to "inflated talk or writing," it can still mean "the study of elements such as content, structure, and cadence in writing or in speech." In short, in the best sense rhetoric is the study of the art of communicating with words.

satire.   A work ridiculing identifiable objects in real life, meant to arouse in the reader contempt for its object. Satire is sometimes distinguished from comedy in that comedy aims simply to evoke amusement, whereas satire aims to bring about moral reform by ridicule. According to Alexander Pope, satire "heals with morals what it hurts with wit." Satire sometimes uses invective (direct abuse), but if the invective is to entertain the reader it must be witty, as in a piling up of ingenious accusations. Invective, however, is probably less common in satire than is irony, a device in which the tone somehow contradicts the words. For instance, a speaker may seem to praise ("well, that's certainly an original idea that you have"), but we perceive that he is ridiculing a crackpot idea. Or the satirist may invent a naive speaker (a persona) who praises, but the praise is really dispraise because a simpleton offers it; the persona is sincere but the writer is ironic and satiric. Or, adopting another strategy, the writer may use an apparently naive persona to represent the voice of reason; the persona dispassionately describes actions that we take for granted (a political campaign), and through this simple, accurate, rational description we see the irrationality of our behavior. (For further comments on irony, see pages 702–703.)

style.   A distinctive way of expression. If we see a picture of a man sitting on a chair, we may say that it looks like a drawing for a comic book, or we may say that it looks like a drawing by Rembrandt or Van Gogh or Andrew Wyeth. We have come to recognize certain ways of expression—independent of the content—as characteristic of certain minds. The content, it can be said, is the same—a man sitting in a chair—but the creator's way of expressing the content is individual.

Similarly, "Four score and seven years ago" and "Eighty-seven years ago" are the same in content; but the styles differ, because "Four score and seven years ago" distinctively reflects a mind familiar with the Bible and an orator speaking solemnly. Many people (we include ourselves) believe that the content is *not* the same if the expression is not the same. The "content" of "Four score and seven years ago" includes suggestions of the Bible and of God-fearing people not present in "eighty-seven years ago." In this view, a difference in style is a difference in content and therefore a difference in meaning. Surely it is true that in the work of the most competent writers, those who make every word count, one cannot separate style and content.

Let C. S. Lewis have the next-to-last word: "The way for a person to develop a style is (a) to know exactly what he wants to say, and (b) to be sure he is saying exactly that. The reader, we must remember, does not start by knowing what we mean. If our words are ambiguous, our meaning will escape him. I sometimes think that writing is like driving sheep down a road. If there is any gate open to the left or the right the readers will most certainly go into it." And let the Austrian writer Karl Kraus have the last word: "There are two kinds of writers, those who are and those who aren't. With the first, content and form belong together like soul and body; with the second, they match each other like body and clothes."

summary.   The word "summary" is related to "sum," to the total something adds up to. (The Greeks and Romans counted upward, and wrote the total at the top.) A summary is a condensation or abridgment briefly giving the reader the gist of a longer work. Here are a few principles that govern summaries:

1. A summary is much briefer than the original. It is *not* a paraphrase—a word-by-word translation of someone's words into your

own—for a paraphrase is usually at least as long as the original, whereas a summary is rarely longer than one-fourth the original, and may even be much briefer, perhaps giving in a sentence or two an entire essay.

2. A summary usually achieves its brevity by omitting almost all the concrete details of the original, presenting only the sum that the details add up to.

3. A summary is accurate; it has no value if it misrepresents the point of the original.

4. The writer of a summary need not make the points in the same order as that of the original. In fact, a reader is occasionally driven to write a summary because the original author does not present the argument in an orderly sequence; the summary is an attempt to disengage the author's argument from the confusing presentation.

5. A summary normally is written in the present tense, because the writer assumes that although the author *wrote* the piece last year or a hundred years ago, the piece speaks to us today. (In other words, the summary is explicitly or implicitly prefaced by "He says," and all that follows is in the present tense.

6. Because a summary is openly based on someone else's views, not your own, you need not use quotation marks around any words that you take from the original.

Here is a summary of this entry on "summary":

A summary is a condensation or abridgment. These are some characteristics: (1) it is rarely more than one-fourth as long as the original; (2) its brevity is usually achieved by leaving out most of the concrete details of the original; (3) it is accurate; (4) it may rearrange the organization of the original, especially if a rearrangement will make things clearer; (5) it normally is in the present tense; (6) quoted words need not be enclosed in quotation marks.

thesis. The writer's position or attitude; the proposition advanced.

thesis statement. A sentence or two summarizing the writer's position or attitude. An essay may or may not have an explicit thesis statement. (See page 14.)

tone. The prevailing spirit of an utterance. The tone may be angry or bitter or joyful or solemn, or expressive of any similar mood or emotion. Tone usually reflects the writer's attitude toward the subject, the audience, and the self. (For further comments on tone, see pages 2–3.)

ACKNOWLEDGMENTS

Woody Allen. "The Colorization of Films Insults Artists and Society," *The New York Times*, 26 June 1987. Copyright © 1987 by The New York Times Company. Reprinted by permission.

Sherwood Anderson. "The Egg" from *The Triumph of the Egg*. Reprinted by permission of Harold Ober Associates Incorporated. Copyright 1921 by B. W. Heubsch, Inc. Copyright renewed 1948 by Eleanor C. Anderson.

Maya Angelou. "Graduation." From *I Know Why the Caged Bird Sings* by Maya Angelou. Copyright © 1969 by Maya Angelou. Reprinted by permission of Random House, Inc.

Anonymous. "Confessions of an Erstwhile Child" from *The New Republic*, 15 June 1974. Reprinted by permission of *The New Republic*, © 1974, The New Republic, Inc.

Anonymous Japanese. "Muddy Road" from *Zen Flesh, Zen Bones*, compiled by Paul Reps. Copyright © 1957 by Charles E. Tuttle Co., Inc. Reprinted by permission of the publisher, Charles E. Tuttle Co., Inc., Tokyo, Japan.

Alexandra Armstrong. "Starting a Business." Reprinted by permission from the March 1988 issue of *Ms.* Magazine.

W. H. Auden. "The Almighty Dollar." Copyright © 1962 by W. H. Auden. Reprinted from *The Dyer's Hand and Other Essays*, by permission of Random House, Inc.

W. H. Auden. "Work, Labor, and Play" from *A Certain World* by W. H. Auden. Copyright © 1970 by W. H. Auden. All rights reserved. Reprinted by permission of Viking Penguin Inc.

Keith H. Basso. "'Stalking with Stories': Names, Places, and Moral Narratives Among the Western Apache" excerpted from *On Nature*, edited by Daniel Halpern, Copyright © 1987. Published by North Point Press and reprinted by permission.

Mary Field Belenky et al., "Toward an Education for Women," From *Women's Ways of Knowing: The Development of Self, Voice, and Mind*, by Mary Field Belenky, Blythe McVicker Clinchy, Nancy Rule Goldberger, and Jill Mattuck Tarule. Copyright © 1986 by Basic Books, Inc. Reprinted by permission of Basic Books, Inc., Publishers.

Warren Bennis. "Time to Hang Up the Old Sports Clichés," *The New York Times*, 5 July 1987. Reprinted by permission of the author.

Barbara R. Bergmann. "Pay Equity—How to Argue Back," *Ms.*, November 1985. Reprinted by permission of the author.

Black Elk. "High Horse's Courting" from John G. Neihart, *Black Elk Speaks*, pp. 67–76. Copyright 1932, © 1959, 1972 by John G. Neihart. Reprinted by permission of the John G. Neihart Trust.

Black Elk. "War Games" from John G. Neihart, *Black Elk Speaks*, pp. 14–15, 59–60. Copyright 1932, © 1959, 1972 by John G. Neihart. Reprinted by permission of the John G. Neihart Trust.

Italo Calvino. "The Aquatic Uncle" from *Cosmi-comics* by Italo Calvino, English translation copyright © 1968 by Harcourt Brace Jovanovich, Inc. and Jonathan Cape Ltd., reprinted by permission of Harcourt Brace Jovanovich, Inc.

Stephen Chapman. "The Prisoner's Dilemma" from *The New Republic*, 8 March 1980. Reprinted by permission of *The New Republic*, © 1980, The New Republic Inc.

Chewing Blackbones. "Old Man and Old Woman" from *Indian Legends from the Northern Rockies*, by Ella E. Clark. Copyright © 1966 by the University of Oklahoma Press. Reprinted by permission.

Robert Coles. "Student Volunteers, Academic Credit," *The New York Times*, 30 April 1988. Copyright © 1988 by The New York Times Company. Reprinted by permission.

Lewis Coser. "The Family." From Lewis A. Coser, *Sociology Through Literature*, © 1963, pp. 250–251. Reprinted by permission of Prentice-Hall, Inc., Englewood Cliffs, New Jersey.

Laura Cunningham. "The Girls' Room" from *The New York Times*, 10 September 1981. Reprinted by permission of William Morris Agency, Inc., on behalf of the author.

Excerpt on pp. 134–135 from pp. 21–22 of *Measuring Growth in English* by Paul Diederich. © 1974 by the National Council of Teachers of English. Reprinted by permission.

Barbara Ehrenreich. "A Step Back to the Workhouse?" from *Ms.*, November 1979. Reprinted by permission of the author.

Letters sent to *Ms.* Magazine in response to "A Step Back to the Workhouse?" and published in the February 1988 issue. Reprinted by permission of the authors.

Barbara Ehrenreich and Annette Fuentes, "Life on the Global Assembly Line" from *Ms.*, June 1981. Reprinted by permission of the authors.

Joseph Epstein. "Obsessed with Sport." Reprinted by permission of Georges Borchardt, Inc. for the author. Copyright © 1976 by Joseph Epstein. Originally appeared in *Harper's* Magazine.

Milton Friedman. "The Social Responsibility of Business Is to Increase Its Profits," *The New York Times* (Magazine), 13 September 1970. Copyright © 1970 by The New York Times Company. Reprinted by permission.

Ernesto Galarza. "Growing into Manhood" from *Barrio Boy* by Ernesto Galarza. Copyright © 1971 University of Notre Dame Press, Notre Dame, IN 46556. Reprinted by permission.

Nathan Glazer. "Some Very Modest Proposals for the Improvement of American Education." Reprinted by permission of *Daedalus*, Journal of the American Academy of Arts and Sciences, 113:4, Fall 1984, Cambridge, MA.

Paul Goodman. "A Proposal to Abolish Grading." Reprinted from *Compulsory Mis-Education* by Paul Goodman, copyright 1964, by permission of the publisher, Horizon Press, New York.

Tipper Gore. "Curbing the Sexploitation Industry," *The New York Times*, 14 March 1988. Copyright © 1988 by The New York Times Company. Reprinted by permission.

Edward T. Hall. "Proxemics in the Arab World." Excerpts from *The Hidden Dimension* by Edward T. Hall. Copyright © 1966 by Edward T. Hall. Reprinted by permission of Doubleday, a division of Bantam, Doubleday, Dell Publishing Group, Inc.

Richard Hawley, "Television and Adolescents: A Teacher's View" from *American Film* Vol. 4, no. 1 (October 1978). Reprinted by permission of the author.

Dolores Hayden. "Advertisements, Pornography, and Public Space." Selection is reprinted from *Redesigning the American Dream: The Future of Housing, Work, and Family Life,* by Dolores Hayden, with the permission of W. W. Norton & Company, Inc. Copyright © 1984 by Dolores Hayden.

Gilbert Highet. "The Gettysburg Address" from *A Clerk of Oxenford*. Reprinted by permission of Curtis Brown, Ltd. Copyright 1954 by Gilbert Highet.

John Holt. "The Right to Control One's Learning" from *Escape from Childhood* by John Holt. Copyright © 1974 by John Holt. Reprinted by permission of Holt Associates, Inc.

Jane Howard. "All Happy Clans Are Alike," from *Families*. Copyright © 1978 by Jane Howard. Reprinted by permission of Simon & Schuster, Inc.

Langston Hughes. "Salvation" from *The Big Sea* by Langston Hughes. Copyright 1940 by Langston Hughes. Copyright renewed © 1968 by Arna Bontemps and George Houston Bass. Reprinted by permission of Hill and Wang, a division of Farrar, Straus and Giroux, Inc.

Lyrics on pp. 167–168 from James Weldon Johnson, "Lift Ev'ry Voice and Sing" (James Weldon Johnson, J. Rosamond Johnson). Used by permission of Edward B. Marks Music Company.

Pauline Kael. "High School and Other Forms of Madness" from *Deeper into Movies* by Pauline Kael. Copyright © 1969 by Pauline Kael. Originally appeared in *The New Yorker*. By permission of Little, Brown and Company.

Robert W. Keidel. "A New Game for Managers to Play," *The New York Times*, 5 December 1985. Copyright © 1985 by The New York Times Company. Reprinted by permission.

Jamaica Kincaid. "Girl" from *At the Bottom of the River* by Jamaica Kincaid. Copyright © 1978, 1979, 1981, 1982, 1983 by Jamaica Kincaid. Reprinted by permission of Farrar, Straus and Giroux, Inc.

Martin Luther King, Jr. "Nonviolent Resistance." From pp. 211–216 in *Stride Toward Freedom* by Martin Luther King, Jr. Copyright © 1958 by Martin Luther King, Jr. By permission of Harper & Row, Publishers.

Stephen King. "Why We Crave Horror Movies." Copyright © 1982 by Stephen King. Originally appeared in *Playboy*. Reprinted by permission of Kirby McCauley Ltd. on behalf of the author.

Edward I. Koch. "Death and Justice: How Capital Punishment Affirms Life" from *The New Republic*, 15 April 1985. Reprinted by permission of *The New Republic*, © 1985, The New Republic, Inc.

Excerpt on p. 138 from *More Lives Than One* by Joseph Wood Krutch. Copyright © 1961 by Joseph Wood Krutch. By permission of William Morrow & Company.

Charles Krauthammer. "The Just Wage: From Bad to Worth" from *The New Republic*, 30 July 1984. Reprinted by permission of *The New Republic*, © 1984, The New Republic, Inc.

Robin Lakoff. "You Are What You Say" from *Ms.* Magazine, July 1974. Reprinted by permission of the author.

Barbara Lawrence. "Four-Letter Words Can Hurt You," *The New York Times*, 27 October 1973. Copyright © 1973 by The New York Times Company. Reprinted by permission.

B. Aisha Lemu. "In Defense of Polygamy" from B. Aisha Lemu and Fatima Heerin, *Women in Islam*. © Islamic Council of Europe, 1978/1398 A.H. Reprinted by permission of The Islamic Foundation, 223 London Road, Leicester LE2 1ZE, U.K.

C. S. Lewis. "What Christians Believe" from *Mere Christianity* by C. S. Lewis. Copyright 1943, 1945, 1952, by Macmillan Publishing Company, Inc. Reprinted by permission of William Collins Sons & Co. Ltd., London.

C. S. Lewis. "Xmas and Christmas" from *God in the Dock* (British edition title, *Undeceptions*) by C. S. Lewis, © The Trustees of the Estate of C. S. Lewis, 1971. Reprinted by permission of Curtis Brown Group Ltd. and William Collins Sons & Co. Ltd., London.

Patricia Nelson Limerick. "The Phenomenon of Phantom Students: Diagnosis and Treatment" from *The Harvard Gazette*, 11 November 1983. Reprinted by permission of the author.

Malcolm X. "The Shoeshine Boy." From *The Autobiography of Malcolm X* by Malcolm X, with Alex Haley. Copyright © 1964 by Alex Haley and Malcolm X, © 1965 by Alex Haley and Betty Shabazz. Reprinted by permission of Random House, Inc.

Marya Mannes. "Television Advertising: The Splitting Image" from *Saturday Review*, 4 November 1970. Copyright © 1970 by Marya Mannes. Reprinted by permission.

Julie Matthaei. "Political Economy and Family Policy." Reprinted from Union for Radical Political Economics, *The Imperiled Economy, Book II: Through the Safety Net*, copyright 1988. Reprinted by permission of the author and the Union for Radical Political Economics.

Stanley Milgram. "Confessions of a News Addict" Copyright © 1977 by The Antioch Review, Inc. First appeared in the *Antioch Review*, Vol. 35, No. 2–3 (Spring/Summer, 1977) with the title "Reflections on News." Reprinted by permission of the editors.

Richard John Neuhaus. "Renting Women, Buying Babies, and Class Struggles." Published by permission of Transaction Publishers, from *Society*, Vol. 25, No. 3, March/April 1988. Copyright © 1988 by Transaction Publishers.

Joyce Carol Oates. "How I Contemplated the World From the Detroit House of Correction and Began My Life Over Again." Reprinted from *The Wheel of Love and Other Stories* by Joyce Carol Oates, by permission of the publisher, Vanguard Press, Inc. Copyright © 1970, 1969, 1968, 1967, 1966, 1965 by Joyce Carol Oates.

George Orwell. "Politics and the English Language," copyright 1946 by Sonia Brownell Orwell, renewed 1974 by Sonia Orwell, reprinted from *Shooting an Elephant and Other Essays* by George Orwell by permission of Harcourt Brace Jovanovich, Inc., the estate of the late Sonia Brownell Orwell, and Martin Secker & Warburg Ltd.

George Orwell. "Shooting an Elephant" from *Shooting an Elephant and Other Essays* by George Orwell, copyright 1950 by Sonia Brownell Orwell, renewed 1978 by Sonia Pitt-Rivers, reprinted by permission of Harcourt Brace Jovanovich, Inc., the estate of the late Sonia Brownell Orwell, and Martin Secker & Warburg Ltd.

J. H. Plumb. "The Dying Family" from *In the Light of History* by J. H. Plumb, published by Houghton Mifflin Company and Penguin Books Ltd. Copyright © 1972 by J. H. Plumb. Reprinted by permission of Sir John Plumb.

Katherine Anne Porter. "The Jilting of Granny Weatherall" from *Flowering Judas and Other Stories* by Katherine Anne Porter, copyright 1930, 1958 by Katherine Anne Porter, reprinted by permission of Harcourt Brace Jovanovich, Inc.

Neil Postman. "Order in the Classroom," (original title, "Teaching as a Conserving Activity") excerpted from the book *Teaching as a Conserving Activity* by Neil Postman. Copyright © 1979 by Neil Postman. Reprinted by permission of Delacorte Press, a division of Bantam, Doubleday, Dell Publishing Group, Inc.

Paul Robinson. "TV Can't Educate" from *The New Republic*, 12 August 1978. Reprinted by permission of *The New Republic*, © 1974, The New Republic, Inc.

Theodore Roethke. "Child on Top of a Greenhouse," copyright 1946 by Editorial Publications, Inc., and "My Papa's Waltz," copyright 1942 by Hearst Magazines, Inc., from *The Collected Poems of Theodore Roethke*. Reprinted by permission of Doubleday, a division of Bantam, Doubleday, Dell Publishing Group, Inc.

Bertrand Russell. "Work." Reprinted from *The Conquest of Happiness* by Bertrand Russell, with the permission of Liveright Publishing Corporation and Unwin Hyman Ltd. Copyright 1930 by Horace Liveright, Inc. Copyright renewed 1958 by Bertrand Russell.

Idries Shah. "Two Islamic Tales" from *Caravan of Dreams* by Idries Shah, pp. 126–127. Copyright Idries Shah 1986. Published by Octagon Press, London, 1986 (hardback) and Octagon Press, London, 1988 (paperback). Reprinted by permission.

Peter Singer. "Animal Liberation" from *The New York Review of Books*, 5 April 1973. Copyright © 1973 by Peter Singer. Reprinted by permission of the author.

Wilfred Cantwell Smith. "Muslims." From *The Faith of Other Men* by Wilfred Cantwell Smith. Copyright © 1962 by Wilfred Cantwell Smith. Printed by arrangement with NAL Penguin Inc., New York, New York.

Stevie Smith. "Not Waving but Drowning." From Stevie Smith, *Collected Poems*. Copyright © 1972 by Stevie Smith. Reprinted by permission of New Directions Publishing Corporation.

Index

To the Student

Part of our job as educational publishers is to try to improve the textbooks we publish. Thus, when revising a book, we take into account the experience of both instructors and students with the previous edition. At some time your instructor will be asked to comment extensively on *The Little, Brown Reader*, Fifth Edition, but right now we want to hear from you. After all, though your instructor assigned this book, you are the one who paid for it.

Please help us by completing this questionnaire and returning it to College English Developmental Group, Scott, Foresman and Company, 1900 East Lake Avenue, Glenview, Illinois 60025.

School _____ Course title _____

Instructor's Name _____

Please rate the selections:

	Liked best				Liked least	Didn't read
1. READING (AND WRITING ABOUT) ESSAYS						
George Orwell, Shooting an Elephant	5	4	3	2	1	—
2. ALL IN THE FAMILY						
Lewis Coser, The Family	5	4	3	2	1	—
J. H. Plumb, The Dying Family	5	4	3	2	1	—
Judy Syfers, Why I Want a Wife	5	4	3	2	1	—
Julie Matthaei, Political Economy and Family Policy	5	4	3	2	1	—
Richard John Neuhaus, Renting Women, Buying Babies and Class Struggles	5	4	3	2	1	—
B. Aisha Lemu, In Defense of Polygamy	5	4	3	2	1	—
Jane Howard, All Happy Clans Are Alike: In Search of the Good Family	5	4	3	2	1	—
Laura Cunningham, The Girls' Room	5	4	3	2	1	—
Black Elk, High Horse's Courting	5	4	3	2	1	—
Anonymous, Confessions of an Erstwhile Child	5	4	3	2	1	—

|---|---|---|---|---|---|---|---|

	Liked best				Liked least	Didn't read
Jonathan Swift, A Modest Proposal	5	4	3	2	1	___
Peter Singer, Animal Liberation	5	4	3	2	1	___
Jamaica Kincaid, Girl	5	4	3	2	1	___
Italo Calvino, The Aquatic Uncle	5	4	3	2	1	___
Theodore Roethke, My Papa's Waltz	5	4	3	2	1	___

3. TEACHING AND LEARNING

	Liked best				Liked least	Didn't read
Plato, The Myth of the Cave	5	4	3	2	1	___
Ernesto Galarza, Growing into Manhood	5	4	3	2	1	___
E. B. White, Education	5	4	3	2	1	___
Maya Angelou, Graduation	5	4	3	2	1	___
Pauline Kael, High School and Other Forms of Madness	5	4	3	2	1	___
Nathan Glazer, Some Very Modest Proposals for the Improvement of American Education	5	4	3	2	1	___
Neil Postman, Order in the Classroom	5	4	3	2	1	___
Merry White, Japanese Education: How Do They Do It?	5	4	3	2	1	___
Robert Coles, Student Volunteers, Academic Credit	5	4	3	2	1	___
John Holt, The Right to Control One's Learning	5	4	3	2	1	___
Paul Goodman, A Proposal to Abolish Grading	5	4	3	2	1	___
Mary Field Belenky, Blythe McVicker Clinchy, Nancy Rule Goldberger, and Jill Mattuck Tarule, Toward an Education for Women	5	4	3	2	1	___
Paul Robinson, TV Can't Educate	5	4	3	2	1	___
Patricia Nelson Limerick, The Phenomenon of Phantom Students: Diagnosis and Treatment	5	4	3	2	1	___
Wu-tsu Fa-yen, Zen and the Art of Burglary	5	4	3	2	1	___

4. WORK AND PLAY

	Liked best				Liked least	Didn't read
Bertrand Russell, Work	5	4	3	2	1	___
W. H. Auden, Work, Labor, and Play	5	4	3	2	1	___
Malcolm X, The Shoeshine Boy	5	4	3	2	1	___
Studs Terkel, Two Workers	5	4	3	2	1	___
Virginia Woolf, Professions for Women	5	4	3	2	1	___
Gloria Steinem, The Importance of Work	5	4	3	2	1	___